Presented to

Tom Sullivan

on the occasion of your

Confirmation

November 2001

St. John the Baptist Church,
Purley

THE JERUSALEM BIBLE

NEW
TESTAMENT

General Editor
ALEXANDER JONES
L.S.S., S.T.L., I.C.B.

THE JERUSALEM BIBLE

NEW
TESTAMENT

With Abridged Introductions
and Notes

DARTON·LONGMAN + TODD

Darton, Longman and Todd Ltd
1 Spencer Court
140–142 Wandsworth High Street
London SW18 4JJ

This edition with abridged introductions and notes first
published 1967

© 1966 and 1967 by Darton, Longman and Todd Ltd
and Doubleday & Company Inc.

The abridged introductions and notes of this Bible are based on
those which appear in *La Bible de Jérusalem* (one volume edition)
published by Les Editions du Cerf, Paris. The English text of this
Bible, though translated from the ancient texts, owes a large debt
to the work of the many scholars who collaborated to produce *La
Bible de Jérusalem*, a debt which the publishers of this English
Bible gratefully acknowledge.

Printed and bound in Great Britain by
The Cromwell Press, Trowbridge, Wiltshire

Not to be sold in or to the U.S.A., Canada or the
Philippine Republic

1A/9

ISBN 0-232-51621-9

EDITOR'S FOREWORD

When the Jerusalem Bible was first published in English in 1966, the Foreword to the complete Standard edition announced its objects: to serve two pressing needs facing the Church, the need to keep abreast of the times and the need to deepen theological thought. This double programme was carried out by translating the ancient texts into the language we use today, and by providing notes to the texts which were neither sectarian nor superficial. In that Foreword also, the dependence of the translators on the original pioneer work of the School of Biblical Studies in Jerusalem was acknowledged, and the English version was offered as an entirely faithful rendering of the original texts which, in doubtful points, preserved the text established and (for the most part) the interpretation adopted by the School in the light of the most recent researches in the fields of history, archaeology and literary criticism. With the text, the Standard edition presented the full explanatory notes that would enable any student to confirm for himself the interpretations that were adopted, to appreciate the theological implications drawn from them, and to understand the complex relations between different parts of the Bible.

However the Bible is not only for students undergoing a formal course of study, and there has been an immediate demand for an edition of the Jerusalem Bible which would bring the modern clarity of the text before the ordinary reader, and open to him the results of modern researches without either justifying them at length in literary and historical notes or linking them with doctrinal studies. For this reason, the present edition has been prepared. The full Introductions of the Standard edition are here greatly abridged, to serve simply as brief explanations of the character of each book or group of books, their dates and their authorship; and the full Notes of the Standard edition have been greatly reduced in number and length, to restrict them to the minimum which are necessary for understanding the primary, literal meaning of the text; to explain terms, places, people and customs; to specify dates, and to identify the sources of quotations. In short, the brief Introductions and Notes are here only to help the ordinary reader to understand what he is reading and do not assume in him any wide literary, historical or theological knowledge or interests.

Christ's College, Liverpool   Alexander Jones
1st March 1967

TYPOGRAPHICAL NOTE

Chapter numbers

The beginning of a chapter is usually marked by a large bold numeral. A smaller bold numeral is used when a chapter begins inside a paragraph.

Verse numbers

The beginning of each verse is indicated in the line by a dot • preceding the first word, except when a verse starts at the beginning of a line or begins a chapter. Where two verses begin in the same line, the verse numbers in the margin are placed one slightly above and the other slightly below the line. In a few places, the text adopted by the Editors differs from the Vulgate, A.V., and other previous versions by omitting a verse which those versions include. The verse numbering of the previous versions has nevertheless been retained for ease of reference; certain verse numbers are therefore omitted from their sequence in the margin, or appear in parentheses.

Italics in the text

Italic type is used in the text to distinguish words which are quotations from or close allusions to another book of the Bible. The origins of such quotations or allusions are given as references in the footnotes (except in cases in which the source is obvious to any Bible-reader), and are not necessarily repeated when the same passage is quoted more than once in a single book.

Punctuation of biblical references

Chapter and verse are separated by a colon, e.g. Ex 20:17. In a succession of references, items are separated by a semi-colon, e.g. Ex 20:17; Lv 9:15. The same practice is followed in a succession of references to different chapters of one book, e.g. Ex 20:17; 21:3 or Ex 15;17;20.

CONTENTS

LIST OF ABBREVIATIONS

The books of the Bible in biblical order

Genesis	Gn	Obadiah		Ob
Exodus	Ex	Jonah		Jon
Leviticus	Lv	Micah		Mi
Numbers	Nb	Nahum		Na
Deuteronomy	Dt	Habakkuk		Hab
Joshua	Jos	Zephaniah		Zp
Judges	Jg	Haggai		Hg
Ruth	Rt	Zechariah		Zc
1 Samuel	1 S	Malachi		Ml
2 Samuel	2 S			
1 Kings	1 K	Matthew		Mt
2 Kings	2 K	Mark		Mk
1 Chronicles	1 Ch	Luke		Lk
2 Chronicles	2 Ch	John		Jn
Ezra	Ezr	Acts		Ac
Nehemiah	Ne	Romans		Rm
Tobit	Tb	1 Corinthians		1 Co
Judith	Jdt	2 Corinthians		2 Co
Esther	Est	Galatians		Ga
1 Maccabees	1 M	Ephesians		Ep
2 Maccabees	2 M	Philippians		Ph
Job	Jb	Colossians		Col
Psalms	Ps	1 Thessalonians		1 Th
Proverbs	Pr	2 Thessalonians		2 Th
Ecclesiastes	Qo	1 Timothy		1 Tm
Song of Songs	Sg	2 Timothy		2 Tm
Wisdom	Ws	Titus		Tt
Ecclesiasticus	Si	Philemon		Phm
Isaiah	Is	Hebrews		Heb
Jeremiah	Jr	James		Jm
Lamentations	Lm	1 Peter		1 P
Baruch	Ba	2 Peter		2 P
Ezekiel	Ezk	1 John		1 Jn
Daniel	Dn	2 John		2 Jn
Hosea	Ho	3 John		3 Jn
Joel	Jl	Jude		Jude
Amos	Am	Revelation		Rv

The books of the Bible in alphabetical order of abbreviations

Ac	Acts	Lk	Luke
Am	Amos	Lm	Lamentations
Ba	Baruch	Lv	Leviticus
1 Ch	1 Chronicles	1 M	1 Maccabees
2 Ch	2 Chronicles	2 M	2 Maccabees
1 Co	1 Corinthians	Mi	Micah
2 Co	2 Corinthians	Mk	Mark
Col	Colossians	Ml	Malachi
Dn	Daniel	Mt	Matthew
Dt	Deuteronomy	Na	Nahum
Ep	Ephesians	Nb	Numbers
Est	Esther	Ne	Nehemiah
Ex	Exodus	Ob	Obadiah
Ezk	Ezekiel	1 P	1 Peter
Ezr	Ezra	2 P	2 Peter
Ga	Galatians	Ph	Philippians
Gn	Genesis	Phm	Philemon
Hab	Habakkuk	Pr	Proverbs
Heb	Hebrews	Ps	Psalms
Hg	Haggai	Qo	Ecclesiastes
Ho	Hosea	Rm	Romans
Is	Isaiah	Rt	Ruth
Jb	Job	Rv	Revelation
Jdt	Judith	1 S	1 Samuel
Jg	Judges	2 S	2 Samuel
Jl	Joel	Sg	Song of Songs
Jm	James	Si	Ecclesiasticus
Jn	John	Tb	·Tobit
1 Jn	1 John	1 Th	1 Thessalonians
2 Jn	2 John	2 Th	2 Thessalonians
3 Jn	3 John	1 Tm	1 Timothy
Jon	Jonah	2 Tm	2 Timothy
Jos	Joshua	Tt	Titus
Jr	Jeremiah	Ws	Wisdom
Jude	Jude	Zc	Zechariah
1 K	1 Kings	Zp	Zephaniah
2 K	2 Kings		

THE NEW TESTAMENT

INTRODUCTION TO
THE SYNOPTIC GOSPELS

The first three gospels are called synoptic ('with the same eye') because their narratives are all built on the same events in the life of Jesus and indeed many passages from all three of them can be placed side by side as evident parallels. From the earliest times, Matthew, Mark and Luke respectively have been named as the writers of them.

According to a tradition dating from the 2nd century, St Matthew was the first to write a gospel and he wrote 'in the Hebrew tongue'. Our Greek 'Gospel according to St Matthew' is not identified with this early Aramaic book, which is lost, though there are times when it appears to represent a more primitive text than Mark.

Some parts of the gospel story assumed a fixed and stereotyped pattern in the oral tradition founded on the preaching of the apostles; the similarity of the Passion in all four gospels suggests a common oral tradition very firmly fixed. But the relationships between the three synoptic gospels are too close and too complex to be explained by a common oral tradition underlying all of them. It is clear that Luke depends on Mark, and although it was held for a long time that Mark depends on Matthew, a number of indications now suggest the reverse. Luke and Matthew also have a number of non-Marcan passages common to both, and these probably have a common source or sources; in addition, each of these gospels includes episodes and sayings not found in the other.

Mark, said to have been Peter's interpreter, is mentioned in St Paul's letters as one of his companions, and described in Acts as a disciple from Jerusalem. Luke is also mentioned in St Paul's letters and when writing Acts incorporated parts of a first-person travel diary. Mark's gospel can be dated before A.D. 70, perhaps about 64. Our Greek Matthew and Luke are later and probably date from 70-80.

The arrangement and presentation of the historical facts in the synoptic gospels are dictated by the purposes of a written gospel: to convert, to edify, to infuse faith, to enlighten it and defend it against its opponents.

Mark

The shortest of the gospels, it is not concerned with elaborating Christ's teaching and it records few of his sayings; the real point of its message is *the manifestation of the crucified Messiah*. While on the one hand Jesus is seen by the writer as the Son of God, acknowledged by the Father and vindicating his power and his mission by miracles, on the other hand he chooses to appear to the world under the mysterious title 'Son of Man', and the gospel puts great emphasis on his apparent frustration and rejection by the people. The 'messianic secret' is a basic idea of Mark's gospel.

Matthew

This gospel is divided into five books, each consisting of a discourse introduced by painstakingly selected narrative matter which follows the same broad outline as in Mark. These are preceded by the story of the Infancy and followed by that of the Passion. The fact that this gospel reports Christ's teaching much more fully than Mark and stresses especially the theme of the 'kingdom of heaven' makes it *a dramatic account in seven acts of the coming of the kingdom.* Matthew, writing for Jewish Christians, makes a special point of demonstrating, by the use of Old Testament quotations, that *the scriptures are fulfilled* in the person and work of Jesus.

Luke

The plan of this gospel follows Mark's outline as a rule, but the narrative is controlled and edited to bring in much teaching, including the longer parables, and to omit episodes that would not interest Luke's non-Jewish readers. The originality of Luke is in *his religious mentality*: he is the faithful recorder of Christ's lovingkindness, he emphasises the necessity for prayer and he is the only one of the synoptic authors to give the Holy Spirit the prominence which we find in Paul and in Acts.

Greek style

Mark's Greek is rough, strongly Aramaic and often faulty, but it is fresh and frank. Matthew's Greek is also rather Aramaic but smoother and more correct than Mark's, though less picturesque. Luke's style is variable: excellent when he is writing independently but at other times incorporating the peculiarities of his sources; as in Acts he suits the style to the subject and occasionally he goes out of his way to give a good imitation of Septuagint Greek.

THE GOSPEL ACCORDING TO
SAINT MATTHEW

I. THE BIRTH AND INFANCY OF JESUS

The ancestry of Jesus

1 **1** A genealogy of Jesus Christ, son of David, son of Abraham:[a]

2   Abraham was the father of Isaac,
Isaac the father of Jacob,
Jacob the father of Judah and his brothers,

3   Judah was the father of Perez and Zerah, Tamar being their mother,
Perez was the father of Hezron,
Hezron the father of Ram,

4   Ram was the father of Amminadab,
Amminadab the father of Nahshon,
Nahshon the father of Salmon,

5   Salmon was the father of Boaz, Rahab being his mother,
Boaz was the father of Obed, Ruth being his mother,
Obed was the father of Jesse;

6   and Jesse was the father of King David.

    David was the father of Solomon, whose mother had been
        Uriah's wife,

7   Solomon was the father of Rehoboam,
Rehoboam the father of Abijah,
Abijah the father of Asa,

8   Asa was the father of Jehoshaphat,
Jehoshaphat the father of Joram,
Joram the father of Azariah,

9   Azariah was the father of Jotham,
Jotham the father of Ahaz,
Ahaz the father of Hezekiah,

10   Hezekiah was the father of Manasseh,
Manasseh the father of Amon,
Amon the father of Josiah;

11   and Josiah was the father of Jechoniah and his brothers.
Then the deportation to Babylon took place.

12   After the deportation to Babylon:

1 a. Showing the descent of Joseph, legally the father of Jesus, from Abraham and David, to whom the messianic promises were made.

Jechoniah was the father of Shealtiel,
Shealtiel the father of Zerubbabel,
Zerubbabel was the father of Abiud,   13
Abiud the father of Eliakim,
Eliakim the father of Azor,
Azor was the father of Zadok,   14
Zadok the father of Achim,
Achim the father of Eliud,
Eliud was the father of Eleazar,   15
Eleazar the father of Matthan,
Matthan the father of Jacob;
and Jacob was the father of Joseph the husband of Mary;   16
of her was born Jesus who is called Christ.

The sum of generations is therefore: fourteen from Abraham to David; 17 fourteen from David to the Babylonian deportation; and fourteen from the Babylonian deportation to Christ.

The virginal conception of Christ

This is how Jesus Christ came to be born. His mother Mary was betrothed 18 to Joseph;[b] but before they came to live together she was found to be with child through the Holy Spirit. •Her husband Joseph, being a man of honour and 19 wanting to spare her publicity, decided to divorce her informally. •He had 20 made up his mind to do this when the angel of the Lord appeared to him in a dream and said, 'Joseph son of David, do not be afraid to take Mary home as your wife, because she has conceived what is in her by the Holy Spirit. •She 21 will give birth to a son and you must name him Jesus, because he is the one who is to save[c] his people from their sins.' •Now all this took place to fulfil the words 22 spoken by the Lord through the prophet:

> *The virgin will conceive and give birth to a son*   23
> *and they will call him Immanuel,*[d]

a name which means 'God-is-with-us'. •When Joseph woke up he did what the 24 angel of the Lord had told him to do: he took his wife to his home •and, though 25 he had not had intercourse with her, she gave birth to a son; and he named him Jesus.

The visit of the Magi

2 After Jesus had been born at Bethlehem in Judaea during the reign of King 1 Herod,[a] some wise men came to Jerusalem from the east. •'Where is the infant 2 king of the Jews?' they asked. 'We saw his star as it rose[b] and have come to do him homage.' •When King Herod heard this he was perturbed, and so was the whole 3 of Jerusalem. •He called together all the chief priests and the scribes of the people, 4 and enquired of them where the Christ was to be born. •'At Bethlehem in Judaea,' 5 they told him 'for this is what the prophet wrote:

> *And you, Bethlehem, in the land of Judah,*   6
> *you are by no means least among the leaders of Judah,*
> *for out of you will come a leader*
> *who will shepherd my people Israel'.*[c]

Then Herod summoned the wise men to see him privately. He asked them the 7

8 exact date on which the star had appeared, •and sent them on to Bethlehem.
'Go and find out all about the child,' he said 'and when you have found him,
9 let me know, so that I too may go and do him homage.' •Having listened to
what the king had to say, they set out. And there in front of them was the star
they had seen rising; it went forward and halted over the place where the child
10/11 was. •The sight of the star filled them with delight, •and going into the house
they saw the child with his mother Mary, and falling to their knees they did him
homage. Then, opening their treasures, they offered him gifts of gold and
12 frankincense and myrrh.[d] •But they were warned in a dream not to go back to
Herod, and returned to their own country by a different way.

The flight into Egypt. The massacre of the Innocents

13 After they had left, the angel of the Lord appeared to Joseph in a dream
and said, 'Get up, take the child and his mother with you, and escape into Egypt,
and stay there until I tell you, because Herod intends to search for the child and
14 do away with him'. •So Joseph got up and, taking the child and his mother
15 with him, left that night for Egypt, •where he stayed until Herod was dead. This
was to fulfil what the Lord had spoken through the prophet:

I called my son out of Egypt.[e]

16 Herod was furious when he realised that he had been outwitted by the
wise men, and in Bethlehem and its surrounding district he had all the male
children killed who were two years old or under, reckoning by the date he
17 had been careful to ask the wise men. •It was then that the words spoken
through the prophet Jeremiah were fulfilled:

18
> *A voice was heard in Ramah,*
> *sobbing and loudly lamenting:*
> *it was Rachel weeping for her children,*
> *refusing to be comforted*
> *because they were no more.*[f]

From Egypt to Nazareth

19 After Herod's death, the angel of the Lord appeared in a dream to Joseph in
20 Egypt •and said, 'Get up, take the child and his mother with you and go back to
21 the land of Israel, for those who wanted to kill the child are dead'. •So Joseph got
up and, taking the child and his mother with him, went back to the land of Israel.
22 But when he learnt that Archelaus[g] had succeeded his father Herod as ruler of
Judaea he was afraid to go there, and being warned in a dream he left for the
23 region of Galilee.[h] •There he settled in a town called Nazareth. In this way the
words spoken through the prophets were to be fulfilled:

He will be called a Nazarene.

---

b. In a Jewish betrothal the man was already called the 'husband' of the woman, and he could
release himself from the engagement only by an act of repudiation, v. 19.   c. 'Jesus' (Hebr.
Yehoshua) means 'Yahweh saves'.   d. Is. 7: 14
2 a. About 5 or 4 B.C. Herod was king of Judaea, Idumaea and Samaria from 37-4 B.C.
b. 'In the east' is an alternative translation, here and in v. 9.   c. Mi 5:1   d. The wealth and
perfumes of Arabia.   e. Ho 11:1   f. Jr 31:15   g. Ethnarch of Judaea, 4 B.C. to A.D. 6.
h. The territory of Herod Antipas.

II. THE KINGDOM OF HEAVEN PROCLAIMED

A. NARRATIVE SECTION

The preaching of John the Baptist

3 In due course John the Baptist appeared; he preached in the wilderness of ₁
Judaea and this was his message: •'Repent, for the kingdom of heaven* is ₂
close at hand'. •This was the man the prophet Isaiah spoke of when he said: ₃

> *A voice cries in the wilderness:*
> *Prepare a way for the Lord,*
> *make his paths straight.*[b]

This man John wore a garment made of camel-hair with a leather belt round his ₄
waist, and his food was locusts and wild honey. •Then Jerusalem and all Judaea ₅
and the whole Jordan district made their way to him, •and as they were baptised ₆
by him in the river Jordan they confessed their sins. •But when he saw a ₇
number of Pharisees and Sadducees[c] coming for baptism he said to them,
'Brood of vipers, who warned you to fly from the retribution that is coming? ₈
But if you are repentant, produce the appropriate fruit, •and do not presume to ₉
tell yourselves, "We have Abraham for our father", because, I tell you, God can
raise children for Abraham from these stones. •Even now the axe is laid to the roots ₁₀
of the trees, so that any tree which fails to produce good fruit will be cut down
and thrown on the fire. •I baptise you in water for repentance, but the one who ₁₁
follows me is more powerful than I am, and I am not fit to carry his sandals; he
will baptise you with the Holy Spirit and fire. •His winnowing-fan is in his hand; ₁₂
he will clear his threshing-floor and gather his wheat into the barn; but the chaff
he will burn in a fire that will never go out.'

Jesus is baptised

Then Jesus appeared: he came from Galilee to the Jordan to be baptised by ₁₃
John. •John tried to dissuade him. 'It is I who need baptism from you' he said ₁₄
'and yet you come to me!' •But Jesus replied, 'Leave it like this for the time being; ₁₅
it is fitting that we should, in this way, do all that righteousness demands'. At this,
John gave in to him.

As soon as Jesus was baptised he came up from the water, and suddenly the ₁₆
heavens opened and he saw the Spirit of God descending like a dove and coming
down on him.   •And a voice spoke from heaven, 'This is my Son, the Beloved; ₁₇
my favour rests on him'.

Temptation in the wilderness

4 Then Jesus was led by the Spirit out into the wilderness to be tempted by the ₁
devil. •He fasted for forty days and forty nights, after which he was very ₂
hungry, •and the tempter came and said to him, 'If you are the Son of God, tell ₃
these stones to turn into loaves'. •But he replied, 'Scripture says: ₄

> *Man does not live on bread alone*
> *but on every word that comes from the mouth of God'.*[a]

The devil then took him to the holy city and made him stand on the parapet of ₅

6 the Temple. •'If you are the Son of God' he said 'throw yourself down; for
scripture says:

> *He will put you in his angels' charge,*
> *and they will support you on their hands*
> *in case you hurt your foot against a stone'.*[b]

7 Jesus said to him, 'Scripture also says:

> *You must not put the Lord your God to the test'.*[c]

8 Next, taking him to a very high mountain, the devil showed him all the kingdoms
9 of the world and their splendour. •'I will give you all these' he said, 'if you fall at
10 my feet and worship me.' •Then Jesus replied, 'Be off, Satan! For scripture says:

> *You must worship the Lord your God,*
> *and serve him alone.'*[d]

11 Then the devil left him, and angels appeared and looked after him.

Return to Galilee

12
13   Hearing that John had been arrested he went back to Galilee, •and leaving
Nazareth he went and settled in Capernaum, a lakeside town on the borders of
14 Zebulun and Naphtali. •In this way the prophecy of Isaiah was to be fulfilled:

15   *Land of Zebulun! Land of Naphtali!*
> *Way of the sea on the far side of Jordan,*
> *Galilee of the nations!*
16 > *The people that lived in darkness*
> *has seen a great light;*
> *on those who dwell in the land and shadow of death*
> *a light has dawned.'*[e]

17 From that moment Jesus began his preaching with the message, 'Repent, for
the kingdom of heaven is close at hand'.

The first four disciples are called

18   As he was walking by the Sea of Galilee he saw two brothers, Simon, who
was called Peter, and his brother Andrew; they were making a cast in the lake
19 with their net, for they were fishermen. •And he said to them, 'Follow me and I
20 will make you fishers of men'. •And they left their nets at once and followed him.
21   Going on from there he saw another pair of brothers, James son of Zebedee
and his brother John; they were in their boat with their father Zebedee, mending
22 their nets, and he called them. •At once, leaving the boat and their father, they
followed him.

Jesus preaches and heals the sick

23   He went round the whole of Galilee teaching in their synagogues, proclaiming
the Good News of the kingdom and curing all kinds of diseases and sickness

3 a. 'kingdom of God'; Mt's phrase reflects the Jewish scruple against using the name of God.
b. Is 40:3   **c.** Pharisees: members of a Jewish sect known for its strict observance of the
Law as it was interpreted and developed by their rabbis. Sadducees: conservatives who
observed the written form of the Law in the scriptures.
4 a. Dt 8:3   **b.** Ps 91:11-12   **c.** Dt 6:16   **d.** Dt 6:13   **e.** Is 8:23-9:1

among the people. •His fame spread throughout Syria,*f* and those who were 24
suffering from diseases and painful complaints of one kind or another, the
possessed, epileptics, the paralysed, were all brought to him, and he cured them.
Large crowds followed him, coming from Galilee, the Decapolis,*g* Jerusalem, 25
Judaea and Transjordania.

B. THE SERMON ON THE MOUNT*a*

The Beatitudes

5 Seeing the crowds, he went up the hill. There he sat down and was joined by 1
his disciples. •Then he began to speak. This is what he taught them: 2

'How happy are the poor in spirit; 3
theirs is the kingdom of heaven.
Happy *the gentle:*b 4
they shall have the earth for their heritage.
Happy those who mourn: 5
they shall be comforted.
Happy those who hunger and thirst for what is right: 6
they shall be satisfied.
Happy the merciful: 7
they shall have mercy shown them.
Happy the pure in heart: 8
they shall see God.
Happy the peacemakers: 9
they shall be called sons of God.
Happy those who are persecuted in the cause of right: 10
theirs is the kingdom of heaven.

'Happy are you when people abuse you and persecute you and speak all kinds 11
of calumny against you on my account. •Rejoice and be glad, for your reward will 12
be great in heaven; this is how they persecuted the prophets before you.

Salt of the earth and light of the world

'You are the salt of the earth. But if salt becomes tasteless, what can make it 13
salty again? It is good for nothing, and can only be thrown out to be trampled
underfoot by men.

'You are the light of the world. A city built on a hill-top cannot be hidden. 14
No one lights a lamp to put it under a tub; they put it on the lamp-stand where 15
it shines for everyone in the house. •In the same way your light must shine in the 16
sight of men, so that, seeing your good works, they may give the praise to your
Father in heaven.

The fulfilment of the Law

'Do not imagine that I have come to abolish the Law or the Prophets. I have 17
come not to abolish but to complete them. •I tell you solemnly, till heaven 18
and earth disappear, not one dot, not one little stroke, shall disappear from
the Law until its purpose is achieved. •Therefore, the man who infringes even 19
one of the least of these commandments and teaches others to do the same will
be considered the least in the kingdom of heaven; but the man who keeps them
and teaches them will be considered great in the kingdom of heaven.

The new standard higher than the old

20 'For I tell you, if your virtue goes no deeper than that of the scribes and Pharisees, you will never get into the kingdom of heaven.

21 'You have learnt how it was said to our ancestors: *You must not kill;*^c and if
22 anyone does kill he must answer for it before the court. •But I say this to you: anyone who is angry with his brother will answer for it before the court; if a man calls his brother "Fool"^d he will answer for it before the Sanhedrin;^e and if a man
23 calls him "Renegade"^f he will answer for it in hell fire. •So then, if you are bringing your offering to the altar and there remember that your brother has something
24 against you, •leave your offering there before the altar, go and be reconciled with
25 your brother first, and then come back and present your offering. •Come to terms with your opponent in good time while you are still on the way to the court with him, or he may hand you over to the judge and the judge to the officer, and you
26 will be thrown into prison. •I tell you solemnly, you will not get out till you have paid the last penny.

27
28 'You have learnt how it was said: *You must not commit adultery.*^g •But I say this to you: if a man looks at a woman lustfully, he has already committed
29 adultery with her in his heart. •If your right eye should cause you to sin, tear it out and throw it away; for it will do you less harm to lose one part of you than to
30 have your whole body thrown into hell. •And if your right hand should cause you to sin, cut it off and throw it away; for it will do you less harm to lose one part of you than to have your whole body go to hell.

31 'It has also been said: *Anyone who divorces his wife must give her a writ of*
32 *dismissal.*^h •But I say this to you: everyone who divorces his wife, except for the case of fornication, makes her an adulteress; and anyone who marries a divorced woman commits adultery.

33 'Again, you have learnt how it was said to our ancestors: *You must not break*
34 *your oath, but must fulfil your oaths to the Lord.*ⁱ •But I say this to you: do not
35 swear at all, either by *heaven*, since that is God's throne; •or by *the earth*, since
36 that is *his footstool;* or by Jerusalem, since that is *the city of the great king.* •Do not swear by your own head either, since you cannot turn a single hair white or black.
37 All you need say is "Yes" if you mean yes, "No" if you mean no; anything more than this comes from the evil one.

38
39 'You have learnt how it was said: *Eye for eye and tooth for tooth.*^j •But I say this to you: offer the wicked man no resistance. On the contrary, if anyone hits
40 you on the right cheek, offer him the other as well; •if a man takes you to law
41 and would have your tunic, let him have your cloak as well. •And if anyone
42 orders you to go one mile, go two miles with him. •Give to anyone who asks, and if anyone wants to borrow, do not turn away.

43 'You have learnt how it was said: *You must love your neighbour* and hate your
44 enemy.^k •But I say this to you: love your enemies and pray for those who
45 persecute you; •in this way you will be sons of your Father in heaven, for he causes his sun to rise on bad men as well as good, and his rain to fall on honest

---

f. I.e. Galilee and the districts listed in v. 25.   g. The 'ten towns', a region south-east of Galilee.
5 a. In this discourse, which occupies three ch. of this gospel, Mt has included sayings which probably originated on other occasions (cf. their parallels in Lk).   **b.** Or 'the lowly'; the word comes from the Greek version of Ps 37.   **c.** Ex 20:13   **d.** Translating an Aramaic term of contempt.   **e.** The High Court at Jerusalem.   **f.** Apostasy was the most repulsive of all sins.   **g.** Ex 20:14   **h.** Dt 24:1   **i.** Ex 20:7   **j.** Ex 21:24   **k.** The quotation is from Lv 19:18; the second part of this commandment, not in the written Law, is an Aramaic way of saying 'You do not have to love your enemy'.

and dishonest men alike. •For if you love those who love you, what right have 46 you to claim any credit? Even the tax collectors[1] do as much, do they not? •And 47 if you save your greetings for your brothers, are you doing anything exceptional? Even the pagans do as much, do they not? •You must therefore be perfect just as 48 your heavenly Father is perfect.

Almsgiving in secret

6 'Be careful not to parade your good deeds before men to attract their notice; 1 by doing this you will lose all reward from your Father in heaven. •So when 2 you give alms, do not have it trumpeted before you; this is what the hypocrites do in the synagogues and in the streets to win men's admiration. I tell you solemnly, they have had their reward. •But when you give alms, your left hand 3 must not know what your right is doing; •your almsgiving must be secret, and 4 your Father who sees all that is done in secret will reward you.

Prayer in secret

'And when you pray, do not imitate the hypocrites: they love to say their 5 prayers standing up in the synagogues and at the street corners for people to see them. I tell you solemnly, they have had their reward. •But when you 6 pray, *go to your private room and, when you have shut your door, pray*[a] to your Father who is in that secret place, and your Father who sees all that is done in secret will reward you.

How to pray. The Lord's Prayer

'In your prayers do not babble as the pagans do, for they think that by using 7 many words they will make themselves heard. •Do not be like them; your Father 8 knows what you need before you ask him. •So you should pray like this: 9

> 'Our Father in heaven,
> may your name be held holy,
> your kingdom come,   10
> your will be done,
> on earth as in heaven.
> Give us today our daily bread.   11
> And forgive us our debts,   12
> as we have forgiven those who are in debt to us.
> And do not put us to the test,   13
> but save us from the evil one.

Yes, if you forgive others their failings, your heavenly Father will forgive you 14 yours; •but if you do not forgive others, your Father will not forgive your 15 failings either.

Fasting in secret

'When you fast do not put on a gloomy look as the hypocrites do: they pull 16 long faces to let men know they are fasting. I tell you solemnly, they have had their reward. •But when you fast, put oil on your head and wash your face, 17 so that no one will know you are fasting except your Father who sees all that is 18 done in secret; and your Father who sees all that is done in secret will reward you.

True treasures

19 'Do not store up treasures for yourselves on earth, where moths and
20 woodworms destroy them and thieves can break in and steal. •But store up
treasures for yourselves in heaven, where neither moth nor woodworms destroy
21 them and thieves cannot break in and steal. •For where your treasure is, there
will your heart be also.

The eye, the lamp of the body

22 'The lamp of the body is the eye. It follows that if your eye is sound, your
23 whole body will be filled with light. •But if your eye is diseased, your whole body
will be all darkness. If then, the light inside you is darkness, what darkness
that will be!

God and money

24 'No one can be the slave of two masters: he will either hate the first and love
the second, or treat the first with respect and the second with scorn. You cannot
be the slave both of God and of money.

Trust in Providence

25 'That is why I am telling you not to worry about your life and what you are to
eat, nor about your body and how you are to clothe it. Surely life means more than
26 food, and the body more than clothing! •Look at the birds in the sky. They do not
sow or reap or gather into barns; yet your heavenly Father feeds them. Are you
27 not worth much more than they are? •Can any of you, for all his worrying, add
28 one single cubit to his span of life? •And why worry about clothing? Think of the
29 flowers growing in the fields; they never have to work or spin; •yet I assure you
30 that not even Solomon in all his regalia was robed like one of these. •Now if that
is how God clothes the grass in the field which is there today and thrown into the
furnace tomorrow, will he not much more look after you, you men of little faith?
31 So do not worry; do not say, "What are we to eat? What are we to drink? How
32 are we to be clothed?" •It is the pagans who set their hearts on all these things.
33 Your heavenly Father knows you need them all. •Set your hearts on his kingdom
first, and on his righteousness, and all these other things will be given you as well.
34 So do not worry about tomorrow: tomorrow will take care of itself. Each day
has enough trouble of its own.

Do not judge

¹₂ **7** 'Do not judge, and you will not be judged; •because the judgements you give
are the judgements you will get, and the amount you measure out is the
3 amount you will be given. •Why do you observe the splinter in your brother's
4 eye and never notice the plank in your own? •How dare you say to your brother,
"Let me take the splinter out of your eye", when all the time there is a plank in
5 your own? •Hypocrite! Take the plank out of your own eye first, and then you
will see clearly enough to take the splinter out of your brother's eye.

---

l. They were employed by the occupying power and this earned them popular contempt.
6 a. Not a direct quotation but an allusion to the practice common in the O.T., see 2 K 4:33.

Do not profane sacred things

'Do not give dogs what is holy;[a] and do not throw your pearls in front of pigs, 6 or they may trample them and then turn on you and tear you to pieces.

Effective prayer

'Ask, and it will be given to you; search, and you will find; knock, and the 7 door will be opened to you. •For the one who asks always receives; the one who 8 searches always finds; the one who knocks will always have the door opened to him. •Is there a man among you who would hand his son a stone when he asked 9 for bread? •Or would hand him a snake when he asked for a fish? •If you, then, 10 11 who are evil, know how to give your children what is good, how much more will your Father in heaven give good things to those who ask him!

The golden rule

'So always treat others as you would like them to treat you; that is the 12 meaning of the Law and the Prophets.

The two ways

'Enter by the narrow gate, since the road that leads to perdition is wide and 13 spacious, and many take it; •but it is a narrow gate and a hard road that leads 14 to life, and only a few find it.

False prophets

'Beware of false prophets[b] who come to you disguised as sheep but underneath 15 are ravenous wolves. •You will be able to tell them by their fruits. Can people 16 pick grapes from thorns, or figs from thistles? •In the same way, a sound tree 17 produces good fruit but a rotten tree bad fruit. •A sound tree cannot bear bad 18 fruit, nor a rotten tree bear good fruit. •Any tree that does not produce good 19 fruit is cut down and thrown on the fire. •I repeat, you will be able to tell them by 20 their fruits.

The true disciple

'It is not those who say to me, "Lord, Lord", who will enter the kingdom of 21 heaven, but the person who does the will of my Father in heaven. •When the day[c] 22 comes many will say to me, "Lord, Lord, did we not prophesy in your name, cast out demons in your name, work many miracles in your name?" •Then 23 I shall tell them to their faces: I have never known you; *away from me, you evil men!*'

'Therefore, everyone who listens to these words of mine and acts on them 24 will be like a sensible man who built his house on rock. •Rain came down, floods 25 rose, gales blew and hurled themselves against that house, and it did not fall: it was founded on rock. •But everyone who listens to these words of mine and does 26 not act on them will be like a stupid man who built his house on sand. •Rain 27 came down, floods rose, gales blew and struck that house, and it fell; and what a fall it had!'

The amazement of the crowds

Jesus had now finished what he wanted to say, and his teaching made a deep 28 impression on the people •because he taught them with authority, and not like 29 their own scribes.[d]

III. THE KINGDOM OF HEAVEN IS PREACHED

A. NARRATIVE SECTION: TEN MIRACLES

Cure of a leper

1 After he had come down from the mountain large crowds followed him.
2 A leper now came up and bowed low in front of him.' Sir,' he said 'if you want
3 to, you can cure me.' •Jesus stretched out his hand, touched him and said, 'Of
4 course I want to! Be cured!' And his leprosy was cured at once. •Then Jesus said
to him, 'Mind you do not tell anyone, but go and show yourself to the priest
and make the offering prescribed by Moses, as evidence for them'.

Cure of the centurion's servant

5   When he went into Capernaum a centurion came up and pleaded with him.
6
7 'Sir,' he said 'my servant is lying at home paralysed, and in great pain.' •'I will
8 come myself and cure him' said Jesus. •The centurion replied, 'Sir, I am not
worthy to have you under my roof; just give the word and my servant will be
9 cured. •For I am under authority myself, and have soldiers under me; and I say
to one man: Go, and he goes; to another: Come here, and he comes; to my
10 servant: Do this, and he does it.' •When Jesus heard this he was astonished and
said to those following him, 'I tell you solemnly, nowhere in Israel have
11 I found faith like this. •And I tell you that many will come from east and west
to take their places with Abraham and Isaac and Jacob at the feast in the kingdom
12 of heaven; •but the subjects of the kingdom[a] will be turned out into the dark,
13 where there will be weeping and grinding of teeth.' •And to the centurion Jesus
said, 'Go back, then; you have believed, so let this be done for you'. And the
servant was cured at that moment.

Cure of Peter's mother-in-law

14   And going into Peter's house Jesus found Peter's mother-in-law in bed with
15 fever. •He touched her hand and the fever left her, and she got up and began
to wait on him.

A number of cures

16   That evening they brought him many who were possessed by devils. He cast
17 out the spirits with a word and cured all who were sick. •This was to fulfil the
prophecy of Isaiah:

He took our sicknesses away and carried our diseases for us.[b]

Hardships of the apostolic calling

18   When Jesus saw the great crowds all about him he gave orders to leave for the
19 other side.[c] •One of the scribes then came up and said to him, 'Master, I will
20 follow you wherever you go'. •Jesus replied, 'Foxes have holes and the birds
of the air have nests, but the Son of Man has nowhere to lay his head'.

7 a. The meat of animals which have been offered in sacrifice in the Temple; the application is
to the parading of holy beliefs and practices in front of those who cannot understand them.
b. Lying teachers of religion.   c. The day of Judgement.   d. Doctors of the law, who but-
tressed their teaching by quotation from the scriptures and traditions.
8 a. The Jews, natural heirs of the promises.   b. Is 53:4   c. The E. bank of Lake Tiberias.

Another man, one of his disciples, said to him, 'Sir, let me go and bury my 21
father first'. •But Jesus replied, 'Follow me, and leave the dead to bury their dead'. 22

The calming of the storm

Then he got into the boat followed by his disciples. •Without warning $^{23}_{24}$
a storm broke over the lake, so violent that the waves were breaking right over
the boat. But he was asleep. •So they went to him and woke him saying, 'Save us, 25
Lord, we are going down!' •And he said to them, 'Why are you so frightened, you 26
men of little faith?' And with that he stood up and rebuked the winds and the
sea; and all was calm again. •The men were astounded and said, 'Whatever kind 27
of man is this? Even the winds and the sea obey him.'

The demoniacs of Gadara

When he reached the country of the Gadarenes on the other side, two 28
demoniacs came towards him out of the tombs—creatures so fierce that no one
could pass that way. •They stood there shouting, 'What do you want with us, 29
Son of God? Have you come here to torture us before the time?'[d] •Now some 30
distance away there was a large herd of pigs feeding, •and the devils pleaded 31
with Jesus, 'If you cast us out, send us into the herd of pigs'. •And he said to them, 32
'Go then', and they came out and made for the pigs; and at that the whole herd
charged down the cliff into the lake and perished in the water. •The swineherds 33
ran off and made for the town, where they told the whole story, including what
had happened to the demoniacs. •At this the whole town set out to meet Jesus; 34
and as soon as they saw him they implored him to leave the neighbourhood.

Cure of a paralytic

9 He got back in the boat, crossed the water and came to his own town.[a] •Then $^{1}_{2}$
some people appeared, bringing him a paralytic stretched out on a bed. Seeing
their faith, Jesus said to the paralytic, 'Courage, my child, your sins are forgiven'.
And at this some scribes said to themselves, 'This man is blaspheming'. •Knowing $^{3}_{4}$
what was in their minds Jesus said, 'Why do you have such wicked thoughts in
your hearts? •Now, which of these is easier: to say, "Your sins are forgiven", 5
or to say, "Get up and walk"? •But to prove to you that the Son of Man has 6
authority on earth to forgive sins,'—he said to the paralytic—'get up, and pick up
your bed and go off home'. •And the man got up and went home. •A feeling of $^{7}_{8}$
awe came over the crowd when they saw this, and they praised God for giving
such power to men.

The call of Matthew

As Jesus was walking on from there he saw a man named Matthew[b] sitting by the 9
customs house, and he said to him, 'Follow me'. And he got up and followed him.

Eating with sinners

While he was at dinner in the house it happened that a number of tax collectors 10
and sinners[c] came to sit at the table with Jesus and his disciples. •When the 11
Pharisees saw this, they said to his disciples, 'Why does your master eat with
tax collectors and sinners?' •When he heard this he replied, 'It is not the healthy 12
who need the doctor, but the sick. •Go and learn the meaning of the words: 13
What I want is mercy, not sacrifice.[d] And indeed I did not come to call the virtuous,
but sinners.'

A discussion on fasting

14   Then John's[e] disciples came to him and said, 'Why is it that we and the
15 Pharisees fast, but your disciples do not?' •Jesus replied, 'Surely the bridegroom's
attendants would never think of mourning as long as the bridegroom is still with
them? But the time will come for the bridegroom to be taken away from them,
16 and then they will fast. •No one puts a piece of unshrunken cloth on to an old
17 cloak, because the patch pulls away from the cloak and the tear gets worse. •Nor
do people put new wine into old wineskins; if they do, the skins burst, the wine
runs out, and the skins are lost. No; they put new wine into fresh skins and both
are preserved.'[f]

Cure of the woman with a haemorrhage. The official's daughter raised to life

18   While he was speaking to them, up came one of the officials, who bowed low
in front of him and said, 'My daughter has just died, but come and lay your hand
19 on her and her life will be saved'. •Jesus rose and, with his disciples, followed him.
20   Then from behind him came a woman, who had suffered from a haemorrhage
21 for twelve years, and she touched the fringe of his cloak, •for she said to herself,
22 'If I can only touch his cloak I shall be well again'. •Jesus turned round and saw
her; and he said to her, 'Courage, my daughter, your faith has restored you to
health'. And from that moment the woman was well again.

23   When Jesus reached the official's house and saw the flute-players, with the
24 crowd making a commotion[g] he said, •'Get out of here; the little girl is not dead,
25 she is asleep'. And they laughed at him. •But when the people had been turned
26 out he went inside and took the little girl by the hand; and she stood up. •And the
news spread all round the countryside.

Cure of two blind men

27   As Jesus went on his way two blind men followed him shouting, 'Take pity
28 on us, Son of David'. •And when Jesus reached the house the blind men came
up with him and he said to them, 'Do you believe I can do this?' They said, 'Sir,
29 we do'. •Then he touched their eyes saying, 'Your faith deserves it, so let this
30 be done for you'. •And their sight returned. Then Jesus sternly warned them,
31 'Take care that no one learns about this'. •But when they had gone, they talked
about him all over the countryside.

Cure of a dumb demoniac

32   They had only just left when a man was brought to him, a dumb demoniac.
33 And when the devil was cast out, the dumb man spoke and the people were
34 amazed. 'Nothing like this has ever been seen in Israel' they said. •But the
Pharisees said, 'It is through the prince of devils that he casts out devils'.

The distress of the crowds

35   Jesus made a tour through all the towns and villages, teaching in their
synagogues, proclaiming the Good News of the kingdom and curing all kinds
of diseases and sickness.

---

d. The day of Judgement, when the reign of God would banish all demons.
9 a. Capernaum, cf. 4:13.   **b.** Called Levi by Mk and Lk.   **c.** Social outcasts, made 'unclean' by breaking religious laws or following a disreputable profession.   **d.** Ho 6:6   **e.** John
the Baptist.   **f.** New devotional exercises, like those which John and the Pharisees add to
the religion of the old order, will not preserve it.   **g.** The loud wailing of the oriental mourner.

And when he saw the crowds he felt sorry for them because they were harassed 36
and dejected, like sheep without a shepherd. •Then he said to his disciples, 37
'The harvest is rich but the labourers are few, so ask the Lord of the harvest to
send labourers to his harvest'.

B. THE INSTRUCTION OF THE APOSTLES

The mission of the Twelve

10 He summoned his twelve disciples, and gave them authority over unclean 1
spirits with power to cast them out and to cure all kinds of diseases and
sickness.

These are the names of the twelve apostles: first, Simon who is called Peter, 2
and his brother Andrew; James the son of Zebedee, and his brother John; •Philip 3
and Bartholomew; Thomas, and Matthew the tax collector; James the son of
Alphaeus, and Thaddaeus; •Simon the Zealot and Judas Iscariot, the one who 4
was to betray him. •These twelve Jesus sent out, instructing them as follows: 5

'Do not turn your steps to pagan territory, and do not enter any Samaritan
town; •go rather to the lost sheep of the House of Israel. •And as you go, ⁶₇
proclaim that the kingdom of heaven is close at hand. •Cure the sick, raise the 8
dead, cleanse the lepers, cast out devils. You received without charge, give without
charge. •Provide yourselves with no gold or silver, not even with a few coppers 9
for your purses, •with no haversack for the journey or spare tunic or footwear 10
or a staff, for the workman deserves his keep.

'Whatever town or village you go into, ask for someone trustworthy and stay 11
with him until you leave. •As you enter his house, salute it, •and if the house ¹²₁₃
deserves it, let your peace descend upon it; if it does not, let your peace come back
to you. •And if anyone does not welcome you or listen to what you have to say, 14
as you walk out of the house or town shake the dust from your feet. •I tell you 15
solemnly, on the day of Judgement it will not go as hard with the land of
Sodom and Gomorrah as with that town. •Remember, I am sending you out 16
like sheep among wolves; so be cunning as serpents and yet as harmless as doves.

The missionaries will be persecuted[a]

'Beware of men: they will hand you over to sanhedrins and scourge you in 17
their synagogues. •You will be dragged before governors and kings for my sake, 18
to bear witness before them and the pagans. •But when they hand you over, do 19
not worry about how to speak or what to say; what you are to say will be given to
you when the time comes; •because it is not you who will be speaking; the Spirit 20
of your Father will be speaking in you.

'Brother will betray brother to death, and the father his child; children will 21
rise against their parents and have them put to death. •You will be hated by all 22
men on account of my name; but the man who stands firm to the end will be saved.
If they persecute you in one town, take refuge in the next; and if they persecute 23
you in that, take refuge in another. I tell you solemnly, you will not have gone
the round of the towns of Israel before the Son of Man comes.

'The disciple is not superior to his teacher, nor the slave to his master. •It is ²⁴₂₅
enough for the disciple that he should grow to be like his teacher, and the slave
like his master. If they have called the master of the house Beelzebul, what will
they not say of his household?

Open and fearless speech

26   'Do not be afraid of them therefore. For everything that is now covered will
27   be uncovered, and everything now hidden will be made clear. •What I say to
you in the dark, tell in the daylight; what you hear in whispers, proclaim from
the housetops.

28   'Do not be afraid of those who kill the body but cannot kill the soul; fear him
29   rather who can destroy both body and soul in hell. •Can you not buy two
sparrows for a penny? And yet not one falls to the ground without your Father
30   knowing. •Why, every hair on your head has been counted. •So there is no
31   need to be afraid; you are worth more than hundreds of sparrows.

32   'So if anyone declares himself for me in the presence of men, I will declare my-
33   self for him in the presence of my Father in heaven. •But the one who disowns
me in the presence of men, I will disown in the presence of my Father in
heaven.

Jesus, the cause of dissension

34   'Do not suppose that I have come to bring peace to the earth: it is not peace I
35   have come to bring, but a sword. •For I have come to set *a man against his father*,
a daughter against her mother, a daughter-in-law against her mother-in-law.
36   *A man's enemies will be those of his own household.* [b]

Renouncing self to follow Jesus

37   'Anyone who prefers father or mother to me is not worthy of me. Anyone
38   who prefers son or daughter to me is not worthy of me. •Anyone who does not
39   take his cross and follow in my footsteps is not worthy of me. •Anyone who
finds his life will lose it; anyone who loses his life for my sake will find it.

Conclusion

40   'Anyone who welcomes you welcomes me; and those who welcome me
welcome the one who sent me.
41   'Anyone who welcomes a prophet because he is a prophet will have
a prophet's reward; and anyone who welcomes a holy man because he is a holy
man will have a holy man's reward.
42   'If anyone gives so much as a cup of cold water to one of these little ones
because he is a disciple, then I tell you solemnly, he will most certainly not lose
his reward.'

IV. THE MYSTERY OF THE KINGDOM OF HEAVEN

A. NARRATIVE SECTION

1   **11** When Jesus had finished instructing his twelve disciples he moved on from
there to teach and preach in their towns. [a]

The Baptist's question. Jesus commends him

2   Now John in his prison had heard what Christ was doing and he sent his
3   disciples to ask him, •'Are you the one who is to come, or have we got to wait for

---

10 a. The conditions described in vv. 17-39 are those of a later time than this first mission
of the Twelve.   **b.** Mi 7:6
11 a. I.e. the Jews' towns.

someone else?' •Jesus answered, 'Go back and tell John what you hear and see; 4
the blind see again, and the lame walk, lepers are cleansed, and the deaf hear, 5
and the dead are raised to life and the Good News is proclaimed to the poor;[b]
and happy is the man who does not lose faith in me'. 6

As the messengers were leaving, Jesus began to talk to the people about John: 7
'What did you go out into the wilderness to see? A reed swaying in the breeze?
No? •Then what did you go out to see? A man wearing fine clothes? Oh no, those 8
who wear fine clothes are to be found in palaces. •Then what did you go out for? 9
To see a prophet? Yes, I tell you, and much more than a prophet: •he is the one 10
of whom scripture says:

> *Look, I am going to send my messenger before you;*
> *he will prepare your way before you.*[c]

'I tell you solemnly, of all the children born of women, a greater than John 11
the Baptist has never been seen; yet the least in the kingdom of heaven is
greater than he is. •Since John the Baptist came, up to this present time, the 12
kingdom of heaven has been subjected to violence and the violent are taking it
by storm. •Because it was towards John that all the prophecies of the prophets 13
and of the Law were leading; •and he, if you will believe me, is the Elijah who 14
was to return.[d] •If anyone has ears to hear, let him listen! 15

Jesus condemns his contemporaries

'What description can I find for this generation? It is like children shouting to 16
each other as they sit in the market place:

> "We played the pipes for you,   17
> and you wouldn't dance;
> we sang dirges,
> and you wouldn't be mourners".

'For John came, neither eating nor drinking, and they say, "He is possessed". 18
The Son of Man came, eating and drinking, and they say, "Look, a glutton and 19
a drunkard, a friend of tax collectors and sinners". Yet wisdom has been proved
right by her actions.'

Lament over the lake-towns

Then he began to reproach the towns in which most of his miracles had been 20
worked, because they refused to repent.

'Alas for you, Chorazin! Alas for you, Bethsaida! For if the miracles done in 21
you had been done in Tyre and Sidon, they would have repented long ago in
sackcloth and ashes. •And still, I tell you that it will not go as hard on Judgement 22
day with Tyre and Sidon as with you. •And as for you, Capernaum, did you 23
want to be exalted as high as heaven? *You shall be thrown down to hell.*[e] For if the
miracles done in you had been done in Sodom, it would have been standing yet.
And still, I tell you that it will not go as hard with the land of Sodom on Judgement 24
day as with you.'

The Good News revealed to the simple. The Father and the Son

At that time Jesus exclaimed, 'I bless you, Father, Lord of heaven and of 25
earth, for hiding these things from the learned and the clever and revealing them
to mere children. •Yes, Father, for that is what it pleased you to do. •Everything 26/27
has been entrusted to me by my Father; and no one knows the Son except the

Father, just as no one knows the Father except the Son and those to whom the Son chooses to reveal him.

The gentle mastery of Christn28 'Come to me, all you who labour and are overburdened, and I will give you
29 rest. •Shoulder my yoke and learn from me, for I am gentle and humble in heart,
30 *and you will find rest for your souls.*[f] •Yes, my yoke is easy and my burden light.'

Picking corn on the sabbath

1 **12** At that time Jesus took a walk one sabbath day through the cornfields.
His disciples were hungry and began to pick ears of corn and eat them.
2 The Pharisees noticed it and said to him, 'Look, your disciples are doing
3 something that is forbidden on the sabbath'. •But he said to them, 'Have you
4 not read what David did when he and his followers were hungry—•how he went
into the house of God and how they ate the loaves of offering which neither he
nor his followers were allowed to eat, but which were for the priests alone?
5 Or again, have you not read in the Law that on the sabbath day the Temple
6 priests break the sabbath without being blamed for it? •Now here, I tell you,
7 is something greater than the Temple. •And if you had understood the meaning
of the words: *What I want is mercy, not sacrifice*, you would not have condemned
8 the blameless. •For the Son of Man is master of the sabbath.'

Cure of the man with a withered hand

9
10 He moved on from there and went to their synagogue, •and a man was there
at the time who had a withered hand. They asked him, 'Is it against the law to
11 cure a man on the sabbath day?' hoping for something to use against him. •But he
said to them, 'If any one of you here had only one sheep and it fell down a hole
12 on the sabbath day, would he not get hold of it and lift it out? •Now a man is far
more important than a sheep, so it follows that it is permitted to do good on the
13 sabbath day.' •Then he said to the man, 'Stretch out your hand'. He stretched it
14 out and his hand was better, as sound as the other one. •At this the Pharisees
went out and began to plot against him, discussing how to destroy him.

Jesus the 'servant of Yahweh'

15 Jesus knew this and withdrew from the district. Many followed him and he
16
17 cured them all, •but warned them not to make him known. •This was to fulfil
the prophecy of Isaiah:

18
Here is my servant whom I have chosen,
my beloved, the favourite of my soul.
I will endow him with my spirit,
and he will proclaim the true faith to the nations.
19
He will not brawl or shout,
nor will anyone hear his voice in the streets.
20
He will not break the crushed reed,
nor put out the smouldering wick
till he has led the truth to victory:
21
in his name the nations will put their hope.[a]

---

b. These are signs of the messianic age in the prophecies of Isaiah.   **c.** Ml 3:1   **d.** According to the last of the prophets, Ml 3:23.   **e.** Is 14   **f.** Jr 6:16
12 a. Is 42:1-4

Jesus and Beelzebul

Then they brought to him a blind and dumb demoniac; and he cured him, 22 so that the dumb man could speak and see. •All the people were astounded and 23 said, 'Can this be the Son of David?' •But when the Pharisees heard this they 24 said, 'The man casts out devils only through Beelzebul,[b] the prince of devils'.

Knowing what was in their minds he said to them, 'Every kingdom divided 25 against itself is heading for ruin; and no town, no household divided against itself can stand. •Now if Satan casts out Satan, he is divided against himself; 26 so how can his kingdom stand? •And if it is through Beelzebul that I cast out 27 devils, through whom do your own experts cast them out? Let them be your judges, then. •But if it is through the Spirit of God that I cast devils out, then 28 know that the kingdom of God has overtaken you.

'Or again, how can anyone make his way into a strong man's house and 29 burgle his property unless he has tied up the strong man first? Only then can he burgle his house.

'He who is not with me is against me, and he who does not gather with me 30 scatters. •And so I tell you, every one of men's sins and blasphemies will be for- 31 given, but blasphemy against the Spirit will not be forgiven. •And anyone who 32 says a word against the Son of Man will be forgiven; but let anyone speak against the Holy Spirit and he will not be forgiven either in this world or in the next.

Words betray the heart

'Make a tree sound and its fruit will be sound; make a tree rotten and its 33 fruit will be rotten. For the tree can be told by its fruit. •Brood of vipers, how 34 can your speech be good when you are evil? For a man's words flow out of what fills his heart. •A good man draws good things from his store of goodness; a bad 35 man draws bad things from his store of badness. •So I tell you this, that for 36 every unfounded word men utter they will answer on Judgement day, •since it 37 is by your words you will be acquitted, and by your words condemned.'

The sign of Jonah

Then some of the scribes and Pharisees spoke up. 'Master,' they said 'we 38 should like to see a sign[c] from you.' •He replied, 'It is an evil and unfaithful 39 generation that asks for a sign! The only sign it will be given is the sign of the prophet Jonah. •For as Jonah *was in the belly of the sea-monster for three* 40 *days and three nights,*[d] so will the Son of Man be in the heart of the earth for three days and three nights. •On Judgement day the men of Nineveh will stand 41 up with this generation and condemn it, because when Jonah preached they repented; and there is something greater than Jonah here. •On Judgement day 42 the Queen of the South will rise up with this generation and condemn it, because she came from the ends of the earth to hear the wisdom of Solomon; and there is something greater than Solomon here.

The return of the unclean spirit

'When an unclean spirit goes out of a man it wanders through waterless 43 country looking for a place to rest, and cannot find one. •Then it says, "I will 44 return to the home I came from". But on arrival, finding it unoccupied, swept and tidied, •it then goes off and collects seven other spirits more evil than itself, and 45 they go in and set up house there, so that the man ends up by being worse than he was before. That is what will happen to this evil generation.'

The true kinsmen of Jesus

46   He was still speaking to the crowds when his mother and his brothers[c] appeared; they were standing outside and were anxious to have a word with
48 him. •But to the man who told him this Jesus replied, 'Who is my mother?
49 Who are my brothers?' •And stretching out his hand towards his disciples he said,
50 'Here are my mother and my brothers. •Anyone who does the will of my Father in heaven, he is my brother and sister and mother.'

B. THE SERMON OF PARABLES

Introduction

¹₂ **13** That same day, Jesus left the house and sat by the lakeside, •but such crowds gathered round him that he got into a boat and sat there. The people
3 all stood on the beach, •and he told them many things in parables.

Parable of the sower

4   He said, 'Imagine a sower going out to sow. •As he sowed, some seeds fell
5 on the edge of the path, and the birds came and ate them up. •Others fell on patches of rock where they found little soil and sprang up straight away, because
6 there was no depth of earth; •but as soon as the sun came up they were scorched
7 and, not having any roots, they withered away. •Others fell among thorns, and
8 the thorns grew up and choked them. •Others fell on rich soil and produced their
9 crop, some a hundredfold, some sixty, some thirty. •Listen, anyone who has ears!'

Why Jesus speaks in parables

10   Then the disciples went up to him and asked, 'Why do you talk to them in
11 parables?' •'Because' he replied 'the mysteries of the kingdom of heaven are
12 revealed to you, but they are not revealed to them. •For anyone who has will be given more, and he will have more than enough; but from anyone who has not,
13 even what he has will be taken away. •The reason I talk to them in parables is
14 that they look without seeing and listen without hearing or understanding. •So in their case this prophecy of Isaiah is being fulfilled:

> *You will listen and listen again, but not understand,*
> *see and see again, but not perceive.*
15 *For the heart of this nation has grown coarse,*
> *their ears are dull of hearing, and they have shut their eyes,*
> *for fear they should see with their eyes,*
> *hear with their ears,*
> *understand with their heart,*
> *and be converted*
> *and be healed by me.*[a]

16   'But happy are your eyes because they see, your ears because they hear!
17 I tell you solemnly, many prophets and holy men longed to see what you see, and never saw it; to hear what you hear, and never heard it.

b. 'prince Baal' often contemptuously changed (e.g. 2 K 1:2f) to 'Beelzebub' 'Lord of the flies'.
c. A miracle to prove his authority.   **d.** Jon 2:1   **e.** In Hebr. and Aramaic (and many other languages), 'brothers' is the word used for cousins or even more distant relations of the same generation.
13 a. Is 6:9-10

The parable of the sower explained

'You, therefore, are to hear the parable of the sower. •When anyone hears 18 19 the word of the kingdom without understanding, the evil one comes and carries off what was sown in his heart: this is the man who received the seed on the edge of the path. •The one who received it on patches of rock is the man who hears 20 the word and welcomes it at once with joy. •But he has no root in him, he does 21 not last; let some trial come, or some persecution on account of the word, and he falls away at once. •The one who received the seed in thorns is the man who 22 hears the word, but the worries of this world and the lure of riches choke the word and so he produces nothing. •And the one who received the seed in rich soil is the 23 man who hears the word and understands it; he is the one who yields a harvest and produces now a hundredfold, now sixty, now thirty.'

Parable of the darnel

He put another parable before them, 'The kingdom of heaven may be 24 compared to a man who sowed good seed in his field. •While everybody was 25 asleep his enemy came, sowed darnel all among the wheat, and made off. •When 26 the new wheat sprouted and ripened, the darnel appeared as well. •The owner's 27 servants went to him and said, "Sir, was it not good seed that you sowed in your field? If so, where does the darnel come from?" •"Some enemy has done this" 28 he answered. And the servants said, "Do you want us to go and weed it out?" But he said, "No, because when you weed out the darnel you might pull up the 29 wheat with it. •Let them both grow till the harvest; and at harvest time I shall 30 say to the reapers: First collect the darnel and tie it in bundles to be burnt, then gather the wheat into my barn." '

Parable of the mustard seed

He put another parable before them, 'The kingdom of heaven is like a mustard 31 seed which a man took and sowed in his field. •It is the smallest of all the seeds, 32 but when it has grown it is the biggest shrub of all and becomes a tree so that the birds of the air come and shelter in its branches.'

Parable of the yeast

He told them another parable, 'The kingdom of heaven is like the yeast 33 a woman took and mixed in with three measures of flour till it was leavened all through'.

The people are taught only in parables

In all this Jesus spoke to the crowds in parables; indeed, he would never speak 34 to them except in parables. •This was to fulfil the prophecy: 35

> *I will speak to you in parables*
> *and expound things hidden since the foundation of the world.*[b]

The parable of the darnel explained

Then, leaving the crowds, he went to the house; and his disciples came to 36 him and said, 'Explain the parable about the darnel in the field to us'. •He said 37 in reply, 'The sower of the good seed is the Son of Man. •The field is the world; 38 the good seed is the subjects of the kingdom; the darnel, the subjects of the evil one; •the enemy who sowed them, the devil; the harvest is the end of the world; 39 the reapers are the angels. •Well then, just as the darnel is gathered up and burnt 40

41 in the fire, so it will be at the end of time. •The Son of Man will send his angels and they will gather out of his kingdom all things that provoke offences and all 42 who do evil, •and throw them into the blazing furnace, where there will be 43 weeping and grinding of teeth. •Then the virtuous will shine like the sun in the kingdom of their Father.[c] Listen, anyone who has ears!

Parables of the treasure and of the pearl

44 'The kingdom of heaven is like treasure hidden in a field which someone has found; he hides it again, goes off happy, sells everything he owns and buys the field.

45 'Again, the kingdom of heaven is like a merchant looking for fine pearls; 46 when he finds one of great value he goes and sells everything he owns and buys it.

Parable of the dragnet

47 'Again, the kingdom of heaven is like a dragnet cast into the sea that brings 48 in a haul of all kinds. •When it is full, the fishermen haul it ashore; then, sitting down, they collect the good ones in a basket and throw away those that are no 49 use. •This is how it will be at the end of time: the angels will appear and separate 50 the wicked from the just •to throw them into the blazing furnace where there will be weeping and grinding of teeth.

Conclusion

51
52 'Have you understood all this?' They said, 'Yes'. •And he said to them, 'Well then, every scribe who becomes a disciple of the kingdom of heaven is like a householder who brings out from his storeroom things both new and old'.[d]

V. THE CHURCH, FIRST-FRUITS
OF THE KINGDOM OF HEAVEN

A. NARRATIVE SECTION

A visit to Nazareth

53
54 When Jesus had finished these parables he left the district; •and, coming to his home town,[e] he taught the people in their synagogue in such a way that they were astonished and said, 'Where did the man get this wisdom and these 55 miraculous powers? •This is the carpenter's son, surely? Is not his mother the woman called Mary, and his brothers James and Joseph and Simon and Jude? 56 His sisters, too, are they not all here with us? So where did the man get it all?' 57 And they would not accept him. But Jesus said to them, 'A prophet is only 58 despised in his own country and in his own house', •and he did not work many miracles there because of their lack of faith.

Herod and Jesus

1
2 **14** At that time Herod the tetrarch heard about the reputation of Jesus, •and said to his court, 'This is John the Baptist himself; he has risen from the dead, and that is why miraculous powers are at work in him'.

---

b. Ps 78:2   **c.** The kingdom of the Son, v. 41, is succeeded by the kingdom of the Father.
d. Perhaps a saying of particular significance to Mt, a 'scribe who became a disciple'.
e. Nazareth, see 2:23.

John the Baptist beheaded

Now it was Herod who had arrested John, chained him up and put him in 3 prison because of Herodias, his brother Philip's*a* wife. ·For John had told him, 4 'It is against the Law for you to have her'. ·He had wanted to kill him but 5 was afraid of the people, who regarded John as a prophet. ·Then, during the 6 celebrations for Herod's birthday, the daughter of Herodias*b* danced before the company, and so delighted Herod ·that he promised on oath to give her anything 7 she asked. ·Prompted by her mother she said, 'Give me John the Baptist's head, 8 here, on a dish'. ·The king was distressed but, thinking of the oaths he had 9 sworn and of his guests, he ordered it to be given her, ·and sent and had John 10 beheaded in the prison. ·The head was brought in on a dish and given to the girl 11 who took it to her mother. ·John's disciples came and took the body and buried 12 it; then they went off to tell Jesus.

First miracle of the loaves

When Jesus received this news he withdrew by boat to a lonely place where 13 they could be by themselves. But the people heard of this and, leaving the towns, went after him on foot. ·So as he stepped ashore he saw a large crowd; and 14 he took pity on them and healed their sick.

When evening came, the disciples went to him and said, 'This is a lonely place, 15 and the time has slipped by; so send the people away, and they can go to the villages to buy themselves some food'. ·Jesus replied, 'There is no need for them 16 to go: give them something to eat yourselves'. ·But they answered, 'All we have 17 with us is five loaves and two fish'. ·'Bring them here to me' he said. ·He gave $^{18}_{19}$ orders that the people were to sit down on the grass; then he took the five loaves and the two fish, raised his eyes to heaven and said the blessing. And breaking the loaves he handed them to his disciples who gave them to the crowds. ·They 20 all ate as much as they wanted, and they collected the scraps remaining, twelve baskets full. ·Those who ate numbered about five thousand men, to say 21 nothing of women and children.

Jesus walks on the water and, with him, Peter

Directly after this he made the disciples get into the boat and go on ahead 22 to the other side while he would send the crowds away. ·After sending the crowds 23 away he went up into the hills by himself to pray. When evening came, he was there alone, ·while the boat, by now far out on the lake, was battling with a heavy 24 sea, for there was a head-wind. ·In the fourth watch of the night*c* he went towards 25 them, walking on the lake, ·and when the disciples saw him walking on the lake 26 they were terrified. 'It is a ghost' they said, and cried out in fear. ·But at once 27 Jesus called out to them, saying, 'Courage! It is I! Do not be afraid.' ·It was Peter 28 who answered. 'Lord,' he said 'if it is you, tell me to come to you across the water.' 'Come' said Jesus. Then Peter got out of the boat and started walking towards 29 Jesus across the water, ·but as soon as he felt the force of the wind, he took fright 30 and began to sink. 'Lord! Save me!' he cried. ·Jesus put out his hand at once and 31 held him. 'Man of little faith,' he said 'why did you doubt?' ·And as they got into 32 the boat the wind dropped. ·The men in the boat bowed down before him and 33 said, 'Truly, you are the Son of God'.

Cures at Gennesaret

34
35 Having made the crossing, they came to land at Gennesaret. •When the local people recognised him they spread the news through the whole neighbourhood
36 and took all that were sick to him, •begging him just to let them touch the fringe of his cloak. And all those who touched it were completely cured.

The traditions of the Pharisees

1
2 **15** Pharisees and scribes from Jerusalem then came to Jesus and said, •'Why do your disciples break away from the tradition of the elders?[a] They do not
3 wash their hands when they eat food.' •'And why do you' he answered 'break
4 away from the commandment of God for the sake of your tradition? •For God said: *Do your duty to[b] your father and mother* and: *Anyone who curses father or*
5 *mother must be put to death.[c]* •But you say, "If anyone says to his father or mother:
6 Anything I have that I might have used to help you is dedicated to God", •he is rid of his duty to father or mother.[d] In this way you have made God's word
7 null and void by means of your tradition. •Hypocrites! It was you Isaiah meant when he so rightly prophesied:

8   *This people honours me only with lip-service,*
            while their hearts are far from me.
9   *The worship they offer me is worthless;*
            the doctrines they teach are only human regulations.'[e]

On clean and unclean

10
11 He called the people to him and said, 'Listen, and understand. •What goes into the mouth does not make a man unclean; it is what comes out of the mouth that makes him unclean.'

12 Then the disciples came to him and said, 'Do you know that the Pharisees
13 were shocked when they heard what you said?' •He replied, 'Any plant my
14 heavenly Father has not planted will be pulled up by the roots. •Leave them alone. They are blind men leading blind men; and if one blind man leads another, both will fall into a pit.'

15
16 At this, Peter said to him, 'Explain the parable for us'. •Jesus replied, 'Do
17 even you not yet understand? •Can you not see that whatever goes into the
18 mouth passes through the stomach and is discharged into the sewer? •But the things that come out of the mouth come from the heart, and it is these that make
19 a man unclean. •For from the heart come evil intentions: murder, adultery,
20 fornication, theft, perjury, slander. •These are the things that make a man unclean. But to eat with unwashed hands does not make a man unclean.'

The daughter of the Canaanite woman healed

21
22 Jesus left that place and withdrew to the region of Tyre and Sidon. •Then out came a Canaanite woman from that district and started shouting, 'Sir, Son
23 of David, take pity on me. My daughter is tormented by a devil.' •But he answered her not a word. And his disciples went and pleaded with him. 'Give
24 her what she wants,' they said 'because she is shouting after us.' •He said in

14 a. Philip, Herod's half-brother, was still alive.   **b.** According to Josephus, the girl's name was Salome.   **c.** 3 to 6 a.m.

15 a. The traditional teaching, including many additions to and extensions of the Law. **b.** Often translated 'honour', but the word implies a respect expressed in practical ways, Ex 20:12.   **c.** Lv 20:9   **d.** Property dedicated in this way could not be passed to another person.   **e.** Is 29:13

reply, 'I was sent only to the lost sheep of the House of Israel'. •But the woman 25 had come up and was kneeling at his feet. 'Lord,' she said 'help me.' •He replied, 26 'It is not fair to take the children's food and throw it to the house-dogs'. •She 27 retorted, 'Ah yes, sir; but even house-dogs can eat the scraps that fall from their master's table'. •Then Jesus answered her, 'Woman, you have great faith. Let 28 your wish be granted.' And from that moment her daughter was well again.

Cures near the lake

Jesus went on from there and reached the shores of the Sea of Galilee, and 29 he went up into the hills. He sat there, •and large crowds came to him bringing 30 the lame, the crippled, the blind, the dumb and many others; these they put down at his feet, and he cured them. •The crowds were astonished to see the 31 dumb speaking, the cripples whole again, the lame walking and the blind with their sight, and they praised the God of Israel.

Second miracle of the loaves

But Jesus called his disciples to him and said, 'I feel sorry for all these people; 32 they have been with me for three days now and have nothing to eat. I do not want to send them off hungry, they might collapse on the way.' •The 33 disciples said to him, 'Where could we get enough bread in this deserted place to feed such a crowd?' •Jesus said to them, 'How many loaves have you?' 'Seven' 34 they said 'and a few small fish.' •Then he instructed the crowd to sit down on the 35 ground, •and he took the seven loaves and the fish, and he gave thanks and 36 broke them and handed them to the disciples who gave them to the crowds. They all ate as much as they wanted, and they collected what was left of the 37 scraps, seven baskets full. •Now four thousand men had eaten, to say nothing 38 of women and children. •And when he had sent the crowds away he got into the 39 boat and went to the district of Magadan.

The Pharisees ask for a sign from heaven

16 The Pharisees and Sadducees came, and to test him they asked if he would 1 show them a sign from heaven. •He replied, 'In the evening you 2 say, "It will be fine; there is a red sky", •and in the morning, "Stormy weather 3 today; the sky is red and overcast". You know how to read the face of the sky, but you cannot read the signs of the times. •It is an evil and unfaithful generation 4 that asks for a sign! The only sign it will be given is the sign of Jonah.' And leaving them standing there, he went away.

The yeast of the Pharisees and Sadducees

The disciples, having crossed to the other shore, had forgotten to take any food. 5 Jesus said to them, 'Keep your eyes open, and be on your guard against the yeast 6 of the Pharisees and Sadducees'. •And they said to themselves, 'It is because we 7 have not brought any bread'. •Jesus knew it, and he said, 'Men of little faith, 8 why are you talking among yourselves about having no bread? •Do you not yet 9 understand? Do you not remember the five loaves for the five thousand and the number of baskets you collected? •Or the seven loaves for the four thousand 10 and the number of baskets you collected? •How could you fail to understand 11 that I was not talking about bread? What I said was: Beware of the yeast of the Pharisees and Sadducees.' •Then they understood that he was telling them to be 12 on their guard, not against the yeast for making bread, but against the teaching of the Pharisees and Sadducees.[a]

Peter's profession of faith; his pre-eminence

13 When Jesus came to the region of Caesarea Philippi he put this question to
14 his disciples, 'Who do people say the Son of Man is?' •And they said, 'Some
say he is John the Baptist, some Elijah, and others Jeremiah or one of the
15,16 prophets'. •'But you,' he said 'who do you say I am?' •Then Simon Peter spoke
17 up, 'You are the Christ,' he said 'the Son of the living God'. •Jesus replied,
'Simon son of Jonah, you are a happy man! Because it was not flesh and blood
18 that revealed this to you but my Father in heaven. •So I now say to you: You
are Peter[b] and on this rock I will build my Church. And the gates of the under-
19 world[c] can never hold out against it. •I will give you the keys of the kingdom
of heaven: whatever you bind on earth shall be considered bound in heaven;
20 whatever you loose on earth shall be considered loosed in heaven.'[d] •Then he
gave the disciples strict orders not to tell anyone that he was the Christ.

First prophecy of the Passion

21 From that time Jesus began to make it clear to his disciples that he was
destined to go to Jerusalem and suffer grievously at the hands of the elders and
chief priests and scribes, to be put to death and to be raised up on the third day.
22 Then, taking him aside, Peter started to remonstrate with him. 'Heaven preserve
23 you, Lord;' he said 'this must not happen to you'. •But he turned and said to
Peter, 'Get behind me, Satan! You are an obstacle in my path, because the way
you think is not God's way but man's.'

The condition of following Christ

24 Then Jesus said to his disciples, 'If anyone wants to be a follower of mine,
25 let him renounce himself and take up his cross and follow me. •For anyone who
wants to save his life will lose it; but anyone who loses his life for my sake will
26 find it. •What, then, will a man gain if he wins the whole world and ruins his
life? Or what has a man to offer in exchange for his life?
27 'For the Son of Man is going to come in the glory of his Father with his
angels, and, when he does, he will reward each one according to his behaviour.
28 I tell you solemnly, there are some of these standing here who will not taste
death before they see the Son of Man coming with his kingdom.'[e]

The transfiguration

1 **17** Six days later, Jesus took with him Peter and James and his brother John
2 and led them up a high mountain where they could be alone. •There in
their presence he was transfigured: his face shone like the sun and his clothes
3 became as white as the light. •Suddenly Moses and Elijah[a] appeared to them;
4 they were talking with him. •Then Peter spoke to Jesus. 'Lord,' he said 'it is
wonderful for us to be here; if you wish, I will make three tents here, one for
5 you, one for Moses and one for Elijah.' •He was still speaking when suddenly
a bright cloud covered them with shadow, and from the cloud there came a voice
which said, 'This is my Son, the Beloved; he enjoys my favour. Listen to him.'

16 a. Yeast, here, is regarded as adulterating pure flour.   **b.** Not, until now, a proper name:
Greek *petros* (as in Engl. saltpetre) represents Aramaic *kepha*, rock.   **c.** The gates symbolise
the power of the underworld to hold captives.   **d.** The keys have become the traditional
insignia of Peter.   **e.** In vv. 27-28, two different sayings have been combined because both
refer to the coming of the kingdom; but the first is about Judgement day, and the second is
about the destruction of Jerusalem, the sign of 'the last days'.

17 a. Representing the Law and the prophets.

When they heard this, the disciples fell on their faces, overcome with fear. •But ⁶₇ Jesus came up and touched them. 'Stand up,' he said 'do not be afraid.' •And 8 when they raised their eyes they saw no one but only Jesus.

The question about Elijah

As they came down from the mountain Jesus gave them this order, 'Tell 9 no one about the vision until the Son of Man has risen from the dead'. •And the 10 disciples put this question to him, 'Why do the scribes say then that Elijah has to come first?' •'True;' he replied 'Elijah is to come to see that everything is 11 once more as it should be; •however, I tell you that Elijah has come already and 12 they did not recognise him but treated him as they pleased; and the Son of Man will suffer similarly at their hands.' •The disciples understood then that he had 13 been speaking of John the Baptist.

The epileptic demoniac

As they were rejoining the crowd a man came up to him and went down on 14 his knees before him. •'Lord,' he said 'take pity on my son: he is a lunatic and 15 in a wretched state; he is always falling into the fire or into the water. •I took 16 him to your disciples and they were unable to cure him.' •'Faithless and perverse 17 generation!' Jesus said in reply 'How much longer must I be with you? How much longer must I put up with you? Bring him here to me.' •And when Jesus rebuked 18 it the devil came out of the boy who was cured from that moment.

Then the disciples came privately to Jesus. 'Why were we unable to cast it 19 out?' they asked. •He answered, 'Because you have little faith. I tell you 20 solemnly, if your faith were the size of a mustard seed you could say to this mountain, "Move from here to there", and it would move; nothing would be impossible for you.'

Second prophecy of the Passion

One day when they were together in Galilee, Jesus said to them, 'The Son 22 of Man is going to be handed over into the power of men; •they will put him to 23 death, and on the third day he will be raised to life again'. And a great sadness came over them.

The Temple tax paid by Jesus and Peter

When they reached Capernaum, the collectors of the half-shekel*ᵇ* came to 24 Peter and said, 'Does your master not pay the half-shekel?' •'Oh yes' he replied, 25 and went into the house. But before he could speak, Jesus said, 'Simon, what is your opinion? From whom do the kings of the earth take toll or tribute? From their sons or from foreigners?' •And when he replied, 'From foreigners', Jesus 26 said, 'Well then, the sons are exempt. •However, so as not to offend these 27 people, go to the lake and cast a hook; take the first fish that bites, open its mouth and there you will find a shekel; take it and give it to them for me and for you.'

B. THE DISCOURSE ON THE CHURCH

Who is the greatest?

18 At this time the disciples came to Jesus and said, 'Who is the greatest in 1 the kingdom of heaven?' •So he called a little child to him and set the child 2 in front of them. •Then he said, 'I tell you solemnly, unless you change and become 3

4 like little children you will never enter the kingdom of heaven. •And so, the one who makes himself as little as this little child is the greatest in the kingdom of heaven.

On leading others astray

5 'Anyone who welcomes a little child like this in my name welcomes me. 6 But anyone who is an obstacle to bring down one of these little ones who have faith in me would be better drowned in the depths of the sea with a great 7 millstone round his neck. •Alas for the world that there should be such obstacles! Obstacles indeed there must be, but alas for the man who provides them!

8 'If your hand or your foot should cause you to sin, cut it off and throw it away: it is better for you to enter into life crippled or lame, than to have two 9 hands or two feet and be thrown into eternal fire. •And if your eye should cause you to sin, tear it out and throw it away: it is better for you to enter into life with one eye, than to have two eyes and be thrown into the hell of fire.

10 'See that you never despise any of these little ones, for I tell you that their angels in heaven are continually in the presence of my Father in heaven.*a*

The lost sheep

12 'Tell me. Suppose a man has a hundred sheep and one of them strays; will 13 he not leave the ninety-nine on the hillside and go in search of the stray? •I tell you solemnly, if he finds it, it gives him more joy than do the ninety-nine that did 14 not stray at all. •Similarly, it is never the will of your Father in heaven that one of these little ones should be lost.

Brotherly correction

15 'If your brother does something wrong, go and have it out with him alone, between your two selves. If he listens to you, you have won back your brother. 16 If he does not listen, take one or two others along with you: *the evidence of two* 17 *or three witnesses is required to sustain any charge.* •But if he refuses to listen to these, report it to the community;*b* and if he refuses to listen to the community, treat him like a pagan or a tax collector.

18 'I tell you solemnly, whatever you bind on earth shall be considered bound in heaven; whatever you loose on earth shall be considered loosed in heaven.

Prayer in common

19 'I tell you solemnly once again, if two of you on earth agree to ask anything 20 at all, it will be granted to you by my Father in heaven. •For where two or three meet in my name, I shall be there with them.'

Forgiveness of injuries

21 Then Peter went up to him and said, 'Lord, how often must I forgive my 22 brother if he wrongs me? As often as seven times?' •Jesus answered, 'Not seven, I tell you, but seventy-seven times.

Parable of the unforgiving debtor

23 'And so the kingdom of heaven may be compared to a king who decided 24 to settle his accounts with his servants. •When the reckoning began, they

b. A tax for the upkeep of the Temple.
18 a. V. 11, at the time when verse numbers were added, consisted of a sentence which is not now accepted as part of the original text.   b. The community of the brothers (the Church).

brought him a man who owed ten thousand talents;^c •but he had no means of 25
paying, so his master gave orders that he should be sold, together with his wife
and children and all his possessions, to meet the debt. •At this, the servant threw 26
himself down at his master's feet. "Give me time" he said "and I will pay the
whole sum." •And the servant's master felt so sorry for him that he let him go 27
and cancelled the debt. •Now as this servant went out, he happened to meet a fellow 28
servant who owed him one hundred denarii;^d and he seized him by the throat
and began to throttle him. "Pay what you owe me" he said. •His fellow servant 29
fell at his feet and implored him, saying, "Give me time and I will pay you".
But the other would not agree; on the contrary, he had him thrown into prison 30
till he should pay the debt. •His fellow servants were deeply distressed when 31
they saw what had happened, and they went to their master and reported the
whole affair to him. •Then the master sent for him. "You wicked servant," he 32
said "I cancelled all that debt of yours when you appealed to me. •Were you not 33
bound, then, to have pity on your fellow servant just as I had pity on you?"
And in his anger the master handed him over to the torturers till he should pay 34
all his debt. •And that is how my. heavenly Father will deal with you unless you 35
each forgive your brother from your heart.'

VI. THE APPROACHING ADVENT
OF THE KINGDOM OF HEAVEN

A. NARRATIVE SECTION

The question about divorce

19 Jesus had now finished what he wanted to say, and he left Galilee and 1
came into the part of Judaea which is on the far side of the Jordan. •Large 2
crowds followed him and he healed them there.

Some Pharisees approached him, and to test him they said, 'Is it against the 3
Law for a man to divorce his wife on any pretext whatever?' •He answered, 'Have 4
you not read that the creator from the beginning *made them male and female* •and 5
that he said: *This is why a man must leave father and mother, and cling to his wife,*
and the two become one body? •They are no longer two, therefore, but one body. 6
So then, what God has united, man must not divide.'

They said to him, 'Then why did Moses command that a writ of dismissal 7
should be given in cases of divorce?' •'It was because you were so unteachable' 8
he said 'that Moses allowed you to divorce your wives, but it was not like this
from the beginning. •Now I say this to you: the man who divorces his wife— 9
I am not speaking of fornication—and marries another, is guilty of adultery.'

Continence

The disciples said to him, 'If that is how things are between husband and wife, 10
it is not advisable to marry'. •But he replied, 'It is not everyone who can accept 11
what I have said, but only those to whom it is granted. •There are eunuchs born 12
that way from their mother's womb, there are eunuchs made so by men and
there are eunuchs who have made themselves that way for the sake of the kingdom
of heaven. Let anyone accept this who can.'

Jesus and the children

13 People brought little children to him, for him to lay his hands on them and
14 say a prayer. The disciples turned them away, •but Jesus said, 'Let the little
children alone, and do not stop them coming to me; for it is to such as these that
15 the kingdom of heaven belongs'. •Then he laid his hands on them and went on
his way.

The rich young man

16 And there was a man who came to him and asked, 'Master, what good deed
17 must I do to possess eternal life?' •Jesus said to him, 'Why do you ask me about
what is good? There is one alone who is good. But if you wish to enter into
18 life, keep the commandments.' •He said, 'Which?' 'These:' Jesus replied '*You
must not kill. You must not commit adultery. You must not bring false witness.*
19 *Honour your father and mother*, and: *you must love your neighbour as yourself.*'[a]
20 The young man said to him, 'I have kept all these. What more do I need to do?'
21 Jesus said, 'If you wish to be perfect, go and sell what you own and give the
money to the poor, and you will have treasure in heaven; then come, follow
22 me'. •But when the young man heard these words he went away sad, for he was
a man of great wealth.

The danger of riches

23 Then Jesus said to his disciples, 'I tell you solemnly, it will be hard for a
24 rich man to enter the kingdom of heaven. •Yes, I tell you again, it is easier
for a camel to pass through the eye of a needle than for a rich man to enter the
25 kingdom of heaven.' •When the disciples heard this they were astonished.
26 'Who can be saved, then?' they said. •Jesus gazed at them. 'For men' he told
them 'this is impossible; for God everything is possible.'

The reward of renunciation

27 Then Peter spoke. 'What about us?' he said to him 'We have left everything
28 and followed you. What are we to have, then?' •Jesus said to him, 'I tell you
solemnly, when all is made new and the Son of Man sits on his throne of glory,
you will yourselves sit on twelve thrones to judge[b] the twelve tribes of Israel.
29 And everyone who has left houses, brothers, sisters, father, mother, children
or land for the sake of my name will be repaid a hundred times over, and also
inherit eternal life.
30 'Many who are first will be last, and the last, first.

Parable of the vineyard labourers

1 **20** 'Now the kingdom of heaven is like a landowner going out at daybreak
2 to hire workers for his vineyard. •He made an agreement with the workers
3 for one denarius a day, and sent them to his vineyard. •Going out at about the
4 third hour he saw others standing idle in the market place •and said to them,
5 "You go to my vineyard too and I will give you a fair wage". •So they went. At
about the sixth hour and again at about the ninth hour, he went out and did the
6 same. •Then at about the eleventh hour he went out and found more men standing
round, and he said to them, "Why have you been standing here idle all day?"

c. 'Millions of pounds'—about £3,000,000.   d. Under £5.
19 a. Ex 20:12-16; Dt 5:16-20   **b.** I.e. to govern.

"Because no one has hired us" they answered. He said to them, "You go into ⁷ my vineyard too". •In the evening, the owner of the vineyard said to his bailiff, ⁸ "Call the workers and pay them their wages, starting with the last arrivals and ending with the first". •So those who were hired at about the eleventh hour came ⁹ forward and received one denarius each. •When the first came, they expected to ¹⁰ get more, but they too received one denarius each. •They took it, but grumbled ¹¹ at the landowner. •"The men who came last" they said "have done only one hour, ¹²· and you have treated them the same as us, though we have done a heavy day's work in all the heat." •He answered one of them and said, "My friend, I am ¹³ not being unjust to you; did we not agree on one denarius? •Take your earnings ¹⁴ and go. I choose to pay the last-comer as much as I pay you. •Have I no right ¹⁵ to do what I like with my own? Why be envious because I am generous?" •Thus ¹⁶ the last will be first, and the first, last.'

Third prophecy of the Passion

Jesus was going up to Jerusalem, and on the way he took the Twelve to one ¹⁷ side and said to them, •'Now we are going up to Jerusalem, and the Son of Man ¹⁸ is about to be handed over to the chief priests and scribes. They will condemn him to death •and will hand him over to the pagans to be mocked and scourged ¹⁹ and crucified; and on the third day he will rise again.'

The mother of Zebedee's sons makes her request

Then the mother of Zebedee's sons came with her sons to make a request of ²⁰ him, and bowed low; •and he said to her, 'What is it you want?' She said to ²¹ him, 'Promise that these two sons of mine may sit one at your right hand and the other at your left in your kingdom'. •'You do not know what you are asking' ²² Jesus answered. 'Can you drink the cup that I am going to drink?' They replied, 'We can'. •'Very well,' he said 'you shall drink my cup,ᵃ but as for seats at ²³ my right hand and my left, these are not mine to grant; they belong to those to whom they have been allotted by my Father.'

Leadership with service

When the other ten heard this they were indignant with the two brothers. ²⁴ But Jesus called them to him and said, 'You know that among the pagans the ²⁵ rulers lord it over them, and their great men make their authority felt. •This is ²⁶ not to happen among you. No; anyone who wants to be great among you must be your servant, •and anyone who wants to be first among you must be your ²⁷ slave, •just as the Son of Man came not to be served but to serve, and to give his ²⁸ life as a ransom for many.'

The two blind men of Jericho

As they left Jericho a large crowd followed him. •Now there were two blind ²⁹₃₀ men sitting at the side of the road. When they heard that it was Jesus who was passing by, they shouted, 'Lord! Have pity on us, Son of David.' •And the crowd ³¹ scolded them and told them to keep quiet, but they only shouted more loudly, 'Lord! Have pity on us, Son of David.' •Jesus stopped, called them over and ³² said, 'What do you want me to do for you?' •They said to him, 'Lord, let us ³³ have our sight back'. •Jesus felt pity for them and touched their eyes, and immed- ³⁴ iately their sight returned and they followed him.

The Messiah enters Jerusalem

1,2 **21** When they were near Jerusalem and had come in sight of Bethphage on the Mount of Olives, Jesus sent two disciples, •saying to them, 'Go to the village facing you, and you will immediately find a tethered donkey and a colt with her.
3 Untie them and bring them to me. •If anyone says anything to you, you are to
4 say, "The Master needs them and will send them back directly".' •This took place to fulfil the prophecy:

5   *Say to the daughter of Zion:*
              Look, your king comes to you;
              he is humble, he rides on a donkey
              and on a colt, the foal of a beast of burden.[a]

6,7 So the disciples went out and did as Jesus had told them. •They brought the donkey and the colt, then they laid their cloaks on their backs and he sat on
8 them. •Great crowds of people spread their cloaks on the road, while others
9 were cutting branches from the trees and spreading them in his path. •The crowds who went in front of him and those who followed were all shouting:

              '*Hosanna*[b] to the Son of David!
              Blessings on him who comes in the name of the Lord![c]
              Hosanna in the highest heavens!'

10 And when he entered Jerusalem, the whole city was in turmoil. 'Who is this?'
11 people asked, •and the crowds answered, 'This is the prophet Jesus from Nazareth in Galilee'.

The expulsion of the dealers from the Temple

12 Jesus then went into the Temple and drove out all those who were selling and buying there; he upset the tables of the money changers and the chairs of those
13 who were selling pigeons.[d] •'According to scripture' he said '*my house will be called*
14 *a house of prayer;*[e] but you are turning it into a *robbers' den.*'[f] •There were also blind
15 and lame people who came to him in the Temple, and he cured them. •At the sight of the wonderful things he did and of the children shouting, 'Hosanna to the
16 Son of David' in the Temple, the chief priests and the scribes were indignant. •'Do you hear what they are saying?' they said to him. 'Yes,' Jesus answered 'have you never read this:

              By the mouths of children, babes in arms,
              you have made sure of praise?'[g]

17 With that he left them and went out of the city to Bethany where he spent the night.

The barren fig tree withers. Faith and prayer

18,19 As he was returning to the city in the early morning, he felt hungry. •Seeing a fig tree by the road, he went up to it and found nothing on it but leaves. And he said to it, 'May you never bear fruit again'; and at that instant the fig tree
20 withered. •The disciples were amazed when they saw it. 'What happened to the

20 a. Perhaps a prophecy of the martyrdom of James and John; James was certainly put to death by Herod Agrippa about 44 A.D., Ac 12:2.
21 a. Is 62:11; Zc 9:9   **b.** Conventional shout of acclaim, like a cheer.   **c.** Ps 118:26
d. Money changers provided Temple currency, and the traders the animals, for making sacrificial offerings.   **e.** Is 56:7   **f.** Jr 7:11   **g.** Ps 8:2 (LXX); Ws 10:21

tree' they said 'that it withered there and then?' •Jesus answered, 'I tell you 21
solemnly, if you have faith and do not doubt at all, not only will you do what
I have done to the fig tree, but even if you say to this mountain, "Get up and throw
yourself into the sea", it will be done. •And if you have faith, everything you ask 22
for in prayer you will receive.'

The authority of Jesus is questioned

He had gone into the Temple and was teaching, when the chief priests and the 23
elders of the people came to him and said, 'What authority have you for acting
like this? And who gave you this authority?' •'And I' replied Jesus 'will ask you 24
a question, only one; if you tell me the answer to it, I will then tell you my
authority for acting like this. •John's baptism: where did it come from: heaven 25
or man?' And they argued it out this way among themselves, 'If we say from
heaven, he will retort, "Then why did you refuse to believe him?"; •but if we say 26
from man, we have the people to fear, for they all hold that John was a prophet'.
So their reply to Jesus was, 'We do not know'. And he retorted, 'Nor will I tell 27
you my authority for acting like this.

Parable of the two sons

'What is your opinion? A man had two sons. He went and said to the first, 28
"My boy, you go and work in the vineyard today". •He answered, "I will not go", 29
but afterwards thought better of it and went. •The man then went and said the 30
same thing to the second who answered, "Certainly, sir", but did not go. •Which 31
of the two did the father's will?' 'The first' they said. Jesus said to them, 'I tell
you solemnly, tax collectors and prostitutes are making their way into
the kingdom of God before you. •For John came to you, a pattern of true 32
righteousness, but you did not believe him, and yet the tax collectors and
prostitutes did. Even after seeing that, you refused to think better of it and
believe in him.

Parable of the wicked husbandmen

'Listen to another parable. There was a man, a landowner, who planted 33
a vineyard; he fenced it round, dug a winepress in it and built a tower; then he
leased it to tenants and went abroad. •When vintage time drew near he sent his 34
servants to the tenants to collect his produce. •But the tenants seized his servants, 35
thrashed one, killed another and stoned a third. •Next he sent some more servants, 36
this time a larger number, and they dealt with them in the same way. •Finally 37
he sent his son to them. "They will respect my son" he said. •But when the tenants 38
saw the son, they said to each other, "This is the heir. Come on, let us kill him and
take over his inheritance." •So they seized him and threw him out of the vineyard 39
and killed him. •Now when the owner of the vineyard comes, what will he do 40
to those tenants?' •They answered,'He will bring those wretches to a wretched end 41
and lease the vineyard to other tenants who will deliver the produce to him when
the season arrives'. •Jesus said to them, 'Have you never read in the scriptures: 42

> *It was the stone rejected by the builders*
> *that became the keystone.*
> *This was the Lord's doing*
> *and it is wonderful to see?*[h]

I tell you, then, that the kingdom of God will be taken from you and given to 43
a people who will produce its fruit.'

45   When they heard his parables, the chief priests and the scribes realised he was
46 speaking about them, ·but though they would have liked to arrest him they were
afraid of the crowds, who looked on him as a prophet.

Parable of the wedding feast

$^1_2$ **22** Jesus began to speak to them in parables once again, ·'The kingdom of
heaven may be compared to a king who gave a feast for his son's wedding.
3 He sent his servants to call those who had been invited, but they would not come.
4 Next he sent some more servants. "Tell those who have been invited" he said
"that I have my banquet all prepared, my oxen and fattened cattle have been
5 slaughtered, everything is ready. Come to the wedding." ·But they were not
6 interested: one went off to his farm, another to his business, ·and the rest seized
7 his servants, maltreated them and killed them. ·The king was furious. He
8 despatched his troops, destroyed those murderers and burnt their town. ·Then
he said to his servants, "The wedding is ready; but as those who were invited
9 proved to be unworthy, ·go to the crossroads in the town and invite everyone
10 you can find to the wedding". ·So these servants went out on to the roads and
collected together everyone they could find, bad and good alike; and the wedding
11 hall was filled with guests. ·When the king came in to look at the guests he noticed
12 one man who was not wearing a wedding garment, ·and said to him, "How did
you get in here, my friend, without a wedding garment?" And the man was silent.
13 Then the king said to the attendants, "Bind him hand and foot and throw him
14 out into the dark, where there will be weeping and grinding of teeth". ·For many
are called, but few are chosen.'

On tribute to Caesar

15   Then the Pharisees went away to work out between them how to trap him
16 in what he said. ·And they sent their disciples to him, together with the
Herodians,^{a} to say, 'Master, we know that you are an honest man and teach
the way of God in an honest way, and that you are not afraid of anyone, because
17 a man's rank means nothing to you. ·Tell us your opinion, then. Is it permissible
18 to pay taxes to Caesar or not?' ·But Jesus was aware of their malice and replied,
19 'You hypocrites! Why do you set this trap for me? ·Let me see the money you
20 pay the tax with.' They handed him a denarius, ·and he said, 'Whose head is this?
21 Whose name?' ·'Caesar's' they replied. He then said to them, 'Very well, give
back to Caesar what belongs to Caesar—and to God what belongs to God'.
22 This reply took them by surprise, and they left him alone and went away.

The resurrection of the dead

23   That day some Sadducees—who deny that there is a resurrection—approached
24 him and they put this question to him, ·'Master, Moses said that if a man
dies childless, his brother is to marry the widow, his sister-in-law, to raise
25 children for his brother. ·Now we had a case involving seven brothers; the first
26 married and then died without children, leaving his wife to his brother; ·the
27 same thing happened with the second and third and so on to the seventh, ·and then
28 last of all the woman herself died. ·Now at the resurrection to which of those
29 seven will she be wife, since she had been married to them all?' ·Jesus answered
them, 'You are wrong, because you understand neither the scriptures nor the

h. Ps 118:22-23
22 a. Supporters of the ruling family, hoping to find a cause for denouncing Jesus to the
Romans.

power of God. •For at the resurrection men and women do not marry; no, they 30
are like the angels in heaven. •And as for the resurrection of the dead, have you 31
never read what God himself said to you: •*I am the God of Abraham, the God of* 32
Isaac and the God of Jacob?[b] God is God, not of the dead, but of the living.'
And his teaching made a deep impression on the people who heard it.   33

The greatest commandment of all

But when the Pharisees heard that he had silenced the Sadducees they got 34
together •and, to disconcert him, one of them put a question, •'Master, which ³⁵₃₆
is the greatest commandment of the Law?' •Jesus said, '*You must love the Lord* 37
your God with all your heart, with all your soul, and with all your mind. •This is 38
the greatest and the first commandment. •The second resembles it: *You must love* 39
your neighbour as yourself. •On these two commandments hang the whole Law, 40
and the Prophets also.'

Christ not only son but also Lord of David

While the Pharisees were gathered round, Jesus put to them this question, 41
'What is your opinion about the Christ? Whose son is he?' 'David's' they told him. 42
'Then how is it' he said 'that David, moved by the Spirit, calls him Lord, where 43
he says:

> *The Lord said to my Lord:*   44
> *Sit at my right hand*
> *and I will put your enemies*
> *under your feet?*[c]

'If David can call him Lord, then how can he be his son?' •Not one could think ⁴⁵₄₆
of anything to say in reply, and from that day no one dared to ask him any
further questions.

The scribes and Pharisees: their hypocrisy and vanity

23 Then addressing the people and his disciples Jesus said, •'The scribes and ¹₂
the Pharisees occupy the chair of Moses. •You must therefore do what they 3
tell you and listen to what they say; but do not be guided by what they do: since
they do not practise what they preach. •They tie up heavy burdens and lay them 4
on men's shoulders, but will they lift a finger to move them? Not they! •Everything 5
they do is done to attract attention, like wearing broader phylacteries and longer
tassels,[a] •like wanting to take the place of honour at banquets and the front 6
seats in the synagogues, •being greeted obsequiously in the market squares and 7
having people call them Rabbi.

'You, however, must not allow yourselves to be called Rabbi, since you have 8
only one Master, and you are all brothers. •You must call no one on earth your 9
father, since you have only one Father, and he is in heaven. •Nor must you allow 10
yourselves to be called teachers, for you have only one Teacher, the Christ.
The greatest among you must be your servant. •Anyone who exalts himself will ¹¹₁₂
be humbled, and anyone who humbles himself will be exalted.

The sevenfold indictment of the scribes and Pharisees

'Alas for you, scribes and Pharisees, you hypocrites! You who shut up the 13
kingdom of heaven in men's faces, neither going in yourselves nor allowing
others to go in[b] who want to.

15 'Alas for you, scribes and Pharisees, you hypocrites! You who travel over sea and land to make a single proselyte, and when you have him you make him twice as fit for hell as you are.

16 'Alas for you, blind guides! You who say, "If a man swears by the Temple, it has no force; but if a man swears by the gold of the Temple, he is bound".

17 Fools and blind! For which is of greater worth, the gold or the Temple that

18 makes the gold sacred? •Or else, "If a man swears by the altar it has no force;

19 but if a man swears by the offering that is on the altar, he is bound". •You blind men! For which is of greater worth, the offering or the altar that makes the

20 offering sacred? •Therefore, when a man swears by the altar he is swearing by

21 that and by everything on it. •And when a man swears by the Temple he

22 is swearing by that and by the One who dwells in it. •And when a man swears by heaven he is swearing by the throne of God and by the One who is seated there.

23 'Alas for you, scribes and Pharisees, you hypocrites! You who pay your tithe of mint and dill and cummin[c] and have neglected the weightier matters of the Law—justice, mercy, good faith! These you should have practised, without

24 neglecting the others. •You blind guides! Straining out gnats and swallowing camels!

25 'Alas for you, scribes and Pharisees, you hypocrites! You who clean the outside of cup and dish and leave the inside full of extortion and intemperance.

26 Blind Pharisee! Clean the inside of cup and dish first so that the outside may become clean as well.

27 'Alas for you, scribes and Pharisees, you hypocrites! You who are like whitewashed tombs that look handsome on the outside, but inside are full of dead

28 men's bones and every kind of corruption. •In the same way you appear to people from the outside like good honest men, but inside you are full of hypocrisy and lawlessness.

29 'Alas for you, scribes and Pharisees, you hypocrites! You who build the

30 sepulchres of the prophets and decorate the tombs of holy men, •saying, "We would never have joined in shedding the blood of the prophets, had we lived in

31 our fathers' day". •So! Your own evidence tells against you! You are the sons of

32 those who murdered the prophets! •Very well then, finish off the work that your fathers began.

Their crimes and approaching punishment

33 'Serpents, brood of vipers, how can you escape being condemned to hell?

34 This is why, in my turn, I am sending you prophets and wise men and scribes: some you will slaughter and crucify, some you will scourge in your synagogues

35 and hunt from town to town; •and so you will draw down on yourselves the blood of every holy man that has been shed on earth, from the blood of Abel the Holy to the blood of Zechariah son of Barachiah[d] whom you murdered between the

36 sanctuary and the altar. •I tell you solemnly, all of this will recoil on this generation.

---

b. Ex 3:6   **c.** Ps 110:1
23 a. Phylacteries: containers for short texts taken from the Law; they were worn on the arm or the forehead in obedience to Ex 13:9,16 and Dt 6:8. The tassels were sewn to the corners of the cloak.   **b.** By interpreting the Law so strictly that nobody could obey all of it.   **c.** The law of paying tithes on crops was extended to include herbs and plants grown for flavouring. **d.** Possibly Zechariah, the last of the prophets to be killed, according to the Jewish scriptures (2 Ch 24:20-22).

Jerusalem admonished

'Jerusalem, Jerusalem, you that kill the prophets and stone those who are 37
sent to you! How often have I longed to gather your children, as a hen gathers
her chicks under her wings, and you refused! •So be it! Your house will be left 38
to you desolate, •for, I promise, you shall not see me any more until you say: 39

Blessings on him who comes in the name of the Lord!' [c]

B. THE SERMON ON THE END

Introduction

24 Jesus left the Temple, and as he was going away his disciples came up to 1
draw his attention to the Temple buildings. •He said to them in reply, 2
'You see all these? I tell you solemnly, not a single stone here will be left
on another: everything will be destroyed.' •And when he was sitting on the 3
Mount of Olives the disciples came and asked him privately, 'Tell us, when is
this going to happen, and what will be the sign of your coming and of the end
of the world?'

The beginning of sorrows

And Jesus answered them, 'Take care that no one deceives you; •because ⁴⁵
many will come using my name and saying, "I am the Christ", and they will
deceive many. •You will hear of wars and rumours of wars; do not be 6
alarmed, for this is something that must happen, but the end will not be yet.
For nation will fight against nation, and kingdom against kingdom. There will 7
be famines and earthquakes here and there. •All this is only the beginning of 8
the birthpangs.

'Then they will hand you over to be tortured and put to death; and you will 9
be hated by all the nations on account of my name. •And then many will fall 10
away; men will betray one another and hate one another. •Many false prophets 11
will arise; they will deceive many, •and with the increase of lawlessness, love in 12
most men will grow cold; •but the man who stands firm to the end will be saved. 13

'This Good News of the kingdom will be proclaimed to the whole world[a] as 14
a witness to all the nations. And then the end[b] will come.

The great tribulation of Jerusalem

'So when you see *the disastrous abomination*, of which the prophet Daniel 15
spoke, set up in the Holy Place (let the reader understand), •then those in 16
Judaea must escape to the mountains; •if a man is on the housetop, he must not 17
come down to collect his belongings; •if a man is in the fields, he must not 18
turn back to fetch his cloak. •Alas for those with child, or with babies at the 19
breast, when those days come! •Pray that you will not have to escape in winter 20
or on a sabbath. •For then there will be *great distress such as, until now, since* 21
the world began, there never *has been*, nor ever will be again. •And if that time 22
had not been shortened, no one would have survived; but shortened that time
shall be, for the sake of those who are chosen.

'If anyone says to you then, "Look, here is the Christ" or, "He is there", 23
do not believe it; •for false Christs and false prophets will arise and produce great 24
signs and portents, enough to deceive even the chosen, if that were possible.
There; I have forewarned you. 25

The coming of the Son of Man will be evident

26 'If, then, they say to you, "Look, he is in the desert", do not go there;
27 "Look, he is in some hiding place", do not believe it; •because the coming of the
Son of Man will be like lightning striking in the east and flashing far into the
28 west. •Wherever the corpse is, there will the vultures gather.

The universal significance of this coming

29 'Immediately after the distress of those days[c] the sun will be darkened, the
moon will lose its brightness, the stars will fall from the sky and the powers of
30 heaven will be shaken. •And then the sign of the Son of Man will appear
in heaven; then too all the peoples of the earth will beat their breasts; and they
will see the Son of Man coming on the clouds of heaven with power and great
31 glory.[d] •And he will send his angels with a loud trumpet to gather his chosen
from the four winds, from one end of heaven to the other.

The time of this coming

32 'Take the fig tree as a parable: as soon as its twigs grow supple and its leaves
33 come out, you know that summer is near. •So with you when you see all these
34 things: know that he is near, at the very gates. •I tell you solemnly, before
35 this generation has passed away all these things will have taken place.[e] •Heaven
36 and earth will pass away, but my words will never pass away. •But as for that day
and hour, nobody knows it, neither the angels of heaven, nor the Son, no one
but the Father only.

Be on the alert

37 'As it was in Noah's day, so will it be when the Son of Man comes. •For in
38
those days before the Flood people were eating, drinking, taking wives, taking
39 husbands, right up to the day Noah went into the ark, •and they suspected nothing
till the Flood came and swept all away. It will be like this when the Son of Man
40 comes. •Then of two men in the fields one is taken, one left; •of two women at
41
the millstone grinding, one is taken, one left.
42 'So stay awake, because you do not know the day when your master is coming.
43 You may be quite sure of this that if the householder had known at what time
of the night the burglar would come, he would have stayed awake and would
44 not have allowed anyone to break through the wall of his house. •Therefore, you
too must stand ready because the Son of Man is coming at an hour you do not
expect.

Parable of the conscientious steward

45 'What sort of servant, then, is faithful and wise enough for the master to
place him over his household to give them their food at the proper time?
46 Happy that servant if his master's arrival finds him at this employment. •I tell
47
48 you solemnly, he will place him over everything he owns. •But as for the
49 dishonest servant who says to himself, "My master is taking his time", •and sets
50 about beating his fellow servants and eating and drinking with drunkards, •his

e. Ps 118:26
24 a. The 'inhabited world' as it was known.   b. The fall and destruction of Jerusalem. A
prophecy of this is combined, in this discourse, with descriptions of the 'last days'.   c. Join
with v. 22. Vv. 23-28 are a digression.   d. As foretold in Dn 7:14.   e. Meaning the fall and
destruction of Jerusalem.

master will come on a day he does not expect and at an hour he does not know. The master will cut him off and send him to the same fate as the hypocrites, where 51 there will be weeping and grinding of teeth.

Parable of the ten bridesmaids

25 'Then the kingdom of heaven will be like this: Ten bridesmaids took their 1 lamps and went to meet the bridegroom. •Five of them were foolish and five 2 were sensible: •the foolish ones did take their lamps, but they brought no oil, 3 whereas the sensible ones took flasks of oil as well as their lamps. •The bride- 4 groom was late, and they all grew drowsy and fell asleep. •But at midnight there 6 was a cry, "The bridegroom is here! Go out and meet him." •At this, all those 7 bridesmaids woke up and trimmed their lamps, •and the foolish ones said to 8 the sensible ones, "Give us some of your oil: our lamps are going out". •But 9 they replied, " There may not be enough for us and for you; you had better go to those who sell it and buy some for yourselves". •They had gone off to buy 10 it when the bridegroom arrived. Those who were ready went in with him to the wedding hall and the door was closed. •The other bridesmaids arrived later. 11 "Lord, Lord," they said "open the door for us." •But he replied, "I tell you 12 solemnly, I do not know you". •So stay awake, because you do not know either 13 the day or the hour.

Parable of the talents

'It is like a man on his way abroad who summoned his servants and entrusted 14 his property to them. •To one he gave five talents, to another two, to a third 15 one; each in proportion to his ability. Then he set out. •The man who had received 16 the five talents promptly went and traded with them and made five more. •The 17 man who had received two made two more in the same way. •But the man who 18 had received one went off and dug a hole in the ground and hid his master's money. •Now a long time after, the master of those servants came back and went 19 through his accounts with them. •The man who had received the five talents came 20 forward bringing five more. "Sir," he said "you entrusted me with five talents; here are five more that I have made." •His master said to him, "Well done, good 21 and faithful servant; you have shown you can be faithful in small things, I will trust you with greater; come and join in your master's happiness". •Next the man 22 with the two talents came forward. " Sir," he said "you entrusted me with two talents; here are two more that I have made." •His master said to him, "Well 23 done, good and faithful servant; you have shown you can be faithful in small things, I will trust you with greater; come and join in your master's happiness". Last came forward the man who had the one talent. "Sir," said he "I had heard 24 you were a hard man, reaping where you have not sown and gathering where you have not scattered; •so I was afraid, and I went off and hid your talent in 25 the ground. Here it is; it was yours, you have it back." •But his master answered 26 him, "You wicked and lazy servant! So you knew that I reap where I have not sown and gather where I have not scattered? •Well then, you should have deposited 27 my money with the bankers, and on my return I would have recovered my capital with interest. •So now, take the talent from him and give it to the man who has 28 the five talents. •For to everyone who has will be given more, and he will have more 29 than enough; but from the man who has not, even what he has will be taken away. As for this good-for-nothing servant, throw him out into the dark, where there 30 will be weeping and grinding of teeth."

The Last Judgement

31 'When the Son of Man comes in his glory, escorted by all the angels, then
32 he will take his seat on his throne of glory. •All the nations will be assembled
before him and he will separate men one from another as the shepherd separates
33 sheep from goats. •He will place the sheep on his right hand and the goats
34 on his left. •Then the King will say to those on his right hand, "Come, you whom
my Father has blessed, take for your heritage the kingdom prepared for you
35 since the foundation of the world. •For I was hungry and you gave me food;
I was thirsty and you gave me drink; I was a stranger and you made me welcome;
36 naked and you clothed me, sick and you visited me, in prison and you came to
37 see me." •Then the virtuous will say to him in reply, "Lord, when did we see
38 you hungry and feed you; or thirsty and give you drink? •When did we see
39 a stranger and make you welcome; naked and clothe you; •sick or in prison and
40 go to see you?" •And the King will answer, "I tell you solemnly, in so far
as you did this to one of the least of these brothers of mine, you did it to me".
41 Next he will say to those on his left hand, "Go away from me, with your curse
42 upon you, to the eternal fire prepared for the devil and his angels. •For I was
hungry and you never gave me food; I was thirsty and you never gave me anything
43 to drink; •I was a stranger and you never made me welcome, naked and you
44 never clothed me, sick and in prison and you never visited me." •Then it will be
their turn to ask, "Lord, when did we see you hungry or thirsty, a stranger or
45 naked, sick or in prison, and did not come to your help?" •Then he will answer,
"'I tell you solemnly, in so far as you neglected to do this to one of the least
46 of these, you neglected to do it to me". •And they will go away to eternal punishment, and the virtuous to eternal life.'

VII. PASSION AND RESURRECTION

The conspiracy against Jesus

1 **26** Jesus had now finished all he wanted to say, and he told his disciples,
2 'It will be Passover, as you know, in two days' time, and the Son of Man
will be handed over to be crucified'.

3   Then the chief priests and the elders of the people assembled in the palace of
4 the high priest, whose name was Caiaphas, •and made plans to arrest Jesus by
5 some trick and have him put to death. •They said, however, 'It must not be during
the festivities; there must be no disturbance among the people'.

The anointing at Bethany

6
7   Jesus was at Bethany in the house of Simon the leper, when •a woman came
to him with an alabaster jar of the most expensive ointment, and poured it on his
8 head as he was at table. •When they saw this, the disciples were indignant; 'Why
9 this waste?' they said. •'This could have been sold at a high price and the money
10 given to the poor.' •Jesus noticed this. 'Why are you upsetting the woman?' he
said to them. 'What she has done for me is one of the good works[a] indeed!
11
12 You have the poor with you always, but you will not always have me. •When she
13 poured this ointment on my body, she did it to prepare me for burial. •I tell you
solemnly, wherever in all the world this Good News is proclaimed, what she has
done will be told also, in remembrance of her.'

26 a. As 'good works', charitable deeds were reckoned superior to almsgiving.

Judas betrays Jesus

Then one of the Twelve, the man called Judas Iscariot, went to the chief 14
priests and said, 'What are you prepared to give me if I hand him over to you?' 15
They paid him thirty silver pieces,[b] and from that moment he looked for an 16
opportunity to betray him.

Preparations for the Passover supper

Now on the first day of Unleavened Bread[c] the disciples came to Jesus to 17
say, 'Where do you want us to make the preparations for you to eat the
passover?' •'Go to so-and-so in the city' he replied 'and say to him, "The Master 18
says: My time is near. It is at your house that I am keeping Passover with my
disciples." ' •The disciples did what Jesus told them and prepared the Passover. 19

The treachery of Judas foretold

When evening came he was at table with the twelve disciples. •And while they ²⁰₂₁
were eating he said, 'I tell you solemnly, one of you is about to betray
me'. •They were greatly distressed and started asking him in turn, 'Not I, Lord, 22
surely?' •He answered, 'Someone who has dipped his hand into the dish with me, 23
will betray me. •The Son of Man is going to his fate, as the scriptures say he 24
will, but alas for that man by whom the Son of Man is betrayed! Better for that
man if he had never been born!' •Judas, who was to betray him, asked in his 25
turn, 'Not I, Rabbi, surely?' 'They are your own words' answered Jesus.

The institution of the Eucharist

Now as they were eating,[d] Jesus took some bread, and when he had said the 26
blessing he broke it and gave it to the disciples. 'Take it and eat;' he said 'this is
my body.' •Then he took a cup, and when he had returned thanks he gave it 27
to them. 'Drink all of you from this,' he said •'for this is my blood, the blood 28
of the covenant, which is to be poured out for many for the forgiveness of
sins. •From now on, I tell you, I shall not drink wine until the day I drink 29
the new wine with you in the kingdom of my Father.'

Peter's denial foretold

After psalms had been sung[e] they left for the Mount of Olives. •Then Jesus said ³⁰₃₁
to them, 'You will all lose faith in me this night,[f] for the scripture says:
I shall strike the shepherd and the sheep of the flock will be scattered,[g]•but after my 32
resurrection I shall go before you to Galilee'. •At this, Peter said, 'Though all 33
lose faith in you, I will never lose faith'. •Jesus answered him, 'I tell you 34
solemnly, this very night, before the cock crows, you will have disowned
me three times'. •Peter said to him, 'Even if I have to die with you, I will never 35
disown you'. And all the disciples said the same.

Gethsemane

Then Jesus came with them to a small estate called Gethsemane; and he said 36
to his disciples, 'Stay here while I go over there to pray'. •He took Peter and the 37
two sons of Zebedee with him. And sadness came over him, and great distress.
Then he said to them, 'My soul is sorrowful to the point of death. Wait here and 38
keep awake with me.' •And going on a little further he fell on his face and prayed. 39
'My Father,' he said 'if it is possible, let this cup pass me by. Nevertheless, let it
be as you, not I, would have it.' •He came back to the disciples and found them 40

sleeping, and he said to Peter, 'So you had not the strength to keep awake with
41 me one hour? •You should be awake, and praying not to be put to the test. The
42 spirit is willing, but the flesh is weak.' •Again, a second time, he went away and
prayed: 'My Father,' he said 'if this cup cannot pass by without my drinking it,
43 your will be done!' •And he came back again and found them sleeping, their eyes
44 were so heavy. •Leaving them there, he went away again and prayed for the
45 third time, repeating the same words. •Then he came back to the disciples and
said to them, 'You can sleep on now and take your rest. Now the hour has
46 come when the Son of Man is to be betrayed into the hands of sinners. •Get up!
Let us go! My betrayer is already close at hand.'

The arrest

47 He was still speaking when Judas, one of the Twelve, appeared, and with him
a large number of men armed with swords and clubs, sent by the chief priests and
48 elders of the people. •Now the traitor had arranged a sign with them. 'The one
49 I kiss,' he had said 'he is the man. Take him in charge .' •So he went straight up to
50 Jesus and said, 'Greetings, Rabbi', and kissed him. •Jesus said to him, 'My friend,
do what you are here for'. Then they came forward, seized Jesus and took him in
51 charge. •At that, one of the followers of Jesus grasped his sword and drew it; he
52 struck out at the high priest's servant, and cut off his ear. •Jesus then said, 'Put your
53 sword back, for all who draw the sword will die by the sword. •Or do you think
that I cannot appeal to my Father who would promptly send more than twelve
54 legions of angels to my defence? •But then, how would the scriptures be fulfilled
55 that say this is the way it must be?' •It was at this time that Jesus said to the
crowds, 'Am I a brigand, that you had to set out to capture me with swords
and clubs? I sat teaching in the Temple day after day and you never laid hands
56 on me.' •Now all this happened to fulfil the prophecies in scripture. Then
all the disciples deserted him and ran away.

Jesus before the Sanhedrin

57 The men who had arrested Jesus led him off to Caiaphas the high priest,
58 where the scribes and the elders were assembled. •Peter followed him at
a distance, and when he reached the high priest's palace, he went in and sat down
with the attendants to see what the end would be.
59 The chief priests and the whole Sanhedrin were looking for evidence against
60 Jesus, however false, on which they might pass the death-sentence. •But they could
not find any, though several lying witnesses came forward. Eventually two
61 stepped forward •and made a statement, 'This man said, "I have power to
62 destroy the Temple of God and in three days build it up"'. •The high priest
then stood up and said to him, 'Have you no answer to that? What is this evidence
63 these men are bringing against you?' •But Jesus was silent. And the high priest
said to him, 'I put you on oath by the living God to tell us if you are the Christ,
64 the Son of God'. •'The words are your own' answered Jesus. 'Moreover, I tell
you that from this time onward you will see the *Son of Man seated at the right*

---

b. 30 shekels, the price fixed for a slave's life, Ex 21:32. c. Unleavened bread was normally
to be eaten during the seven days which followed the Passover supper; here the writer
appears to mean the first day of the whole Passover celebration. d. The Passover supper
itself, for which exact rules for the blessing of bread and wine were laid down. The 'eating' of
v. 21 is the first course, which came before the Passover itself. e. The psalms of praise which
end the Passover supper. f. 'be brought down': the regular expression for the losing of faith
through a difficulty or blow to it. g. Zc 13:7

hand of the Power and *coming on the clouds of heaven.*' •At this, the high priest 65
tore his clothes and said, 'He has blasphemed. What need of witnesses have
we now? There! You have just heard the blasphemy. •What is your opinion?' 66
They answered, 'He deserves to die'.

Then they spat in his face and hit him with their fists; others said as they 67
struck him, •'Play the prophet, Christ! Who hit you then?' 68

Peter's denials

Meanwhile Peter was sitting outside in the courtyard, and a servant-girl came 69
up to him and said, 'You too were with Jesus the Galilean'. •But he denied it in 70
front of them all. 'I do not know what you are talking about' he said. •When he 71
went out to the gateway another servant-girl saw him and said to the people there,
'This man was with Jesus the Nazarene'. •And again, with an oath, he denied 72
it, 'I do not know the man'. •A little later the bystanders came up and said to 73
Peter, 'You are one of them for sure! Why, your accent gives you away.' •Then 74
he started calling down curses on himself and swearing, 'I do not know the man'.
At that moment the cock crew, •and Peter remembered what Jesus had said, 75
'Before the cock crows you will have disowned me three times'. And he went
outside and wept bitterly.

Jesus is taken before Pilate

27 When morning came, all the chief priests and the elders of the people met 1
in council to bring about the death of Jesus. •They had him bound, and 2
led him away to hand him over to Pilate,ᵃ the governor.

The death of Judas

When he found that Jesus had been condemned, Judas his betrayer was filled 3
with remorse and took the thirty silver pieces back to the chief priests and elders.
'I have sinned;' he said 'I have betrayed innocent blood.' 'What is that to us?' 4
they replied 'That is your concern.' •And flinging down the silver pieces in the 5
sanctuary he made off, and went and hanged himself. •The chief priests picked 6
up the silver pieces and said, 'It is against the Law to put this into the treasury;
it is blood-money'. •So they discussed the matter and bought the potter's field 7
with it as a graveyard for foreigners, •and this is why the field is called the Field 8
of Blood today. •The words of the prophet Jeremiahᵇ were then fulfilled: *And* 9
they took the thirty silver pieces, the sum at which the precious One was priced
by children of Israel, •*and they gave them for the potter's field, just as the Lord* 10
directed me.

Jesus before Pilate

Jesus, then, was brought before the governor, and the governor put to him 11
this question, 'Are you the king of the Jews?' Jesus replied, 'It is you who say
it'. •But when he was accused by the chief priests and the elders he refused to 12
answer at all. •Pilate then said to him, 'Do you not hear how many charges they 13
have brought against you?' •But to the governor's complete amazement, he 14
offered no reply to any of the charges.

At festival time it was the governor's practice to release a prisoner for the 15
people, anyone they chose. •Now there was at that time a notorious prisoner 16
whose name was Barabbas. •So when the crowd gathered, Pilate said to them, 17
'Which do you want me to release for you: Barabbas, or Jesus who is called
Christ?' •For Pilate knew it was out of jealousy that they had handed him over. 18

19   Now as he was seated in the chair of judgement, his wife sent him a message, 'Have nothing to do with that man; I have been upset all day by a dream I had about him'.

20   The chief priests and the elders, however, had persuaded the crowd to demand
21 the release of Barabbas and the execution of Jesus. •So when the governor spoke and asked them, 'Which of the two do you want me to release for you?' they
22 said, 'Barabbas'. •'But in that case,' Pilate said to them 'what am I to do with Jesus
23 who is called Christ?' They all said, 'Let him be crucified!' •'Why?' he asked 'What harm has he done?' But they shouted all the louder, 'Let him be crucified!'
24 Then Pilate saw that he was making no impression, that in fact a riot was imminent. So he took some water, washed his hands in front of the crowd and
25 said, 'I am innocent of this man's blood. It is your concern.' •And the people,
26 to a man, shouted back, 'His blood be on us and on our children!' •Then he released Barabbas for them. He ordered Jesus to be first scourged^c and then handed over to be crucified.

Jesus is crowned with thorns

27   The governor's soldiers took Jesus with them into the Praetorium and
28 collected the whole cohort round him. •Then they stripped him and made
29 him wear a scarlet cloak, •and having twisted some thorns into a crown they put this on his head and placed a reed in his right hand. To make fun of him they
30 knelt to him saying, 'Hail, king of the Jews!' •And they spat on him and took
31 the reed and struck him on the head with it. •And when they had finished making fun of him, they took off the cloak and dressed him in his own clothes and led him away to crucify him.

The crucifixion

32   On their way out, they came across a man from Cyrene, Simon by name,
33 and enlisted him to carry his cross. •When they had reached a place called
34 Golgotha,^{d} that is, the place of the skull, •they gave him wine to drink mixed
35 with gall, which he tasted but refused to drink. •When they had finished
36 crucifying him they shared out his clothing by casting lots, •and then sat down and stayed there keeping guard over him.

37   Above his head was placed the charge against him; it read: 'This is Jesus,
38 the King of the Jews'. •At the same time two robbers were crucified with him, one on the right and one on the left.

The crucified Christ is mocked

39
40   The passers-by jeered at him; they shook their heads •and said, 'So you would destroy the Temple and rebuild it in three days! Then save yourself! If
41 you are God's son, come down from the cross!' •The chief priests with the
42 scribes and elders mocked him in the same way. •'He saved others;' they said 'he cannot save himself. He is the king of Israel; let him come down from the
43 cross now, and we will believe in him. •He puts his trust in God; now let God
44 rescue him if he wants him. For he did say, "I am the son of God".' •Even the robbers who were crucified with him taunted him in the same way.

27 a. The Jews had to approach the Roman governor for confirmation and execution of any sentence of death.   b. Actually a free quotation from Zc 11:12-13.   c. The normal prelude to crucifixion.   d. The Aramaic form of the name of which Calvary is the more familiar Latin equivalent.

The death of Jesus

From the sixth hour there was darkness over all the land until the ninth hour.*ᵉ* 45 And about the ninth hour, Jesus cried out in a loud voice, 'Eli, Eli, lama sabach- 46 thani?' that is, '*My God, my God, why have you deserted me?*'*ᶠ* • When some of 47 those who stood there heard this, they said, 'The man is calling on Elijah', and one of them quickly ran to get a sponge which he dipped in vinegar*ᵍ* and, 48 putting it on a reed, gave it him to drink. •'Wait!' said the rest of them 'and 49 see if Elijah will come to save him.' •But Jesus, again crying out in a loud 50 voice, yielded up his spirit.

At that, the veil of the Temple *ʰ* was torn in two from top to bottom; the earth 51 quaked; the rocks were split; •the tombs opened and the bodies of many holy men 52 rose from the dead, •and these, after his resurrection, came out of the tombs, 53 entered the Holy City and appeared to a number of people. •Meanwhile the centur- 54 ion, together with the others guarding Jesus, had seen the earthquake and all that was taking place, and they were terrified and said, 'In truth this was a son of God.'

And many women were there, watching from a distance, the same 55 women who had followed Jesus from Galilee and looked after him. •Among 56 them were Mary of Magdala, Mary the mother of James and Joseph, and the mother of Zebedee's sons.

The burial

When it was evening, there came a rich man of Arimathaea, called Joseph, 57 who had himself become a disciple of Jesus. •This man went to Pilate and asked 58 for the body of Jesus. Pilate thereupon ordered it to be handed over. •So Joseph 59 took the body, wrapped it in a clean shroud •and put it in his own new tomb 60 which he had hewn out of the rock. He then rolled a large stone across the entrance of the tomb and went away. •Now Mary of Magdala and the other Mary were 61 there, sitting opposite the sepulchre.

The guard at the tomb

Next day, that is, when Preparation Day*ⁱ* was over, the chief priests and the 62 Pharisees went in a body to Pilate •and said to him, 'Your Excellency, we 63 recall that this impostor said, while he was still alive, "After three days I shall rise again". •Therefore give the order to have the sepulchre kept secure until the 64 third day, for fear his disciples come and steal him away and tell the people, "He has risen from the dead". This last piece of fraud would be worse than what went before.' •'You may have your guard' said Pilate to them. 'Go and make 65 all as secure as you know how.' •So they went and made the sepulchre secure, 66 putting seals on the stone and mounting a guard.

The empty tomb. The angel's message

28 After the sabbath, and towards dawn on the first day of the week, Mary of 1 Magdala and the other Mary went to visit the sepulchre. •And all at once 2 there was a violent earthquake, for the angel of the Lord, descending from heaven, came and rolled away the stone and sat on it. •His face was like lightning, 3 his robe white as snow. •The guards were so shaken, so frightened of him, that 4 they were like dead men. •But the angel spoke; and he said to the women, 5 'There is no need for you to be afraid. I know you are looking for Jesus, who was crucified. •He is not here, for he has risen, as he said he would. Come and see 6 the place where he lay, •then go quickly and tell his disciples, "He has risen 7

from the dead and now he is going before you to Galilee; it is there you will
8 see him". Now I have told you.' •Filled with awe and great joy the women came
quickly away from the tomb and ran to tell the disciples.

Appearance to the women

9   And there, coming to meet them, was Jesus. 'Greetings' he said. And the
10 women came up to him and, falling down before him, clasped his feet. •Then
Jesus said to them, 'Do not be afraid; go and tell my brothers that they must leave
for Galilee; they will see me there'.

Precautions taken by the leaders of the people

11   While they were on their way, some of the guard went off into the city to tell
12 the chief priests all that had happened. •These held a meeting with the elders
and, after some discussion, handed a considerable sum of money to the soldiers
13 with these instructions, 'This is what you must say, "His disciples came during
14 the night and stole him away while we were asleep". •And should the governor
come to hear of this, we undertake to put things right with him ourselves and
15 to see that you do not get into trouble.' •The soldiers took the money and carried
out their instructions, and to this day that is the story among the Jews.

Appearance in Galilee. The mission to the world

16   Meanwhile the eleven disciples set out for Galilee, to the mountain where
17 Jesus had arranged to meet them. •When they saw him they fell down before
18 him, though some hesitated. •Jesus came up and spoke to them. He said, 'All
19 authority in heaven and on earth has been given to me. •Go, therefore, make
disciples of all the nations; baptise them in the name of the Father and of the
20 Son and of the Holy Spirit,ᵃ •and teach them to observe all the commands I
gave you. And know that I am with you always; yes, to the end of time.'

e. From mid-day to 3 p.m.   f. Ps 22:1   g. The rough wine drunk by Roman soldiers.
h. There were two curtains in the Temple; most probably this was the inner curtain which
guarded the Most Holy Place.   i. The day before the sabbath.
28 a. This formula is perhaps a reflection of the liturgical usage of the writer's own time.

THE GOSPEL ACCORDING TO
SAINT MARK

I. PRELUDE TO THE PUBLIC MINISTRY OF JESUS

The preaching of John the Baptist

1 The beginning of the Good News about Jesus Christ, the Son of God. •It is ¹⁄₂ written in the book of the prophet Isaiah:

> *Look, I am going to send my messenger before you;*
> *he will prepare your way.*
> *A voice cries in the wilderness:*   3
> *Prepare a way for the Lord,*
> *make his paths straight,ᵃ*

and so it was that John the Baptist appeared in the wilderness, proclaiming 4 a baptism of repentance for the forgiveness of sins. •All Judaea and all the people 5 of Jerusalem made their way to him, and as they were baptised by him in the river Jordan they confessed their sins. •John wore a garment of camel-skin, and 6 he lived on locusts and wild honey. •In the course of his preaching he said, 7 'Someone is following me, someone who is more powerful than I am, and I am not fit to kneel down and undo the strap of his sandals. •I have baptised you 8 with water, but he will baptise you with the Holy Spirit.'

Jesus is baptised

It was at this time that Jesus came from Nazareth in Galilee and was baptised 9 in the Jordan by John. •No sooner had he come up out of the water than he 10 saw the heavens torn apart and the Spirit, like a dove, descending on him. And a voice came from heaven, 'You are my Son, the Beloved; my favour rests 11 on you'.

Temptation in the wilderness

Immediately afterwards the Spirit drove him out into the wilderness •and he ¹²⁄₁₃ remained there for forty days, and was tempted by Satan. He was with the wild beasts, and the angels looked after him.

II. THE GALILEAN MINISTRY

Jesus begins to preach

After John had been arrested, Jesus went into Galilee. There he proclaimed 14 the Good News from God. •'The time has come' he said 'and the kingdom of 15 God is close at hand. Repent, and believe the Good News.'

The first four disciples are called

16 As he was walking along by the Sea of Galilee he saw Simon and his brother
17 Andrew casting a net in the lake — for they were fishermen. •And Jesus said to
18 them, 'Follow me and I will make you into fishers of men'. •And at once they
left their nets and followed him.

19 Going on a little further, he saw James son of Zebedee and his brother John;
20 they too were in their boat, mending their nets. He called them at once •and,
leaving their father Zebedee in the boat with the men he employed, they went
after him.

Jesus teaches in Capernaum and cures a demoniac

21 They went as far as Capernaum, and as soon as the sabbath came he went
22 to the synagogue and began to teach. •And his teaching made a deep impression
on them because, unlike the scribes, he taught them with authority.

23 In their synagogue just then there was a man possessed by an unclean spirit,
24 and it shouted, •'What do you want with us, Jesus of Nazareth? Have you come
25 to destroy us? I know who you are: the Holy One of God.' •But Jesus said
26 sharply, 'Be quiet! Come out of him!' •And the unclean spirit threw the man into
27 convulsions and with a loud cry went out of him. •The people were so astonished
that they started asking each other what it all meant. 'Here is a teaching that is
new' they said 'and with authority behind it: he gives orders even to unclean
28 spirits and they obey him.' •And his reputation rapidly spread everywhere,
through all the surrounding Galilean countryside.

Cure of Simon's mother-in-law

29 On leaving the synagogue, he went with James and John straight to the house
30 of Simon and Andrew. •Now Simon's mother-in-law had gone to bed with fever,
31 and they told him about her straightaway. •He went to her, took her by the hand
and helped her up. And the fever left her and she began to wait on them.

A number of cures

32 That evening, after sunset, they brought to him all who were sick and those
33 who were possessed by devils. •The whole town came crowding round the door,
34 and he cured many who were suffering from diseases of one kind or another;
he also cast out many devils, but he would not allow them to speak, because they
knew who he was.[b]

Jesus quietly leaves Capernaum and travels through Galilee

35 In the morning, long before dawn, he got up and left the house, and went
36 off to a lonely place and prayed there. •Simon and his companions set out in
37 search of him, •and when they found him they said, 'Everybody is looking for
38 you'. •He answered, 'Let us go elsewhere, to the neighbouring country towns,
39 so that I can preach there too, because that is why I came'. •And he went all
through Galilee, preaching in their synagogues and casting out devils.

Cure of a leper

40 A leper came to him and pleaded on his knees: 'If you want to' he said 'you
41 can cure me'. •Feeling sorry for him, Jesus stretched out his hand and touched

---

1 a. Is 40:3   b. Throughout this gospel, Jesus never explicitly claims to be the Messiah and
he forbids others to speak of the fact.

him. 'Of course I want to!' he said. 'Be cured!' •And the leprosy left him at once 42 and he was cured. •Jesus immediately sent him away and sternly ordered him, 43 'Mind you say nothing to anyone, but go and show yourself to the priest, and 44 make the offering for your healing prescribed by Moses as evidence of your recovery'. •The man went away, but then started talking about it freely and 45 telling the story everywhere, so that Jesus could no longer go openly into any town, but had to stay outside in places where nobody lived. Even so, people from all around would come to him.

Cure of a paralytic

2 When he returned to Capernaum some time later, word went round that he 1 was back; •and so many people collected that there was no room left, even 2 in front of the door. He was preaching the word to them •when some people 3 came bringing him a paralytic carried by four men, •but as the crowd made 4 it impossible to get the man to him, they stripped the roof over the place where Jesus was; and when they had made an opening, they lowered the stretcher on which the paralytic lay. •Seeing their faith, Jesus said to the paralytic, 'My child, 5 your sins are forgiven'. •Now some scribes were sitting there, and they thought 6 to themselves, •'How can this man talk like that? He is blaspheming. Who can 7 forgive sins but God?' •Jesus, inwardly aware that this was what they were 8 thinking, said to them, 'Why do you have these thoughts in your hearts? Which of these is easier: to say to the paralytic, "Your sins are forgiven" or to 9 say, "Get up, pick up your stretcher and walk"? •But to prove to you that the 10 Son of Man has authority on earth to forgive sins,'—•he said to the paralytic— 11 'I order you: get up, pick up your stretcher, and go off home.' •And the man 12 got up, picked up his stretcher at once and walked out in front of everyone, so that they were all astounded and praised God saying, 'We have never seen anything like this'.

The call of Levi

He went out again to the shore of the lake;ᵃ and all the people came to him, 13 and he taught them. •As he was walking on he saw Levi the son of Alphaeus, 14 sitting by the customs house, and he said to him, 'Follow me'. And he got up and followed him.

Eating with sinners

When Jesus was at dinner in his house, a number of tax collectors and sinners 15 were also sitting at the table with Jesus and his disciples; for there were many of them among his followers. •When the scribes of the Pharisee party saw him eating 16 with sinners and tax collectors, they said to his disciples, 'Why does he eat with tax collectors and sinners?' •When Jesus heard this he said to them, 'It is not the 17 healthy who need the doctor, but the sick. I did not come to call the virtuous, but sinners.'

A discussion on fasting

One day when John's disciples and the Pharisees were fasting, some people 18 came and said to him, 'Why is it that John's disciples and the disciples of the Pharisees fast, but your disciples do not?' •Jesus replied, 'Surely the bridegroom's 19 attendants would never think of fasting while the bridegroom is still with them? As long as they have the bridegroom with them, they could not think of fasting. But the time will come for the bridegroom to be taken away from them, and then, 20

21 on that day, they will fast. •No one sews a piece of unshrunken cloth on an old cloak; if he does, the patch pulls away from it, the new from the old, and the tear
22 gets worse. •And nobody puts new wine into old wineskins; if he does, the wine will burst the skins, and the wine is lost and the skins too. No! New wine, fresh skins!'

Picking corn on the sabbath

23   One sabbath day he happened to be taking a walk through the cornfields, and
24 his disciples began to pick ears of corn as they went along. •And the Pharisees said to him, 'Look, why are they doing something on the sabbath day that is
25 forbidden?' •And he replied, 'Did you never read what David did in his time of
26 need when he and his followers were hungry—•how he went into the house of God when Abiathar[b] was high priest, and ate the loaves of offering which only the priests are allowed to eat, and how he also gave some to the men with him?'
27   And he said to them, 'The sabbath was made for man, not man for the
28 sabbath; •so the Son of Man is master even of the sabbath'.

Cure of the man with a withered hand

1 3 He went again into a synagogue, and there was a man there who had a withered
2   hand. •And they were watching him to see if he would cure him on the sabbath
3 day, hoping for something to use against him. •He said to the man with the
4 withered hand, 'Stand up out in the middle!' •Then he said to them, 'Is it against the law on the sabbath day to do good, or to do evil; to save life, or to
5 kill?' But they said nothing. •Then, grieved to find them so obstinate, he looked angrily round at them, and said to the man, 'Stretch out your hand'. He stretched
6 it out and his hand was better. •The Pharisees went out and at once began to plot with the Herodians against him, discussing how to destroy him.

The crowds follow Jesus

7   Jesus withdrew with his disciples to the lakeside, and great crowds from
8 Galilee followed him. From Judaea, •Jerusalem, Idumaea, Transjordania and the region of Tyre and Sidon, great numbers who had heard of all he was doing
9 came to him. •And he asked his disciples to have a boat ready for him because
10 of the crowd, to keep him from being crushed. •For he had cured so many that all
11 who were afflicted in any way were crowding forward to touch him. •And the unclean spirits, whenever they saw him, would fall down before him and shout,
12 'You are the Son of God!' •But he warned them strongly not to make him known.

The appointment of the Twelve

13   He now went up into the hills and summoned those he wanted. So they came
14 to him •and he appointed twelve; they were to be his companions and to be sent
15
16 out to preach, •with power to cast out devils. •And so he appointed the Twelve:
17 Simon to whom he gave the name Peter, •James the son of Zebedee and John the brother of James, to whom he gave the name Boanerges or 'Sons of Thunder';
18 then Andrew, Philip, Bartholomew, Matthew, Thomas, James the son of
19 Alphaeus, Thaddaeus, Simon the Zealot •and Judas Iscariot, the man who was to betray him.

---

2 a. Tiberias, the 'Sea of Galilee'.   **b.** See 1 S 21:1-7. Abiathar was the better known as high priest in David's reign, but Ahimelech is named in this source.

His relatives are concerned about Jesus

He went home again, and once more such a crowd collected that they could 20 not even have a meal. •When his relatives heard of this, they set out to take 21 charge of him, convinced he was out of his mind.

Allegations of the scribes

The scribes who had come down from Jerusalem were saying, 'Beelzebul is 22 in him' and, 'It is through the prince of devils that he casts devils out'. •So he called 23 them to him and spoke to them in parables, 'How can Satan cast out Satan? If a kingdom is divided against itself, that kingdom cannot last. •And if $^{24}_{25}$ a household is divided against itself, that household can never stand. •Now if 26 Satan has rebelled against himself and is divided, he cannot stand either—it is the end of him. •But no one can make his way into a strong man's house and 27 burgle his property unless he has tied up the strong man first. Only then can he burgle his house.

'I tell you solemnly, all men's sins will be forgiven, and all their 28 blasphemies; •but let anyone blaspheme against the Holy Spirit and he will never 29 have forgiveness: he is guilty of an eternal sin.' •This was because they were 30 saying, 'An unclean spirit is in him'.

The true kinsmen of Jesus

His mother and brothers now arrived and, standing outside, sent in a message 31 asking for him. •A crowd was sitting round him at the time the message was passed 32 to him, 'Your mother and brothers and sisters are outside asking for you'. He replied, 'Who are my mother and·my brothers?' •And looking round at $^{33}_{34}$ those sitting in a circle about him, he said, 'Here are my mother and my brothers. Anyone who does the will of God, that person is my brother and sister and 35 mother.'

Parable of the sower

4 Again he began to teach by the lakeside, but such a huge crowd gathered 1 round him that he got into a boat on the lake and sat there. The people were all along the shore, at the water's edge. •He taught them many things in parables, 2 and in the course of his teaching he said to them, •'Listen! Imagine a sower 3 going out to sow. •Now it happened that, as he sowed, some of the seed fell on 4 the edge of the path, and the birds came and ate it up. •Some seed fell on rocky 5 ground where it found little soil and sprang up straightaway, because there was no depth of earth; •and when the sun came up it was scorched and, not having 6 any roots, it withered away. •Some seed fell into thorns, and the thorns 7 grew up and choked it, and it produced no crop. •And some seeds fell into rich 8 soil and, growing tall and strong, produced crop; and yielded thirty, sixty, even a hundredfold.' •And he said, 'Listen, anyone who has ears to hear!' 9

Why Jesus speaks in parables

When he was alone, the Twelve, together with the others who formed his 10 company, asked what the parables meant. •He told them, 'The secret of the 11 kingdom of God is given to you, but to those who are outside everything comes in parables, •so that *they may see and see again, but not perceive; may hear and* 12 *hear again, but not understand; otherwise they might be converted and be forgiven'.*[a]

The parable of the sower explained

13 He said to them, 'Do you not understand this parable? Then how will you
14 understand any of the parables? •What the sower is sowing is the word. •Those
15 on the edge of the path where the word is sown are people who have no sooner
heard it than Satan comes and carries away the word that was sown in them.
16 Similarly, those who receive the seed on patches of rock are people who, when
17 first they hear the word, welcome it at once with joy. •But they have no root
in them, they do not last; should some trial come, or some persecution on
18 account of the word, they fall away at once. •Then there are others who receive
19 the seed in thorns. These have heard the word, •but the worries of this world,
the lure of riches and all the other passions come in to choke the word, and so
20 it produces nothing. •And there are those who have received the seed in rich
soil: they hear the word and accept it and yield a harvest, thirty and sixty and a
hundredfold.'

Parable of the lamp

21 He also said to them, 'Would you bring in a lamp to put it under a tub or
22 under the bed? Surely you will put it on the lamp-stand? •For there is nothing
hidden but it must be disclosed, nothing kept secret except to be brought to light.
23 If anyone has ears to hear, let him listen to this.'

Parable of the measure

24 He also said to them, 'Take notice of what you are hearing. The amount you
25 measure out is the amount you will be given—and more besides; •for the man
who has will be given more; from the man who has not, even what he has will be
taken away.'

Parable of the seed growing by itself

26 He also said, 'This is what the kingdom of God is like. A man throws seed on
27 the land. •Night and day, while he sleeps, when he is awake, the seed is sprouting
28 and growing; how, he does not know. •Of its own accord the land produces first
29 the shoot, then the ear, then the full grain in the ear. •And when the crop is ready,
he loses no time: he starts to reap because the harvest has come.'

Parable of the mustard seed

30 He also said, 'What can we say the kingdom of God is like? What parable can
31 we find for it? •It is like a mustard seed which at the time of its sowing in the
32 soil is the smallest of all the seeds on earth; •yet once it is sown it grows into the
biggest shrub of them all and puts out big branches so that the birds of the air
can shelter in its shade.'

The use of parables

33 Using many parables like these, he spoke the word to them, so far as they were
34 capable of understanding it. •He would not speak to them except in parables,
but he explained everything to his disciples when they were alone.

The calming of the storm

35 With the coming of evening that same day, he said to them, 'Let us cross over
36 to the other side'. •And leaving the crowd behind they took him, just as he was,
37 in the boat; and there were other boats with him. •Then it began to blow a gale

4 a. Is 6:9-10

and the waves were breaking into the boat so that it was almost swamped. •But 38
he was in the stern, his head on the cushion, asleep. •They woke him and said 39
to him, 'Master, do you not care? We are going down!' And he woke up and
rebuked the wind and said to the sea, 'Quiet now! Be calm!' And the wind
dropped, and all was calm again. •Then he said to them, 'Why are you so 40
frightened? How is it that you have no faith?' •They were filled with awe and said 41
to one another, 'Who can this be? Even the wind and the sea obey him.'

The Gerasene demoniac

5 They reached the country of the Gerasenes*a* on the other side of the lake, •and ½
no sooner had he left the boat than a man with an unclean spirit came out
from the tombs towards him. •The man lived in the tombs and no one could 3
secure him any more, even with a chain; •because he had often been secured 4
with fetters and chains but had snapped the chains and broken the fetters, and no
one had the strength to control him. •All night and all day, among the tombs 5
and in the mountains, he would howl and gash himself with stones. •Catching 6
sight of Jesus from a distance, he ran up and fell at his feet •and shouted at the 7
top of his voice, 'What do you want with me, Jesus, son of the Most High God?
Swear by God you will not torture me!' •—For Jesus had been saying to him, 8
'Come out of the man, unclean spirit'. •'What is your name?' Jesus asked. 'My 9
name is legion,' he answered 'for there are many of us.' •And he begged him 10
earnestly not to send them out of the district. •Now there was there on the 11
mountainside a great herd of pigs feeding, •and the unclean spirits begged 12
him, 'Send us to the pigs, let us go into them'. •So he gave them leave. With that, 13
the unclean spirits came out and went into the pigs, and the herd of about two
thousand pigs charged down the cliff into the lake, and there they were drowned.
The swineherds ran off and told their story in the town and in the country round 14
about; and the people came to see what had really happened. •They came to 15
Jesus and saw the demoniac sitting there, clothed and in his full senses—the very
man who had had the legion in him before—and they were afraid. •And those 16
who had witnessed it reported what had happened to the demoniac and what had
become of the pigs. •Then they began to implore Jesus to leave the neighbourhood. 17
As he was getting into the boat, the man who had been possessed begged to be 18
allowed to stay with him. •Jesus would not let him but said to him, 'Go home 19
to your people and tell them all that the Lord in his mercy has done for you'.
So the man went off and proceeded to spread throughout the Decapolis all that 20
Jesus had done for him. And everyone was amazed.

Cure of the woman with a haemorrhage. The daughter of Jairus raised to life

When Jesus had crossed again in the boat to the other side, a large crowd 21
gathered round him and he stayed by the lakeside. •Then one of the synagogue 22
officials came up, Jairus by name, and seeing him, fell at his feet •and pleaded 23
with him earnestly, saying, 'My little daughter is desperately sick. Do come and
lay your hands on her to make her better and save her life.' •Jesus went with him 24
and a large crowd followed him; they were pressing all round him.

Now there was a woman who had suffered from a haemorrhage for 25
twelve years; •after long and painful treatment under various doctors, she had 26
spent all she had without being any the better for it, in fact, she was getting
worse. •She had heard about Jesus, and she came up behind him through the crowd 27
and touched his cloak. •'If I can touch even his clothes,' she had told herself 28
'I shall be well again.' •And the source of the bleeding dried up instantly, and she 29

30 felt in herself that she was cured of her complaint. •Immediately aware that power had gone out from him, Jesus turned round in the crowd and said, 'Who 31 touched my clothes?' •His disciples said to him, 'You see how the crowd is 32 pressing round you and yet you say, "Who touched me?" ' •But he continued 33 to look all round to see who had done it. •Then the woman came forward, frightened and trembling [b] because she knew what had happened to her, and she 34 fell at his feet and told him the whole truth. •'My daughter,' he said 'your faith has restored you to health; go in peace and be free from your complaint.'

35   While he was still speaking some people arrived from the house of the synagogue official to say, 'Your daughter is dead: why put the Master to any 36 further trouble?' •But Jesus had overheard this remark of theirs and he said to 37 the official, 'Do not be afraid; only have faith'. •And he allowed no one to go 38 with him except Peter and James and John the brother of James. •So they came to the official's house and Jesus noticed all the commotion, with people weeping 39 and wailing unrestrainedly. •He went in and said to them, 'Why all this 40 commotion and crying? The child is not dead, but asleep.' •But they laughed at him. So he turned them all out and, taking with him the child's father and mother and his own companions, he went into the place where the child lay. 41 And taking the child by the hand he said to her, 'Talitha, kum!' which means, 42 'Little girl, I tell you to get up'. •The little girl got up at once and began to walk about, for she was twelve years old. At this they were overcome with astonishment, 43 and he ordered them strictly not to let anyone know about it, and told them to give her something to eat.

A visit to Nazareth

1 **6** Going from that district, he went to his home town and his disciples accompa- 2 nied him. •With the coming of the sabbath he began teaching in the synagogue and most of them were astonished when they heard him. They said, 'Where did the man get all this? What is this wisdom that has been granted him, and these 3 miracles that are worked through him? •This is the carpenter, surely, the son of Mary, the brother of James and Joset and Jude and Simon? His sisters, too, are 4 they not here with us?' And they would not accept him. •And Jesus said to them, 'A prophet is only despised in his own country, among his own relations and 5 in his own house'; •and he could work no miracle there, though he cured a few 6 sick people by laying his hands on them. •He was amazed at their lack of faith.

The mission of the Twelve

7   He made a tour round the villages, teaching. •Then he summoned the Twelve and began to send them out in pairs giving them authority over the unclean spirits. 8 And he instructed them to take nothing for the journey except a staff —no bread, 9 no haversack, no coppers for their purses. •They were to wear sandals but, he 10 added, 'Do not take a spare tunic'. •And he said to them, 'If you enter a house 11 anywhere, stay there until you leave the district. •And if any place does not welcome you and people refuse to listen to you, as you walk away shake off 12 the dust from under your feet as a sign to them.' •So they set off to preach 13 repentance; •and they cast out many devils, and anointed many sick people with oil and cured them.

---

5 a. 'Gadarenes' in some versions.   **b.** According to the Law, she was unclean, and to be touched by her would be defilement.

Herod and Jesus

Meanwhile King Herod had heard about him, since by now his name was well- 14
known. Some were saying, 'John the Baptist has risen from the dead, and that
is why miraculous powers are at work in him'. •Others said, 'He is Elijah'; 15
others again, 'He is a prophet, like the prophets we used to have'. •But when 16
Herod heard this he said, 'It is John whose head I cut off; he has risen from the
dead'.

John the Baptist beheaded

Now it was this same Herod who had sent to have John arrested, and had 17
him chained up in prison because of Herodias, his brother Philip's wife whom he
had married. •For John had told Herod, 'It is against the law for you to have 18
your brother's wife'. •As for Herodias, she was furious with him and wanted to 19
kill him; but she was not able to, •because Herod was afraid of John, knowing 20
him to be a good and holy man, and gave him his protection. When he had heard
him speak he was greatly perplexed, and yet he liked to listen to him.

An opportunity came on Herod's birthday when he gave a banquet for the 21
nobles of his court, for his army officers and for the leading figures in Galilee.
When the daughter of this same Herodias came in and danced, she delighted 22
Herod and his guests; so the king said to the girl, 'Ask me anything you like
and I will give it you'. •And he swore her an oath, 'I will give you anything you 23
ask, even half my kingdom'. •She went out and said to her mother, 'What shall 24
I ask for?' She replied, 'The head of John the Baptist'. •The girl hurried straight 25
back to the king and made her request, 'I want you to give me John the Baptist's
head, here and now, on a dish'. •The king was deeply distressed but, thinking 26
of the oaths he had sworn and of his guests, he was reluctant to break his word
to her. •So the king at once sent one of the bodyguard with orders to bring 27
John's head. •The man went off and beheaded him in prison; then he brought 28
the head on a dish and gave it to the girl, and the girl gave it to her mother.
When John's disciples heard about this, they came and took his body and laid 29
it in a tomb.

First miracle of the loaves

The apostles rejoined Jesus and told him all they had done and taught. 30
Then he said to them, 'You must come away to some lonely place all by yourselves 31
and rest for a while'; for there were so many coming and going that the apostles
had no time even to eat. •So they went off in a boat to a lonely place where they 32
could be by themselves. •But people saw them going, and many could guess where; 33
and from every town they all hurried to the place on foot and reached it before
them. •So as he stepped ashore he saw a large crowd; and he took pity on them 34
because they were like sheep without a shepherd, and he set himself to teach them
at some length. •By now it was getting very late, and his disciples came up to him 35
and said, 'This is a lonely place and it is getting very late, •so send them away, 36
and they can go to the farms and villages round about, to buy themselves
something to eat'. •He replied, 'Give them something to eat yourselves'. They 37
answered, 'Are we to go and spend two hundred denarii on bread for them to
eat?' •'How many loaves have you?' he asked 'Go and see.' And when they had 38
found out they said, 'Five, and two fish'. •Then he ordered them to get all the 39
people together in groups on the green grass, •and they sat down on the ground 40
in squares of hundreds and fifties. •Then he took the five loaves and the two fish, 41

raised his eyes to heaven and said the blessing; then he broke the loaves and handed them to his disciples to distribute among the people. He also shared out
⁴²/₄₃ the two fish among them all. •They all ate as much as they wanted. •They
⁴⁴ collected twelve basketfuls of scraps of bread and pieces of fish. •Those who had eaten the loaves numbered five thousand men.

Jesus walks on the water

⁴⁵   Directly after this he made his disciples get into the boat and go on ahead to
⁴⁶ Bethsaida, while he himself sent the crowd away. •After saying good-bye to
⁴⁷ them he went off into the hills to pray. •When evening came, the boat was far out
⁴⁸ on the lake, and he was alone on the land. •He could see they were worn out with rowing, for the wind was against them; and about the fourth watch of the night he came towards them, walking on the lake. He was going to pass them by,
⁴⁹ but when they saw him walking on the lake they thought it was a ghost and cried
⁵⁰ out; •for they had all seen him and were terrified. But he at once spoke to them,
⁵¹ and said, 'Courage! It is I! Do not be afraid.' •Then he got into the boat with them,
⁵² and the wind dropped. They were utterly and completely dumbfounded, •because they had not seen what the miracle of the loaves meant; their minds were closed.

Cures at Gennesaret

⁵³/₅₄   Having made the crossing, they came to land at Gennesaret and tied up. •No
⁵⁵ sooner had they stepped out of the boat than people recognised him, •and started hurrying all through the countryside and brought the sick on stretchers to wherever
⁵⁶ they heard he was. •And wherever he went, to village, or town, or farm, they laid down the sick in the open spaces, begging him to let them touch even the fringe of his cloak. And all those who touched him were cured.

The traditions of the Pharisees

¹ **7** The Pharisees and some of the scribes who had come from Jerusalem gathered
²   round him, •and they noticed that some of his disciples were eating with
³ unclean hands, that is, without washing them. •For the Pharisees, and the Jews in general, follow the tradition of the elders and never eat without washing their
⁴ arms as far as the elbow; •and on returning from the market place they never eat without first sprinkling themselves. There are also many other observances which have been handed down to them concerning the washing of cups and pots
⁵ and bronze dishes. •So these Pharisees and scribes asked him, 'Why do your disciples not respect the tradition of the elders but eat their food with unclean
⁶ hands?' •He answered, 'It was of you hypocrites that Isaiah so rightly prophesied in this passage of scripture:

> *This people honours me only with lip-service,*
> *while their hearts are far from me.*
⁷ *The worship they offer me is worthless,*
> *the doctrines they teach are only human regulations.*ᵃ

⁸/₉ You put aside the commandment of God to cling to human traditions.' •And he said to them, 'How ingeniously you get round the commandment of God
¹⁰ in order to preserve your own tradition! •For Moses said: *Do your duty to your father and your mother*, and, *Anyone who curses father or mother must be put to*
¹¹ *death*. •But you say, "If a man says to his father or mother: Anything I have
¹² that I might have used to help you is Corbanᵇ (that is, dedicated to God), •then

7 a. Is 29:13   **b.** See note on Mt 15:6.

he is forbidden from that moment to do anything for his father or mother".
In this way you make God's word null and void for the sake of your tradition 13
which you have handed down. And you do many other things like this.'

On clean and unclean

He called the people to him again and said, 'Listen to me, all of you, and 14
understand. •Nothing that goes into a man from outside can make him unclean; 15
it is the things that come out of a man that make him unclean. •If anyone has 16
ears to hear, let him listen to this.'

When he had gone back into the house, away from the crowd, his disciples 17
questioned him about the parable. •He said to them, 'Do you not understand 18
either? Can you not see that whatever goes into a man from outside cannot
make him unclean, •because it does not go into his heart but through his stomach 19
and passes out into the sewer?' (Thus he pronounced all foods clean.) •And he 20
went on, 'It is what comes out of a man that makes him unclean. •For it is from 21
within, from men's hearts, that evil intentions emerge: fornication, theft, murder,
adultery, •avarice, malice, deceit, indecency, envy, slander, pride, folly. •All these $\frac{22}{23}$
evil things come from within and make a man unclean.'

III. JOURNEYS OUTSIDE GALILEE

The daughter of the Syrophoenician woman healed

He left that place and set out for the territory of Tyre. There he went into 24
a house and did not want anyone to know he was there, but he could not pass
unrecognised. •A woman whose little daughter had an unclean spirit heard about 25
him straightaway and came and fell at his feet. •Now the woman was a pagan, 26
by birth a Syrophoenician, and she begged him to cast the devil out of her
daughter. •And he said to her, 'The children should be fed first, because it is not 27
fair to take the children's food and throw it to the house-dogs'. •But she spoke 28
up: 'Ah yes, sir,' she replied 'but the house-dogs under the table can eat the
children's scraps'. •And he said to her, 'For saying this, you may go home happy: 29
the devil has gone out of your daughter'. •So she went off to her home and found 30
the child lying on the bed and the devil gone.

Healing of the deaf man

Returning from the district of Tyre, he went by way of Sidon towards the Sea 31
of Galilee, right through the Decapolis region. •And they brought him a deaf 32
man who had an impediment in his speech; and they asked him to lay his hand on
him. •He took him aside in private, away from the crowd, put his fingers into the 33
man's ears and touched his tongue with spittle. •Then looking up to heaven he 34
sighed; and he said to him, 'Ephphatha', that is, 'Be opened'. •And his ears were 35
opened, and the ligament of his tongue was loosened and he spoke clearly.
And Jesus ordered them to tell no one about it, but the more he insisted, the 36
more widely they published it. •Their admiration was unbounded. 'He has done 37
all things well,' they said 'he makes the deaf hear and the dumb speak.'

Second miracle of the loaves

8 And now once again a great crowd had gathered, and they had nothing to eat. 1
So he called his disciples to him and said to them, •'I feel sorry for all these 2
people; they have been with me for three days now and have nothing to eat.

3 If I send them off home hungry they will collapse on the way; some have come
4 a great distance.' •His disciples replied, 'Where could anyone get bread to feed
5 these people in a deserted place like this?' •He asked them, 'How many loaves
6 have you?' 'Seven' they said. •Then he instructed the crowd to sit down on the
ground, and he took the seven loaves, and after giving thanks he broke them and
handed them to his disciples to distribute; and they distributed them among the
7 crowd. •They had a few small fish as well, and over these he said a blessing and
8 ordered them to be distributed also. •They ate as much as they wanted, and they
9 collected seven basketfuls of the scraps left over. •Now there had been about four
10 thousand people. He sent them away •and immediately, getting into the boat
with his disciples, went to the region of Dalmanutha.

The Pharisees ask for a sign from heaven

11 The Pharisees came up and started a discussion with him; they demanded
12 of him a sign from heaven, to test him. •And with a sigh that came straight from
the heart he said, 'Why does this generation demand a sign? I tell you solemnly,
13 no sign shall be given to this generation.' •And leaving them again and re-em-
barking he went away to the opposite shore.

The yeast of the Pharisees and of Herod

14 The disciples had forgotten to take any food and they had only one loaf with
15 them in the boat. •Then he gave them this warning, 'Keep your eyes open; be
16 on your guard against the yeast of the Pharisees and the yeast of Herod'. •And
17 they said to one another, 'It is because we have no bread'. •And Jesus knew it,
and he said to them, 'Why are you talking about having no bread? Do you not
18 yet understand? Have you no perception? Are your minds closed? •Have you
19 *eyes that do not see, ears that do not hear*?[a] Or do you not remember? •When
I broke the five loaves among the five thousand, how many baskets full of scraps
20 did you collect?' They answered, 'Twelve'. •'And when I broke the seven loaves
for the four thousand, how many baskets full of scraps did you collect?'
21 And they answered, 'Seven'. •Then he said to them, 'Are you still without
perception?'

Cure of a blind man at Bethsaida

22 They came to Bethsaida, and some people brought to him a blind man whom
23 they begged him to touch. •He took the blind man by the hand and led him outside
the village. Then putting spittle on his eyes and laying his hands on him, he asked,
24 'Can you see anything?' •The man, who was beginning to see, replied, 'I can see
25 people; they look like trees to me, but they are walking about'. •Then he laid
his hands on the man's eyes again and he saw clearly; he was cured, and he could
26 see everything plainly and distinctly. •And Jesus sent him home, saying, 'Do
not even go into the village'.

Peter's profession of faith

27 Jesus and his disciples left for the villages round Caesarea Philippi. On the
28 way he put this question to his disciples, 'Who do people say I am?' •And they
told him. 'John the Baptist,' they said 'others Elijah; others again, one of the
29 prophets.' •'But you,' he asked 'who do you say I am?' Peter spoke up and said

8 a. Jr 5:21; Ezk 12:2

to him, 'You are the Christ'. •And he gave them strict orders not to tell anyone 30 about him.

First prophecy of the Passion

And he began to teach them that the Son of Man was destined to suffer 31 grievously, to be rejected by the elders and the chief priests and the scribes, and to be put to death, and after three days to rise again; •and he said all this quite 32 openly. Then, taking him aside, Peter started to remonstrate with him. •But, 33 turning and seeing his disciples, he rebuked Peter and said to him, 'Get behind me, Satan! Because the way you think is not God's way but man's.'

The condition of following Christ

He called the people and his disciples to him and said, 'If anyone wants to be 34 a follower of mine, let him renounce himself and take up his cross and follow me. •For anyone who wants to save his life will lose it; but anyone who loses his 35 life for my sake, and for the sake of the gospel, will save it. •What gain, then, is 36 it for a man to win the whole world and ruin his life? •And indeed what can 37 a man offer in exchange for his life? •For if anyone in this adulterous and sinful 38 generation is ashamed of me and of my words, the Son of Man will also be ashamed of him when he comes in the glory of his Father with the holy angels.' 9 And he said to them, 'I tell you solemnly, there are some standing here who 1 will not taste death before they see the kingdom of God come with power'.

The transfiguration

Six days later, Jesus took with him Peter and James and John and led them 2 up a high mountain where they could be alone by themselves. There in their presence he was transfigured: •his clothes became dazzlingly white, whiter 3 than any earthly bleacher could make them. •Elijah appeared to them with 4 Moses; and they were talking with Jesus. •Then Peter spoke to Jesus: 'Rabbi,' 5 he said 'it is wonderful for us to be here; so let us make three tents, one for you, one for Moses and one for Elijah'. •He did not know what to say; they were 6 so frightened. •And a cloud came, covering them in shadow; and there came 7 a voice from the cloud, 'This is my Son, the Beloved. Listen to him.' •Then 8 suddenly, when they looked round, they saw no one with them any more but only Jesus.

The question about Elijah

As they came down from the mountain he warned them to tell no one 9 what they had seen, until after the Son of Man had risen from the dead. They observed the warning faithfully, though among themselves they discussed 10 what 'rising from the dead' could mean. •And they put this question to him, 11 'Why do the scribes say that Elijah has to come first?' •'True,' he said 'Elijah 12 is to come first and to see that everything is as it should be; yet how is it that the scriptures say about the Son of Man that he is to suffer grievously and be treated with contempt? •However, I tell you that Elijah has come and they have 13 treated him as they pleased, just as the scriptures say about him.'

The epileptic demoniac

When they rejoined the disciples they saw a large crowd round them and 14 some scribes arguing with them. •The moment they saw him the whole crowd 15 were struck with amazement and ran to greet him. •'What are you arguing about 16

17 with them?' he asked. •A man answered him from the crowd, 'Master, I have
18 brought my son to you; there is a spirit of dumbness in him, •and when it
takes hold of him it throws him to the ground, and he foams at the mouth and
grinds his teeth and goes rigid. And I asked your disciples to cast it out and
19 they were unable to.' •'You faithless generation' he said to them in reply. 'How
much longer must I be with you? How much longer must I put up with you?
20 Bring him to me.' •They brought the boy to him, and as soon as the spirit
saw Jesus it threw the boy into convulsions, and he fell to the ground and
21 lay writhing there, foaming at the mouth. •Jesus asked the father, 'How
22 long has this been happening to him?' 'From childhood,' he replied •'and it
has often thrown him into the fire and into the water, in order to destroy him.
23 But if you can do anything, have pity on us and help us.' •'If you can?' retorted
24 Jesus. 'Everything is possible for anyone who has faith.' •Immediately the
25 father of the boy cried out, 'I do have faith. Help the little faith I have!' •And
when Jesus saw how many people were pressing round him, he rebuked the
unclean spirit. 'Deaf and dumb spirit,' he said 'I command you: come out of him
26 and never enter him again.' •Then throwing the boy into violent convulsions it
came out shouting, and the boy lay there so like a corpse that most of them
27 said, 'He is dead'. •But Jesus took him by the hand and helped him up, and he
28 was able to stand. •When he had gone indoors his disciples asked him privately,
29 'Why were we unable to cast it out?' •'This is the kind' he answered 'that can
only be driven out by prayer.'

Second prophecy of the Passion

30   After leaving that place they made their way through Galilee; and he did
31 not want anyone to know, •because he was instructing his disciples; he was telling
them, 'The Son of Man will be delivered into the hands of men; they will put
him to death; and three days after he has been put to death he will rise again'.
32 But they did not understand what he said and were afraid to ask him.

Who is the greatest?

33   They came to Capernaum, and when he was in the house he asked them,
34 'What were you arguing about on the road?' •They said nothing because they
35 had been arguing which of them was the greatest. •So he sat down, called the
Twelve to him and said, 'If anyone wants to be first, he must make himself last
36 of all and servant of all'. •He then took a little child, set him in front of them,
37 put his arms round him, and said to them, •'Anyone who welcomes one of
these little children in my name, welcomes me; and anyone who welcomes me
welcomes not me but the one who sent me'.

On using the name of Jesus

38   John said to him, 'Master, we saw a man who is not one of us casting out
devils in your name; and because he was not one of us we tried to stop him'.
39 But Jesus said, 'You must not stop him: no one who works a miracle in my name
40 is likely to speak evil of me. •Anyone who is not against us is for us.

Charity shown to Christ's disciples

41   'If anyone gives you a cup of water to drink just because you belong to Christ,
then I tell you solemnly, he will most certainly not lose his reward.

On leading others astray

'But anyone who is an obstacle to bring down one of these little ones who 42 have faith, would be better thrown into the sea with a great millstone round his neck. •And if your hand should cause you to sin, cut it off; it is better for you 43 to enter into life crippled, than to have two hands and go to hell, into the fire that cannot be put out. •And if your foot should cause you to sin, cut it off; it is 45 better for you to enter into life lame, than to have two feet and be thrown into hell. •And if your eye should cause you to sin, tear it out; it is better for you to 47 enter into the kingdom of God with one eye, than to have two eyes and be thrown into hell •where *their worm does not die nor their fire go out.*ᵃ •For everyone will 48 49 be salted with fire. •Salt is a good thing, but if salt has become insipid, how can 50 you season it again? Have salt in yourselves and be at peace with one another.'

The question about divorce

10 Leaving there, he came to the district of Judaea and the far side of the 1 Jordan. And again crowds gathered round him, and again he taught them, as his custom was. •Some Pharisees approached him and asked, 'Is it against 2 the law for a man to divorce his wife?' They were testing him. •He answered 3 them, 'What did Moses command you?' •'Moses allowed us' they said 'to draw 4 up a writ of dismissal and so to divorce.' •Then Jesus said to them, 'It was 5 because you were so unteachable that he wrote this commandment for you. But from the beginning of creation *God made them male and female.* •*This is why* 6 7 *a man must leave father and mother,* •*and the two become one body.*ᵃ They are no 8 longer two, therefore, but one body. •So then, what God has united, man must not 9 divide.' •Back in the house the disciples questioned him again about this, •and 10 11 he said to them, 'The man who divorces his wife and marries another is guilty of adultery against her. •And if a woman divorces her husband and marries 12 another she is guilty of adultery too.'

Jesus and the children

People were bringing little children to him, for him to touch them. The 13 disciples turned them away, •but when Jesus saw this he was indignant and said 14 to them, 'Let the little children come to me; do not stop them; for it is to such as these that the kingdom of God belongs. •I tell you solemnly, anyone who 15 does not welcome the kingdom of God like a little child will never enter it.' Then he put his arms round them, laid his hands on them and gave them his 16 blessing.

The rich young man

He was setting out on a journey when a man ran up, knelt before him and 17 put this question to him, 'Good master, what must I do to inherit eternal life?' Jesus said to him, 'Why do you call me good? No one is good but God alone. 18 You know the commandments: *You must not kill; You must not commit adultery;* 19 *You must not steal; You must not bring false witness;* You must not defraud; *Honour your father and mother.*' •And he said to him, 'Master, I have kept all 20 these from my earliest days'. •Jesus looked steadily at him and loved him, and 21 he said, 'There is one thing you lack. Go and sell everything you own and give the money to the poor, and you will have treasure in heaven; then come, follow me.' •But his face fell at these words and he went away sad, for he was a man 22 of great wealth.

The danger of riches

23 Jesus looked round and said to his disciples, 'How hard it is for those who
24 have riches to enter the kingdom of God!' •The disciples were astounded by
these words, but Jesus insisted, 'My children,' he said to them 'how hard it is to
25 enter the kingdom of God! •It is easier for a camel to pass through the eye of
26 a needle than for a rich man to enter the kingdom of God.' •They were more
astonished than ever. 'In that case' they said to one another 'who can be saved?'
27 Jesus gazed at them. 'For men' he said 'it is impossible, but not for God: because
everything is possible for God.'

The reward of renunciation

28 Peter took this up. 'What about us?' he asked him. 'We have left everything
29 and followed you.' •Jesus said, 'I tell you solemnly, there is no one who has left
house, brothers, sisters, father, children or land for my sake and for the sake of
30 the gospel •who will not be repaid a hundred times over, houses, brothers, sisters,
mothers, children and land—not without persecutions—now in this present time
and, in the world to come, eternal life.
31 'Many who are first will be last, and the last first.'

Third prophecy of the Passion

32 They were on the road, going up to Jerusalem; Jesus was walking on ahead
of them; they were in a daze, and those who followed were apprehensive. Once
more taking the Twelve aside he began to tell them what was going to happen
33 to him: •'Now we are going up to Jerusalem, and the Son of Man is about
to be handed over to the chief priests and the scribes. They will condemn him
34 to death and will hand him over to the pagans, •who will mock him and spit at
him and scourge him and put him to death; and after three days he will
rise again.'

The sons of Zebedee make their request

35 James and John, the sons of Zebedee, approached him. 'Master,' they said
36 to him 'we want you to do us a favour.' •He said to them, 'What is it you want
37 me to do for you?' •They said to him, 'Allow us to sit one at your right hand
38 and the other at your left in your glory'. •'You do not know what you are asking'
Jesus said to them. 'Can you drink the cup that I must drink, or be baptised
39 with the baptism with which I must be baptised?' •They replied, 'We can'.
Jesus said to them, 'The cup that I must drink you shall drink, and with the
40 baptism with which I must be baptised you shall be baptised, •but as for seats
at my right hand or my left, these are not mine to grant; they belong to those
to whom they have been allotted'.

Leadership with service

41 When the other ten heard this they began to feel indignant with James and
42 John, •so Jesus called them to him and said to them, 'You know that among the
pagans their so-called rulers lord it over them, and their great men make their
43 authority felt. •This is not to happen among you. No; anyone who wants to become
44 great among you must be your servant, •and anyone who wants to be first
45 among you must be slave to all. •For the Son of Man himself did not come to
be served but to serve, and to give his life as a ransom for many.'

9 a. Is 66:24   **10 a.** Gn 1:27; 2:24

The blind man of Jericho

They reached Jericho; and as he left Jericho with his disciples and a large 46 crowd, Bartimaeus (that is, the son of Timaeus), a blind beggar, was sitting at the side of the road. •When he heard that it was Jesus of Nazareth, he began to shout 47 and to say, 'Son of David, Jesus, have pity on me'. •And many of them scolded 48 him and told him to keep quiet, but he only shouted all the louder, 'Son of David, have pity on me'. •Jesus stopped and said, 'Call him here'. So they called the 49 blind man. 'Courage,' they said 'get up; he is calling you.' •So throwing off his 50 cloak, he jumped up and went to Jesus. •Then Jesus spoke, 'What do you want 51 me to do for you?' 'Rabbuni,'* the blind man said to him 'Master, let me see again.' •Jesus said to him, 'Go; your faith has saved you'. And immediately his sight returned and he followed him along the road.

IV. THE JERUSALEM MINISTRY

The Messiah enters Jerusalem

11 When they were approaching Jerusalem, in sight of Bethphage and Bethany, 1 close by the Mount of Olives, he sent two of his disciples •and said to them, 2 'Go off to the village facing you, and as soon as you enter it you will find a tethered colt that no one has yet ridden. Untie it and bring it here. •If anyone says to 3 you, "What are you doing?" say, "The Master needs it and will send it back here directly".' •They went off and found a colt tethered near a door in 4 the open street. As they untied it, •some men standing there said, 'What are you 5 doing, untying that colt?' •They gave the answer Jesus had told them, and the 6 men let them go. •Then they took the colt to Jesus and threw their cloaks on its 7 back, and he sat on it. •Many people spread their cloaks on the road, others green- 8 ery which they had cut in the fields. •And those who went in front and those who 9 followed were all shouting, '*Hosanna! Blessings on him who comes in the name of the Lord!*ᵃ•Blessings on the coming kingdom of our father David! *Hosanna* 10 in the highest heavens!' •He entered Jerusalem and went into the Temple. He 11 looked all round him, but as it was now late, he went out to Bethany with the Twelve.

The barren fig tree

Next day as they were leaving Bethany, he felt hungry. •Seeing a fig tree in ¹²/₁₃ leaf some distance away, he went to see if he could find any fruit on it, but when he came up to it he found nothing but leaves; for it was not the season for figs. And he addressed the fig tree. 'May no one ever eat fruit from you again' he 14 said. And his disciples heard him say this.

The expulsion of the dealers from the Temple

So they reached Jerusalem and he went into the Temple and began driving 15 out those who were selling and buying there; he upset the tables of the money changers and the chairs of those who were selling pigeons. •Nor would he allow 16 anyone to carry anything through the Temple. •And he taught them and said, 17 'Does not scripture say: *My house will be called a house of prayer for all the peoples?*ᵇ·But you have turned it into *a robbers' den.*ᶜ•This came to the ears 18

of the chief priests and the scribes, and they tried to find some way of doing
away with him; they were afraid of him because the people were carried away
19 by his teaching. ·And when evening came he went out of the city.

The fig tree withered. Faith and prayer

20   Next morning, as they passed by, they saw the fig tree withered to the roots.
21 Peter remembered. 'Look, Rabbi,' he said to Jesus 'the fig tree you cursed has
$^{22}_{23}$ withered away.' ·Jesus answered, 'Have faith in God. ·I tell you solemnly,
if anyone says to this mountain, "Get up and throw yourself into the sea", with no
hesitation in his heart but believing that what he says will happen, it will be done
24 for him. ·I tell you therefore: everything you ask and pray for, believe that you
25 have it already, and it will be yours. ·And when you stand in prayer, forgive
whatever you have against anybody, so that your Father in heaven may forgive
your failings too.'

The authority of Jesus is questioned

27   They came to Jerusalem again, and as Jesus was walking in the Temple, the
28 chief priests and the scribes and the elders came to him, ·and they said to him,
'What authority have you for acting like this? Or who gave you authority to do
29 these things?' ·Jesus said to them, 'I will ask you a question, only one; answer
30 me and I will tell you my authority for acting like this. ·John's baptism: did it
31 come from heaven, or from man? Answer me that.' ·And they argued it out
this way among themselves: 'If we say from heaven, he will say, "Then why did
32 you refuse to believe him?" ·But dare we say from man?'—they had the people
33 to fear, for everyone held that John was a real prophet. ·So their reply to Jesus
was, 'We do not know'. And Jesus said to them, 'Nor will I tell you my authority
for acting like this'.

Parable of the wicked husbandmen

1 **12** He went on to speak to them in parables, 'A man planted a vineyard; he
fenced it round, dug out a trough for the winepress and built a tower; then
2 he leased it to tenants and went abroad. ·When the time came, he sent a servant
to the tenants to collect from them his share of the produce from the vineyard.
$^{3}_{4}$ But they seized the man, thrashed him and sent him away empty-handed. ·Next
he sent another servant to them; him they beat about the head and treated
5 shamefully. ·And he sent another and him they killed; then a number of others,
6 and they thrashed some and killed the rest. ·He had still someone left: his beloved
7 son. He sent him to them last of all. "They will respect my son" he said. ·But
those tenants said to each other, "This is the heir. Come on, let us kill him, and the
8 inheritance will be ours." ·So they seized him and killed him and threw him out
9 of the vineyard. ·Now what will the owner of the vineyard do? He will come and
10 make an end of the tenants and give the vineyard to others. ·Have you not read
this text of scripture:

> *It was the stone rejected by the builders*
> *that became the keystone.*
11 > *This was the Lord's doing*
> *and it is wonderful to see*?[a]

b. Aramaic: 'My master'.
11 a. Ps 118:25-26   **b.** Is 56:7   **c.** Jr 7:11
12 a. Ps 118:22-23

And they would have liked to arrest him, because they realised that the parable 12 was aimed at them, but they were afraid of the crowds. So they left him alone and went away.

On tribute to Caesar

Next they sent to him some Pharisees and some Herodians to catch him out 13 in what he said. •These came and said to him, 'Master, we know you are an honest 14 man, that you are not afraid of anyone, because a man's rank means nothing to you, and that you teach the way of God in all honesty. Is it permissible to pay taxes to Caesar or not? Should we pay, yes or no?' •Seeing through their 15 hypocrisy he said to them, 'Why do you set this trap for me? Hand me a denarius and let me see it.' •They handed him one and he said, 'Whose head 16 is this? Whose name?' 'Caesar's' they told him. •Jesus said to them, 'Give back 17 to Caesar what belongs to Caesar—and to God what belongs to God'. This reply took them completely by surprise.

The resurrection of the dead

Then some Sadducees—who deny that there is a resurrection—came to 18 him and they put this question to him, •'Master, we have it from Moses in 19 writing, if a man's brother dies leaving a wife but no child, the man must marry the widow to raise up children for his brother. •Now there were seven 20 brothers. The first married a wife and then died leaving no children. •The second 21 married the widow, and he too died leaving no children; with the third it was the same, •and none of the seven left any children. Last of all the woman herself 22 died. •Now at the resurrection, when they rise again, whose wife will she be, 23 since she had been married to all seven?'

Jesus said to them, 'Is not the reason why you go wrong, that you understand 24 neither the scriptures nor the power of God? •For when they rise from the dead, 25 men and women do not marry; no, they are like the angels in heaven. •Now 26 about the dead rising again, have you never read in the Book of Moses, in the passage about the Bush, how God spoke to him and said: *I am the God of Abraham, the God of Isaac and the God of Jacob*?[b] •He is God, not of the dead, 27 but of the living. You are very much mistaken.'

The greatest commandment of all

One of the scribes who had listened to them debating and had observed how 28 well Jesus had answered them, now came up and put a question to him, 'Which is the first of all the commandments?' •Jesus replied, 'This is the first: *Listen,* 29 *Israel, the Lord our God is the one Lord,* •*and you must love the Lord your God with* 30 *all your heart, with all your soul,* with all your mind and *with all your strength.*[c] The second is this: *You must love your neighbour as yourself.*[d] There is no com- 31 mandment greater than these.' •The scribe said to him, 'Well spoken, Master; 32 what you have said is true: that he is one and there is no other. •To love him with 33 all your heart, with all your understanding and strength, and to love your neighbour as yourself, this is far more important than any holocaust or sacrifice.' Jesus, seeing how wisely he had spoken, said, 'You are not far from the kingdom 34 of God'. And after that no one dared to question him any more.

Christ not only son but also Lord of David

Later, while teaching in the Temple, Jesus said, 'How can the scribes maintain 35 that the Christ is the son of David? •David himself, moved by the Holy Spirit, 36 said:

> *The Lord said to my Lord:*
> *Sit at my right hand*
> *and I will put your enemies*
> *under your feet.*[c]

37 David himself calls him Lord, in what way then can he be his son?' And the great majority of the people heard this with delight.

The scribes condemned by Jesus

38   In his teaching he said, 'Beware of the scribes who like to walk about
39 in long robes, to be greeted obsequiously in the market squares, •to take
40 the front seats in the synagogues and the places of honour at banquets; •these are the men who swallow the property of widows, while making a show of lengthy prayers. The more severe will be the sentence they receive.'

The widow's mite

41   He sat down opposite the treasury and watched the people putting money
42 into the treasury, and many of the rich put in a great deal. •A poor widow came
43 and put in two small coins, the equivalent of a penny. •Then he called his disciples and said to them, 'I tell you solemnly, this poor widow has
44 put more in than all who have contributed to the treasury; •for they have all put in money they had over, but she from the little she had has put in everything she possessed, all she had to live on'.

The eschatological discourse: introduction

1 **13** As he was leaving the Temple one of his disciples said to him, 'Look at the
2 size of those stones, Master! Look at the size of those buildings!' •And Jesus said to him, 'You see these great buildings? Not a single stone will be left on another: everything will be destroyed.'

3   And while he was sitting facing the Temple, on the Mount of Olives, Peter,
4 James, John and Andrew questioned him privately, •'Tell us, when is this going to happen, and what sign will there be that all this is about to be fulfilled?'

The beginning of sorrows

5
6   Then Jesus began to tell them, 'Take care that no one deceives you. •Many will
7 come using my name and saying, "I am he", and they will deceive many. •When you hear of wars and rumours of wars, do not be alarmed, this is something that
8 must happen, but the end will not be yet. •For nation will fight against nation, and kingdom against kingdom. There will be earthquakes here and there; there will be famines. This is the beginning of the birthpangs.

9   'Be on your guard: they will hand you over to sanhedrins; you will be beaten in synagogues; and you will stand before governors and kings for my sake,
10 to bear witness before them, •since the Good News must first be proclaimed to all the nations.

11   'And when they lead you away to hand you over, do not worry beforehand about what to say; no, say whatever is given to you when the time comes, because
12 it is not you who will be speaking: it will be the Holy Spirit. •Brother will betray brother to death, and the father his child; children will rise against their parents

---

b. Ex 3:6   **c.** Dt 6:4-5   **d.** Lv 19:18   **e.** Ps 110:1

and have them put to death. •You will be hated by all men on account of my 13
name; but the man who stands firm to the end will be saved.

The great tribulation of Jerusalem

'When you see *the disastrous abomination*[a] set up where it ought not to be 14
(let the reader understand), then those in Judaea must escape to the mountains;
if a man is on the housetop, he must not come down to go into the house to 15
collect any of his belongings; •if a man is in the fields, he must not turn back 16
to fetch his cloak. •Alas for those with child, or with babies at the breast, when 17
those days come! •Pray that this may not be in winter. •For in those days there 18
will be *such distress as, until now, has not been*[b] equalled since the beginning when 19
God created the world, nor ever will be again. •And if the Lord had not shortened 20
that time, no one would have survived; but he did shorten the time, for the sake
of the elect whom he chose.

'And if anyone says to you then, "Look, here is the Christ" or, "Look, he 21
is there", do not believe it; •for false Christs and false prophets will arise and 22
produce signs and portents to deceive the elect, if that were possible. •You 23
therefore must be on your guard. I have forewarned you of everything.

The coming of the Son of Man

'But in those days, after that time of distress, the sun will be darkened, the 24
moon will lose its brightness, •the stars will come falling from heaven and the 25
powers in the heavens will be shaken. •And then they will see the Son of Man 26
coming in the clouds with great power and glory; •then too he will send the angels 27
to gather his chosen from the four winds, from the ends of the world to the ends
of heaven.

The time of this coming

'Take the fig tree as a parable: as soon as its twigs grow supple and its leaves 28
come out, you know that summer is near. •So with you when you see these things 29
happening: know that he is near, at the very gates. •I tell you solemnly, 30
before this generation has passed away all these things will have taken
place. •Heaven and earth will pass away, but my words will not pass away. 31

'But as for that day or hour, nobody knows it, neither the angels of heaven, 32
nor the Son; no one but the Father.

Be on the alert

'Be on your guard, stay awake, because you never know when the time will 33
come. •It is like a man travelling abroad: he has gone from home, and left his 34
servants in charge, each with his own task; and he has told the doorkeeper to
stay awake. •So stay awake, because you do not know when the master of the 35
house is coming, evening, midnight, cockcrow, dawn; •if he comes unexpectedly, 36
he must not find you asleep. •And what I say to you I say to all: Stay awake!' 37

V. PASSION AND RESURRECTION

The conspiracy against Jesus

14 It was two days before the Passover and the feast of Unleavened Bread, and 1
the chief priests and the scribes were looking for a way to arrest Jesus by

2 some trick and have him put to death. •For they said, 'It must not be during the festivities, or there will be a disturbance among the people'.

The anointing at Bethany

3 Jesus was at Bethany in the house of Simon the leper; he was at dinner when a woman came in with an alabaster jar of very costly ointment, pure nard. She
4 broke the jar and poured the ointment on his head. •Some who were there said
5 to one another indignantly, 'Why this waste of ointment? •Ointment like this could have been sold for over three hundred denarii and the money given to the
6 poor'; and they were angry with her. •But Jesus said, 'Leave her alone. Why are you upsetting her? What she has done for me is one of the good works.
7 You have the poor with you always, and you can be kind to them whenever you
8 wish, but you will not always have me. •She has done what was in her power to
9 do: she has anointed my body beforehand for its burial. •I tell you solemnly, wherever throughout all the world the Good News is proclaimed, what she has done will be told also, in remembrance of her.'

Judas betrays Jesus

10 Judas Iscariot, one of the Twelve, approached the chief priests with an offer
11 to hand Jesus over to them. •They were delighted to hear it, and promised to give him money; and he looked for a way of betraying him when the opportunity should occur.

Preparations for the Passover supper

12 On the first day of Unleavened Bread, when the Passover lamb was sacrificed, his disciples said to him, 'Where do you want us to go and make the preparations
13 for you to eat the passover?' •So he sent two of his disciples, saying to them, 'Go into the city and you will meet a man carrying a pitcher of water. Follow him,
14 and say to the owner of the house which he enters, "The Master says: Where
15 is my dining room in which I can eat the passover with my disciples?" •He will show you a large upper room furnished with couches, all prepared. Make the
16 preparations for us there.' •The disciples set out and went to the city and found everything as he had told them, and prepared the Passover.

The treachery of Judas foretold

17
18 When evening came he arrived with the Twelve. •And while they were at table eating, Jesus said, 'I tell you solemnly, one of you is about to betray
19 me, one of you eating with me'. •They were distressed and asked him, one after
20 another, 'Not I, surely?' •He said to them, 'It is one of the Twelve, one who is
21 dipping into the same dish with me. •Yes, the Son of Man is going to his fate, as the scriptures say he will, but alas for that man by whom the Son of Man is betrayed! Better for that man if he had never been born!'

The institution of the Eucharist

22 And as they were eating he took some bread, and when he had said the blessing
23 he broke it and gave it to them. 'Take it,' he said 'this is my body.' •Then he took a cup, and when he had returned thanks he gave it to them, and all drank from
24 it, •and he said to them, 'This is my blood, the blood of the covenant, which is
25 to be poured out for many. •I tell you solemnly, I shall not drink any more wine until the day I drink the new wine in the kingdom of God.'

13 a. Dn 9:27, and ch. 11,12   **b.** Dn 12:1

Peter's denial foretold

After psalms had been sung they left for the Mount of Olives. •And Jesus ²⁶₂₇
said to them, 'You will all lose faith, for the scripture says: *I shall strike
the shepherd and the sheep will be scattered*,ᵃ•however after my resurrection I shall 28
go before you to Galilee'. •Peter said, 'Even if all lose faith, I will not'. •And ²⁹₃₀
Jesus said to him, 'I tell you solemnly, this day, this very night, before
the cock crows twice, you will have disowned me three times'. •But he repeated 31
still more earnestly, 'If I have to die with you, I will never disown you'. And
they all said the same.

Gethsemane

They came to a small estate called Gethsemane, and Jesus said to his disciples, 32
'Stay here while I pray'. •Then he took Peter and James and John with him. 33
And a sudden fear came over him, and great distress. •And he said to them, 'My 34
soul is sorrowful to the point of death. Wait here, and keep awake.' •And going 35
on a little further he threw himself on the ground and prayed that, if it were
possible, this hour might pass him by. •'Abba (Father)!' he said 'Everything 36
is possible for you. Take this cup away from me. But let it be as you, not I, would
have it.' •He came back and found them sleeping, and he said to Peter, 'Simon, 37
are you asleep? Had you not the strength to keep awake one hour? •You should 38
be awake, and praying not to be put to the test. The spirit is willing, but the flesh
is weak.' •Again he went away and prayed, saying the same words. •And ³⁹₄₀
once more he came back and found them sleeping, their eyes were so heavy; and
they could find no answer for him. •He came back a third time and said to them, 41
'You can sleep on now and take your rest. It is all over. The hour has come. Now
the Son of Man is to be betrayed into the hands of sinners. •Get up! Let us go! 42
My betrayer is close at hand already.'

The arrest

Even while he was still speaking, Judas, one of the Twelve, came up with 43
a number of men armed with swords and clubs, sent by the chief priests and
the scribes and the elders. •Now the traitor had arranged a signal with them. 44
'The one I kiss,' he had said 'he is the man. Take him in charge, and see he is
well guarded when you lead him away.' •So when the traitor came, he went 45
straight up to Jesus and said, 'Rabbi!' and kissed him. •The others seized him 46
and took him in charge. •Then one of the bystanders drew his sword and struck 47
out at the high priest's servant, and cut off his ear.

Then Jesus spoke. 'Am I a brigand' he said 'that you had to set out to 48
capture me with swords and clubs? •I was among you teaching in the Temple day 49
after day and you never laid hands on me. But this is to fulfil the scriptures.'
And they all deserted him and ran away. •A young man who followed him had ⁵⁰₅₁
nothing on but a linen cloth. They caught hold of him, •but he left the cloth 52
in their hands and ran away naked.

Jesus before the Sanhedrin

They led Jesus off to the high priest; and all the chief priests and the elders 53
and the scribes assembled there. •Peter had followed him at a distance, right 54
into the high priest's palace, and was sitting with the attendants warming himself
at the fire.

55 The chief priests and the whole Sanhedrin were looking for evidence against
Jesus on which they might pass the death-sentence. But they could not find any.
56 Several, indeed, brought false evidence against him, but their evidence was
57 conflicting. •Some stood up and submitted this false evidence against him,
58 'We heard him say, "I am going to destroy this Temple made by human hands,
59 and in three days build another, not made by human hands" '. •But even on
60 this point their evidence was conflicting. •The high priest then stood up before
the whole assembly and put this question to Jesus, 'Have you no answer to that?
61 What is this evidence these men are bringing against you?' •But he was silent
and made no answer at all. The high priest put a second question to him, 'Are
62 you the Christ,' he said 'the Son of the Blessed One?' •'I am,' said Jesus 'and
you will see *the Son of Man seated at the right hand of the Power* and *coming with*
63 *the clouds of heaven.*'[b] •The high priest tore his robes, 'What need of witnesses have
64 we now?' he said. •'You heard the blasphemy. What is your finding?' And they
all gave their verdict: he deserved to die.
65 Some of them started spitting at him and, blindfolding him, began hitting
him with their fists and shouting, 'Play the prophet!' And the attendants rained
blows on him.

Peter's denials

66 While Peter was down below in the courtyard, one of the high priest's
67 servant-girls came up. •She saw Peter warming himself there, stared at him and
68 said, 'You too were with Jesus, the man from Nazareth'. •But he denied it.
'I do not know, I do not understand, what you are talking about' he said. And
69 he went out into the forecourt. •The servant-girl saw him and again started
70 telling the bystanders, 'This fellow is one of them'. •But again he denied it.
A little later the bystanders themselves said to Peter, 'You are one of them for
71 sure! Why, you are a Galilean.' •But he started calling down curses on himself
72 and swearing, 'I do not know the man you speak of'. •At that moment the
cock crew for the second time, and Peter recalled how Jesus had said to him,
'Before the cock crows twice, you will have disowned me three times'. And
he burst into tears.

Jesus before Pilate

1 **15** First thing in the morning, the chief priests together with the elders and
scribes, in short the whole Sanhedrin, had their plan ready. They had
Jesus bound and took him away and handed him over to Pilate.

2 Pilate questioned him, 'Are you the king of the Jews?' 'It is you who say it'
3 he answered. •And the chief priests brought many accusations against him.
4 Pilate questioned him again, 'Have you no reply at all? See how many accusations
5 they are bringing against you!' •But, to Pilate's amazement, Jesus made no
further reply.

6 At festival time Pilate used to release a prisoner for them, anyone they asked
7 for. •Now a man called Barabbas was then in prison with the rioters who had
8 committed murder during the uprising. •When the crowd went up and began to
9 ask Pilate the customary favour, •Pilate answered them, 'Do you want me to
10 release for you the king of the Jews?' •For he realised it was out of jealousy that
11 the chief priests had handed Jesus over. •The chief priests, however, had incited
12 the crowd to demand that he should release Barabbas for them instead. •Then

14 a. Zc 13:7　　b. Dn 7:13; Ps 110:1

Pilate spoke again. 'But in that case,' he said to them 'what am I to do with the
man you call king of the Jews?' •They shouted back, 'Crucify him!' •'Why?' Pilate 13
asked them 'What harm has he done?' But they shouted all the louder, 'Crucify 14
him!' •So Pilate, anxious to placate the crowd, released Barabbas for them and, 15
having ordered Jesus to be scourged, handed him over to be crucified.

Jesus crowned with thorns

The soldiers led him away to the inner part of the palace, that is, the Prae- 16
torium, and called the whole cohort together. •They dressed him up in purple, 17
twisted some thorns into a crown and put it on him. •And they began saluting 18
him, 'Hail, king of the Jews!' •They struck his head with a reed and spat on him; 19
and they went down on their knees to do him homage. •And when they had 20
finished making fun of him, they took off the purple and dressed him in his own
clothes.

The way of the cross

They led him out to crucify him. •They enlisted a passer-by, Simon of Cyrene, 21
father of Alexander and Rufus,*a* who was coming in from the country, to carry
his cross. •They brought Jesus to the place called Golgotha, which means the 22
place of the skull.

The crucifixion

They offered him wine mixed with myrrh, but he refused it. •Then they 23
crucified him, and shared out his clothing, casting lots to decide what each should 24
get. •It was the third hour*b* when they crucified him. •The inscription giving the 25
charge against him read: 'The King of the Jews'. •And they crucified two robbers 26
with him, one on his right and one on his left. 27

The crucified Christ is mocked

The passers-by jeered at him; they shook their heads and said, 'Aha! So you 29
would destroy the Temple and rebuild it in three days! •Then save yourself: 30
come down from the cross!' •The chief priests and the scribes mocked him among 31
themselves in the same way. 'He saved others,' they said 'he cannot save
himself. •Let the Christ, the king of Israel, come down from the cross now, for 32
us to see it and believe.' Even those who were crucified with him taunted him.

The death of Jesus

When the sixth hour came there was darkness over the whole land until the 33
ninth hour. •And at the ninth hour Jesus cried out in a loud voice, 'Eloi, Eloi, 34
lama sabachthani?' which means, '*My God, my God, why have you deserted me?*'*c*
When some of those who stood by heard this, they said, 'Listen, he is calling on 35
Elijah'. •Someone ran and soaked a sponge in vinegar and, putting it on a reed, 36
gave it him to drink saying, 'Wait and see if Elijah will come to take him down'.
But Jesus gave a loud cry and breathed his last. •And the veil of the Temple was 37
torn in two from top to bottom. •The centurion, who was standing in front of 38
him, had seen how he had died, and he said, 'In truth this man was a son of 39
God'.

The women on Calvary

There were some women watching from a distance. Among them were Mary 40
of Magdala, Mary who was the mother of James the younger and Joset, and

41 Salome. •These used to follow him and look after him when he was in Galilee. And there were many other women there who had come up to Jerusalem with him.

The burial

42 It was now evening, and since it was Preparation Day (that is, the vigil of the
43 sabbath), •there came Joseph of Arimathaea, a prominent member of the Council, who himself lived in the hope of seeing the kingdom of God, and he
44 boldly went to Pilate and asked for the body of Jesus. •Pilate, astonished that he should have died so soon, summoned the centurion and enquired if he was
45 already dead. •Having been assured of this by the centurion, he granted the
46 corpse to Joseph •who bought a shroud, took Jesus down from the cross, wrapped him in the shroud and laid him in a tomb which had been hewn out
47 of the rock. He then rolled a stone against the entrance to the tomb. •Mary of Magdala and Mary the mother of Joset were watching and took note of where he was laid.

The empty tomb. The angel's message

1 **16** When the sabbath was over, Mary of Magdala, Mary the mother of James,
2 and Salome, bought spices with which to go and anoint him. •And very early in the morning on the first day of the week they went to the tomb, just as the sun was rising.
3 They had been saying to one another, 'Who will roll away the stone for us
4 from the entrance to the tomb?' •But when they looked they could see that the
5 stone—which was very big—had already been rolled back. •On entering the tomb they saw a young man in a white robe seated on the right-hand side;
6 they were struck with amazement. •But he said to them, 'There is no need for alarm. You are looking for Jesus of Nazareth, who was crucified: he has risen,
7 he is not here. See, here is the place where they laid him. •But you must go and tell his disciples and Peter, "He is going before you to Galilee; it is there
8 you will see him, just as he told you".' •And the women came out and ran away from the tomb because they were frightened out of their wits; and they said nothing to a soul, for they were afraid...

Appearances of the risen Christ[a]

9 Having risen in the morning on the first day of the week, he appeared first to
10 Mary of Magdala from whom he had cast out seven devils. •She then went to those who had been his companions, and who were mourning and in tears, and told
11 them. •But they did not believe her when they heard her say that he was alive and that she had seen him.
12 After this, he showed himself under another form to two of them as they
13 were on their way into the country. •These went back and told the others, who did not believe them either.
14 Lastly, he showed himself to the Eleven themselves while they were at table. He reproached them for their incredulity and obstinacy, because they had refused
15 to believe those who had seen him after he had risen. •And he said to them,

15 a. Alexander and Rufus were doubtless known to the Roman circle in which Mark wrote his gospel. Cf. Rm 16:13.   b. 9 a.m.   c. Ps 22:1
16 a. Many MSS omit vv. 9-20 and this ending to the gospel may not have been written by Mark, though it is old enough.

'Go out to the whole world; proclaim the Good News to all creation. •He who 16 believes and is baptised will be saved; he who does not believe will be condemned. These are the signs that will be associated with believers: in my name they will cast 17 out devils; they will have the gift of tongues; •they will pick up snakes in their 18 hands, and be unharmed should they drink deadly poison; they will lay their hands on the sick, who will recover.'

And so the Lord Jesus, after he had spoken to them, was taken up into heaven: 19 there at the right hand of God he took his place, •while they, going out, preached 20 everywhere, the Lord working with them and confirming the word by the signs that accompanied it.

THE GOSPEL ACCORDING TO
SAINT LUKE

Prologue

1 Seeing that many others have undertaken to draw up accounts of the events
2 that have taken place among us, •exactly as these were handed down to us by
3 those who from the outset were eyewitnesses and ministers of the word, •I in my
turn, after carefully going over the whole story from the beginning, have decided
4 to write an ordered account for you, Theophilus, •so that your Excellency may
learn how well founded the teaching is that you have received.

I. THE BIRTH AND HIDDEN LIFE
OF JOHN THE BAPTIST AND OF JESUS

The birth of John the Baptist foretold

5 In the days of King Herod of Judaea there lived a priest called Zechariah
who belonged to the Abijah section of the priesthood, and he had a wife,
6 Elizabeth by name, who was a descendant of Aaron. •Both were worthy in the
sight of God, and scrupulously observed all the commandments and observances
7 of the Lord. •But they were childless: Elizabeth was barren and they were
both getting on in years.

8 Now it was the turn of Zechariah's section* to serve, and he was exercising
9 his priestly office before God •when it fell to him by lot, as the ritual custom
10 was, to enter the Lord's sanctuary and burn incense there.*b* •And at the hour of
incense the whole congregation was outside, praying.

11 Then there appeared to him the angel of the Lord, standing on the right
12 of the altar of incense. •The sight disturbed Zechariah and he was overcome with
13 fear. •But the angel said to him, 'Zechariah, do not be afraid, your prayer
has been heard. Your wife Elizabeth is to bear you a son and you must name
14 him John.*c* •He will be your joy and delight and many will rejoice at his birth,
15 for he will be great in the sight of the Lord; he must drink no wine, no strong
16 drink.*d* Even from his mother's womb he will be filled with the Holy Spirit, •and
17 he will bring back many of the sons of Israel to the Lord their God. •With the
spirit and power of Elijah, he will go before him *to turn the hearts of fathers*

---

1 a. The 24 families of the 'sons of Aaron' were responsible in rotation for service in the
Temple, and in each class or family the individual was chosen by lot. See 1 Ch 24.   **b.** The
priest tended the brazier on the altar of incense in front of the Most Holy Place.   **c.** The
meaning of the name is 'Yahweh is gracious'.   **d.** See Nb 6:1, where this abstinence is required
in anyone performing a vow to the Lord.

*towards their children*ᶠ and the disobedient back to the wisdom that the virtuous have, preparing for the Lord a people fit for him.' •Zechariah said to the angel, 18 '*How can I be sure of this?*ᶠ I am an old man and my wife is getting on in years.' The angel replied, 'I am Gabriel who stand in God's presence, and I have been 19 sent to speak to you and bring you this good news. •Listen! Since you have not 20 believed my words, which will come true at their appointed time, you will be silenced and have no power of speech until this has happened.' •Meanwhile 21 the people were waiting for Zechariah and were surprised that he stayed in the sanctuary so long. •When he came out he could not speak to them, and they 22 realised that he had received a vision in the sanctuary. But he could only make signs to them, and remained dumb.

When his time of service came to an end he returned home. •Some time later ²³₂₄ his wife Elizabeth conceived, and for five months she kept to herself. •'The Lord 25 has done this for me' she said 'now that it has pleased him to take away the humiliation I suffered among men.'

The annunciation

In the sixth month the angel Gabriel was sent by God to a town in Galilee 26 called Nazareth, •to a virgin betrothed to a man named Joseph, of the House 27 of David; and the virgin's name was Mary. •He went in and said to her, 'Rejoice, 28 so highly favoured! The Lord is with you.' •She was deeply disturbed by these 29 words and asked herself what this greeting could mean, •but the angel said 30 to her, 'Mary, do not be afraid; you have won God's favour. •Listen! You are 31 to conceive and bear a son, and you must name him Jesus. •He will be great and 32 will be called Son of the Most High. The Lord God will give him the throne of his ancestor David; •he will rule over the House of Jacob for ever and his reign 33 will have no end.' •Mary said to the angel, 'But how can this come about, since 34 I am a virgin?'ᵍ •'The Holy Spirit will come upon you' the angel answered 'and 35 the power of the Most High will cover you with its shadow. And so the child will be holy and will be called Son of God. •Know this too: your kinswoman 36 Elizabeth has, in her old age, herself conceived a son, and she whom people called barren is now in her sixth month, •*for nothing is impossible to God*.'ʰ •'I am the ³⁷₃₈ handmaid of the Lord,' said Mary 'let what you have said be done to me.' And the angel left her.

The visitation

Mary set out at that time and went as quickly as she could to a town in the 39 hill country of Judah. •She went into Zechariah's house and greeted Elizabeth. 40 Now as soon as Elizabeth heard Mary's greeting, the child leapt in her womb 41 and Elizabeth was filled with the Holy Spirit. •She gave a loud cry and said, 42 'Of all women you are the most blessed, and blessed is the fruit of your womb. Why should I be honoured with a visit from the mother of my Lord? •For the ⁴³₄₄ moment your greeting reached my ears, the child in my womb leapt for joy. Yes, blessed is she who believed that the promise made her by the Lord would 45 be fulfilled.'

The Magnificat

And Maryⁱ said: 46

'My soul proclaims the greatness of the Lord
and my spirit *exults in God my saviour;*   47

48   because *he has looked upon his lowly handmaid.*
      Yes, from this day forward all generations will call me blessed,
49   for the Almighty has done great things for me.
      Holy is his name,
50   and *his mercy reaches from age to age for those who fear him.*
51   He has shown the power of his arm,
      he has routed the proud of heart.
52   *He has pulled down princes* from their thrones *and exalted the lowly.*
53   *The hungry he has filled with good things,* the rich sent empty away.
54   *He has come to the help of Israel his servant, mindful of his mercy*
55   —according to the promise he made to our ancestors—
      of his mercy to Abraham and to his descendants for ever.'

56   Mary stayed with Elizabeth about three months and then went back home.

The birth of John the Baptist and visit of the neighbours

57   Meanwhile the time came for Elizabeth to have her child, and she gave birth
58 to a son; •and when her neighbours and relations heard that the Lord had shown
her so great a kindness, they shared her joy.

The circumcision of John the Baptist

59   Now on the eighth day they came to circumcise the child; they were going
60 to call[j] him Zechariah after his father, •but his mother spoke up. 'No,' she
61 said 'he is to be called John.' •They said to her, 'But no one in your family has
62 that name', •and made signs to his father to find out what he wanted him called.
63 The father asked for a writing-tablet and wrote, 'His name is John'. And they
64 were all astonished. •At that instant his power of speech returned and he spoke
65 and praised God. •All their neighbours were filled with awe and the whole affair
66 was talked about throughout the hill country of Judaea. •All those who heard
of it treasured it in their hearts. 'What will this child turn out to be?'
they wondered. And indeed the hand of the Lord was with him.

The Benedictus

67   His father Zechariah was filled with the Holy Spirit and spoke this prophecy:

68   '*Blessed be the Lord, the God of Israel,*[k]
          for he has visited his people, he has come to their rescue
69   and he has raised up for us a power for salvation
          in the House of his servant David,
70   even as he proclaimed,
          by the mouth of his holy prophets from ancient times,
71   that he would save us from our enemies
          and from the hands of all who hate us.
72   Thus he shows mercy to our ancestors,
          thus *he remembers* his holy *covenant,*[l]
73   the oath he swore
          to our father Abraham

e. Ml 3:23-24   f. Zechariah asks for a sign in a way reminiscent of Abram, Gn 15:8.
g. Lit. 'since I do not know man'.   h. Gn 8:14   i. Mary's canticle is reminiscent of
Hannah's, 1 S 2:1-10. Other quotations and allusions in the Magnificat are: 1 S 1:11; Ps 103:17;
Ps 111:9; Jb 5:11 and 12:19; Ps 98:3; Ps 107:9; Is 41:8-9.   j. The name was normally given at
the time of circumcision.   **k.** Ps 41:13   **l.** Lv 26:42

that he would grant us, free from fear,　　　　　　　74
to be delivered from the hands of our enemies,
to serve him in holiness and virtue　　　　　　　　75
in his presence, all our days.
And you, little child,　　　　　　　　　　　　76
you shall be called Prophet of the Most High,
for you will go before the Lord
to prepare the way for him.
To give his people knowledge of salvation　　　　77
through the forgiveness of their sins;
this by the tender mercy of our God　　　　　　　78
who from on high will bring the rising Sun to visit us,
to give light to *those who live*　　　　　　　79
in darkness and the shadow of death, *ᵐ*
and to guide our feet
into the way of peace.'

The hidden life of John the Baptist

Meanwhile the child grew up and his spirit matured.　And　he　lived out in　80
the wilderness until the day he appeared openly to Israel.

The birth of Jesus and visit of the shepherds

2 Now at this time Caesar Augustus*ᵃ* issued a decree for a census of the whole　1
world to be taken. •This census—the first *ᵇ*—took place while Quirinius was　2
governor of Syria, •and everyone went to his own town to be registered. •So Joseph　³₄
set out from the town of Nazareth in Galilee and travelled up to Judaea, to the
town of David called Bethlehem, since he was of David's House and line, •in　5
order to be registered together with Mary, his betrothed, who was with child.
While they were there the time came for her to have her child, •and she gave birth　⁶₇
to a son, her first-born.*ᶜ* She wrapped him in swaddling clothes, and laid him in a
manger because there was no room for them at the inn. •In the countryside　8
close by there were shepherds who lived in the fields and took it in turns to watch
their flocks during the night. •The angel of the Lord appeared to them　and　9
the glory of the Lord shone round them. They were terrified, •but the angel　10
said, 'Do not be afraid. Listen, I bring you news of great joy, a joy to be shared
by the whole people. •Today in the town of David a saviour has been born to　11
you; he is Christ the Lord.　•And here is a sign for you: you will find a baby　12
wrapped in swaddling clothes and lying in a manger.' •And suddenly with the　13
angel there was a great throng of the heavenly host, praising God and singing:

'Glory to God in the highest heaven,　　　　　　14
and peace to men who enjoy his favour'.

Now when the angels had gone from them into heaven, the shepherds said　15
to one another, 'Let us go to Bethlehem and see this thing that has happened
which the Lord has made known to us'. •So they hurried away and found　16
Mary and Joseph, and the baby lying in the manger. •When they saw the child　17
they repeated what they had been told about him, •and everyone who heard　18
it was astonished at what the shepherds had to say. •As for Mary, she treasured　19
all these things and pondered them in her heart. •And the shepherds went　20
back glorifying and praising God for all they had heard and seen; it was exactly
as they had been told.

The circumcision of Jesus

21   When the eighth day came and the child was to be circumcised, they gave
him the name Jesus, the name the angel had given him before his conception.

Jesus is presented in the Temple

22   And when the day came for them to be purified[d] as laid down by the Law
23 of Moses, they took him up to Jerusalem to present him to the Lord —•observing
what stands written in the Law of the Lord: *Every first-born male must be con-*
24 *secrated to the Lord[e]*—•and also to offer in sacrifice, in accordance with what
25 is said in the Law of the Lord, *a pair of turtledoves or two young pigeons.[f]* •Now
in Jerusalem there was a man named Simeon. He was an upright and devout
man; he looked forward to Israel's comforting and the Holy Spirit rested on
26 him. •It had been revealed to him by the Holy Spirit that he would not see death
27 until he had set eyes on the Christ of the Lord.[g] •Prompted by the Spirit he
came to the Temple; and when the parents brought in the child Jesus to do for
28 him what the Law required, •he took him into his arms and blessed God; and he
said:

The Nunc Dimittis

29   'Now, Master, you can let your servant go in peace,
                      just as you promised;
30   because my eyes have seen the salvation
31   which you have prepared for all the nations to see,
32   a light to enlighten the pagans
                      and the glory of your people Israel'.

The prophecy of Simeon

33   As the child's father and mother stood there wondering at the things that
34 were being said about him, •Simeon blessed them and said to Mary his mother,
'You see this child: he is destined for the fall and for the rising of many in Israel,
35 destined to be a sign that is rejected—•and a sword will pierce your own soul
too—so that the secret thoughts of many may be laid bare'.

The prophecy of Anna

36   There was a prophetess also, Anna the daughter of Phanuel, of the tribe
of Asher. She was well on in years. Her days of girlhood over, she had been
37 married for seven years •before becoming a widow. She was now eighty-four
years old and never left the Temple, serving God night and day with fasting
38 and prayer. •She came by just at that moment and began to praise God; and
she spoke of the child to all who looked forward to the deliverance of Jerusalem.[h]

The hidden life of Jesus at Nazareth

39   When they had done everything the Law of the Lord required, they went back
40 to Galilee, to their own town of Nazareth. •Meanwhile the child grew to maturity,
and he was filled with wisdom; and God's favour was with him.

---

m. Is 9:1
2 a. Emperor of Rome 30 B.C to 14 A.D.   **b.** About 8-6 B.C.   **c.** The term does not necessarily imply younger brothers.   **d.** The mother needed to be 'purified'; the child had to be
'redeemed'.   **e.** Ex 13:2   **f.** The offering of the poor, Lv 5:7.   **g.** 'The anointed one of God'.
h. I.e. Israel. Jerusalem is the holy city.

Jesus among the doctors of the Law

Every year his parents used to go to Jerusalem for the feast of the Passover. 41
When he was twelve years old, they went up for the feast as usual. •When they $^{42}_{43}$
were on their way home after the feast, the boy Jesus stayed behind in Jerusalem
without his parents knowing it. •They assumed he was with the caravan, and 44
it was only after a day's journey that they went to look for him among their
relations and acquaintances. •When they failed to find him they went back to 45
Jerusalem looking for him everywhere.

Three days later, they found him in the Temple, sitting among the doctors, 46
listening to them, and asking them questions; •and all those who heard him 47
were astounded at his intelligence and his replies. •They were overcome 48
when they saw him, and his mother said to him, 'My child, why have
you done this to us? See how worried your father and I have been, looking for
you.' •'Why were you looking for me?' he replied 'Did you not know that I must 49
be busy with my Father's affairs?' •But they did not understand what he meant. 50

The hidden life at Nazareth resumed

He then went down with them and came to Nazareth and lived under their 51
authority. His mother stored up all these things in her heart. •And Jesus increased 52
in wisdom, in stature, and in favour with God and men.

II. PRELUDE TO THE PUBLIC MINISTRY OF JESUS

The preaching of John the Baptist

3 In the fifteenth year of Tiberius Caesar's reign,^{a} when Pontius Pilate^b was 1
governor of Judaea, Herod^c tetrarch of Galilee, his brother Philip^d tetrarch
of the lands of Ituraea and Trachonitis, Lysanias tetrarch of Abilene, •during 2
the pontificate of Annas and Caiaphas,^{e} the word of God came to John son of
Zechariah, in the wilderness. •He went through the whole Jordan district pro- 3
claiming a baptism of repentance for the forgiveness of sins, •as it is written 4
in the book of the sayings of the prophet Isaiah:

> *A voice cries in the wilderness:*
> *Prepare a way for the Lord,*
> *make his paths straight.*
> *Every valley will be filled in,*   5
> *every mountain and hill be laid low,*
> *winding ways will be straightened*
> *and rough roads made smooth.*
> *And all mankind shall see the salvation of God.* ^{f} 6

He said, therefore, to the crowds who came to be baptised by him, 'Brood of 7
vipers, who warned you to fly from the retribution that is coming? •But if you are 8
repentant, produce the appropriate fruits, and do not think of telling yourselves,
"We have Abraham for our father" because, I tell you, God can raise children for
Abraham from these stones. •Yes, even now the axe is laid to the roots of the 9
trees, so that any tree which fails to produce good fruit will be cut down and
thrown on the fire.'

When all the people asked him, 'What must we do, then?' •he answered, $^{10}_{11}$
'If anyone has two tunics he must share with the man who has none, and the
one with something to eat must do the same'. •There were tax collectors too 12

13 who came for baptism, and these said to him, 'Master, what must we do?' •He
14 said to them, 'Exact no more than your rate'. •Some soldiers asked him in their
turn, 'What about us? What must we do?' He said to them, 'No intimidation!
No extortion! Be content with your pay!'

15 A feeling of expectancy had grown among the people, who were beginning
16 to think that John might be the Christ, •so John declared before them all, 'I
baptise you with water, but someone is coming, someone who is more powerful
than I am, and I am not fit to undo the strap of his sandals; he will baptise
17 you with the Holy Spirit and fire. •His winnowing-fan is in his hand to clear
his threshing-floor and to gather the wheat into his barn; but the chaff he will
18 burn in a fire that will never go out.' •As well as this, there were many other
things he said to exhort the people and to announce the Good News to them.

John the Baptist imprisoned

19 But Herod the tetrarch, whom he criticised for his relations with his brother's
20 wife Herodias and for all the other crimes Herod had committed, •added a further
crime to all the rest by shutting John up in prison.

Jesus is baptised

21 Now when all the people had been baptised and while Jesus after his own
22 baptism was at prayer, heaven opened •and the Holy Spirit descended on him
in bodily shape, like a dove. And a voice came from heaven, 'You are my Son,
the Beloved; my favour rests on you'.

The ancestry of Jesus

23 When he started to teach, Jesus was about thirty years old, being the son,
24 as it was thought, of Joseph son of Heli, •son of Matthat, son of Levi, son
25 of Melchi, son of Jannai, son of Joseph, •son of Mattathias, son of Amos, son
26 of Nahum, son of Esli, son of Naggai, •son of Maath, son of Mattathias, son
27 of Semein, son of Josech, son of Joda, •son of Joanan, son of Rhesa, son of
28 Zerubbabel, son of Shealtiel, son of Neri, •son of Melchi, son of Addi, son of
29 Cosam, son of Elmadam, son of Er, •son of Joshua, son of Eliezer, son
30 of Jorim, son of Matthat, son of Levi, •son of Symeon, son of Judah, son
31 of Joseph, son of Jonam, son of Eliakim, •son of Melea, son of Menna, son of
32 Mattatha, son of Nathan, son of David, •son of Jesse, son of Obed, son of Boaz,
33 son of Sala, son of Nahshon, •son of Amminadab, son of Admin, son of Arni,
34 son of Hezron, son of Perez, son of Judah, •son of Jacob, son of Isaac, son
35 of Abraham, son of Terah, son of Nahor, •son of Serug, son of Reu, son of
36 Peleg, son of Eber, son of Shelah, •son of Cainan, son of Arphaxad, son of
37 Shem, son of Noah, son of Lamech, •son of Methuselah, son of Enoch, son of
38 Jared, son of Mahalaleel, son of Cainan, •son of Enos, son of Seth, son of Adam,
son of God.

3 a. By Roman dating, the 15th year of Tiberius Caesar's reign was August 28 A.D. to August
29 A.D.; by the Syrian method, it was Sept.-Oct. 27 A.D. to Sept.-Oct. 28 A.D. At that time,
Jesus was between 33 and 36 years old. The mistake in calculating 'the Christian era' results
from taking Lk 3:23 as an exact statement. **b.** Procurator of Judaea 26-36 A.D. **c.** Herod
Antipas, tetrarch of Galilee and Peraea 4 B.C. to 39 A.D. **d.** Tetrarch from 4 B.C. to 34 A.D.
e. Caiaphas was high priest from 18 to 36 A.D. His father-in-law, Annas, is associated with
him here and elsewhere; he had been high priest earlier and presumably still had great influence.
f. Is 40:3-5

Temptation in the wilderness

4 Filled with the Holy Spirit, Jesus left the Jordan and was led by the Spirit 1 through the wilderness, •being tempted there by the devil for forty days. 2 During that time he ate nothing and at the end he was hungry. •Then the devil 3 said to him, 'If you are the Son of God, tell this stone to turn into a loaf'. •But 4 Jesus replied, 'Scripture says: *Man does not live on bread alone*'. *ᵃ*

Then leading him to a height, the devil showed him in a moment of time all 5 the kingdoms of the world •and said to him, 'I will give you all this power and 6 the glory of these kingdoms, for it has been committed to me and I give it to anyone I choose. •Worship me, then, and it shall all be yours.' •But Jesus 7⁄8 answered him, 'Scripture says:

> *You must worship the Lord your God,*
> *and serve him alone'.* *ᵇ*

Then he led him to Jerusalem and made him stand on the parapet of the 9 Temple. 'If you are the Son of God,' he said to him 'throw yourself down from here, •for scripture says: 10

> *He will put his angels in charge of you*
> *to guard you,*

and again:

> *They will hold you up on their hands* 11
> *in case you hurt your foot against a stone'.* *ᶜ*

But Jesus answered him, 'It has been said: 12

> *You must not put the Lord your God to the test'.* *ᵈ*

Having exhausted all these ways of tempting him, the devil left him, to return 13 at the appointed time.

III. THE GALILEAN MINISTRY

Jesus begins to preach

Jesus, with the power of the Spirit in him, returned to Galilee; and his 14 reputation spread throughout the countryside. •He taught in their synagogues 15 and everyone praised him.

Jesus at Nazareth

He came to Nazara, where he had been brought up, and went into the 16 synagogue on the sabbath day as he usually did. He stood up to read,*ᶜ* •and they 17 handed him the scroll of the prophet Isaiah. Unrolling the scroll he found the place where it is written:

> *The spirit of the Lord has been given to me,* 18
> *for he has anointed me.*
> *He has sent me to bring the good news to the poor,*
> *to proclaim liberty to captives*
> *and to the blind new sight,*
> *to set the downtrodden free,*
> *to proclaim the Lord's year of favour.* *ᶠ* 19

20 He then rolled up the scroll, gave it back to the assistant and sat down. And all
21 eyes in the synagogue were fixed on him. •Then he began to speak to them, 'This
22 text is being fulfilled today even as you listen'. •And he won the approval of all,
and they were astonished by the gracious words that came from his lips.

23 They said, 'This is Joseph's son, surely?' •But he replied, 'No doubt you will
quote me the saying, "Physician, heal yourself," and tell me, "We have heard all
that happened in Capernaum, do the same here in your own countryside" '.
24 And he went on, 'I tell you solemnly, no prophet is ever accepted in his own
country.

25 'There were many widows in Israel, I can assure you, in Elijah's day, when
heaven remained shut for three years and six months and a great famine raged
26 throughout the land, •but Elijah was not sent to any one of these: he was sent
27 *to a widow at Zarephath, a Sidonian town.*ᵍ •And in the prophet Elisha's time
there were many lepers in Israel, but none of these was cured, except the Syrian,
Naaman.'

28 When they heard this everyone in the synagogue was enraged. •They sprang
29 to their feet and hustled him out of the town; and they took him up to the brow
30 of the hill their town was built on, intending to throw him down the cliff, •but
he slipped through the crowd and walked away.

Jesus teaches in Capernaum and cures a demoniac

31 He went down to Capernaum, a town in Galilee, and taught them on the
32 sabbath. •And his teaching made a deep impression on them because he spoke
with authority.

33 In the synagogue there was a man who was possessed by the spirit of an
34 unclean devil, and it shouted at the top of its voice, •'Ha! What do you want
with us, Jesus of Nazareth? Have you come to destroy us? I know who you are:
35 the Holy One of God.' •But Jesus said sharply, 'Be quiet! Come out of him!'
And the devil, throwing the man down in front of everyone, went out of him
36 without hurting him at all. •Astonishment seized them and they were all saying
to one another, 'What teaching! He gives orders to unclean spirits with authority
37 and power and they come out.' •And reports of him went all through the
surrounding countryside.

Cure of Simon's mother-in-law

38 Leaving the synagogue he went to Simon's house. Now Simon's mother-in-law
was suffering from a high fever and they asked him to do something for her.
39 Leaning over her he rebuked the fever and it left her. And she immediately got
up and began to wait on them.

A number of cures

40 At sunset all those who had friends suffering from diseases of one kind or
41 another brought them to him, and laying his hands on each he cured them. •Devils
too came out of many people, howling, 'You are the Son of God'. But he rebuked
them and would not allow them to speak because they knew that he was the
Christ.

---

4 a. Dt 8:3   **b.** Dt 6:13   **c.** Ps 91:11-12   **d.** Dt 6:16   **e.** Any adult man could be permitted by the president to read the scriptures.   **f.** Is 61:1-2   **g.** 1K 17:9

Jesus quietly leaves Capernaum and travels through Judaea

When daylight came he left the house and made his way to a lonely place. 42 The crowds went to look for him, and when they had caught up with him they wanted to prevent him leaving them, •but he answered, 'I must proclaim the 43 Good News of the kingdom of God to the other towns too, because that is what I was sent to do'. •And he continued his preaching in the synagogues of Judaea. 44

The first four disciples are called

5 Now he was standing one day by the Lake of Gennesaret, with the crowd 1 pressing round him listening to the word of God, •when he caught sight of two 2 boats close to the bank. The fishermen had gone out of them and were washing their nets. •He got into one of the boats—it was Simon's —and asked him to put 3 out a little from the shore. Then he sat down and taught the crowds from the boat.

When he had finished speaking he said to Simon, 'Put out into deep water 4 and pay out your nets for a catch'. •'Master,' Simon replied 'we worked hard all 5 night long and caught nothing, but if you say so, I will pay out the nets.' •And 6 when they had done this they netted such a huge number of fish that their nets began to tear, •so they signalled to their companions in the other boat to come 7 and help them; when these came, they filled the two boats to sinking point.

When Simon Peter saw this he fell at the knees of Jesus saying, 'Leave me, 8 Lord; I am a sinful man'. •For he and all his companions were completely 9 overcome by the catch they had made; •so also were James and John, sons of 10 Zebedee, who were Simon's partners. But Jesus said to Simon, 'Do not be afraid; from now on it is men you will catch'. •Then, bringing their boats back to land, 11 they left everything and followed him.

Cure of a leper

Now Jesus was in one of the towns when a man appeared, covered with 12 leprosy. Seeing Jesus he fell on his face and implored him. 'Sir,' he said 'if you want to, you can cure me.' •Jesus stretched out his hand, touched him and said, 13 'Of course I want to! Be cured!' And the leprosy left him at once. •He ordered 14 him to tell no one, 'But go and show yourself to the priest and make the offering for your healing as Moses prescribed it, as evidence for them'.

His reputation continued to grow, and large crowds would gather to hear him 15 and to have their sickness cured, •but he would always go off to some place where 16 he could be alone and pray.

Cure of a paralytic

Now he was teaching one day, and among the audience there were Pharisees 17 and doctors of the Law who had come from every village in Galilee, from Judaea and from Jerusalem. And the Power of the Lord was behind his works of healing. •Then some men appeared, carrying on a bed a paralysed man whom 18 they were trying to bring in and lay down in front of him. •But as the crowd 19 made it impossible to find a way of getting him in, they went up on to the flat roof and lowered him and his stretcher down through the tiles into the middle of the gathering, in front of Jesus. •Seeing their faith he said, 'My friend, your sins 20 are forgiven you'. •The scribes and the Pharisees began to think this over. 'Who is 21 this man talking blasphemy? Who can forgive sins but God alone?' •But Jesus, 22 aware of their thoughts, made them this reply, 'What are these thoughts you have in your hearts? •Which of these is easier: to say, "Your sins are forgiven you" 23 or to say, "Get up and walk"? •But to prove to you that the Son of Man has 24

authority on earth to forgive sins,'—he said to the paralysed man—'I order you:
25 get up, and pick up your stretcher and go home.' •And immediately before
their very eyes he got up, picked up what he had been lying on and went home
praising God.

26 They were all astounded and praised God, and were filled with awe,
saying, 'We have seen strange things today'.

The call of Levi

27 When he went out after this, he noticed a tax collector, Levi by name, sitting
28 by the customs house, and said to him, 'Follow me'. •And leaving everything he
got up and followed him.

Eating with sinners in Levi's house

29 In his honour Levi held a great reception in his house, and with them at table
30 was a large gathering of tax collectors and others. •The Pharisees and their scribes
complained to his disciples and said, 'Why do you eat and drink with tax collectors
31 and sinners?' •Jesus said to them in reply, 'It is not those who are well who need
32 the doctor, but the sick. •I have not come to call the virtuous, but sinners to
repentance.'

Discussion on fasting

33 They then said to him, 'John's disciples are always fasting and saying prayers,
and the disciples of the Pharisees too, but yours go on eating and drinking'.
34 Jesus replied, 'Surely you cannot make the bridegroom's attendants fast while
35 the bridegroom is still with them?' •But the time will come, the time for the bridegroom to be taken away from them; that will be the time when they will fast.'

36 He also told them this parable, 'No one tears a piece from a new cloak to put
it on an old cloak; if he does, not only will he have torn the new one, but the
piece taken from the new will not match the old.

37 'And nobody puts new wine into old skins; if he does, the new wine will burst
38 the skins and then run out, and the skins will be lost. •No; new wine must be put
39 into fresh skins. •And nobody who has been drinking old wine wants new. "The
old is good" he says.'

Picking corn on the sabbath

1 6 Now one sabbath he happened to be taking a walk through the cornfields,
and his disciples were picking ears of corn, rubbing them in their hands
2 and eating them. •Some of the Pharisees said, 'Why are you doing something
3 that is forbidden on the sabbath day?' •Jesus answered them, 'So you have not
4 read what David did when he and his followers were hungry—•how he went into
the house of God, took the loaves of offering and ate them and gave them to his
5 followers, loaves which only the priests are allowed to eat?' •And he said to them,
'The Son of Man is master of the sabbath'.

Cure of the man with a withered hand

6 Now on another sabbath he went into the synagogue and began to teach, and
7 a man was there whose right hand was withered. •The scribes and the Pharisees
were watching him to see if he would cure a man on the sabbath, hoping to
8 find something to use against him. •But he knew their thoughts; and he said to the
man with the withered hand, 'Stand up! Come out into the middle.' And he came
9 out and stood there. •Then Jesus said to them, 'I put it to you: is it against the
10 law on the sabbath to do good, or to do evil; to save life, or to destroy it?' •Then

he looked round at them all and said to the man, 'Stretch out your hand'. He did so, and his hand was better. •But they were furious, and began to discuss the 11 best way of dealing with Jesus.

The choice of the Twelve

Now it was about this time that he went out into the hills to pray; and he spent 12 the whole night in prayer to God. •When day came he summoned his disciples 13 and picked out twelve of them; he called them 'apostles': •Simon whom he 14 called Peter, and his brother Andrew; James, John, Philip, Bartholomew, Matthew, Thomas, James son of Alphaeus, Simon called the Zealot, •Judas son 15 16 of James," and Judas Iscariot who became a traitor.

The crowds follow Jesus

He then came down with them and stopped at a piece of level ground where 17 there was a large gathering of his disciples with a great crowd of people from all parts of Judaea and from Jerusalem and from the coastal region of Tyre and Sidon who had come to hear him and to be cured of their diseases. People tormented 18 by unclean spirits were also cured, •and everyone in the crowd was trying to touch 19 him because power came out of him that cured them all.

The inaugural discourse. The Beatitudes

Then fixing his eyes on his disciples he said: 20

    'How happy are you who are poor: yours is the kingdom of God.
    Happy you who are hungry now: you shall be satisfied.   21
    Happy you who weep now: you shall laugh.

'Happy are you when people hate you, drive you out, abuse you, denounce 22 your name as criminal, on account of the Son of Man. •Rejoice when that day 23 comes and dance for joy, for then your reward will be great in heaven. This was the way their ancestors treated the prophets.

The curses

    'But alas for you who are rich: you are having your consolation now.   24
    Alas for you who have your fill now: you shall go hungry.   25
    Alas for you who laugh now: you shall mourn and weep.

'Alas for you when the world speaks well of you! This was the way their 26 ancestors treated the false prophets.

Love of enemies

'But I say this to you who are listening: Love your enemies, do good to those 27 who hate you, •bless those who curse you, pray for those who treat you badly. 28 To the man who slaps you on one cheek, present the other cheek too; to the man 29 who takes your cloak from you, do not refuse your tunic. •Give to everyone who 30 asks you, and do not ask for your property back from the man who robs you. Treat others as you would like them to treat you. •If you love those who love 31 32 you, what thanks can you expect? Even sinners love those who love them. •And if 33 you do good to those who do good to you, what thanks can you expect? For even sinners do that much. •And if you lend to those from whom you hope to receive, 34 what thanks can you expect? Even sinners lend to sinners to get back the same amount. •Instead, love your enemies and do good, and lend without any hope 35 of return. You will have a great reward, and you will be sons of the Most High, for he himself is kind to the ungrateful and the wicked.

Compassion and generosity

³⁶³⁷ 'Be compassionate as your Father is compassionate. •Do not judge, and you will not be judged yourselves; do not condemn, and you will not be condemned ³⁸ yourselves; grant pardon, and you will be pardoned. •Give, and there will be gifts for you: a full measure, pressed down, shaken together, and running over, will be poured into your lap; because the amount you measure out is the amount you will be given back.'

Integrity

³⁹ He also told a parable to them, 'Can one blind man guide another? Surely ⁴⁰ both will fall into a pit? •The disciple is not superior to his teacher; the fully ⁴¹ trained disciple will always be like his teacher. •Why do you observe the splinter ⁴² in your brother's eye and never notice the plank in your own? •How can you say to your brother, "Brother, let me take out the splinter that is in your eye", when you cannot see the plank in your own? Hypocrite! Take the plank out of your own eye first, and then you will see clearly enough to take out the splinter that is in your brother's eye.

⁴³ 'There is no sound tree that produces rotten fruit, nor again a rotten tree that ⁴⁴ produces sound fruit. •For every tree can be told by its own fruit: people do not ⁴⁵ pick figs from thorns, nor gather grapes from brambles. •A good man draws what is good from the store of goodness in his heart; a bad man draws what is bad from the store of badness. For a man's words flow out of what fills his heart.

The true disciple

⁴⁶ 'Why do you call me, "Lord, Lord" and not do what I say?

⁴⁷ 'Everyone who comes to me and listens to my words and acts on them—I will ⁴⁸ show you what he is like. •He is like the man who when he built his house dug, and dug deep, and laid the foundations on rock; when the river was in flood it ⁴⁹ bore down on that house but could not shake it, it was so well built. •But the one who listens and does nothing is like the man who built his house on soil, with no foundations: as soon as the river bore down on it, it collapsed; and what a ruin that house became!'

Cure of the centurion's servant

¹ **7**When he had come to the end of all he wanted the people to hear, he went into ² Capernaum. •A centurion there had a servant, a favourite of his, who was ³ sick and near death. •Having heard about Jesus he sent some Jewish elders ⁴ to him to ask him to come and heal his servant. •When they came to Jesus they ⁵ pleaded earnestly with him. 'He deserves this of you' they said •'because he is friendly towards our people; in fact, he is the one who built the synagogue.' ⁶ So Jesus went with them, and was not very far from the house when the centurion sent word to him by some friends: 'Sir,' he said 'do not put yourself to trouble; ⁷ because I am not worthy to have you under my roof; •and for this same reason I did not presume to come to you myself; but give the word and let my servant ⁸ be cured. •For I am under authority myself, and have soldiers under me; and I say to one man: Go, and he goes; to another: Come here, and he comes; to my ⁹ servant: Do this, and he does it.' •When Jesus heard these words he was astonished at him and, turning round, said to the crowd following him, 'I tell

6 a. Or possibly 'brother of James'.

you, not even in Israel have I found faith like this'. •And when the messengers 10
got back to the house they found the servant in perfect health.

The son of the widow of Nain restored to life

Now soon afterwards he went to a town called Nain, accompanied by his 11
disciples and a great number of people. •When he was near the gate of the town 12
it happened that a dead man was being carried out for burial, the only son of his
mother, and she was a widow. And a considerable number of the townspeople
were with her. •When the Lord*a* saw her he felt sorry for her. 'Do not cry' he 13
said. •Then he went up and put his hand on the bier and the bearers stood still, 14
and he said, 'Young man, I tell you to get up'. •And the dead man sat up and 15
began to talk, and Jesus *gave him to his mother.b* •Everyone was filled with awe 16
and praised God saying, 'A great prophet has appeared among us; God has
visited his people'. •And this opinion of him spread throughout Judaea and all 17
over the countryside.

The Baptist's question. Jesus commends him

The disciples of John gave him all this news, and John, summoning two of his 18
disciples, •sent them to the Lord to ask, 'Are you the one who is to come, or must 19
we wait for someone else?' •When the men reached Jesus they said, 'John the 20
Baptist has sent us to you, to ask, "Are you the one who is to come or have we
to wait for someone else?" ' •It was just then that he cured many people of 21
diseases and afflictions and of evil spirits, and gave the gift of sight to many who
were blind. •Then he gave the messengers their answer, 'Go back and tell John 22
what you have seen and heard: the blind see again, the lame walk, lepers are
cleansed, and the deaf hear, the dead are raised to life, the Good News is proclaimed to the poor •and happy is the man who does not lose faith in me'. 23

When John's messengers had gone he began to talk to the people about John, 24
'What did you go out into the wilderness to see? A reed swaying in the breeze? 25
No? Then what did you go out to see? A man dressed in fine clothes?
Oh no, those who go in for fine clothes and live luxuriously are to be found at
court! •Then what did you go out to see? A prophet? Yes, I tell you, and much 26
more than a prophet: •he is the one of whom scripture says: 27

> *See, I am going to send my messenger before you;*
> *he will prepare the way before you.c*

'I tell you, of all the children born of women, there is no one greater than John; 28
yet the least in the kingdom of God is greater than he is. •All the people who 29
heard him, and the tax collectors too, acknowledged God's plan by accepting
baptism from John; •but by refusing baptism from him the Pharisees and the 30
lawyers had thwarted what God had in mind for them.

Jesus condemns his contemporaries

'What description, then, can I find for the men of this generation? What are 31
they like? •They are like children shouting to one another while they sit in the 32
market place:

> "We played the pipes for you,
> and you wouldn't dance;
> we sang dirges,
> and you wouldn't cry".

33 'For John the Baptist comes, not eating bread, not drinking wine, and you
34 say, "He is possessed". •The Son of Man comes, eating and drinking, and you
say, "Look, a glutton and a drunkard, a friend of tax collectors and sinners".
35 Yet Wisdom has been proved right by all her children.'

The woman who was a sinner

36 One of the Pharisees invited him to a meal. When he arrived at the Pharisee's
37 house and took his place at table, •a woman came in, who had a bad name in
the town. She had heard he was dining with the Pharisee and had brought with her
38 an alabaster jar of ointment. •She waited behind him at his feet, weeping, and her
tears fell on his feet, and she wiped them away with her hair; then she covered
his feet with kisses and anointed them with the ointment.

39 When the Pharisee who had invited him saw this, he said to himself, 'If this
man were a prophet, he would know who this woman is that is touching him and
40 what a bad name she has'. •Then Jesus took him up and said, 'Simon, I have
41 something to say to you'. 'Speak, Master' was the reply. •'There was once a
creditor who had two men in his debt; one owed him five hundred denarii, the
42 other fifty. •They were unable to pay, so he pardoned them both. Which of them
43 will love him more?' •'The one who was pardoned more, I suppose' answered
Simon. Jesus said, 'You are right'.

44 Then he turned to the woman. 'Simon,' he said 'you see this woman? I came
into your house, and you poured no water over my feet, but she has poured out her
45 tears over my feet and wiped them away with her hair. •You gave me no kiss, but
46 she has been covering my feet with kisses ever since I came in. •You did not
47 anoint my head with oil, but she has anointed my feet with ointment. •For this
reason I tell you that her sins, her many sins, must have been forgiven her, or she
would not have shown such great love. It is the man who is forgiven little who
48/49 shows little love.' •Then he said to her, 'Your sins are forgiven'. •Those who
were with him at table began to say to themselves, 'Who is this man, that he even
50 forgives sins?' •But he said to the woman, 'Your faith has saved you; go in peace'.

The women accompanying Jesus

1 **8** Now after this he made his way through towns and villages preaching, and
proclaiming the Good News of the kingdom of God. With him went the
2 Twelve, •as well as certain women who had been cured of evil spirits and ailments:
Mary surnamed the Magdalene, from whom seven demons had gone out,
3 Joanna the wife of Herod's steward Chuza, Susanna, and several others who
provided for them out of their own resources.

Parable of the sower

4 With a large crowd gathering and people from every town finding their way
to him, he used this parable:
5 'A sower went out to sow his seed. As he sowed, some fell on the edge of the
6 path and was trampled on; and the birds of the air ate it up. •Some seed fell on
7 rock, and when it came up it withered away, having no moisture. •Some seed fell
8 amongst thorns and the thorns grew with it and choked it. •And some seed fell
into rich soil and grew and produced its crop a hundredfold.' Saying this he
cried, 'Listen, anyone who has ears to hear!'

---

7 a. For the first time in the gospel narrative Jesus is given the title hitherto reserved for God.
b. 1 K 17:23   **c.** Ml 3:1

Why Jesus speaks in parables

His disciples asked him what this parable might mean, •and he said, 'The $^9_{10}$ mysteries of the kingdom of God are revealed to you; for the rest there are only parables, so that

> *they may see but not perceive,*
> *listen but not understand.* [a]

The parable of the sower explained

'This, then, is what the parable means: the seed is the word of God. •Those $^{11}_{12}$ on the edge of the path are people who have heard it, and then the devil comes and carries away the word from their hearts in case they should believe and be saved. •Those on the rock are people who, when they first hear it, welcome the 13 word with joy. But these have no root; they believe for a while, and in time of trial they give up. •As for the part that fell into thorns, this is people who have 14 heard, but as they go on their way they are choked by the worries and riches and pleasures of life and do not reach maturity. •As for the part in the rich soil, this 15 is people with a noble and generous heart who have heard the word and take it to themselves and yield a harvest through their perseverance.

Parable of the lamp

'No one lights a lamp to cover it with a bowl or to put it under a bed. No, he 16 puts it on a lamp-stand so that people may see the light when they come in. For nothing is hidden but it will be made clear, nothing secret but it will be 17 known and brought to light. •So take care how you hear; for anyone who has 18 will be given more; from anyone who has not, even what he thinks he has will be taken away.'

The true kinsmen of Jesus

His mother and his brothers came looking for him, but they could not get to 19 him because of the crowd. •He was told, 'Your mother and brothers are standing 20 outside and want to see you'. •But he said in answer, 'My mother and my 21 brothers are those who hear the word of God and put it into practice'.

The calming of the storm

One day, he got into a boat with his disciples and said to them, 'Let us cross 22 over to the other side of the lake'. So they put to sea, •and as they sailed he fell 23 asleep. When a squall came down on the lake the boat started taking in water and they found themselves in danger. •So they went to rouse him saying, 'Master! 24 Master! We are going down!' Then he woke up and rebuked the wind and the rough water; and they subsided and it was calm again. •He said to them, 'Where 25 is your faith?' They were awestruck and astonished and said to one another, 'Who can this be, that gives orders even to winds and waves and they obey him?'

The Gerasene demoniac

They came to land in the country of the Gerasenes, [b] which is opposite Galilee. 26 He was stepping ashore when a man from the town who was possessed by devils 27 came towards him; for a long time the man had worn no clothes, nor did he live in a house, but in the tombs.

Catching sight of Jesus he gave a shout, fell at his feet and cried out at the 28

top of his voice, 'What do you want with me, Jesus, son of the Most High God?
29 I implore you, do not torture me.'•—For Jesus had been telling the unclean
spirit to come out of the man. It was a devil that had seized on him a great many
times, and then they used to secure him with chains and fetters to restrain him,
but he would always break the fastenings, and the devil would drive him out into
30 the wilds. •'What is your name?' Jesus asked. 'Legion' he said—because
31 many devils had gone into him. •And these pleaded with him not to order them
to depart into the Abyss.ᶜ

32 Now there was a large herd of pigs feeding there on the mountain, and the
33 devils pleaded with him to let them go into these. So he gave them leave. •The
devils came out of the man and went into the pigs, and the herd charged down
the cliff into the lake and were drowned.

34 When the swineherds saw what had happened they ran off and told their story
35 in the town and in the country round about; •and the people went out to see what
had happened. When they came to Jesus they found the man from whom the
devils had gone out sitting at the feet of Jesus, clothed and in his full
36 senses; and they were afraid. •Those who had witnessed it told them how the
37 man who had been possessed came to be healed. •The entire population of the
Gerasene territory was in a state of panic and asked Jesus to leave them. So he
got into the boat and went back.

38 The man from whom the devils had gone out asked to be allowed to stay with
39 him, but he sent him away. •'Go back home,' he said 'and report all that God has
done for you.' So the man went off and spread throughout the town all that
Jesus had done for him.

Cure of the woman with a haemorrhage. Jairus' daughter raised to life

40 On his return Jesus was welcomed by the crowd, for they were all there waiting
41 for him. •And now there came a man named Jairus, who was an official of the
synagogue. He fell at Jesus' feet and pleaded with him to come to his house,
42 because he had an only daughter about twelve years old, who was dying. And the
crowds were almost stifling Jesus as he went.

43 Now there was a woman suffering from a haemorrhage for twelve years,
44 whom no one had been able to cure. •She came up behind him and touched
45 the fringe of his cloak; and the haemorrhage stopped at that instant. •Jesus said,
'Who touched me?' When they all denied that they had, Peter and his companions
46 said, 'Master, it is the crowds round you, pushing'. •But Jesus said, 'Somebody
47 touched me. I felt that power had gone out from me.' •Seeing herself discovered, the
woman came forward trembling, and falling at his feet explained in front of all the
48 people why she had touched him and how she had been cured at that very moment.
'My daughter,' he said 'your faith has restored you to health; go in peace.'

49 While he was still speaking, someone arrived from the house of the synagogue
official to say, 'Your daughter has died. Do not trouble the Master any further.'
50 But Jesus had heard this, and he spoke to the man, 'Do not be afraid, only have
51 faith and she will be safe'. •When he came to the house he allowed no one to go
in with him except Peter and John and James, and the child's father and mother.
52 They were all weeping and mourning for her, but Jesus said, 'Stop crying; she is
53 not dead, but asleep'. •But they laughed at him, knowing she was dead. •But
54
55 taking her by the hand he called to her, 'Child, get up'. •And her spirit returned and
56 she got up at once. Then he told them to give her something to eat. •Her parents
were astonished, but he ordered them not to tell anyone what had happened.

8 a. Is 6:9   b. 'Gadarenes' in some versions.   c. The underworld.

The mission of the Twelve

9 He called the Twelve together and gave them power and authority over all 1 devils and to cure diseases, ·and he sent them out to proclaim the kingdom of 2 God and to heal. ·He said to them, 'Take nothing for the journey: neither staff, 3 nor haversack, nor bread, nor money; and let none of you take a spare tunic. Whatever house you enter, stay there; and when you leave, let it be from there. 4 As for those who do not welcome you, when you leave their town shake the 5 dust from your feet as a sign to them.' ·So they set out and went from village 6 to village proclaiming the Good News and healing everywhere.

Herod and Jesus

Meanwhile Herod the tetrarch had heard about all that was going on; and 7 he was puzzled, because some people were saying that John had risen from the dead, ·others that Elijah had reappeared, still others that one of the ancient 8 prophets had come back to life. ·But Herod said, 'John? I beheaded him. So who 9 is this I hear such reports about?' And he was anxious to see him.

The return of the apostles. Miracle of the loaves

On their return the apostles gave him an account of all they had done. Then 10 he took them with him and withdrew to a town called Bethsaida where they could be by themselves. ·But the crowds got to know and they went after him. 11 He made them welcome and talked to them about the kingdom of God; and he cured those who were in need of healing.

It was late afternoon when the Twelve came to him and said, 'Send the 12 people away, and they can go to the villages and farms round about to find lodging and food; for we are in a lonely place here'. ·He replied, 'Give them some- 13 thing to eat yourselves'. But they said, 'We have no more than five loaves and two fish, unless we are to go ourselves and buy food for all these people'. ·For there 14 were about five thousand men. But he said to his disciples, 'Get them to sit down in parties of about fifty'. ·They did so and made them all sit down. ·Then he took $^{15}_{16}$ the five loaves and the two fish, raised his eyes to heaven, and said the blessing over them; then he broke them and handed them to his disciples to distribute among the crowd. ·They all ate as much as they wanted, and when the scraps 17 remaining were collected they filled twelve baskets.

Peter's profession of faith

Now one day when he was praying alone in the presence of his disciples he 18 put this question to them, 'Who do the crowds say I am?' ·And they answered, 19 'John the Baptist; others Elijah; and others say one of the ancient prophets come back to life'. ·'But you,' he said 'who do you say I am?' It was Peter who spoke 20 up. 'The Christ of God' he said. ·But he gave them strict orders not to tell 21 anyone anything about this.

First prophecy of the Passion

'The Son of Man' he said 'is destined to suffer grievously, to be rejected by the 22 elders and chief priests and scribes and to be put to death, and to be raised up on the third day.'

The condition of following Christ

Then to all he said, 'If anyone wants to be a follower of mine, let him renounce 23 himself and take up his cross every day and follow me. ·For anyone who wants 24 to save his life will lose it; but anyone who loses his life for my sake, that man

25 will save it. •What gain, then, is it for a man to have won the whole world and to
26 have lost or ruined his very self? •For if anyone is ashamed of me and of my
words, of him the Son of Man will be ashamed when he comes in his own glory
and in the glory of the Father and the holy angels.

The kingdom will come soon

27   'I tell you truly, there are some standing here who will not taste death before
they see the kingdom of God.'

The transfiguration

28   Now about eight days after this had been said, he took with him Peter and
29 John and James and went up the mountain to pray. •As he prayed, the aspect of
30 his face was changed and his clothing became brilliant as lightning. •Suddenly
31 there were two men there talking to him; they were Moses and Elijah •appearing
in glory, and they were speaking of his passing which he was to accomplish in
32 Jerusalem. •Peter and his companions were heavy with sleep, but they kept awake
33 and saw his glory and the two men standing with him. •As these were leaving
him, Peter said to Jesus, 'Master, it is wonderful for us to be here; so let us make
three tents, one for you, one for Moses and one for Elijah'.—He did not know
34 what he was saying. •As he spoke, a cloud came and covered them with shadow;
35 and when they went into the cloud the disciples were afraid. •And a voice came
36 from the cloud saying, 'This is my Son, the Chosen One. Listen to him.' •And
after the voice had spoken, Jesus was found alone. The disciples kept silence and,
at that time, told no one what they had seen.

The epileptic demoniac

37   Now on the following day when they were coming down from the mountain
38 a large crowd came to meet him. •Suddenly a man in the crowd cried out. 'Master,'
39 he said 'I implore you to look at my son: he is my only child. •All at once a spirit
will take hold of him, and give a sudden cry and throw the boy into convulsions
with foaming at the mouth; it is slow to leave him, but when it does it leaves the
40 boy worn out. •I begged your disciples to cast it out, and they could not.'
41 'Faithless and perverse generation!'Jesus said in reply 'How much longer must I be
42 among you and put up with you? Bring your son here.' •The boy was still moving
towards Jesus when the devil threw him to the ground in convulsions. But Jesus
rebuked the unclean spirit and cured the boy and gave him back to his father,
43 and everyone was awestruck by the greatness of God.

Second prophecy of the Passion

     At a time when everyone was •full of admiration for all he did, he said to
44 his disciples, •'For your part, you must have these words constantly in your
mind: The Son of Man is going to be handed over into the power of men'.
45 But they did not understand him when he said this; it was hidden from them
so that they should not see the meaning of it, and they were afraid to ask him
about what he had just said.

Who is the greatest?

46   An argument started between them about which of them was the greatest.
47 Jesus knew what thoughts were going through their minds, and he took a
48 little child and set him by his side •and then said to them, 'Anyone who

welcomes this little child in my name welcomes me; and anyone who welcomes
me welcomes the one who sent me. For the least among you all, that is the one
who is great.'

On using the name of Jesus

John spoke up. 'Master,' he said 'we saw a man casting out devils in your 49
name, and because he is not with us we tried to stop him.'. •But Jesus said 50
to him, 'You must not stop him: anyone who is not against you is for you'.

IV. THE JOURNEY TO JERUSALEM

A Samaritan village is inhospitable

Now as the time drew near for him to be taken up to heaven, he resolutely 51
took the road for Jerusalem •and sent messengers ahead of him. These set out, 52
and they went into a Samaritan village to make preparations for him, •but the 53
people would not receive him because he was making for Jerusalem.*ª* •Seeing 54
this, the disciples James and John said, 'Lord, do you want us to call down fire
from heaven to burn them up?' •But he turned and rebuked them, •and they 55,56
went off to another village.

Hardships of the apostolic calling

As they travelled along they met a man on the road who said to him, 'I will 57
follow you wherever you go'. •Jesus answered, 'Foxes have holes and the birds 58
of the air have nests, but the Son of Man has nowhere to lay his head'.

Another to whom he said, 'Follow me', replied, 'Let me go and bury my 59
father first'. •But he answered, 'Leave the dead to bury their dead; your duty 60
is to go and spread the news of the kingdom of God'.

Another said, 'I will follow you, sir, but first let me go and say good-bye 61
to my people at home'. •Jesus said to him, 'Once the hand is laid on the plough, 62
no one who looks back is fit for the kingdom of God'.

The mission of the seventy-two disciples

10 After this the Lord appointed seventy-two others and sent them out ahead 1
of him, in pairs, to all the towns and places he himself was to visit.
He said to them, 'The harvest is rich but the labourers are few, so ask the Lord 2
of the harvest to send labourers to his harvest. •Start off now, but remember, 3
I am sending you out like lambs among wolves. •Carry no purse, no haversack, 4
no sandals. Salute no one on the road. •Whatever house you go into, let your 5
first words be, "Peace to this house!" •And if a man of peace lives there, your 6
peace will go and rest on him; if not, it will come back to you. •Stay in the same 7
house, taking what food and drink they have to offer, for the labourer deserves
his wages; do not move from house to house. •Whenever you go into a town where 8
they make you welcome, eat what is set before you. •Cure those in it who are 9
sick, and say, "The kingdom of God is very near to you". •But whenever you enter 10
a town and they do not make you welcome, go out into its streets and say, •"We 11
wipe off the very dust of your town that clings to our feet, and leave it with you.
Yet be sure of this: the kingdom of God is very near." •I tell you, on that day 12
it will not go as hard with Sodom as with that town.

'Alas for you, Chorazin! Alas for you, Bethsaida! For if the miracles done 13
in you had been done in Tyre and Sidon, they would have repented long ago, sitting

14 in sackcloth and ashes. •And still, it will not go as hard with Tyre and Sidon at the
15 Judgement as with you. •And as for you, Capernaum, did you want to be exalted
high as heaven? *You shall be thrown down to hell.*[a]

16   'Anyone who listens to you listens to me; anyone who rejects you rejects me,
and those who reject me reject the one who sent me.'

True cause for the apostles to rejoice

17   The seventy-two came back rejoicing. 'Lord,' they said 'even the devils
18 submit to us when we use your name.' •He said to them, 'I watched Satan fall
19 like lightning from heaven. •Yes, I have given you power to tread underfoot
serpents and scorpions and the whole strength of the enemy; nothing shall ever
20 hurt you. •Yet do not rejoice that the spirits submit to you; rejoice rather that
your names are written in heaven.'

The Good News revealed to the simple. The Father and the Son

21   It was then that, filled with joy by the Holy Spirit, he said, 'I bless
you, Father, Lord of heaven and of earth, for hiding these things from the learned
and the clever and revealing them to mere children. Yes, Father, for that is what
22 it pleased you to do. • Everything has been entrusted to me by my Father; and
no one knows who the Son is except the Father, and who the Father is except
the Son and those to whom the Son chooses to reveal him.'

The privilege of the disciples

23   Then turning to his disciples he spoke to them in private, 'Happy the eyes
24 that see what you see, •for I tell you that many prophets and kings wanted to see
what you see, and never saw it; to hear what you hear, and never heard it'.

The great commandment

25   There was a lawyer who, to disconcert him, stood up and said to him, 'Master,
26 what must I do to inherit eternal life?' •He said to him, 'What is written in the
27 Law? What do you read there?' •He replied, '*You must love the Lord your God
with all your heart, with all your soul, with all your strength,* and with all your
28 mind, *and your neighbour as yourself* '.[b] •'You have answered right,' said Jesus
'do this and life is yours.'

Parable of the good Samaritan

29   But the man was anxious to justify himself and said to Jesus, 'And who is
30 my neighbour?' •Jesus replied, 'A man was once on his way down from Jerusalem
to Jericho and fell into the hands of brigands; they took all he had, beat him
31 and then made off, leaving him half dead. •Now a priest happened to be travelling
down the same road, but when he saw the man, he passed by on the other side.
32 In the same way a Levite who came to the place saw him, and passed by on the
33 other side. •But a Samaritan traveller who came upon him was moved with
34 compassion when he saw him. •He went up and bandaged his wounds, pouring
oil and wine on them. He then lifted him on to his own mount, carried him to the
35 inn and looked after him. •Next day, he took out two denarii and handed them
to the innkeeper. "Look after him," he said "and on my way back I will make

9 a. The hatred of Samaritans for Jews would show itself particularly towards those who were
on pilgrimage to Jerusalem.
10 a. See Is 14:13,15.   b. Dt 6:5 and Lv 19:18

good any extra expense you have." •Which of these three, do you think, proved 36
himself a neighbour to the man who fell into the brigands' hands?' •'The one 37
who took pity on him' he replied. Jesus said to him, 'Go, and do the same
yourself'.

Martha and Mary

In the course of their journey he came to a village, and a woman named 38
Martha welcomed him into her house. •She had a sister called Mary, who sat 39
down at the Lord's feet and listened to him speaking. •Now Martha who was 40
distracted with all the serving said, 'Lord, do you not care that my sister is leaving
me to do the serving all by myself? Please tell her to help me.' •But the Lord 41
answered: 'Martha, Martha,' he said 'you worry and fret about so many things,
and yet few are needed, indeed only one. It is Mary who has chosen the better 42
part; it is not to be taken from her.'

The Lord's prayer

11 Now once he was in a certain place praying, and when he had finished 1
one of his disciples said, 'Lord, teach us to pray, just as John taught his
disciples'. •He said to them, 'Say this when you pray: 2

> "Father, may your name be held holy,
> your kingdom come;
> give us each day our daily bread, 3
> and forgive us our sins,
> for we ourselves forgive each one who is in debt to us. 4
> And do not put us to the test." '

The importunate friend

He also said to them, 'Suppose one of you has a friend and goes to him in 5
the middle of the night to say, "My friend, lend me three loaves, •because a friend 6
of mine on his travels has just arrived at my house and I have nothing to offer
him"; •and the man answers from inside the house, "Do not bother me. The 7
door is bolted now, and my children and I are in bed; I cannot get up to give
it you". •I tell you, if the man does not get up and give it him for friendship's 8
sake, persistence will be enough to make him get up and give his friend all he
wants.

Effective prayer

'So I say to you: Ask, and it will be given to you; search, and you will find; 9
knock, and the door will be opened to you. •For the one who asks always receives; 10
the one who searches always finds; the one who knocks will always have the door
opened to him. •What father among you would hand his son a stone when he 11
asked for bread? Or hand him a snake instead of a fish? •Or hand him a 12
scorpion if he asked for an egg? •If you then, who are evil, know how to give 13
your children what is good, how much more will the heavenly Father give
the Holy Spirit to those who ask him!'

Jesus and Beelzebul

He was casting out a devil and it was dumb; but when the devil had gone 14
out the dumb man spoke, and the people were amazed. •But some of them 15
said, 'It is through Beelzebul, the prince of devils, that he casts out devils'. •Others 16

17 asked him, as a test, for a sign from heaven; •but, knowing what they were thinking, he said to them, 'Every kingdom divided against itself is heading for
18 ruin, and a household divided against itself collapses. •So too with Satan: if he is divided against himself, how can his kingdom stand?—Since you assert that
19 it is through Beelzebul that I cast out devils. •Now if it is through Beelzebul that I cast out devils, through whom do your own experts cast them out? Let
20 them be your judges, then. •But if it is through the finger of God that I cast
21 out devils, then know that the kingdom of God has overtaken you. •So long as a strong man fully armed guards his own palace, his goods are undisturbed;
22 but when someone stronger than he is attacks and defeats him, the stronger man takes away all the weapons he relied on and shares out his spoil.

No compromise

23   'He who is not with me is against me; and he who does not gather with me scatters.

Return of the unclean spirit

24   'When an unclean spirit goes out of a man it wanders through waterless country looking for a place to rest, and not finding one it says, "I will go back to
25
26 the home I came from". •But on arrival, finding it swept and tidied, •it then goes off and brings seven other spirits more wicked than itself, and they go in and set up house there, so that the man ends up by being worse than he was before.'

The truly happy

27   Now as he was speaking, a woman in the crowd raised her voice and said,
28 'Happy the womb that bore you and the breasts you sucked!' •But he replied, 'Still happier those who hear the word of God and keep it!'

The sign of Jonah

29   The crowds got even bigger and he addressed them, 'This is a wicked generation; it is asking for a sign. The only sign it will be given is the sign of Jonah.
30 For just as Jonah became a sign to the Ninevites, so will the Son of Man be to this
31 generation. •On Judgement day the Queen of the South will rise up with the men of this generation and condemn them, because she came from the ends of the earth to hear the wisdom of Solomon; and there is something greater than
32 Solomon here. •On Judgement day the men of Nineveh will stand up with this generation and condemn it, because when Jonah preached they repented; and there is something greater than Jonah here.

The parable of the lamp repeated

33   'No one lights a lamp and puts it in some hidden place or under a tub, but
34 on the lamp-stand so that people may see the light when they come in. •The lamp of your body is your eye. When your eye is sound, your whole body too is filled with
35 light; but when it is diseased your body too will be all darkness. •See to it then that
36 the light inside you is not darkness. •If, therefore, your whole body is filled with light, and no trace of darkness, it will be light entirely, as when the lamp shines on you with its rays.'

The Pharisees and the lawyers attacked

He had just finished speaking when a Pharisee invited him to dine at his 37 house. He went in and sat down at the table. •The Pharisee saw this and was 38 surprised that he had not first washed before the meal. •But the Lord said to him, 39 'Oh, you Pharisees! You clean the outside of cup and plate, while inside yourselves you are filled with extortion and wickedness. •Fools! Did not he who made the 40 outside make the inside too? •Instead, give alms from what you have and then 41 indeed everything will be clean for you. •But alas for you Pharisees! You who pay 42 your tithe of mint and rue and all sorts of garden herbs and overlook justice and the love of God! These you should have practised, without leaving the others undone. •Alas for you Pharisees who like taking the seats of honour in the 43 synagogues and being greeted obsequiously in the market squares! •Alas for 44 you, because you are like the unmarked tombs that men walk on without knowing it!*a*

A lawyer then spoke up. 'Master,' he said 'when you speak like this you 45 insult us too.' •'Alas for you lawyers also,' he replied 'because you load on men 46 burdens that are unendurable, burdens that you yourselves do not move a finger to lift.

'Alas for you who build the tombs of the prophets, the men your ancestors 47 killed! •In this way you both witness what your ancestors did and approve it; they 48 did the killing, you do the building.

'And that is why the Wisdom of God said, "I will send them prophets and 49 apostles; some they will slaughter and persecute, •so that this generation will have 50 to answer for every prophet's blood that has been shed since the foundation of the world, •from the blood of Abel to the blood of Zechariah, who was 51 murdered between the altar and the sanctuary". Yes, I tell you, this generation will have to answer for it all.

'Alas for you lawyers who have taken away the key of knowledge! You have 52 not gone in yourselves, and have prevented others going in who wanted to.'

When he left the house, the scribes and the Pharisees began a furious attack 53 on him and tried to force answers from him on innumerable questions, •setting 54 traps to catch him out in something he might say.

Open and fearless speech

12 Meanwhile the people had gathered in their thousands so that they were 1 treading on one another. And he began to speak, first of all to his disciples. 'Be on your guard against the yeast of the Pharisees—that is, their hypocrisy. Everything that is now covered will be uncovered, and everything now hidden 2 will be made clear. •For this reason, whatever you have said in the dark will 3 be heard in the daylight, and what you have whispered in hidden places will be proclaimed on the housetops.

'To you my friends I say: Do not be afraid of those who kill the body and 4 after that can do no more. •I will tell you whom to fear: fear him who, after he 5 has killed, has the power to cast into hell. Yes, I tell you, fear him. •Can you 6 not buy five sparrows for two pennies? And yet not one is forgotten in God's sight. •Why, every hair on your head has been counted. There is no need to be 7 afraid: you are worth more than hundreds of sparrows.

'I tell you, if anyone openly declares himself for me in the presence of men, the 8 Son of Man will declare himself for him in the presence of God's angels. •But 9 the man who disowns me in the presence of men will be disowned in the presence of God's angels.

10 'Everyone who says a word against the Son of Man will be forgiven, but he who blasphemes against the Holy Spirit will not be forgiven.

11 'When they take you before synagogues and magistrates and authorities, 12 do not worry about how to defend yourselves or what to say, •because when the time comes, the Holy Spirit will teach you what you must say.'

On hoarding possessions

13 A man in the crowd said to him, 'Master, tell my brother to give me a share 14 of our inheritance'. •'My friend,' he replied 'who appointed me your judge, or 15 the arbitrator of your claims?' •Then he said to them, 'Watch, and be on your guard against avarice of any kind, for a man's life is not made secure by what he owns, even when he has more than he needs'.

16 Then he told them a parable: 'There was once a rich man who, having had 17 a good harvest from his land, •thought to himself, "What am I to do? I have 18 not enough room to store my crops." •Then he said, "This is what I will do: I will pull down my barns and build bigger ones, and store all my grain and my 19 goods in them, •and I will say to my soul: My soul, you have plenty of good things laid by for many years to come; take things easy, eat, drink, have a good 20 time". •But God said to him, "Fool! This very night the demand will be made 21 for your soul; and this hoard of yours, whose will it be then?" •So it is when a man stores up treasure for himself in place of making himself rich in the sight of God.'

Trust in Providence

22 Then he said to his disciples, 'That is why I am telling you not to worry about your life and what you are to eat, nor about your body and how you are 23 to clothe it. •For life means more than food, and the body more than clothing. 24 Think of the ravens. They do not sow or reap; they have no storehouses and no barns; yet God feeds them. And how much more are you worth than the 25 birds! •Can any of you, for all his worrying, add a single cubit to his span of 26 life? •If the smallest things, therefore, are outside your control, why worry 27 about the rest? •Think of the flowers; they never have to spin or weave; yet, I assure you, not even Solomon in all his regalia was robed like one of these. 28 Now if that is how God clothes the grass in the field which is there today and thrown into the furnace tomorrow, how much more will he look after you, you 29 men of little faith! •But you, you must not set your hearts on things to eat and 30 things to drink; nor must you worry. •It is the pagans of this world who set their 31 hearts on all these things. Your Father well knows you need them. •No; set your hearts on his kingdom, and these other things will be given you as well.

32 'There is no need to be afraid, little flock, for it has pleased your Father to give you the kingdom.

On almsgiving

33 'Sell your possessions and give alms. Get yourselves purses that do not wear out, treasure that will not fail you, in heaven where no thief can reach it and 34 no moth destroy it. •For where your treasure is, there will your heart be also.

---

11 a. Thus contracting legal impurity, Nb 19:16.

On being ready for the Master's return

'See that you are dressed for action and have your lamps lit. •Be like men 35 36
waiting for their master to return from the wedding feast, ready to open the
door as soon as he comes and knocks. •Happy those servants whom the master 37
finds awake when he comes. I tell you solemnly, he will put on an apron, sit
them down at table and wait on them. •It may be in the second watch he comes, 38
or in the third, but happy those servants if he finds them ready. •You may be 39
quite sure of this, that if the householder had known at what hour the burglar
would come, he would not have let anyone break through the wall of his house.
You too must stand ready, because the Son of Man is coming at an hour you 40
do not expect.'

Peter said, 'Lord, do you mean this parable for us, or for everyone?' •The 41 42
Lord replied, 'What sort of steward,[a] then, is faithful and wise enough for the
master to place him over his household to give them their allowance of food at
the proper time? •Happy that servant if his master's arrival finds him at this 43
employment. •I tell you truly, he will place him over everything he owns. •But 44 45
as for the servant who says to himself, "My master is taking his time coming",
and sets about beating the menservants and the maids, and eating and drinking
and getting drunk, •his master will come on a day he does not expect and at 46
an hour he does not know. The master will cut him off and send him to the same
fate as the unfaithful.

'The servant who knows what his master wants, but has not even started to 47
carry out those wishes, will receive very many strokes of the lash. •The one who 48
did not know, but deserves to be beaten for what he has done, will receive
fewer strokes. When a man has had a great deal given him, a great deal will be
demanded of him; when a man has had a great deal given him on trust, even
more will be expected of him.

Jesus and his Passion

'I have come to bring fire to the earth, and how I wish it were blazing 49
already! •There is a baptism I must still receive, and how great is my distress till 50
it is over!

Jesus the cause of dissension

'Do you suppose that I am here to bring peace on earth? No, I tell you, but 51
rather division. •For from now on a household of five will be divided: three 52
against two and two against three; •the father divided against the son, son 53
against father, mother against daughter, daughter against mother, mother-in-law
against daughter-in-law, daughter-in-law against mother-in-law.'

On reading the signs of the times

He said again to the crowds, 'When you see a cloud looming up in the west 54
you say at once that rain is coming, and so it does. •And when the wind is from 55
the south you say it will be hot, and it is. •Hypocrites! You know how to 56
interpret the face of the earth and the sky. How is it you do not know how to
interpret these times?

'Why not judge for yourselves what is right? •For example: when you go 57 58
to court with your opponent, try to settle with him on the way, or he may drag
you before the judge and the judge hand you over to the bailiff and the bailiff
have you thrown into prison. •I tell you, you will not get out till you have paid 59
the very last penny.'

Examples inviting repentance

1 **13** It was just about this time that some people arrived and told him about the Galileans whose blood Pilate had mingled with that of their sacrifices. [a]
2 At this he said to them, 'Do you suppose these Galileans who suffered like that
3 were greater sinners than any other Galileans? •They were not, I tell you. No;
4 but unless you repent you will all perish as they did. •Or those eighteen on whom the tower at Siloam fell and killed them? Do you suppose that they were more
5 guilty than all the other people living in Jerusalem? •They were not, I tell you. No; but unless you repent you will all perish as they did.'

Parable of the barren fig tree

6 He told this parable: 'A man had a fig tree planted in his vineyard, and he
7 came looking for fruit on it but found none. •He said to the man who looked after the vineyard, "Look here, for three years now I have been coming to look for fruit on this fig tree and finding none. Cut it down: why should it be taking
8 up the ground?" •"Sir," the man replied "leave it one more year and give me
9 time to dig round it and manure it: •it may bear fruit next year; if not, then you can cut it down." '

Healing of the crippled woman on a sabbath

10
11 One sabbath day he was teaching in one of the synagogues, •and a woman was there who for eighteen years had been possessed by a spirit that left her
12 enfeebled; she was bent double and quite unable to stand upright. •When Jesus saw her he called her over and said, 'Woman, you are rid of your infirmity'
13 and he laid his hands on her. And at once she straightened up, and she glorified God.
14 But the synagogue official was indignant because Jesus had healed on the sabbath, and he addressed the people present. 'There are six days' he said 'when work is to be done. Come and be healed on one of those days and not on the
15 sabbath.' •But the Lord answered him. 'Hypocrites!' he said 'Is there one of you who does not untie his ox or his donkey from the manger on the sabbath
16 and take it out for watering? •And this woman, a daughter of Abraham whom Satan has held bound these eighteen years—was it not right to untie her bonds
17 on the sabbath day?' •When he said this, all his adversaries were covered with confusion, and all the people were overjoyed at all the wonders he worked.

Parable of the mustard seed

18 He went on to say, 'What is the kingdom of God like? What shall I compare
19 it with? •It is like a mustard seed which a man took and threw into his garden: it grew and became a tree, and the birds of the air sheltered in its branches.'

Parable of the yeast

20 Another thing he said, 'What shall I compare the kingdom of God with?
21 It is like the yeast a woman took and mixed in with three measures of flour till it was leavened all through.'

---

12 a. I.e. a servant or employee with authority to act as his master's deputy in his absence.
13 a. The author expects this incident, and that mentioned in v.4, to be known to his readers; no other evidence of them remains.

The narrow door; rejection of the Jews, call of the gentiles

Through towns and villages he went teaching, making his way to Jerusalem. 22 Someone said to him, 'Sir, will there be only a few saved?' He said to them, 23 'Try your best to enter by the narrow door, because, I tell you, many will try 24 to enter and will not succeed.

'Once the master of the house has got up and locked the door, you may find 25 yourself knocking on the door, saying, "Lord, open to us" but he will answer, "I do not know where you come from". •Then you will find yourself saying, 26 "We once ate and drank in your company; you taught in our streets" •but he 27 will reply, "I do not know where you come from. *Away from me, all you wicked men!*" [b]

'Then there will be weeping and grinding of teeth, when you see Abraham 28 and Isaac and Jacob and all the prophets in the kingdom of God, and yourselves turned outside. •And men from east and west, from north and south, will come 29 to take their places at the feast in the kingdom of God.

'Yes, there are those now last who will be first, and those now first who will 30 be last.'

Herod the fox

Just at this time some Pharisees came up. 'Go away' they said. 'Leave this 31 place, because Herod means to kill you.' •He replied, 'You may go and give 32 that fox this message: Learn that today and tomorrow I cast out devils and on the third day [c] attain my end. •But for today and tomorrow and the next day 33 I must go on, since it would not be right for a prophet to die outside Jerusalem.

Jerusalem admonished

'Jerusalem, Jerusalem, you that kill the prophets and stone those who are 34 sent to you! How often have I longed to gather your children, as a hen gathers her brood under her wings, and you refused! •So be it! Your house will be left 35 to you. Yes, I promise you, you shall not see me till the time comes when you say:

Blessings on him who comes in the name of the Lord! [d]

Healing of a dropsical man on the sabbath

14 Now on a sabbath day he had gone for a meal to the house of one of the 1 leading Pharisees; and they watched him closely. •There in front of him was 2 a man with dropsy, •and Jesus addressed the lawyers and Pharisees. 'Is it 3 against the law' he asked 'to cure a man on the sabbath, or not?' •But they 4 remained silent, so he took the man and cured him and sent him away. •Then 5 he said to them, 'Which of you here, if his son falls into a well, or his ox, will not pull him out on a sabbath day without hesitation?' •And to this they could 6 find no answer.

On choosing places at table

He then told the guests a parable, because he had noticed how they 7 picked the places of honour. He said this, •'When someone invites you to a 8 wedding feast, do not take your seat in the place of honour. A more distinguished person than you may have been invited, •and the person who invited you both 9 may come and say, "Give up your place to this man". And then, to your embarrassment, you would have to go and take the lowest place. •No; when you 10

are a guest, make your way to the lowest place and sit there, so that, when your
host comes, he may say, "My friend, move up higher". In that way, everyone
11 with you at the table will see you honoured. •For everyone who exalts himself
will be humbled, and the man who humbles himself will be exalted.'

On choosing guests to be invited

12   Then he said to his host, 'When you give a lunch or a dinner, do not ask
your friends, brothers, relations or rich neighbours, for fear they repay your
13 courtesy by inviting you in return. •No; when you have a party, invite the poor,
14 the crippled, the lame, the blind; •that they cannot pay you back means that
you are fortunate, because repayment will be made to you when the virtuous
rise again.'

The invited guests who made excuses

15   On hearing this, one of those gathered round the table said to him, 'Happy
16 the man who will be at the feast in the kingdom of God!' •But he said to him,
'There was a man who gave a great banquet, and he invited a large number of
17 people. •When the time for the banquet came, he sent his servant to say to those
18 who had been invited, "Come along: everything is ready now". •But all alike
started to make excuses. The first said, "I have bought a piece of land and must
19 go and see it. Please accept my apologies." •Another said, "I have bought five
yoke of oxen and am on my way to try them out. Please accept my apologies."
20 Yet another said,"I have just got married and so am unable to come".

21   'The servant returned and reported this to his master. Then the householder,
in a rage, said to his servant, "Go out quickly into the streets and alleys of the
22 town and bring in here the poor, the crippled, the blind and the lame". •"Sir,"
said the servant "your orders have been carried out and there is still room."
23 Then the master said to his servant, "Go to the open roads and the hedgerows
24 and force people to come in to make sure my house is full; •because, I tell you,
not one of those who were invited shall have a taste of my banquet". '

Renouncing all that one holds dear

25   Great crowds accompanied him on his way and he turned and spoke to
26 them. •'If any man comes to me without hating[a] his father, mother, wife, children,
27 brothers, sisters, yes and his own life too, he cannot be my disciple. •Anyone
who does not carry his cross and come after me cannot be my disciple.

Renouncing possessions

28   'And indeed, which of you here, intending to build a tower, would not first
29 sit down and work out the cost to see if he had enough to complete it? •Otherwise,
if he laid the foundation and then found himself unable to finish the work, the
30 onlookers would all start making fun of him and saying, •"Here is a man who
31 started to build and was unable to finish". •Or again, what king marching to
war against another king would not first sit down and consider whether with
ten thousand men he could stand up to the other who advanced against him with
32 twenty thousand? •If not, then while the other king was still a long way off, he
33 would send envoys to sue for peace. •So in the same way, none of you can be
my disciple unless he gives up all his possessions.

b. Ps 6:8   **c.** 'after a short time'.   **d.** Ps 118:26
14 a. Hebraism: an emphatic way of expressing a total detachment.

On loss of enthusiasm in a disciple

'Salt is a useful thing. But if the salt itself loses its taste, how can it be ₃₄ seasoned again? •It is good for neither soil nor manure heap. People throw it ₃₅ out. Listen, anyone who has ears to hear!'

The three parables of God's mercy

15 The tax collectors and the sinners, meanwhile, were all seeking his company ₁ to hear what he had to say, •and the Pharisees and the scribes complained. ₂ 'This man' they said 'welcomes sinners and eats with them.' •So he spoke this ₃ parable to them:

The lost sheep

'What man among you with a hundred sheep, losing one, would not leave ₄ the ninety-nine in the wilderness and go after the missing one till he found it? And when he found it, would he not joyfully take it on his shoulders •and then, ⁵₆ when he got home, call together his friends and neighbours? "Rejoice with me," he would say "I have found my sheep that was lost." •In the same way, I tell you, ₇ there will be more rejoicing in heaven over one repentant sinner than over ninety-nine virtuous men who have no need of·repentance.

The lost drachma

'Or again, what woman with ten drachmas would not, if she lost one, light ₈ a lamp and sweep out the house and search thoroughly till she found it? •And ₉ then, when she had found it, call together her friends and neighbours? "Rejoice with me," she would say "I have found the drachma I lost." •In the same way, ₁₀ I tell you, there is rejoicing among the angels of God over one repentant sinner.'

The lost son (the 'prodigal') and the dutiful son

He also said, 'A man had two sons. •The younger said to his father, "Father, ¹¹₁₂ let me have the share of the estate that would come to me". So the father divided the property between them. •A few days later, the younger son got together ₁₃ everything he had and left for a distant country where he squandered his money on a life of debauchery.

'When he had spent it all, that country experienced a severe famine, and now ₁₄ he began to feel the pinch, •so he hired himself out to one of the local inhabitants ₁₅ who put him on his farm to feed the pigs. •And he would willingly have filled ₁₆ his belly with the husks the pigs were eating but no one offered him anything. Then he came to his senses and said, "How many of my father's paid servants ₁₇ have more food than they want, and here am I dying of hunger! •I will leave ₁₈ this place and go to my father and say: Father, I have sinned against heaven and against you; •I no longer deserve to be called your son; treat me as one of your ₁₉ paid servants." •So he left the place and went back to his father. ₂₀

'While he was still a long way off, his father saw him and was moved with pity. He ran to the boy, clasped him in his arms and kissed him tenderly. •Then his ₂₁ son said, "Father, I have sinned against heaven and against you. I no longer deserve to be called your son." •But the father said to his servants, "Quick! ₂₂ Bring out the best robe and put it on him; put a ring on his finger and sandals on his feet. •Bring the calf we have been fattening, and kill it; we are going to ₂₃ have a feast, a celebration, •because this son of mine was dead and has come ₂₄ back to life; he was lost and is found." And they began to celebrate.

25 'Now the elder son was out in the fields, and on his way back, as he drew
26 near the house, he could hear music and dancing. •Calling one of the servants
27 he asked what it was all about. •"Your brother has come" replied the servant
"and your father has killed the calf we had fattened because he has got him back
28 safe and sound." •He was angry then and refused to go in, and his father came
29 out to plead with him; •but he answered his father, "Look, all these years
I have slaved for you and never once disobeyed your orders, yet you never
30 offered me so much as a kid for me to celebrate with my friends. •But, for this
son of yours, when he comes back after swallowing up your property—he and
his women—you kill the calf we had been fattening."

31 'The father said, "My son, you are with me always and all I have is yours.
32 But it was only right we should celebrate and rejoice, because your brother
here was dead and has come to life; he was lost and is found." '

The crafty steward

1 **16** He also said to his disciples, 'There was a rich man and he had a steward
2 who was denounced to him for being wasteful with his property. •He called
for the man and said, "What is this I hear about you? Draw me up an account of
3 your stewardship because you are not to be my steward any longer." •Then the
steward said to himself, "Now that my master is taking the stewardship from me,
what am I to do? Dig? I am not strong enough. Go begging? I should be too
4 ashamed. •Ah, I know what I will do to make sure that when I am dismissed
from office there will be some to welcome me into their homes."

5 'Then he called his master's debtors one by one. To the first he said, "How
6 much do you owe my master?" •"One hundred measures of oil" was the reply.
The steward said, "Here, take your bond; sit down straight away and write fifty".
7 To another he said, "And you, sir, how much do you owe?" "One hundred
measures of wheat" was the reply. The steward said, "Here, take your bond and
write eighty".

8 'The master praised the dishonest steward for his astuteness.[a] For the children
of this world are more astute in dealing with their own kind than are the children
of light.'

The right use of money

9 'And so I tell you this: use money, tainted as it is, to win you friends, and
thus make sure that when it fails you, they will welcome you into the tents of
10 eternity. •The man who can be trusted in little things can be trusted in great;
11 the man who is dishonest in little things will be dishonest in great. •If then you
cannot be trusted with money, that tainted thing, who will trust you with genuine
12 riches? •And if you cannot be trusted with what is not yours, who will give
you what is your very own?

13 'No servant can be the slave of two masters: he will either hate the first and
love the second, or treat the first with respect and the second with scorn. You
cannot be the slave both of God and of money.'

Against the Pharisees and their love of money

14
15 The Pharisees, who loved money, heard all this and laughed at him. •He
said to them, 'You are the very ones who pass yourselves off as virtuous in
people's sight, but God knows your hearts. For what is thought highly of by men
is loathsome in the sight of God.

16 a. Not for his dishonesty.

The kingdom stormed

'Up to the time of John it was the Law and the Prophets; since then, the 16 kingdom of God has been preached, and by violence everyone is getting in.

The Law remains

'It is easier for heaven and earth to disappear than for one little stroke to drop 17 out of the Law.

Marriage indissoluble

'Everyone who divorces his wife and marries another is guilty of adultery, and 18 the man who marries a woman divorced by her husband commits adultery.

The rich man and Lazarus

'There was a rich man who used to dress in purple and fine linen and feast 19 magnificently every day. •And at his gate there lay a poor man called Lazarus, 20 covered with sores, •who longed to fill himself with the scraps that fell from 21 the rich man's table. Dogs even came and licked his sores. •Now the poor man 22 died and was carried away by the angels to the bosom of Abraham. The rich man also died and was buried.

'In his torment in Hades he looked up and saw Abraham a long way off 23 with Lazarus in his bosom. •So he cried out, "Father Abraham, pity me and 24 send Lazarus to dip the tip of his finger in water and cool my tongue, for I am in agony in these flames". •"My son," Abraham replied "remember that during 25 your life good things came your way, just as bad things came the way of Lazarus. Now he is being comforted here while you are in agony. •But that is not all: 26 between us and you a great gulf has been fixed, to stop anyone, if he wanted to, crossing from our side to yours, and to stop any crossing from your side to ours."

'The rich man replied, "Father, I beg you then to send Lazarus to my father's 27 house, •since I have five brothers, to give them warning so that they do not 28 come to this place of torment too". •"They have Moses and the prophets," 29 said Abraham "let them listen to them." •"Ah no, father Abraham," said the 30 rich man "but if someone comes to them from the dead, they will repent." •Then 31 Abraham said to him, "If they will not listen either to Moses or to the prophets, they will not be convinced even if someone should rise from the dead". '

On leading others astray

17 He said to his disciples, 'Obstacles are sure to come, but alas for the one 1 who provides them! •It would be better for him to be thrown into the sea 2 with a millstone put round his neck than that he should lead astray a single one of these little ones. •Watch yourselves!   3

Brotherly correction

'If your brother does something wrong, reprove him and, if he is sorry, forgive him. •And if he wrongs you seven times a day and seven times comes 4 back to you and says, "I am sorry", you must forgive him.'

The power of faith

The apostles said to the Lord, 'Increase our faith'. •The Lord replied, 'Were ⁵⁄₆ your faith the size of a mustard seed you could say to this mulberry tree, "Be uprooted and planted in the sea", and it would obey you.

Humble service

7   'Which of you, with a servant ploughing or minding sheep, would say to him
when he returned from the fields, "Come and have your meal immediately"?
8 Would he not be more likely to say, "Get my supper laid; make yourself tidy
and wait on me while I eat and drink. You can eat and drink yourself afterwards"?
10 Must he be grateful to the servant for doing what he was told? •So with you:
9

when you have done all you have been told to do, say, "We are merely servants:
we have done no more than our duty".'

The ten lepers

11   Now on the way to Jerusalem he travelled along the border between Samaria
12 and Galilee.* •As he entered one of the villages, ten lepers came to meet him.
13 They stood some way off •and called to him, 'Jesus! Master! Take pity on us.'
14 When he saw them he said, 'Go and show yourselves to the priests'. Now as they
15 were going away they were cleansed. •Finding himself cured, one of them
16 turned back praising God at the top of his voice •and threw himself at the feet
17 of Jesus and thanked him. The man was a Samaritan. •This made Jesus say,
18 'Were not all ten made clean? The other nine, where are they? •It seems that no
19 one has come back to give praise to God, except this foreigner.' •And he said to
the man, 'Stand up and go on your way. Your faith has saved you.'

The coming of the kingdom of God

20   Asked by the Pharisees when the kingdom of God was to come, he gave them
this answer, 'The coming of the kingdom of God does not admit of observation
21 and there will be no one to say, "Look here! Look there!" For, you must know,
the kingdom of God is among you.'

The day of the Son of Man

22   He said to the disciples, 'A time will come when you will long to see one of
23 the days of the Son of Man and will not see it. •They will say to you, "Look
24 there!" or, "Look here!" Make no move; do not set off in pursuit; •for as the
lightning flashing from one part of heaven lights up the other, so will be the Son
25 of Man when his day comes. •But first he must suffer grievously and be rejected
by this generation.
26   'As it was in Noah's day, so will it also be in the days of the Son of Man.
27 People were eating and drinking, marrying wives and husbands, right up to the
28 day Noah went into the ark, and the Flood came and destroyed them all. •It
will be the same as it was in Lot's day: people were eating and drinking, buying
29 and selling, planting and building, •but the day Lot left Sodom, God rained fire
30 and brimstone from heaven and it destroyed them all. •It will be the same when
the day comes for the Son of Man to be revealed.
31   'When that day comes, anyone on the housetop, with his possessions in the
house, must not come down to collect them, nor must anyone in the fields turn
32 back either. •Remember Lot's wife. •Anyone who tries to preserve his life will lose
33
34 it; and anyone who loses it will keep it safe. •I tell you, on that night two will be
35 in one bed: one will be taken, the other left; •two women will be grinding corn
37 together: one will be taken, the other left.'   •The disciples interrupted. 'Where,
Lord?' they asked. He said, 'Where the body is, there too will the vultures gather'.

17 a. Making for the Jordan valley and Jericho; from there he goes up to Jerusalem.

The unscrupulous judge and the importunate widow

18 Then he told them a parable about the need to pray continually and never 1 lose heart. •'There was a judge in a certain town' he said 'who had neither 2 fear of God nor respect for man. •In the same town there was a widow who kept 3 on coming to him and saying, "I want justice from you against my enemy!" For a long time he refused, but at last he said to himself, "Maybe I have neither 4 fear of God nor respect for man, •but since she keeps pestering me I must give 5 this widow her just rights, or she will persist in coming and worry me to death". '

And the Lord said, 'You notice what the unjust judge has to say? •Now will $^6_7$ not God see justice done to his chosen who cry to him day and night even when he delays to help them? •I promise you, he will see justice done to them, and 8 done speedily. But when the Son of Man comes, will he find any faith on earth?'

The Pharisee and the publican

He spoke the following parable to some people who prided themselves on being 9 virtuous and despised everyone else, •'Two men went up to the Temple to pray, 10 one a Pharisee, the other a tax collector. •The Pharisee stood there and said this 11 prayer to himself, "I thank you, God, that I am not grasping, unjust, adulterous like the rest of mankind, and particularly that I am not like this tax collector here. I fast twice a week; I pay tithes on all I get." •The tax collector stood some $^{12}_{13}$ distance away, not daring even to raise his eyes to heaven; but he beat his breast and said, "God, be merciful to me, a sinner". •This man, I tell you, went home 14 again at rights with God; the other did not. For everyone who exalts himself will be humbled, but the man who humbles himself will be exalted.'

Jesus and the children

People even brought little children to him, for him to touch them; but 15 when the disciples saw this they turned them away. •But Jesus called the children 16 to him and said, 'Let the little children come to me, and do not stop them; for it is to such as these that the kingdom of God belongs. •I tell you solemnly, anyone 17 who does not welcome the kingdom of God like a little child will never enter it.'

The rich aristocrat

A member of one of the leading families put this question to him, 'Good 18 Master, what have I to do to inherit eternal life?' •Jesus said to him, 'Why do you 19 call me good? No one is good but God alone. •You know the commandments: 20 *You must not commit adultery; You must not kill; You must not steal; You must not bring false witness; Honour your father and mother.*' •He replied, 'I have kept 21 all these from my earliest days till now'. •And when Jesus heard this he said, 22 'There is still one thing you lack. Sell all that you own and distribute the money to the poor, and you will have treasure in heaven; then come, follow me.' •But 23 when he heard this he was filled with sadness, for he was very rich.

The danger of riches

Jesus looked at him and said, 'How hard it is for those who have riches to 24 make their way into the kingdom of God! •Yes, it is easier for a camel to pass 25 through the eye of a needle than for a rich man to enter the kingdom of God.' 'In that case' said the listeners 'who can be saved?' •'Things that are impossible $^{26}_{27}$ for men' he replied 'are possible for God.'

The reward of renunciation

28
29   Then Peter said, 'What about us? We left all we had to follow you.' •He said
to them, 'I tell you solemnly, there is no one who has left house, wife, brothers,
30 parents or children for the sake of the kingdom of God •who will not be given
repayment many times over in this present time and, in the world to come,
eternal life'.

Third prophecy of the Passion

31   Then taking the Twelve aside he said to them, 'Now we are going up to
Jerusalem, and everything that is written by the prophets about the Son of Man
32 is to come true. •For he will be handed over to the pagans and will be mocked,
33 maltreated and spat on, •and when they have scourged him they will put him
34 to death; and on the third day he will rise again.' •But they could make nothing
of this; what he said was quite obscure to them, they had no idea what it meant.

Entering Jericho: the blind man

35   Now as he drew near to Jericho there was a blind man sitting at the side of the
36 road begging. •When he heard the crowd going past he asked what it was all about,
37
38 and they told him that Jesus the Nazarene was passing by. •So he called out,
39 'Jesus, Son of David, have pity on me'. •The people in front scolded him and told
him to keep quiet, but he shouted all the louder, 'Son of David, have pity on me'.
40 Jesus stopped and ordered them to bring the man to him, and when he came up,
41 asked him, •'What do you want me to do for you?' 'Sir,' he replied 'let me see
42 again.' •Jesus said to him, 'Receive your sight. Your faith has saved you.'
43 And instantly his sight returned and he followed him praising God, and all the
people who saw it gave praise to God for what had happened.

Zacchaeus

1
2   **19** He entered Jericho and was going through the town •when a man whose
name was Zacchaeus made his appearance; he was one of the senior tax
3 collectors and a wealthy man. •He was anxious to see what kind of man Jesus
4 was, but he was too short and could not see him for the crowd; •so he ran ahead
and climbed a sycamore tree to catch a glimpse of Jesus who was to pass that
5 way. •When Jesus reached the spot he looked up and spoke to him: 'Zacchaeus,
6 come down. Hurry, because I must stay at your house today.' •And he hurried
7 down and welcomed him joyfully. •They all complained when they saw what
8 was happening. 'He has gone to stay at a sinner's house' they said. •But Zacchaeus
stood his ground and said to the Lord, 'Look, sir, I am going to give half my
property to the poor, and if I have cheated anybody I will pay him back four
9 times the amount'.[a] •And Jesus said to him, 'Today salvation has come to this
10 house, because this man too is a son of Abraham;[b] •for the Son of Man has come
to seek out and save what was lost'.

Parable of the pounds

11   While the people were listening to this he went on to tell a parable, because
he was near Jerusalem and they imagined that the kingdom of God was going
12 to show itself then and there. •Accordingly he said, 'A man of noble birth went

19 a. I.e. at the highest rate known to Jewish law (Ex 21:37) or the rate imposed by Roman
law on convicted thieves.   **b.** Although he belongs to a profession generally ranked with
pagans.

to a distant country to be appointed king and afterwards return.' •He summoned 13
ten of his servants and gave them ten pounds. "Do business with these" he told
them "until I get back." •But his compatriots detested him and sent a delegation 14
to follow him with this message, "We do not want this man to be our king".

'Now on his return, having received his appointment as king, he sent for those 15
servants to whom he had given the money, to find out what profit each had made.
The first came in and said, "Sir, your one pound has brought in ten". •"Well done, ¹⁶₁₇
my good servant!" he replied "Since you have proved yourself faithful in a very
small thing, you shall have the government of ten cities." •Then came the second 18
and said, "Sir, your one pound has made five". •To this one also he said, "And 19
you shall be in charge of five cities". •Next came the other and said, "Sir, here 20
is your pound. I put it away safely in a piece of linen •because I was afraid of you; 21
for you are an exacting man: you pick up what you have not put down and reap
what you have not sown." •"You wicked servant!" he said "Out of your own 22
mouth I condemn you. So you knew I was an exacting man, picking up what
I have not put down and reaping what I have not sown? •Then why did you not 23
put my money in the bank? On my return I could have drawn it out with
interest." •And he said to those standing by, "Take the pound from him and 24
give it to the man who has ten pounds". •And they said to him, "But, sir, he has 25
ten pounds . . ." •"I tell you, to everyone who has will be given more; but 26
from the man who has not, even what he has will be taken away.

"But as for my enemies who did not want me for their king, bring them here 27
and execute them in my presence." '

V. THE JERUSALEM MINISTRY

The Messiah enters Jerusalem

When he had said this he went on ahead, going up to Jerusalem. •Now when ²⁸₂₉
he was near Bethphage and Bethany, close by the Mount of Olives as it is called,
he sent two of the disciples, telling them, •'Go off to the village opposite, and 30
as you enter it you will find a tethered colt that no one has yet ridden. Untie it
and bring it here. •If anyone asks you, "Why are you untying it?" you are to say 31
this, "The Master needs it". ' •The messengers went off and found everything just 32
as he had told them. •As they were untying the colt, its owner said, 'Why are 33
you untying that colt?' •and they answered, 'The Master needs it'. 34

So they took the colt to Jesus, and throwing their garments over its back they 35
helped Jesus on to it. •As he moved off, people spread their cloaks in the road, 36
and now, as he was approaching the downward slope of the Mount of Olives, 37
the whole group of disciples joyfully began to praise God at the top of their
voices for all the miracles they had seen. •They cried out: 38

> '*Blessings on the King who comes,*
> *in the name of the Lord!*
> Peace in heaven
> and glory in the highest heavens!'

Jesus defends his disciples for acclaiming him

Some Pharisees in the crowd said to him, 'Master, check your disciples', 39
but he answered, 'I tell you, if these keep silence the stones will cry out'. 40

Lament for Jerusalem

⁴¹⁴² As he drew near and came in sight of the city he shed tears over it •and said, 'If you in your turn had only understood on this day the message of peace! ⁴³ But, alas, it is hidden from your eyes! •Yes, a time is coming when your enemies will raise fortifications all round you, when they will encircle you and hem you ⁴⁴ in on every side; •they will dash you and the children inside your walls to the ground; they will leave not one stone standing on another within you—and all because you did not recognise your opportunity when God offered it!'

The expulsion of the dealers from the Temple

⁴⁵ Then he went into the Temple and began driving out those who were selling. ⁴⁶ 'According to scripture,' he said *'my house will be a house of prayer.*^d But you have turned it into *a robbers' den.'*^e

Jesus teaches in the Temple

⁴⁷ He taught in the Temple every day. The chief priests and the scribes, with ⁴⁸ the support of the leading citizens, tried to do away with him, •but they did not see how they could carry this out because the people as a whole hung on his words.

The Jews question the authority of Jesus

¹ **20** Now one day while he was teaching the people in the Temple and proclaiming the Good News, the chief priests and the scribes came up, ² together with the elders, •and spoke to him. 'Tell us' they said 'what authority ³ have you for acting like this? Or who is it that gave you this authority?' •'And ⁴ I' replied Jesus 'will ask you a question. Tell me: •John's baptism: did it come ⁵ from heaven, or from man?' •And they argued it out this way among themselves, ⁶ 'If we say from heaven, he will say, "Why did you refuse to believe him?"; •and if we say from man, the people will all stone us, for they are convinced that John ⁷ was a prophet'. •So their reply was that they did not know where it came from. ⁸ And Jesus said to them, 'Nor will I tell you my authority for acting like this'.

Parable of the wicked husbandmen

⁹ And he went on to tell the people this parable: 'A man planted a vineyard ¹⁰ and leased it to tenants, and went abroad for a long while. •When the time came, he sent a servant to the tenants to get his share of the produce of the vineyard from them. But the tenants thrashed him, and sent him away ¹¹ empty-handed. •But he persevered and sent a second servant; they thrashed ¹² him too and treated him shamefully and sent him away empty-handed. •He still persevered and sent a third; they wounded this one also, and threw him out. ¹³ Then the owner of the vineyard said, "What am I to do? I will send them my ¹⁴ dear son. Perhaps they will respect him." •But when the tenants saw him they put their heads together. "This is the heir," they said "let us kill him so that ¹⁵ the inheritance will be ours." •So they threw him out of the vineyard and killed him.

¹⁶ 'Now what will the owner of the vineyard do to them? •He will come and make an end of these tenants and give the vineyard to others.' Hearing this they

c. Probably alluding to the journey of Archelaus to Rome in 4 B.C. to have the will of Herod the Great confirmed in his favour. A deputation of Jews followed him there to contest his claim. **d.** Is 56:7 **e.** Jr 7:11

said, 'God forbid!' •But he looked hard at them and said, 'Then what does this 17
text in the scriptures mean:

> *It was the stone rejected by the builders*
> *that became the keystone?*[a]

Anyone who falls on that stone will be dashed to pieces; anyone it falls on will 18
be crushed.'

But for their fear of the people, the scribes and the chief priests would have 19
liked to lay hands on him that very moment, because they realised that this
parable was aimed at them.

On tribute to Caesar

So they waited their opportunity and sent agents to pose as men devoted to 20
the Law, and to fasten on something he might say and so enable them to hand
him over to the jurisdiction and authority of the governor. •They put to him 21
this question, 'Master, we know that you say and teach what is right; you favour
no one, but teach the way of God in all honesty. •Is it permissible for us to pay 22
taxes to Caesar or not?' •But he was aware of their cunning and said, •'Show 23 24
me a denarius. Whose head and name are on it?' 'Caesar's' they said. •'Well 25
then,' he said to them 'give back to Caesar what belongs to Caesar—and to
God what belongs to God.'

As a result, they were unable to find fault with anything he had to say in 26
public; his answer took them by surprise and they were silenced.

The resurrection of the dead

Some Sadducees—those who say that there is no resurrection—approached 27
him and they put this question to him, •'Master, we have it from Moses in 28
writing, that if a man's married brother dies childless, the man must marry the
widow to raise up children for his brother. •Well then, there were seven brothers. 29
The first, having married a wife, died childless. •The second •and then the third 30 31
married the widow. And the same with all seven, they died leaving no children.
Finally the woman herself died. •Now, at the resurrection, to which of them 32 33
will she be wife since she had been married to all seven?'

Jesus replied, 'The children of this world take wives and husbands, •but 34 35
those who are judged worthy of a place in the other world and in the resurrection
from the dead do not marry •because they can no longer die, for they are the 36
same as the angels, and being children of the resurrection they are sons of
God. •And Moses himself implies that the dead rise again, in the passage 37
about the bush where he calls the Lord *the God of Abraham, the God of Isaac*
and the God of Jacob.[b] •Now he is God, not of the dead, but of the living; for 38
to him all men are in fact alive.'

Some scribes[c] then spoke up. 'Well put, Master' they said•—because they 39 40
would not dare to ask him any more questions.

Christ, not only son but also Lord of David

He then said to them, 'How can people maintain that the Christ is son of 41
David? •Why, David himself says in the Book of Psalms: 42

> *The Lord said to my Lord:*
> *Sit at my right hand*
> *and I will make your enemies* 43
> *a footstool for you.*[d]

44 David here calls him Lord; how then can he be his son?'

The scribes condemned by Jesus

45
46　　While all the people were listening he said to the disciples, •'Beware of the scribes who like to walk about in long robes and love to be greeted obsequiously in the market squares, to take the front seats in the synagogues and the places
47 of honour at banquets, •who swallow the property of widows, while making a show of lengthy prayers. The more severe will be the sentence they receive.'

The widow's mite

1 **21** As he looked up he saw rich people putting their offerings into the
2 treasury; •then he happened to notice a poverty-stricken widow putting
3 in two small coins, •and he said, 'I tell you truly, this poor widow has put in
4 more than any of them; •for these have all contributed money they had over, but she from the little she had has put in all she had to live on'.

Discourse on the destruction of Jerusalem:*ᵃ* Introduction

5　　When some were talking about the Temple, remarking how it was adorned
6 with fine stonework and votive offerings, he said, •'All these things you are staring at now—the time will come when not a single stone will be left on another:
7 everything will be destroyed'. •And they put to him this question: 'Master,' they said 'when will this happen, then, and what sign will there be that this is about to take place?'

The warning signs

8　　'Take care not to be deceived,' he said 'because many will come using my name and saying, "I am he" and, "The time is near at hand". Refuse to join them.
9 And when you hear of wars and revolutions, do not be frightened, for this is some-
10 thing that must happen but the end is not so soon.' •Then he said to them, 'Nation
11 will fight against nation, and kingdom against kingdom. •There will be great earthquakes and plagues and famines here and there; there will be fearful sights and great signs from heaven.
12　　'But before all this happens, men will seize you and persecute you; they will hand you over to the synagogues and to imprisonment, and bring you before
13 kings and governors because of my name•—and that will be your opportunity
14 to bear witness. •Keep this carefully in mind: you are not to prepare your defence,
15 because I myself shall give you an eloquence and a wisdom that none of your
16 opponents will be able to resist or contradict. •You will be betrayed even by parents and brothers, relations and friends; and some of you will be put to death.
17
18 You will be hated by all men on account of my name, •but not a hair of your
19 head will be lost. •Your endurance will win you your lives.

The siege

20　　'When you see Jerusalem surrounded by armies, you must realise that she will
21 soon be laid desolate. •Then those in Judaea must escape to the mountains, those inside the city must leave it, and those in country districts must not take refuge

20 a. Ps 118:22　　**b.** Ex 3:6　　**c.** Most scribes were Pharisees and believed in the resurrection of the dead.　　**d.** Ps 110:1
21 a. This passage on the End Time also includes some elements of a prophecy of the destruction of Jerusalem.

in it. •For this is the time of vengeance when all that scripture says[b] must be 22
fulfilled. •Alas for those with child, or with babies at the breast, when those days 23
come!

The disaster and the age of the pagans

'For great misery will descend on the land and wrath on this people. •They 24
will fall by the edge of the sword and be led captive to every pagan country; and
Jerusalem will be trampled down by the pagans until the age of the pagans is
completely over.

Cosmic disasters and the coming of the Son of Man

'There will be signs in the sun and moon and stars; on earth nations in agony, 25
bewildered by the clamour of the ocean and its waves; •men dying of fear as they 26
await what menaces the world, for the powers of heaven will be shaken. •And 27
then they will see the Son of Man coming in a cloud with power and great glory.
When these things begin to take place, stand erect, hold your heads high, because 28
your liberation[c] is near at hand.'

The time of this coming

And he told them a parable, 'Think of the fig tree and indeed every tree. •As 29 30
soon as you see them bud, you know that summer is now near. •So with you 31
when you see these things happening: know that the kingdom of God is near.
I tell you solemnly, before this generation has passed away all will have 32
taken place. •Heaven and earth will pass away, but my words will never pass 33
away.

Be on the alert

'Watch yourselves, or your hearts will be coarsened with debauchery and 34
drunkenness and the cares of life, and that day will be sprung on you suddenly,
like a trap. For it will come down on every living man on the face of the earth. 35
Stay awake, praying at all times for the strength to survive all that is going to 36
happen, and to stand with confidence before the Son of Man.'

The last days of Jesus

In the daytime he would be in the Temple teaching, but would spend the night 37
on the hill called the Mount of Olives. •And from early morning the people 38
would gather round him in the Temple to listen to him.

VI. THE PASSION

The conspiracy against Jesus: Judas betrays him

22 The feast of Unleavened Bread, called the Passover, was now drawing near, 1
and the chief priests and the scribes were looking for some way of doing 2
away with him, because they mistrusted the people.

Then Satan entered into Judas, surnamed Iscariot, who was numbered among 3
the Twelve. •He went to the chief priests and the officers of the guard[a] to discuss 4
a scheme for handing Jesus over to them. •They were delighted and agreed to give 5
him money. •He accepted, and looked for an opportunity to betray him to them 6
without the people knowing.

Preparation for the Passover supper

7 The day of Unleavened Bread came round, the day on which the passover
8 had to be sacrificed, •and he sent Peter and John, saying, 'Go and make the
9 preparations for us to eat the passover'. •'Where do you want us to prepare it?'
10 they asked. •'Listen,' he said 'as you go into the city you will meet a man
11 carrying a pitcher of water. Follow him into the house he enters •and tell the
owner of the house, "The Master has this to say to you: Where is the dining room
12 in which I can eat the passover with my disciples?" •The man will show you a large
13 upper room furnished with couches. Make the preparations there.' •They set off
and found everything as he had told them, and prepared the Passover.

The supper

14 When the hour came he took his place at table, and the apostles with him.
15 And he said to them, 'I have longed to eat this passover with you before I suffer;
16 because, I tell you, I shall not eat it again until it is fulfilled in the kingdom of
God'.
17 Then, taking a cup,[b] he gave thanks and said, 'Take this and share it among
18 you, •because from now on, I tell you, I shall not drink wine until the kingdom of God comes'.

The institution of the Eucharist

19 Then he took some bread, and when he had given thanks, broke it and gave it
to them, saying, 'This is my body which will be given for you; do this as a memorial
20 of me'. •He did the same with the cup after supper, and said, 'This cup is the new
covenant in my blood which will be poured out for you.

The treachery of Judas foretold

21 'And yet, here with me on the table is the hand of the man who betrays me.
22 The Son of Man does indeed go to his fate even as it has been decreed, but alas for
23 that man by whom he is betrayed!' •And they began to ask one another which of
them it could be who was to do this thing.

Who is the greatest?

24 A dispute arose also between them about which should be reckoned the
25 greatest, •but he said to them, 'Among pagans it is the kings who lord it over them,
26 and those who have authority over them are given the title Benefactor. •This must
not happen with you. No; the greatest among you must behave as if he were the
27 youngest, the leader as if he were the one who serves. •For who is the greater:
the one at table or the one who serves? The one at table, surely? Yet here am I
among you as one who serves!

The reward promised to the apostles

28
29 'You are the men who have stood by me faithfully in my trials; •and now
30 I confer a kingdom on you, just as my Father conferred one on me: •you will
eat and drink at my table in my kingdom, and you will sit on thrones to judge the
twelve tribes of Israel.

---

b. Possibly alluding to Dn 9:27.   c. Or 'redemption'.
22 a. The Temple police, chosen from among the Levites.   **b.** Luke distinguishes the
Passover and the cup of vv. 15-18 from the bread and the cup of vv. 19-20.

Peter's denial and repentance foretold

'Simon, Simon! Satan, you must know, has got his wish to sift you all like 31
wheat; •but I have prayed for you, Simon, that your faith may not fail, and once 32
you have recovered, you in your turn must strengthen your brothers.' •'Lord,' 33
he answered 'I would be ready to go to prison with you, and to death.' •Jesus 34
replied, 'I tell you, Peter, by the time the cock crows today you will have denied
three times that you know me'.

A time of crisis

He said to them, 'When I sent you out without purse or haversack or sandals, 35
were you short of anything? •'No' they said. He said to them, 'But now if you have 36
a purse, take it; if you have a haversack, do the same; if you have no sword, sell
your cloak and buy one, •because I tell you these words of scripture have to 37
be fulfilled in me: *He let himself be taken for a criminal.*' Yes, what scripture says
about me is even now reaching its fulfilment.' •'Lord,' they said 'there are two 38
swords here now.' He said to them, 'That is enough!'

The Mount of Olives

He then left to make his way as usual to the Mount of Olives, with the 39
disciples following. •When they reached the place he said to them, 'Pray not to be 40
put to the test'.

Then he withdrew from them, about a stone's throw away, and knelt down 41
and prayed. •'Father,' he said 'if you are willing, take this cup away from me. 42
Nevertheless, let your will be done, not mine.' •Then an angel appeared to 43
him, coming from heaven to give him strength. •In his anguish he prayed even 44
more earnestly, and his sweat fell to the ground like great drops of blood.

When he rose from prayer he went to the disciples and found them sleeping 45
for sheer grief. •'Why are you asleep?' he said to them. 'Get up and pray not to 46
be put to the test.'

The arrest

He was still speaking when a number of men appeared, and at the head of 47
them the man called Judas, one of the Twelve, who went up to Jesus to kiss him.
Jesus said, 'Judas, are you betraying the Son of Man with a kiss?' •His followers, 48 49
seeing what was happening, said, 'Lord, shall we use our swords?' •And one of 50
them struck out at the high priest's servant, and cut off his right ear. •But at 51
this Jesus spoke. 'Leave off!' he said 'That will do!' And touching the man's ear
he healed him.

Then Jesus spoke to the chief priests and captains of the Temple guard and 52
elders who had come for him. 'Am I a brigand' he said 'that you had to set out
with swords and clubs? •When I was among you in the Temple day after day 53
you never moved to lay hands on me. But this is your hour; this is the reign of
darkness.'

Peter's denials

They seized him then and led him away, and they took him to the high 54
priest's house. Peter followed at a distance. •They had lit a fire in the middle of 55
the courtyard and Peter sat down among them, •and as he was sitting there by 56
the blaze a servant-girl saw him, peered at him, and said, 'This person was with
him too'. •But he denied it. 'Woman,' he said 'I do not know him.' •Shortly 57 58
afterwards someone else saw him and said, 'You are another of them'. But Peter

59 replied, 'I am not, my friend'. •About an hour later another man insisted,
60 saying, 'This fellow was certainly with him. Why, he is a Galilean.' •'My
friend,' said Peter 'I do not know what you are talking about.' At that instant,
61 while he was still speaking, the cock crew, •and the Lord turned and looked
straight at Peter, and Peter remembered what the Lord had said to him, 'Before
62 the cock crows today, you will have disowned me three times'. •And he went
outside and wept bitterly.

Jesus mocked by the guards

63   Meanwhile the men who guarded Jesus were mocking and beating him.
64 They blindfolded him and questioned him. 'Play the prophet' they said. 'Who
65 hit you then?' •And they continued heaping insults on him.

Jesus before the Sanhedrin

66   When day broke there was a meeting of the elders of the people, attended
67 by the chief priests and scribes. He was brought before their council, •and they
said to him, 'If you are the Christ, tell us'. 'If I tell you,' he replied 'you will not
68
69 believe me, •and if I question you, you will not answer. •But from now on, the
70 Son of Man will be *seated at the right hand* of the Power *of God*.'[d] •Then they
all said, 'So you are the Son of God then?' He answered, 'It is you who say I am'.
71 'What need of witnesses have we now?' they said. 'We have heard it for ourselves
1 from his own lips.' **23** The whole assembly then rose, and they brought him
before Pilate.

Jesus before Pilate

2   They began their accusation by saying, 'We found this man inciting our
people to revolt, opposing payment of the tribute to Caesar, and claiming to be
3 Christ, a king'. •Pilate put to him this question, 'Are you the king of the Jews?'
4 'It is you who say it' he replied. •Pilate then said to the chief priests and the crowd,
5 'I find no case against this man'. •But they persisted, 'He is inflaming the people
with his teaching all over Judaea; it has come all the way from Galilee, where he
6 started, down to here'. •When Pilate heard this, he asked if the man were a
7 Galilean; •and finding that he came under Herod's jurisdiction he passed him
over to Herod who was also in Jerusalem at that time.

Jesus before Herod

8   Herod was delighted to see Jesus; he had heard about him and had
been wanting for a long time to set eyes on him; moreover, he was hoping to see
9 some miracle worked by him. •So he questioned him at some length; but without
10 getting any reply. •Meanwhile the chief priests and the scribes were there, violently
11 pressing their accusations. •Then Herod, together with his guards, treated him
with contempt and made fun of him; he put a rich cloak[a] on him and sent him
12 back to Pilate. •And though Herod and Pilate had been enemies before, they
were reconciled that same day.

Jesus before Pilate again

13   Pilate then summoned the chief priests and the leading men and the people.
14 'You brought this man before me' he said 'as a political agitator. Now I have

c. Is 53:12   **d.** Ps 110:1
23 a. Ceremonial dress of a prince.

gone into the matter myself in your presence and found no case against the man
in respect of all the charges you bring against him. •Nor has Herod either, since 15
he has sent him back to us. As you can see, the man has done nothing that
deserves death, •so I shall have him flogged and then let him go.' •But as one ¹⁶₁₈
man they howled, 'Away with him! Give us Barabbas!' •(This man had been 19
thrown into prison for causing a riot in the city and for murder.)

Pilate was anxious to set Jesus free and addressed them again, •but they ²⁰₂₁
shouted back, 'Crucify him! Crucify him!' •And for the third time he spoke 22
to them, 'Why? What harm has this man done? I have found no case against
him that deserves death, so I shall have him punished and then let him go.' •But 23
they kept on shouting at the top of their voices, demanding that he should be
crucified. And their shouts were growing louder.

Pilate then gave his verdict: their demand was to be granted. •He released ²⁴₂₅
the man they asked for, who had been imprisoned for rioting and murder, and
handed Jesus over to them to deal with as they pleased.

The way to Calvary

As they were leading him away they seized on a man, Simon from Cyrene, 26
who was coming in from the country, and made him shoulder the cross and
carry it behind Jesus. •Large numbers of people followed him, and of women 27
too,ᵇ who mourned and lamented for him. •But Jesus turned to them and said, 28
'Daughters of Jerusalem, do not weep for me; weep rather for yourselves and for
your children. •For the days will surely come when people will say, "Happy are 29
those who are barren, the wombs that have never borne, the breasts that have
never suckled!" •Then they will begin to *say to the mountains,*"*Fall on us !*"; *to the* 30
hills, "Cover us !"ᶜ •For if men use the green wood like this, what will happen 31
when it is dry?' •Now with him they were also leading out two other criminals 32
to be executed.

The crucifixion

When they reached the place called The Skull, they crucified him there and the 33
two criminals also, one on the right, the other on the left. • Jesus said, 'Father, 34
forgive them; they do not know what they are doing'. Then they cast lots to
share out his clothing.

The crucified Christ is mocked

The people stayed there watching him. As for the leaders, they jeered at him. 35
'He saved others,' they said 'let him save himself if he is the Christ of God, the
Chosen One.' •The soldiers mocked him too, and when they approached to offer 36
him vinegar •they said, 'If you are the king of the Jews, save yourself'. •Above ³⁷₃₈
him there was an inscription: 'This is the King of the Jews'.

The good thief

One of the criminals hanging there abused him. 'Are you not the Christ?' 39
he said. 'Save yourself and us as well.' •But the other spoke up and rebuked him. 40
'Have you no fear of God at all?' he said. 'You got the same sentence as he did,
but in our case we deserved it: we are paying for what we did. But this man has 41
done nothing wrong. •Jesus,' he said 'remember me when you come into your 42
kingdom.' •'Indeed, I promise you,' he replied 'today you will be with me in 43
paradise.'

The death of Jesus

44   It was now about the sixth hour and, with the sun eclipsed, a darkness came
45 over the whole land until the ninth hour. •The veil of the Temple was torn right
46 down the middle; •and when Jesus had cried out in a loud voice, He said, 'Father,
into your hands I commit my spirit'.[d] With these words he breathed his last.

After the death

47   When the centurion saw what had taken place, he gave praise to God and
48 said, 'This was a great and good man'. •And when all the people who had gathered
for the spectacle saw what had happened, they went home beating their breasts.
49   All his friends stood at a distance; so also did the women who had accompanied
him from Galilee, and they saw all this happen.

The burial

50   Then a member of the council arrived, an upright and virtuous man named
51 Joseph. •He had not consented to what the others had planned and carried out.
He came from Arimathaea, a Jewish town, and he lived in the hope of seeing the
52 kingdom of God. •This man went to Pilate and asked for the body of Jesus.
53 He then took it down, wrapped it in a shroud and put him in a tomb which was
54 hewn in stone in which no one had yet been laid. •It was Preparation Day and
the sabbath was imminent.
55   Meanwhile the women who had come from Galilee with Jesus were following
behind. They took note of the tomb and of the position of the body.
56   Then they returned and prepared spices and ointments. And on the sábbath
day they rested, as the Law required.

VII. AFTER THE RESURRECTION

The empty tomb. The angel's message

1 **24** On the first day of the week, at the first sign of dawn, they went to the
2 tomb with the spices they had prepared. •They found that the stone had
3 been rolled away from the tomb, •but on entering discovered that the body of the
4 Lord Jesus was not there. •As they stood there not knowing what to think, two
5 men in brilliant clothes suddenly appeared at their side. •Terrified, the women
lowered their eyes. But the two men said to them, 'Why look among the dead
6 for someone who is alive? •He is not here; he has risen. Remember what he told
7 you when he was still in Galilee: •that the Son of Man had to be handed over
into the power of sinful men and be crucified, and rise again on the third day.'
8 And they remembered his words.

The apostles refuse to believe the women

9   When the women returned from the tomb they told all this to the Eleven and
10 to all the others. •The women were Mary of Magdala, Joanna, and Mary the
11 mother of James. The other women with them also told the apostles, •but this
story of theirs seemed pure nonsense, and they did not believe them.

b. The Talmud records that noblewomen of Jerusalem used to give soothing drinks to condemned criminals.   **c.** Ho 10:8   **d.** Ps 31:5

Peter at the tomb

Peter, however, went running to the tomb. He bent down and saw the binding 12 cloths but nothing else; he then went back home, amazed at what had happened.

The road to Emmaus

That very same day, two of them were on their way to a village called Emmaus, 13 seven miles*ᵃ* from Jerusalem, •and they were talking together about all that had 14 happened. •Now as they talked this over, Jesus himself came up and walked by 15 their side; •but something prevented them from recognising him. •He said to ¹⁶₁₇ them, 'What matters are you discussing as you walk along?' They stopped short, their faces downcast.

Then one of them, called Cleopas, answered him, 'You must be the only 18 person staying in Jerusalem who does not know the things that have been happening there these last few days'. •'What things?' he asked. 'All about Jesus 19 of Nazareth' they answered 'who proved he was a great prophet by the things he said and did in the sight of God and of the whole people; •and how our chief 20 priests and our leaders handed him over to be sentenced to death, and had him crucified. •Our own hope had been that he would be the one to set Israel free. 21 And this is not all: two whole days have gone by since it all happened; •and some 22 women from our group have astounded us: they went to the tomb in the early morning, •and when they did not find the body, they came back to tell us they 23 had seen a vision of angels who declared he was alive. •Some of our friends 24 went to the tomb and found everything exactly as the women had reported, but of him they saw nothing.'

Then he said to them, 'You foolish men! So slow to believe the full message 25 of the prophets! •Was it not ordained that the Christ should suffer and so enter 26 into his glory?' •Then, starting with Moses and going through all the prophets, 27 he explained to them the passages throughout the scriptures that were about himself.

When they drew near to the village to which they were going, he made as if 28 to go on; •but they pressed him to stay with them. 'It is nearly evening' they said 29 'and the day is almost over.' So he went in to stay with them. •Now while he was 30 with them at table, he took the bread and said the blessing; then he broke it and handed it to them. •And their eyes were opened and they recognised him; but he 31 had vanished from their sight. •Then they said to each other, 'Did not our hearts 32 burn within us as he talked to us on the road and explained the scriptures to us?'

They set out that instant and returned to Jerusalem. There they found the 33 Eleven assembled together with their companions, •who said to them, 'Yes, it is 34 true. The Lord has risen and has appeared to Simon.' •Then they told their 35 story of what had happened on the road and how they had recognised him at the breaking of bread.

Jesus appears to the apostles

They were still talking about all this when he himself stood among them 36 and said to them, 'Peace be with you!' •In a state of alarm and fright, they thought 37 they were seeing a ghost. •But he said, 'Why are you so agitated, and why are 38 these doubts rising in your hearts? •Look at my hands and feet; yes, it is I indeed. 39 Touch me and see for yourselves; a ghost has no flesh and bones as you can see I have.' •And as he said this he showed them his hands and feet. •Their joy ⁴⁰₄₁ was so great that they still could not believe it, and they stood there dumbfounded;

42 so he said to them, 'Have you anything here to eat?' •And they offered him a piece
43 of grilled fish, •which he took and ate before their eyes.

Last instructions to the apostles

44 Then he told them, 'This is what I meant when I said, while I was still with
you, that everything written about me in the Law of Moses, in the Prophets and
45 in the Psalms, has to be fulfilled'. •He then opened their minds to understand the
46 scriptures, •and he said to them, 'So you see how it is written that the Christ would
47 suffer and on the third day rise from the dead, •and that, in his name, repentance
for the forgiveness of sins would be preached to all the nations, beginning
48 from Jerusalem. •You are witnesses to this.
49 'And now I am sending down to you what the Father has promised. Stay in the
city then, until you are clothed with the power from on high.'

The ascension

50 Then he took them out as far as the outskirts of Bethany, and lifting up his
51 hands he blessed them. •Now as he blessed them, he withdrew from them and
52 was carried up to heaven. •They worshipped him and then went back to
53 Jerusalem full of joy; •and they were continually in the Temple praising God.

24 a. The identity of the village is disputed.

INTRODUCTION TO
THE GOSPEL AND LETTERS OF SAINT JOHN

Date, authorship and form of the gospel

Tradition almost unanimously names John the apostle, the son of Zebedee, as the author. Before A.D. 150 the book was known and used by Ignatius of Antioch, Papias, Justin and the author of the *Odes of Solomon*, and the first explicit testimony is by Irenaeus, c. 180: 'Last of all John, too, the disciple of the Lord who leant against his breast, himself brought out a gospel while he was in Ephesus'. The gospel itself has much supporting evidence, apart from its claim to be the work of an eye-witness who was a beloved disciple of the Lord: its vocabulary and style betray its semitic origin, it is familiar with Jewish customs and with the topography of Palestine, and its author is evidently a close friend of Peter.

It was published not by John himself but by his disciples after his death, and it is possible that in this gospel we have the end-stage of a slow process that has brought together not only component parts of different ages but also corrections, additions and sometimes more than one revision of the same discourse. The arrangement of the gospel is not always easy to explain, but it is clear that the author attaches special importance to the Jewish liturgical feasts which punctuate his narrative; the following analysis can be made:

> *Prologue* (1:1-18)
> I. *First week* of the messianic ministry, ending with the first miracle at Cana (1:19–2:11)
> II. *First Passover* with accompanying events, ending with the second miracle at Cana (2:12–4:54)
> III. *Sabbath 'of the paralytic'* (5:1–47)
> IV. *The Passover 'of the bread of life'* and its discourse (6:1-71)
> V. *The feast of Tabernacles* and the man born blind (7:1–10:21)
> VI. *The feast of Dedication* and the raising of Lazarus (10:22–11:54)
> VII. *Week of the Passion* and the crucifixion Passover (11:55–19:42)
> VIII. *The resurrection* and week of appearances (20:1-29)
> IX. *Appendix:* the Church and Christ's return (ch. 21)

This division suggests that Christ not only fulfilled the Jewish liturgy but in doing so brought it to an end.

Special characteristics of the gospel

The fourth gospel is concerned to bring out the significance of all that Christ did and said. The things that he did were 'signs', and the meaning of them, hidden at first, could be understood only after his glorification; the things he said had a deeper meaning not perceived at the time but understood only after the Spirit who spoke in the name of the risen Christ had come to 'lead' his disciples 'into all truth'. The gospel is revelation at this stage of development.

The whole of John's thought is dominated by the mystery of the Incarnation, from the Prologue with which the book opens. Here the revelation of Christ's glory, which in the synoptic gospels is associated primarily with his return at the end of time, has a new interpretation: judgement is working here and now in the soul, and eternal life (John's counterpart to the 'kingdom' of the synoptic gospels) is made to be something actually present, already in the possession of those who have faith. God's victory over evil, his salvation of the world, is already guaranteed by Christ's resurrection in glory.

The letters

The three letters are like the gospel in style and doctrine. The first, an encyclical letter to the Christian communities of 'Asia', summarises the whole content of John's religious experience and develops themes from the gospel, for churches threatened with disintegration under the impact of the early heresies. The second letter was written to a church in answer to some who had denied the reality of the Incarnation. The third, which is probably the earliest in date, was written to settle a dispute on jurisdiction in one of the churches acknowledging John's authority.

THE GOSPEL ACCORDING TO
SAINT JOHN

PROLOGUE

1

In the beginning was the Word: 1
the Word was with God
and the Word was God.
He was with God in the beginning.   2
Through him all things came to be,   3
not one thing had its being but through him.
All that came to be had life in him   4
and that life was the light of men,
a light that shines in the dark,   5
a light that darkness could not overpower.[a]

A man came, sent by God.   6
His name was John.
He came as a witness,   7
as a witness to speak for the light,
so that everyone might believe through him.
He was not the light,   8
only a witness to speak for the light.

The Word was the true light   9
that enlightens all men;
and he was coming into the world.
He was in the world   10
that had its being through him,
and the world did not know him.
He came to his own domain   11
and his own people did not accept him.
But to all who did accept him   12
he gave power to become children of God,
to all who believe in the name of him
who was born not out of human stock   13
or urge of the flesh
or will of man
but of God himself.
The Word was made flesh,   14
he lived among us,[b]

and we saw his glory,
the glory that is his as the only Son of the Father,
full of grace and truth.

15   John appears as his witness. He proclaims:
'This is the one of whom I said:
He who comes after me
ranks before me
because he existed before me'.

16   Indeed, from his fulness we have, all of us, received—
yes, grace in return for grace,
17   since, though the Law was given through Moses,
grace and truth have come through Jesus Christ.
18   No one has ever seen God;
it is the only Son, who is nearest to the Father's heart,
who has made him known.

I. THE FIRST PASSOVER

A. THE OPENING WEEK

The witness of John

19   This is how John appeared as a witness. When the Jews[c] sent priests and
20 Levites from Jerusalem to ask him, 'Who are you?' •he not only declared, but
21 he declared quite openly, 'I am not the Christ'. •'Well then,' they asked 'are you
22 Elijah?'[d] 'I am not' he said. 'Are you the Prophet?'[e] He answered, 'No'. •So they
said to him, 'Who are you? We must take back an answer to those who sent us.
23 What have you to say about yourself?' •So John said, 'I am, as Isaiah prophesied:

a voice that cries in the wilderness:
Make a straight way for the Lord'.[f]

24   Now these men had been sent by the Pharisees, •and they put this further
25 question to him, 'Why are you baptising if you are not the Christ, and not Elijah,
26 and not the prophet?' •John replied, 'I baptise with water; but there stands
27 among you—unknown to you—•the one who is coming after me; and I am
28 not fit to undo his sandal-strap'. •This happened at Bethany, on the far side of
the Jordan, where John was baptising.

29   The next day, seeing Jesus coming towards him, John said, 'Look, there is
30 the lamb of God that takes away the sin of the world. •This is the one I spoke
of when I said: A man is coming after me who ranks before me because he
31 existed before me. •I did not know him myself, and yet it was to reveal him to
32 Israel that I came baptising with water.' •John also declared, 'I saw the Spirit
33 coming down on him from heaven like a dove and resting on him. •I did not
know him myself, but he who sent me to baptise with water had said to me,

---

1 a. Or 'grasp', in the sense of 'enclose' or 'understand'.   b. 'pitched his tent among us'.
c. In Jn this usually indicates the Jewish religious authorities who were hostile to Jesus; but
occasionally the Jews as a whole.   d. Whose return was expected, Ml 3:23-24.   e. The
Prophet greater than Moses who was expected as Messiah, on an interpretation of Dt 18:15.
f. Is 40:3

"The man on whom you see the Spirit come down and rest is the one who is going to baptise with the Holy Spirit". •Yes, I have seen and I am the witness 34 that he is the Chosen One of God.'

The first disciples

On the following day as John stood there again with two of his disciples, 35 Jesus passed, and John stared hard at him and said, 'Look, there is the lamb of 36 God'. •Hearing this, the two disciples followed Jesus. •Jesus turned round, saw $^{37}_{38}$ them following and said, 'What do you want?' They answered, 'Rabbi,'—which means Teacher—'where do you live?' •'Come and see' he replied; so they went 39 and saw where he lived, and stayed with him the rest of that day. It was about the tenth hour.^{g}

One of these two who became followers of Jesus after hearing what John had 40 said was Andrew, the brother of Simon Peter. •Early next morning, Andrew 41 met his brother and said to him, 'We have found the Messiah'—which means the Christ—•and he took Simon to Jesus. Jesus looked hard at him and said, 42 'You are Simon son of John; you are to be called Cephas'—meaning Rock.

The next day, after Jesus had decided to leave for Galilee, he met Philip and 43 said, 'Follow me'. •Philip came from the same town, Bethsaida, as Andrew and 44 Peter. •Philip found Nathanael ^{h} and said to him, 'We have found the one 45 Moses wrote about in the Law, the one about whom the prophets wrote: he is Jesus son of Joseph, from Nazareth'. •'From Nazareth?' said Nathanael 'Can 46 anything good come from that place?' 'Come and see' replied Philip. •When 47 Jesus saw Nathanael coming he said of him, 'There is an Israelite who deserves the name, incapable of deceit'. •'How do you know me?' said Nathanael. 48 'Before Philip came to call you,' said Jesus 'I saw you under the fig tree.' •Na- 49 thanael answered, 'Rabbi, you are the Son of God, you are the King of Israel'. Jesus replied, 'You believe that just because I said: I saw you under the fig tree. 50 You will see greater things than that.' •And then he added, 'I tell you most 51 solemnly, you will see heaven laid open and, above the Son of Man, the angels of God ascending and descending'.

The wedding at Cana

2 Three days later there was a wedding at Cana in Galilee. The mother of 1 Jesus was there, •and Jesus and his disciples had also been invited. •When $^2_3$ they ran out of wine, since the wine provided for the wedding was all finished, the mother of Jesus said to him, 'They have no wine'. •Jesus said, 'Woman, why 4 turn to me? My hour has not come yet.' •His mother said to the servants, 5 '*Do whatever he tells you*'.^{a} •There were six stone water jars standing there, meant 6 for the ablutions that are customary among the Jews: each could hold twenty or thirty gallons. •Jesus said to the servants, 'Fill the jars with water', and they 7 filled them to the brim. •'Draw some out now' he told them 'and take it to the 8 steward.' •They did this; the steward tasted the water, and it had turned into 9 wine. Having no idea where it came from—only the servants who had drawn the water knew—the steward called the bridegroom •and said, 'People generally 10 serve the best wine first, and keep the cheaper sort till the guests have had plenty to drink; but you have kept the best wine till now'.

This was the first of the signs given by Jesus: it was given at Cana in Galilee. 11 He let his glory be seen, and his disciples believed in him. •After this he went 12 down to Capernaum with his mother and the brothers, but they stayed there only a few days.

B. THE PASSOVER

The cleansing of the Temple

¹³₁₄　　Just before the Jewish Passover Jesus went up to Jerusalem, •and in the Temple he found people selling cattle and sheep and pigeons, and the money
15 changers sitting at their counters there. •Making a whip out of some cord, he drove them all out of the Temple, cattle and sheep as well, scattered the money
16 changers' coins, knocked their tables over •and said to the pigeon-sellers, 'Take
17 all this out of here and stop turning my Father's house into a market'. •Then his disciples remembered the words of scripture: *Zeal for your house will devour me.*[b]
18 The Jews intervened and said, 'What sign can you show us to justify what you
19 have done?' •Jesus answered, 'Destroy this sanctuary, and in three days I will
20 raise it up'. •The Jews replied, 'It has taken forty-six years to build this
21 sanctuary:[c] are you going to raise it up in three days?' •But he was speaking of
22 the sanctuary that was his body, •and when Jesus rose from the dead, his disciples remembered that he had said this, and they believed the scripture and the words he had said.

23　　During his stay in Jerusalem for the Passover many believed in his name
24 when they saw the signs that he gave, •but Jesus knew them all and did not trust
25 himself to them; •he never needed evidence about any man; he could tell what a man had in him.

C. THE MYSTERY OF THE SPIRIT REVEALED
TO A MASTER IN ISRAEL

The conversation with Nicodemus

¹₂　**3** There was one of the Pharisees called Nicodemus, a leading Jew, •who came to Jesus by night and said, 'Rabbi, we know that you are a teacher who comes from God; for no one could perform the signs that you do unless God were with
3 him'. •Jesus answered:

> 'I tell you most solemnly,
> unless a man is born from above,
> he cannot see the kingdom of God'.

4 Nicodemus said, 'How can a grown man be born? Can he go back into his
5 mother's womb and be born again?' •Jesus replied:

> 'I tell you most solemnly,
> unless a man is born through water and the Spirit,
> he cannot enter the kingdom of God:
6 > what is born of the flesh is flesh;
> what is born of the Spirit is spirit.
7 > Do not be surprised when I say:
> You must be born from above.

g. 4 p.m.　　h. Probably the Bartholomew of the other gospels.
2 a. Gn 41:55　　**b.** Ps 69:9　　**c.** Reconstruction work on the Temple began in 19 B.C. This is therefore the Passover of 28 A.D.

The wind   blows wherever it pleases;   8
you hear its sound,
but you cannot tell where it comes from or where it is going.
That is how it is with all who are born of the Spirit.'

'How can that be possible?' asked Nicodemus. •'You, a teacher in Israel, ⁹₁₀
and you do not know these things!' replied Jesus.

'I tell you most solemnly,   11
we speak only about what we know
and witness only to what we have seen
and yet you people reject our evidence.
If you do not believe me   12
when I speak about things in this world,
how are you going to believe me
when I speak to you about heavenly things?
No one has gone up to heaven   13
except the one who came down from heaven,
the Son of Man who is in heaven;
and the Son of Man must be lifted up
as Moses lifted up the serpent in the desert,   14
so that everyone who believes may have eternal life in him.   15
Yes, God loved the world so much   16
that he gave his only Son,
so that everyone who believes in him may not be lost
but may have eternal life.
For God sent his Son into the world   17
not to condemn the world,
but so that through him the world might be saved.
No one who believes in him will be condemned;   18
but whoever refuses to believe is condemned already,
because he has refused to believe
in the name of God's only Son.
On these grounds is sentence pronounced: 19
that though the light has come into the world
men have shown they prefer
darkness to the light
because their deeds were evil.
And indeed, everybody who does wrong   20
hates the light and avoids it,
for fear his actions should be exposed;
but the man who lives by the truth   21
comes out into the light,
so that it may be plainly seen that what he does is done in God.'

II. JOURNEYS IN SAMARIA AND GALILEE

John bears witness for the last time

After this, Jesus went with his disciples into the Judaean countryside and 22
stayed with them there and baptised. •At the same time John was baptising at 23

Aenon[a] near Salim, where there was plenty of water, and people were going
24 there to be baptised. •This was before John had been put in prison.

25   Now some of John's disciples had opened a discussion with a Jew about
26 purification, •so they went to John and said, 'Rabbi, the man who was with
you on the far side of the Jordan, the man to whom you bore witness, is baptising
27 now; and everyone is going to him'. •John replied:

> 'A man can lay claim
> only to what is given him from heaven.

28 'You yourselves can bear me out: I said: I myself am not the Christ; I am
the one who has been sent in front of him.

29   'The bride is only for the bridegroom;
and yet the bridegroom's friend,
who stands there and listens,
is glad when he hears the bridegroom's voice.
This same joy I feel, and now it is complete.
30   He must grow greater,
I must grow smaller.
31   He who comes from above
is above all others;
he who is born of the earth
is earthly himself and speaks in an earthly way.
He who comes from heaven
32   bears witness to the things he has seen and heard,
even if his testimony is not accepted;
33   though all who do accept his testimony
are attesting the truthfulness of God,
34   since he whom God has sent
speaks God's own words:
God gives him the Spirit without reserve.
35   The Father loves the Son
and has entrusted everything to him.
36   Anyone who believes in the Son has eternal life,
but anyone who refuses to believe in the Son will never see life:
the anger of God stays on him.'

The saviour of the world revealed to the Samaritans

1 **4** When Jesus heard that the Pharisees had found out that he was making
2 and baptising more disciples than John—•though in fact it was his disciples
3 who baptised, not Jesus himself—•he left Judaea and went back to Galilee.
4 This meant that he had to cross Samaria.

5   On the way he came to the Samaritan town called Sychar,[a] near the land
6 that Jacob gave to his son Joseph. •Jacob's well is there and Jesus, tired by the
7 journey, sat straight down by the well. It was about the sixth hour.[b] •When
a Samaritan woman came to draw water, Jesus said to her, 'Give me a drink'.
⁸₉ His disciples had gone into the town to buy food. •The Samaritan woman said

---

3 a. A tradition locates Aenon ('Springs') in the Jordan valley 7 m. from Scythopolis.
4 a. Either Shechem (Aramaic: Sichara), or Askar at the foot of Mt Ebal. 'Jacob's Well' is
not mentioned in Gn.   b. Noon.

to him, 'What? You are a Jew and you ask me, a Samaritan, for a drink?'—Jews, in fact, do not associate with Samaritans. •Jesus replied: 10

'If you only knew what God is offering
and who it is that is saying to you:
Give me a drink,
you would have been the one to ask,
and he would have given you living water'.

'You have no bucket, sir,' she answered 'and the well is deep: how could 11 you get this living water? •Are you a greater man than our father Jacob who 12 gave us this well and drank from it himself with his sons and his cattle?' •Jesus 13 replied:

'Whoever drinks this water
will get thirsty again;
but anyone who drinks the water that I shall give   14
will never be thirsty again:
the water that I shall give
will turn into a spring inside him, welling up to eternal life'.

'Sir,' said the woman 'give me some of that water, so that I may never get 15 thirsty and never have to come here again to draw water.' •'Go and call your 16 husband' said Jesus to her 'and come back here.' •The woman answered, 'I have 17 no husband'. He said to her, 'You are right to say, "I have no husband"; •for 18 although you have had five, the one you have now is not your husband. You spoke the truth there.' •'I see you are a prophet, sir' said the woman. •'Our 19 20 fathers worshipped on this mountain,ᶜ while you say that Jerusalem is the place where one ought to worship.' •Jesus said: 21

'Believe me, woman, the hour is coming
when you will worship the Father
neither on this mountain nor in Jerusalem.
You worship what you do not know;   22
we worship what we do know;
for salvation comes from the Jews.
But the hour will come—in fact it is here already—   23
when true worshippers will worship the Father in spirit and truth:
that is the kind of worshipper
the Father wants.
God is spirit,   24
and those who worship
must worship in spirit and truth.'

The woman said to him, 'I know that Messiah—that is, Christ—is coming; 25 and when he comes he will tell us everything'. •'I who am speaking to you,' 26 said Jesus 'I am he.'

At this point his disciples returned, and were surprised to find him speaking 27 to a woman, though none of them asked, 'What do you want from her?' or, 'Why are you talking to her?' •The woman put down her water jar and hurried 28 back to the town to tell the people, •'Come and see a man who has told me 29 everything I ever did; I wonder if he is the Christ?' •This brought people out of 30 the town and they started walking towards him.

Meanwhile, the disciples were urging him, 'Rabbi, do have something to 31

$^{32}_{33}$ eat'; •but he said, 'I have food to eat that you do not know about'. •So the
34 disciples asked one another, 'Has someone been bringing him food?' •But Jesus
said:

> 'My food
> is to do the will of the one who sent me,
> and to complete his work.
35 Have you not got a saying:
> Four months and then the harvest?
> Well, I tell you:
> Look around you, look at the fields;
> already they are white, ready for harvest!
36 Already •the reaper is being paid his wages,
> already he is bringing in the grain for eternal life,
> and thus sower and reaper rejoice together.
37 For here the proverb holds good:
> one sows, another reaps;
38 I sent you to reap
> a harvest you had not worked for.
> Others worked for it;
> and you have come into the rewards of their trouble.'

39 Many Samaritans of that town had believed in him on the strength of the
40 woman's testimony when she said, 'He told me all I have ever done', •so, when
the Samaritans came up to him, they begged him to stay with them. He stayed
$^{41}_{42}$ for two days, and •when he spoke to them many more came to believe; •and
they said to the woman, 'Now we no longer believe because of what you told us;
we have heard him ourselves and we know that he really is the saviour of the
world'.

The cure of the nobleman's son

$^{43}_{44}$ When the two days were over Jesus left for Galilee. •He himself had declared
45 that there is no respect for a prophet in his own country, •but on his arrival the
Galileans received him well, having seen all that he had done at Jerusalem
during the festival which they too had attended.

46 He went again to Cana in Galilee, where he had changed the water into wine.
47 Now there was a court official there whose son was ill at Capernaum •and,
hearing that Jesus had arrived in Galilee from Judaea, he went and asked him
48 to come and cure his son as he was at the point of death. •Jesus said, 'So you will
49 not believe unless you see signs and portents!' •'Sir,' answered the official 'come
50 down before my child dies.' •'Go home,' said Jesus 'your son will live.' The man
51 believed what Jesus had said and started on his way; •and while he was still on
52 the journey back his servants met him with the news that his boy was alive. •He
asked them when the boy had begun to recover. 'The fever left him yesterday'
53 they said 'at the seventh hour.' •The father realised that this was exactly the time
when Jesus had said, 'Your son will live'; and he and all his household believed.
54 This was the second sign given by Jesus, on his return from Judaea to Galilee.

c. Gerizim, the mountain on which the Samaritans built a rival to the Jerusalem Temple; it was
destroyed by Hyrcanus, 129 B.C.

III. THE SECOND FEAST AT JERUSALEM

The cure of a sick man at the Pool of Bethzatha

5 Some time after this there was a Jewish festival, and Jesus went up to Jeru- 1 salem. •Now at the Sheep Pool in Jerusalem there is a building, called Beth- 2 zatha in Hebrew, consisting of five porticos; •and under these were crowds of 3 sick people—blind, lame, paralysed—waiting for the water to move; •for at 4 intervals the angel of the Lord came down into the pool, and the water was disturbed, and the first person to enter the water after this disturbance was cured of any ailment he suffered from. •One man there had an illness which had lasted 5 thirty-eight years, •and when Jesus saw him lying there and knew he had been in 6 this condition for a long time, he said, 'Do you want to be well again?' •'Sir,' 7 replied the sick man 'I have no one to put me into the pool when the water is disturbed; and while I am still on the way, someone else gets there before me.' Jesus said, 'Get up, pick up your sleeping-mat and walk'. •The man was cured ⁸₉ at once, and he picked up his mat and walked away.

Now that day happened to be the sabbath, •so the Jews said to the man who 10 had been cured, 'It is the sabbath; you are not allowed to carry your sleeping- mat'. •He replied, 'But the man who cured me told me, "Pick up your mat and 11 walk" '. •They asked, 'Who is the man who said to you, "Pick up your mat and 12 walk"?' •The man had no idea who it was, since Jesus had disappeared into the 13 crowd that filled the place. •After a while Jesus met him in the Temple and said, 14 'Now you are well again, be sure not to sin any more, or something worse may happen to you'. •The man went back and told the Jews that it was Jesus who 15 had cured him. •It was because he did things like this on the sabbath that the 16 Jews began to persecute Jesus. •His answer to them was, 'My Father goes on 17 working, and so do I'. •But that only made the Jews even more intent on killing 18 him, because, not content with breaking the sabbath, he spoke of God as his own Father, and so made himself God's equal.

To this accusation Jesus replied: 19

'I tell you most solemnly,
the Son can do nothing by himself;
he can do only what he sees the Father doing:
and whatever the Father does the Son does too.
For the Father loves the Son   20
and shows him everything he does himself,
and he will show him even greater things than these,
works that will astonish you.
Thus, as the Father raises the dead and gives them life,   21
so the Son gives life to anyone he chooses;
for the Father judges no one;   22
he has entrusted all judgement to the Son,
so that all may honour the Son   23
as they honour the Father.
Whoever refuses honour to the Son
refuses honour to the Father who sent him.
I tell you most solemnly,   24
whoever listens to my words,
and believes in the one who sent me,

has eternal life;
without being brought to judgement
he has passed from death to life.

25   I tell you most solemnly,
the hour will come—in fact it is here already—
when the dead will hear the voice of the Son of God,
and all who hear it will live.

26   For the Father, who is the source of life,
has made the Son the source of life;

27   and, because he is the Son of Man,
has appointed him supreme judge.

28   Do not be surprised at this,
for the hour is coming
when the dead will leave their graves
at the sound of his voice:

29   those who did good
will rise again to life;
and those who did evil, to condemnation.

30   I can do nothing by myself;
I can only judge as I am told to judge,
and my judging is just,
because my aim is to do not my own will,
but the will of him who sent me.

31   'Were I to testify on my own behalf,
my testimony would not be valid;

32   but there is another witness who can speak on my behalf,
and I know that his testimony is valid.

33   You sent messengers to John,
and he gave his testimony to the truth:

34   not that I depend on human testimony;
no, it is for your salvation that I speak of this.

35   John was a lamp alight and shining
and for a time you were content to enjoy the light that he gave.

36   But my testimony is greater than John's:
the works my Father has given me to carry out,
these same works of mine
testify that the Father has sent me.

37   Besides, the Father who sent me
bears witness to me himself.
You have never heard his voice,
you have never seen his shape,

38   and his word finds no home in you
because you do not believe
in the one he has sent.

39   'You study the scriptures,
believing that in them you have eternal life;
now these same scriptures testify to me,

40   and yet you refuse to come to me for life!

41   As for human approval, this means nothing to me.

Besides, I know you too well: 42
you have no love of God in you.
I have come in the name of my Father   43
and you refuse to accept me;
if someone else comes in his own name
you will accept him.

How can you believe,   44
since you look to one another for approval
and are not concerned
with the approval that comes from the one God?
Do not imagine that I am going to accuse you before the Father: 45
you place your hopes on Moses,
and Moses will be your accuser.
If you really believed him   46
you would believe me too,
since it was I that he was writing about;
but if you refuse to believe what he wrote,   47
how can you believe what I say?'

IV. ANOTHER PASSOVER, THE BREAD OF LIFE

The miracle of the loaves

6 Some time after this, Jesus went off to the other side of the Sea of Galilee— 1
or of Tiberias—•and a large crowd followed him, impressed by the signs he 2
gave by curing the sick. •Jesus climbed the hillside, and sat down there with his 3
disciples. •It was shortly before the Jewish feast of Passover.   4
    Looking up, Jesus saw the crowds approaching and said to Philip, 'Where 5
can we buy some bread for these people to eat?' •He only said this to test Philip; 6
he himself knew exactly what he was going to do. •Philip answered, 'Two hundred 7
denarii would only buy enough to give them a small piece each'. •One of his 8
disciples, Andrew, Simon Peter's brother, said, •'There is a small boy here 9
with five barley loaves and two fish; but what is that between so many?' •Jesus 10
said to them, 'Make the people sit down'. There was plenty of grass there, and
as many as five thousand men sat down. •Then Jesus took the loaves, gave 11
thanks, and gave them out to all who were sitting ready; he then did the same with
the fish, giving out as much as was wanted. •When they had eaten enough he 12
said to the disciples, 'Pick up the pieces left over, so that nothing gets wasted'.
So they picked them up, and filled twelve hampers with scraps left over from the 13
meal of five barley loaves. •The people, seeing this sign that he had given, said, 14
'This really is the prophet who is to come into the world'. •Jesus, who could see 15
they were about to come and take him by force and make him king, escaped
back to the hills by himself.

Jesus walks on the waters

    That evening the disciples went down to the shore of the lake and •got into 16/17
a boat to make for Capernaum on the other side of the lake. It was getting
dark by now and Jesus had still not rejoined them. •The wind was strong, and 18
the sea was getting rough, •They had rowed three or four miles when they saw 19
Jesus walking on the lake and coming towards the boat. This frightened them,

²⁰₂₁ but he said, 'It is I. Do not be afraid.' •They were for taking him into the boat, but in no time it reached the shore at the place they were making for.

The discourse in the synagogue at Capernaum

22 Next day, the crowd that had stayed on the other side saw that only one boat had been there, and that Jesus had not got into the boat with his disciples, but 23 that the disciples had set off by themselves. •Other boats, however, had put in 24 from Tiberias, near the place where the bread had been eaten. •When the people saw that neither Jesus nor his disciples were there, they got into those 25 boats and crossed to Capernaum to look for Jesus. •When they found him on 26 the other side, they said to him, 'Rabbi, when did you come here?' •Jesus answered:

> 'I tell you most solemnly,
> you are not looking for me
> because you have seen the signs
> but because you had all the bread you wanted to eat.
27 > Do not work for food that cannot last,
> but work for food that endures to eternal life,
> the kind of food the Son of Man is offering you,
> for on him the Father, God himself, has set his seal.'

28 Then they said to him, 'What must we do if we are to do the works that God 29 wants?' •Jesus gave them this answer, 'This is working for God: you must 30 believe in the one he has sent'. •So they said, 'What sign will you give to show us 31 that we should believe in you? What work will you do? •Our fathers had manna to eat in the desert; as scripture says: *He gave them bread from heaven to eat.*[a]

32 Jesus answered:

> 'I tell you most solemnly,
> it was not Moses who gave you bread from heaven,
> it is my Father who gives you the bread from heaven,
> the true bread;
33 > for the bread of God
> is that which comes down from heaven
> and gives life to the world'.

³⁴₃₅ 'Sir,' they said 'give us that bread always.' •Jesus answered:

> 'I am the bread of life.
> He who comes to me will never be hungry;
> he who believes in me will never thirst.
36 > But, as I have told you,
> you can see me and still you do not believe.
37 > All that the Father gives me will come to me,
> and whoever comes to me
> I shall not turn him away;
38 > because I have come from heaven,
> not to do my own will,
> but to do the will of the one who sent me.
39 > Now the will of him who sent me

6 a. Ex 16:4f

is that I should lose nothing
of all that he has given to me,
and that I should raise it up on the last day.
Yes, it is my Father's will   40
that whoever sees the Son and believes in him
shall have eternal life,
and that I shall raise him up on the last day.'

Meanwhile the Jews were complaining to each other about him, because he 41
had said, 'I am the bread that came down from heaven'. •'Surely this is Jesus 42
son of Joseph' they said. 'We know his father and mother. How can he now say,
"I have come down from heaven"?' •Jesus said in reply, 'Stop complaining to 43
each other.

'No one can come to me   44
unless he is drawn by the Father who sent me,
and I will raise him up at the last day.
It is written in the prophets: 45
They will all be taught by God,[b]
and to hear the teaching of the Father,
and learn from it,
is to come to me.
Not that anybody has seen the Father,   46
except the one who comes from God:
he has seen the Father.
I tell you most solemnly,   47
everybody who believes has eternal life.
I am the bread of life.   48
Your fathers ate the manna in the desert   49
and they are dead;
but this is the bread that comes down from heaven,   50
so that a man may eat it and not die.
I am the living bread which has come down from heaven.   51
Anyone who eats this bread will live for ever;
and the bread that I shall give
is my flesh, for the life of the world.'

Then the Jews started arguing with one another: 'How can this man give 52
us his flesh to eat?' they said. •Jesus replied: 53

'I tell you most solemnly,
if you do not eat the flesh of the Son of Man
and drink his blood,
you will not have life in you.
Anyone who does eat my flesh and drink my blood   54
has eternal life,
and I shall raise him up on the last day.
For my flesh is real food   55
and my blood is real drink.
He who eats my flesh and drinks my blood   56
lives in me
and I live in him.
As I, who am sent by the living Father,   57

myself draw life from the Father,
so whoever eats me will draw life from me.
58 This is the bread come down from heaven;
not like the bread our ancestors ate:
they are dead,
but anyone who eats this bread will live for ever.'

59
60 He taught this doctrine at Capernaum, in the synagogue. •After hearing it, many of his followers said, 'This is intolerable language. How could anyone 61 accept it?' •Jesus was aware that his followers were complaining about it and 62 said, 'Does this upset you? •What if you should see the Son of Man ascend to where he was before?

63 'It is the spirit that gives life,
the flesh has nothing to offer.
The words I have spoken to you are spirit
and they are life.

64 'But there are some of you who do not believe.' For Jesus knew from the outset 65 those who did not believe, and who it was that would betray him. •He went on, 'This is why I told you that no one could come to me unless the Father allows 66 him'. •After this, many of his disciples left him and stopped going with him.

Peter's profession of faith

67 Then Jesus said to the Twelve, 'What about you, do you want to go away too?' 68 Simon Peter answered, 'Lord, who shall we go to? You have the message of 69 eternal life, • and we believe; we know that you are the Holy One of God.' 70 Jesus replied, 'Have I not chosen you, you Twelve? Yet one of you is a devil.' 71 He meant Judas son of Simon Iscariot, since this was the man, one of the Twelve, who was going to betray him.

V. THE FEAST OF TABERNACLES

Jesus goes up to Jerusalem for the feast and teaches there

1 7 After this Jesus stayed in Galilee; he could not stay in Judaea, because the Jews were out to kill him.
2
3 As the Jewish feast of Tabernacles drew near, •his brothers[a] said to him, 'Why not leave this place and go to Judaea, and let your disciples[b] see the works 4 you are doing; •if a man wants to be known he does not do things in secret; since 5 you are doing all this, you should let the whole world see'. • Not even his brothers, 6 in fact, had faith in him. •Jesus answered, 'The right time for me has not come yet, 7 but any time is the right time for you. •The world cannot hate you, but it does 8 hate me, because I give evidence that its ways are evil. •Go up to the festival yourselves: I am not going to this festival, because for me the time is not ripe 9 yet.' • Having said that, he stayed behind in Galilee.
10 However, after his brothers had left for the festival, he went up as well, but 11 quite privately, without drawing attention to himself. •At the festival the Jews

b. Is 54:13
7 a. In the wide sense, as in Mt 12:46: relations of his own generation.   b. Those in Jerusalem and Judaea.

were on the look-out for him: 'Where is he?' they said. •People stood in groups 12
whispering^c about him. Some said, 'He is a good man'; others, 'No, he is leading
the people astray'. •Yet no one spoke about him openly, for fear of the Jews. 13

When the festival was half over, Jesus went to the Temple and began to 14
teach. •The Jews were astonished and said, 'How did he learn to read? He has 15
not been taught.' •Jesus answered them: 16

> 'My teaching is not from myself:
> it comes from the one who sent me;
> and if anyone is prepared to do his will, 17
> he will know whether my teaching is from God
> or whether my doctrine is my own.
> When a man's doctrine is his own 18
> he is hoping to get honour for himself;
> but when he is working for the honour of one who sent him,
> then he is sincere
> and by no means an impostor.
> Did not Moses give you the Law? 19
> And yet not one of you keeps the Law!

'Why do you want to kill me?' •The crowd replied, 'You are mad! Who wants 20
to kill you?' •Jesus answered, 'One work I did, and you are all surprised by it. 21
Moses ordered you to practise circumcision—not that it began with him, it goes 22
back to the patriarchs—and you circumcise on the sabbath. •Now if a man 23
can be circumcised on the sabbath so that the Law of Moses is not broken,
why are you angry with me for making a man whole and complete on a sabbath?
Do not keep judging according to appearances; let your judgement be according 24
to what is right.'

The people discuss the origin of the Messiah

Meanwhile some of the people of Jerusalem were saying, 'Isn't this the man 25
they want to kill? •And here he is, speaking freely, and they have nothing to 26
say to him! Can it be true the authorities have made up their minds that he is
the Christ? •Yet we all know where he comes from, but when the Christ appears 27
no one will know where he comes from.'^d

Then, as Jesus taught in the Temple, he cried out: 28

> 'Yes, you know me and you know where I came from.
> Yet I have not come of myself:
> no, there is one who sent me and I really come from him,
> and you do not know him,
> but I know him 29
> because I have come from him
> and it was he who sent me.'

They would have arrested him then, but because his time had not yet come 30
no one laid a hand on him.

Jesus foretells his approaching departure

There were many people in the crowds, however, who believed in him; they 31
were saying, 'When the Christ comes, will he give more signs than this man?'
Hearing that rumours like this about him were spreading among the people, 32

the Pharisees sent the Temple police to arrest him.

33   Then Jesus said:

> 'I shall remain with you for only a short time now;
> then I shall go back to the one who sent me.

34
> You will look for me and will not find me:
> where I am
> you cannot come.'

35   The Jews then said to one another, 'Where is he going that we shan't be
able to find him? Is he going abroad to the people who are dispersed among
36 the Greeks and will he teach the Greeks? •What does he mean when he says:

> "You will look for me and will not find me:
> where I am,
> you cannot come"?'

The promise of living water

37   On the last day and greatest day of the festival, Jesus stood there and cried
out:

> 'If any man is thirsty, let him come to me!

38
> Let the man come and drink •who believes in me!'

As scripture says: From his breast shall flow fountains of living water.ᶜ

39   He was speaking of the Spirit which those who believed in him were to receive;
for there was no Spirit as yet because Jesus had not yet been glorified.

Fresh discussions on the origin of the Messiah

40   Several people who had been listening said, 'Surely he must be the prophet',
41 and some said, 'He is the Christ', but others said, 'Would the Christ be from
42 Galilee? •Does not scripture say that the Christ must be descended from David
43 and come from the town of Bethlehem?' •So the people could not agree about
44 him. •Some would have liked to arrest him, but no one actually laid hands on
him.

45   The police went back to the chief priests and Pharisees who said to them,
46 'Why haven't you brought him?' •The police replied, 'There has never been
47 anybody who has spoken like him'. •'So' the Pharisees answered 'you have been
48 led astray as well? •Have any of the authorities believed in him? Any of the
49 Pharisees? •This rabble knows nothing about the Law—they are damned.'
50 One of them, Nicodemus—the same man who had come to Jesus earlier—said to
51 them, •'But surely the Law does not allow us to pass judgement on a man without
52 giving him a hearing and discovering what he is about?' •To this they answered,
'Are you a Galilean too? Go into the matter, and see for yourself: prophets do
not come out of Galilee.'

c. Or 'In the crowds there was whispering about him'.   d. Although the prophecy that
the Messiah would be born in Bethlehem was well known, it was commonly believed that
he would appear suddenly from some secret place.   e. Life-giving water for Zion was a
theme of the readings from scripture on the feast of Tabernacles (Zc 14:8, Ezk 47:1f);
the liturgy included prayers for rain and the commemoration of the miracle of Moses and the
water, Ex 17.

The adulterous woman[1]

They all went home, **8** and Jesus went to the Mount of Olives. ⁵³₁

At daybreak he appeared in the Temple again; and as all the people came 2 to him, he sat down and began to teach them.

The scribes and Pharisees brought a woman along who had been caught 3 committing adultery; and making her stand there in full view of everybody, they said to Jesus, 'Master, this woman was caught in the very act of committing 4 adultery, •and Moses has ordered us in the Law to condemn women like this to 5 death by stoning. What have you to say?' •They asked him this as a test, looking 6 for something to use against him. But Jesus bent down and started writing on the ground with his finger. •As they persisted with their question, he looked 7 up and said, 'If there is one of you who has not sinned, let him be the first to throw a stone at her'. •Then he bent down and wrote on the ground again. 8 When they heard this they went away one by one, beginning with the eldest, 9 until Jesus was left alone with the woman, who remained standing there. •He 10 looked up and said, 'Woman, where are they? Has no one condemned you?' 'No one, sir' she replied. 'Neither do I condemn you,' said Jesus 'go away, and 11 don't sin any more.'

Jesus, the light of the world

When Jesus spoke to the people again, he said: 12

'I am the light of the world;
anyone who follows me will not be walking in the dark;
he will have the light of life'.

A discussion on the testimony of Jesus to himself

At this the Pharisees said to him, 'You are testifying on your own behalf; 13 your testimony is not valid'. •Jesus replied: 14

'It is true that I am testifying on my own behalf,
but my testimony is still valid,
because I know
where I came from and where I am going;
but you do not know
where I come from or where I am going.
You judge by human standards; 15
I judge no one,
but if I judge, 16
my judgement will be sound,
because I am not alone:
the one who sent me is with me;
and in your Law it is written 17
that the testimony of two witnesses is valid.
I may be testifying on my own behalf, 18
but the Father who sent me is my witness too.'

They asked him, 'Where is your Father?' Jesus answered: 19

'You do not know me, nor do you know my Father;
if you did know me, you would know my Father as well'.

He spoke these words in the Treasury, while teaching in the Temple. No one 20 arrested him, because his time had not yet come.

The unbelieving Jews warned

21 Again he said to them:

> 'I am going away; you will look for me
> and you will die in your sin.
> Where I am going, you cannot come.'

22 The Jews said to one another, 'Will he kill himself? Is that what he means by
23 saying, "Where I am going, you cannot come"?' •Jesus went on:

> 'You are from below;
> I am from above.
> You are of this world;
> I am not of this world.
24 > I have told you already: You will die in your sins.
> Yes, if you do not believe that I am He,
> you will die in your sins.'

25 So they said to him, 'Who are you?' Jesus answered:

> 'What I have told you from the outset.
26 > About you I have much to say
> and much to condemn;
> but the one who sent me is truthful,
> and what I have learnt from him
> I declare to the world.'

27 They failed to understand that he was talking to them about the Father.
28 So Jesus said:

> 'When you have lifted up the Son of Man,
> then you will know that I am He
> and that I do nothing of myself:
> what the Father has taught me
> is what I preach;
29 > he who sent me is with me,
> and has not left me to myself,
> for I always do what pleases him'.

30 As he was saying this, many came to believe in him.

Jesus and Abraham

31 To the Jews who believed in him Jesus said:

> 'If you make my word your home
> you will indeed be my disciples,
32 > you will learn the truth
> and the truth will make you free'.

33 They answered, 'We are descended from Abraham and we have never been
34 the slaves of anyone; what do you mean, "You will be made free"?' •Jesus replied:

> 'I tell you most solemnly,
> everyone who commits sin is a slave.

f. The author of this passage is not John; the oldest MSS do not include it or place it elsewhere. The style is that of the Synoptics.

Now the slave's place in the house is not assured,   35
but the son's place is assured.
So if the Son makes you free,   36
you will be free indeed.
I know that you are descended from Abraham;   37
but in spite of that you want to kill me
because nothing I say has penetrated into you.
What I, for my part, speak of   38
is what I have seen with my Father;
but you, you put into action
the lessons learnt from your father.'

They repeated, 'Our father is Abraham'. Jesus said to them: 39

'If you were Abraham's children,
you would do as Abraham did.
As it is, you want to kill me   40
when I tell you the truth
as I have learnt it from God;
that is not what Abraham did.
What you are doing is what your father does.'   41

'We were not born of prostitution,'[a] they went on 'we have one father: God.'
Jesus answered: 42

'If God were your father, you would love me,
since I have come here from God; yes, I have come from him;
not that I came because I chose,
no, I was sent, and by him.
Do you know why you cannot take in what I say?   43
It is because you are unable to understand my language.
The devil is your father,   44
and you prefer to do
what your father wants.

He was a murderer from the start;
he was never grounded in the truth;
there is no truth in him at all:
when he lies
he is drawing on his own store,
because he is a liar, and the father of lies.
But as for me, I speak the truth   45
and for that very reason,
you do not believe me.
Can one of you convict me of sin?   46
If I speak the truth, why do you not believe me?
A child of God   47
listens to the words of God;
if you refuse to listen,
it is because you are not God's children.'

The Jews replied, 'Are we not right in saying that you are a Samaritan and 48
possessed by a devil?' Jesus answered:

49 'I am not possessed;
no, I honour my Father,
but you want to dishonour me.
50 Not that I care for my own glory,
there is someone who takes care of that and is the judge of it.
51 I tell you most solemnly,
whoever keeps my word
will never see death.'

52 The Jews said, 'Now we know for certain that you are possessed. Abraham is dead, and the prophets are dead, and yet you say, "Whoever keeps my word
53 will never know the taste of death". •Are you greater than our father Abraham,
54 who is dead? The prophets are dead too. Who are you claiming to be?' •Jesus answered:

'If I were to seek my own glory
that would be no glory at all;
my glory is conferred by the Father,
by the one of whom you say, "He is our God"
55 although you do not know him.
But I know him,
and if I were to say: I do not know him,
I should be a liar, as you are liars yourselves.
But I do know him, and I faithfully keep his word.
56 Your father Abraham rejoiced
to think that he would see my Day;
he saw it and was glad.'

57 The Jews then said, 'You are not fifty yet, and you have seen Abraham!'
58 Jesus replied:

'I tell you most solemnly,
before Abraham ever was,
I Am'.

59 At this they picked up stones to throw at him;[b] but Jesus hid himself and left the Temple.

The cure of the man born blind

1 9 As he went along, he saw a man who had been blind from birth. •His disciples
2 asked him, 'Rabbi, who sinned, this man or his parents, for him to have been
3 born blind?' •'Neither he nor his parents sinned,' Jesus answered 'he was born blind so that the works of God might be displayed in him.

4 'As long as the day lasts
I must carry out the work of the one who sent me;
the night will soon be here when no one can work.
5 As long as I am in the world
I am the light of the world.'

6 Having said this, he spat on the ground, made a paste with the spittle, put
7 this over the eyes of the blind man, •and said to him, 'Go and wash in the Pool

8 a. By 'prostitution' the prophets often mean religious infidelity, cf. Ho 1:2.   **b.** Stoning was the penalty for blasphemy. Cf. 10:33.

of Siloam*ᵃ* (a name that means 'sent'). So the blind man went off and washed himself, and came away with his sight restored.

His neighbours and people who earlier had seen him begging said, 'Isn't 8 this the man who used to sit and beg?' ·Some said, 'Yes, it is the same one'. 9 Others said, 'No, he only looks like him'. The man himself said, 'I am the man'. So they said to him, 'Then how do your eyes come to be open?' ·'The man called ¹⁰₁₁ Jesus' he answered 'made a paste, daubed my eyes with it and said to me, "Go and wash at Siloam"; so I went, and when I washed I could see.' ·They asked, 12 'Where is he?' 'I don't know' he answered.

They brought the man who had been blind to the Pharisees. ·It had been a ¹³₁₄ sabbath day when Jesus made the paste and opened the man's eyes, ·so when 15 the Pharisees asked him how he had come to see, he said, 'He put a paste on my eyes, and I washed, and I can see'. ·Then some of the Pharisees said, 'This 16 man cannot be from God: he does not keep the sabbath'. Others said, 'How could a sinner produce signs like this?' And there was disagreement among them. So they spoke to the blind man again, 'What have you to say about him yourself, 17 now that he has opened your eyes?' 'He is a prophet' replied the man.

However, the Jews would not believe that the man had been blind and had 18 gained his sight, without first sending for his parents and ·asking them, 'Is this 19 man really your son who you say was born blind? If so, how is it that he is now able to see?' ·His parents answered, 'We know he is our son and we know he 20 was born blind, ·but we don't know how it is that he can see now, or who 21 opened his eyes. He is old enough: let him speak for himself.' ·His parents 22 spoke like this out of fear of the Jews, who had already agreed to expel from the synagogue anyone who should acknowledge Jesus as the Christ. ·This was why 23 his parents said, 'He is old enough; ask him'.

So the Jews again sent for the man and said to him, 'Give glory to God!*ᵇ* 24 For our part, we know that this man is a sinner.' ·The man answered, 'I don't 25 know if he is a sinner; I only know that I was blind and now I can see'. ·They 26 said to him, 'What did he do to you? How did he open your eyes?' ·He replied, 27 'I have told you once and you wouldn't listen. Why do you want to hear it all again? Do you want to become his disciples too?' ·At this they hurled abuse 28 at him: 'You can be his disciple,' they said 'we are disciples of Moses: ·we 29 know that God spoke to Moses, but as for this man, we don't know where he comes from'. ·The man replied, 'Now here is an astonishing thing! He has 30 opened my eyes, and you don't know where he comes from! ·We know that God 31 doesn't listen to sinners, but God does listen to men who are devout and do his will. ·Ever since the world began it is unheard of for anyone to open the eyes 32 of a man who was born blind; ·if this man were not from God, he couldn't do 33 a thing.' ·'Are you trying to teach us,' they replied 'and you a sinner through 34 and through, since you were born!' And they drove him away.

Jesus heard they had driven him away, and when he found him he said to 35 him, 'Do you believe in the Son of Man?' ·'Sir,' the man replied 'tell me who 36 he is so that I may believe in him.' ·Jesus said, 'You are looking at him; he is 37 speaking to you'. · The man said, 'Lord, I believe', and worshipped him. 38
Jesus said: 39

　　　　'It is for judgement
　　　　that I have come into this world,
　　　　so that those without sight may see
　　　　and those with sight turn blind'.

40 Hearing this, some Pharisees who were present said to him, 'We are not blind,
41 surely?' •Jesus replied:

> 'Blind? If you were,
> you would not be guilty,
> but since you say, "We see",
> your guilt remains.

The good shepherd

1   **10** 'I tell you most solemnly, anyone who does not enter the sheepfold
through the gate, but gets in some other way is a thief and a brigand.
2/3 The one who enters through the gate is the shepherd of the flock; •the
gatekeeper lets him in, the sheep hear his voice, one by one he calls his
4 own sheep and leads them out. •When he has brought out his flock, he goes
5 ahead of them, and the sheep follow because they know his voice. •They never
follow a stranger but run away from him: they do not recognise the voice of
strangers.'

6   Jesus told them*a* this parable but they failed to understand what he meant
by telling it to them.

7   So Jesus spoke to them again:

> 'I tell you most solemnly,
> I am the gate of the sheepfold.
8   All others who have come
> are thieves and brigands;
> but the sheep took no notice of them.
9   I am the gate.
> Anyone who enters through me will be safe:
> he will go freely in and out
> and be sure of finding pasture.
10   The thief comes
> only to steal and kill and destroy.
> I have come
> so that they may have life
> and have it to the full.
11   I am the good shepherd:
> the good shepherd is one who lays down his life for his sheep.
12   The hired man, since he is not the shepherd
> and the sheep do not belong to him,
> abandons the sheep and runs away
> as soon as he sees a wolf coming,
> and then the wolf attacks and scatters the sheep;
13   this is because he is only a hired man
> and has no concern for the sheep.
14   I am the good shepherd;
> I know my own
> and my own know me,
15   just as the Father knows me

---

9 a. Water from this pool was drawn during the feast of Tabernacles to symbolise the waters of
blessing.   **b.** I.e. putting the man on oath.
10 a. The Pharisees.

> and I know the Father;
> and I lay down my life for my sheep.
> And there are other sheep I have   16
> that are not of this fold,
> and these I have to lead as well.
> They too will listen to my voice,
> and there will be only one flock,
> and one shepherd.
> The Father loves me,   17
> because I lay down my life
> in order to take it up again.
> No one takes it from me;   18
> I lay it down of my own free will,
> and as it is in my power to lay it down,
> so it is in my power to take it up again;
> and this is the command I have been given by my Father.'

These words caused disagreement   among the Jews. •Many said, 'He is 19 20 possessed, he is raving; why bother to listen to him?' •Others said, 'These are 21 not the words of a man possessed by a devil: could a devil open the eyes of the blind?'

VI. THE FEAST OF DEDICATION

Jesus claims to be the Son of God

It was the time when the feast of Dedication was being celebrated in Jerusalem. 22 It was winter, •and Jesus was in the Temple walking up and down in the Portico 23 of Solomon. •The Jews gathered round him and said, 'How much longer are 24 you going to keep us in suspense? If you are the Christ, tell us plainly.' •Jesus 25 replied:

> 'I have told you, but you do not believe.
> The works I do in my Father's name are my witness;
> but you do not believe,   26
> because you are no sheep of mine.
> The sheep that belong to me listen to my voice;   27
> I know them and they follow me.
> I give them eternal life;   28
> they will never be lost
> and no one will ever steal them from me.
> The Father who gave them to me is greater than anyone,   29
> and no one can steal   from the Father.
> The Father and I are one.'   30

The Jews fetched stones to stone him, •so Jesus said to them, 'I have done 31 32 many good works for you to see, works from my Father; for which of these are you stoning me?' •The Jews answered him, 'We are not stoning you for doing 33 a good work but for blasphemy: you are only a man and you claim to be God'. Jesus answered: 34

> 'Is it not written in your Law:
> *I said, you are gods?* [b]

35 So the Law uses the word gods
of those to whom the word of God was addressed,
and scripture cannot be rejected.

36 Yet you say to someone the Father has consecrated and sent
into the world,
"You are blaspheming",
because he says, "I am the Son of God".

37 If I am not doing my Father's work,
there is no need to believe me;

38 but if I am doing it,
then even if you refuse to believe in me,
at least believe in the work I do;
then you will know for sure
that the Father is in me and I am in the Father.'

39 They wanted to arrest him then, but he eluded them.

Jesus withdraws to the other side of the Jordan

40 He went back again to the far side of the Jordan to stay in the district where
41 John had once been baptising. •Many people who came to him there said, 'John
42 gave no signs, but all he said about this man was true'; •and many of them
believed in him.

The resurrection of Lazarus

1   **11**   There was a man named Lazarus who lived in the village of Bethany with
2   the two sisters, Mary and Martha, and he was ill.—•It was the same
Mary, the sister of the sick man Lazarus, who anointed the Lord with
3 ointment and wiped his feet with her hair. •The sisters sent this message to
4 Jesus, 'Lord, the man you love is ill'. •On receiving the message, Jesus said,
'This sickness will end not in death but in God's glory, and through it the Son
of God will be glorified'.

5 Jesus loved Martha and her sister and Lazarus, •yet when he heard that
6
7 Lazarus was ill he stayed where he was for two more days •before saying to the
8 disciples, 'Let us go to Judaea'. •The disciples said, 'Rabbi, it is not long since
9 the Jews wanted to stone you; are you going back again?' •Jesus replied:

'Are there not twelve hours in the day?
A man can walk in the daytime without stumbling
because he has the light of this world to see by;
10 but if he walks at night he stumbles,
because there is no light to guide him.'

11 He said that and then added, 'Our friend Lazarus is resting, I am going to
12 wake him'. •The disciples said to him, 'Lord, if he is able to rest he is sure to get
13 better'. •The phrase Jesus used referred to the death of Lazarus, but they thought
14 that by 'rest' he meant 'sleep', so •Jesus put it plainly, 'Lazarus is dead; •and
15
for your sake I am glad I was not there because now you will believe. But let
16 us go to him.' •Then Thomas—known as the Twin—said to the other disciples,
'Let us go too, and die with him'.

17 On arriving, Jesus found that Lazarus had been in the tomb for four days
18 already. •Bethany is only about two miles from Jerusalem, •and many Jews had
19

b. Ps 82:6

come to Martha and Mary to sympathise with them over their brother. •When 20 Martha heard that Jesus had come she went to meet him. Mary remained sitting in the house. •Martha said to Jesus, 'If you had been here, my brother would 21 not have died, •but I know that, even now, whatever you ask of God, he will 22 grant you'. •'Your brother' said Jesus to her 'will rise again.' •Martha said, 23 24 'I know he will rise again at the resurrection on the last day'. •Jesus said: 25

> 'I am the resurrection.
> If anyone believes in me, even though he dies he will live,
> and whoever lives and believes in me 26
> will never die.
> Do you believe this?'

'Yes, Lord,' she said 'I believe that you are the Christ, the Son of God, the one 27 who was to come into this world.'

When she had said this, she went and called her sister Mary, saying in a low 28 voice, 'The Master is here and wants to see you'. •Hearing this, Mary got up 29 quickly and went to him. •Jesus had not yet come into the village; he was still 30 at the place where Martha had met him. •When the Jews who were in the house 31 sympathising with Mary saw her get up so quickly and go out, they followed her, thinking that she was going to the tomb to weep there.

Mary went to Jesus, and as soon as she saw him she threw herself at his 32 feet, saying, 'Lord, if you had been here, my brother would not have died'. •At 33 the sight of her tears, and those of the Jews who followed her, Jesus said in great distress, with a sigh that came straight from the heart, •'Where have you put 34 him?' They said, 'Lord, come and see'. •Jesus wept; •and the Jews said, 'See 35 36 how much he loved him!' •But there were some who remarked, 'He opened the 37 eyes of the blind man, could he not have prevented this man's death?' •Still 38 sighing, Jesus reached the tomb: it was a cave with a stone to close the opening. Jesus said, 'Take the stone away'. Martha said to him, 'Lord, by now he will 39 smell; this is the fourth day'. •Jesus replied, 'Have I not told you that if you 40 believe you will see the glory of God?' •So they took away the stone. Then 41 Jesus lifted up his eyes and said:

> 'Father, I thank you for hearing my prayer.
> I knew indeed that you always hear me, 42
> but I speak
> for the sake of all these who stand round me,
> so that they may believe it was you who sent me.'

When he had said this, he cried in a loud voice, 'Lazarus, here! Come out!' 43 The dead man came out, his feet and hands bound with bands of stuff and a 44 cloth round his face. Jesus said to them, 'Unbind him, let him go free'.

The Jewish leaders decide on the death of Jesus

Many of the Jews who had come to visit Mary and had seen what he did 45 believed in him, •but some of them went to tell the Pharisees what Jesus had 46 done. •Then the chief priests and Pharisees called a meeting. 'Here is this man 47 working all these signs' they said 'and what action are we taking? •If we let 48 him go on in this way everybody will believe in him, and the Romans will come and destroy the Holy Place and our nation.' •One of them, Caiaphas, the 49 high priest that year, said, 'You don't seem to have grasped the situation at all;

50 you fail to see that it is better for one man to die for the people, than for the
51 whole nation to be destroyed'. •He did not speak in his own person, it was as
high priest that he made this prophecy that Jesus was to die for the nation—
52 and not for the nation only, but to gather together in unity the scattered children
53
54 of God. •From that day they were determined to kill him. •So Jesus no longer
went about openly among the Jews, but left the district for a town called
Ephraim, in the country bordering on the desert, and stayed there with his
disciples.

VII. THE LAST PASSOVER

A. BEFORE THE PASSION

The Passover draws near

55   The Jewish Passover drew near, and many of the country people who had
56 gone up to Jerusalem to purify themselves •looked out for Jesus, saying to one
another as they stood about in the Temple, 'What do you think? Will he come
57 to the festival or not?' •The chief priests and Pharisees had by now given their
orders: anyone who knew where he was must inform them so that they could
arrest him.

The anointing at Bethany

1 **12** Six days before the Passover, Jesus went to Bethany, where Lazarus
2 was, whom he had raised from the dead. •They gave a dinner for him
3 there; Martha waited on them and Lazarus was among those at table. •Mary
brought in a pound of very costly ointment, pure nard, and with it anointed the
feet of Jesus, wiping them with her hair; the house was full of the scent of the
4 ointment. •Then Judas Iscariot—one of his disciples, the man who was to betray
5 him—said, •'Why wasn't this ointment sold for three hundred denarii, and the
6 money given to the poor?' •He said this, not because he cared about the poor,
but because he was a thief; he was in charge of the common fund and used to
7 help himself to the contributions. •So Jesus said, 'Leave her alone; she had to
8 keep this scent for the day of my burial. •You have the poor with you always,
you will not always have me.'
9   Meanwhile a large number of Jews heard that he was there and came not
only on account of Jesus but also to see Lazarus whom he had raised from the
10
11 dead. •Then the chief priests decided to kill Lazarus as well, •since it was on his
account that many of the Jews were leaving them and believing in Jesus.

The Messiah enters Jerusalem

12   The next day the crowds who had come up for the festival heard that Jesus
13 was on his way to Jerusalem. •They took branches of palm and went out to
meet him, shouting, '*Hosanna! Blessings on* the King of Israel, *who comes in the*
14 *name of the Lord.*'[a]•Jesus found a young donkey and mounted it—as scripture
15 says: • *Do not be afraid, daughter of Zion; see, your king is coming, mounted on*
16 *the colt of a donkey.*[b]•At the time his disciples did not understand this, but later,
after Jesus had been glorified, they remembered that this had been written

12 a. Ps 118:26   **b.** Zc 9:9f

about him and that this was in fact how they had received him. •All who had 17
been with him when he called Lazarus out of the tomb and raised him from the
dead were telling how they had witnessed it; •it was because of this, too, that 18
the crowd came out to meet him: they had heard that he had given this sign.
Then the Pharisees said to one another, 'You see, there is nothing you can do; 19
look, the whole world is running after him!'

Jesus foretells his death and subsequent glorification

Among those who went up to worship at the festival were some Greeks.*c* 20
These approached Philip, who came from Bethsaida in Galilee, and put this 21
request to him, 'Sir, we should like to see Jesus'. •Philip went to tell Andrew, 22
and Andrew and Philip together went to tell Jesus.

Jesus replied to them: 23

> 'Now the hour has come
> for the Son of Man to be glorified.
> I tell you, most solemnly,   24
> unless a wheat grain falls on the ground and dies,
> it remains only a single grain;
> but if it dies,
> it yields a rich harvest.
> Anyone who loves his life loses it;   25
> anyone who hates his life in this world
> will keep it for the eternal life.
> If a man serves me, he must follow me,   26
> wherever I am, my servant will be there too.
> If anyone serves me, my Father will honour him.
> Now my soul is troubled.   27
> What shall I say:
> Father, save me from this hour?
> But it was for this very reason that I have come to this hour.
> Father, glorify your name!'   28

A voice came from heaven, 'I have glorified it, and I will glorify it again'.

People standing by, who heard this, said it was a clap of thunder; others 29
said, 'It was an angel speaking to him'. •Jesus answered, 'It was not for my sake 30
that this voice came, but for yours.

> 'Now sentence is being passed on this world;   31
> now the prince of this world is to be overthrown.*d*
> And when I am lifted up from the earth,   32
> I shall draw all men to myself.'

By these words he indicated the kind of death he would die. •The crowd $^{33}_{34}$
answered, 'The Law has taught us that the Christ will remain for ever. How can
you say, "The Son of Man must be lifted up"? Who is this Son of Man?' •Jesus 35
then said:

> 'The light will be with you only a little longer now.
> Walk while you have the light,
> or the dark will overtake you;
> he who walks in the dark does not know where he is going.

36 While you still have the light,
believe in the light
and you will become sons of light.'

Having said this, Jesus left them and kept himself hidden.

Conclusion: the unbelief of the Jews

37 Though they had been present when he gave so many signs, they did not
38 believe in him; •this was to fulfil the words of the prophet Isaiah: *Lord, who
could believe what we have heard said, and to whom has the power of the Lord
39 been revealed?*[e] •Indeed, they were unable to believe because, as Isaiah says
40 again: •*He has blinded their eyes, he has hardened their heart, for fear they should
see with their eyes and understand with their heart, and turn to me for healing.*[f]
41 Isaiah said this when he saw his glory,[g] and his words referred to Jesus.
42 And yet there were many who did believe in him, even among the leading
men, but they did not admit it, through fear of the Pharisees and fear of being
43 expelled from the synagogue: •they put honour from men before the honour
that comes from God.
44 Jesus declared publicly:

'Whoever believes in me
believes not in me
but in the one who sent me,
45 and whoever sees me,
sees the one who sent me.
46 I, the light, have come into the world,
so that whoever believes in me
need not stay in the dark any more.
47 If anyone hears my words and does not keep them faithfully,
it is not I who shall condemn him,
since I have come not to condemn the world,
but to save the world:
48 he who rejects me and refuses my words
has his judge already:
the word itself that I have spoken
will be his judge on the last day.
49 For what I have spoken does not come from myself;
no, what I was to say, what I had to speak,
was commanded by the Father who sent me,
50 and I know that his commands mean eternal life.
And therefore what the Father has told me
is what I speak.'

c. The 'God-fearing men' of Ac 10:2: converts who observed certain specific Mosaic observances.
d. Satan.   e. Is 53:1   f. Is 6:9f   g. Isaiah's vision in the Temple, Is 6:4, interpreted as a
prophetic vision of Christ's glory.

B. THE LAST SUPPER

Jesus washes his disciples' feet

13 It was before the festival of the Passover, and Jesus knew that the hour 1 had come for him to pass from this world to the Father. He had always loved those who were his in the world, but now he showed how perfect his love was.

They were at supper, and the devil had already put it into the mind of 2 Judas Iscariot son of Simon, to betray him. •Jesus knew that the Father had 3 put everything into his hands, and that he had come from God and was returning to God, •and he got up from table, removed his outer garment and, taking a 4 towel, wrapped it round his waist; •he then poured water into a basin and 5 began to wash the disciples' feet *a* and to wipe them with the towel he was wearing.

He came to Simon Peter, who said to him, 'Lord, are you going to wash my 6 feet?' •Jesus answered, 'At the moment you do not know what I am doing, but 7 later you will understand'. •'Never!' said Peter 'You shall never wash my feet.' 8 Jesus replied, 'If I do not wash you, you can have nothing in common with me'. 'Then, Lord,' said Simon Peter 'not only my feet, but my hands and my head 9 as well!' •Jesus said, 'No one who has taken a bath needs washing, he is clean 10 all over. You too are clean, though not all of you are.' •He knew who was 11 going to betray him, that was why he said, 'though not all of you are'.

When he had washed their feet and put on his clothes again he went back 12 to the table. 'Do you understand' he said 'what I have done to you? •You call 13 me Master and Lord, and rightly; so I am. •If I, then, the Lord and Master, 14 have washed your feet, you should wash each other's feet. •I have given you 15 an example so that you may copy what I have done to you.

> 'I tell you most solemnly, 16
> no servant is greater than his master,
> no messenger is greater than the man who sent him.

'Now that you know this, happiness will be yours if you behave accordingly. 17 I am not speaking about all of you: I know the ones I have chosen; but what 18' scripture says must be fulfilled: *Someone who shares my table rebels against me.* *b*

> 'I tell you this now, before it happens, 19
> so that when it does happen
> you may believe that I am He.
> I tell you most solemnly, 20
> whoever welcomes the one I send welcomes me,
> and whoever welcomes me welcomes the one who sent me.'

The treachery of Judas foretold

Having said this, Jesus was troubled in spirit and declared, 'I tell you most 21 solemnly, one of you will betray me'. •The disciples looked at one another, 22 wondering which he meant. •The disciple Jesus loved was reclining next 23 to Jesus; •Simon Peter signed to him and said, 'Ask who it is he means', •so $\frac{24}{25}$ leaning back on Jesus' breast he said, 'Who is it, Lord?' •'It is the one' replied 26 Jesus 'to whom I give the piece of bread that I shall dip in the dish.' He dipped the piece of bread and gave it to Judas son of Simon Iscariot. •At that instant, 27

after Judas had taken the bread, Satan entered him. Jesus then said, 'What you
28 are going to do, do quickly'. •None of the others at table understood the reason
29 he said this. •Since Judas had charge of the common fund, some of them thought
Jesus was telling him, 'Buy what we need for the festival', or telling him to give
30 something to the poor. •As soon as Judas had taken the piece of bread he went
out. Night had fallen.

31   When he had gone Jesus said:

> 'Now has the Son of Man been glorified,
> and in him God has been glorified.
32   If God has been glorified in him,
> God will in turn glorify him in himself,[c]
> and will glorify him very soon.

Farewell discourses

33   'My little children,
> I shall not be with you much longer.
> You will look for me,
> and, as I told the Jews,
> where I am going,
> you cannot come.
34   I give you a new commandment:
> love one another;
> just as I have loved you,
> you also must love one another.
35   By this love you have for one another,
> everyone will know that you are my disciples.'

36   Simon Peter said, 'Lord, where are you going?' Jesus replied, 'Where I am
37 going you cannot follow me now; you will follow me later'. •Peter said to him,
38 'Why can't I follow you now? I will lay down my life for you.' •'Lay down your
life for me?' answered Jesus. 'I tell you most solemnly, before the cock crows
you will have disowned me three times.

1 **14**   'Do not let your hearts be troubled.
> Trust in God still, and trust in me.
2   There are many rooms in my Father's house;
> if there were not, I should have told you.
> I am going now to prepare a place for you,
3   and after I have gone and prepared you a place,
> I shall return to take you with me;
> so that where I am
> you may be too.
4   You know the way to the place where I am going.'

5   Thomas said, 'Lord, we do not know where you are going, so how can we
6 know the way?' •Jesus said:

> 'I am the Way, the Truth and the Life.
> No one can come to the Father except through me.

---

13 a. The dress and the duty are those of a slave.   **b.** Ps 41:9   **c.** I.e. the Father will take
the Son of Man to himself in glory.

If you know me, you know my Father too.   7
From this moment you know him and have seen him.'

Philip said, 'Lord, let us see the Father and then we shall be satisfied'.   8
'Have I been with you all this time, Philip,' said Jesus to him 'and you still do   9
not know me?

'To have seen me is to have seen the Father,
so how can you say, "Let us see the Father"?
Do you not believe   10
that I am in the Father and the Father is in me?
The words I say to you I do not speak as from myself:
it is the Father, living in me, who is doing this work.
You must believe me when I say   11
that I am in the Father and the Father is in me;
believe it on the evidence of this work, if for no other reason.
I tell you most solemnly,   12
whoever believes in me
will perform the same works as I do myself,
he will perform even greater works,
because I am going to the Father.
Whatever you ask for in my name I will do,   13
so that the Father may be glorified in the Son.
If you ask for anything in my name,   14
I will do it.
If you love me you will keep my commandments.   15
I shall ask the Father,   16
and he will give you another Advocate[a]
to be with you for ever,
that Spirit of truth   17
whom the world can never receive
since it neither sees nor knows him;
but you know him,
because he is with you, he is in you.
I will not leave you orphans;   18
I will come back to you.
In a short time the world will no longer see me;   19
but you will see me,
because I live and you will live.
On that day   20
you will understand that I am in my Father
and you in me and I in you.
Anybody who receives my commandments and keeps them   21
will be one who loves me;
and anybody who loves me will be loved by my Father,
and I shall love him and show myself to him.'

Judas[b]—this was not Judas Iscariot—said to him, 'Lord, what is all this   22
about? Do you intend to show yourself to us and not to the world?' •Jesus   23
replied:

'If anyone loves me he will keep my word,

and my Father will love him,
and we shall come to him
and make our home with him.

24   Those who do not love me do not keep my words.
And my word   is not my own:
it is the word of the one who sent me.

25   I have said these things to you
while still with you;

26   but the Advocate, the Holy Spirit,
whom the Father will send in my name,
will teach you everything
and remind you of all I have said to you.

27   Peace‹ I bequeath to you,
my own peace I give you,
a peace the world cannot give, this is my gift to you.
Do not let your hearts be troubled or afraid.

28   You heard me say:
I am going away, and shall return.
If you loved me you would have been glad to know that I am
   going to the Father,
for the Father is greater than I.

29   I have told you this now before it happens,
so that when it does happen you may believe.

30   I shall not talk with you any longer,
because the prince of this world is on his way.
He has no power over me,

31   but the world must be brought to know that I love the Father
and that I am doing exactly what the Father told me.
Come now, let us go.

The true vine

1 **15**   'I am the true vine,
and my Father is the vinedresser.

2   Every branch in me that bears no fruit
he cuts away,
and every branch that does bear fruit he prunes
to make it bear even more.

3   You are pruned already,
by means of the word that I have spoken to you.

4   Make your home in me, as I make mine in you.
As a branch cannot bear fruit all by itself,
but must remain part of the vine,
neither can you unless you remain in me.

5   I am the vine,
you are the branches.
Whoever remains in me, with me in him,
bears fruit in plenty;

14 a. Greek *parakletos*: advocate or counsellor or protector.   **b.** 'Judas, brother of James' in
Lk 6:16 and Ac 1:13; the Thaddaeus of Mt 10:3 and Mk 3:18.   **c.** The customary Jewish
farewell.

for cut off from me you can do nothing.
Anyone who does not remain in me   6
is like a branch that has been thrown away
—he withers;
these branches are collected and thrown on the fire,
and they are burnt.
If you remain in me   7
and my words remain in you,
you may ask what you will
and you shall get it.
It is to the glory of my Father that you should bear much fruit,   8
and then you will be my disciples.
As the Father has loved me,   9
so I have loved you.
Remain in my love,
If you keep my commandments   10
you will remain in my love,
just as I have kept my Father's commandments
and remain in his love.
I have told you this   11
so that my own joy may be in you
and your joy be complete.
This is my commandment: 12
love one another,
as I have loved you.
A man can have no greater love   13
than to lay down his life for his friends.
You are my friends,   14
if you do what I command you.
I shall not call you servants any more,   15
because a servant does not know
his master's business;
I call you friends,
because I have made known to you
everything I have learnt from my Father.
You did not choose me,   16
no, I chose you;
and I commissioned you
to go out and to bear fruit,
fruit that will last;
and then the Father will give you
anything you ask him in my name.
What I command you   17
is to love one another.

The hostile world

'If the world hates you,   18
remember that it hated me before you.
If you belonged to the world,   19
the world would love you as its own;

but because you do not belong to the world,
because my choice withdrew you from the world,
therefore the world hates you.

20 Remember the words I said to you:
A servant is not greater than his master.
If they persecuted me,
they will persecute you too;
if they kept my word,
they will keep yours as well.

21 But it will be on my account that they will do all this,
because they do not know the one who sent me.

22 If I had not come,
if I had not spoken to them,
they would have been blameless;
but as it is they have no excuse for their sin.

23 Anyone who hates me hates my Father.

24 If I had not performed such works among them
as no one else has ever done,
they would be blameless;
but as it is, they have seen all this,
and still they hate both me and my Father.

25 But all this was only to fulfil the words written in their Law:
They hated me for no reason.[a]

26 When the Advocate comes,
whom I shall send to you from the Father,
the Spirit of truth who issues from the Father,
he will be my witness.

27 And you too will be witnesses,
because you have been with me from the outset.

1 **16** 'I have told you all this
so that your faith may not be shaken.

2 They will expel you from the synagogues,
and indeed the hour is coming
when anyone who kills you will think he is doing a holy duty for God.

3 They will do these things
because they have never known either the Father or myself.

4 But I have told you all this,
so that when the time for it comes
you may remember that I told you.

The coming of the Advocate

'I did not tell you this from the outset,
because I was with you;

5 but now I am going to the one who sent me.
Not one of you has asked, "Where are you going?"

6 Yet you are sad at heart because I have told you this.

7 Still, I must tell you the truth:
it is for your own good that I am going

15 a. Ps 35: 19

because unless I go,
the Advocate will not come to you;
but if I do go,
I will send him to you.
And when he comes,   8
he will show the world how wrong it was,
about sin,
and about who was in the right,
and about judgement:
about sin: 9
proved by their refusal to believe in me;
about who was in the right: 10
proved by my going to the Father
and your seeing me no more;
about judgement: 11
proved by the prince of this world being already condemned.
I still have many things to say to you   12
but they would be too much for you now.
But when the Spirit of truth comes   13
he will lead you to the complete truth,
since he will not be speaking as from himself
but will say only what he has learnt;
and he will tell you of the things to come.
He will glorify me,   14
since all he tells you
will be taken from what is mine.
Everything the Father has is mine;   15
that is why I said:
All he tells you
will be taken from what is mine.

Jesus to return very soon

'In a short time you will no longer see me,   16
and then a short time later you will see me again.'

Then some of his disciples said to one another, 'What does he mean, "In a 17
short time you will no longer see me, and then a short time later you will see me
again" and, "I am going to the Father"? •What is this "short time"? We don't 18
know what he means.' •Jesus knew that they wanted to question him, so he 19
said, 'You are asking one another what I meant by saying: In a short time you
will no longer see me, and then a short time later you will see me again.

'I tell you most solemnly,   20
you will be weeping and wailing
while the world will rejoice;
you will be sorrowful,
but your sorrow will turn to joy.
A woman in childbirth suffers,   21
because her time has come;
but when she has given birth to the child she forgets the suffering
in her joy that a man has been born into the world.

22 So it is with you: you are sad now,
but I shall see you again, and your hearts will be full of joy,
and that joy no one shall take from you.

23 When that day comes,
you will not ask me any questions.
I tell you most solemnly,
anything you ask for from the Father
he will grant in my name.

24 Until now you have not asked for anything in my name.
Ask and you will receive,
and so your joy will be complete.

25 I have been telling you all this in metaphors,
the hour is coming
when I shall no longer speak to you in metaphors;
but tell you about the Father in plain words.

26 When that day comes
you will ask in my name;
and I do not say that I shall pray to the Father for you,

27 because the Father himself loves you
for loving me
and believing that I came from God.

28 I came from the Father and have come into the world
and now I leave the world to go to the Father.'

29 His disciples said, 'Now you are speaking plainly and not using metaphors!
30 Now we see that you know everything, and do not have to wait for questions to
31 be put into words; because of this we believe that you came from God.' •Jesus
answered them:

'Do you believe at last?

32 Listen; the time will come—in fact it has come already—
when you will be scattered, each going his own way
and leaving me alone.
And yet I am not alone,
because the Father is with me.

33 I have told you all this
so that you may find peace in me.
In the world you will have trouble,
but be brave:
I have conquered the world.'

The priestly prayer of Christ

17 After saying this, Jesus raised his eyes to heaven and said:

1 'Father, the hour has come:
glorify your Son
so that your Son may glorify you;

2 and, through the power over all mankind*a* that you have given him,
let him give eternal life to all those you have entrusted to him.

3 And eternal life is this:

17 a. Lit. 'all flesh'.

to know you,
the only true God,
and Jesus Christ whom you have sent.
I have glorified you on earth   4
and finished the work
that you gave me to do.
Now, Father, it is time for you to glorify me   5
with that glory I had with you
before ever the world was.
I have made your name known   6
to the men you took from the world to give me.
They were yours and you gave them to me,
and they have kept your word.
Now at last they know   7
that all you have given me comes indeed from you;
for I have given them   8
the teaching you gave to me,
and they have truly accepted this, that I came from you,
and have believed that it was you who sent me.
I pray for them;   9
I am not praying for the world
but for those you have given me,
because they belong to you:
all I have is yours   10
and all you have is mine,
and in them I am glorified.
I am not in the world any longer,   11
but they are in the world,
and I am coming to you.
Holy Father,
keep those you have given me true to your name,
so that they may be one like us.
While I was with them,   12
I kept those you had given me true to your name.
I have watched over them and not one is lost
except the one who chose to be lost,*b*
and this was to fulfil the scriptures.
But now I am coming to you   13
and while still in the world I say these things
to share my joy with them to the full.
I passed your word on to them,   14
and the world hated them,
because they belong to the world
no more than I belong to the world.
I am not asking you to remove them from the world,   15
but to protect them from the evil one.
They do not belong to the world   16
any more than I belong to the world.
Consecrate them in the truth;   17
your word is truth.

18 As you sent me into the world,
    I have sent them into the world,
19 and for their sake I consecrate myself
    so that they too may be consecrated in truth.
20 I pray not only for these,
    but for those also
    who through their words will believe in me.
21 May they all be one.
    Father, may they be one in us,
    as you are in me and I am in you,
    so that the world may believe it was you who sent me.
22 I have given them the glory you gave to me,
    that they may be one as we are one.
23 With me in them and you in me,
    may they be so completely one
    that the world will realise that it was you who sent me
    and that I have loved them   as much as you loved me.
24 Father,
    I want those you have given me
    to be with me where I am,
    so that they may always see the glory
    you have given me
    because you loved me
    before the foundation of the world.
25 Father, Righteous One,
    the world has not known you,
    but I have known you,
    and these have known
    that you have sent me.
26 I have made your name known to them
    and will continue to make it known,
    so that the love with which you loved me may be in them,
    and so that I may be in them.'

C. THE PASSION

The arrest of Jesus

1 **18** After he had said all this Jesus left with his disciples and crossed the Kedron valley. There was a garden there, and he went into it with his 2 disciples. •Judas the traitor knew the place well, since Jesus had often met his 3 disciples there, •and he brought the cohort*a* to this place together with a detachment of guards sent by the chief priests and the Pharisees, all with lanterns and 4 torches and weapons. •Knowing everything that was going to happen to him, 5 Jesus then came forward and said, 'Who are you looking for?' •They answered, 'Jesus the Nazarene'. He said, 'I am he'. Now Judas the traitor was standing 6 among them. •When Jesus said, 'I am he', they moved back and fell to the ground. 7 He asked them a second time, 'Who are you looking for?' They said, 'Jesus the

b. Lit. 'the son of perdition'.
18 a. A detachment from the Roman garrison in Jerusalem.

Nazarene'. •'I have told you that I am he' replied Jesus. 'If I am the one you 8
are looking for, let these others go.' •This was to fulfil the words he had spoken, 9
'Not one of those you gave me have I lost'.

Simon Peter, who carried a sword, drew it and wounded the high priest's ser- 10
vant, cutting off his right ear. The servant's name was Malchus. •Jesus said to 11
Peter, 'Put your sword back in its scabbard; am I not to drink the cup that the
Father has given me?'

Jesus before Annas and Caiaphas. Peter disowns him

The cohort and its captain and the Jewish guards seized Jesus and bound 12
him. •They took him first to Annas, because Annas was the father-in-law of 13
Caiaphas, who was high priest that year. •It was Caiaphas who had suggested 14
to the Jews, 'It is better for one man to die for the people'.

Simon Peter, with another disciple, followed Jesus. This disciple, who was 15
known to the high priest, went with Jesus into the high priest's palace, •but 16
Peter stayed outside the door. So the other disciple, the one known to the high
priest, went out, spoke to the woman who was keeping the door and brought
Peter in. •The maid on duty at the door said to Peter, 'Aren't you another of 17
that man's disciples?' He answered, 'I am not'. •Now it was cold, and the servants 18
and guards had lit a charcoal fire and were standing there warming themselves;
so Peter stood there too, warming himself with the others.

The high priest questioned Jesus about his disciples and his teaching. •Jesus ¹⁹₂₀
answered, 'I have spoken openly for all the world to hear; I have always taught
in the synagogue and in the Temple where all the Jews meet together: I have said
nothing in secret. •But why ask me? Ask my hearers what I taught: they know 21
what I said.' •At these words, one of the guards standing by gave Jesus a slap 22
in the face, saying, 'Is that the way to answer the high priest?' •Jesus replied, 'If 23
there is something wrong in what I said, point it out; but if there is no offence
in it, why do you strike me?' •Then Annas sent him, still bound, to Caiaphas 24
the high priest.

As Simon Peter stood there warming himself, someone said to him, 'Aren't 25
you another of his disciples?' He denied it saying, 'I am not'. •One of the high 26
priest's servants, a relation of the man whose ear Peter had cut off, said, 'Didn't
I see you in the garden with him?' •Again Peter denied it; and at once a cock 27
crew.

Jesus before Pilate

They then led Jesus from the house of Caiaphas to the Praetorium.ᵇ It was 28
now morning. They did not go into the Praetorium themselves or they would be
defiledᶜ and unable to eat the passover. •So Pilate came outside to them and 29
said, 'What charge do you bring against this man?' They replied, •'If he were 30
not a criminal, we should not be handing him over to you'. •Pilate said, 'Take 31
him yourselves, and try him by your own Law'. The Jews answered, 'We are not
allowed to put a man to death'. •This was to fulfil the words Jesus had spoken 32
indicating the way he was going to die.

So Pilate went back into the Praetorium and called Jesus to him, 'Are you 33
the king of the Jews?' he asked. •Jesus replied, 'Do you ask this of your own 34
accord, or have others spoken to you about me?' •Pilate answered, 'Am I a Jew? 35
It is your own people and the chief priests who have handed you over to me:
what have you done?' •Jesus replied, 'Mine is not a kingdom of this world; if 36
my kingdom were of this world, my men would have fought to prevent my being

37 surrendered to the Jews. But my kingdom is not of this kind.' •'So you are a king then?' said Pilate. 'It is you who say it' answered Jesus. 'Yes, I am a king. I was born for this, I came into the world for this: to bear witness to the truth;
38 and all who are on the side of truth listen to my voice.' •'Truth?' said Pilate 'What is that?'; and with that he went out again to the Jews and said, 'I find
39 no case against him. •But according to a custom of yours I should release one prisoner at the Passover; would you like me, then, to release the king of the
40 Jews?' •At this they shouted: 'Not this man,' they said 'but Barabbas'. Barabbas was a brigand.

${}^{1}_{2}$ **19** Pilate then had Jesus taken away and scourged; •and after this, the soldiers twisted some thorns into a crown and put it on his head, and dressed him
3 in a purple robe. •They kept coming up to him and saying, 'Hail, king of the Jews!'; and they slapped him in the face.

4   Pilate came outside again and said to them, 'Look, I am going to bring
5 him out to you to let you see that I find no case'. •Jesus then came out wearing
6 the crown of thorns and the purple robe. Pilate said, 'Here is the man'. •When they saw him the chief priests and the guards shouted, 'Crucify him! Crucify him!' Pilate said, 'Take him yourselves and crucify him: I can find no case against him'.
7 'We have a Law,' the Jews replied 'and according to that Law he ought to die, because he has claimed to be the Son of God.'

${}^{8}_{9}$ When Pilate heard them say this his fears increased. •Re-entering the Praetorium, he said to Jesus, 'Where do you come from?' But Jesus made no answer.
10 Pilate then said to him, 'Are you refusing to speak to me? Surely you know I
11 have power to release you and I have power to crucify you?' •'You would have no power over me' replied Jesus 'if it had not been given you from above; that is why the one who handed me over to you has the greater guilt.'

Jesus is condemned to death

12   From that moment Pilate was anxious to set him free, but the Jews shouted, 'If you set him free you are no friend of Caesar's; anyone who makes himself
13 king is defying Caesar'. •Hearing these words, Pilate had Jesus brought out, and seated himself on the chair of judgement at a place called the Pavement, in
14 Hebrew Gabbatha. •It was Passover Preparation Day, about the sixth hour.^{a}
15 'Here is your king' said Pilate to the Jews. •'Take him away, take him away!' they said. 'Crucify him!' 'Do you want me to crucify your king?' said Pilate.
16 The chief priests answered, 'We have no king except Caesar'. •So in the end Pilate handed him over to them to be crucified.

The crucifixion

17   They then took charge of Jesus, •and carrying his own cross he went out of the city to the place of the skull or, as it was called in Hebrew, Golgotha,
18 where they crucified him with two others, one on either side with Jesus in the
19 middle. •Pilate wrote out a notice and had it fixed to the cross; it ran: 'Jesus
20 the Nazarene, King of the Jews'. •This notice was read by many of the Jews, because the place where Jesus was crucified was not far from the city, and the
21 writing was in Hebrew, Latin and Greek. •So the Jewish chief priests said to

b. The judicial court of the Roman procurator.   **c.** By entering the house of a pagan. Cf. Lk 7:6.
19 a. On Preparation Day, the Passover supper was made ready for eating after sunset. The sixth hour is midday, by which time all leaven had to be removed from the house; during the feast only unleavened bread was eaten.

Pilate, 'You should not write "King of the Jews", but "This man said: I am King of the Jews" '. •Pilate answered, 'What I have written, I have written'.　　22

Christ's garments divided

When the soldiers had finished crucifying Jesus they took his clothing and 23 divided it into four shares, one for each soldier. His undergarment was seamless, woven in one piece from neck to hem; •so they said to one another, 'Instead of 24 tearing it, let's throw dice to decide who is to have it'. In this way the words of scripture were fulfilled:

> *They shared out my clothing among them.*
> *They cast lots for my clothes.*[b]

This is exactly what the soldiers did.

Jesus and his mother

Near the cross of Jesus stood his mother and his mother's sister, Mary the 25 wife of Clopas, and Mary of Magdala. •Seeing his mother and the disciple 26 he loved standing near her, Jesus said to his mother, 'Woman, this is your son'. Then to the disciple he said, 'This is your mother'. And from that moment the 27 disciple made a place for her in his home.

The death of Jesus

After this, Jesus knew that everything had now been completed, and to 28 fulfil the scripture perfectly he said:

> *'I am thirsty'.*[c]

A jar full of vinegar stood there, so putting a sponge soaked in the vinegar on 29 a hyssop stick they held it up to his mouth. •After Jesus had taken the vinegar 30 he said, 'It is accomplished'; and bowing his head he gave up his spirit.

The pierced Christ

It was Preparation Day, and to prevent the bodies remaining on the cross 31 during the sabbath—since that sabbath was a day of special solemnity—the Jews asked Pilate to have the legs broken[d] and the bodies taken away. •Consequently 32 the soldiers came and broke the legs of the first man who had been crucified with him and then of the other. •When they came to Jesus, they found he was already 33 dead, and so instead of breaking his legs •one of the soldiers pierced his side 34 with a lance; and immediately there came out blood and water. •This is the 35 evidence of one who saw it —trustworthy evidence, and he knows he speaks the truth—and he gives it so that you may believe as well. •Because all this happened 36 to fulfil the words of scripture:

> *Not one bone of his will be broken;*[e]

and again, in another place scripture says:　　　　　　　　　　　　　　　37

> *They will look on the one whom they have pierced.*[f]

The burial

After this, Joseph of Arimathaea, who was a disciple of Jesus—though a 38 secret one because he was afraid of the Jews—asked Pilate to let him remove the body of Jesus. Pilate gave permission, so they came and took it away.

39 Nicodemus came as well—the same one who had first come to Jesus at night-time
   —and he brought a mixture of myrrh and aloes, weighing about a hundred
40 pounds. •They took the body of Jesus and wrapped it with the spices in linen
41 cloths, following the Jewish burial custom. •At the place where he had been
   crucified there was a garden, and in this garden a new tomb in which no one
42 had yet been buried. •Since it was the Jewish Day of Preparation and the tomb
   was near at hand, they laid Jesus there.

VIII. THE DAY OF CHRIST'S RESURRECTION

The empty tomb

1 **20** It was very early on the first day of the week   and still dark, when Mary
         of Magdala came to the tomb. She saw that the stone had been moved
2 away from the tomb •and came running to Simon Peter and the other disciple,
   the one Jesus loved. 'They have taken the Lord out of the tomb' she said 'and
   we don't know where they have put him.'
3
4   So Peter set out with the other disciple to go to the tomb. •They ran together,
5 but the other disciple, running faster than Peter, reached the tomb first; •he bent
6 down and saw the linen cloths lying on the ground, but did not go in.   •Simon
   Peter who was following now came up, went right into the tomb, saw the linen
7 cloths on the ground, •and also the cloth that had been over his head; this was
8 not with the linen cloths but rolled up in a place by itself. •Then the other disciple
9 who had reached the tomb first also went in; he saw and he believed. •Till this
   moment they had failed to understand the teaching of scripture, that he must
10 rise from the dead. •The disciples then went home again.

The appearance to Mary of Magdala

11   Meanwhile Mary stayed outside near the tomb, weeping. Then, still weeping,
12 she stooped to look inside, •and saw two angels in white sitting where the body
13 of Jesus had been, one at the head, the other at the feet. •They said, 'Woman,
   why are you weeping?' 'They have taken my Lord away' she replied 'and I
14 don't know where they have put him.' •As she said this she turned round and
15 saw Jesus standing there, though she did not recognise him. •Jesus said, 'Woman,
   why are you weeping? Who are you looking for?' Supposing him to be the
   gardener, she said, 'Sir, if you have taken him away, tell me where you have put
16 him, and I will go and remove him'. •Jesus said, 'Mary!' She knew him then
17 and said to him in Hebrew, 'Rabbuni!'—which means Master. •Jesus said to
   her, 'Do not cling to me, because I have not yet ascended to the Father. But
   go and find the brothers, and tell them: I am ascending to my Father and your
18 Father, to my God and your God.' •So Mary of Magdala went and told the
   disciples that she had seen the Lord and that he had said these things to her.

Appearances to the disciples

19   In the evening of that same day, the first day of the week, the doors were
   closed in the room where the disciples were, for fear of the Jews. Jesus came
20 and stood among them. He said to them, 'Peace be with you', •and showed

b. Ps 22:18   c. Ps 22:15   d. To hasten death.   e. Two texts are here combined: Ps 34:20 and
Ex 12:46. The allusion is both to God protecting the good man, and to the ritual for preparing
the Passover lamb.   f. Zc 12:10

them his hands and his side. The disciples were filled with joy when they saw the Lord, •and he said to them again, 'Peace be with you. 21

'As the Father sent me,
so am I sending you.'

After saying this he breathed on them and said: 22

'Receive the Holy Spirit.
For those whose sins you forgive, 23
they are forgiven;
for those whose sins you retain,
they are retained.'

Thomas, called the Twin, who was one of the Twelve, was not with them 24 when Jesus came. •When the disciples said, 'We have seen the Lord', he ans- 25 wered, 'Unless I see the holes that the nails made in his hands and can put my finger into the holes they made, and unless I can put my hand into his side, I refuse to believe'. •Eight days later the disciples were in the house again and 26 Thomas was with them. The doors were closed, but Jesus came in and stood among them. 'Peace be with you' he said. •Then he spoke to Thomas, 'Put 27 your finger here; look, here are my hands. Give me your hand; put it into my side. Doubt no longer but believe.' •Thomas replied, 'My Lord and my God!' 28 Jesus said to him: 29

'You believe because you can see me.
Happy are those who have not seen and yet believe.'

CONCLUSION

There were many other signs that Jesus worked and the disciples saw, but 30 they are not recorded in this book. •These are recorded so that you may believe 31 that Jesus is the Christ, the Son of God, and that believing this you may have life through his name.

APPENDIX[a]

The appearance on the shore of Tiberias

21 Later on, Jesus showed himself again to the disciples. It was by the Sea 1 of Tiberias, and it happened like this: •Simon Peter, Thomas called the 2 Twin, Nathanael from Cana in Galilee, the sons of Zebedee and two more of his disciples were together. •Simon Peter said, 'I'm going fishing'. They replied, 3 'We'll come with you'. They went out and got into the boat but caught nothing that night.

It was light by now and there stood Jesus on the shore, though the disciples 4 did not realise that it was Jesus. •Jesus called out, 'Have you caught anything, 5 friends?' And when they answered, 'No', •he said, 'Throw the net out to starboard 6 and you'll find something'. So they dropped the net, and there were so many fish that they could not haul it in. •The disciple Jesus loved said to Peter, 'It is 7 the Lord'. At these words 'It is the Lord', Simon Peter, who had practically nothing on, wrapped his cloak round him and jumped into the water. •The 8 other disciples came on in the boat, towing the net and the fish; they were only about a hundred yards from land.

9 As soon as they came ashore they saw that there was some bread there, and
10 a charcoal fire with fish cooking on it. •Jesus said, 'Bring some of the fish you
11 have just caught'. •Simon Peter went aboard and dragged the net to the shore, full of big fish, one hundred and fifty-three of them; and in spite of there being
12 so many the net was not broken. •Jesus said to them, 'Come and have breakfast'. None of the disciples was bold enough to ask, 'Who are you?'; they knew quite
13 well it was the Lord. •Jesus then stepped forward, took the bread and gave it
14 to them, and the same with the fish. •This was the third time that Jesus showed himself to the disciples after rising from the dead.

15 After the meal Jesus said to Simon Peter, 'Simon son of John, do you love me more than these others do?' He answered, 'Yes Lord, you know I love you'.
16 Jesus said to him, 'Feed my lambs'. •A second time he said to him, 'Simon son of John, do you love me?' He replied, 'Yes, Lord, you know I love you'. Jesus
17 said to him, 'Look after my sheep'. •Then he said to him a third time, 'Simon son of John, do you love me?' Peter was upset that he asked him the third time, 'Do you love me?' and said, 'Lord, you know everything; you know I love you'. Jesus said to him, 'Feed my sheep.

18   'I tell you most solemnly,
             when you were young
             you put on your own belt
             and walked where you liked;
             but when you grow old
             you will stretch out your hands,
             and somebody else will put a belt round you
             and take you where you would rather not go.'

19 In these words he indicated the kind of death by which Peter would give glory to God. After this he said, 'Follow me'.
20 Peter turned and saw the disciple Jesus loved following them—the one who had leaned on his breast at the supper and had said to him, 'Lord, who is it that
21 will betray you?' •Seeing him, Peter said to Jesus, 'What about him, Lord?'
22 Jesus answered, 'If I want him to stay behind till I come, what does it matter
23 to you? You are to follow me.' •The rumour then went out among the brothers that this disciple would not die. Yet Jesus had not said to Peter, 'He will not die', but, 'If I want him to stay behind till I come'.

Conclusion

24 This disciple is the one who vouches for these things and has written them down, and we know that his testimony is true.
25 There were many other things that Jesus did; if all were written down, the world itself, I suppose, would not hold all the books that would have to be written.

21 a. Added either by the evangelist or by a disciple of his.

INTRODUCTION TO
THE ACTS OF THE APOSTLES

St Luke's Gospel and The Acts of the Apostles are the two volumes of a single work that today we should call 'a history of the rise of Christianity'. The two books are inseparably linked by their Prologues and by their style. From the text of Acts it is evident that the author was a Christian of the apostolic age, either a thoroughly hellenised Jew or more probably a well-educated 'Greek' with a thorough knowledge of the Septuagint and of Jewish culture and traditions. No other name has ever been suggested than that of Luke, the close friend of Paul, who according to an ancient tradition was a Syrian from Antioch, a doctor and a convert from paganism.

Acts is in the form of a single continuous narrative. It begins with the birth and growth of the primitive Christian community in Jerusalem and tells of the founding of the community in Antioch by hellenist Jews and the conversion of St Paul; it goes on to show the spread of the Church outside Palestine through the missionary travels of Paul and ends with his captivity in Rome in A.D. 61-63. The narrative can be seen to be made up of separate episodes of varying lengths, all containing a great deal of circumstantial detail and commonly joined to each other by editorial formulae.

For the later journeys of Paul, Luke appears to have his own notes; the rest of the book confirms the claim made in the Prologue of the first volume (Lk 1:1-4) that the author collected a large quantity of evidence from a variety of sources. In the editing of this, and the chronological arranging of it, a certain amount of repetition, fusion and anomalies in the order of incidents was unavoidable, but the basic reliability of the work may be seen by checking Luke's account of Paul's missionary activities with Paul's own letters, which were not among his sources. The historical worth of Acts is high, since it not only includes a major section which is an eye-witness account of the events described, but gives much detailed factual information which we should otherwise lack. Although Luke, like any other classical historian, took the freedom to reconstruct speeches which he had not himself heard, there is every evidence that he went back to true sources and treated them with respect: notice, for instance, the archaisms and semitisms left in the reported speeches of Peter and Stephen, and the remarkable distinction between the simple theological background of the earliest Christian sermons and that of Paul's later teaching. It is also to be noticed that he can include a speech which failed to convince its hearers.

Thus Acts is a principal source for much of our knowledge of life in the earliest Christian communities, of the first impact made by the Christian faith on pagan nations, of the primitive beginnings of church organisation, of the early developments of Christology, of the personalities of the apostolic age. Luke is, however, not interested in presenting a formal history of the spread of Christianity. What he is interested in is: 1. The spiritual energy inside Christianity that motivates its expansion, and 2. the spiritual doctrine that he can show by object lessons with the facts at his disposal.

THE ACTS
OF THE APOSTLES

Prologue

1 In my earlier work,*a* Theophilus, I dealt with everything Jesus had done and 1
taught from the beginning •until the day he gave his instructions to the 2
apostles he had chosen through the Holy Spirit, and was taken up to heaven.
He had shown himself alive to them after his Passion by many demonstrations: 3
for forty days he had continued to appear to them and tell them about the
kingdom of God. •When he had been at table with them, he had told them not 4
to leave Jerusalem, but to wait there for what the Father had promised. 'It is'
he had said 'what you have heard me speak about: •John baptised with water but 5
you, not many days from now, will be baptised with the Holy Spirit.'

The ascension

Now having met together,*b* they asked him, 'Lord, has the time come? Are 6
you going to restore the kingdom to Israel?' •He replied, 'It is not for you to 7
know times or dates that the Father has decided by his own authority, •but 8
you will receive power when the Holy Spirit comes on you, and then you will be
my witnesses not only in Jerusalem but throughout Judaea and Samaria, and
indeed to the ends of the earth'.

As he said this he was lifted up while they looked on, and a cloud took him 9
from their sight. •They were still staring into the sky when suddenly two men 10
in white were standing near them •and they said, 'Why are you men from Galilee 11
standing here looking into the sky? Jesus who has been taken up from you into
heaven, this same Jesus will come back in the same way as you have seen him
go there.'

I. THE JERUSALEM CHURCH

The group of apostles

So from the Mount of Olives, as it is called, they went back to Jerusalem, 12
a short distance away, no more than a sabbath walk; •and when they reached 13
the city they went to the upper room where they were staying; there were Peter
and John, James and Andrew, Philip and Thomas, Bartholomew and Matthew,
James son of Alphaeus and Simon the Zealot, and Jude son of James.*c* •All 14
these joined in continuous prayer, together with several women, including
Mary the mother of Jesus, and with his brothers.*d*

The election of Matthias

15 One day Peter stood up to speak to the brothers*^c*—there were about a
16 hundred and twenty persons in the congregation: •'Brothers, the passage of
scripture had to be fulfilled in which the Holy Spirit, speaking through David,
foretells the fate of Judas, who offered himself as a guide to the men who
17 arrested Jesus—•after having been one of our number and actually sharing this
18 ministry of ours. •As you know, he bought a field with the money he was paid
for his crime. He fell headlong and burst open, and all his entrails poured out.
19 Everybody in Jerusalem heard about it and the field came to be called the Bloody
20 Acre, in their language Hakeldama. •Now in the Book of Psalms it says:

> *Let his camp be reduced to ruin,*
> *Let there be no one to live in it.*^f

And again:

> *Let someone else take his office.*^g

21 'We must therefore choose someone who has been with us the whole time that
22 the Lord Jesus was travelling round with us, •someone who was with us right
from the time when John was baptising until the day when he was taken up from
us—and he can act with us as a witness to his resurrection.'

23 Having nominated two candidates, Joseph known as Barsabbas, whose
24 surname was Justus, and Matthias, •they prayed, 'Lord, you can read everyone's
25 heart; show us therefore which of these two you have chosen •to take over this
ministry and apostolate, which Judas abandoned to go to his proper place'.
26 They then drew lots for them, and as the lot fell to Matthias, he was listed as
one of the twelve apostles.

Pentecost

¹₂ 2 When Pentecost day came round, they had all met in one room, •when
suddenly they heard what sounded like a powerful wind from heaven, the
3 noise of which filled the entire house in which they were sitting; •and something
4 appeared to them that seemed like tongues of fire; these separated and came
to rest on the head of each of them. •They were all filled with the Holy Spirit,
and began to speak foreign languages as the Spirit gave them the gift of speech.
5 Now there were devout men living in Jerusalem from every nation under
6 heaven, •and at this sound they all assembled, each one bewildered to hear these
7 men speaking his own language. •They were amazed and astonished. 'Surely'
8 they said 'all these men speaking are Galileans? •How does it happen that each
9 of us hears them in his own native language? •Parthians, Medes and Elamites;
10 people from Mesopotamia, Judaea and Cappadocia, Pontus and Asia, •Phrygia
and Pamphylia, Egypt and the parts of Libya round Cyrene; as well as visitors
11 from Rome—•Jews and proselytes*^a* alike—Cretans and Arabs; we hear them
12 preaching in our own language about the marvels of God.' •Everyone was
amazed and unable to explain it; they asked one another what it all meant.

---

1 a. The gospel according to Luke.   **b.** This verse takes up the narrative broken off in
Lk 24:49.   **c.** 'Son' (of Alphaeus, of James) is not in the Greek. This Jude is not the Jude
'brother' of Jesus, Mt 13:55 and Mk 6:3, and brother of James (Jude 1). Nor is it likely that
'James of Alphaeus' was James brother of the Lord.   **d.** Cousins, as in the gospels.   **e.** The
term for Christians, usually the laity as distinct from apostles and elders.   **f.** Ps 69:25
g. Ps 109:8
2 a. Converts from paganism.

Some, however, laughed it off. 'They have been drinking too much new wine' 13 they said.

Peter's address to the crowd

Then Peter stood up with the Eleven and addressed them in a loud voice: 14
'Men of Judaea, and all you who live in Jerusalem, make no mistake about this, but listen carefully to what I say. •These men are not drunk, as you 15 imagine; why, it is only the third hour of the day.[b] •On the contrary, this is 16 what the prophet[c] spoke of:

In the days to come —it is the Lord who speaks— 17
I will pour out my spirit on all mankind.
Their sons and daughters shall prophesy,
your young men shall see visions,
your old men shall dream dreams.
Even on my slaves, men and women, 18
in those days, I will pour out my spirit.
I will display portents in heaven *above* 19
and *signs* on earth *below*.
The sun will be turned into darkness 20
and the moon into blood
before the great Day of the Lord dawns.
All who call on the name of the Lord will be saved. 21

'Men of Israel, listen to what I am going to say: Jesus the Nazarene was a 22 man commended to you by God by the miracles and portents and signs that God worked through him when he was among you, as you all know. •This 23 man, who was put into your power by the deliberate intention and foreknowledge of God, you took and had crucified by men outside the Law.[d] You killed him, but God raised him to life, freeing him from the pangs of Hades; for it was 24 impossible for him to be held in its power since, •as David says of him: 25

I saw the Lord before me always,
for with him at my right hand nothing can shake me.
So my heart was glad 26
and my tongue cried out with joy;
my body, too, will rest in the hope
that you will not abandon my soul to Hades 27
nor allow your holy one to experience corruption.
You have made known the way of life to me, 28
you will fill me with gladness through your presence.[e]

'Brothers, no one can deny that the patriarch David himself is dead and 29 buried: his tomb is still with us. •But since he was a prophet, and knew that 30 God *had sworn him* an oath *to make one of his descendants succeed him on the throne,[f]* •what he foresaw and spoke about was the resurrection of the Christ: 31 he is the one who was *not abandoned to Hades*, and whose body did not *experience corruption.* •God raised this man Jesus to life, and all of us are witnesses to that. 32 Now raised to the heights by God's right hand, he has received from the Father 33 the Holy Spirit, who was promised, and what you see and hear is the outpouring of that Spirit. •For David himself never went up to heaven; and yet these 34 words are his:

> *The Lord said to my Lord:*
> *Sit at my right hand*
35   *until I make your enemies*
> *a footstool for you.*[g]

36 'For this reason the whole House of Israel can be certain that God has made this Jesus whom you crucified both Lord and Christ.'

The first conversions

37 Hearing this, they were cut to the heart and said to Peter and the apostles,
38 'What must we do, brothers?' •You must repent,' Peter answered 'and every one of you must be baptised in the name of Jesus Christ for the forgiveness of
39 your sins, and you will receive the gift of the Holy Spirit. •The promise that was made is for you and your children, and for all *those who are far away, for all*
40 *those whom the Lord* our God *will call to himself.*'[h] •He spoke to them for a long time using many arguments, and he urged them, 'Save yourselves from this
41 perverse generation'. •They were convinced by his arguments, and they accepted what he said and were baptised. That very day about three thousand were added to their number.

The early Christian community

42 These remained faithful to the teaching of the apostles, to the brotherhood, to the breaking of bread and to the prayers.
43 The many miracles and signs worked through the apostles made a deep impression on everyone.
44
45 The faithful all lived together and owned everything in common; •they sold their goods and possessions and shared out the proceeds among themselves according to what each one needed.
46 They went as a body to the Temple every day but met in their houses for the
47 breaking of bread; they shared their food gladly and generously; •they praised God and were looked up to by everyone. Day by day the Lord added to their community those destined to be saved.

The cure of a lame man

1 **3** Once, when Peter and John were going up to the Temple for the prayers at
2 the ninth hour,[a] •it happened that there was a man being carried past. He was a cripple from birth; and they used to put him down every day near the Temple entrance called the Beautiful Gate so that he could beg from the people
3 going in. •When this man saw Peter and John on their way into the Temple he
4 begged from them. •Both Peter and John looked straight at him and said, 'Look
5 at us'. •He turned to them expectantly, hoping to get something from them,
6 but Peter said, 'I have neither silver nor gold, but I will give you what I have:
7 in the name of Jesus Christ the Nazarene, walk!' •Peter then took him by the hand and helped him to stand up. Instantly his feet and ankles became firm,
8 he jumped up, stood, and began to walk, and he went with them into the Temple,
9 walking and jumping and praising God. •Everyone could see him walking and

b. About 9 a.m.   **c.** Joel. See Jl 3:1-5.   **d.** The Romans.   **e.** Ps 16:8-11; quoted according to the LXX.   **f.** 2 S 7:12 and Ps 132:11   **g.** Ps 110:1   **h.** Is 57:19
3 a. The time of evening sacrifice.

praising God, •and they recognised him as the man who used to sit begging at 10 the Beautiful Gate of the Temple. They were all astonished and unable to explain what had happened to him.

Peter's address to the people

Everyone came running towards them in great excitement, to the Portico of 11 Solomon, as it is called, where the man was still clinging to Peter and John. When Peter saw the people he addressed them, 'Why are you so surprised at 12 this? Why are you staring at us as though we had made this man walk by our own power or holiness? •You are Israelites, and it is *the God of Abraham, Isaac* 13 *and Jacob, the God of our ancestors, who has glorified his servant*[b] Jesus, the same Jesus you handed over and then disowned in the presence of Pilate after Pilate had decided to release him. •It was you who accused the Holy One, the Just 14 One, you who demanded the reprieve of a murderer •while you killed the prince 15 of life. God, however, raised him from the dead, and to that fact we are the witnesses; •and it is the name of Jesus which, through our faith in it, has 16 brought back the strength of this man whom you see here and who is well known to you. It is faith in that name that has restored this man to health, as you can all see.

'Now I know, brothers, that neither you nor your leaders had any idea what 17 you were really doing; •this was the way God carried out what he had foretold, 18 when he said through all his prophets that his Christ would suffer. •Now you 19 must repent and turn to God, so that your sins may be wiped out, •and so 20 that the Lord may send the time of comfort. Then he will send you the Christ he has predestined, that is Jesus, •whom heaven must keep till the universal 21 restoration comes which God proclaimed, speaking through his holy prophets. Moses, for example, said: *The Lord God will raise up a prophet like myself for you,* 22 *from among your own brothers; you must listen to whatever he tells you. •The* 23 *man who does not listen to that prophet is to be cut off from the people.*[c] •In fact, 24 all the prophets that have ever spoken, from Samuel onwards, have predicted these days.

'You are the heirs of the prophets, the heirs of the covenant God made with 25 our ancestors when he told Abraham: *in your offspring all the families of the earth* *will be blessed.*[d] •It was for you in the first place that God raised up his servant 26 and sent him to bless you by turning every one of you from your wicked ways.'

Peter and John before the Sanhedrin

4 While they were still talking to the people the priests came up to them, accom- 1 panied by the captain of the Temple and the Sadducees.[a] •They were extremely 2 annoyed at their teaching the people the doctrine of the resurrection from the dead by proclaiming the resurrection of Jesus. •They arrested them, but as it 3 was already late, they held them till the next day. •But many of those who had 4 listened to their message became believers, the total number of whom had now risen to something like five thousand.

The next day the rulers, elders and scribes[b] had a meeting in Jerusalem •with 5/6 Annas the high priest, Caiaphas, Jonathan, Alexander and all the members of the high-priestly families. •They made the prisoners stand in the middle and 7 began to interrogate them, 'By what power, and by whose name have you men done this?' •Then Peter, filled with the Holy Spirit, addressed them, 'Rulers of 8

9 the people, and elders! •If you are questioning us today about an act of kindness
10 to a cripple, and asking us how he was healed, •then I am glad to tell you all,
and would indeed be glad to tell the whole people of Israel, that it was by the
name of Jesus Christ the Nazarene, the one you crucified, whom God raised
from the dead, by this name and by no other that this man is able to stand up
11 perfectly healthy, here in your presence, today. •This is *the stone rejected by you*
12 *the builders, but which has proved to be the keystone.*^c •For of all the names in the
world given to men, this is the only one by which we can be saved.'

13   They were astonished at the asssurance shown by Peter and John, considering
they were uneducated laymen; and they recognised them as associates of Jesus;
14 but when they saw the man who had been cured standing by their side, they could
15 find no answer. •So they ordered them to stand outside while the Sanhedrin had
16 a private discussion. •'What are we going to do with these men?' they asked.
'It is obvious to everybody in Jerusalem that a miracle has been worked through
17 them in public, and we cannot deny it. •But to stop the whole thing spreading
any further among the people, let us caution them never to speak to anyone in
this name again.'

18   So they called them in and gave them a warning on no account to make
19 statements or to teach in the name of Jesus. •But Peter and John retorted, 'You
20 must judge whether in God's eyes it is right to listen to you and not to God. •We
21 cannot promise to stop proclaiming what we have seen and heard.' •The court
repeated the warnings and then released them; they could not think of any way
to punish them, since all the people were giving glory to God for what
22 had happened. •The man who had been miraculously cured was over forty years
old.

The apostles' prayer under persecution

23   As soon as they were released they went to the community and told them
24 everything the chief priests and elders had said to them. •When they heard it
they lifted up their voice to God all together. 'Master,' they prayed 'it is you
25 who made heaven and earth and sea, and everything in them; •you it is who said
through the Holy Spirit and speaking through our ancestor David, your servant:

> *Why this arrogance among the nations,*
> *these futile plots among the peoples?*
26 > *Kings on earth setting out to war,*
> *princes making an alliance,*
> *against the Lord and against his Anointed.*^d

27   'This is what has come true: in this very city Herod and Pontius Pilate *made*
an alliance with the pagan *nations* and the *peoples* of Israel, against your holy
28 servant Jesus whom you *anointed*,^e •but only to bring about the very thing that you
29 in your strength and your wisdom had predetermined should happen. •And
now, Lord, take note of their threats and help your servants to proclaim your
30 message with all boldness, •by stretching out your hand to heal and to work
31 miracles and marvels through the name of your holy servant Jesus.' •As they
prayed, the house where they were assembled rocked; they were all filled with
the Holy Spirit and began to proclaim the word of God boldly.

b. Ex 3:6,15 and Is 52:13   c. Dt 18:18,19   d. Gn 12:3+
4 a. The Sadducees (see note on Mt 3:7) are always represented as denying the doctrine of the
resurrection, e.g. Ac 23.   **b.** I.e. the Sanhedrin, explained for the non-Jewish reader.
c. Ps 118:22   **d.** Ps 2:1-2   **e.** I.e. made the Christ, the anointed Messiah.

The early Christian community

The whole group of believers was united, heart and soul; no one claimed for 32 his own use anything that he had, as everything they owned was held in common.

The apostles continued to testify to the resurrection of the Lord Jesus with 33 great power, and they were all given great respect.

None of their members was ever in want, as all those who owned land or 34 houses would sell them, and bring the money from them, •to present it to the 35 apostles; it was then distributed to any members who might be in need.

The generosity of Barnabas

There was a Levite of Cypriot origin called Joseph whom the apostles surnamed 36 Barnabas (which means 'son of encouragement'). •He owned a piece of land 37 and he sold it and brought the money, and presented it to the apostles.

The fraud of Ananias and Sapphira

5 There was another man, however, called Ananias. He and his wife, Sapphira, 1 agreed to sell a property; •but with his wife's connivance he kept back part of 2 the proceeds, and brought the rest and presented it to the apostles. •'Ananias,' Peter 3 said 'how can Satan have so possessed you that you should lie to the Holy Spirit and keep back part of the money from the land? •While you still owned the land, 4 wasn't it yours to keep, and after you had sold it wasn't the money yours to do with as you liked? What put this scheme into your mind? It is not to men that you have lied, but to God.' •When he heard this Ananias fell down dead. This 5 made a profound impression on everyone present. •The younger men got up, 6 wrapped the body in a sheet, carried it out and buried it.

About three hours later his wife came in, not knowing what had taken place. 7 Peter challenged her, 'Tell me, was this the price you sold the land for?' 'Yes,' 8 she said 'that was the price.' •Peter then said, 'So you and your husband have 9 agreed to put the Spirit of the Lord to the test! What made you do it? You hear those footsteps? They have just been to bury your husband; they will carry you out, too.' •Instantly she dropped dead at his feet. When the young men came in they 10 found she was dead, and they carried her out and buried her by the side of her husband. •This made a profound impression on the whole Church and on all 11 who heard it.

The general situation

They all used to meet by common consent in the Portico of Solomon. •No one 12b / 13 else ever dared to join them, but the people were loud in their praise •and the 14 numbers of men and women who came to believe in the Lord increased steadily. So many signs and wonders were worked among the people at the hands of the 12a apostles •that the sick were even taken out into the streets and laid on beds and 15 sleeping-mats in the hope that at least the shadow of Peter might fall across some of them as he went past. •People even came crowding in from the towns round 16 about Jerusalem, bringing with them their sick and those tormented by unclean spirits, and all of them were cured.

The apostles' arrest and miraculous deliverance

Then the high priest intervened with all his supporters from the party of the 17 Sadducees. Prompted by jealousy, •they arrested the apostles and had them put 18 in the common gaol.

19 But at night the angel of the Lord opened the prison gates and said as he led
20 them out, ·'Go and stand in the Temple, and tell the people all about this new
21 Life'. ·They did as they were told; they went into the Temple at dawn and
began to preach.

A summons to appear before the Sanhedrin

When the high priest arrived, he and his supporters convened the Sanhedrin
—this was the full Senate of Israel—and sent to the gaol for them to be brought.
22 But when the officials arrived at the prison they found they were not inside, so
23 they went back and reported, ·'We found the gaol securely locked and the warders
on duty at the gates, but when we unlocked the door we found no one inside'.
24 When the captain of the Temple and the chief priests heard this news they
25 wondered what this could mean. ·Then a man arrived with fresh news.
'At this very moment' he said 'the men you imprisoned are in the Temple.
26 They are standing there preaching to the people.' ·The captain went with his
men and fetched them. They were afraid to use force in case the people stoned
them.
27 When they had brought them in to face the Sanhedrin, the high priest
28 demanded an explanation. ·'We gave you a formal warning' he said 'not to
preach in this name, and what have you done? You have filled Jerusalem with
your teaching, and seem determined to fix the guilt of this man's death on us.'
29 In reply Peter and the apostles said, 'Obedience to God comes before obedience
30 to men; ·it was the God of our ancestors who raised up Jesus, but it was you
31 who had him executed by hanging on a tree.*a* ·By his own right hand God has
now raised him up to be leader and saviour, to give repentance and forgiveness
32 of sins through him to Israel. ·We are witnesses to all this, we and the Holy
33 Spirit whom God has given to those who obey him.' ·This so infuriated them
that they wanted to put them to death.

Gamaliel's intervention

34 One member of the Sanhedrin, however, a Pharisee called Gamaliel, who was
a doctor of the Law and respected by the whole people,*b* stood up and asked
35 to have the men taken outside for a time. ·Then he addressed the Sanhedrin,
36 'Men of Israel, be careful how you deal with these people. ·There was Theudas
who became notorious not so long ago. He claimed to be someone important,
and he even collected about four hundred followers; but when he was killed,
37 all his followers scattered and that was the end of them. ·And then there was
Judas the Galilean, at the time of the census, who attracted crowds of supporters;
38 but he got killed too, and all his followers dispersed. ·What I suggest, therefore,
is that you leave these men alone and let them go. If this enterprise, this movement
39 of theirs, is of human origin it will break up of its own accord; ·but if it does in
fact come from God you will not only be unable to destroy them, but you might
find yourselves fighting against God.'
40 His advice was accepted; ·and they had the apostles called in, gave orders
for them to be flogged, warned them not to speak in the name of Jesus and
41 released them. ·And so they left the presence of the Sanhedrin glad to have had
the honour of suffering humiliation for the sake of the name.

5 a. The phrase recalls Dt 21:23.   **b.** Gamaliel I, a Pharisee of the school of Hillel; he was
Paul's teacher.

They preached every day both in the Temple and in private houses, and their 42
proclamation of the Good News of Christ Jesus was never interrupted.

II. THE EARLIEST MISSIONS

The institution of the Seven

6 About this time, when the number of disciples was increasing, the Hellenists 1
made a complaint against the Hebrews:[a] in the daily distribution their own
widows were being overlooked. •So the Twelve called a full meeting of the 2
disciples and addressed them, 'It would not be right for us to neglect the word
of God so as to give out food; •you, brothers, must select from among yourselves 3
seven men of good reputation, filled with the Spirit and with wisdom; we will
hand over this duty to them, •and continue to devote ourselves to prayer and 4
to the service of the word'. •The whole assembly approved of this proposal and 5
elected Stephen, a man full of faith and of the Holy Spirit, together with Philip,
Prochorus, Nicanor, Timon, Parmenas, and Nicolaus of Antioch, a convert to
Judaism. •They presented these to the apostles, who prayed and laid their hands 6
on them.[b]

The word of the Lord continued to spread: the number of disciples in Jeru- 7
salem was greatly increased, and a large group of priests made their submission
to the faith.

Stephen's arrest

Stephen was filled with grace and power and began to work miracles and 8
great signs among the people. •But then certain people came forward to debate 9
with Stephen, some from Cyrene and Alexandria who were members of the
synagogue called the Synagogue of Freedmen,[c] and others from Cilicia and Asia.
They found they could not get the better of him because of his wisdom, and 10
because it was the Spirit that prompted what he said. •So they procured some 11
men to say, 'We heard him using blasphemous language against Moses and against
God'. •Having in this way turned the people against him as well as the elders 12
and scribes, they took Stephen by surprise, and arrested him and brought him
before the Sanhedrin. •There they put up false witnesses to say, 'This man 13
is always making speeches against this Holy Place and the Law. •We have heard 14
him say that Jesus the Nazarene is going to destroy this Place and alter the
traditions that Moses handed down to us.' •The members of the Sanhedrin all 15
looked intently at Stephen, and his face appeared to them like the face of an
angel.

Stephen's speech

7 The high priest asked, 'Is this true?' •He replied, 'My brothers, my fathers, 1
listen to what I have to say. The God of glory appeared to our ancestor Abraham, 2
while he was in Mesopotamia before settling in Haran, •*and said to him*, "*Leave* 3
your country and your family and go to the land I will show you".[a] •So he left 4
Chaldaea and settled in Haran; and after his father died God made him leave
Haran and come to this land where you are living today. •God did not give him 5
a single square foot of this land to call his own, yet he promised to *give it to him
and after him to his descendants, childless*[b] though he was. •The actual words God 6
used when he spoke to him are that *his descendants would be exiles in a foreign land,*

7 *where they would be slaves and oppressed for four hundred years.* •*"But I will pass judgement on the nation that enslaves them"* God said *"and after this they will leave,*
8 *and worship me in this* place."ᶜ •Then he made the covenant of circumcision: so when his son Isaac was born he circumcised him on the eighth day. Isaac did the same for Jacob, and Jacob for the twelve patriarchs.

9   'The patriarchs were *jealous of Joseph and sold him into slavery in Egypt.*ᵈ But
10 *God was with him,*ᵉ •and rescued him from all his miseries by making him wise enough to attract the attention of Pharaoh king of Egypt, who *made him governor*
11 *of Egypt*ᶠ and put him in charge of the royal household. •*Then a famine came* that caused much suffering *throughout Egypt and Canaan,* and our ancestors could
12 find nothing to eat. •When Jacob *heard that there was grain for sale in Egypt,*
13 he sent our ancestors there on a first visit, •but it was on the second that *Joseph*
14 *made himself known to his brothers,* and told Pharaoh about his family. •Joseph then sent for his father Jacob and his whole family, a total of *seventy-five people.*
15 Jacob went down into Egypt and after he and our ancestors had died there,
16 their bodies were brought back to Shechem and buried in the tomb that Abraham had bought and paid for from the sons of Hamor, the father of Shechem.

17   'As the time drew near for God to fulfil the promise he had solemnly made
18 to Abraham, our nation in Egypt *grew larger and larger,* •*until a new king came*
19 *to power in Egypt who knew nothing of*ᵍ Joseph. •*He exploited* our race, and ill-treated our ancestors, forcing them to expose their babies to prevent their
20 surviving. •It was at this period that Moses was born, *a fine child* and favoured
21 by God. He was looked after for three months in his father's house, •and after he had been exposed, *Pharaoh's daughter* adopted him and *brought him up*
22 *as her own son.* •So Moses was taught all the wisdom of the Egyptians and became a man with power both in his speech and his actions.

23
24   'At the age of forty he decided to visit *his countrymen, the sons of Israel.* •When he saw one of them being ill-treated he went to his defence and rescued the man by
25 *killing the Egyptian.* •He thought his brothers realised that through him God
26 would liberate them, but they did not. •The next day, when he came across some of them fighting, he tried to reconcile them. 'Friends,' he said 'you are
27 brothers; why are you hurting each other?' •But *the man who was attacking his fellow countryman* pushed him aside. '*And who appointed you*' he said '*to be our*
28 *leader and judge?* • *Do you intend to kill me as you killed the Egyptian yesterday?*'
29 Moses fled when he heard thisʰ and *he went to stay in the land of Midian,* where he became the father of two sons.

30   'Forty years later, *in the wilderness* near Mount Sinai, *an angel appeared to him*
31 *in the flames of a bush* that was on fire. •Moses was amazed by what he saw.
32 *As he went nearer to look at it the voice of the Lord was heard,* •"*I am the God of your ancestors, the God of Abraham, Isaac and Jacob*". Moses trembled and *did not*
33 *dare to look any more.* •The Lord said to him, "*Take off your shoes; the place where*
34 *you are standing is holy ground.* •*I have seen the way my people are ill-treated in*

6 a. 'Hellenists': Jews from outside Palestine; they had their own synagogues in Jerusalem, where the scriptures were read in Greek. The 'Hebrews' were Palestinian Jews and in their synagogues scriptures were read in Hebrew.   b. 'and they prayed and laid their hands on them'; probably meaning the apostles, handing over their duties as in v.3.   c. Probably the descendants of Jews carried off to Rome, 63 B.C. and sold as slaves but later released.
7 a. Gn 12:1   b. Gn 15:2   c. Gn 15:2,13,14; Ex 3:12   d. Gn 37   e. Gn 39   f. Gn 41. Other direct quotations and allusions in this paragraph are from Gn 42-50.   g. O.T. quotations from here to v. 35 are from Ex 1-3.   h. In Ex 2:15 Moses runs away because he is afraid of Pharaoh.

Egypt, I have heard their groans, and I have come down to liberate them. So come here and let me send you into Egypt."

'It was the same Moses that they had disowned when they said, "*Who 35 appointed you to be our leader and judge?*" who was now sent to be both leader and redeemer through the angel who had appeared to him in the bush. •It was 36 Moses who, after performing *miracles and signs in Egypt*, led them out across the Red Sea and *through the wilderness for forty years.*[i] •It was Moses who told the 37 sons of Israel, "*God will raise up a prophet like myself for you from among your own brothers*".[j] •When they held the assembly in the wilderness it was only 38 through Moses that our ancestors could communicate with the angel who had spoken to him on Mount Sinai; it was he who was entrusted with words of life to hand on to us. •This is the man that our ancestors refused to listen to: they 39 pushed him aside, *turned back to Egypt* in their thoughts, •*and said to Aaron,* 40 "*Make some gods to be our leaders; we do not understand what has come over this Moses who led us out of Egypt*"[k] •It was then that *they made a bull calf and offered* 41 *sacrifice* to the idol. They were perfectly happy with something they had made for themselves. •God turned away from them and abandoned them to the 42 worship of the army of heaven,[l] as scripture says in the book of the prophets:

> *Did you bring me victims and sacrifices in the wilderness*
> *for all those forty years, you House of Israel?*
> *No, you carried the tent of Moloch on your shoulders*   43
> *and the star of the god Rephan,*
> *those idols that you had made to adore.*
> *So now I will exile you even further than Babylon.*[m]

'While they were in the desert our ancestors possessed the Tent of Testimony 44 that had been constructed according to the instructions God gave Moses, telling him to *make an exact copy of the pattern*[n] he had been shown. •It was handed 45 down from one ancestor of ours to another until Joshua brought it into the country we had conquered from the nations which were driven out by God as we advanced. Here it stayed until the time of David. •He won God's favour and 46 asked permission *to have a temple built for* the House of *Jacob*, •though it was 47 *Solomon* who actually *built God's house*[o] for him. •Even so the Most High does 48 not live in a house that human hands have built: for as the prophet says:

> *With heaven my throne*   49
> *and earth my footstool,*
> *what house could you build me,*
> *what place could you make for my rest?*
> *Was not all this made by my hand?*[p]   50

'You stubborn people, with your pagan hearts and pagan ears. You are always 51 resisting the Holy Spirit, just as your ancestors used to do. •Can you name 52 a single prophet your ancestors never persecuted? In the past they killed those who foretold the coming of the Just One, and now you have become his betrayers, his murderers. •You who had the Law brought to you by angels are 53 the very ones who have not kept it.'

They were infuriated when they heard this, and ground their teeth at him.   54

The stoning of Stephen. Saul as persecutor

But Stephen, filled with the Holy Spirit, gazed into heaven and saw the glory 55 of God, and Jesus standing at God's right hand. •'I can see heaven thrown open' 56

57 he said 'and the Son of Man standing at the right hand of God.' ·At this all the members of the council shouted out and stopped their ears with their hands; then 58 they all rushed at him, ·sent him out of the city and stoned him. The wit- 59 nesses[q] put down their clothes at the feet of a young man called Saul. ·As they were stoning him, Stephen said in invocation, 'Lord Jesus, receive my spirit'. 60 Then he knelt down and said aloud, 'Lord, do not hold this sin against them'; 1 and with these words he fell asleep. **8** Saul entirely approved of the killing.

That day a bitter persecution started against the church in Jerusalem, and everyone[a] except the apostles fled to the country districts of Judaea and Samaria.

2 There were some devout people, however, who buried Stephen and made great mourning for him.

3 Saul then worked for the total destruction of the Church; he went from house to house arresting both men and women and sending them to prison.

Philip in Samaria

4 Those who had escaped went from place to place preaching the Good News. 5 One of them was Philip who went to a Samaritan town and proclaimed the 6 Christ to them. ·The people united in welcoming the message Philip preached, either because they had heard of the miracles he worked or because they saw 7 them for themselves. ·There were, for example, unclean spirits that came shrieking out of many who were possessed, and several paralytics and cripples were cured. 8 As a result there was great rejoicing in that town.

Simon the magician

9 Now a man called Simon had already practised magic arts in the town and astounded the Samaritan people. He had given it out that he was someone 10 momentous, ·and everyone believed what he said; eminent citizens and ordinary 11 people alike had declared, 'He is the divine power that is called Great'. ·They had only been won over to him because of the long time he had spent working 12 on them with his magic. ·But when they believed Philip's preaching of the Good News about the kingdom of God and the name of Jesus Christ, they were 13 baptised, both men and women, ·and even Simon himself became a believer. After his baptism Simon, who went round constantly with Philip, was astonished when he saw the wonders and great miracles that took place.

14 When the apostles in Jerusalem heard that Samaria had accepted the word 15 of God, they sent Peter and John to them, ·and they went down there, and 16 prayed for the Samaritans to receive the Holy Spirit, ·for as yet he had not come down on any of them: they had only been baptised in the name of the Lord Jesus. 17 Then they laid hands on them, and they received the Holy Spirit.

18 When Simon saw that the Spirit was given through the imposition of hands 19 by the apostles, he offered them some money. ·'Give me the same power' he said 20 'so that anyone I lay my hands on will receive the Holy Spirit.' ·Peter answered, 'May your silver be lost forever, and you with it, for thinking that money could 21 buy what God has given for nothing! ·You have no share, no rights, in this: 22 God can see how your heart is warped. ·Repent of this wickedness of yours, and 23 pray to the Lord; you may still be forgiven for thinking as you did; ·it is plain

---

i. Nb 14:33   j. Dt 18:15,18   k. Ex 32:1,23 and 32:4,6   l. The stars and planets.   m. Am 5:25-27 (LXX)   n. Ex 25:40   o. 1 K 6:2   p. Is 66:1-2   q. By the Law, the accusers had to begin the execution of the sentence.

8 a. The persecution seems to have been directed principally against the Hellenists. .

to me that you are trapped in the bitterness of gall and the chains of sin.'
'Pray to the Lord for me yourselves' Simon replied ' so that none of the things 24
you have spoken about may happen to me.'

Having given their testimony and proclaimed the word of the Lord, they went 25
back to Jerusalem, preaching the Good News to a number of Samaritan villages.

Philip baptises a eunuch

The angel of the Lord spoke to Philip saying, 'Be ready to set out at noon 26
along the road that goes from Jerusalem down to Gaza, the desert road'. •So he 27
set off on his journey. Now it happened that an Ethiopian had been on pilgrimage
to Jerusalem; he was a eunuch and an officer at the court of the kandake, or
queen, of Ethiopia, and was in fact her chief treasurer. •He was now on his way 28
home; and as he sat in his chariot he was reading the prophet Isaiah. •The 29
Spirit said to Philip, 'Go up and meet that chariot'. •When Philip ran up, he 30
heard him reading Isaiah the prophet and asked, 'Do you understand what you
are reading?' •'How can I' he replied 'unless I have someone to guide me?' So 31
he invited Philip to get in and sit by his side. •Now the passage of scripture he 32
was reading was this:

> *Like a sheep that is led to the slaughter-house,*
> *like a lamb that is dumb in front of its shearers,*
> *like these he never opens his mouth.*
> *He has been humiliated and has no one to defend him.*   33
> *Who will ever talk about his descendants,*
> *since his life on earth has been cut short !* [b]

The eunuch turned to Philip and said, 'Tell me, is the prophet referring to 34
himself or someone else?' •Starting, therefore, with this text of scripture Philip 35
proceeded to explain the Good News of Jesus to him.

Further along the road they came to some water, and the eunuch said, 'Look, 36
there is some water here; is there anything to stop me being baptised?[c] •He 38
ordered the chariot to stop, then Philip and the eunuch both went down into
the water and Philip baptised him. •But after they had come up out of the water 39
again Philip was taken away by the Spirit of the Lord, and the eunuch never
saw him again but went on his way rejoicing. •Philip found that he had reached 40
Azotus and continued his journey proclaiming the Good News in every town as far
as Caesarea.

The conversion of Saul

9 Meanwhile Saul was still breathing threats to slaughter the Lord's disciples. 1
He had gone to the high priest •and asked for letters addressed to the 2
synagogues in Damascus, that would authorise him to arrest and take to Jerusalem
any followers of the Way, men or women, that he could find.

Suddenly, while he was travelling to Damascus and just before he reached 3
the city, there came a light from heaven all round him. •He fell to the ground, 4
and then he heard a voice saying, 'Saul, Saul, why are you persecuting me?'
'Who are you, Lord?' he asked, and the voice answered, 'I am Jesus, and you 5
are persecuting me. •Get up now and go into the city, and you will be told what 6
you have to do.' •The men travelling with Saul stood there speechless, for 7
though they heard the voice they could see no one. •Saul got up from the ground, 8
but even with his eyes wide open he could see nothing at all, and they had to lead

9 him into Damascus by the hand. •For three days he was without his sight, and took neither food nor drink.

10 A disciple called Ananias who lived in Damascus had a vision in which he
11 heard the Lord say to him, 'Ananias!' When he replied, 'Here I am, Lord', •the Lord said, 'You must go to Straight Street and ask at the house of Judas for someone called Saul, who comes from Tarsus. At this moment he is praying,
12 having had a vision of a man called Ananias coming in and laying hands on him to give him back his sight.'

13 When he heard that, Ananias said, 'Lord, several people have told me about
14 this man and all the harm he has been doing to your saints in Jerusalem. •He has only come here because he holds a warrant from the chief priests to arrest
15 everybody who invokes your name.' •The Lord replied, 'You must go all the same, because this man is my chosen instrument to bring my name before pagans
16 and pagan kings and before the people of Israel; •I myself will show him how
17 much he himself must suffer for my name'. •Then Ananias went. He entered the house, and at once laid his hands on Saul and said, 'Brother Saul, I have been sent by the Lord Jesus who appeared to you on your way here so that you may
18 recover your sight and be filled with the Holy Spirit'. •Immediately it was as though scales fell away from Saul's eyes and he could see again. So he was
19 baptised there and then, •and after taking some food he regained his strength.

Saul's preaching at Damascus

20 After he had spent only a few days with the disciples in Damascus, •he began
21 preaching in the synagogues, 'Jesus is the Son of God'. •All his hearers were amazed. 'Surely' they said 'this is the man who organised the attack in Jerusalem against the people who invoke this name, and who came here for the sole
22 purpose of arresting them to have them tried by the chief priests?' •Saul's power increased steadily, and he was able to throw the Jewish colony at Damascus into complete confusion by the way he demonstrated that Jesus was the Christ.

23
24 Some time passed,[a] and the Jews worked out a plot to kill him, •but news of it reached Saul. To make sure of killing him they kept watch on the gates day
25 and night, •but when it was dark the disciples took him and let him down from the top of the wall, lowering him in a basket.

Saul's visit to Jerusalem

26 When he got to Jerusalem he tried to join the disciples, but they were all
27 afraid of him: they could not believe he was really a disciple. •Barnabas, however, took charge of him, introduced him to the apostles, and explained how the Lord had appeared to Saul and spoken to him on his journey, and how he
28 had preached boldly at Damascus in the name of Jesus. •Saul now started to go round with them in Jerusalem, preaching fearlessly in the name of the Lord.
29 But after he had spoken to the Hellenists, and argued with them, they became
30 determined to kill him. •When the brothers knew, they took him to Caesarea, and sent him off from there to Tarsus.

---

b. Is 53:7-8, quoted from the LXX version.   c. At the time when verse numbers were introduced, there was a gloss, numbered v. 37, at this point.
9 a. Three years, according to Ga 1:17-18.

A lull

The churches throughout Judaea, Galilee and Samaria were now left in peace, 31 building themselves up, living in the fear of the Lord, and filled with the consolation of the Holy Spirit.

Peter cures a paralytic at Lydda

Peter visited one place after another and eventually came to the saints living 32 down in Lydda. •There he found a man called Aeneas, a paralytic who had been 33 bedridden for eight years. •Peter said to him, 'Aeneas, Jesus Christ cures you: 34 get up and fold up your sleeping mat'. Aeneas got up immediately; •everybody 35 who lived in Lydda and Sharon saw him, and they were all converted to the Lord.

Peter raises a woman to life at Jaffa

At Jaffa there was a woman disciple called Tabitha, or Dorcas in Greek,[b] 36 who never tired of doing good or giving in charity. •But the time came when she 37 got ill and died, and they washed her and laid her out in a room upstairs. •Lydda 38 is not far from Jaffa, so when the disciples heard that Peter was there, they sent two men with an urgent message for him, 'Come and visit us as soon as possible'.

Peter went back with them straightaway, and on his arrival they took him 39 to the upstairs room, where all the widows stood round him in tears, showing him tunics and other clothes Dorcas had made when she was with them. •Peter 40 sent them all out of the room and knelt down and prayed. Then he turned to the dead woman and said, 'Tabitha, stand up'. She opened her eyes, looked at Peter and sat up. •Peter helped her to her feet, then he called in the saints and 41 widows and showed them she was alive. •The whole of Jaffa heard about it and 42 many believed in the Lord.

Peter stayed on some time in Jaffa, lodging with a leather-tanner called Simon. 43

Peter visits a Roman centurion

10 One of the centurions of the Italica cohort stationed in Caesarea was 1 called Cornelius. •He and the whole of his household were devout and 2 God-fearing, and he gave generously to Jewish causes and prayed constantly to God.

One day at about the ninth hour he had a vision in which he distinctly saw 3 the angel of God come into his house and call out to him, 'Cornelius!' •He stared 4 at the vision in terror and exclaimed, 'What is it, Lord?' 'Your offering of prayers and alms' the angel answered 'has been accepted by God. •Now you must send 5 someone to Jaffa and fetch a man called Simon, known as Peter, •who is lodging 6 with Simon the tanner whose house is by the sea.' •When the angel who said 7 this had gone, Cornelius called two of the slaves and a devout soldier of his staff, told them what had happened, and sent them off to Jaffa. 8

Next day, while they were still on their journey and had only a short distance 9 to go before reaching Jaffa, Peter went to the housetop at about the sixth hour to pray. •He felt hungry and was looking forward to his meal, but before it was 10 ready he fell into a trance •and saw heaven thrown open and something like a big 11 sheet being let down to earth by its four corners; •it contained every possible 12 sort of animal and bird, walking, crawling or flying ones. •A voice then said 13 to him, 'Now, Peter; kill and eat!' •But Peter answered, 'Certainly not, Lord; 14 I have never yet eaten anything profane or unclean'. •Again, a second time, the 15 voice spoke to him, 'What God has made clean, you have no right to call

16 profane'. •This was repeated three times, and then suddenly the container was
drawn up to heaven again.

17   Peter was still worrying over the meaning of the vision he had seen, when the
men sent by Cornelius arrived. They had asked where Simon's house was and
18 they were now standing at the door, •calling out to know if the Simon known as
19 Peter was lodging there. •Peter's mind was still on the vision and the Spirit had
20 to tell him, 'Some men have come to see you. •Hurry down, and do not hesitate
21 about going back with them; it was I who told them to come.' •Peter went down
22 and said to them, 'I am the man you are looking for; why have you come?' •They
said, 'The centurion Cornelius, who is an upright and God-fearing man, highly
regarded by the entire Jewish people, was directed by a holy angel to send for you
23 and bring you to his house and to listen to what you have to say'. •So Peter
asked them in and gave them lodging.

Next day, he was ready to go off with them, accompanied by some of the
24 brothers from Jaffa. •They reached Caesarea the following day, and Cornelius
was waiting for them. He had asked his relations and close friends to be there,
25 and as Peter reached the house Cornelius went out to meet him, knelt at his feet
26 and prostrated himself. •But Peter helped him up. 'Stand up,' he said 'I am only
27 a man after all!' •Talking together they went in to meet all the people assembled
28 there, •and Peter said to them, 'You know it is forbidden for Jews to mix with
people of another race and visit them, but God has made it clear to me that
29 I must not call anyone profane or unclean. •That is why I made no objection
to coming when I was sent for; but I should like to know exactly why you
30 sent for me.' •Cornelius replied, 'Three days ago I was praying in my house
at the ninth hour, when I suddenly saw a man in front of me in shining robes.
31 He said, "Cornelius, your prayer has been heard and your alms have been
32 accepted as a sacrifice in the sight of God; •so now you must send to Jaffa and
fetch Simon known as Peter who is lodging in the house of Simon the tanner, by
33 the sea". •So I sent for you at once, and you have been kind enough to come.
Here we all are, assembled in front of you to hear what message God has given
you for us.'

Peter's address in the house of Cornelius

34   Then Peter addressed them: 'The truth I have now come to realise' he said
35 'is that God does not have favourites, •but that anybody of any nationality who
fears God and does what is right is acceptable to him.

36   'It is true, God sent his word to the people of Israel, and it was to them that
the good news of peace was brought[a] by Jesus Christ—but Jesus Christ is Lord of
37 all men. •You must have heard about the recent happenings in Judaea; about
Jesus of Nazareth and how he began in Galilee, after John had been preaching
38 baptism. •*God had anointed him with the Holy Spirit*[b] and with power, and because
God was with him, Jesus went about doing good and curing all who had fallen
39 into the power of the devil. •Now I, and those with me, can witness to everything
he did throughout the countryside of Judaea and in Jerusalem itself: and also
40 to the fact that they killed him by hanging him on a tree, •yet three days afterwards
41 God raised him to life and allowed him to be seen, •not by the whole people
but only by certain witnesses God had chosen beforehand. Now we are those
witnesses—we have eaten and drunk with him after his resurrection from the

b. I.e. 'Gazelle'.
10 a. Is 52:7   b. Is 61:1

dead—•and he has ordered us to proclaim this to his people and to tell them 42
that God has appointed him to judge everyone, alive or dead. •It is to him that 43
all the prophets bear this witness: that all who believe in Jesus will have their sins
forgiven through his name.'

Baptism of the first pagans

While Peter was still speaking the Holy Spirit came down on all the listeners. 44
Jewish believers who had accompanied Peter were all astonished that the gift 45
of the Holy Spirit should be poured out on the pagans too, •since they could 46
hear them speaking strange languages and proclaiming the greatness of God.
Peter himself then said, •'Could anyone refuse the water of baptism to these 47
people, now they have received the Holy Spirit just as much as we have?' •He 48
then gave orders for them to be baptised in the name of Jesus Christ. Afterwards they begged him to stay on for some days.

Jerusalem: Peter justifies his conduct

11 The apostles and the brothers in Judaea heard that the pagans too had 1
accepted the word of God, •and when Peter came up to Jerusalem the 2
Jews criticised him •and said, 'So you have been visiting the uncircumcised 3
and eating with them, have you?' •Peter in reply gave them the details point by 4
point: •'One day, when I was in the town of Jaffa,' he began 'I fell into a trance as 5
I was praying and had a vision of something like a big sheet being let down from
heaven by its four corners. This sheet reached the ground quite close to me.
I watched it intently and saw all sorts of animals and wild beasts—everything 6
possible that could walk, crawl or fly. •Then I heard a voice that said to me, "Now, 7
Peter; kill and eat!" •But I answered: Certainly not, Lord; nothing profane or 8
unclean has ever crossed my lips. •And a second time the voice spoke from 9
heaven, "What God has made clean, you have no right to call profane". •This 10
was repeated three times, before the whole of it was drawn up to heaven again.

'Just at that moment, three men stopped outside the house where we were 11
staying; they had been sent from Caesarea' to fetch me, •and the Spirit told me 12
to have no hesitation about going back with them. The six brothers here came
with me as well, and we entered the man's house. •He told us he had seen an angel 13
standing in his house who said, "Send to Jaffa and fetch Simon known as Peter;
he has a message for you that will save you and your entire household".   14

'I had scarcely begun to speak when the Holy Spirit came down on them 15
in the same way as it came on us at the beginning, •and I remembered that the 16
Lord had said, "John baptised with water, but you will be baptised with the Holy
Spirit". •I realised then that God was giving them the identical thing he gave to us 17
when we believed in the Lord Jesus Christ; and who was I to stand in God's way?'

This account satisfied them, and they gave glory to God. 'God' they said 'can 18
evidently grant even the pagans the repentance that leads to life.'

Foundation of the church of Antioch

Those who had escaped during the persecution that happened because of
Stephen travelled as far as Phoenicia and Cyprus and Antioch,*ᵃ* but they usually 19
proclaimed the message only to Jews. •Some of them, however, who came from
Cyprus and Cyrene, went to Antioch where they started preaching to the Greeks, 20
proclaiming the Good News of the Lord Jesus to them as well. •The Lord helped
them, and a great number believed and were converted to the Lord.   21

The church[b] in Jerusalem heard about this and they sent Barnabas to Antioch.
22 There he could see for himself that God had given grace, and this pleased him,
23 and he urged them all to remain faithful to the Lord with heartfelt devotion;
for he was a good man, filled with the Holy Spirit and with faith. And a large
24 number of people were won over to the Lord.
25
26 Barnabas then left for Tarsus to look for Saul, •and when he found him he
brought him to Antioch. As things turned out they were to live together in that
church a whole year, instructing a large number of people. It was at Antioch
that the disciples were first called 'Christians'.

Barnabas and Saul sent as deputies to Jerusalem

27 While they were there some prophets[b] came down to Antioch from Jerusalem,
28 and one of them whose name was Agabus, seized by the Spirit, stood up and
predicted that a famine would spread over the whole empire. This in fact happened
29 before the reign of Claudius came to an end.[c] •The disciples decided to send
relief, each to contribute what he could afford, to the brothers living in Judaea.
30 They did this and delivered their contributions to the elders in the care of
Barnabas and Saul.

Peter's arrest and miraculous deliverance[a]

1 **12** It was about this time that King Herod started persecuting certain members
2
3 of the Church. •He beheaded James the brother of John, •and when he
4 saw that this pleased the Jews he decided to arrest Peter as well. •This was during
the days of Unleavened Bread, and he put Peter in prison, assigning four squads
of four soldiers each to guard him in turns. Herod meant to try Peter in public
5 after the end of Passover week. •All the time Peter was under guard the Church
prayed to God for him unremittingly.
6 On the night before Herod was to try him, Peter was sleeping between two
soldiers, fastened with double chains, while guards kept watch at the main
7 entrance to the prison. •Then suddenly the angel of the Lord stood there, and
the cell was filled with light. He tapped Peter on the side and woke him. 'Get up!'
8 he said 'Hurry!'—and the chains fell from his hands. •The angel then said, 'Put
on your belt and sandals'. After he had done this, the angel next said, 'Wrap
9 your cloak round you and follow me'. •Peter followed him, but had no idea that
what the angel did was all happening in reality; he thought he was seeing a vision.
10 They passed through two guard posts one after the other, and reached the iron
gate leading to the city. This opened of its own accord; they went through it
and had walked the whole length of one street when suddenly the angel left him.
11 It was only then that Peter came to himself. 'Now I know it is all true' he said.
'The Lord really did send his angel and has saved me from Herod and from all
that the Jewish people were so certain would happen to me.'
12 As soon as he realised this he went straight to the house of Mary the mother
13 of John Mark,[b] where a number of people had assembled and were praying. •He

11 a. Antioch on the Orontes, capital of Syria. **b.** Christian prophets, inspired speakers,
generally ranked second to the apostles in the lists of the persons 'gifted by the Spirit'.
c. Claudius reigned until 54 A.D.
12 a. Herod Agrippa I was king of Judaea and Samaria, 41-44 A.D. This episode, though
fitted in the book between 11:30 and 12:25, must have taken place before Barnabas and Saul
visited Jerusalem. **b.** Mark is mentioned in ch. 12,13 and 15: also in Col 4 and Phm 24 and
2 Tim 4. Tradition names him as author of the second gospel.

knocked at the outside door and a servant called Rhoda came to answer it. •She 14
recognised Peter's voice and was so overcome with joy that, instead of opening
the door, she ran inside with the news that Peter was standing at the main entrance.
They said to her, 'You are out of your mind', but she insisted that it was true. 15
Then they said, 'It must be his angel!' •Peter, meanwhile, was still knocking, 16
so they opened the door and were amazed to see that it really was Peter himself.
With a gesture of his hand he stopped them talking, and described to them how 17
the Lord had led him out of prison. He added, 'Tell James and the brothers'.
Then he left and went to another place.

When daylight came there was a great commotion among the soldiers, who 18
could not imagine what had become of Peter. •Herod put out an unsuccessful 19
search for him; he had the guards questioned, and before leaving Judaea to take
up residence in Caesarea he gave orders for their execution.

The death of the persecutor

Now Herod was on bad terms with the Tyrians and Sidonians. However, they 20
sent a joint deputation which managed to enlist the support of Blastus, the king's
chamberlain, and through him negotiated a treaty, since their country depended
for its food supply on King Herod's territory. •A day was fixed, and Herod, 21
wearing his robes of state and enthroned on a dais, made a speech to them.
The people acclaimed him with, 'It is a god speaking, not a man!', •and at ²²₂₃
that moment the angel of the Lord struck him down, because he had not given
the glory to God. He was eaten away with worms and died.

Barnabas and Saul return to Antioch

The word of God continued to spread and to gain followers. •Barnabas and ²⁴₂₅
Saul completed their task and came back from Jerusalem, bringing John Mark
with them.

III. THE MISSION OF BARNABAS AND PAUL
THE COUNCIL OF JERUSALEM

The mission sent out

13 In the church at Antioch the following were prophets and teachers: Bar- 1
nabas, Simeon called Niger, and Lucius of Cyrene, Manaen, who had
been brought up with Herod the tetrarch, and Saul. •One day while they were 2
offering worship to the Lord and keeping a fast, the Holy Spirit said, 'I want
Barnabas and Saul set apart for the work to which I have called them'. •So it was 3
that after fasting and prayer they laid their hands on them and sent them off.

Cyprus: the magician Elymas

So these two, sent on their mission by the Holy Spirit, went down to Seleucia 4
and from there sailed to Cyprus. •They landed at Salamis and proclaimed the 5
word of God in the synagogues of the Jews; John acted as their assistant.

They travelled the whole length of the island, and at Paphos they came in 6
contact with a Jewish magician called Bar-jesus. •This false prophet was one 7
of the attendants of the proconsul Sergius Paulus who was an extremely intelligent
man. The proconsul summoned Barnabas and Saul and asked to hear the word

8 of God, •but Elymas Magos—as he was called in Greek—tried to stop them
9 so as to prevent the proconsul's conversion to the faith. •Then Saul, whose other
10 name is Paul, looked him full in the face •and said, 'You utter fraud, you
impostor, you son of the devil, you enemy of all true religion, why don't you
11 stop twisting the straightforward ways of the Lord? •Now watch how the hand
of the Lord will strike you: you will be blind, and for a time you will not see the
sun.' That instant, everything went misty and dark for him, and he groped about
12 to find someone to lead him by the hand. •The proconsul, who had watched
everything, became a believer, being astonished by what he had learnt about
the Lord.

They arrive at Antioch in Pisidia

13 Paul and his friends went by sea from Paphos to Perga in Pamphylia where
14 John left them to go back to Jerusalem. •The others carried on from Perga till they
reached Antioch in Pisidia. Here they went to synagogue on the sabbath and took
15 their seats. •After the lessons from the Law and the Prophets had been read,
the presidents of the synagogue sent them a message: 'Brothers, if you would
like to address some words of encouragement to the congregation, please do so'.
16 Paul stood up, held up a hand for silence and began to speak:

Paul's preaching before the Jews

17 'Men of Israel, and fearers of God, listen! •The God of our nation Israel
chose our ancestors, and made our people great when they were living as foreigners
18 in Egypt; then by divine power he led them out, •and for about forty years *took*
19 *care of them in the wilderness.* • *When he had destroyed seven nations in Canaan,*
20 *he put them in possession*[a] of their land •for about four hundred and fifty years.
21 After this he gave them judges, down to the prophet Samuel. •Then they
demanded a king, and God gave them Saul son of Kish, a man of the tribe of
22 Benjamin. After forty years, •he deposed him and made David their king, of
whom he approved in these words, "*I have selected David son of Jesse, a man after*
23 *my own heart, who will carry out my whole purpose*".[b] •To keep his promise, God
24 has raised up for Israel one of David's descendants, Jesus, as Saviour, •whose
coming was heralded by John when he proclaimed a baptism of repentance for the
25 whole people of Israel. •Before John ended his career he said, "I am not the one
you imagine me to be; that one is coming after me and I am not fit to undo his
sandal".

26 'My brothers, sons of Abraham's race, and all you who fear God, this message
27 of salvation is meant for you. •What the people of Jerusalem and their rulers
did, though they did not realise it, was in fact to fulfil the prophecies read on every
28 sabbath. •Though they found nothing to justify his death, they condemned him
29 and asked Pilate to have him executed. •When they had carried out everything
that scripture foretells about him they took him down from the tree and buried
30 31 him in a tomb. •But God raised him from the dead, •and for many days he
appeared to those who had accompanied him from Galilee to Jerusalem: and
it is these same companions of his who are now his witnesses before our people.
32 'We have come here to tell you the Good News. It was to our ancestors that
33 God made the promise but •it is to us, their children, that he has fulfilled it,
by raising Jesus from the dead. As scripture says in the first psalm: *You are my*

13 a. Dt 1:31; 7:1   **b.** 1 S 13:14

son: today I have become your father. •The fact that God raised him from the 34
dead, never to return to corruption, is no more than what he had declared: *To
you I shall give the sure and holy things promised to David.*[c] •This is explained by 35
another text: *You will not allow your holy one to experience corruption.*[d] •Now when 36
David in his own time had served God's purposes he died; he was buried with
his ancestors and has certainly *experienced corruption.* •The one whom God has 37
raised up, however, has not *experienced corruption.*

'My brothers, I want you to realise that it is through him that forgiveness of 38
your sins is proclaimed. Through him justification from all sins which the Law
of Moses was unable to justify •is offered to every believer. 39

'So be careful—or what the prophets say will happen to you. 40

> *Cast your eyes around you, mockers;* 41
> *be amazed, and.perish!*
> *For I am doing something in your own days*
> *that you would not believe if you were to be told of it.*[e]

As they left they were asked to preach on the same theme the following 42
sabbath. •When the meeting broke up many Jews and devout converts joined 43
Paul and Barnabas, and in their talks with them Paul and Barnabas urged
them to remain faithful to the grace God had given them.

Paul and Barnabas preach to the pagans

The next sabbath almost the whole town assembled to hear the word of God. 44
When they saw the crowds, the Jews, prompted by jealousy, used blasphemies 45
and contradicted everything Paul said. •Then Paul and Barnabas spoke out 46
boldly. 'We had to proclaim the word of God to you first, but since you have
rejected it, since you do not think yourselves worthy of eternal life, we must turn
to the pagans. •For this is what the Lord commanded us to do when he said: 47

> *I have made you a light for the nations,*
> *so that my salvation may reach the ends of the earth.*[f]

It made the pagans very happy to hear this and they thanked the Lord for his 48
message; all who were destined for eternal life became believers. •Thus the 49
word of the Lord spread through the whole countryside.

But the Jews worked upon some of the devout women of the upper 50
classes and the leading men of the city and persuaded them to turn against Paul
and Barnabas and expel them from their territory. •So they shook the dust 51
from their feet in defiance and went off to Iconium; •but the disciples were filled 52
with joy and the Holy Spirit.

Iconium evangelised

14 At Iconium they went to the Jewish synagogue, as they had at Antioch, 1
and they spoke so effectively that a great many Jews and Greeks became
believers.

Some of the Jews, however, refused to believe, and they poisoned the minds 2
of the pagans against the brothers.[a]

Accordingly Paul and Barnabas stayed on for some time, preaching fearlessly 3
for the Lord; and the Lord supported all they said about his gift of grace, allowing
signs and wonders to be performed by them.

The people in the city were divided, some supported the Jews, others the 4

5 apostles, •but eventually with the connivance of the authorities a move was
made by pagans as well as Jews to make attacks on them and to stone them.
6 When the apostles came to hear of this, they went off for safety to Lycaonia where,
7 in the towns of Lystra and Derbe and in the surrounding country, •they preached
the Good News.

Healing of a cripple

8 A man sat there[b] who had never walked in his life, because his feet were
9 crippled from birth; •and as he listened to Paul preaching, he managed to catch
10 his eye. Seeing that the man had the faith to be cured, •Paul said in a loud voice,
'Get to your feet—stand up', and the cripple jumped up and began to walk.
11 When the crowd saw what Paul had done they shouted in the language of
Lycaonia, 'These people are gods who have come down to us disguised as men'.
12 They addressed Barnabas as Zeus, and since Paul was the principal speaker they
13 called him Hermes.[c] •The priests of Zeus-outside-the-Gate, proposing that all
the people should offer sacrifice with them, brought garlanded oxen to the gates.
14 When the apostles Barnabas and Paul heard what was happening they tore their
15 clothes,[d] and rushed into the crowd, shouting, •'Friends, what do you think you
are doing? We are only human beings like you. We have come with good news
to make you turn from these empty idols to the living God who made heaven
16 and earth and the sea and all that these hold. •In the past he allowed each nation
17 to go its own way; •but even then he did not leave you without evidence of himself
in the good things he does for you: he sends you rain from heaven, he makes your
18 crops grow when they should, he gives you food and makes you happy.' •Even
this speech, however, was scarcely enough to stop the crowd offering them
sacrifice.

The mission is disrupted

19 Then some Jews arrived from Antioch and Iconium, and turned the people
against the apostles. They stoned Paul and dragged him outside the town,
20 thinking he was dead. •The disciples came crowding round him but, as they did
so, he stood up and went back to the town. The next day he and Barnabas went
off to Derbe.
21 Having preached the Good News in that town and made a considerable number
22 of disciples, they went back through Lystra and Iconium to Antioch. •They put
fresh heart into the disciples, encouraging them to persevere in the faith. 'We
all have to experience many hardships' they said 'before we enter the kingdom
23 of God.' •In each of these churches they appointed elders, and with prayer and
fasting they commended them to the Lord in whom they had come to believe.
24 They passed through Pisidia and reached Pamphylia. •Then after proclaiming
25
26 the word at Perga they went down to Attalia •and from there sailed for Antioch,
where they had originally been commended to the grace of God for the work
they had now completed.
27 On their arrival they assembled the church and gave an account of all that
God had done with them, and how he had opened the door of faith to the pagans.
28 They stayed there with the disciples for some time.

c. Is 55:3   d. Ps 16:9   e. Hab 1:5   f. Is 49:6, quoted freely from the LXX.
14 a. This sentence is a parenthesis. V.3 continues from v.1.   b. In Lystra.   c. Mercury,
the messenger or herald of the gods.   d. Conventional sign of despair.

Controversy at Antioch

15 Then some men came down from Judaea[a] and taught the brothers, 'Unless 1
you have yourselves circumcised in the tradition of Moses you cannot be
saved'.•This led to disagreement, and after Paul and Barnabas had had a long 2
argument with these men it was arranged that Paul and Barnabas and others of
the church should go up to Jerusalem and discuss the problem with the apostles
and elders.

All the members of the church saw them off, and as they passed through 3
Phoenicia and Samaria they told how the pagans had been converted, and this
news was received with the greatest satisfaction by the brothers. •When they 4
arrived in Jerusalem they were welcomed by the church and by the apostles and
elders, and gave an account of all that God had done with them.

Controversy at Jerusalem

But certain members of the Pharisees' party who had become believers 5
objected, insisting that the pagans should be circumcised and instructed to keep
the Law of Moses. •The apostles and elders met to look into the matter, •and ⁶⁄₇
after the discussion had gone on a long time, Peter stood up and addressed them.

Peter's speech

'My brothers,' he said 'you know perfectly well that in the early days God
made his choice among you: the pagans were to learn the Good News from me
and so become believers. •In fact God, who can read everyone's heart, showed his 8
approval of them by giving the Holy Spirit to them just as he had to us. •God 9
made no distinction between us and them, since he purified their hearts by faith.
It would only provoke God's anger now, surely, if you imposed on the disciples 10
the very burden that neither we nor our ancestors were strong enough to support?
Remember, we believe that we are saved in the same way as they are: through 11
the grace of the Lord Jesus.'

This silenced the entire assembly, and they listened to Barnabas and Paul 12
describing all the signs and wonders God had worked through them among the
pagans.

James' speech

When they had finished it was James who spoke. 'My brothers,' he said 13
'listen to me. •Simeon[b] has described how God first arranged to enlist a people 14
for his name out of the pagans. •This is entirely in harmony with the words of the 15
prophets, since the scriptures say:

> *After that I shall return* 16
> *and rebuild the fallen House of David;*
> *I shall rebuild it from its ruins*
> *and restore it.*
> *Then the rest of mankind,* 17
> *all the pagans who are consecrated to my name,*
> *will look for the Lord,*
> *says the Lord who made this •known so long ago.[c]* 18

'I rule, then, that instead of making things more difficult for pagans who 19
turn to God, •we send them a letter telling them merely to abstain from anything 20
polluted by idols,[d] from fornication,[e] from the meat of strangled animals and

21 from blood. •For Moses has always had his preachers in every town, and is read aloud in the synagogues every sabbath.'

The apostolic letter

22 Then the apostles and elders decided to choose delegates to send to Antioch with Paul and Barnabas; the whole church concurred with this. They chose Judas known as Barsabbas and Silas,*f* both leading men in the brotherhood, 23 and gave them this letter to take with them:

'The apostles and elders, your brothers, send greetings to the brothers of pagan 24 birth in Antioch, Syria and Cilicia. •We hear that some of our members have disturbed you with their demands and have unsettled your minds. They acted 25 without any authority from us, •and so we have decided unanimously to elect delegates and to send them to you with Barnabas and Paul, men we highly respect 26/27 who have dedicated their lives to the name of our Lord Jesus Christ. •Accordingly we are sending you Judas and Silas, who will confirm by word of mouth 28 what we have written in this letter. •It has been decided by the Holy Spirit and by 29 ourselves not to saddle you with any burden beyond these essentials: •you are to abstain from food sacrificed to idols, from blood, from the meat of strangled animals and from fornication. Avoid these, and you will do what is right. Farewell.'

The delegates at Antioch

30 The party left and went down to Antioch, where they summoned the whole 31 community and delivered the letter. •The community read it and were delighted 32 with the encouragement it gave them. •Judas and Silas, being themselves prophets, 33 spoke for a long time, encouraging and strengthening the brothers. •These two spent some time there, and then the brothers wished them peace and they went 35 back to those who had sent them. •Paul and Barnabas, however, stayed on in Antioch, and there with many others they taught and proclaimed the Good News, the word of the Lord.

IV PAUL'S MISSIONS

Paul separates from Barnabas and recruits Silas

36 On a later occasion Paul said to Barnabas, 'Let us go back and visit all the towns where we preached the word of the Lord, so that we can see how 37/38 the brothers are doing' •Barnabas suggested taking John Mark, •but Paul was not in favour of taking along the very man who had deserted them in Pamphylia and had refused to share in their work.

39 After a violent quarrel they parted company, and Barnabas sailed off with 40 Mark to Cyprus. •Before Paul left, he chose Silas to accompany him and was commended by the brothers to the grace of God.

15 a. In the allusion to this incident in Ga, they are said to have come 'from James', Ga 2:12. b. Semitic form of Simon Peter's name.   c. Am 9:11,12, quoted according to the LXX. d. I.e. which has been offered in sacrifice to false gods.   e. Perhaps all the irregular marriages listed in Lv 18.   f. Silas, also mentioned in Ac 18; 1 Th, 2 Th, 2 Co, 1 P.

Lycaonia: Paul recruits Timothy

He travelled through Syria and Cilicia, consolidating the churches.   41

16 From there he went to Derbe, and then on to Lystra. Here there was a 1
disciple called Timothy, whose mother was a Jewess who had become a
believer; but his father was a Greek. •The brothers at Lystra and Iconium spoke 2
well of Timothy, •and Paul, who wanted to have him as a travelling companion, 3
had him circumcised. This was on account of the Jews in the locality where
everyone knew his father was a Greek.

As they visited one town after another, they passed on the decisions reached 4
by the apostles and elders in Jerusalem, with instructions to respect them.

So the churches grew strong in the faith, as well as growing daily in numbers. 5

The crossing into Asia Minor

They travelled through Phrygia and the Galatian country, having been told 6
by the Holy Spirit not to preach the word in Asia. •When they reached the frontier 7
of Mysia they thought to cross it into Bithynia, but as the Spirit of Jesus would
not allow them, •they went through Mysia and came down to Troas.   8

One night Paul had a vision: a Macedonian appeared and appealed to him 9
in these words, 'Come across to Macedonia and help us'. •Once he had seen this 10
vision we lost no time in arranging a passage to Macedonia, convinced that God
had called us to bring them the Good News.

Arrival at Philippi

Sailing from Troas we made a straight run for Samothrace; the next day for 11
Neapolis, •and from there for Philippi, a Roman colony and the principal city 12
of that particular district of Macedonia. After a few days in this city •we went 13
along the river outside the gates as it was the sabbath and this was a customary
place for prayer.*a* We sat down and preached to the women who had come to the
meeting. •One of these women was called Lydia, a devout woman from the town 14
of Thyatira who was in the purple-dye trade. She listened to us, and the Lord
opened her heart to accept what Paul was saying. •After she and her household 15
had been baptised she sent us an invitation: 'If you really think me a true believer
in the Lord,' she said 'come and stay with us'; and she would take no refusal.

Imprisonment of Paul and Silas

One day as we were going to prayer, we met a slave-girl who was a soothsayer 16
and made a lot of money for her masters by telling fortunes. •This girl started 17
following Paul and the rest of us and shouting, 'Here are the servants of the Most
High God; they have come to tell you how to be saved!' •She did this every day 18
afterwards until Paul lost his temper one day and turned round and said to the
spirit, 'I order you in the name of Jesus Christ to leave that woman'. The spirit
went out of her then and there.

When her masters saw that there was no hope of making any more money 19
out of her, they seized Paul and Silas and dragged them to the law courts in the
market place •where they charged them before the magistrates and said, 'These 20
people are causing a disturbance in our city. They are Jews •and are advocating 21
practices which it is unlawful for us as Romans to accept or follow.'*b* •The crowd 22
joined in and showed its hostility to them, so the magistrates had them stripped
and ordered them to be flogged. •They were given many lashes and then thrown 23
into prison, and the gaoler was told to keep a close watch on them. •So, following 24

his instructions, he threw them into the inner prison and fastened their feet in the stocks.

The miraculous deliverance of Paul and Silas

25 Late that night Paul and Silas were praying and singing God's praises, while
26 the other prisoners listened. •Suddenly there was an earthquake that shook the prison to its foundations. All the doors flew open and the chains fell from all the
27 prisoners. •When the gaoler woke and saw the doors wide open he drew his sword
28 and was about to commit suicide, presuming that the prisoners had escaped. •But Paul shouted at the top of his voice, 'Don't do yourself any harm; we are all here'.
29 The gaoler called for lights, then rushed in, threw himself trembling at the
30 feet of Paul and Silas, •and escorted them out, saying, 'Sirs, what must I do to be
31 saved?' •They told him, 'Become a believer in the Lord Jesus, and you will be
32 saved, and your household too'. •Then they preached the word of the Lord to
33 him and to all his family. •Late as it was, he took them to wash their wounds,
34 and was baptised then and there with all his household. •Afterwards he took them home and gave them a meal, and the whole family celebrated their conversion to belief in God.

35 When it was daylight the magistrates sent the officers with the order: 'Release
36 those men'. •The gaoler reported the message to Paul, 'The magistrates have
37 sent an order for your release; you can go now and be on your way'. •'What!' Paul replied 'They flog Roman citizens in public and without trial and throw us into prison, and then think they can push us out on the quiet! Oh no! They must come and escort us out themselves.'

38 The officers reported this to the magistrates, who were horrified to hear the
39 men were Roman citizens. •They came and begged them to leave the town.
40 From the prison they went to Lydia's house where they saw all the brothers and gave them some encouragement; then they left.

Thessalonika: difficulties with the Jews

1 **17** Passing through Amphipolis and Apollonia, they eventually reached
2 Thessalonika, where there was a Jewish synagogue. •Paul as usual introduced himself and for three consecutive sabbaths developed the arguments from
3 scripture for them, •explaining and proving how it was ordained that the Christ should suffer and rise from the dead. 'And the Christ' he said 'is this Jesus whom
4 I am proclaiming to you.' •Some of them were convinced and joined Paul and Silas, and so did a great many God-fearing people and Greeks, as well as a number of rich women.

5 The Jews, full of resentment, enlisted the help of a gang from the market place, stirred up a crowd, and soon had the whole city in an uproar. They made for Jason's house, hoping to find them there and drag them off to the People's
6 Assembly; •however, they only found Jason and some of the brothers, and these they dragged before the city council, shouting, 'The people who have been
7 turning the whole world upside down have come here now; •they have been staying at Jason's. They have broken every one of Caesar's edicts by claiming
8 that there is another emperor, Jesus.' •This accusation alarmed the citizens
9 and the city councillors •and they made Jason and the rest give security before setting them free.

16 a. There was no synagogue in this Latin city; the Jews met by the river for ritual ablutions.
b. The Jews had no right to proselytise Romans.

Fresh difficulties at Beroea

When it was dark the brothers immediately sent Paul and Silas away to Beroea, 10 where they visited the Jewish synagogue as soon as they arrived. •Here the Jews 11 were more open-minded than those in Thessalonika, and they welcomed the word very readily; every day they studied the scriptures to check whether it was true. Many Jews became believers, and so did many Greek women from the upper 12 classes and a number of the men.

When the Jews of Thessalonika heard that the word of God was being preached 13 by Paul in Beroea as well, they went there to make trouble and stir up the people. So the brothers arranged for Paul to go immediately as far as the coast, leaving 14 Silas and Timothy behind. •Paul's escort took him as far as Athens, and went 15 back with instructions for Silas and Timothy to rejoin Paul as soon as they could.

Paul in Athens

Paul waited for them in Athens and there his whole soul was revolted at the 16 sight of a city given over to idolatry. •In the synagogue he held debates with the 17 Jews and the God-fearing, but in the market place he had debates every day with anyone who would face him. •Even a few Epicurean and Stoic philosophers 18 argued with him. Some said, 'Does this parrot know what he's talking about?' And, because he was preaching about Jesus and the resurrection, others said, 'He sounds like a propagandist for some outlandish gods .[a]

They invited him to accompany them to the Council of the Areopagus, where 19 they said to him, 'How much of this new teaching you were speaking about are we allowed to know? •Some of the things you said seemed startling to us and we 20 would like to find out what they mean.' •The one amusement the Athenians and 21 the foreigners living there seem to have, apart from discussing the latest ideas, is listening to lectures about them.

So Paul stood before the whole Council of the Areopagus and made this 22 speech:

Paul's speech before the Council of the Areopagus

'Men of Athens, I have seen for myself how extremely scrupulous you are in all religious matters, •because I noticed, as I strolled round admiring your 23 sacred monuments, that you had an altar inscribed: To An Unknown God. Well, the God whom I proclaim is in fact the one whom you already worship without knowing it.

'Since the God who made the world and everything in it is himself Lord of 24 heaven and earth, he does not make his home in shrines made by human hands. Nor is he dependent on anything that human hands can do for him, since he can 25 never be in need of anything; on the contrary, it is he who gives everything— including life and breath—to everyone. •From one single stock he not only 26 created the whole human race so that they could occupy the entire earth, but he decreed how long each nation should flourish and what the boundaries of its territory should be. •And he did this so that all nations might seek the deity 27 and, by feeling their way towards him, succeed in finding him. Yet in fact he is not far from any of us, •since it is in him that we live, and move, and exist,[b] as indeed 28 some of your own writers have said:

"We are all his children".[c]

29   'Since we are the children of God, we have no excuse for thinking that the deity looks like anything in gold, silver or stone that has been carved and designed by a man.

30   'God overlooked that sort of thing when men were ignorant, but now he is
31   telling everyone everywhere that they must repent, •because he has fixed a day when the whole world will be judged, and judged in righteousness, and he has appointed a man to be the judge. And God has publicly proved this by raising this man from the dead.'

32   At this mention of rising from the dead, some of them burst out laughing;
33   others said, 'We would like to hear you talk about this again'. •After that Paul
34   left them, •but there were some who attached themselves to him and became believers, among them Dionysius the Areopagite and a woman called Damaris, and others besides.

Foundation of the church of Corinth

$\frac{1}{2}$ **18** After this Paul left Athens and went to Corinth, •where he met a Jew called Aquila whose family came from Pontus. He and his wife Priscilla[a] had recently left Italy because an edict of Claudius had expelled all the Jews from
3   Rome.[b] Paul went to visit them, •and when he found they were tentmakers, of the
4   same trade as himself, he lodged with them, and they worked together. •Every sabbath he used to hold debates in the synagogues, trying to convert Jews as well as Greeks.

5   After Silas and Timothy had arrived from Macedonia, Paul devoted all his
6   time to preaching, declaring to the Jews that Jesus was the Christ. •When they turned against him and started to insult him, he took his cloak and shook it out in front of them, saying, 'Your blood be on your own heads; from now on I can
7   go to the pagans with a clear conscience'. •Then he left the synagogue and moved to the house next door that belonged to a worshipper of God called Justus.
8   Crispus, president of the synagogue, and his whole household, all became believers in the Lord. A great many Corinthians who had heard. him became believers and
9   were baptised. •One night the Lord spoke to Paul in a vision, 'Do not be afraid
10   to speak out, nor allow yourself to be silenced: •I am with you. I have so many
11   people on my side in this city that no one will even attempt to hurt you.' •So Paul stayed there preaching the word of God among them for eighteen months.

The Jews take Paul to court

12   But while Gallio was proconsul of Achaia,[c] the Jews made a concerted attack
13   on Paul and brought him before the tribunal. •'We accuse this man' they said
14   'of persuading people to worship God in a way that breaks the Law.' •Before Paul could open his mouth, Gallio said to the Jews, 'Listen, you Jews. If this were
15   a misdemeanour or a crime, I would not hesitate to attend to you; •but if it is only quibbles about words and names, and about your own Law, then you must deal with it yourselves—I have no intention of making legal decisions about things
$\frac{16}{17}$ like that.' •Then he sent them out of the court, •and at once they all turned on Sosthenes, the synagogue president, and beat him in front of the court house. Gallio refused to take any notice at all.

---

17 a. They assumed that *Anastasis* ('Resurrection') was the name of a goddess.   **b.** Expression suggested by the poet Epimenides.   **c.** From the *Phainomena* of Aratus.
18 a. Also called Prisca, Rm 16:3; 1 Co 16:19; 2 Tm 4:19.   **b.** This edict was issued in 49 or 50.   **c.** In 52, according to an inscription from Delphi.

Return to Antioch and departure for the third journey

After staying on for some time, Paul took leave of the brothers and sailed for 18 Syria, [d] accompanied by Priscilla and Aquila. At Cenchreae he had his hair cut off, because of a vow he had made.

When they reached Ephesus, he left them, but first he went alone to the 19 synagogue to debate with the Jews. •They asked him to stay longer but he declined, 20 though when he left he said, 'I will come back another time, God willing'. Then 21 he sailed from Ephesus.

He landed at Caesarea, and went up to greet the church. Then he came down 22 to Antioch •where he spent a short time before continuing his journey 23 through the Galatian country and then through Phrygia, encouraging all the followers.

Apollos

An Alexandrian Jew named Apollos now arrived in Ephesus. He was an 24 eloquent man, with a sound knowledge of the scriptures, and yet, •though he had 25 been given instruction in the Way of the Lord and preached with great spiritual earnestness and was accurate in all the details he taught about Jesus, he had only experienced the baptism of John. •When Priscilla and Aquila heard him speak 26 boldly in the synagogue, they took an interest in him and gave him further instruction about the Way.

When Apollos thought of crossing over to Achaia, the brothers encouraged 27 him and wrote asking the disciples to welcome him. When he arrived there he was able by God's grace to help the believers considerably •by the energetic way he 28 refuted the Jews in public and demonstrated from the scriptures that Jesus was the Christ.

The disciples of John at Ephesus

19 While Apollos was in Corinth, Paul made his way overland as far as 1 Ephesus, where he found a number of disciples. •When he asked, 'Did 2 you receive the Holy Spirit when you became believers?' they answered, 'No, we were never even told there was such a thing as a Holy Spirit'. •'Then how 3 were you baptised?' he asked. 'With John's baptism' they replied. •'John's 4 baptism' said Paul 'was a baptism of repentance; but he insisted that the people should believe in the one who was to come after him—in other words Jesus.' When they heard this, they were baptised in the name of the Lord Jesus, •and $\frac{5}{6}$ the moment Paul had laid hands on them the Holy Spirit came down on them, and they began to speak with tongues and to prophesy.•There were about twelve 7 of these men.

Foundation of the church of Ephesus

He began by going to the synagogue, where he spoke out boldly and argued 8 persuasively about the kingdom of God. He did this for three months, •till the 9 attitude of some of the congregation hardened into unbelief. As soon as they began attacking the Way in front of the others, he broke with them and took his disciples apart to hold daily discussions in the lecture room of Tyrannus. •This 10 went on for two years, with the result that people from all over Asia, [a] both Jews and Greeks, were able to hear the word of the Lord.

The Jewish exorcists

¹¹₁₂ So remarkable were the miracles worked by God at Paul's hands •that handkerchiefs or aprons which had touched him were taken to the sick, and they were cured of their illnesses, and the evil spirits came out of them.

13 But some itinerant Jewish exorcists tried pronouncing the name of the Lord Jesus over people who were possessed by evil spirits; they used to say, 'I command
14 you by the Jesus whose spokesman is Paul'. •Among those who did this were
15 seven sons of Sceva, a Jewish chief priest. •The evil spirit replied, 'Jesus
16 I recognise, and I know who Paul is, but who are you?' •and the man with the evil spirit hurled himself at them and overpowered first one and then another, and handled them so violently that they fled from that house naked and badly
17 mauled. •Everybody in Ephesus, both Jews and Greeks, heard about this episode; they were all greatly impressed, and the name of the Lord Jesus came to be held in great honour.

18 Some believers, too, came forward to admit in detail how they had used spells
19 and a number of them who had practised magic collected their books and made a bonfire of them in public. The value of these was calculated to be fifty thousand silver pieces.

20 In this impressive way the word of the Lord spread more and more widely and successfully.

V. A PRISONER FOR CHRIST

Paul's plans

21 When all this was over Paul made up his mind to go back to Jerusalem through Macedonia and Achaia. 'After I have been there' he said 'I must go on to see
22 Rome as well.' •So he sent two of his helpers, Timothy and Erastus, ahead of him to Macedonia, while he remained for a time in Asia.

Ephesus: the silversmiths' riot

23 It was during this time that a rather serious disturbance broke out in connection
24 with the Way. •A silversmith called Demetrius, who employed a large number
25 of craftsmen making silver shrines of Diana, •called a general meeting of his own men with others in the same trade. 'As you men know,' he said 'it is on this
26 industry that we depend for our prosperity. •Now you must have seen and heard how, not just in Ephesus but nearly everywhere in Asia, this man Paul has persuaded and converted a great number of people with his argument that gods made
27 by hand are not gods at all. •This threatens not only to discredit our trade, but also to reduce the sanctuary of the great goddess Diana to unimportance. It could end up by taking away all the prestige of a goddess venerated all over Asia, yes,
28 and everywhere in the civilised world.' •This speech roused them to fury, and they
29 started to shout, 'Great is Diana of the Ephesians!' •The whole town was in an uproar and the mob rushed to the theatre dragging along two of Paul's
30 Macedonian travelling companions, Gaius and Aristarchus. •Paul wanted to
31 make an appeal to the people, but the disciples refused to let him; •in fact, some

d. To Antioch.
19 a. I.e. the region round Ephesus, including the seven towns of Rv 1:11.

of the Asiarchs,[b] who were friends of his, sent messages imploring him not to take the risk of going into the theatre.

By now everybody was shouting different things till the assembly itself had 32 no idea what was going on; most of them did not even know why they had been summoned. •The Jews pushed Alexander to the front, and when some of the 33 crowd shouted encouragement he raised his hand for silence in the hope of being able to explain things to the people. •When they realised he was a Jew, they all 34 started shouting in unison, 'Great is Diana of the Ephesians!' and they kept this up for two hours. •When the town clerk eventually succeeded in calming the 35 crowd, he said, 'Citizens of Ephesus! Is there anybody alive who does not know that the city of the Ephesians is the guardian of the temple of great Diana and of her statue that fell from heaven? •Nobody can contradict this and there is no 36 need for you to get excited or do anything rash. •These men you have brought 37 here are not guilty of any sacrilege or blasphemy against our goddess. •If Deme- 38 trius and the craftsmen he has with him want to complain about anyone, there are the assizes and the proconsuls; let them take the case to court. •And if you want 39 to ask any more questions you must raise them in the regular assembly. •We could 40 easily be charged with rioting for today's happenings: there was no ground for it all, and we can give no reason for this gathering.' •When he had finished this 41 speech he dismissed the assembly.

Paul leaves Ephesus

20 When the disturbance was over, Paul sent for the disciples and, after 1 speaking words of encouragement to them, said good-bye and set out for Macedonia. •On his way through those areas he said many words of encourage- 2 ment to them and then made his way into Greece, •where he spent three months. 3 He was leaving by ship for Syria[a] when a plot organised against him by the Jews made him decide to go back by way of Macedonia. •He was accompanied by 4 Sopater, son of Pyrrhus, who came from Beroea; Aristarchus and Secundus who came from Thessalonika; Gaius from Doberus, and Timothy, as well as Tychicus and Trophimus who were from Asia. •They all went on to Troas where they 5 waited for us. •We ourselves left Philippi by ship after the days of Unleavened 6 Bread and met them five days later at Troas, where we stopped for a week.

Troas: Paul raises a dead man to life

On the first day of the week[b] we met to break bread. Paul was due to leave 7 the next day, and he preached a sermon that went on till the middle of the night. A number of lamps were lit in the upstairs room where we were assembled, •and 8/9 as Paul went on and on, a young man called Eutychus who was sitting on the window-sill grew drowsy and was overcome by sleep and fell to the ground three floors below. He was picked up dead. •Paul went down and stooped to clasp the 10 boy to him. 'There is no need to worry,' he said 'there is still life in him.' •Then 11 he went back upstairs where he broke bread and ate and carried on talking till he left at daybreak. •They took the boy away alive, and were greatly 12 encouraged.

From Troas to Miletus

We were now to go on ahead by sea, so we set sail for Assos, where we were 13 to take Paul on board; this was what he had arranged, for he wanted to go by road. When he rejoined us at Assos we took him aboard and went on to Mitylene. •The 14/15 next day we sailed from there and arrived opposite Chios. The second day we touched at Samos and, after stopping at Trogyllium, made Miletus the next day.

16 Paul had decided to pass wide of Ephesus so as to avoid spending time in Asia, since he was anxious to be in Jerusalem, if possible, for the day of Pentecost.

Farewell to the elders of Ephesus

17
18 From Miletus he sent for the elders of the church of Ephesus. •When they arrived he addressed these words to them:

'You know what my way of life has been ever since the first day I set foot
19 among you in Asia, •how I have served the Lord in all humility, with all the
20 sorrows and trials that came to me through the plots of the Jews. •I have not hesitated to do anything that would be helpful to you; I have preached to you,
21 and instructed you both in public and in your homes, •urging both Jews and Greeks to turn to God and to believe in our Lord Jesus.

22 'And now you see me a prisoner already in spirit; I am on my way to Jeru-
23 salem, but have no idea what will happen to me there, •except that the Holy Spirit, in town after town, has made it clear enough that imprisonment and persecution
24 await me. •But life to me is not a thing to waste words on, provided that when I finish my race I have carried out the mission the Lord Jesus gave me—and that was to bear witness to the Good News of God's grace.

25 'I now feel sure that none of you among whom I have gone about proclaiming
26 the kingdom will ever see my face again. •And so here and now I swear that my
27 conscience is clear as far as all of you are concerned, •for I have without faltering put before you the whole of God's purpose.

28 'Be on your guard for yourselves and for all the flock of which the Holy Spirit has made you the overseers, to feed the Church of God which he bought with
29 his own blood. •I know quite well that when I have gone fierce wolves will invade
30 you and will have no mercy on the flock. •Even from your own ranks there will be men coming forward with a travesty of the truth on their lips to induce the
31 disciples to follow them. •So be on your guard, remembering how night and day for three years I never failed to keep you right, shedding tears over each one of
32 you. •And now I commend you to God, and to the word of his grace that has power to build you up and to give you your inheritance among all the sanctified.
33
34 'I have never asked anyone for money or clothes; •you know for yourselves that the work I did earned enough to meet my needs and those of my compan-
35 ions. •I did this to show you that this is how we must exert ourselves to support the weak, remembering the words of the Lord Jesus, who himself said, "There is more happiness in giving than in receiving". '

36
37 When he had finished speaking he knelt down with them all and prayed. •By now they were all in tears; they put their arms round Paul's neck and kissed him;
38 what saddened them most was his saying they would never see his face again. Then they escorted him to the ship.

The journey to Jerusalem

1 **21** When we had at last torn ourselves away from them and put to sea, we set a straight course and arrived at Cos; the next day we reached Rhodes, and

b. Local leaders of the official state worship.
20 a. Taking to Jerusalem the proceeds of the collection, Rm 15:25.   **b.** The day was reckoned in the Jewish fashion; the Lord's day began on the evening of Saturday and it was then that this meeting was held.

from there went on to Patara. •Here we found a ship bound for Phoenicia, so we 2
went on board and sailed in her. •After sighting Cyprus and leaving it to port, 3
we sailed to Syria and put in at Tyre, since the ship was to unload her cargo there.
We sought out the disciples and stayed there a week. Speaking in the Spirit, 4
they kept telling Paul not to go on to Jerusalem, •but when our time was up we set 5
off. Together with the women and children they all escorted us on our way till we
were out of the town. When we reached the beach, we knelt down and prayed;
then, after saying good-bye to each other, we went aboard and they returned 6
home.

The end of our voyage from Tyre came when we landed at Ptolemais, where 7
we greeted the brothers and stayed one day with them. •The next day we left and 8
came to Caesarea. Here we called on Philip the evangelist, one of the Seven, and
stayed with him. •He had four virgin daughters who were prophets. •When we $^9_{10}$
had been there several days a prophet called Agabus arrived from Judaea •to see 11
us. He took Paul's girdle, and tied up his own feet and hands, and said, 'This
is what the Holy Spirit says, "The man this girdle belongs to will be bound like
this by the Jews in Jerusalem, and handed over to the pagans" '. •When we heard 12
this, we and everybody there implored Paul not to go on to Jerusalem. •To 13
this he replied, 'What are you trying to do—weaken my resolution by your tears?
For my part, I am ready not only to be tied up but even to die in Jerusalem for
the name of the Lord Jesus.' •And so, as he would not be persuaded, we gave up 14
the attempt, saying, 'The Lord's will be done'.

Paul's arrival in Jerusalem

After this we packed and went on up to Jerusalem. •Some of the disciples $^{15}_{16}$
from Caesarea accompanied us and took us to the house of a Cypriot with whom
we were to lodge; he was called Mnason and had been one of the earliest disciples.

On our arrival in Jerusalem the brothers gave us a very warm welcome. •The $^{17}_{18}$
next day Paul went with us to visit James, and all the elders were present. •After 19
greeting them he gave a detailed account of all that God had done among the
pagans through his ministry. •They gave glory to God when they heard this. 20
'But you see, brother,' they said 'how thousands of Jews have now become
believers, all of them staunch upholders of the Law, and •they have heard that 21
you instruct all Jews living among the pagans to break away from Moses,
authorising them not to circumcise their children or to follow the customary
practices. •What is to be done? Inevitably there will be a meeting of the whole 22
body, since they are bound to hear that you have come. •So do as we suggest. 23
We have four men here who are under a vow; •take these men along and be 24
purified with them and pay all the expenses connected with the shaving of their
heads.^{a} This will let everyone know there is no truth in the reports they have heard
about you and that you still regularly observe the Law. •The pagans who have 25
become believers, as we wrote when we told them our decisions, must abstain from
things sacrificed to idols, from blood, from the meat of strangled animals and
from fornication.'

So the next day Paul took the men along and was purified with them, and he 26
visited the Temple to give notice of the time when the period of purification would
be over and the offering would have to be presented on behalf of each of them.

Paul's arrest

The seven days were nearly over when some Jews from Asia caught sight of 27
him in the Temple and stirred up the crowd and seized him, •shouting, 'Men of 28

Israel, help! This is the man who preaches to everyone everywhere against our
people, against the Law and against this place. Now he has profaned this Holy
29 Place by bringing Greeks into the Temple.' •They had, in fact, previously seen
Trophimus the Ephesian in the city with him, and thought that Paul had brought
him into the Temple.
30   This roused the whole city; people came running from all sides; they seized
Paul and dragged him out of the Temple, and the gates were closed behind them.
31 They would have killed him if a report had not reached the tribune of the cohort[b]
32 that there was rioting all over Jerusalem. •He immediately called out soldiers
and centurions, and charged down on the crowd, who stopped beating Paul when
33 they saw the tribune and the soldiers. •When the tribune came up he arrested
Paul, had him bound with two chains and enquired who he was and what he had
34 done. •People in the crowd called out different things, and since the noise made
it impossible for him to get any positive information, the tribune ordered Paul
35 to be taken into the fortress. •When Paul reached the steps, the crowd became
36 so violent that he had to be carried by the soldiers; •and indeed the whole mob
was after them, shouting, 'Kill him!'
37   Just as Paul was being taken into the fortress, he asked the tribune if he could
38 have a word with him. The tribune said, 'You speak Greek, then? •So you are
not the Egyptian who started the recent revolt and led those four thousand cut-
39 throats[c] out into the desert?' •'I?' said Paul 'I am a Jew and a citizen of the well-
known city of Tarsus in Cilicia. Please give me permission to speak to the people.'
40 The man gave his consent and Paul, standing at the top of the steps, gestured to
the people with his hand. When all was quiet again he spoke to them in Hebrew.[d]

Paul's address to the Jews of Jerusalem

1 **22** 'My brothers, my fathers, listen to what I have to say to you in my defence.'
2   When they realised he was speaking in Hebrew, the silence was even greater
3 than before. •'I am a Jew,' Paul said 'and was born at Tarsus in Cilicia. I was
brought up here in this city. I studied under Gamaliel and was taught the exact
observance of the Law of our ancestors. In fact, I was as full of duty towards God
4 as you are today. •I even persecuted this Way to the death, and sent women as
5 well as men to prison in chains •as the high priest and the whole council of elders
can testify, since they even sent me with letters to their brothers in Damascus.
When I set off it was with the intention of bringing prisoners back from there
to Jerusalem for punishment.
6   'I was on that journey and nearly at Damascus when about midday a bright
7 light from heaven suddenly shone round me. •I fell to the ground and heard a voice
8 saying, "Saul, Saul, why are you persecuting me?" •I answered: Who are you,
Lord? and he said to me, "I am Jesus the Nazarene, and you are persecuting
9 me". •The people with me saw the light but did not hear his voice as he spoke
10 to me. •I said: What am I to do, Lord? The Lord answered, "Stand up and go
into Damascus, and there you will be told what you have been appointed to do".
11 The light had been so dazzling that I was blind and my companions had to take
me by the hand; and so I came to Damascus.
12   'Someone called Ananias, a devout follower of the Law and highly thought

21 a. For the duration of a nazirite vow, the hair was not to be cut. Discharge from the vow,
on fulfilment, had to be celebrated with expensive sacrifices.   **b.** Commanding officer of
the Roman garrison.   **c.** Nationalist extremists.   **d.** I.e. Aramaic.

of by all the Jews living there, •came to see me; he stood beside me and said, 13 "Brother Saul, receive your sight". Instantly my sight came back and I was able to see him. •Then he said, "The God of our ancestors has chosen you to know 14 his will, to see the Just One and hear his own voice speaking, •because you are 15 to be his witness before all mankind, testifying to what you have seen and heard. And now why delay? It is time you were baptised and had your sins washed away 16 while invoking his name."

'Once, after I had got back to Jerusalem, when I was praying in the Temple, 17 I fell into a trance •and then I saw him. "Hurry," he said "leave Jerusalem at 18 once; they will not accept the testimony you are giving about me." •Lord, 19 I answered, it is because they know that I used to go from synagogue to synagogue, imprisoning and flogging those who believed in you; •and that when the 20 blood of your witness*a* Stephen was being shed, I was standing by in full agreement with his murderers, and minding their clothes. •Then he said to me, "Go! I am 21 sending you out to the pagans far away." '

Paul the Roman citizen

So far they had listened to him, but at these words they began to shout, 'Rid 22 the earth of the man! He is not fit to live!' •They were yelling, waving their 23 cloaks and throwing dust into the air, •and so the tribune had him brought into 24 the fortress and ordered him to be examined under the lash, to find out the reason for the outcry against him. •But when they had strapped him down Paul said 25 to the centurion on duty, 'Is it legal for you to flog a man who is a Roman citizen and has not been brought to trial?' •When he heard this the centurion went and 26 told the tribune; 'Do you realise what you are doing?' he said 'This man is a Roman citizen'. •So the tribune came and asked him, 'Tell me, are you a 27 Roman citizen?' 'I am' Paul said. •The tribune replied, 'It cost me a large sum to 28 acquire this citizenship'. 'But I was born to it' said Paul. •Then those who were 29 about to examine him hurriedly withdrew, and the tribune himself was alarmed when he realised that he had put a Roman citizen in chains.

His appearance before the Sanhedrin

The next day, since he wanted to know what precise charge the Jews were 30 bringing, he freed Paul and gave orders for a meeting of the chief priests and the entire Sanhedrin; then he brought Paul down and stood him in front of them.

23 Paul looked steadily at the Sanhedrin and began to speak, 'My brothers, 1 to this day I have conducted myself before God with a perfectly clear conscience'. •At this the high priest Ananias ordered his attendants to strike him 2 on the mouth. •Then Paul said to him, 'God will surely strike you, you 3 whitewashed wall! How can you sit there to judge me according to the Law, and then break the Law by ordering a man to strike me?' •The attendants said, 'It is 4 God's high priest you are insulting!' •Paul answered, 'Brothers, I did not realise 5 it was the high priest, for scripture says: *You must not curse a ruler of your people*.*a*

Now Paul was well aware that one section was made up of Sadducees and the 6 other of Pharisees, so he called out in the Sanhedrin, 'Brothers, I am a Pharisee and the son of Pharisees. It is for our hope in the resurrection of the dead that I am on trial.' •As soon as he said this a dispute broke out between the Pharisees 7 and Sadducees, and the assembly was split between the two parties. •For the 8 Sadducees say there is neither resurrection, nor angel, nor spirit, while the

9   Pharisees accept all three. ·The shouting grew louder, and some of the scribes
from the Pharisees' party stood up and protested strongly, 'We find nothing wrong
10   with this man. Suppose a spirit has spoken to him, or an angel?' ·Feeling was
running high, and the tribune, afraid that they would tear Paul to pieces, ordered
his troops to go down and haul him out and bring him into the fortress.
11   Next night, the Lord appeared to him and said, 'Courage! You have borne
witness for me in Jerusalem, now you must do the same in Rome.'

The conspiracy of the Jews against Paul

12   When it was day, the Jews held a secret meeting at which they made a vow
13   not to eat or drink until they had killed Paul. ·There were more than forty who
14   took part in this conspiracy, ·and they went to the chief priests and elders, and
told them, 'We have made a solemn vow to let nothing pass our lips until we have
15   killed Paul. ·Now it is up to you and the Sanhedrin together to apply to the
tribune to bring him down to you, as though you meant to examine his case more
closely; we, on our side, are prepared to dispose of him before he reaches you.'
16   But the son of Paul's sister heard of the ambush they were laying and made
17   his way into the fortress and told Paul, ·who called one of the centurions and
18   said, 'Take this young man to the tribune; he has something to tell him'. ·So the
man took him to the tribune, and reported, 'The prisoner Paul summoned me and
19   requested me to bring this young man to you; he has something to tell you'. ·Then
the tribune took him by the hand and drew him aside and asked, 'What is it you
20   have to tell me?' ·He replied, 'The Jews have made a plan to ask you to take Paul
down to the Sanhedrin tomorrow, as though they meant to inquire more closely
21   into his case. ·Do not let them persuade you. There are more than forty of them
lying in wait for him, and they have vowed not to eat or drink until they have
got rid of him. They are ready now and only waiting for your order to be given.'
22   The tribune let the young man go with this caution, 'Tell no one that you have
given me this information'.

Paul transferred to Caesarea

23   Then he summoned two of the centurions and said, 'Get two hundred soldiers
ready to leave for Caesarea by the third hour of the night with seventy cavalry and
24   two hundred auxiliaries; ·provide horses for Paul, and deliver him unharmed
25
26   to Felix the governor'.[b] ·He also wrote a letter in these terms: ·'Claudius Lysias
27   to his Excellency the governor Felix, greetings. ·This man had been seized by the
Jews and would have been murdered by them but I came on the scene with my
troops and got him away, having discovered that he was a Roman citizen.
28   Wanting to find out what charge they were making against him, I brought him
29   before their Sanhedrin. ·I found that the accusation concerned disputed points
of their Law, but that there was no charge deserving death or imprisonment.
30   My information is that there is a conspiracy against the man, so I hasten to send
him to you, and have notified his accusers that they must state their case against
him in your presence.'
31   The soldiers carried out their orders; they took Paul and escorted him by night
32   to Antipatris. ·Next day they left the mounted escort to go on with him and
33   returned to the fortress. ·On arriving at Caesarea the escort delivered the letter
34   to the governor and handed Paul over to him. ·The governor read the letter

22 a. *Martyr:* the word had not yet acquired its restricted meaning.
23 a. Ex 22:27   b. Antoninus Felix, procurator of Judaea from 52 to 59-60.

and asked him what province he came from. Learning that he was from Cilicia he said, •'I will hear your case as soon as your accusers are here too'. Then he 35 ordered him to be held in Herod's praetorium.

The case before Felix

24 Five days later the high priest Ananias came down with some of the 1 elders and an advocate named Tertullus, and they laid information against Paul before the governor. •Paul was called, and Tertullus opened for the 2 prosecution, 'Your Excellency, Felix, the unbroken peace we enjoy and the reforms this nation owes to your foresight •are matters we accept, always 3 and everywhere, with all gratitude. •I do not want to take up too much of your 4 time, but I beg you to give us a brief hearing. •The plain truth is that we find 5 this man a perfect pest; he stirs up trouble among Jews the world over, and is a ringleader of the Nazarene sect. •He has even attempted to profane the Temple. 6 We placed him under arrest, intending to judge him according to our Law, •but 7 the tribune Lysias intervened and took him out of our hands by force, •ordering 8 his accusers to appear before you; if you ask him*a* you can find out for yourself the truth of all our accusations against this man.' •The Jews supported him, 9 asserting that these were the facts.

When the governor motioned him to speak, Paul answered: 10

Paul's speech before the Roman governor

'I know that you have administered justice over this nation for many years, and I can therefore speak with confidence in my defence. •As you can verify for 11 yourself, it is no more than twelve days since I went up to Jerusalem on pilgrimage, •and it is not true that they ever found me arguing with anyone or 12 stirring up the mob, either in the Temple, in the synagogues, or about the town; neither can they prove any of the accusations they are making against me now. 13

'What I do admit to you is this: it is according to the Way which they describe 14 as a sect that I worship the God of my ancestors, retaining my belief in all points of the Law and in what is written in the prophets; •and I hold the same hope 15 in God as they do that there will be a resurrection of good men and bad men alike. •In these things, I, as much as they, do my best to keep a clear conscience 16 at all times before God and man.

'After several years I came to bring alms to my nation and to make offerings; 17 it was in connection with these that they found me in the Temple; I had been 18 purified, and there was no crowd involved, and no disturbance. •But some Jews 19 from Asia...—these are the ones who should have appeared before you and accused me of whatever they had against me. •At least let those who are present 20 say what crime they found me guilty of when I stood before the Sanhedrin, •unless 21 it were to do with this single outburst, when I stood up among them and called out: It is about the resurrection of the dead that I am on trial before you today.'

Paul's captivity at Caesarea

At this, Felix, who knew more about the Way than most people, adjourned 22 the case, saying, 'When Lysias the tribune has come down I will go into your case'. •He then gave orders to the centurion that Paul should be kept under arrest 23 but free from restriction, and that none of his own people should be prevented from seeing to his needs.

Some days later Felix came with his wife Drusilla who was a Jewess.*b* He sent 24

25 for Paul and gave him a hearing on the subject of faith in Christ Jesus. •But when he began to treat of righteousness, self-control and the coming Judgement, Felix took fright and said, 'You may go for the present; I will send for you when I find 26 it convenient'. •At the same time he had hopes of receiving money from Paul, and for this reason he sent for him frequently and had talks with him.

27 When the two years' came to an end, Felix was succeeded by Porcius Festus and, being anxious to gain favour with the Jews, Felix left Paul in custody.

Paul appeals to Caesar

1 **25** Three days after his arrival in the province, Festus went up to Jerusalem 2 from Caesarea. •The chief priests and leaders of the Jews informed him of 3 the case against Paul, urgently •asking him to support them rather than Paul, and to have him transferred to Jerusalem. They were, in fact, preparing an ambush 4 to murder him on the way. •But Festus replied that Paul would remain in custody 5 in Caesarea, and that he would be going back there shortly himself. •'Let your authorities come down with me' he said 'and if there is anything wrong about the man, they can bring a charge against him.'

6 After staying with them for eight or ten days at the most, he went down to Caesarea and the next day he took his seat on the tribunal and had Paul brought 7 in. •As soon as Paul appeared, the Jews who had come down from Jerusalem surrounded him, making many serious accusations which they were unable to 8 substantiate. •Paul's defence was this, 'I have committed no offence whatever 9 against either Jewish law, or the Temple, or Caesar'. •Festus was anxious to gain favour with the Jews, so he said to Paul, 'Are you willing to go up to Jerusalem 10 and be tried on these charges before me there?' •But Paul replied, 'I am standing before the tribunal of Caesar and this is where I should be tried. I have done the 11 Jews no wrong, as you very well know. •If I am guilty of committing any capital crime, I do not ask to be spared the death penalty. But if there is no substance in the accusations these persons bring against me, no one has a right to surrender 12 me to them. I appeal to Caesar.' •Then Festus conferred with his advisers and replied, 'You have appealed to Caesar; to Caesar you shall go'.

Paul appears before King Agrippa

13 Some days later King Agrippa and Bernice[a] arrived in Caesarea and paid 14 their respects to Festus. •Their visit lasted several days, and Festus put Paul's case before the king. 'There is a man here' he said 'whom Felix left behind in 15 custody, •and while I was in Jerusalem the chief priests and elders of the Jews 16 laid information against him, demanding his condemnation. •But I told them that Romans are not in the habit of surrendering any man, until the accused confronts his accusers and is given an opportunity to defend himself against the 17 charge. •So they came here with me, and I wasted no time but took my seat on 18 the tribunal the very next day and had the man brought in. •When confronted with him, his accusers did not charge him with any of the crimes I had expected; 19 but they had some argument or other with him about their own religion and about 20 a dead man called Jesus whom Paul alleged to be alive. •Not feeling qualified to deal with questions of this sort, I asked him if he would be willing to go to 21 Jerusalem to be tried there on this issue. •But Paul put in an appeal for his case

24 a. Lysias.   b. Youngest daughter of Herod Agrippa.   c. The maximum length of protective custody; Felix was breaking the law by continuing to detain Paul.
25 a. Agrippa, Bernice and Drusilla (24:24) were children of Herod Agrippa I.

to be reserved for the judgement of the august emperor, so I ordered him to be remanded until I could send him to Caesar.' •Agrippa said to Festus, 'I should 22 like to hear the man myself'. 'Tomorrow' he answered 'you shall hear him.'

So the next day Agrippa and Bernice arrived in great state and entered the 23 audience chamber attended by the tribunes and the city notables; and Festus ordered Paul to be brought in. •Then Festus said, 'King Agrippa, and all here 24 present with us, you see before you the man about whom the whole Jewish community has petitioned me, both in Jerusalem and here, loudly protesting that he ought not to be allowed to remain alive. •For my own part I am satisfied 25 that he has committed no capital crime, but when he himself appealed to the august emperor I decided to send him. •But I have nothing definite that I can 26 write to his Imperial Majesty about him; that is why I have produced him before you all, and before you in particular, King Agrippa, so that after the examination I may have something to write. •It seems to me pointless to send a prisoner 27 without indicating the charges against him.'

26 Then Agrippa said to Paul, 'You have leave to speak on your own behalf'. 1 And Paul held up his hand and began his defence:

Paul's speech before King Agrippa

'I consider myself fortunate, King Agrippa, in that it is before you I am to 2 answer today all the charges made against me by the Jews, •the more so because 3 you are an expert in matters of custom and controversy among the Jews. So I beg you to listen to me patiently.

'My manner of life from my youth, a life spent from the beginning among 4 my own people and in Jerusalem, is common knowledge among the Jews. •They 5 have known me for a long time and could testify, if they would, that I followed the strictest party in our religion and lived as a Pharisee. •And now it is for my 6 hope in the promise made by God to our ancestors that I am on trial, •the promise 7 that our twelve tribes, constant in worship night and day, hope to attain. For that hope, Sire, I am actually put on trial by Jews! •Why does it seem incredible 8 to you that God should raise the dead?

'As for me, I once thought it was my duty to use every means to oppose the 9 name of Jesus the Nazarene. •This I did in Jerusalem; I myself threw many of the 10 saints into prison, acting on authority from the chief priests, and when they were sentenced to death I cast my vote against them. •I often went round the 11 synagogues inflicting penalties, trying in this way to force them to renounce their faith; my fury against them was so extreme that I even pursued them into foreign cities.

'On one such expedition I was going to Damascus, armed with full powers 12 and a commission from the chief priests, •and at midday as I was on my way, 13 your Majesty, I saw a light brighter than the sun come down from heaven. It shone brilliantly round me and my fellow travellers. •We all fell to the ground, 14 and I heard a voice saying to me in Hebrew, "Saul, Saul, why are you persecuting me? It is hard for you, kicking like this against the goad."*a* •Then I said: Who 15 are you, Lord? And the Lord answered, "I am Jesus, and you are persecuting me. •But get up and stand on your feet, for I have appeared to you for this 16 reason: to appoint you as my servant and as witness of this vision in which you have seen me, and of others in which I shall appear to you. •*I shall deliver you* 17 from the people and *from the pagans, to whom I am sending you* •*to open their* 18 *eyes*, so that they may turn *from darkness to light*,*b* from the dominion of Satan to God, and receive, through faith in me, forgiveness of their sins and a share in the inheritance of the sanctified."

19
20 'After that, King Agrippa, I could not disobey the heavenly vision. •On the contrary I started preaching, first to the people of Damascus, then to those of Jerusalem and all the countryside of Judaea, and also to the pagans, urging them
21 to repent and turn to God, proving their change of heart by their deeds. •This was why the Jews laid hands on me in the Temple and tried to do away with me.
22 But I was blessed with God's help, and so I have stood firm to this day, testifying to great and small alike, saying nothing more than what the prophets and Moses
23 himself said would happen: •that the Christ was to suffer and that, as the first to rise from the dead, he was to proclaim that light now shone for our people and for the pagans too.'

His hearers' reactions

24 He had reached this point in his defence when Festus shouted out, 'Paul, you
25 are out of your mind; all that learning of yours is driving you mad'. •'Festus, your Excellency,' answered Paul 'I am not mad: I am speaking nothing but the
26 sober truth. •The king understands these matters, and to him I now speak with assurance, confident that nothing of all this is lost on him; after all, these things
27 were not done in a corner. •King Agrippa, do you believe in the prophets? I know
28 you do.' •At this Agrippa said to Paul, 'A little more, and your arguments would
29 make a Christian of me'. •'Little or more,' Paul replied 'I wish before God that not only you but all who have heard me today would come to be as I am —except for these chains.'

30 At this the king rose to his feet, with the governor and Bernice and those who
31 sat there with them. •When they had retired they talked together and agreed,
32 'This man is doing nothing that deserves death or imprisonment'. •And Agrippa remarked to Festus, 'The man could have been set free if he had not appealed to Caesar'.

The departure for Rome

1 **27** When it had been decided that we should sail for Italy, Paul and some other prisoners were handed over to a centurion called Julius, of the
2 Augustan cohort. •We boarded a vessel from Adramyttium bound for ports on the Asiatic coast, and put to sea; we had Aristarchus with us, a Macedonian of
3 Thessalonika. •Next day we put in at Sidon, and Julius was considerate enough to allow Paul to go to his friends to be looked after.
4 From there we put to sea again, but as the winds were against us we sailed
5 under the lee of Cyprus, •then across the open sea off Cilicia and Pamphylia,
6 taking a fortnight to reach Myra in Lycia. •There the centurion found an Alexandrian ship leaving for Italy and put us aboard.
7 For some days we made little headway, and we had difficulty in making Cnidus. The wind would not allow us to touch there, so we sailed under the lee
8 of Crete off Cape Salmone •and struggled along the coast until we came to a place called Fair Havens, near the town of Lasea.

26 a. Greek proverbial expression for useless resistance. **b.** Quotations from Jr 1; Is 42; Is 9.

Storm and shipwreck

A great deal of time had been lost, and navigation was already hazardous 9 since it was now well after the time of the Fast,[a] so Paul gave them this warning, 'Friends, I can see this voyage will be dangerous and that we run the risk of losing 10 not only the cargo and the ship but also our lives as well'. • But the centurion 11 took more notice of the captain and the ship's owner than of what Paul was saying; • and since the harbour was unsuitable for wintering, the majority were 12 for putting out from there in the hope of wintering at Phoenix—a harbour in Crete, facing south-west and north-west.

A southerly breeze sprang up and, thinking their objective as good as reached, 13 they weighed anchor and began to sail past Crete, close inshore. • But it was not 14 long before a hurricane, the 'north-easter' as they call it, burst on them from across the island. • The ship was caught and could not be turned head-on to the wind, 15 so we had to give way to it and let ourselves be driven. • We ran under the lee of 16 a small island called Cauda and managed with some difficulty to bring the ship's boat under control. • They hoisted it aboard and with the help of tackle bound 17 cables round the ship; then, afraid of running aground on the Syrtis banks, they floated out the sea-anchor and so let themselves drift. • As we were making very 18 heavy weather of it, the next day they began to jettison the cargo, • and the third 19 day they threw the ship's gear overboard with their own hands. • For a number 20 of days both the sun and the stars were invisible and the storm raged unabated until at last we gave up all hope of surviving.

Then, when they had been without food for a long time, Paul stood up among 21 the men. 'Friends,' he said 'if you had listened to me and not put out from Crete, you would have spared yourselves all this damage and loss. • But now I ask you 22 not to give way to despair. There will be no loss of life at all, only of the ship. Last night there was standing beside me an angel of the God to whom I belong 23 and whom I serve, • and he said, "Do not be afraid, Paul. You are destined to 24 appear before Caesar, and for this reason God grants you the safety of all who are sailing with you." • So take courage, friends; I trust in God that things will 25 turn out just as I was told; • but we are to be stranded on some island.' 26

On the fourteenth night we were being driven one way and another in the 27 Adriatic,[b] when about midnight the crew sensed that land of some sort was near. They took soundings and found twenty fathoms; after a short interval they 28 sounded again and found fifteen fathoms. • Then, afraid that we might run 29 aground somewhere on a reef, they dropped four anchors from the stern and prayed for daylight. • When some of the crew tried to escape from the ship and 30 lowered the ship's boat into the sea as though to lay out anchors from the bows, Paul said to the centurion and his men, 'Unless those men stay on board you 31 cannot hope to be saved'. • So the soldiers cut the boat's ropes and let it drop 32 away.

Just before daybreak Paul urged them all to have something to eat. 'For 33 fourteen days' he said 'you have been in suspense, going hungry and eating nothing. • Let me persuade you to have something to eat; your safety is not in 34 doubt. Not a hair of your heads will be lost.' • With these words he took some 35 bread, gave thanks to God in front of them all, broke it and began to eat. • Then 36 they all plucked up courage and took something to eat themselves. • We were 37 in all two hundred and seventy-six souls on board that ship. • When they had 38 eaten what they wanted they lightened the ship by throwing the corn overboard into the sea.

39 When day came they did not recognise the land, but they could make out a kind of bay with a beach; they planned to run the ship aground on this if they 40 could. •They slipped the anchors and left them to the sea, and at the same time loosened the lashings of the rudders; then, hoisting the foresail to the wind, they 41 headed for the beach. •But the cross-currents carried them into a shoal and the vessel ran aground. The bows were wedged in and stuck fast, while the stern began to break up with the pounding of the waves.

42 The soldiers planned to kill the prisoners for fear that any should swim off 43 and escape. •But the centurion was determined to bring Paul safely through, and would not let them do what they intended. He gave orders that those who could 44 swim should jump overboard first and so get ashore, •and the rest follow either on planks or on pieces of wreckage. In this way all came safe and sound to land.

Waiting in Malta

1 28 Once we had come safely through, we discovered that the island was 2 called Malta. •The inhabitants treated us with unusual kindness. They made us all welcome, and they lit a huge fire because it had started to rain and 3 the weather was cold. •Paul had collected a bundle of sticks and was putting them on the fire when a viper brought out by the heat attached itself to his hand. 4 When the natives saw the creature hanging from his hand they said to one another, 'That man must be a murderer; he may have escaped the sea, but divine 5 vengeance would not let him live'. •However, he shook the creature off into the 6 fire and came to no harm, •although they were expecting him at any moment to swell up or drop dead on the spot. After they had waited a long time without seeing anything out of the ordinary happen to him, they changed their minds and began to say he was a god.

7 In that neighbourhood there were estates belonging to the prefect of the island, whose name was Publius. He received us and entertained us hospitably 8 for three days. •It so happened that Publius' father was in bed, suffering from feverish attacks and dysentery. Paul went in to see him, and after a prayer he laid 9 his hands on the man and healed him. •When this happened, the other sick 10 people on the island came as well and were cured;•they honoured us with many . marks of respect, and when we sailed they put on board the provisions we needed.

From Malta to Rome

11 At the end of three months we set sail in a ship that had wintered in the 12 island; she came from Alexandria and her figurehead was the Twins. •We put in 13 at Syracuse and spent three days there; •from there we followed the coast up to Rhegium. After one day there a south wind sprang up and on the second day we 14 made Puteoli, [a] •where we found some brothers and were much rewarded by staying a week with them. And so we came to Rome.

15 When the brothers there heard of our arrival they came to meet us, as far as the Forum of Appius and the Three Taverns. When Paul saw them he thanked 16 God and took courage. •On our arrival in Rome Paul was allowed to stay in lodgings of his own with the soldier who guarded him.

---

27 a. 'the Fast', the feast of Atonement, was kept about the time of the autumn equinox; winter was coming on. **b.** The term includes the seas between Greece, Italy and Africa.
28 a. Pozzuoli, on the Gulf of Naples.

Paul makes contact with the Roman Jews

After three days he called together the leading Jews. When they had assembled, 17 he said to them, 'Brothers, although I have done nothing against our people or the customs of our ancestors, I was arrested in Jerusalem and handed over to the Romans. •They examined me and would have set me free, since they found 18 me guilty of nothing involving the death penalty; •but the Jews lodged an objec- 19 tion, and I was forced to appeal to Caesar, not that I had any accusation to make against my own nation. •That is why I have asked to see you and talk to you, 20 for it is on account of the hope of Israel that I wear this chain.'

They answered, 'We have received no letters from Judaea about you, nor has 21 any countryman of yours arrived here with any report or story of anything to your discredit. •We think it would be as well to hear your own account of 22 your position; all we know about this sect is that opinion everywhere condemns it.'

Paul's declaration to the Roman Jews

So they arranged a day with him and a large number of them visited him at his 23 lodgings. He put his case to them, testifying to the kingdom of God and trying to persuade them about Jesus, arguing from the Law of Moses and the prophets. This went on from early morning until evening, •and some were convinced by 24 what he said, while the rest were sceptical. •So they disagreed among themselves 25 and, as they went away, Paul had one last thing to say to them, 'How aptly the Holy Spirit spoke when he told your ancestors through the prophet Isaiah:

> *Go to this nation and say:*   26
> *You will hear and hear again but not understand,*
> *see and see again, but not perceive.*
> *For the heart of this nation has grown coarse,*   27
> *their ears are dull of hearing and they have shut their eyes,*
> *for fear they should see with their eyes,*
> *hear with their ears,*
> *understand with their heart,*
> *and be converted*
> *and be healed by me.*[b]

'Understand, then, that this salvation of God has been sent to the pagans; 28 they will listen to it.'

Epilogue

Paul spent the whole of the two years[c] in his own rented lodging. He welcomed 30 all who came to visit him, •proclaiming the kingdom of God and teaching the 31 truth about the Lord Jesus Christ with complete freedom and without hindrance from anyone.

b. Is 6:9-10   c. See note on 24:27

INTRODUCTION TO
THE LETTERS OF SAINT PAUL

Paul was born about A.D. 10, of a Jewish family living among 'the Greeks' at Tarsus, a Roman municipality in Cilicia. He was educated as a Pharisee in Jerusalem. He was converted to belief in Christ about A.D. 34, and many particulars of his life as an apostle can be found in his letters and in Acts. The letters may be dated from A.D. 50-65. Paul was imprisoned in Rome, A.D. 61-63, and set free for want of evidence; a second imprisonment in Rome ended, according to a very ancient tradition, in martyrdom by execution, probably in the year 67.

Paul's letters show him as a man of sensitive temperament and warm emotions, completely dedicated to the spreading of the 'Good News' that Christ by his death and resurrection was proved tq be the one universal saviour of Jew and 'Greek' alike. Crises and controversies led him to explain the message of the gospel in ways adapted to the needs of his readers and so to bring into play his remarkable powers of theological analysis and his grasp of profundities. His letters, in a fluent Greek which was his second mother-tongue, were generally a response to a particular situation in a particular church, and although some passages in them were obviously written after long and careful thought, more often the style suggests spontaneity and urgency. The letters were usually dictated, and then signed by Paul with a short personal greeting.

The order in which the letters are printed in this Bible is the traditional one which arranges them in order of diminishing length. If they are read in the order in which they were written, the development in Paul's theological thinking can be seen as he finds expression for further depths and implications in the gospel.

1 and 2 Thessalonians. A.D. 50-51

1 Thessalonians was written from Corinth, when Paul's companion Timothy had come back from a second visit to Thessalonika and reported to Paul on the state of the church there. Besides a series of practical recommendations, it includes Paul's teaching on death and the 'second coming' of Christ, expressed in the terms of contemporary apocalyptic writing.

2 Thessalonians, written about a year later, shows that Paul's thought on the same subject had deepened. Parts of the two letters show some close

correspondences, and some critics have doubted the authenticity of 2 Thessalonians. However, the earliest authorities accepted them as both by Paul.

1 and 2 Corinthians. A.D. 57

Corinth, a great and populous port, was a magnet to every sort of philosophy and religion and was also a notorious centre of immorality. Paul's converts in the city were particularly in need of instruction and guidance, both about the Good News itself and about the Christian life which it implied. Paul appears to have written four letters to the church in Corinth, of which we now have only two.

His first letter to Corinth has not survived, and the earliest we have was written from Ephesus sometime near Easter, 57. Shortly afterwards, Paul had to pay a brief visit to Corinth in which he had to take painful disciplinary measures, and when later he sent a representative to Corinth instead of going himself, the Corinthians did not accept his authority, and Paul wrote a third letter which was very severe. In Macedonia, towards the end of 57, Paul heard from Titus that the 'severe letter' had had the desired effect, and then he wrote the letter which we know as 2 Corinthians.

However, 2 Corinthians is not a single consistent letter; it has been suggested that it includes part of the lost first letter (2 Co 6:14–7:1) and part of the 'severe letter' (2 Co 10-13).

The two letters to the Corinthians contain much information about urgent problems that faced the church and the important decisions which were made to meet them: questions of morality, about the liturgy and the holding of assemblies, the recognition of spiritual gifts and the avoidance of contamination from pagan religions. It was Paul's religious genius to turn what might have remained textbook cases of conscience into the means of exploring the profound doctrines of Christian liberty, the sanctification of the body, the supremacy of love, and union with Christ.

Galatians. Romans. A.D. 57-58

These two letters analyse the same problem, but while Galatians is Paul's immediate response to a particular situation, Romans is more like a systematic treatise and gives a methodical arrangement to all the new ideas that had emerged from the argument.

Paul had not himself founded the church at Rome. It was a mixed community in which there was a danger that Jewish and non-Jewish converts might look down on each other, and Paul, before visiting the church, sent this considered examination of how Judaism and Christianity were related to one another, using the ideas which he had developed in the Galatian crisis and further refining them. In both these letters we can see Paul correcting the unbalance of the Greek outlook which relied too exclusively on human reason, just as in earlier letters he had corrected the unbalance of the Jewish outlook which relied too heavily on the Law.

Philippians. A.D. 56-57

This is a letter without a lot of doctrinal exposition in it, giving some news to his converts at Philippi and warning them of some enemies who had worked against Paul elsewhere and might turn to them next. At the time of writing, Paul was under arrest, but it is unlikely that this letter was written from Rome during his imprisonment there in 61-63 and it may have been written from Ephesus.

Ephesians. Colossians. Philemon. A.D. 61-63

All three letters are closely related and were written while Paul was under arrest in Rome. It appears that the relation between Ephesians and Colossians is like that between Romans and Galatians. The news of a crisis at Colossae led Paul to write a letter to the Christians there against the growing belief and trust in celestial and cosmic powers. Paul accepts these powers as the angels of Jewish tradition, but he shows that in the great scheme of salvation they have only a preparatory and subordinate part and now there is a new order in which Christ is all. About the same time, he wrote a fuller and more systematic treatment of the same ideas and this is the letter that we know as 'Ephesians' though it was probably written for circulation through all the churches.

Some critics have questioned the authorship of both these letters, and particularly of Ephesians, since it seems to borrow ideas from Colossians and not always to digest them smoothly. But we know nothing of any other person capable of writing them; in parts of them, Paul is at his most personal and characteristic, and they represent a further reconsideration of themes which he had already explored in his earlier letters.

The short letter to Philemon is a personal message which was written in Paul's own handwriting.

1 Timothy. Titus. 2 Timothy. A.D. 65

These are letters of advice and instruction to two of Paul's most loyal followers in their work of organising and leading the communities to which he had sent them. It is possible that 1 Timothy and Titus were written from Macedonia about A.D. 65, but by the time he wrote 2 Timothy, Paul was a prisoner in Rome awaiting death. From the details of his recent movements given in this letter, this must have been a second imprisonment, and not that of 61-63.

Hebrews. A.D. 67

The question who wrote this letter to Jewish Christians has been a subject of debate from the earliest times. It is ranked with Paul's letters in importance, its doctrine has Pauline overtones, and it was written from Italy, perhaps from Rome; but while there may be a strong presumption that its author had come under the influence of Paul, the letter can hardly be attributed to Paul himself.

It is a sustained argument from Old Testament texts, to keep its readers firm under persecution. The theme is that the ineffectual sacrifices of the levitical priests are replaced by the one uniquely efficacious sacrifice of Christ, and that his priesthood is of an altogether higher order than that of the Jewish priests, derived from Aaron.

ROMANS

THE LETTER OF PAUL
TO THE CHURCH IN ROME

Address

1 From Paul, a servant of Christ Jesus who has been called to be an apostle,
2 and specially chosen to preach the Good News that God ·promised long
ago through his prophets in the scriptures.

3 This news is about the Son of God who, according to the human nature he
4 took, was a descendant of David: ·it is about Jesus Christ our Lord who, in the
order of the spirit, the spirit of holiness that was in him, was proclaimed Son
5 of God in all his power through his resurrection from the dead. ·Through him
we received grace and our apostolic mission to preach the obedience of faith
6 to all pagan nations in honour of his name. ·You are one of these nations, and
7 by his call belong to Jesus Christ. ·To you all, then, who are God's beloved in
Rome, called to be saints, may God our Father and the Lord Jesus Christ send
grace and peace.

Thanksgiving and prayer

8 First I thank my God through Jesus Christ for all of you and for the way in
9 which your faith is spoken of all over the world. ·The God I worship spiritually
by preaching the Good News of his Son knows that I never fail to mention you
10 in my prayers, ·and to ask to be allowed at long last the opportunity to visit
11 you, if he so wills. ·For I am longing to see you either to strengthen you by
12 sharing a spiritual gift with you, ·or what is better, to find encouragement
13 among you from our common faith. ·I want you to know, brothers, that I have
often planned to visit you—though until now I have always been prevented—
in the hope that I might work as fruitfully among you as I have done among the
14 other pagans. ·I owe a duty to Greeks*a* just as much as to barbarians, to the
15 educated just as much as to the uneducated, ·and it is this that makes me want
to bring the Good News to you too in Rome.

1 a. When contrasted with 'barbarians' (as here), 'Greeks' means the inhabitants of the
hellenic world, including the Romans; when contrasted with 'Jews', it means the pagans in
general.

SALVATION BY FAITH
I. JUSTIFICATION

The theme stated

For I am not ashamed of the Good News: it is the power of God saving all 16
who have faith—Jews first, but Greeks as well— • since this is what reveals the 17
justice of God to us: it shows how faith leads to faith, or as scripture says:
The upright man finds life through faith.[b]

A. GOD'S ANGER AGAINST PAGAN AND JEW

God's anger against the pagans

The anger of God is being revealed from heaven against all the impiety and 18
depravity of men who keep truth imprisoned in their wickedness. • For what can 19
be known about God is perfectly plain to them since God himself has made it
plain. • Ever since God created the world his everlasting power and deity— 20
however invisible—have been there for the mind to see in the things he has
made. That is why such people are without excuse: • they knew God and yet 21
refused to honour him as God or to thank him; instead, they made nonsense
out of logic and their empty minds were darkened. • The more they called 22
themselves philosophers, the more stupid they grew, • until *they exchanged the* 23
glory[c] of the immortal God for a worthless imitation, *for the image* of mortal man,
of birds, of quadrupeds and reptiles. • That is why God left them to their filthy 24
enjoyments and the practices with which they dishonour their own bodies,
since they have given up divine truth for a lie and have worshipped and served 25
creatures instead of the creator, who is blessed for ever. Amen!

That is why God has abandoned them to degrading passions: why their women 26
have turned from natural intercourse to unnatural practices • and why their 27
menfolk have given up natural intercourse to be consumed with passion for each
other, men doing shameless things with men and getting an appropriate reward
for their perversion.

In other words, since they refused to see it was rational to acknowledge God, 28
God has left them to their own irrational ideas and to their monstrous behaviour.
And so they are steeped in all sorts of depravity, rottenness, greed and malice, 29
and addicted to envy, murder, wrangling, treachery and spite. • Libellers, 30
slanderers, enemies of God, rude, arrogant and boastful, enterprising in sin,
rebellious to parents, • without brains, honour, love or pity. • They know what $^{31}_{32}$
God's verdict is: that those who behave like this deserve to die—and yet they
do it; and what is worse, encourage others to do the same.

The Jews are not exempt from God's anger

2 So no matter who you are, if you pass judgement you have no excuse. 1
In judging others you condemn yourself, since you behave no differently
from those you judge. • We know that God condemns that sort of behaviour 2
impartially: • and when you judge those who behave like this while you are 3
doing exactly the same, do you think you will escape God's judgement? • Or are 4
you abusing his abundant goodness, patience and toleration, not realising that

5 this goodness of God is meant to lead you to repentance? •Your stubborn refusal
to repent is only adding to the anger God will have towards you on that day of
6 anger when his just judgements will be made known. •*He will repay each one as*
7 *his works deserve.*[a] •For those who sought renown and honour and immortality
8 by always doing good there will be eternal life; •for the unsubmissive who
refused to take truth for their guide and took depravity instead, there will be
9 anger and fury. •Pain and suffering will come to every human being who employs
10 himself in evil—Jews first, but Greeks as well; •renown, honour and peace will
11 come to everyone who does good—Jews first, but Greeks as well. •God has
no favourites.

The Law will not save them

12 Sinners who were not subject to the Law will perish all the same, without
that Law; sinners who were under the Law will have that Law to judge them.
13 It is not listening to the Law but keeping it that will make people holy in the
14 sight of God. •For instance, pagans who never heard of the Law but are led
by reason to do what the Law commands, may not actually 'possess' the Law,
15 but they can be said to 'be' the Law. •They can point to the substance of the
Law engraved on their hearts—they can call a witness, that is, their own
conscience—they have accusation and defence, that is, their own inner mental
16 dialogue.[b] •...on the day when, according to the Good News I preach, God,
through Jesus Christ, judges the secrets of mankind.

17 If you call yourself a Jew, if you really trust in the Law and are proud of
18 your God, •if you know God's will through the Law and can tell what is right,
19 if you are convinced you can guide the blind and be a beacon to those in the
20 dark, •if you can teach the ignorant and instruct the unlearned because your Law
21 embodies all knowledge and truth, •then why not teach yourself as well as the
22 others? You preach against stealing, yet you steal; •you forbid adultery, yet you
23 commit adultery; you despise idols, yet you rob their temples. •By boasting about
24 the Law and then disobeying it, you bring God into contempt. •As scripture
says: *It is your fault that the name of God is blasphemed among the pagans.*

Circumcision will not save them

25 It is a good thing to be circumcised if you keep the Law; but if you break the
26 Law, you might as well have stayed uncircumcised. •If a man who is not
circumcised obeys the commandments of the Law, surely that makes up for not
27 being circumcised? •More than that, the man who keeps the Law, even though
he has not been physically circumcised, is a living condemnation of the way you
disobey the Law in spite of being circumcised and having it all written down.
28 To be a Jew is not just to look like a Jew, and circumcision is more than a physical
29 operation. •The real Jew is the one who is inwardly a Jew, and the real circumcision is in the heart—something not of the letter but of the spirit. A Jew like that
may not be praised by man, but he will be praised by God.

God's promises will not save them

1 3 Well then, is a Jew any better off? Is there any advantage in being circum-
2 cised? •A great advantage in every way. First, the Jews are the people to

b. Hab 2:4   **c.** Ps 106:20
2 a. Ps 6:12   **b.** This verse follows on from v.13.

whom God's message was entrusted. •What if some of them were unfaithful? 3
Will their lack of fidelity cancel God's fidelity? •That would be absurd. God will 4
always be true even though *everyone* proves to be *false*;[a] so scripture says: *In all
you say your justice shows, and when you are judged you win your case.*[b] •But if our 5
lack of holiness makes God demonstrate his integrity, how can we say God is
unjust when—to use a human analogy—he gets angry with us in return? •That 6
would be absurd, it would mean God could never judge the world. •You might 7
as well say that since my untruthfulness makes God demonstrate his truthfulness
and thus gives him glory, I should not be judged to be a sinner at all. •That 8
would be the same as saying: Do evil as a means to good. Some slanderers have
accused us of teaching this, but they are justly condemned.

All are guilty

Well: are we any better off? Not at all: as we said before, Jews and Greeks 9
are all under sin's dominion. •As scripture says: 10

> *There is not a good man left, no, not one;*
> *there is not one who understands,* 11
> *not one who looks for God.*
> *All have turned aside, tainted all alike;* 12
> *there is not one good man left, not a single one.*
> *Their throats are yawning graves;* 13
> *their tongues are full of deceit.*
> *Vipers' venom is on their lips,*
> *bitter curses fill their mouths.* 14
> *Their feet are swift when blood is to be shed,* 15
> *wherever they go there is havoc and ruin.* 16
> *They know nothing of the way of peace,* 17
> *there is no fear of God before their eyes.*[c] 18

Now all this that the Law says is said, as we know, for the benefit of those 19
who are subject to the Law, but it is meant to silence everyone and to lay the
whole world open to God's judgement; •and this is because *no one can be justified* 20
in the sight[d] of God by keeping the Law: all that law does is to tell us what is
sinful.

B. FAITH AND THE JUSTICE OF GOD

The revelation of God's justice

God's justice that was made known through the Law and the Prophets has 21
now been revealed outside the Law, •since it is the same justice of God that 22
comes through faith to everyone, Jew and pagan alike, who believes in Jesus
Christ. •Both Jew and pagan sinned and forfeited God's glory, •and both are $^{23}_{24}$
justified through the free gift of his grace by being redeemed in Christ Jesus
who was appointed by God to sacrifice his life so as to win reconciliation through 25
faith. In this way God makes his justice known; first, for the past, when sins went
unpunished because he held his hand, •then, for the present age, by showing 26
positively that he is just, and that he justifies everyone who believes in Jesus.

What faith does

27   So what becomes of our boasts? There is no room for them. What sort of
law excludes them? The sort of law that tells us what to do? On the contrary,
28 it is the law of faith, •since, as we see it, a man is justified by faith and not
29 by doing something the Law tells him to do. •Is God the God of Jews alone and
30 not of the pagans too? Of the pagans too, most certainly, •since there is only one
God, and he is the one who will justify the circumcised because of their faith
31 and justify the uncircumcised through their faith. •Do we mean that faith makes
the Law pointless? Not at all: we are giving the Law its true value.

C. THE EXAMPLE OF ABRAHAM

Abraham justified by faith

1   **4** Apply this to Abraham, the ancestor from whom we are all descended.
2   If Abraham was justified as a reward for doing something, he would really
3   have had something to boast about, though not in God's sight •because scripture
says: *Abraham put his faith in God, and this faith was considered as justifying him.*[a]
4   If a man has work to show, his wages are not considered as a favour but as his
5   due; •but when a man has nothing to show except faith in the one who justifies
6   sinners, then his faith is considered as justifying him. •And David says the same:
a man is happy if God considers him righteous, irrespective of good deeds:

7   *Happy those whose crimes are forgiven,*
whose sins are blotted out;
8   *happy the man whom the Lord considers sinless.*[b]

Justified before circumcision

9   Is this happiness meant only for the circumcised, or is it meant for others as
well? Think of Abraham again: *his faith*, we say, *was considered as justifying him*,
10 but when was this done? When he was already circumcised or before he had been
11 circumcised? It was before he had been circumcised, not after; •and when he was
circumcised later it was only *as a sign* and guarantee that the faith he had before
his circumcision justified him. In this way Abraham became the ancestor of all
12 uncircumcised believers, so that they too might be considered righteous; •and
ancestor, also, of those who though circumcised do not rely on that fact alone,
but follow our ancestor Abraham along the path of faith he trod before he had
been circumcised.

Not justified by obedience to the Law

13 The promise of inheriting the world was not made to Abraham and his
descendants on account of any law but on account of the righteousness which
14 consists in faith. •If the world is only to be inherited by those who submit to
15 the Law, then faith is pointless and the promise worth nothing. •Law
involves the possibility of punishment for breaking the law—only where there
16 is no law can that be avoided. •That is why what fulfils the promise depends on
faith, so that it may be a free gift and be available to all of Abraham's

3 a. Ps 116:11   **b.** Ps 51:4 (LXX)   **c.** Quotations from Ps 14, Ps 5, Ps 140, Ps 10, Is 59,
Ps 36.   **d.** Ps 143:2
4 a. Gn 15:6   **b.** Ps 32:1-2

descendants, not only those who belong to the Law but also those who belong to the faith of Abraham who is the father of all of us. •As scripture says: *I have* 17 *made you the ancestor of many nations*ʳ—Abraham is our father in the eyes of God, in whom he put his faith, and who brings the dead to life and calls into being what does not exist.

Abraham's faith, a model of Christian faith

Though it seemed Abraham's hope could not be fulfilled, he hoped and he 18 believed, and through doing so he did become *the father of many nations* exactly as he had been promised: *Your descendants will be as many as the stars.*ᵈ •Even 19 the thought that his body was past fatherhood —he was about a hundred years old—and Sarah too old to become a mother, did not shake his belief. •Since God 20 had promised it, Abraham refused either to deny it or even to doubt it, but drew strength from faith and gave glory to God, •convinced that God had power 21 to do what he had promised. •This is the faith that was '*considered as justi-* 22 *fying him*'. •Scripture however does not refer only to him but to us as well 23 when it says that his faith was thus 'considered'; •our faith too will be 'considered' 24 if we believe in him who raised Jesus our Lord from the dead, •Jesus who was 25 *put to death for our sins*ᵉ and raised to life to justify us.

II. SALVATION

Faith guarantees salvation

5 So far then we have seen that, through our Lord Jesus Christ, by faith we are 1 judged righteous and at peace with God, •since it is by faith and through 2 Jesus that we have entered this state of grace in which we can boast about looking forward to God's glory. •But that is not all we can boast about; we can 3 boast about our sufferings. These sufferings bring patience, as we know, •and 4 patience brings perseverance, and perseverance brings hope, •and this hope is 5 not deceptive, because the love of God has been poured into our hearts by the Holy Spirit which has been given us. •We were still helpless when at his appointed 6 moment Christ died for sinful men. •It is not easy to die even for a good man— 7 though of course for someone really worthy, a man might be prepared to die— but what proves that God loves us is that Christ died for us while we were still 8 sinners. •Having died to make us righteous, is it likely that he would now fail 9 to save us from God's anger? •When we were reconciled to God by the death of 10 his Son, we were still enemies; now that we have been reconciled, surely we may count on being saved by the life of his Son? •Not merely because we have been 11 reconciled but because we are filled with joyful trust in God, through our Lord Jesus Christ, through whom we have already gained our reconciliation.

A. DELIVERANCE FROM SIN AND DEATH AND LAW

Adam and Jesus Christ

Well then, sin *entered the world* through one man, and through sin death, and 12 thus death has spread through the whole human race because everyone has sinned. •Sin existed in the world long before the Law was given. There was no 13 law and so no one could be accused of the sin of 'law-breaking', •yet death reigned 14 over all from Adam to Moses, even though their sin, unlike that of Adam, was not a matter of breaking a law.

15   Adam prefigured the One to come, •but the gift itself considerably outweighed the fall. If it is certain that through one man's fall so many died, it is even more certain that divine grace, coming through the one man, Jesus Christ, came to so
16   many as an abundant free gift. •The results of the gift also outweigh the results of one man's sin: for after one single fall came judgement with a verdict of condem-
17   nation, now after many falls comes grace with its verdict of acquittal. •If it is certain that death reigned over everyone as the consequence of one man's fall, it is even more certain that one man, Jesus Christ, will cause everyone to reign in life who receives the free gift that he does not deserve, of being made righteous.
18   Again, as one man's fall brought condemnation on everyone, so the good act of
19   one man brings everyone life and makes them justified. •As by one man's disobed-ience many were made sinners, so by one man's obedience many will be made
20   righteous. •When law came, it was to multiply the opportunities of falling,
21   but however great the number of sins committed, grace was even greater; •and so, just as sin reigned wherever there was death, so grace will reign to bring eternal life thanks to the righteousness that comes through Jesus Christ our Lord.

Baptism

1   **6** Does it follow that we should remain in sin so as to let grace have greater
2   scope? •Of course not. We are dead to sin, so how can we continue to live
3   in it? •You have been taught that when we were baptised in Christ Jesus we were
4   baptised in his death; •in other words, when we were baptised we went into the tomb with him and joined him in death, so that as Christ was raised from the dead by the Father's glory, we too might live a new life.
5   If in union with Christ we have imitated his death, we shall also imitate him
6   in his resurrection. •We must realise that our former selves have been crucified
7   with him to destroy this sinful body and to free us from the slavery of sin. •When a man dies, of course, he has finished with sin.
8   But we believe that having died with Christ we shall return to life with him:
9   Christ, as we know, having been raised from the dead will never die again. Death
10 has no power over him any more. •When he died, he died, once for all, to sin,
11 so his life now is life with God; •and in that way, you too must consider yourselves to be dead to sin but alive for God in Christ Jesus.

Holiness, not sin, to be the master

12 That is why you must not let sin reign in your mortal bodies or command
13 your obedience to bodily passions, •why you must not let any part of your body turn into an unholy weapon fighting on the side of sin; you should, instead, offer yourselves to God, and consider yourselves dead men brought back to life; you should make every part of your body into a weapon fighting on the side of
14 God; •and then sin will no longer dominate your life, since you are living by grace and not by law.

The Christian is freed from the slavery of sin

15 Does the fact that we are living by grace and not by law mean that we are
16 free to sin? Of course not. •You know that if you agree to serve and obey a

c. Gn 17:5 (the same chapter to which allusion is made in v. 11, above).   **d.** Gn 15:5
e. Is 53:5,6

master you become his slaves. You cannot be slaves of sin that leads to death
and at the same time slaves of obedience that leads to righteousness. •You were 17
once slaves of sin, but thank God you submitted without reservation to the
creed you were taught. •You may have been freed from the slavery of sin, but only 18
to become 'slaves' of righteousness. •If I may use human terms to help your 19
natural weakness: as once you put your bodies at the service of vice and immorality, so now you must put them at the service of righteousness for your sanctification.

The reward of sin and the reward of holiness

When you were slaves of sin, you felt no obligation to righteousness, •and $^{20}_{21}$
what did you get from this? Nothing but experiences that now make you blush,
since that sort of behaviour ends in death. •Now, however, you have been set 22
free from sin, you have been made slaves of God, and you get a reward leading
to your sanctification and ending in eternal life. •For the wage paid by sin is 23
death; the present given by God is eternal life in Christ Jesus our Lord.

The Christian is not bound by the Law

7 Brothers, those of you who have studied law will know that laws affect 1
a person only during his lifetime. •A married woman, for instance, has legal 2
obligations to her husband while he is alive, but all these obligations come to
an end if the husband dies. •So if she gives herself to another man while her 3
husband is still alive, she is legally an adulteress; but after her husband is dead
her legal obligations come to an end, and she can marry someone else without
becoming an adulteress. •That is why you, my brothers, who through the body 4
of Christ are now dead to the Law, can now give yourselves to another husband,
to him who rose from the dead to make us productive for God. •Before our 5
conversion*a* our sinful passions, quite unsubdued by the Law, fertilised our
bodies to make them give birth to death. •But now we are rid of the Law, freed 6
by death from our imprisonment, free to serve in the new spiritual way and not
the old way of a written law.

The function of the Law

Does it follow that the Law itself is sin? Of course not. What I mean is that 7
I should not have known what sin was except for the Law. I should not for
instance have known what it means to covet if the Law had not said *You shall
not covet.* •But it was this commandment that sin took advantage of to produce 8
all kinds of covetousness in me, for when there is no Law, sin is dead.

Once, when there was no Law, I*b* was alive; but when the commandment 9
came, sin came to life •and I died: the commandment was meant to lead me to 10
life but it turned out to mean death for me, •because sin took advantage of the 11
commandment to mislead me, and so sin, through that commandment, killed me.
The Law is sacred, and what it commands is sacred, just and good. •Does $^{12}_{13}$
that mean that something good killed me? Of course not. But sin, to show itself
in its true colours, used that good thing to kill me; and thus sin, thanks to the
commandment, was able to exercise all its sinful power.

The inward struggle

The Law, of course, as we all know, is spiritual; but I am unspiritual; I have 14
been sold as a slave to sin. •I cannot understand my own behaviour. I fail to carry 15
out the things I want to do, and I find myself doing the very things I hate. •When 16

I act against my own will, that means I have a self that acknowledges that the
17 Law is good, ·and so the thing behaving in that way is not my self but sin living
18 in me. ·The fact is, I know of nothing good living in me—living, that is, in my
unspiritual self—for though the will to do what is good is in me, the performance
19 is not, ·with the result that instead of doing the good things I want to do, I carry
20 out the sinful things I do not want. ·When I act against my will, then, it is not
my true self doing it, but sin which lives in me.

21 In fact, this seems to be the rule, that every single time I want to do good
22 it is something evil that comes to hand. ·In my inmost self I dearly love God's
23 Law, but ·I can see that my body follows a different law that battles against
the law which my reason dictates. This is what makes me a prisoner of that law
of sin which lives inside my body.

24 What a wretched man I am! Who will rescue me from this body doomed to
25 death? ·Thanks be to God through Jesus Christ our Lord!

In short, it is I who with my reason serve the Law of God, and no less I who
serve in my unspiritual self the law of sin.

B. THE CHRISTIAN'S SPIRITUAL LIFE

The life of the spirit

1 **8** The reason, therefore, why those who are in Christ Jesus are not condemned,
2 is that the law of the spirit of life in Christ Jesus has set you free from the
3 law of sin and death. ·God has done what the Law, because of our unspiritual
nature,[a] was unable to do. God dealt with sin by sending his own Son in a body
4 as physical as any sinful body, and in that body God condemned sin. ·He did
· this in order that the Law's just demands might be satisfied in us, who behave
not as our unspiritual nature but as the spirit dictates.

5 The unspiritual are interested only in what is unspiritual, but the spiritual
6 are interested in spiritual things. ·It is death to limit oneself to what is unspiritual;
7 life and peace can only come with concern for the spiritual. ·That is because to
limit oneself to what is unspiritual is to be at enmity with God: such a limitation
8 never could and never does submit to God's law. ·People who are interested
9 only in unspiritual things can never be pleasing to God. ·Your interests, however,
are not in the unspiritual, but in the spiritual, since the Spirit of God has made
his home in you. In fact, unless you possessed the Spirit of Christ you would not
10 belong to him. ·Though your body may be dead it is because of sin, but if Christ
11 is in you then your spirit is life itself because you have been justified; ·and if the
Spirit of him who raised Jesus from the dead is living in you, then he who raised
Jesus from the dead will give life to your own mortal bodies through his Spirit
living in you.

12 So then, my brothers, there is no necessity for us to obey our unspiritual
13 selves or to live unspiritual lives. ·If you do live in that way, you are doomed to
die; but if by the Spirit you put an end to the misdeeds of the body you will live.

Children of God

14
15 Everyone moved by the Spirit is a son of God. ·The spirit you received
is not the spirit of slaves bringing fear into your lives again; it is the spirit of

7 a. 'While we were in the flesh'.　　**b.** Rhetorical figure; Paul speaks in the person of mankind.
8 a. 'flesh'.

sons, and it makes us cry out, 'Abba, Father!'[b] •The Spirit himself and our spirit 16
bear united witness that we are children of God. •And if we are children we 17
are heirs as well: heirs of God and coheirs with Christ, sharing his sufferings
so as to share his glory.

Glory as our destiny

I think that what we suffer in this life can never be compared to the glory, 18
as yet unrevealed, which is waiting for us. •The whole creation is eagerly 19
waiting for God to reveal his sons. •It was not for any fault on the part of 20
creation that it was made unable to attain its purpose, it was made so by God;
but creation still retains the hope •of being freed, like us, from its slavery to 21
decadence, to enjoy the same freedom and glory as the children of God. •From 22
the beginning till now the entire creation, as we know, has been groaning in
one great act of giving birth; •and not only creation, but all of us who possess 23
the first-fruits of the Spirit, we too groan inwardly as we wait for our bodies
to be set free. •For we must be content to hope that we shall be saved—our 24
salvation is not in sight, we should not have to be hoping for it if it were—•but, 25
as I say, we must hope to be saved since we are not saved yet—it is something
we must wait for with patience.

The Spirit too comes to help us in our weakness. For when we cannot choose 26
words in order to pray properly, the Spirit himself expresses our plea in a way
that could never be put into words, •and God who knows everything in our 27
hearts knows perfectly well what he means, and that the pleas of the saints
expressed by the Spirit are according to the mind of God.

God has called us to share his glory

We know that by turning everything to their good God co-operates with all 28
those who love him, with all those that he has called according to his purpose.
They are the ones he chose specially long ago and intended to become true 29
images of his Son, so that his Son might be the eldest of many brothers. •He 30
called those he intended for this; those he called he justified, and with those he
justified he shared his glory.

A hymn to God's love

After saying this, what can we add? With God on our side who can be against 31
us? •Since God did not spare his own Son, but gave him up to benefit us all, 32
we may be certain, after such a gift, that he will not refuse anything he can give.
Could anyone accuse those that God has chosen? When God acquits, •could 33
anyone condemn? Could Christ Jesus? No! He not only died for us—he rose 34
from the dead, and there at God's right hand he stands and pleads for us.

Nothing therefore can come between us and the love of Christ, even if we are 35
troubled or worried, or being persecuted, or lacking food or clothes, or being
threatened or even attacked. •As scripture promised: *For your sake we are being* 36
massacred daily, and reckoned as sheep for the slaughter.[c] •These are the trials 37
through which we triumph, by the power of him who loved us.

For I am certain of this: neither death nor life, no angel, no prince, nothing 38
that exists, nothing still to come, not any power, •or height or depth,[d] nor any 39
created thing, can ever come between us and the love of God made visible in
Christ Jesus our Lord.

C. THE PLACE OF ISRAEL

The privileges of Israel

1 9 What I want to say now is no pretence; I say it in union with Christ—it is the truth—my conscience in union with the Holy Spirit assures me of it too.
2 What I want to say is this: my sorrow is so great, my mental anguish so endless,
3 I would willingly be condemned *a* and be cut off from Christ if it could help my
4 brothers of Israel, my own flesh and blood. •They were adopted as sons, they were given the glory and the covenants; the Law and the ritual were drawn up
5 for them, and the promises were made to them. •They are descended from the patriarchs and from their flesh and blood came Christ who is above all, God for ever blessed! Amen.

God has kept his promise

6   Does this mean that God has failed to keep his promise? Of course not.
7 Not all those who descend from Israel are Israel; •not all the descendants of Abraham are his true children. Remember: *It is through Isaac that your name will*
8 *be carried on,*[b] •which means that it is not physical descent that decides who are the children of God; it is only the children of the promise who will count as the
9 true descendants. •The actual words in which the promise was made were: *I shall*
10 *visit you* at such and such a time, *and Sarah will have a son.*[c] •Even more to the point is what was said to Rebecca when she was pregnant by our ancestor Isaac,
11 but before her twin children were born and before either had done good or evil.
12 In order to stress that God's choice is free, •since it depends on the one who calls, not on human merit, Rebecca was told: *the elder shall serve the younger,*[d]
13 or as scripture says elsewhere: *I showed my love for Jacob and my hatred for Esau.*[e]

God is not unjust

14
15   Does it follow that God is unjust? Of course not. •Take what God said to
16 Moses: *I have mercy on whom I will, and I show pity to whom I please.*[f] •In other words, the only thing that counts is not what human beings want or try to do,
17 but the mercy of God. •For in scripture he says to Pharaoh: *It was for this I raised you up, to use you as a means of showing my power and to make my name known*
18 *throughout the world.*[g] •In other words, when God wants to show mercy he does, and when he wants to harden someone's heart he does so.

19   You will ask me, 'In that case, how can God ever blame anyone, since no one
20 can oppose his will?' •But what right have you, a human being, to cross-examine God? *The pot has no right to say to the potter: Why did you make me this shape?*[h]
21 Surely a potter can do what he likes with the clay? It is surely for him to decide whether he will use a particular lump of clay to make a special pot or an ordinary one?
22   Or else imagine that although God is ready to show his anger and display his power, yet he patiently puts up with the people who make him angry,
23 however much they deserve to be destroyed. •He puts up with them for the sake

b. The prayer of Christ in Gethsemane.   c. Ps 44:11   d. 'powers', 'heights' and 'depths' are probably cosmic forces hostile to mankind.
9 a. *Anathema,* cursed and excommunicated.   b. Gn 21:12   c. Gn 18:10   d. Gn 25:23
e. Ml 1:2-3   f. Ex 33:19   g. Ex 9:16   h. Is 29:16

of those other people, to whom he wants to be merciful, to whom he wants to reveal the richness of his glory, people he had prepared for this glory long ago. Well, we are those people; whether we were Jews or pagans we are the ones he 24 has called.

All has been foretold in the Old Testament

That is exactly what God says in Hosea: *I shall say to a people that was not* 25 *mine,* '*You are my people*', *and to a nation I never loved,* '*I love you*'. •*Instead of* 26 *being told,* '*You are no people of mine*', *they will now be called the sons of the living God.*[i] •Referring to Israel Isaiah had this to say: *Though Israel should have as* 27 *many descendants as there are grains of sand on the seashore, only a remnant will be saved,* •*for without hesitation or delay the Lord will execute his sentence on the* 28 *earth.*[j] •As Isaiah foretold: *Had the Lord of hosts not left us some descendants we* 29 *should now be like Sodom, we should be like Gomorrah.*[k]

From this it follows that the pagans who were not looking for righteousness 30 found it all the same, a righteousness that comes of faith, •while Israel, looking 31 for a righteousness derived from law failed to do what that law required. •Why 32 did they fail? Because they relied on good deeds instead of trusting in faith. In other words, they *stumbled over the stumbling-stone*[l] •mentioned in scripture: 33 *See how I lay in Zion a stone to stumble over, a rock to trip men up— only those who believe in him will have no cause for shame.*[m]

Israel fails to see that it is God who makes us holy

10 Brothers, I have the very warmest love for the Jews, and I pray to God for 1 them to be saved. •I can swear to their fervour for God, but their zeal is 2 misguided. •Failing to recognise the righteousness that comes from God, they 3 try to promote their own idea of it, instead of submitting to the righteousness of God. •But now the Law has come to an end with Christ, and everyone who has 4 faith may be justified.

The testimony of Moses

When Moses refers to being justified by the Law, he writes: *those who keep* 5 *the Law will draw life from it.*[a] •But the righteousness that comes from faith says 6 this: Do not tell yourself you have to bring Christ down—as in the text: *Who will go up to heaven?*[b] •or that you have to bring Christ back from the dead—as 7 in the text: *Who will go down to the underworld?* •On the positive side it says: 8 *The word,* that is the faith we proclaim, *is very near to you, it is on your lips and in your heart.* •If your lips confess that Jesus is Lord and if you believe in your 9 heart that God raised him from the dead, then you will be saved. •By believing 10 from the heart you are made righteous; by confessing with your lips you are saved. •When scripture says: *those who believe in him will have no cause for shame,*[c] 11 it makes no distinction between Jew and Greek: all belong to the same Lord who 12 is rich enough, however many ask his help, •*for everyone who calls on the name* 13 *of the Lord will be saved.*[d]

Israel has no excuse

But they will not ask his help unless they believe in him, and they will not 14 believe in him unless they have heard of him, and they will not hear of him unless they get a preacher, •and they will never have a preacher unless one is sent, but 15 as scripture says: *The footsteps of those who bring good news is a welcome sound.*[c] Not everyone, of course, listens to the Good News. As Isaiah says: *Lord, how many* 16

17 *believed what we proclaimed?*[*j*] •So faith comes from what is preached, and what is preached comes from the word of Christ.

18　　　Let me put the question: is it possible that they did not hear? Indeed they did; in the words of the psalm, *their voice has gone out through all the earth, and*
19 *their message to the ends of the world.*[*g*] •A second question: is it possible that Israel did not understand? Moses answered this long ago: *I will make you jealous of people who are not even a nation; I will make you angry with an irreligious people.*[*h*]
20 Isaiah said more clearly: *I have been found by those who did not seek me, and have*
21 *revealed myself to those who did not consult me;*[*i*]•and referring to Israel he goes on: *Each day I stretched out my hand to a disobedient and rebellious people.*

The remnant of Israel

1　 **11** Let me put a further question then: is it possible that *God has rejected his people*?[*a*] Of course not. I, an Israelite, descended from Abraham through
2 the tribe of Benjamin, •could never agree that God had rejected his people, the people he chose specially long ago. Do you remember what scripture says of
3 Elijah—how he complained to God about Israel's behaviour? •*Lord, they have killed your prophets and broken down your altars. I, and I only, remain, and they*
4 *want to kill me.*[*b*]•What did God say to that? *I have kept for myself seven*
5 *thousand men who have not bent the knee to Baal.*[*c*] •Today the same thing
6 has happened: there is a remnant, chosen by grace. •By grace, you notice, nothing therefore to do with good deeds, or grace would not be grace at all!

7　　　What follows? It was not Israel as a whole that found what it was seeking,
8 but only the chosen few. The rest were not allowed to see the truth; •as scripture says: *God has given them a sluggish spirit, unseeing eyes and inattentive ears, and*
9 *they are still like that today.*[*d*] •And David says: *May their own table prove a trap*
10 *for them, a snare and a pitfall—let that be their punishment; •may their eyes be struck incurably blind, their backs bend for ever.*[*e*]

The Jews to be restored in the future

11　　　Let me put another question then: have the Jews fallen for ever, or have they just stumbled? Obviously they have not fallen for ever: their fall, though, has
12 saved the pagans in a way the Jews may now well emulate. •Think of the extent to which the world, the pagan world, has benefited from their fall and defection—
13 then think how much more it will benefit from the conversion of them all. •Let me tell you pagans[*f*] this: I have been sent to the pagans as their apostle, and I am
14 proud of being sent, •but the purpose of it is to make my own people envious
15 of you, and in this way save some of them. •Since their rejection meant the reconciliation of the world, do you know what their admission will mean? Nothing less than a resurrection from the dead!

The Jews are still the chosen people

16　　　A whole batch of bread is made holy if the first handful of dough is made
17 holy; all the branches are holy if the root is holy. •No doubt some of the branches have been cut off, and, like shoots of wild olive, you have been grafted among
18 the rest to share with them the rich sap provided by the olive tree itself, •but still,

i. Ho 2:25 and 2:1　　j. Is 10:22:23　　k. Is 1:9　　l. Is 8:14　　m. Is 28:16
10 a. Lv 18:5　　b. This quotation, and the two following, are a free rendering of Dt 30:12-14.
c. Is 28:16　　d. Jl 3:5　　e. Is 52:7　　f. Is 53:1　　g. Ps 19:4　　h. Dt 32:21　　i. Is 65:1,2
11 a. Ps 94:14　　b. 1 K 19:10.14　　c. 1 K 19:18　　d. Is 29:10　　e. Ps 69:22f　　f. Converts from paganism.

even if you think yourself superior to the other branches, remember that you do not support the root; it is the root that supports you. •You will say, 'Those 19 branches were cut off on purpose to let me be grafted in!' True, •they were cut off, 20 but through their unbelief; if you still hold firm, it is only thanks to your faith. Rather than making you proud, that should make you afraid. •God did not 21 spare the natural branches, and he is not likely to spare you. •Do not forget 22 that God can be severe as well as kind: he is severe to those who fell, and he is kind to you, but only for as long as he chooses to be, otherwise you will find yourself cut off too, •and the Jews, if they give up their unbelief, grafted back in 23 your place. God is perfectly able to graft them back again; •after all, if you were 24 cut from your natural wild olive to be grafted unnaturally on to a cultivated olive, it will be much easier for them, the natural branches, to be grafted back on the tree they came from.

The conversion of the Jews

There is a hidden reason for all this, brothers, of which I do not want you 25 to be ignorant, in case you think you know more than you do. One section of Israel has become blind, but this will last only until the whole pagan world has entered, •and then after this the rest of Israel will be saved as well. As scripture 26 says: *The liberator will come from Zion, he will banish godlessness from Jacob. And this is the covenant I will make with them when I take their sins away.*[g] 27

The Jews are enemies of God only with regard to the Good News, and 28 enemies only for your sake; but as the chosen people, they are still loved by God, loved for the sake of their ancestors. •God never takes back his gifts or revokes 29 his choice.

Just as you changed from being disobedient to God, and now enjoy mercy 30 because of their disobedience, •so those who are disobedient now—and only 31 because of the mercy shown to you—will also enjoy mercy eventually. •God has 32 imprisoned all men in their own disobedience only to show mercy to all mankind.

A hymn to God's mercy and wisdom

How rich are the depths of God—how deep his wisdom and knowledge— 33 and how impossible to penetrate his motives or understand his methods! *Who could ever know the mind of the Lord? Who could ever be his counsellor?* •*Who* 34 *could ever give him anything or lend him anything?*[h] •All that exists comes from him; 36 all is by him and for him. To him be glory for ever! Amen.

EXHORTATION

Spiritual worship

12 Think of God's mercy, my brothers, and worship him, I beg you, in a way 1 that is worthy of thinking beings, by offering your living bodies as a holy sacrifice, truly pleasing to God. •Do not model yourselves on the behaviour 2 of the world around you, but let your behaviour change, modelled by your new mind. This is the only way to discover the will of God and know what is good, what it is that God wants, what is the perfect thing to do.

Humility and charity

In the light of the grace I have received I want to urge each one among you 3 not to exaggerate his real importance. Each of you must judge himself soberly by

4 the standard of the faith God has given him. •Just as each of our bodies has
5 several parts and each part has a separate function, •so all of us, in union with
6 Christ, form one body, and as parts of it we belong to each other. •Our gifts
differ according to the grace given us. If your gift is prophecy, then use it as your
7 faith suggests; •if administration, then use it for administration; if teaching,
8 then use it for teaching. •Let the preachers deliver sermons, the almsgivers give
freely, the officials be diligent, and those who do works of mercy do them
cheerfully.
9
10   Do not let your love be a pretence, but sincerely prefer good to evil. •Love
each other as much as brothers should, and have a profound respect for each
11 other. •Work for the Lord with untiring effort and with great earnestness of
12 spirit. •If you have hope, this will make you cheerful. Do not give up if trials
13 come; and keep on praying. •If any of the saints are in need you must share with
them; and you should make hospitality your special care.

Charity to everyone, including enemies

14
15   Bless those who persecute you: never curse them, bless them. •Rejoice with
16 those who rejoice and be sad with those in sorrow. •Treat everyone with equal
kindness; never be condescending but make real friends with the poor. Do not
17 allow yourself to become self-satisfied. •Never repay evil with evil but let everyone
18 see that you are interested only in the highest ideals. •Do all you can to live at
19 peace with everyone. •Never try to get revenge; leave that, my friends, to God's
anger. As scripture says: *Vengeance is mine—I will pay them back,*[a] the Lord
20 promises. •But there is more: *If your enemy is hungry, you should give him food,*
21 *and if he is thirsty, let him drink. Thus you heap red-hot coals on his head.*[b] •Resist
evil and conquer it with good.

Submission to civil authority

1 **13** You must all obey the governing authorities. Since all government comes
2 from God, the civil authorities were appointed by God, •and so anyone who
resists authority is rebelling against God's decision, and such an act is bound
3 to be punished. •Good behaviour is not afraid of magistrates; only criminals
have anything to fear. If you want to live without being afraid of authority, you
4 must live honestly and authority may even honour you. •The state is there to
serve God for your benefit. If you break the law, however, you may well have
fear: the bearing of the sword has its significance. The authorities are there to
5 serve God: they carry out God's revenge by punishing wrongdoers. •You must
obey, therefore, not only because you are afraid of being punished, but also
6 for conscience' sake. •This is also the reason why you must pay taxes, since all
government officials are God's officers. They serve God by collecting taxes.
7 Pay every government official what he has a right to ask—whether it be direct
tax or indirect, fear or honour.

Love and law

8   Avoid getting into debt, except the debt of mutual love. If you love your fellow
9 men you have carried out your obligations. •All the commandments: *You shall*
not commit adultery, you shall not kill, you shall not steal, you shall not covet,[a]

g. Is 27:9   **h.** Is 40:13
12 a. Dt 32:35   **b.** Pr 25:21-22
13 a. From the Commandments in Ex 20 and Dt 17.

and so on, are summed up in this single command: *You must love your neighbour as yourself.*[b] •Love is the one thing that cannot hurt your neighbour; that is why 10 it is the answer to every one of the commandments.

Children of the light

Besides, you know 'the time' has come: you must wake up now: our salvation 11 is even nearer than it was when we were converted. •The night is almost over, it 12 will be daylight soon—let us give up all the things we prefer to do under cover of the dark; let us arm ourselves and appear in the light. •Let us live decently 13 as people do in the daytime: no drunken orgies, no promiscuity or licentiousness, and no wrangling or jealousy. •Let your armour be the Lord Jesus Christ; forget 14 about satisfying your bodies with all their cravings.

Charity towards the scrupulous

14 If a person's faith is not strong enough, welcome him all the same without 1 starting an argument. •People range from those who believe they may eat 2 any sort of meat to those whose faith is so weak they dare not eat anything except vegetables. •Meat-eaters must not despise the scrupulous. On the other 3 hand, the scrupulous must not condemn those who feel free to eat anything they choose, since God has welcomed them. •It is not for you to condemn someone 4 else's servant: whether he stands or falls it is his own master's business; he will stand, you may be sure, because the Lord has power to make him stand. •If 5 one man keeps certain days as holier than others, and another considers all days to be equally holy, each must be left free to hold his own opinion. •The one who 6 observes special days does so in honour of the Lord. The one who eats meat also does so in honour of the Lord, since he gives thanks to God; but then the man who abstains does that too in honour of the Lord, and so he also gives God thanks. The life and death of each of us has its influence on others; •if we live, we live $^7_8$ for the Lord; and if we die, we die for the Lord, so that alive or dead we belong to the Lord. •This explains why Christ both died and came to life, it was so that 9 he might be Lord both of the dead and of the living. •This is also why you should 10 never pass judgement on a brother or treat him with contempt, as some of you have done. We shall all have to stand before the judgement seat of God; •as 11 scripture says: *By my life—it is the Lord who speaks—every knee shall bend before me, and every tongue shall praise God.*[a] •It is to God, therefore, that each of us 12 must give an account of himself.

Far from passing judgement on each other, therefore, you should make up 13 your mind never to be the cause of your brother tripping or falling. •Now I am 14 perfectly well aware, of course, and I speak for the Lord Jesus, that no food is unclean in itself; however, if someone thinks that a particular food is unclean, then it is unclean for him. •And indeed if your attitude to food is upsetting your 15 brother, then you are hardly being guided by charity. You are certainly not free to eat what you like if that means the downfall of someone for whom Christ died.

In short, you must not compromise your privilege, •because the kingdom $^{16}_{17}$ of God does not mean eating or drinking this or that, it means righteousness and peace and joy brought by the Holy Spirit. •If you serve Christ in this way you 18 will please God and be respected by men. •So let us adopt any custom that leads 19 to peace and our mutual improvement; •do not wreck God's work over a 20 question of food. Of course all food is clean, but it becomes evil if by eating it you make somebody else fall away. •In such cases the best course is to abstain 21 from meat and wine and anything else that would make your brother trip or fall or weaken in any way.

22 Hold on to your own belief, as between yourself and God —and consider the man fortunate who can make his decision without going against his conscience.

23 But anybody who eats in a state of doubt is condemned, because he is not in good faith; and every act done in bad faith is a sin.

1 **15** We who are strong have a duty to put up with the qualms of the weak
2 without thinking of ourselves. •Each of us should think of his neighbours and
3 help them to become stronger Christians. •Christ did not think of himself: the words
4 of scripture—*the insults of those who insult you fall on me*[a]—apply to him. •And indeed everything that was written long ago in the scriptures was meant to teach us something about hope from the examples scripture gives of how people who
5 did not give up were helped by God. •And may he who helps us when we refuse to give up, help you all to be tolerant with each other, following the example
6 of Christ Jesus, •so that united in mind and voice you may give glory to the God and Father of our Lord Jesus Christ.

An appeal for unity

7 It can only be to God's glory, then, for you to treat each other in the same
8 friendly way as Christ treated you. •The reason Christ became the servant of circumcised Jews was not only so that God could faithfully carry out the promises
9 made to the patriarchs, •it was also to get the pagans to give glory to God for his mercy, as scripture says in one place: *For this I shall praise you among the*
10 *pagans and sing to your name.*[b] •And in another place: *Rejoice, pagans, with his*
11 *people,*[c] •and in a third place: *Let all the pagans praise the Lord, let all the peoples*
12 *sing his praises.*[d] •Isaiah too has this to say: *The root of Jesse will appear, rising up to rule the pagans, and in him the pagans will put their hope.*[e]
13 May the God of hope bring you such joy and peace in your faith that the power of the Holy Spirit will remove all bounds to hope.

EPILOGUE

Paul's ministry

14 It is not because I have any doubts about you, my brothers; on the contrary I am quite certain that you are full of good intentions, perfectly well instructed
15 and able to advise each other. •The reason why I have written to you, and put some things rather strongly, is to refresh your memories, since God has given me
16 this special position. •He has appointed me as a priest of Jesus Christ, and I am to carry out my priestly duty by bringing the Good News from God to the pagans, and so make them acceptable as an offering, made holy by the Holy Spirit.

17 I think I have some reason to be proud of what I, in union with Christ Jesus,
18 have been able to do for God. •What I am presuming to speak of, of course, is only what Christ himself has done to win the allegiance of the pagans, using
19 what I have said and done •by the power of signs and wonders, by the power of the Holy Spirit. Thus, all the way along, from Jerusalem to Illyricum,[f] I have

b. Lv 19:18
14 a. Is 45:23
15 a. Ps 69:9   b. Ps 18:50   c. Dt 32:43 (LXX)   d. Ps 117:1   e. Is 11:10; 11:1   f. The two extremes of Paul's missionary journeys.

preached Christ's Good News to the utmost of my capacity. •I have always, 20 however, made it an unbroken rule never to preach where Christ's name has already been heard. The reason for that was that I had no wish to build on other men's foundations; •on the contrary, my chief concern has been to fulfil the 21 text: *Those who have never been told about him will see him, and those who have never heard about him will understand.*[g]

Paul's plans

That is the reason why I have been kept from visiting you so long, •though 22 23 for many years I have been longing to pay you a visit. Now, however, having no more work to do here, •I hope to see you on my way to Spain and, after 24 enjoying a little of your company, to complete the rest of the journey with your good wishes. •First, however, I must take a present of money to the saints in 25 Jerusalem, •since Macedonia and Achaia have decided to send a generous 26 contribution to the poor among the saints at Jerusalem. •A generous contribution 27 as it should be, since it is really repaying a debt: the pagans who share the spiritual possessions of these poor people have a duty to help them with temporal possessions. •So when I have done this and officially handed over what has been raised, 28 I shall set out for Spain and visit you on the way. •I know that when I reach you 29 I shall arrive with rich blessings from Christ.

But I beg you, brothers, by our Lord Jesus Christ and the love of the Spirit, 30 to help me through my dangers by praying to God for me. •Pray that I may 31 escape the unbelievers in Judaea, and that the aid I carry to Jerusalem may be accepted by the saints. •Then, if God wills, I shall be feeling very happy when 32 I come to enjoy a period of rest among you. •May the God of peace be with you 33 all! Amen.

Greetings and good wishes

16 I commend to you our sister Phoebe,[a] a deaconess of the church at 1 Cenchreae. •Give her, in union with the Lord, a welcome worthy of saints, 2 and help her with anything she needs: she has looked after a great many people, myself included.

My greetings to Prisca and Aquila, my fellow workers in Christ Jesus, •who 3 4 risked death to save my life:[b] I am not the only one to owe them a debt of gratitude, all the churches among the pagans do as well. •My greetings also 5 to the church that meets at their house.

Greetings to my friend Epaenetus, the first of Asia's gifts to Christ; greetings 6 to Mary who worked so hard for you; •to those outstanding apostles Andronicus 7 and Junias, my compatriots and fellow prisoners who became Christians before me; •to Ampliatus, my friend in the Lord; •to Urban, my fellow worker in 8 9 Christ; to my friend Stachys; •to Apelles who has gone through so much for 10 Christ; to everyone who belongs to the household of Aristobulus; •to my 11 compatriot Herodion; to those in the household of Narcissus who belong to the Lord; •to Tryphaena and Tryphosa, who work hard for the Lord; to my friend 12 Persis who has done so much for the Lord; •to Rufus, a chosen servant of 13 the Lord, and to his mother who has been a mother to me too. •Greetings to 14 Asyncritus, Phlegon, Hermes, Patrobas, Hermas, and all the brothers who are with them; •to Philologus and Julia, Nereus and his sister, and Olympas and all 15 the saints who are with them. •Greet each other with a holy kiss. All the churches 16 of Christ send greetings.

A warning and first postscript

17 I implore you, brothers, be on your guard against anybody who encourages trouble or puts difficulties in the way of the doctrine you have been taught. Avoid
18 them. •People like that are not slaves of Jesus Christ, they are slaves of their own appetites, confusing the simple-minded with their pious and persuasive
19 arguments. •Your fidelity to Christ, anyway, is famous everywhere, and that makes me very happy about you. I only hope that you are also wise in what is
20 good, and innocent of what is bad. •The God of peace will soon crush Satan beneath your feet. The grace of our Lord Jesus Christ be with you.

Last greetings and second postscript

21 Timothy, who is working with me, sends his greetings; so do my compatriots,
22 Jason and Sosipater. •I, Tertius, who wrote out this letter, greet you in the Lord.
23 Greetings from Gaius, who is entertaining me and from the whole church that meets in his house. Erastus, the city treasurer, sends his greetings; so does our brother Quartus.

Doxology

25 Glory to him who is able to give you the strength to live according to the Good News I preach, and in which I proclaim Jesus Christ, the revelation of a
26 mystery kept secret for endless ages, •but now so clear that it must be broadcast to pagans everywhere to bring them to the obedience of faith. This is only what scripture has predicted, and it is all part of the way the eternal God wants things
27 to be. •He alone is wisdom; give glory therefore to him through Jesus Christ for ever and ever. Amen.

g. Is 52:15
16 a. Probably the bearer of the letter.   b. Probably in Ephesus, either at the time of the riot described in Ac 19 or during Paul's imprisonment there.

1 CORINTHIANS

THE FIRST LETTER OF PAUL
TO THE CHURCH AT CORINTH

INTRODUCTION

Address and greetings. Thanksgiving

1 I, Paul, appointed by God to be an apostle, together with brother Sosthenes, 1 send greetings •to the church of God in Corinth, to the holy people of Jesus 2 Christ, who are called to take their place among all the saints everywhere who pray to our Lord Jesus Christ; for he is their Lord no less than ours. •May God 3 our Father and the Lord Jesus Christ send you grace and peace.

I never stop thanking God for all the graces you have received through 4 Jesus Christ. •I thank him that you have been enriched in so many ways, especial- 5 ly in your teachers and preachers; •the witness to Christ has indeed been strong 6 among you •so that you will not be without any of the gifts of the Spirit while 7 you are waiting for our Lord Jesus Christ to be revealed; •and he will keep you 8 steady and without blame until the last day, the day of our Lord Jesus Christ, because God by calling you has joined you to his Son, Jesus Christ; and God 9 is faithful.

I. DIVISIONS AND SCANDALS

A. FACTIONS IN THE CORINTHIAN CHURCH

Dissensions among the faithful

All the same, I do appeal to you, brothers, for the sake of our Lord Jesus 10 Christ, to make up the differences between you, and instead of disagreeing among yourselves, to be united again in your belief and practice. •From what 11 Chloe's people have been telling me, my dear brothers, it is clear that there are serious differences among you. •What I mean are all these slogans that you have, 12 like: 'I am for Paul', 'I am for Apollos', 'I am for Cephas',[a] 'I am for Christ'. Has Christ been parcelled out? Was it Paul that was crucified for you? Were you 13 baptised in the name of Paul? •I am thankful that I never baptised any of you 14 after Crispus and Gaius •so none of you can say he was baptised in my name. 15 Then there was the family of Stephanas, of course, that I baptised too, but no one 16 else as far as I can remember.

The true wisdom and the false

17   For Christ did not send me to baptise, but to preach the Good News, and not to preach that in the terms of philosophy *b* in which the crucifixion of Christ
18 cannot be expressed. •The language of the cross may be illogical to those who are not on the way to salvation, but those of us who are on the way see it as God's
19 power to save. •As scripture says: *I shall destroy the wisdom of the wise and bring*
20 *to nothing all the learning of the learned.* • *Where are the philosophers now? Where are the scribes?* *c* Where are any of our thinkers today? Do you see now how God
21 has shown up the foolishness of human wisdom? •If it was God's wisdom that human wisdom should not know God, it was because God wanted to save those who have faith through the foolishness of the message that we preach.
22 And so, while the Jews demand miracles and the Greeks look for wisdom, •here
23 are we preaching a crucified Christ; to the Jews an obstacle that they cannot
24 get over, to the pagans madness, •but to those who have been called, whether
25 they are Jews or Greeks, a Christ who is the power and the wisdom of God. •For God's foolishness is wiser than human wisdom, and God's weakness is stronger than human strength.

26   Take yourselves for instance, brothers, at the time when you were called: how many of you were wise in the ordinary sense of the word, how many were
27 influential people, or came from noble families? •No, it was to shame the wise that God chose what is foolish by human reckoning, and to shame what is strong
28 that he chose what is weak by human reckoning; •those whom the world thinks common and contemptible are the ones that God has chosen—those who are
29 nothing at all to show up those who are everything. •The human race has nothing
30 to boast about to God, •but you, God has made members of Christ Jesus and by God's doing he has become our wisdom, and our virtue, and our holiness, and
31 our freedom. •As scripture says: *if anyone wants to boast, let him boast about the Lord.* *d*

1   **2** As for me, brothers, when I came to you, it was not with any show of oratory
2   or philosophy, but simply to tell you what God had guaranteed. •During my stay with you, the only knowledge I claimed to have was about Jesus, and
3 only about him as the crucified Christ. •Far from relying on any power of my
4 own, I came among you in great 'fear and trembling' *a* •and in my speeches and the sermons that I gave, there were none of the arguments that belong to philo-
5 sophy; only a demonstration of the power of the Spirit. •And I did this so that your faith should not depend on human philosophy but on the power of God.
6   But still we have a wisdom to offer those who have reached maturity: not a philosophy of our age, it is true, still less of the masters of our age, which
7 are coming to their end. •The hidden wisdom of God which we teach in our mysteries is the wisdom that God predestined to be for our glory before the ages
8 began. •It is a wisdom that none of the masters of this age have ever known, or
9 they would not have crucified the Lord of Glory; •we teach what scripture calls: *the things that no eye has seen and no ear has heard, things beyond the mind of man, all that God has prepared for those who love him.* *b*

10   These are the very things that God has revealed to us through the Spirit, for
11 the Spirit reaches the depths of everything, even the depths of God. •After all,

---

1 a. Peter.   b. 'wisdom', the term used by Paul for the human wisdom of philosophy and rhetoric.   c. Quotations from Is 29:14, Ps 33:10 and Is 33:18 (LXX).   d. Jr 9:22-23
2 a. A scriptural cliché frequently used by Paul.   b. A free combination of Is 64:3 and Jr 3:16.

the depths of a man can only be known by his own spirit, not by any other man, and in the same way the depths of God can only be known by the Spirit of God. Now instead of the spirit of the world, we have received the Spirit that comes 12 from God, to teach us to understand the gifts that he has given us. •Therefore 13 we teach, not in the way in which philosophy is taught, but in the way that the Spirit teaches us: we teach spiritual things spiritually. •An unspiritual person 14 is one who does not accept anything of the Spirit of God: he sees it all as nonsense; it is beyond his understanding because it can only be understood by means of the Spirit. •A spiritual man, on the other hand, is able to judge the value of everything, 15 and his own value is not to be judged by other men. •As scripture says: *Who* 16 *can know the mind of the Lord, so who can teach him?*[c] But we are those who have the mind of Christ.

3 Brothers, I myself was unable to speak to you as people of the Spirit: I treated 1 you as sensual men, still infants in Christ. •What I fed you with was milk, 2 not solid food, for you were not ready for it; and indeed, you are still not ready for it •since you are still unspiritual. Isn't that obvious from all the jealousy 3 and wrangling that there is among you, from the way that you go on behaving like ordinary people? •What could be more unspiritual than your slogans, 'I am 4 for Paul' and 'I am for Apollos'?

The place of the Christian preacher

After all, what is Apollos and what is Paul? They are servants who brought 5 the faith to you. Even the different ways in which they brought it were assigned to them by the Lord. •I did the planting, Apollos did the watering, but God 6 made things grow. •Neither the planter nor the waterer matters: only God, who 7 makes things grow. •It is all one who does the planting and who does the watering, 8 and each will duly be paid according to his share in the work. •We are fellow 9 workers with God; you are God's farm, God's building.

By the grace God gave me, I succeeded as an architect and laid the foundations, 10 on which someone else is doing the building. Everyone doing the building must work carefully. •For the foundation, nobody can lay any other than the one 11 which has already been laid, that is Jesus Christ. •On this foundation you can 12 build in gold, silver and jewels, or in wood, grass and straw, •but whatever the 13 material, the work of each builder is going to be clearly revealed when the day comes. That day will begin with fire, and the fire will test the quality of each man's work. •If his structure stands up to it, he will get his wages; •if it is burnt down, ${14 \atop 15}$ he will be the loser, and though he is saved himself, it will be as one who has gone through fire.

Didn't you realise that you were God's temple and that the Spirit of God was 16 living among you? •If anybody should destroy the temple of God, God 17 will destroy him, because the temple of God is sacred; and you are that temple.

Conclusions

Make no mistake about it: if any one of you thinks of himself as wise, in the 18 ordinary sense of the word, then he must learn to be a fool before he really can be wise. •Why? Because the wisdom of this world is foolishness to God. As scripture 19 says: *The Lord knows wise men's thoughts: he knows how useless they are:*[a] or again: *God is not convinced by the arguments of the wise.*[b] •So there is ${20 \atop 21}$ nothing to boast about in anything human: •Paul, Apollos, Cephas, the world, 22 life and death, the present and the future, are all your servants; •but you belong 23 to Christ and Christ belongs to God.

1 **4** People must think of us as Christ's servants, stewards entrusted with the
2 mysteries of God. •What is expected of stewards is that each one should be
3 found worthy of his trust. •Not that it makes the slightest difference to me
whether you, or indeed any human tribunal, find me worthy or not. I will not
4 even pass judgement on myself. •True, my conscience does not reproach me at
all, but that does not prove that I am acquitted: the Lord alone is my judge.
5 There must be no passing of premature judgement. Leave that until the Lord
comes: he will light up all that is hidden in the dark and reveal the secret intentions
of men's hearts. Then will be the time for each one to have whatever praise he
deserves, from God.

6 Now in everything I have said here, brothers, I have taken Apollos and
myself as an example (remember the maxim: 'Keep to what is written'); it is not
for you, so full of your own importance, to go taking sides for one man against
7 another. •In any case, brother, has anybody given you some special right? What
do you have that was not given to you? And if it was given, how can you boast
8 as though it were not? •Is it that you have everything you want—that you are
rich already, in possession of your kingdom, with us left outside? Indeed I wish
9 you were really kings, and we could be kings with you! •But instead, it seems to
me, God has put us apostles at the end of his parade, with the men sentenced
to death; it is true—we have been put on show in front of the whole universe,
10 angels as well as men. •Here we are, fools for the sake of Christ, while you are
the learned men in Christ; we have no power, but you are influential; you are
11 celebrities, we are nobodies. •To this day, we go without food and drink and
12 clothes; we are beaten and have no homes; •we work for our living with our own
hands. When we are cursed, we answer with a blessing; when we are hounded,
13 we put up with it; •we are insulted and we answer politely. We are treated as
the offal of the world, still to this day, the scum of the earth.

An appeal

14 I am saying all this not just to make you ashamed but to bring you, as my
15 dearest children, to your senses. •You might have thousands of guardians in
Christ, but not more than one father and it was I who begot you in Christ Jesus
16 by preaching the Good News. •That is why I beg you to copy me •and why I have
17
sent you Timothy, my dear and faithful son in the Lord: he will remind you of the
way that I live in Christ, as I teach it everywhere in all the churches.

18 When it seemed that I was not coming to visit you, some of you became self-
19 important, •but I will be visiting you soon, the Lord willing, and then I shall
want to know not what these self-important people have to say, but what they
20 can do, •since the kingdom of God is not just words, it is power. •It is for you
21
to decide: do I come with a stick in my hand or in a spirit of love and goodwill?

B. INCEST IN CORINTH

1 **5** I have been told as an undoubted fact that one of you is living with his father's
wife.[a] This is a case of sexual immorality among you that must be unparal-
2 leled even among pagans. •How can you be so proud of yourselves? You should
be in mourning. A man who does a thing like that ought to have been expelled

c. Is 40:13
3 a. Jb 5:13   b. Ps 94:11
5 a. Stepmother. Lv 18:8 forbids sexual relations with 'your father's wife'.

from the community. •Though I am far away in body, I am with you in spirit, 3
and have already condemned the man who did this thing as if I were actually
present. •When you are assembled together in the name of the Lord Jesus, 4
and I am spiritually present with you, then with the power of our Lord Jesus
he is to be handed over to Satan so that his sensual body may be destroyed and 5
his spirit saved on the day of the Lord.

The pride that you take in yourselves is hardly to your credit. You must know 6
how even a small amount of yeast is enough to leaven all the dough, •so get rid 7
of all the old yeast, and make yourselves into a completely new batch of bread,
unleavened as you are meant to be. Christ, our passover, has been sacrificed;
let us celebrate the feast, then, by getting rid of all the old yeast of evil and wick- 8
edness, having only the unleavened bread of sincerity and truth.[b]

When I wrote in my letter to you not to associate with people living immoral 9
lives, •I was not meaning to include all the people in the world who are sexually 10
immoral, any more than I meant to include all usurers and swindlers or idol-
worshippers. To do that, you would have to withdraw from the world altogether.
What I wrote was that you should not associate with a brother Christian who 11
is leading an immoral life, or is a usurer, or idolatrous, or a slanderer, or a drunkard, or is dishonest; you should not even eat a meal with people like that. •It is 12
not my business to pass judgement on those outside. Of those who are inside,
you can surely be the judges. •But of those who are outside, God is the judge. 13
You must drive out this evil-doer from among you.[c]

C. RECOURSE TO THE PAGAN COURTS

6 How dare one of your members take up a complaint against another in the 1
lawcourts of the unjust[a] instead of before the saints? •As you know, it is the 2
saints who are to 'judge the world'; and if the world is to be judged by you, how
can you be unfit to judge trifling cases? •Since we are also to judge angels, it follows 3
that we can judge matters of everyday life; •but when you have had cases of that 4
kind, the people you appointed to try them were not even respected in the
Church. •You should be ashamed: is there really not one reliable man among 5
you to settle differences between brothers •and so one brother brings a court 6
case against another in front of unbelievers? •It is bad enough for you to have 7
lawsuits at all against one another: oughtn't you to let yourselves be wronged,
and let yourselves be cheated? •But you are doing the wronging and the cheating, 8
and to your own brothers.

You know perfectly well that people who do wrong will not inherit the 9
kingdom of God: people of immoral lives, idolaters, adulterers, catamites,
sodomites, •thieves, usurers, drunkards, slanderers and swindlers will never 10
inherit the kingdom of God. •These are the sort of people some of you were 11
once, but now you have been washed clean, and sanctified, and justified through
the name of the Lord Jesus Christ and through the Spirit of our God.

D. FORNICATION

'For me there are no forbidden things';[b] maybe, but not everything does good. 12
I agree there are no forbidden things for me, but I am not going to let anything
dominate me. •Food is only meant for the stomach, and the stomach for food; 13
yes, and God is going to do away with both of them. But the body—this is not

14 meant for fornication; it is for the Lord, and the Lord for the body. •God, who raised the Lord from the dead, will by his power raise us up too.

15 You know, surely, that your bodies are members making up the body of Christ; do you think I can take parts of Christ's body and join them to the body 16 of a prostitute? Never! •As you know, a man who goes with a prostitute is one 17 body with her, since *the two*, as it is said, *become one flesh.* •But anyone who is joined to the Lord is one spirit with him.

18 Keep away from fornication. All the other sins are committed outside the 19 body; but to fornicate is to sin against your own body. •Your body, you know, is the temple of the Holy Spirit, who is in you since you received him from God. 20 You are not your own property; •you have been bought and paid for. That is why you should use your body for the glory of God.

II. ANSWERS TO VARIOUS QUESTIONS

A. MARRIAGE AND VIRGINITY

1 **7** Now for the questions about which you wrote. Yes, it is a good thing for 2 a man not to touch a woman; •but since sex is always a danger, let each 3 man have his own wife and each woman her own husband. •The husband must give his wife what she has the right to expect, and so too the wife to the husband. 4 The wife has no rights over her own body; it is the husband who has them. In the 5 same way, the husband has no rights over his body; the wife has them. •Do not refuse each other except by mutual consent, and then only for an agreed time, to leave yourselves free for prayer; then come together again in case Satan should 6 take advantage of your weakness to tempt you. •This is a suggestion, not a rule: 7 I should like everyone to be like me, but everybody has his own particular gifts from God, one with a gift for one thing and another with a gift for the opposite.

8 There is something I want to add for the sake of widows and those who are 9 not married: it is a good thing for them to stay as they are, like me, •but if they cannot control the sexual urges, they should get married, since it is better to be married than to be tortured.

10 For the married I have something to say, and this is not from me but from 11 the Lord: a wife must not leave her husband —•or if she does leave him, she must either remain unmarried or else make it up with her husband—nor must a husband send his wife away.

12 The rest is from me and not from the Lord. If a brother has a wife who is an unbeliever, and she is content to live with him, he must not send her away; 13 and if a woman has an unbeliever for her husband, and he is content to live with 14 her, she must not leave him. •This is because the unbelieving husband is made one with the saints through his wife, and the unbelieving wife is made one with the saints through her husband. If this were not so, your children would be 15 unclean, whereas in fact they are holy. •However, if the unbelieving partner does not consent, they may separate; in these circumstances, the brother or 16 sister is not tied: God has called you to a life of peace. •If you are a wife, it

---

b. See note *a* to Jn 19, on the Passover practice.　　c. Dt 13:6

6 a. The pagan magistrates of Corinth.　　**b.** Probably one of Paul's own sayings which has been misapplied by false teachers: this section of the letter is directed against the libertines, who had been teaching that sexual intercourse was as necessary for the body as food and drink.

may be your part to save your husband, for all you know; if a husband, for all you know, it may be your part to save your wife.

For the rest, what each one has is what the Lord has given him and he should 17 continue as he was when God's call reached him. This is the ruling that I give in all the churches. •If anyone had already been circumcised at the time of 18 his call, he need not disguise it, and anyone who was uncircumcised at the time of his call need not be circumcised; •because to be circumcised or 19 uncircumcised means nothing: what does matter is to keep the commandments of God. •Let everyone stay as he was at the time of his call. •If, when you were $^{20}_{21}$ called, you were a slave, do not let this bother you; but if you should have the chance of being free, accept it. •A slave, when he is called in the Lord, becomes 22 the Lord's freedman, and a freeman called in the Lord becomes Christ's slave. You have all been bought and paid for; do not be slaves of other men. •Each $^{23}_{24}$ one of you, my brothers, should stay as he was before God at the time of his call.

About remaining celibate, I have no directions from the Lord but give my 25 own opinion as one who, by the Lord's mercy, has stayed faithful. •Well then, 26 I believe that in these present times of stress this is right: that it is good for a man to stay as he is. •If you are tied to a wife, do not look for freedom; if you are 27 free of a wife, then do not look for one. •But if you marry, it is no sin, and it is 28 not a sin for a young girl to get married. They will have their troubles, though, in their married life, and I should like to spare you that.

Brothers, this is what I mean: our time is growing short. Those who have 29 wives should live as though they had none, •and those who mourn should live as 30 though they had nothing to mourn for; those who are enjoying life should live as though there were nothing to laugh about; those whose life is buying things should live as though they had nothing of their own; •and those who have to 31 deal with the world should not become engrossed in it. I say this because the world as we know it is passing away.

I would like to see you free from all worry. An unmarried man can devote 32 himself to the Lord's affairs, all he need worry about is pleasing the Lord; •but 33 a married man has to bother about the world's affairs and devote himself to pleasing his wife: •he is torn two ways. In the same way an unmarried woman, 34 like a young girl, can devote herself to the Lord's affairs; all she need worry about is being holy in body and spirit. The married woman, on the other hand, has to worry about the world's affairs and devote herself to pleasing her husband. I say this only to help you, not to put a halter round your necks, but simply to 35 make sure that everything is as it should be, and that you give your undivided attention to the Lord.

Still, if there is anyone who feels that it would not be fair to his daughter to 36 let her grow too old for marriage, and that he should do something about it, he is free to do as he likes: he is not sinning if there is a marriage. •On the other 37 hand, if someone has firmly made his mind up, without any compulsion and in complete freedom of choice, to keep his daughter as she is, he will be doing a good thing. •In other words, the man who sees that his daughter is married 38 has done a good thing but the man who keeps his daughter unmarried has done something even better.*ª*

A wife is tied as long as her husband is alive. But if the husband dies, she is 39 free to marry anybody she likes, only it must be in the Lord. •She would be 40 happier, in my opinon, if she stayed as she is—and I too have the Spirit of God, I think.

B. FOOD OFFERED TO IDOLS

General principles

1 **8** Now about food sacrificed to idols. 'We all have knowledge'; yes, that is so, but knowledge gives self-importance—it is love that makes the building grow.
2 A man may imagine he understands something, but still not understand anything
3 in the way that he ought to. •But any man who loves God is known by him.
4 Well then, about eating food sacrificed to idols:[a] we know that idols do not really
5 exist in the world and that there is no god but the One. •And even if there were things called gods, either in the sky or on earth—where there certainly seem to
6 be 'gods' and 'lords' in plenty—•still for us there is one God, the Father, from whom all things come and for whom we exist; and there is one Lord, Jesus Christ, through whom all things come and through whom we exist.

The claims of love

7 Some people, however, do not have this knowledge. There are some who have been so long used to idols that they eat this food as though it really had been sacrificed to the idol, and their conscience, being weak, is defiled
8 by it. •Food, of course, cannot bring us in touch with God: we lose nothing
9 if we refuse to eat, we gain nothing if we eat. •Only be careful that you do not make use of this freedom in a way that proves a pitfall for the weak.
10 Suppose someone sees you, a man who understands, eating in some temple of an idol; his own conscience, even if it is weak, may encourage him
11 to eat food which has been offered to idols. •In this way your knowledge could become the ruin of someone weak, of a brother for whom Christ
12 died. •By sinning in this way against your brothers, and injuring their weak
13 consciences, it would be Christ against whom you sinned. •That is why, since food can be the occasion of my brother's downfall, I shall never eat meat again in case I am the cause of a brother's downfall.

Paul invokes his own example

1 **9** I, personally, am free: I am an apostle and I have seen Jesus our Lord. You
2 are all my work in the Lord. •Even if I were not an apostle to others, I should
3 still be an apostle to you who are the seal of my apostolate in the Lord. •My
4 answer to those who want to interrogate me is this: •Have we not every right
5 to eat and drink?[a] •And the right to take a Christian woman round with us, like all the other apostles and the brothers of the Lord and Cephas?
6/7 Are Barnabas and I the only ones who are not allowed to stop working? •Nobody ever paid money to stay in the army, and nobody ever planted a vineyard and refused to eat the fruit of it. Who has there ever been that kept a flock and did not feed on the milk from his flock?
8 These may be only human comparisons, but does not the Law itself say the
9 same thing? •It is written in the Law of Moses: *You must not put a muzzle on the*

7 a. 'daughter' is not the only possible word; this passage has been read as alluding to the practice of a man and a woman living together under vows of chastity; a practice for which there is evidence of a later date.

8 a. At feasts and public ceremonies, portions of the food were 'sacrificed' and went to the gods, the priests and the donors; the whole of the food was regarded as dedicated, whether it was eaten at a ceremonial meal or part of it sold in the markets.

9 a. At the expense of the Christian congregations.

ox when it is treading out the corn.[b] Is it about oxen that God is concerned, •or is 10 there not an obvious reference to ourselves? Clearly this was written for our sake to show that the ploughman ought to plough in expectation, and the thresher to thresh in the expectation of getting his share. •If we have sown spiritual things 11 for you, why should you be surprised if we harvest your material things? •Others 12 are allowed these rights over you and our right is surely greater? In fact we have never exercised this right. On the contrary we have put up with anything rather than obstruct the Good News of Christ in any way.•Remember that the ministers 13 serving in the Temple get their food from the Temple and those serving at the altar can claim their share from the altar itself. •In the same sort of way the Lord 14 directed that those who preach the gospel should get their living from the gospel.

However, I have not exercised any of these rights, and I am not writing all 15 this to secure this treatment for myself. I would rather die than let anyone take away something that I can boast of. •Not that I do boast of preaching the gospel, 16 since it is a duty which has been laid on me; I should be punished if I did not preach it! •If I had chosen this work myself, I might have been paid for it, but 17 as I have not, it is a responsibility which has been put into my hands. •Do you 18 know what my reward is? It is this: in my preaching, to be able to offer the Good News free, and not insist on the rights which the gospel gives me.

So though I am not a slave of any man I have made myself the slave of 19 everyone so as to win as many as I could. •I made myself a Jew to the Jews, to 20 win the Jews; that is, I who am not a subject of the Law made myself a subject of the Law to those who are the subjects of the Law, to win those who are subject to the Law. •To those who have no Law, I was free of the Law myself (though 21 not free from God's law, being under the law of Christ) to win those who have no Law. •For the weak I made myself weak. I made myself all things to all men in 22 order to save some at any cost; •and I still do this, for the sake of the gospel, 23 to have a share in its blessings.

All the runners at the stadium are trying to win, but only one of them gets 24 the prize. You must run in the same way, meaning to win. •All the fighters at 25 the games go into strict training; they do this just to win a wreath that will wither away, but we do it for a wreath that will never wither. •That is how I run, intent 26 on winning; that is how I fight, not beating the air. •I treat my body hard and 27 make it obey me, for, having been an announcer myself, I should not want to be disqualified.

A warning, and the lessons of Israel's history

10 I want to remind you, brothers, how our fathers were all guided by a cloud 1 above them and how they all passed through the sea. •They were all 2 baptised into Moses in this cloud and in this sea; •all ate the same spiritual 3 food •and all drank the same spiritual drink, since they all drank from the 4 spiritual rock that followed them as they went, and that rock was Christ. •In 5 spite of this, most of them failed to please God and their corpses littered the desert.

These things all happened as warnings[a] for us, not to have the wicked lusts 6 for forbidden things that they had. •Do not become idolaters as some of them 7 did, for scripture says: *After sitting down to eat and drink, the people got up to amuse themselves.*[b] •We must never fall into sexual immorality: some of them did, 8 and twenty-three thousand met their downfall in one day. •We are not to put 9 the Lord to the test: some of them did, and they were killed by snakes. •You 10

must never complain: some of them did, and they were killed by the Destroyer.
11 All this happened to them as a warning, and it was written down to be a lesson
12 for us who are living at the end of the age. •The man who thinks he is safe must
13 be careful that he does not fall. •The trials that you have had to bear are no more than people normally have. You can trust God not to let you be tried beyond your strength, and with any trial he will give you a way out of it and the strength to bear it.

Sacrificial feasts. No compromise with idolatry

14 This is the reason, my dear brothers, why you must keep clear of idolatry.
15
16 I say to you as sensible people: judge for yourselves what I am saying. •The blessing-cup that we bless is a communion with the blood of Christ, and the
17 bread that we break is a communion with the body of Christ. •The fact that there is only one loaf means that, though there are many of us, we form a single body
18 because we all have a share in this one loaf. •Look at the other Israel, the race,
19 where those who eat the sacrifices are in communion with the altar. •Does this mean that the food sacrificed to idols has a real value, or that the idol itself is
20 real? •Not at all. It simply means that the sacrifices that they offer *they sacrifice to demons who are not God.*[c] I have no desire to see you in communion with
21 demons. •You cannot drink the cup of the Lord and the cup of demons. You
22 cannot take your share at the table of the Lord and at the table of demons. •Do we want to make the Lord angry; are we stronger than he is?

Food sacrificed to idols. Practical solutions

23 'For me there are no forbidden things', but not everything does good. True, there are no forbidden things, but it is not everything that helps the building to
24 grow. •Nobody should be looking for his own advantage, but everybody for the
25 other man's. •Do not hesitate to eat anything that is sold in butchers' shops:
26 there is no need to raise questions of conscience; •for *the earth and everything*
27 *that is in it belong to the Lord.*[d] •If an unbeliever invites you to his house, go if you want to, and eat whatever is put in front of you, without asking questions
28 just to satisfy conscience. •But if someone says to you, 'This food was offered in sacrifice', then, out of consideration for the man that told you, you should
29 not eat it, for the sake of his scruples; •his scruples, you see, not your own. Why
30 should my freedom depend on somebody else's conscience? •If I take my share with thankfulness, why should I be blamed for food for which I have thanked God?

Conclusion

31 Whatever you eat, whatever you drink, whatever you do at all, do it for the
32 glory of God. •Never do anything offensive to anyone—to Jews or Greeks or to
33 the Church of God; •just as I try to be helpful to everyone at all times, not anxious for my own advantage but for the advantage of everybody else, so that they may be saved.

11 ¹ Take me for your model, as I take Christ.

---

b. Dt 25:4
10 a. Lit. 'types'; events prefiguring in the history of Israel the spiritual realities of the messianic age.   **b.** Ex 32:6   **c.** Dt 32:17   **d.** Ps 24:1

C. DECORUM IN PUBLIC WORSHIP

Women's behaviour at services

You have done well in remembering me so constantly and in maintaining 2 the traditions just as I passed them on to you. •However, what I want you to 3 understand is that Christ is the head of every man, man is the head of woman, and God is the head of Christ. •For a man to pray or prophesy with his head 4 covered is a sign of disrespect to his head.[a] •For a woman, however, it is a sign 5 of disrespect to her head[b] if she prays or prophesies unveiled; she might as well have her hair shaved off. •In fact, a woman who will not wear a veil ought to have 6 her hair cut off. If a woman is ashamed to have her hair cut off or shaved, she ought to wear a veil.

A man should certainly not cover his head, since he is the image of God and 7 reflects God's glory; but woman is the reflection of man's glory. •For man did 8 not come from woman; no, woman came from man; •and man was not created 9 for the sake of woman, but woman was created for the sake of man. •That is the 10 argument for women's covering their heads with a symbol of the authority over them, out of respect for the angels.[c] •However, though woman cannot do 11 without man, neither can man do without woman, in the Lord; •woman may 12 come from man, but man is born of woman—both come from God.

Ask yourselves if it is fitting for a woman to pray to God without a veil; 13 and whether nature itself does not tell you that long hair on a man is nothing 14 to be admired, •while a woman, who was given her hair as a covering, thinks 15 long hair her glory?

To anyone who might still want to argue: it is not the custom with us, nor in 16 the churches of God.

The Lord's Supper

Now that I am on the subject of instructions, I cannot say that you have done 17 well in holding meetings that do you more harm than good. •In the first place, 18 I hear that when you all come together as a community, there are separate factions among you, and I half believe it—•since there must no doubt be separate 19 groups among you, to distinguish those who are to be trusted. •The point is, 20 when you hold these meetings, it is not the Lord's Supper[d] that you are eating, since when the time comes to eat, everyone is in such a hurry to start his own 21 supper that one person goes hungry while another is getting drunk. •Surely you 22 have homes for eating and drinking in? Surely you have enough respect for the community of God not to make poor people embarrassed? What am I to say to you? Congratulate you? I cannot congratulate you on this.

For this is what I received from the Lord, and in turn passed on to you: that 23 on the same night that he was betrayed, the Lord Jesus took some bread, •and 24 thanked God for it and broke it, and he said, 'This is my body, which is for you; do this as a memorial of me'. •In the same way he took the cup after supper, 25 and said, 'This cup is the new covenant in my blood. Whenever you drink it, do this as a memorial of me.' •Until the Lord comes, therefore, every time you eat 26 this bread and drink this cup, you are proclaiming his death, •and so anyone 27 who eats the bread or drinks the cup of the Lord unworthily will be behaving unworthily towards the body and blood of the Lord.

Everyone is to recollect himself before eating this bread and drinking this 28

29 cup; •because a person who eats and drinks without recognising the Body
30 is eating and drinking his own condemnation. •In fact that is why many of you
31 are weak and ill and some of you have died. •If only we recollected ourselves,
32 we should not be punished like that. •But when the Lord does punish us like that,
it is to correct us and stop us from being condemned with the world.

33   So to sum up, my dear brothers, when you meet for the Meal, wait for one
34 another. •Anyone who is hungry should eat at home, and then your meeting
will not bring your condemnation. The other matters I shall adjust when I come.

Spiritual gifts

1   **12** Now my dear brothers, I want to clear up a wrong impression about
2   spiritual gifts. •You remember that, when you were pagans, whenever
3 you felt irresistibly drawn, it was towards dumb idols? •It is for that reason that
I want you to understand that on the one hand no one can be speaking under the
influence of the Holy Spirit and say, 'Curse Jesus', and on the other hand, no one
can say, 'Jesus is Lord' unless he is under the influence of the Holy Spirit.

The variety and the unity of gifts

4
5   There is a variety of gifts but always the same Spirit; •there are all sorts of
6 service to be done, but always to the same Lord; •working in all sorts of different
7 ways in different people, it is the same God who is working in all of them. •The
particular way in which the Spirit is given to each person is for a good purpose.
8 One may have the gift of preaching with wisdom given him by the Spirit; another
9 may have the gift of preaching instruction given him by the same Spirit; •and
another the gift of faith given by the same Spirit; another again the gift of healing,
10 through this one Spirit; •one, the power of miracles; another, prophecy;
another the gift of recognising spirits; another the gift of tongues and another
11 the ability to interpret them. •All these are the work of one and the same Spirit,
who distributes different gifts to different people just as he chooses.

The analogy of the body

12   Just as a human body, though it is made up of many parts, is a single unit
13 because all these parts, though many, make one body, so it is with Christ. •In
the one Spirit we were all baptised, Jews as well as Greeks, slaves as well as
citizens, and one Spirit was given to us all to drink.
14
15   Nor is the body to be identified with any one of its many parts. •If the foot
were to say, 'I am not a hand and so I do not belong to the body', would that
16 mean that it stopped being part of the body? •If the ear were to say, 'I am not
an eye, and so I do not belong to the body', would that mean that it was not a part
17 of the body? •If your whole body was just one eye, how would you hear anything?
If it was just one ear, how would you smell anything?
18
19   Instead of that, God put all the separate parts into the body on purpose. •If
20 all the parts were the same, how could it be a body? •As it is, the parts are many
21 but the body is one. •The eye cannot say to the hand, 'I do not need you', nor can
the head say to the feet, 'I do not need you'.

22   What is more, it is precisely the parts of the body that seem to be the weakest
23 which are the indispensable ones; •and it is the least honourable parts of the

---

11 a. His leader, a Greek pun.   **b.** Her husband, who is her head; she is claiming equality.
c. The guardians of due order in public worship.   **d.** The *agapē*, or love feast, preceding the
liturgical meal.

body that we clothe with the greatest care. So our more improper parts get decorated •in a way that our more proper parts do not need. God has arranged 24 the body so that more dignity is given to the parts which are without it, •and so 25 that there may not be disagreements inside the body, but that each part may be equally concerned for all the others. •If one part is hurt, all parts are hurt with 26 it. If one part is given special honour, all parts enjoy it.

Now you together are Christ's body; but each of you is a different part of it. 27 In the Church, God has given the first place to apostles, the second to prophets, 28 the third to teachers; after them, miracles, and after them the gift of healing; helpers, good leaders, those with many languages. •Are all of them apostles, 29 or all of them prophets, or all of them teachers? Do they all have the gift of miracles, •or all have the gift of healing? Do all speak strange languages, and 30 all interpret them?

The order of importance in spiritual gifts. Love

Be ambitious for the higher gifts. And I am going to show you a way that is 31 better than any of them.

13 If I have all the eloquence of men or of angels, but speak without love, 1 I am simply a gong booming or a cymbal clashing. •If I have the gift of 2 prophecy, understanding all the mysteries there are, and knowing everything, and if I have faith in all its fulness, to move mountains, but without love, then I am nothing at all. •If I give away all that I possess, piece by piece, and if I even 3 let them take my body to burn it, but am without love, it will do me no good whatever.

Love is always patient and kind; it is never jealous; love is never boastful 4 or conceited; •it is never rude or selfish; it does not take offence, and is not 5 resentful. •Love takes no pleasure in other people's sins but delights in the truth; 6 it is always ready to excuse, to trust, to hope, and to endure whatever comes. 7

Love does not come to an end. But if there are gifts of prophecy, the time 8 will come when they must fail; or the gift of languages, it will not continue for ever; and knowledge—for this, too, the time will come when it must fail. For our knowledge is imperfect and our prophesying is imperfect; •but once $^9_{10}$ perfection comes, all imperfect things will disappear. •When I was a child, I used 11 to talk like a child, and think like a child, and argue like a child, but now I am a man, all childish ways are put behind me. •Now we are seeing a dim reflection 12 in a mirror; but then we shall be seeing face to face. The knowledge that I have now is imperfect; but then I shall know as fully as I am known.

In short, there are three things that last: faith, hope and love; and the 13 greatest of these is love.

Spiritual gifts: their respective importance in the community

14 You must want love more than anything else; but still hope for the spiritual 1 gifts as well, especially prophecy. •Anybody with the gift of tongues speaks 2 to God, but not to other people; because nobody understands him when he talks in the spirit about mysterious things. •On the other hand, the man who 3 prophesies does talk to other people, to their improvement, their encouragement and their consolation. •The one with the gift of tongues talks for his own 4 benefit, but the man who prophesies does so for the benefit of the community. While I should like you all to have the gift of tongues, I would much rather you 5 could prophesy, since the man who prophesies is of greater importance than the

man with the gift of tongues, unless of course the latter offers an interpretation so that the church may get some benefit.

6 Now suppose, my dear brothers, I am someone with the gift of tongues, and I come to visit you, what use shall I be if all my talking reveals nothing new, tells
7 you nothing, and neither inspires you nor instructs you? •Think of a musical instrument, a flute or a harp: if one note on it cannot be distinguished
8 from another, how can you tell what tune is being played? •Or if no one can be sure which call the trumpet has sounded, who will be ready for the attack?
9 It is the same with you: if your tongue does not produce intelligible speech, how
10 can anyone know what you are saying? You will be talking to the air. •There are any number of different languages in the world, and not one of them is meaning-
11 less, •but if I am ignorant of what the sounds mean, I am a savage to the man
12 who is speaking, and he is a savage to me. •It is the same in your own case: since you aspire to spiritual gifts, concentrate on those which will grow to benefit the community.

13 That is why anybody who has the gift of tongues must pray for the power
14 of interpreting them. •For if I use this gift in my prayers, my spirit may be praying
15 but my mind is left barren. •What is the answer to that? Surely I should pray not only with the spirit but with the mind as well? And sing praises not only with
16 the spirit but with the mind as well? •Any uninitiated person will never be able to say Amen to your thanksgiving, if you only bless God with the spirit, for he
17 will have no idea what you are saying. •However well you make your thanks-
18 giving, the other gets no benefit from it. •I thank God that I have a greater gift
19 of tongues than all of you, •but when I am in the presence of the community I would rather say five words that mean something than ten thousand words in a tongue.

20 Brothers, you are not to be childish in your outlook. You can be babies as
21 far as wickedness is concerned, but mentally you must be adult. •In the written Law it says: *Through men speaking strange languages and through the lips of foreigners, I shall talk to the nation, and still they will not listen to me, says the*
22 *Lord.*[a] •You see then, that the strange languages are meant to be a sign not for believers but for unbelievers, while on the other hand, prophecy is a sign not for
23 unbelievers but for believers. •So that any uninitiated people or unbelievers, coming into a meeting of the whole church where everybody was speaking in
24 tongues, would say you were all mad; •but if you were all prophesying and an unbeliever or uninitiated person came in, he would find himself analysed and
25 judged by everyone speaking; •he would find his secret thoughts laid bare, and then fall on his face and worship God, declaring that *God is among you indeed.*[b]

Regulating spiritual gifts

26 So, my dear brothers, what conclusion is to be drawn? At all your meetings, let everyone be ready with a psalm or a sermon or a revelation, or ready to use his gift of tongues or to give an interpretation; but it must always be for the
27 common good. •If there are people present with the gift of tongues, let only two or three, at the most, be allowed to use it, and only one at a time, and there must
28 be someone to interpret. •If there is no interpreter present, they must keep quiet
29 in church and speak only to themselves and to God. •As for prophets, let two

14 a. A free version of Is 28:11-12.   **b.** Is 45:14

or three of them speak, and the others attend to them. •If one of the listeners 30 receives a revelation, then the man who is already speaking should stop. •For 31 you can all prophesy in turn, so that everybody will learn something and everybody will be encouraged. •Prophets can always control their prophetic 32 spirits, •since God is not a God of disorder but of peace. 33

As in all the churches of the saints, •women are to remain quiet at meetings 34 since they have no permission to speak; they must keep in the background as the Law itself lays it down. •If they have any questions to ask, they should ask 35 their husbands at home: it does not seem right for a woman to raise her voice at meetings.

Do you think the word of God came out of yourselves? Or that it has come 36 only to you? •Anyone who claims to be a prophet or inspired ought to recognise 37 that what I am writing to you is a command from the Lord. •Unless he recognises 38 this, you should not recognise him.

And so, my dear brothers, by all means be ambitious to prophesy, do not 39 suppress the gift of tongues, •but let everything be done with propriety and in order. 40

III. THE RESURRECTION OF THE DEAD

The fact of the resurrection

15 Brothers, I want to remind you of the gospel I preached to you, the gospel 1 that you received and in which you are firmly established; •because the 2 gospel will save you only if you keep believing exactly what I preached to you— believing anything else will not lead to anything.

Well then, in the first place, I taught you what I had been taught myself, 3 namely that Christ died for our sins, in accordance with the scriptures; •that he 4 was buried; and that he was raised to life on the third day, in accordance with the scriptures; •that he appeared first to Cephas and secondly to the Twelve. 5 Next he appeared to more than five hundred of the brothers at the same time, 6 most of whom are still alive, though some have died; •then he appeared to 7 James, and then to all the apostles; •and last of all he appeared to me too; it was 8 as though I was born when no one expected it.

I am the least of the apostles; in fact, since I persecuted the Church of God, 9 I hardly deserve the name apostle; •but by God's grace that is what I am, and 10 the grace that he gave me has not been fruitless. On the contrary, I, or rather the grace of God that is with me, have worked harder than any of the others; •but 11 what matters is that I preach what they preach, and this is what you all believed.

Now if Christ raised from the dead is what has been preached, how can 12 some of you be saying that there is no resurrection of the dead? •If there is no 13 resurrection of the dead, Christ himself cannot have been raised, •and if Christ 14 has not been raised then our preaching is useless and your believing it is useless; indeed, we are shown up as witnesses who have committed perjury before God, 15 because we swore in evidence before God that he had raised Christ to life. •For 16 if the dead are not raised, Christ has not been raised, •and if Christ has not been 17 raised, you are still in your sins. •And what is more serious, all who have died in 18 Christ have perished. •If our hope in Christ has been for this life only, we are 19 the most unfortunate of all people.

But Christ has in fact been raised from the dead, the first-fruits of all who 20 have fallen asleep. •Death came through one man and in the same way the 21

22 resurrection·of the dead has come through one man. ·Just as all·men die in Adam,
23 so all men will be brought to life in Christ; ·but all of them in their proper order:
Christ as the first-fruits and then, after the coming of Christ, those who belong
24 to him. ·After that will come the end, when he hands over the kingdom to God
the Father, having done away with every sovereignty, authority and power.
25
26 For he must be king *until he has put all his enemies under his feet*[a] ·and the last
of the enemies to be destroyed is death, for everything is to be *put under his feet*.
27 —Though when it is said that *everything is subjected*, this clearly cannot include
28 the One who subjected everything to him. ·And when everything is subjected to
him, then the Son himself will be subject in his turn to the One who subjected
all things to him, so that God may be all in all.

29   If this were not true, what do people hope to gain by being baptised for
the dead? If the dead are not ever going to be raised, why be baptised on their
30 behalf? ·What about ourselves? Why are we living under a constant threat?
31 I face death every day, brothers, and I can swear it by the pride that I take in you
32 in Christ Jesus our Lord. ·If my motives were only human ones, what good would
33 it do me to fight the wild animals at Ephesus? ·You say: *Let us eat and drink
today; tomorrow we shall be dead.*[b] You must stop being led astray: 'Bad friends
34 ruin the noblest people'.[c] ·Come to your senses, behave properly, and leave sin
alone; there are some of you who seem not to know God at all; you should be
ashamed.

The manner of the resurrection

35   Someone may ask,'How are dead people raised,and what sort of body do they
36 have when they come back?' ·They are stupid questions. Whatever you sow in the
37 ground has to die before it is given new life ·and the thing that you sow is not
what is going to come; you sow a bare grain, say of wheat or something like that,
38 and then God gives it the sort of body that he has chosen: each sort of seed gets
its own sort of body.

39   Everything that is flesh is not the same flesh: there is human flesh, animals'
40 flesh, the flesh of birds and the flesh of fish. ·Then there are heavenly bodies and
there are earthly bodies; but the heavenly bodies have a beauty of their own and
41 the earthly bodies a different one. ·The sun has its brightness, the moon a different
brightness, and the stars a different brightness, and the stars differ from each
42 other in brightness. ·It is the same with the resurrection of the dead: the thing
43 that is sown is perishable but what is raised is imperishable; ·the thing that is
sown is contemptible but what is raised is glorious; the thing that is sown is weak
44 but what is raised is powerful; ·when it is sown it embodies the soul, when it is
raised it embodies the spirit.

    If the soul has its own embodiment, so does the spirit have its own embodiment.
45 The first *man*, Adam, as scripture says, *became a living soul*; but the last Adam
46 has become a life-giving spirit. ·That is, first the one with the soul, not the spirit,
47 and after that, the one with the spirit. ·The first man, being from the earth, is
48 earthly by nature; the second man is from heaven. ·As this earthly man was, so
49 are we on earth; and as the heavenly man is, so are we in heaven. ·And we, who
have been modelled on the earthly man, will be modelled on the heavenly man.
50   Or else, brothers, put it this way: flesh and blood cannot inherit the kingdom
51 of God: and the perishable cannot inherit what lasts for ever. ·I will tell you

15 a. Ps 110:1   **b.** Is 22:13   **c.** This quotation from Menander's *Thais* may have become a
proverb.

something that has been secret: that we are not all going to die, but we shall all be changed. •This will be instantaneous, in the twinkling of an eye, when the 52 last trumpet sounds. It will sound, and the dead will be raised, imperishable, and we shall be changed as well, •because our present perishable nature must 53 put on imperishability and this mortal nature must put on immortality.

A hymn of triumph. Conclusion

When this perishable nature has put on imperishability, and when this 54 mortal nature has put on immortality, then the words of scripture will come true: *Death is swallowed up in victory.* • *Death, where is your* victory? *Death, where* 55 *is your sting?[d]* •Now the sting of death is sin, and sin gets its power from the Law. 56 So let us thank God for giving us the victory through our Lord Jesus Christ.   57

Never give in then, my dear brothers, never admit defeat; keep on working 58 at the Lord's work always, knowing that, in the Lord, you cannot be labouring in vain.

CONCLUSION

Commendations. Greetings

16 Now about the collection made for the saints: you are to do as I told the 1 churches in Galatia to do. •Every Sunday, each one of you must put 2 aside what he can afford, so that collections need not be made after I have come. When I am with you, I will send your offering to Jerusalem by the hand 3 of whatever men you give letters of reference to; •if it seems worth while for me 4 to go too, they can travel with me.

I shall be coming to you after I have passed through Macedonia—and I am 5 doing no more than pass through Macedonia—•and I may be staying with you, 6 perhaps even passing the winter, to make sure that it is you who send me on my way wherever my travels take me. •As you see, I do not want to make it only 7 a passing visit to you and I hope to spend some time with you, the Lord permitting. •In any case I shall be staying at Ephesus until Pentecost •because a big 8,9 and important door has opened for my work and there is a great deal of opposition.

If Timothy comes, show him that he has nothing to be afraid of in you: like 10 me, he is doing the Lord's work, •and nobody is to be scornful of him. Send 11 him happily on his way to come back to me; the brothers and I are waiting for him. •As for our brother Apollos, I begged him to come to you with the brothers 12 but he was quite firm that he did not want to go yet and he will come as soon as he can.

Be awake to all the dangers; stay firm in the faith; be brave and be strong. 13 Let everything you do be done in love.   14

There is something else to ask you, brothers. You know how the Stephanas 15 family, who were the first-fruits of Achaia, have really worked hard to help the saints. •Well, I want you in your turn to put yourselves at the service of people 16 like this, and anyone who helps and works with them. •I am delighted that 17 Stephanas, Fortunatus and Achaicus have arrived; they make up for your absence. •They have settled my mind, and yours too; I hope you appreciate men 18 like this.

All the churches of Asia send you greetings. Aquila and Prisca, with the 19 church that meets at their house, send you their warmest wishes, in the Lord.

20 All the brothers send you their greetings. Greet one another with a holy kiss.

21   This greeting is in my own hand—Paul.

22   If anyone does not love the Lord, a curse on him. 'Maran atha.'[a]

23   The grace of the Lord Jesus be with you.

24   My love is with you all in Christ Jesus.

---

d. A free version; see Ho 13:J4.
16 a. Aramaic. 'The Lord is coming', or 'Lord, come'.

2 CORINTHIANS

THE SECOND LETTER OF PAUL
TO THE CHURCH AT CORINTH

INTRODUCTION

Address and greetings. Thanksgiving

1 From Paul, appointed by God to be an apostle of Christ Jesus, and from 1
Timothy, one of the brothers, to the church of God at Corinth and to all the
saints in the whole of Achaia. •Grace and peace to you from God our Father and 2
the Lord Jesus Christ.

Blessed be the God and Father of our Lord Jesus Christ, a gentle Father and 3
the God of all consolation, •who comforts us in all our sorrows, so that we can 4
offer others, in their sorrows, the consolation that we have received from God
ourselves. •Indeed, as the sufferings of Christ overflow to us, so, through Christ, 5
does our consolation overflow. •When we are made to suffer, it is for your 6
consolation and salvation. When, instead, we are comforted, this should be a
consolation to you, supporting you in patiently bearing the same sufferings as
we bear. •And our hope for you is confident, since we know that, sharing our 7
sufferings, you will also share our consolations.

For we should like you to realise, brothers, that the things we had to undergo 8
in Asia were more of a burden than we could carry, so that we despaired of
coming through alive. •Yes, we were carrying our own death warrant with us, 9
and it has taught us not to rely on ourselves but only on God, who raises the
dead to life. •And he saved us from dying, as he will save us again; yes, that is our 10
firm hope in him, that in the future he will save us again. •You must all join in the 11
prayers for us: the more people there are asking for help for us, the more will be
giving thanks when it is granted to us.

I. SOME RECENT EVENTS REVIEWED

Why Paul changed his plans

There is one thing we are proud of, and our conscience tells us it is true: that 12
we have always treated everybody, and especially you, with the reverence   and
sincerity which come from God, and by the grace of God we have done this
without ulterior motives. •There are no hidden meanings in our letters besides 13
what you can read for yourselves and understand. •And I hope that, although 14
you do not know us very well yet, you will have come to recognise, when the day

of our Lord Jesus comes, that you can be as proud of us as we are of you.

15 Because I was so sure of this, I had meant to come to you first, so that you
16 would benefit doubly; •staying with you before going to Macedonia and coming
back to you again on the way back from Macedonia, for you to see me on my way
17 to Judaea. •Do you think I was not sure of my own intentions when I planned
this? Do you really think that when I am making my plans, my motives are
ordinary human ones, and that I say Yes, yes, and No, no, at the same time?
18
19 I swear by God's truth, there is no Yes and No about what we say to you. •The
Son of God, the Christ Jesus that we proclaimed among you— I mean Silvanus
20 and Timothy and I—was never Yes and No: with him it was always Yes, •and
however many the promises God made, the Yes to them all is in him. That is
21 why it is 'through him' that we answer Amen to the praise of God. •Remember
it is God himself who assures us all, and you, of our standing in Christ, and has
22 anointed us, •marking us with his seal and giving us the pledge, the Spirit, that
we carry in our hearts.

23 By my life, I call God to witness that the reason why I did not come to Corinth
24 after all was to spare your feelings. •We are not dictators over your faith, but are
fellow workers with you for your happiness; in the faith you are steady enough.
1 **2** Well then, I made up my mind not to pay you a second distressing visit.
2 I may have hurt you, but if so I have hurt the only people who could give me any
3 pleasure. •I wrote as I did to make sure that, when I came, I should not be distressed by the very people who should have made me happy. I am sure you all
4 know that I could never be happy unless you were. •When I wrote to you, in deep
distress and anguish of mind, and in tears, it was not to make you feel hurt but
to let you know how much love I have for you.

5 Someone has been the cause of pain; and the cause of pain not to me, but to
6 some degree—not to overstate it--to all of you. •The punishment already imposed
7 by the majority on the man in question is enough; •and the best thing now is to
give him your forgiveness and encouragement, or he might break down from so
8 much misery. •So I am asking you to give some definite proof of your love for
9 him. •What I really wrote for, after all, was to test you and see whether you are
10 completely obedient. •Anybody that you forgive, I forgive; and as for my
forgiving anything—if there has been anything to be forgiven, I have forgiven
11 it for your sake in the presence of Christ. •And so we will not be outwitted by
Satan—we know well enough what his intentions are.

From Troas to Macedonia. The apostolate: its importance

12 When I went up to Troas to preach the Good News of Christ, and the door
13 was wide open for my work there in the Lord, •I was so continually uneasy in
mind at not meeting brother Titus there, I said good-bye to them and went
on to Macedonia.

14 Thanks be to God who, wherever he goes, makes us, in Christ, partners of his
triumph,[a] and through us is spreading the knowledge of himself, like a sweet smell,
15 everywhere. •We are Christ's incense to God for those who are being saved and
16 for those who are not; •for the last, the smell of death that leads to death, for the
first the sweet smell of life that leads to life. And who could be qualified for work
17 like this? •At least we do not go round offering the word of God for sale, as many
other people do. In Christ, we speak as men of sincerity, as envoys of God and
in God's presence.

2 a. Like a victorious general making his ceremonial entry into Rome.

3 Does this sound like a new attempt to commend ourselves to you? Unlike ¹ other people, we need no letters of recommendation either to you or from you, ·because you are yourselves our letter, written in our hearts, that anybody ² can see and read, ·and it is plain that you are a letter from Christ, drawn up by ³ us, and written not with ink but with the Spirit of the living God, not on stone tablets but on the tablets of your living hearts.

Before God, we are confident of this through Christ: ·not that we are qualified ⁴₅ in ourselves to claim anything as our own work: all our qualifications come from God. ·He is the one who has given us the qualifications to be the administrators ⁶ of this new covenant, which is not a covenant of written letters but of the Spirit: the written letters bring death, but the Spirit gives life. ·Now if the administering ⁷ of death, in the written letters engraved on stones, was accompanied by such a brightness that the Israelites could not bear looking at the face of Moses, though it was a brightness that faded, ·then how much greater will be the brightness that ⁸ surrounds the administering of the Spirit! ·For if there was any splendour in ⁹ administering condemnation, there must be very much greater splendour in administering justification. ·In fact, compared with this greater splendour, the ¹⁰ thing that used to have such splendour now seems to have none; ·and if what ¹¹ was so temporary had any splendour, there must be much more in what is going to last for ever.

Having this hope, we can be quite confident; ·not like Moses, who put a veil ¹²₁₃ over his face so that the Israelites would not notice the ending of what had to fade.ᵃ ·And anyway, their minds had been dulled; indeed, to this very day, that ¹⁴ same veil is still there when the old covenant is being read, a veil never lifted, since Christ alone can remove it. ·Yes, even today, whenever Moses is read, the veil is ¹⁵ over their minds. ·It will not be removed until they turn to the Lord. ·Now this ¹⁶₁₇ Lord is the Spirit, and where the Spirit of the Lord is, there is freedom. ·And ¹⁸ we, with our unveiled faces reflecting like mirrors the brightness of the Lord, all grow brighter and brighter as we are turned into the image that we reflect; this is the work of the Lord who is Spirit.

4 Since we have by an act of mercy been entrusted with this work of adminis- ¹ tration, there is no weakening on our part. ·On the contrary, we will have ² none of the reticence of those who are ashamed, no deceitfulness or watering down the word of God; but the way we commend ourselves to every human being with a conscience is by stating the truth openly in the sight of God. ·If our ³ gospel does not penetrate the veil, then the veil is on those who are not on the way to salvation; ·the unbelievers whose minds the god of this world has blinded, ⁴ to stop them seeing the light shed by the Good News of the glory of Christ, who is the image of God. ·For it is not ourselves that we are preaching, but Christ ⁵ Jesus as the Lord, and ourselves as your servants for Jesus' sake. ·It is the same ⁶ God that said, 'Let there be light shining out of darkness', who has shone in our minds to radiate the light of the knowledge of God's glory, the glory on the face of Christ.

The trials and hopes of the apostolate

We are only the earthenware jars that hold this treasure, to make it clear ⁷ that such an overwhelming power comes from God and not from us. ·We are in ⁸ difficulties on all sides, but never cornered; we see no answer to our problems, but never despair; ·we have been persecuted, but never deserted; knocked down, ⁹ but never killed; ·always, wherever we may be, we carry with us in our body

the death of Jesus, so that the life of Jesus, too, may always be seen in our body.
11 Indeed, while we are still alive, we are consigned to our death every day, for the sake of Jesus, so that in our mortal flesh the life of Jesus, too, may be openly
12 shown. •So death is at work in us, but life in you.

13   But as we have the same spirit of faith that is mentioned in scripture— *I believed, and therefore I spoke*[a]—we too believe and therefore we too speak,
14 knowing that he who raised the Lord Jesus to life will raise us with Jesus in our
15 turn, and put us by his side and you with us. •You see, all this is for your benefit, so that the more grace is multiplied among people, the more thanksgiving there will be, to the glory of God.

16   That is why there is no weakening on our part, and instead, though this outer man of ours may be falling into decay, the inner man is renewed day by day.
17 Yes, the troubles which are soon over, though they weigh little, train us for the
18 carrying of a weight of eternal glory which is out of all proportion to them. •And so we have no eyes for things that are visible, but only for things that are invisible; for visible things last only for a time, and the invisible things are eternal.

1   5 For we know that when the tent that we live in on earth is folded up, there is a house built by God for us, an everlasting home not made by human hands,
2 in the heavens. •In this present state, it is true, we groan as we wait with longing
3 to put on our heavenly home over the other; •we should like to be found wearing
4 clothes and not without them. •Yes, we groan and find it a burden being still in this tent, not that we want to strip it off, but to put the second garment over it
5 and to have what must die taken up into life. •This is the purpose for which God made us, and he has given us the pledge of the Spirit.

6   We are always full of confidence, then, when we remember that to live in the
7 body means to be exiled from the Lord, •going as we do by faith and not by sight
8 —we are full of confidence, I say, and actually want to be exiled from the body
9 and make our home with the Lord. •Whether we are living in the body or exiled
10 from it, we are intent on pleasing him. •For all the truth about us will be brought out in the law court of Christ, and each of us will get what he deserves for the things he did in the body, good or bad.

The apostolate in action

11   And so it is with the fear of the Lord in mind that we try to win people over. God knows us for what we really are, and I hope that in your consciences you
12 know us too. •This is not another attempt to commend ourselves to you: we are simply giving you reasons to be proud of us, so that you will have an answer ready for the people who can boast more about what they seem than what they are.
13 If we seemed out of our senses, it was for God; but if we are being reasonable
14 now, it is for your sake. •And this is because the love of Christ overwhelms us when we reflect that if one man has died for all, then all men should be dead;
15 and the reason he died for all was so that living men should live no longer for themselves, but for him who died and was raised to life for them.

16   From now onwards, therefore, we do not judge anyone by the standards of the flesh. Even if we did once know Christ in the flesh, that is not how we know him
17 now. •And for anyone who is in Christ, there is a new creation; the old creation
18 has gone, and now the new one is here. •It is all God's work. It was God who

3 a. See Ex 34:33.
4 a. Ps 116:10

reconciled us to himself through Christ and gave us the work of handing on this reconciliation. •In other words, God in Christ was reconciling the world to 19 himself, not holding men's faults against them, and he has entrusted to us the news that they are reconciled. •So we are ambassadors for Christ; it is as though 20 God were appealing through us, and the appeal that we make in Christ's name is: be reconciled to God. •For our sake God made the sinless one into sin, so 21 that in him we might become the goodness of God. 6 As his fellow workers, we 1 beg you once again not to neglect the grace of God that you have received. •For 2 he says: *At the favourable time, I have listened to you; on the day of salvation I came to your help.*[a] Well, now is the favourable time; this is the day of salvation.

We do nothing that people might object to, so as not to bring discredit on our 3 function as God's servants. •Instead, we prove we are servants of God by great 4 fortitude in times of suffering: in times of hardship and distress; •when we are 5 flogged, or sent to prison, or mobbed; labouring, sleepless, starving. •We prove 6 we are God's servants by our purity, knowledge, patience and kindness; by a spirit of holiness, by a love free from affectation; •by the word of truth and by 7 the power of God; by being armed with the weapons of righteousness in the right hand and in the left, •prepared for honour or disgrace, for blame or praise; taken 8 for impostors while we are genuine; •obscure yet famous; said to be dying and 9 here are we alive; rumoured to be executed before we are sentenced; •thought 10 most miserable and yet we are always rejoicing; taken for paupers though we make others rich, for people having nothing though we have everything.

Paul opens his heart. A warning

Corinthians, we have spoken to you very frankly; our mind has been opened 11 in front of you. •Any constraint that you feel is not on our side; the constraint 12 is in your own selves. •I speak as if to children of mine: as a fair exchange, open 13 your minds in the same way.

Do not harness yourselves in an uneven team with unbelievers. Virtue is no 14 companion for crime. Light and darkness have nothing in common. •Christ is 15 not the ally of Beliar, nor has a believer anything to share with an unbeliever. The temple of God has no common ground with idols, and that is what we 16 are—the temple of the living God. We have God's word for it: *I will make my home among them and live with them; I will be their God and they shall be my people.*[b] •Then *come away from them and keep aloof, says the Lord. Touch nothing that is unclean,*[c] *and I will welcome you •and be your father, and you shall be my* 17 *sons and daughters, says the Almighty Lord.*[d] 18

7 With promises like these made to us, dear brothers, let us wash off all that 1 can soil either body or spirit, to reach perfection of holiness in the fear of God.

Keep a place for us in your hearts. We have not injured anyone, or ruined 2 anyone, or exploited anyone. •I am not saying this to put any blame on you; 3 as I have already told you, you are in our hearts—together we live or together we die. •I have the very greatest confidence in you, and I am so proud of you that 4 in all our trouble I am filled with consolation and my joy is overflowing.

Paul in Macedonia; he is joined by Titus

Even after we had come to Macedonia, however, there was no rest for this 5 body of ours. Far from it; we found trouble on all sides: quarrels outside, mis- givings inside. •But God comforts the miserable, and he comforted us, by the 6

7 arrival of Titus, •and not only by his arrival but also by the comfort which he had gained from you. He has told us all about how you want to see me, how sorry you were, and how concerned for me, and so I am happier now than I was before.

8 But to tell the truth, even if I distressed you by my letter, I do not regret it. I did regret it before, and I see that that letter did distress you, at least for a time;

9 but I am happy now—not because I made you suffer, but because your suffering led you into repentance. Yours has been a kind of suffering that God approves,

10 and so you have come to no kind of harm from us. •To suffer in God's way means changing for the better and leaves no regrets, but to suffer as the world

11 knows suffering brings death. •Just look at what suffering in God's way has brought you: what keenness, what explanations, what indignation, what alarm! Yes, and what aching to see me, what concern for me, and what justice done!

12 In every way you have shown yourselves blameless in this affair. •So then, though I wrote the letter to you, it was not written for the sake either of the offender or of the one offended; it was to make you realise, in the sight of God, your own

13 concern for us. •That is what we have found so encouraging.

With this encouragement, too, we had the even greater happiness of finding

14 Titus so happy; thanks to you all, he has no more worries; •I had rather boasted to him about you, and now I have not been made to look foolish; in fact, our boasting to Titus has proved to be as true as anything that we ever said to you.

15 His own personal affection for you is all the greater when he remembers how

16 willing you have all been, and with what deep respect you welcomed him. •I am very happy knowing that I can rely on you so completely.

II. ORGANISATION OF THE COLLECTION

Why the Corinthians should be generous

1 ⑧ Now here, brothers, is the news of the grace of God which was given in the

2 churches in Macedonia; •and of how, throughout great trials by suffering, their constant cheerfulness and their intense poverty have overflowed in a wealth

3 of generosity. •I can swear that they gave not only as much as they could afford,

4 but far more, and quite spontaneously, •begging and begging us for the favour

5 of sharing in this service to the saints •and, what was quite unexpected, they offered their own selves first to God and, under God, to us.

6 Because of this, we have asked Titus, since he has already made a beginning,

7 to bring this work of mercy to the same point of success among you. •You always have the most of everything—of faith, of eloquence, of understanding, of keenness for any cause, and the biggest share of our affection—so we expect

8 you to put the most into this work of mercy too. •It is not an order that I am giving you; I am just testing the genuineness of your love against the keenness of

9 others. •Remember how generous the Lord Jesus was: he was rich, but he

10 became poor for your sake, to make you rich out of his poverty. •As I say, I am only making a suggestion; it is only fair to you, since you were the first, a year

11 ago, not only in taking action but even in deciding to. •So now finish the work and let the results be worthy, as far as you can afford it, of the decision you made

12 so promptly. •As long as the readiness is there, a man is acceptable with whatever

13 he can afford; never mind what is beyond his means. •This does not mean that

6 a. Is 49:8   **b.** Lv 26:11-12   **c.** Is 52:11   **d.** Is 43:6

to give relief to others you ought to make things difficult for yourselves: it is a question of balancing ⋅what happens to be your surplus now against their 14 present need, and one day they may have something to spare that will supply your own need. That is how we strike a balance: ⋅as scripture says: *The man who* 15 *gathered much had none too much, the man who gathered little did not go short.*[a]

The delegates recommended to the Corinthians

I thank God for putting into Titus' heart the same concern for you that I have 16 myself. ⋅He did what we asked him; indeed he is more concerned than ever, and 17 is visiting you on his own initiative. ⋅As his companion we are sending the 18 brother who is famous in all the churches for spreading the gospel. ⋅More than 19 that, he happens to be the same brother who has been elected by the churches to be our companion on this errand of mercy that, for the glory of God, we have undertaken to satisfy our impatience to help. ⋅We hope that in this way there 20 will be no accusations made about our administering such a large fund; ⋅for *we* 21 *are trying to do right* not only *in the sight of God* but *also* in the sight of *men.*[b] ⋅To 22 accompany these, we are sending a third brother, of whose keenness we have often had proof in many different ways, and who is particularly keen about this, because he has great confidence in you. ⋅Titus, perhaps I should add, is my own 23 colleague and fellow worker in your interests; the other two brothers, who are delegates of the churches, are a real glory to Christ. ⋅So then, in front of all the 24 churches, give them a proof of your love, and prove to them that we are right to be proud of you.

9 There is really no need for me to write to you on the subject of offering 1 your services to the saints, ⋅since I know how anxious you are to help; in 2 fact, I boast about you to the Macedonians, telling them, 'Achaia has been ready since last year'. So your zeal has been a spur to many more. ⋅I am sending the 3 brothers all the same, to make sure that our boasting about you does not prove to have been empty this time, and that you really are ready as I said you would be. ⋅If some of the Macedonians who are coming with me found you unprepared, 4 we should be humiliated—to say nothing of yourselves—after being so confident. That is why I have thought it necessary to ask these brothers to go on to you 5 ahead of us, and make sure in advance that the gift you promised is all ready, and that it all comes as a gift out of your generosity and not by being extorted from you.

Blessings to be expected from the collection

Do not forget: thin sowing means thin reaping; the more you sow, the more 6 you reap. ⋅Each one should give what he has decided in his own mind, not 7 grudgingly or because he is made to, for *God loves a cheerful giver.*[a] ⋅And there 8 is no limit to the blessings which God can send you—he will make sure that you will always have all you need for yourselves in every possible circumstance, and still have something to spare for all sorts of good works. ⋅As scripture says: *He* 9 *was free in almsgiving, and gave to the poor: his good deeds will never be forgotten.*[b]

The one who provides *seed for the sower and bread for food* will provide you with 10 all the seed you want and make *the harvest of your good deeds* a larger one, ⋅and, 11 made richer in every way, you will be able to do all the generous things which, through us, are the cause of thanksgiving to God. ⋅For doing this holy service 12 is not only supplying all the needs of the saints, but it is also increasing the amount of thanksgiving that God receives. ⋅By offering this service, you show 13 them what you are, and that makes them give glory to God for the way you accept and profess the gospel of Christ, and for your sympathetic generosity to them

14 and to all. •And their prayers for you, too, show how they are drawn to you on

15 account of all the grace that God has given you. •Thanks be to God for his inexpressible gift!

III. PAUL'S APOLOGIA

Paul's reply to accusations of weakness

1 **10** This is a personal matter; this is Paul himself appealing to you by the gentleness and patience of Christ—I, the man who is so humble when he

2 is facing you, but bullies you when he is at a distance. •I only ask that I do not have to bully you when I come, with all the confident assurance I mean to show when I come face to face with people I could name who think we go by ordinary

3 human motives. •We live in the flesh, of course, but the muscles that we fight

4 with are not flesh. •Our war is not fought with weapons of flesh, yet they are strong enough, in God's cause, to demolish fortresses. We demolish sophistries,

5 and the arrogance that tries to resist the knowledge of God; every thought is

6 our prisoner, captured to be brought into obedience to Christ. •Once you have given your complete obedience, we are prepared to punish any disobedience.

7 Face plain facts. Anybody who is convinced that he belongs to Christ must

8 go on to reflect that we all belong to Christ no less than he does. •Maybe I do boast rather too much about our authority, but the Lord gave it to me for building

9 you up and not for pulling you down, and I shall not be ashamed of it. •I do not

10 want you to think of me as someone who only frightens you by letter. •Someone said, 'He writes powerful and strongly-worded letters but when he is with you

11 you see only half a man and no preacher at all'. •The man who said that can remember this: whatever we are like in the words of our letters when we are absent, that is what we shall be like in our actions when we are present.

His reply to the accusation of ambition

12 We are not being so bold as to rank ourselves, or invite comparison, with certain people who write their own references. Measuring themselves against themselves, and comparing themselves to themselves, they are simply foolish.

13 We, on the other hand, are not going to boast without a standard to measure against: taking for our measure the yardstick which God gave us to measure

14 with, which is long enough to reach to you. •We are not stretching further than we ought; otherwise we should not have reached you, as we did come all the

15 way to you with the gospel of Christ. •So we are not boasting without any measure, about work that was done by other people; in fact, we trust that, as your faith

16 grows, we shall get taller and taller, when judged by our own standard. •I mean, we shall be carrying the gospel to places far beyond you, without encroaching on

17 anyone else's field, not boasting of the work already done. •*If anyone wants to*

18 *boast, let him boast of the Lord.*[a] •It is not the man who commends himself that can be accepted, but the man who is commended by the Lord.

---

8 a. Ex 16:18   **b.** Pr 3:4 (LXX)
9 a. Pr 22:8 (LXX)   **b.** Ps 112:9
10 a. Jr 9:23

Paul is driven to sound his own praises

11 I only wish you were able to tolerate a little foolishness from me. But of course: you are tolerant towards me. •You see, the jealousy that I feel for you is God's own jealousy: I arranged for you to marry Christ so that I might give you away as a chaste virgin to this one husband. •But the serpent, with his cunning, seduced Eve, and I am afraid that in the same way your ideas may get corrupted and turned away from simple devotion to Christ. •Because any new-comer has only to proclaim a new Jesus, different from the one that we preached, or you have only to receive a new spirit, different from the one you have already received, or a new gospel, different from the one you have already accepted—and you welcome it with open arms. •As far as I can tell, these arch-apostles have nothing more than I have. •I may not be a polished speechmaker, but as for knowledge, that is a different matter; surely we have made this plain, speaking on every subject in front of all of you.

Or was I wrong, lowering myself so as to lift you high, by preaching the gospel of God to you and taking no fee for it? •I was robbing other churches living on them so that I could serve you. •When I was with you and ran out of money, I was no burden to anyone; the brothers who came from Macedonia provided me with everything I wanted. I was very careful, and I always shall be, not to be a burden to you in any way, •and by Christ's truth in me, this cause of boasting will never be taken from me in the regions of Achaia. •Would I do that if I did not love you? God knows I do. •I intend to go on doing what I am doing now—leaving no opportunity for those people who are looking for an opportunity to claim equality with us in what they boast of. •These people are counterfeit apostles, they are dishonest workmen disguised as apostles of Christ. •There is nothing unexpected about that; if Satan himself goes disguised as an angel of light, there is no need to be surprised when his servants, too, disguise themselves as the servants of righteousness. They will come to the end that they deserve.

As I said before, let no one take me for a fool; but if you must, then treat me as a fool and let me do a little boasting of my own. •What I am going to say now is not prompted by the Lord, but said as if in a fit of folly, in the certainty that I have something to boast about. •So many others have been boasting of their worldly achievements, that I will boast myself. •You are all wise men and can cheerfully tolerate fools, •yes, even to tolerating somebody who makes slaves of you, makes you feed him, imposes on you, orders you about and slaps you in the face. •I hope you are ashamed of us for being weak with you instead!

But if anyone wants some brazen speaking—I am still talking as a fool—then I can be as brazen as any of them, and about the same things. •Hebrews, are they? So am I. Israelites? So am I. Descendants of Abraham? So am I. •The servants of Christ? I must be mad to say this, but so am I, and more than they: more, because I have worked harder, I have been sent to prison more often, and whipped so many times more, often almost to death. •Five times I had the thirty-nine lashes from the Jews; •three times I have been beaten with sticks; once I was stoned; three times I have been shipwrecked and once adrift in the open sea for a night and a day. •Constantly travelling, I have been in danger from rivers and in danger from brigands, in danger from my own people and in danger from pagans; in danger in the towns, in danger in the open country, danger at sea and danger from so-called brothers. •I have worked and laboured, often without sleep; I have been hungry and thirsty and often starving; I have been in the cold without clothes. •And, to leave out much more, there is my daily preoccupation:

29 my anxiety for all the churches. •When any man has had scruples, I have had scruples with him; when any man is made to fall, I am tortured.

30
31 If I am to boast, then let me boast of my own feebleness. •The God and Father
32 of the Lord Jesus—bless him for ever—knows that I am not lying. •When I was in Damascus, the ethnarch of King Aretas put guards round the city to catch
33 me, •and I had to be let down over the wall in a hamper, through a window, in order to escape.

1 **12** Must I go on boasting, though there is nothing to be gained by it? But I will move on to the visions and revelations I have had from the Lord.
2 I know a man in Christ who, fourteen years ago, was caught up—whether still in the body or out of the body, I do not know; God knows—right into the third
3 heaven.[a] •I do know, however, that this same person—whether in the body or
4 out of the body, I do not know; God knows—•was caught up into paradise and
5 heard things which must not and cannot be put into human language. •I will boast about a man like that, but not about anything of my own except my weak-
6 nesses. •If I should decide to boast, I should not be made to look foolish, because I should only be speaking the truth; but I am not going to, in case anyone should begin to think I am better than he can actually see and hear me to be.

7 In view of the extraordinary nature of these revelations, to stop me from getting too proud I was given a thorn in the flesh, an angel of Satan to beat me
8 and stop me from getting too proud! •About this thing, I have pleaded with the
9 Lord three times for it to leave me, •but he has said, 'My grace is enough for you: my power is at its best in weakness'. So I shall be very happy to make my
10 weaknesses my special boast so that the power of Christ may stay over me, •and that is why I am quite content with my weaknesses, and with insults, hardships, persecutions, and the agonies I go through for Christ's sake. For it is when I am weak that I am strong.

11 I have been talking like a fool, but you forced me to do it: you are the ones who should have been commending me. Though I am a nobody, there is not
12 a thing these arch-apostles have that I do not have as well. •You have seen done among you all the things that mark the true apostle, unfailingly produced: the
13 signs, the marvels, the miracles. •Is there anything of which you have had less than the other churches have had, except that I have not myself been a burden on
14 you? For this unfairness, please forgive me. •I am all prepared now to come to you for the third time, and I am not going to be a burden on you: it is you I want, not your possessions. Children are not expected to save up for their parents, but
15 parents for children. •I am perfectly willing to spend what I have, and to be expended, in the interests of your souls. Because I love you more, must I be loved the less?

16 All very well, you say: I personally put no pressure on you, but like the cunning
17 fellow that I am, I took you in by a trick. •So we exploited you, did we, through
18 one of the men that I have sent to you? •Well, Titus went at my urging, and I sent the brother that came with him. Can Titus have exploited you? You know that he and I have always been guided by the same spirit and trodden in the same tracks.

Paul's fears and anxieties

19 All this time you have been thinking that our defence is addressed to you, but it is before God that we, in Christ, are speaking; and it is all, my dear

12 a. I.e. the highest heaven.

brothers, for your benefit. •What I am afraid of is that when I come I may find 20
you different from what I want you to be, and you may find that I am not as you
would like me to be; and then there will be wrangling, jealousy, and tempers
roused, intrigues and backbiting and gossip, obstinacies and disorder. •I am 21
afraid that on my next visit, my God may make me ashamed on your account
and I shall be grieving over all those who sinned before and have still not repented
of the impurities, fornication and debauchery they committed.

13 This will be the third time I have come to you. *The evidence of three, or at* 1
least two, witnesses is necessary to sustain the charge.[a] •I gave warning when 2
I was with you the second time and I give warning now, too, before I come, to
those who sinned before and to any others, that when I come again, I shall have
no mercy. •You want proof, you say, that it is Christ speaking in me: you have 3
known him not as a weakling, but as a power among you? •Yes, but he was 4
crucified through weakness, and still he lives now through the power of God.
So then, we are weak, as he was, but we shall live with him, through the power
of God, for your benefit.

Examine yourselves to make sure you are in the faith; test yourselves. Do 5
you acknowledge that Jesus Christ is really in you? If not, you have failed the
test, •but we, as I hope you will come to see, have not failed it. •We pray to God 6 7
that you will do nothing wrong: not that we want to appear as the ones who have
been successful—we would rather that you did well even though we failed. •We 8
have no power to resist the truth; only to further it. •We are only too glad to be 9
weak provided you are strong. ˙ What we ask in our prayers is for you to be made
perfect. •That is why I am writing this from a distance, so that when I am with 10
you I shall not need to be strict, with the authority which the Lord gave me for
building up and not for destroying.

CONCLUSION

Recommendations. Greetings. Final good wishes

In the meantime, brothers, we wish you happiness; try to grow perfect; help 11
one another. Be united; live in peace, and the God of love and peace will be with
you.

Greet one another with the holy kiss. All the saints send you greetings.   12

The grace of the Lord Jesus Christ, the love of God and the fellowship of the 13
Holy Spirit be with you all.

13 a. Dt 19:15

GALATIANS

THE LETTER OF PAUL
TO THE CHURCH IN GALATIA

Address

1 1 From Paul to the churches of Galatia, and from all the brothers who are here
2 with me, an apostle who does not owe his authority to men or his appointment
to any human being but who has been appointed by Jesus Christ and by God the
3 Father who raised Jesus from the dead. •We wish you the grace and peace of
4 God our Father and of the Lord Jesus Christ, •who in order to rescue us from
this present wicked world sacrificed himself for our sins, in accordance with
5 the will of God our Father, •to whom be glory for ever and ever. Amen.

A warning

6 I am astonished at the promptness with which you have turned away from the
one who called you and have decided to follow a different version of the Good
7 News. •Not that there can be more than one Good News; it is merely that some
8 troublemakers among you want to change the Good News of Christ; •and let
me warn you that if anyone preaches a version of the Good News different from
the one we have already preached to you, whether it be ourselves or an angel
9 from heaven, he is to be condemned. •I am only repeating what we told you
before: if anyone preaches a version of the Good News different from the one
10 you have already heard, he is to be condemned. •So now whom am I trying to
please—man, or God? Would you say it is men's approval I am looking for?[a] If
I still wanted that, I should not be what I am—a servant of Christ.

I. PAUL'S APOLOGIA

God's call

11 The fact is, brothers, and I want you to realise this, the Good News I
12 preached is not a human message •that I was given by men, it is something
13 I learnt only through a revelation of Jesus Christ. •You must have heard of
my career as a practising Jew, how merciless I was in persecuting the Church of
14 God, how much damage I did to it, •how I stood out among other Jews of my
generation, and how enthusiastic I was for the traditions of my ancestors.

---

1 a. Probably a rejoinder to an accusation by the judaisers that Paul was trying to make the
pagans' conversion easy by not insisting on circumcision.

Then God, who had specially *chosen* me while I was *still in my mother's* 15
womb,[b] called me through his grace and chose •to reveal his Son in me, so that 16
I might preach the Good News about him to the pagans. I did not stop to discuss
this with any human being, •nor did I go up to Jerusalem to see those who were 17
already apostles before me, but I went off to Arabia[c] at once and later went
straight back from there to Damascus. •Even when after three years I went up 18
to Jerusalem to visit Cephas and stayed with him for fifteen days, •I did not see 19
any of the other apostles; I only saw James, the brother of the Lord, •and I 20
swear before God that what I have just written is the literal truth. •After that 21
I went to Syria and Cilicia, •and was still not known by sight to the churches of 22
Christ in Judaea, •who had heard nothing except that their one-time persecutor 23
was now preaching the faith he had previously tried to destroy; •and they gave 24
glory to God for me.

The meeting at Jerusalem

2 It was not till fourteen years had passed that I went up to Jerusalem again. 1
I went with Barnabas and took Titus with me. •I went there as the result of 2
a revelation, and privately I laid before the leading men the Good News as I
proclaim it among the pagans; I did so for fear the course I was adopting or had
already adopted would not be allowed. •And what happened? Even though Titus 3
who had come with me is a Greek, he was not obliged to be circumcised. •The 4
question came up only because some who do not really belong to the brotherhood
have furtively crept in to spy on the liberty we enjoy in Christ Jesus, and want
to reduce us all to slavery. •I was so determined to safeguard for you the true 5
meaning of the Good News, that I refused even out of deference to yield to
such people for one moment. •As a result, these people who are acknowledged 6
leaders—not that their importance matters to me, since God has no favourites—
these leaders, as I say, had nothing to add to the Good News as I preach it. •On 7
the contrary, they recognised that I had been commissioned to preach the Good
News to the uncircumcised just as Peter had been commissioned to preach it to
the circumcised. •The same person whose action had made Peter the apostle of 8
the circumcised had given me a similar mission to the pagans. •So, James, 9
Cephas and John, these leaders, these pillars, shook hands with Barnabas and
me as a sign of partnership: we were to go to the pagans and they to the
circumcised.[a] •The only thing they insisted on was that we should remember to 10
help the poor, as indeed I was anxious to do.

Peter and Paul at Antioch

When Cephas came to Antioch, however, I opposed him to his face, since 11
he was manifestly in the wrong. •His custom had been to eat with the pagans,[b] 12
but after certain friends of James arrived he stopped doing this and kept away
from them altogether for fear of the group that insisted on circumcision. •The 13
other Jews joined him in this pretence, and even Barnabas felt himself obliged
to copy their behaviour.

When I saw they were not respecting the true meaning of the Good News, 14
I said to Cephas in front of everyone, 'In spite of being a Jew, you live like the
pagans and not like the Jews, so you have no right to make the pagans copy
Jewish ways'.

The Good News as proclaimed by Paul

15 16 'Though we were born Jews and not pagan sinners, •we acknowledge that what makes a man righteous is not obedience to the Law, but faith in Jesus Christ. We had to become believers in Christ Jesus no less than you had, and now we hold that faith in Christ rather than fidelity to the Law is what justifies 17 us, and that *no one can be justified*[c] by keeping the Law. •Now if we were to admit that the result of looking to Christ to justify us is to make us sinners like the rest, it would follow that Christ had induced us to sin, which would be 18 absurd. •If I were to return to a position I had already abandoned, I should be 19 admitting I had done something wrong. •In other words, through the Law I am dead to the Law, so that now I can live for God. I have been crucified with 20 Christ, •and I live now not with my own life but with the life of Christ who lives in me. The life I now live in this body I live in faith: faith in the Son of 21 God who loved me and who sacrificed himself for my sake. •I cannot bring myself to give up God's gift: if the Law can justify us, there is no point in the death of Christ.'

II. DOCTRINAL MATTERS

Justification by faith

1 **3** Are you people in Galatia mad? Has someone put a spell on you, in spite of the plain explanation you have had of the crucifixion of Jesus Christ? 2 Let me ask you one question: was it because you practised the Law that you 3 received the Spirit, or because you believed what was preached to you? •Are you foolish enough to end in outward observances what you began in the Spirit? 4 Have all the favours you received been wasted? And if this were so, they would 5 most certainly have been wasted. •Does God give you the Spirit so freely and work miracles among you because you practise the Law, or because you believed what was preached to you?

6 Take Abraham for example: *he put his faith in God, and this faith was* 7 *considered as justifying him.*[a] •Don't you see that it is those who rely on faith who 8 are the sons of Abraham? •Scripture foresaw that God was going to use faith to justify the pagans, and proclaimed the Good News long ago when Abraham 9 was told: *In you all the pagans will be blessed.*[b] •Those therefore who rely on faith receive the same blessing as Abraham, the man of faith.

The curse brought by the Law

10 On the other hand, those who rely on the keeping of the Law are under a curse, since scripture says: *Cursed be everyone who does not persevere in observing* 11 *everything prescribed in the book of the Law.*[c] •The Law will not justify anyone in the sight of God, because we are told: *the righteous man finds life through faith.*[d] 12 The Law is not even based on faith, since we are told: *The man who practises* 13 *these precepts finds life through practising them.*[e] •Christ redeemed us from the curse of the Law by being cursed for our sake, since scripture says: *Cursed be* 14 *everyone who is hanged on a tree.*[f] •This was done so that in Christ Jesus the

b. Is 49:1   c. Probably the kingdom of the Nabataean Arabs, to the S. of Damascus.
2 a. The distinction is geographical rather than racial; when Paul went among the Gentiles the resident Jews were his first concern.   b. Converts from paganism.   c. Ps 143:2
3 a. Gn 15:6   b. Gn 12:3   c. Dt 27:26   d. Hab 2:4   e. Lv 18:5   f. Dt 21:23

blessing of Abraham might include the pagans, and so that through faith we might receive the promised Spirit.

The Law did not cancel the promise

Compare this, brothers, with what happens in ordinary life. If a will has 15 been drawn up in due form, no one is allowed to disregard it or add to it. •Now 16 the promises were addressed to Abraham *and to his descendants*—notice, in passing, that scripture does not use a plural word as if there were several descendants, it uses the singular: to his posterity, which is Christ. •But my 17 point is this: once God had expressed his will in due form, no law that came four hundred and thirty years later could cancel that and make the promise meaningless. •If you inherit something as a legal right, it does not come to you 18 as the result of a promise, and it was precisely in the form of a promise that God made his gift to Abraham.

The purpose of the Law

What then was the purpose of adding the Law? This was done to specify 19 crimes, until the posterity came to whom the promise was addressed. The Law was promulgated by angels,ᵍ assisted by an intermediary. •Now there can only 20 be an intermediary between two parties, yet God is one. •Does this mean that 21 there is opposition between the Law and the promises of God? Of course not. We could have been justified by the Law if the Law we were given had been capable of giving life, •but it is not: scripture makes no exceptions when it says 22 that sin is master everywhere. In this way the promise can only be given through faith in Jesus Christ and can only be given to those who have this faith.

The coming of faith

Before faith came, we were allowed no freedom by the Law; we were being 23 looked after till faith was revealed. •The Law was to be our guardian until the 24 Christ came and we could be justified by faith. •Now that that time has come 25 we are no longer under that guardian, •and you are, all of you, sons of God 26 through faith in Christ Jesus. •All baptised in Christ, you have all clothed 27 yourselves in Christ, •and there are no more distinctions between Jew and 28 Greek, slave and free, male and female, but all of you are one in Christ Jesus. Merely by belonging to Christ you are the posterity of Abraham, the heirs he 29 was promised.

Sons of God

4 Let me put this another way: an heir, even if he has actually inherited 1 everything, is no different from a slave for as long as he remains a child. He is under the control of guardians and administrators until he reaches the 2 age fixed by his father. •Now before we came of age we were as good as slaves to 3 the elemental principles of this world,ᵃ •but when the appointed time came, 4 God sent his Son, born of a woman, born a subject of the Law, •to redeem the 5 subjects of the Law and to enable us to be adopted as sons. •The proof that you 6 are sons is that God has sent the Spirit of his Son into our hearts: the Spirit that cries, 'Abba, Father', •and it is this that makes you a son, you are not a 7 slave any more; and if God has made you son, then he has made you heir.

Once you were ignorant of God, and enslaved to 'gods' who are not really 8 gods at all; •but now that you have come to acknowledge God—or rather, now 9

that God has acknowledged you—how can you want to go back to elemental
10 things like these, that can do nothing and give nothing, and be their slaves? •You
11 and your special days and months and seasons and years! •You make me feel I
have wasted my time with you.

A personal appeal

12   Brothers, all I ask is that you should copy me as I copied you. You have
13 never treated me in an unfriendly way before; •even at the beginning, when that
14 illness gave me the opportunity to preach the Good News to you, •you never
showed the least sign of being revolted or disgusted by my disease that was such
a trial to you; instead you welcomed me as an angel of God, as if I were Christ
15 Jesus himself. •What has become of this enthusiasm you had? I swear that you
16 would even have gone so far as to pluck out your eyes and give them to me. •Is it
17 telling you the truth that has made me your enemy? •The blame lies in the way
they have tried to win you over: by separating you from me, they want to win
18 you over to themselves. •It is always a good thing to win people over—and
19 I do not have to be there with you—but it must be for a good purpose, •my
children! I must go through the pain of giving birth to you all over again, until
20 Christ is formed in you. •I wish I were with you now so that I could know exactly
what to say; as it is, I have no idea what to do for the best.

The two covenants: Hagar and Sarah

21
22   You want to be subject to the Law? Then listen to what the Law says. •It
says, if you remember, that Abraham had two sons, one by the slave-girl, and one
23 by his free-born wife. •The child of the slave-girl was born in the ordinary way;
24 the child of the free woman was born as the result of a promise. •This can be
regarded as an allegory: the women stand for the two covenants. The first who
25 comes from Mount Sinai, and whose children are slaves, is Hagar—•since Sinai
is in Arabia—and she corresponds to the present Jerusalem that is a slave like
26
27 her children. •The Jerusalem above, however, is free and is our mother, •since
scripture says: *Shout for joy, you barren women who bore no children! Break into
shouts of joy and gladness, you who were never in labour. For there are more sons of*
28 *the forsaken one than sons of the wedded wife.*[b] •Now you, my brothers, like Isaac,
29 are children of the promise, •and as at that time the child born in the ordinary
30 way persecuted the child born in the Spirit's way, so also now. •Does not
scripture say: *Drive away that slave-girl and her son; this slave-girl's son is not to*
31 *share the inheritance with the son*[c] of the free woman? •So, my brothers, we are
the children, not of the slave-girl, but of the free-born wife.

III. EXHORTATION

Christian liberty

1 **5** When Christ freed us, he meant us to remain free. Stand firm, therefore,
2 and do not submit again to the yoke of slavery. •It is I, Paul, who tell you
this: if you allow yourselves to be circumcised, Christ will be of no benefit to
3 you at all. •With all solemnity I repeat my warning: Everyone who accepts

---

g. In Jewish tradition angels were present at Sinai; the 'intermediary' is Moses.
4 a. The principles that make up the physical universe; Paul has related the Law to 'outward
observances', 3:3.   **b.** Is 54:1   **c.** Gn 21:10

circumcision is obliged to keep the whole Law. •But if you do look to the Law 4
to make you justified, then you have separated yourselves from Christ, and have
fallen from grace. •Christians are told by the Spirit to look to faith for those 5
rewards that righteousness hopes for, •since in Christ Jesus whether you are 6
circumcised or not makes no difference—what matters is faith that makes its
power felt through love.

You began your race well: who made you less anxious to obey the truth? 7
You were not prompted by him who called you! •The yeast seems to be spreading ⁸₉
through the whole batch of you. •I feel sure that, united in the Lord, you· will 10
agree with me, and anybody who troubles you in future will be condemned,
no matter who he is. •As for me, my brothers, if I still preach circumcision,ᵃ 11
why am I still persecuted? If I did that now, would there be any scandal of the
cross? •Tell those who are disturbing you I would like to see the knife slip. 12

Liberty and charity

My brothers, you were called, as you know, to liberty; but be careful, or this 13
liberty will provide an opening for self-indulgence. Serve one another, rather, in
works of love, •since the whole of the Law is summarised in a single command: 14
*Love your neighbour as yourself.*ᵇ •If you go snapping at each other and tearing 15
each other to pieces, you had better watch or you will destroy the whole
community.

Let me put it like this: if you are guided by the Spirit you will be in no danger 16
of yielding to self-indulgence, •since self-indulgence is the opposite of the Spirit, 17
the Spirit is totally against such a thing, and it is precisely because the two are
so opposed that you do not always carry out your good intentions. •If you are 18
led by the Spirit, no law can touch you. •When self-indulgence is at work the 19
results are obvious: fornication, gross indecency and sexual irresponsibility;
idolatry and sorcery; feuds and wrangling, jealousy, bad temper and quarrels; 20
disagreements, factions, •envy; drunkenness, orgies and similar things. I warn 21
you now, as I warned you before: those who behave like this will not inherit the
kingdom of God. •What the Spirit brings is very different: love, joy, peace, 22
patience, kindness, goodness, trustfulness, •gentleness and self-control. There 23
can be no law against things like that, of course. •You cannot belong to Christ 24
Jesus unless you crucify all self-indulgent passions and desires.

Since the Spirit is our life, let us be directed by the Spirit. •We must stop ²⁵₂₆
being conceited, provocative and envious.

On kindness and perseverance

6 Brothers, if one of you misbehaves, the more spiritual of you who set him 1
right should do so in a spirit of gentleness, not forgetting that you may be
tempted yourselves. •You should carry each other's troubles and fulfil the 2
law of Christ. •It is the people who are not important who often make the 3
mistake of thinking that they are. •Let each of you examine his own conduct; 4
if you find anything to boast about, it will at least be something of your own, not
just something better than your neighbour has. •Everyone has his own burden 5
to carry.

People under instruction should always contribute something to the support 6
of the man who is instructing them.

Don't delude yourself into thinking God can be cheated: where a man sows, 7
there he reaps: •if he sows in the field of self-indulgence he will get a harvest of 8
corruption out of it; if he sows in the field of the Spirit he will get from it a

9 harvest of eternal life. •We must never get tired of doing good because if we
10 don't give up the struggle we shall get our harvest at the proper time. •While
we have the chance, we must do good to all, and especially to our brothers
in the faith.

Epilogue

11 Take good note of what I am adding in my own handwriting and in large
12 letters. •It is only self-interest that makes them want to force circumcision on
13 you—they want to escape persecution for the cross of Christ—•they accept
circumcision but do not keep the Law themselves; they only want you to be
14 circumcised so that they can boast of the fact. •As for me, the only thing I can
boast about is the cross of our Lord Jesus Christ, through whom the world is
15 crucified to me, and I to the world. •It does not matter if a person is circumcised
16 or not; what matters is for him to become an altogether new creature. •Peace
and mercy to all who follow this rule, who form the Israel of God.

17 I want no more trouble from anybody after this; the marks on my body are
18 those of Jesus. •The grace of our Lord Jesus Christ be with your spirit, my
brothers. Amen.

5 a. As Paul's enemies were apparently claiming.   **b.** Lv 19:18

EPHESIANS

THE LETTER OF PAUL
TO THE CHURCH AT EPHESUS

Address and Greetings

1 From Paul, appointed by God to be an apostle of Christ Jesus, to the saints 1
who are faithful to Christ Jesus: ·Grace and peace to you from God our 2
Father and from the Lord Jesus Christ.

I. THE MYSTERY OF SALVATION AND OF THE CHURCH

God's plan of salvation

Blessed be God the Father of our Lord Jesus Christ,   3
who has blessed us with all the spiritual blessings of heaven in Christ.
Before the world was made, he chose us, chose us in Christ,   4
to be holy and spotless, and to live through love in his presence,
determining that we should become his adopted sons, through 5
    Jesus Christ
for his own kind purposes,
to make us praise the glory of his grace,   6
his free gift to us in the Beloved,
in whom, through his blood, we gain our freedom, the forgiveness 7
    of our sins.
Such is the richness of the grace
which he has showered on us   8
in all wisdom and insight.
He has let us know the mystery of his purpose,   9
the hidden plan he so kindly made in Christ from the beginning
to act upon when the times had run their course to the end: 10
that he would bring everything together under Christ, as head,
everything in the heavens and everything on earth.
And it is in him that we were claimed as God's own,   11
chosen from the beginning,
under the predetermined plan of the one who guides all things
as he decides by his own will;
chosen to be,   12
for his greater glory,
the people who would put their hopes in Christ before he came.
Now you too, in him,   13

have heard the message of the truth and the good news of your
salvation,

and have believed it;

and you too have been stamped with the seal of the Holy Spirit
of the Promise,

14   the pledge of our inheritance

which brings freedom for those whom God has taken for his own,

to make his glory praised.

The triumph and the supremacy of Christ

15   That will explain why I, having once heard about your faith in the Lord Jesus,
16 and the love that you show towards all the saints, •have never failed to remember
17 you in my prayers and to thank God for you. •May the God of our
Lord Jesus Christ, the Father of glory, give you a spirit of wisdom and perception
18 of what is revealed, to bring you to full knowledge of him. •May he enlighten
the eyes of your mind so that you can see what hope his call holds for you, what
19 rich glories he has promised the saints will inherit •and how infinitely great is
the power that he has exercised for us believers. This you can tell from the strength
20 of his power •at work in Christ, when he used it to raise him from the dead and
21 to make him sit at his right hand, in heaven, •far above every Sovereignty,
Authority, Power, or Domination,[a] or any other name that can be named, not
22 only in this age but also in the age to come. •*He has put all things under his feet*,[b]
23 and made him, as the ruler of everything, the head of the Church; •which is his
body, the fullness of him who fills the whole creation.

Salvation in Christ a free gift

$\frac{1}{2}$ 2 And you were dead, through the crimes and the sins •in which you used to live
when you were following the way of this world, obeying the ruler who governs
3 the air,[a] the spirit who is at work in the rebellious. •We all were among them
too in the past, living sensual lives, ruled entirely by our own physical desires
and our own ideas; so that by nature we were as much under God's anger as the
4 rest of the world. •But God loved us with so much love that he was generous
5 with his mercy: •when we were dead through our sins, he brought us to life
6 with Christ—it is through grace that you have been saved—•and raised us up
with him and gave us a place with him in heaven, in Christ Jesus.

7   This was to show for all ages to come, through his goodness towards us in
8 Christ Jesus, how infinitely rich he is in grace. •Because it is by grace that you
have been saved, through faith; not by anything of your own, but by a gift from
9 God; •not by anything that you have done, so that nobody can claim the credit.
10 We are God's work of art, created in Christ Jesus to live the good life as from the
beginning he had meant us to live it.

Reconciliation of the Jews and the pagans with each other and with God

11   Do not forget, then, that there was a time when you who were pagans
physically, termed the Uncircumcised by those who speak of themselves as the
12 Circumcision by reason of a physical operation, •do not forget, I say, that
you had no Christ and were excluded from membership of Israel, aliens with
no part in the covenants with their Promise; you were immersed in this world,

1 a. Orders of the angelic hierarchy in Jewish literature.   b. Ps 8:6
2 a. Satan.

without hope and without God. •But now in Christ Jesus, you that used to be ₁₃
so far apart from us have been brought very close, by the blood of Christ.
For he is the peace between us, and has made the two into one and broken ₁₄
down the barrier which used to keep them apart, actually destroying in his
own person the hostility •caused by the rules and decrees of the Law. This ₁₅
was to create one single New Man in himself out of the two of them and by
restoring peace •through the cross, to unite them both in a single Body and ₁₆
reconcile them with God. In his own person he killed the hostility. •Later he ₁₇
came to bring the good news of peace, *peace to you who were far away and peace
to those who were near at hand.*ᵇ •Through him, both of us have in the one Spirit ₁₈
our way to come to the Father.

So you are no longer aliens or foreign visitors: you are citizens like all the ₁₉
saints, and part of God's household. •You are part of a building that has the ₂₀
apostles and prophets ͨ for its foundations, and Christ Jesus himself for its main
cornerstone. •As every structure is aligned on him, all grow into one holy temple ₂₁
in the Lord; •and you too, in him, are being built into a house where God lives, ₂₂
in the Spirit.

Paul, a servant of the mystery

3 So I, Paul, a prisoner of Christ Jesus for the sake of you pagans.... •You have ₁ ₂
probably heard how I have been entrusted by God with the grace he meant
for you, •and that it was by a revelation that I was given the knowledge of the ₃
mystery, as I have just described it very shortly. •If you read my words, you will ₄
have some idea of the depths that I see in the mystery of Christ. •This mystery ₅
that has now been revealed through the Spirit to his holy apostles and prophets
was unknown to any men in past generations; •it means that pagans now share ₆
the same inheritance, that they are parts of the same body, and that the same
promise has been made to them, in Christ Jesus, through the gospel. •I have ₇
been made the servant of that gospel by a gift of grace from God who gave it to
me by his own power. •I, who am less than the least of all the saints, have been ₈
entrusted with this special grace, not only of proclaiming to the pagans the
infinite treasure of Christ •but also of explaining how the mystery is to be ₉
dispensed. Through all the ages, this has been kept hidden in God, the creator
of everything. Why? •So that the Sovereignties and Powers should learn ₁₀
only now, through the Church, how comprehensive God's wisdom really is,
exactly according to the plan which he had had from all eternity in Christ Jesus ₁₁
our Lord. •This is why we are bold enough to approach God in complete ₁₂
confidence, through our faith in him; •so, I beg you, never lose confidence just ₁₃
because of the trials that I go through on your account: they are your glory.

Paul's prayer

This, then, is what I pray, kneeling before the Father, •from whom every ₁₄ ₁₅
family,ᵈ whether spiritual or natural, takes its name:

Out of his infinite glory, may he give you the power through his Spirit ₁₆
for your hidden self to grow strong, •so that Christ may live in your hearts ₁₇
through faith, and then, planted in love and built on love, •you will with all ₁₈
the saints have strength to grasp the breadth and the length, the height and
the depth; •until, knowing the love of Christ, which is beyond all knowledge, ₁₉
you are filled with the utter fullness of God.

Glory be to him whose power, working in us, can do infinitely more than we ₂₀

21 can ask or imagine; •glory be to him from generation to generation in the Church and in Christ Jesus for ever and ever. Amen.

II. EXHORTATION

A call to unity

1 4 I, the prisoner in the Lord, implore you therefore to lead a life worthy of your
2 vocation. •Bear with one another charitably, in complete selflessness,
3 gentleness and patience. •Do all you can to preserve the unity of the Spirit by the
4 peace that binds you together. •There is one Body, one Spirit, just as you were all
5 called into one and the same hope when you were called. •There is one Lord, one
6 faith, one baptism, •and one God who is Father of all, over all, through all and within all.

7 Each one of us, however, has been given his own share of grace, given as
8 Christ allotted it. •It was said that he would:

> *When he ascended to the height, he captured prisoners,*
> *he gave gifts to men.*[a]

9 When it says, 'he ascended', what can it mean if not that he descended right
10 down to the lower regions of the earth? •The one who rose higher than all the
11 heavens to fill all things is none other than the one who descended. •And to
some, his gift was that they should be apostles; to some, prophets; to some,
12 evangelists; to some, pastors and teachers; •so that the saints together make
13 a unity in the work of service, building up the body of Christ. •In this way we
are all to come to unity in our faith and in our knowledge of the Son of God, until
we become the perfect Man, fully mature with the fullness of Christ himself.

14 Then we shall not be children any longer, or tossed one way and another and
carried along by every wind of doctrine, at the mercy of all the tricks men play
15 and their cleverness in practising deceit. •If we live by the truth and in love, we
16 shall grow in all ways into Christ, who is the head •by whom the whole body
is fitted and joined together, every joint adding its own strength, for each
separate part to work according to its function. So the body grows until it has
built itself up, in love.

The new life in Christ

17 In particular, I want to urge you in the name of the Lord, not to go on living
18 the aimless kind of life that pagans live. •Intellectually they are in the dark,
and they are estranged from the life of God, without knowledge because they
19 have shut their hearts to it. •Their sense of right and wrong once dulled, they
have abandoned themselves to sexuality and eagerly pursue a career of indecency
20 of every kind. •Now that is hardly the way you have learnt from Christ, •unless
21 you failed to hear him properly when you were taught what the truth is in Jesus.
22 You must give up your old way of life; you must put aside your old self, which
23 gets corrupted by following illusory desires. •Your mind must be renewed by a
24 spiritual revolution •so that you can put on the new self that has been created in
God's way, in the goodness and holiness of the truth.

b. Is 57:19   c. The N.T. prophets.
3 a. A pun on the words 'Father' and 'family' (clan or tribe) is lost in translation; traces of it survive in *paternity* and *patriotism.*
4 a. Ps 68:18

So from now on, there must be no more lies: *You must speak the truth to one* [25] *another*,[b] since we are all parts of one another. •*Even if you are angry, you must not* [26] *sin:*[c] never let the sun set on your anger •or else you will give the devil a foothold. [27] Anyone who was a thief must stop stealing; he should try to find some useful [28] manual work instead, and be able to do some good by helping others that are in need. •Guard against foul talk; let your words be for the improvement of [29] others, as occasion offers, and do good to your listeners, •otherwise you will [30] only be grieving the Holy Spirit of God who has marked you with his seal for you to be set free when the day comes. •Never have grudges against others, or [31] lose your temper, or raise your voice to anybody, or call each other names, or allow any sort of spitefulness. •Be friends with one another, and kind, [32] forgiving each other as readily as God forgave you in Christ.

5 Try, then, to imitate God, as children of his that he loves, •and follow Christ [1/2] by loving as he loved you, giving himself up in our place *as a fragrant offering and a sacrifice to God.*[a] •Among you there must be not even a mention of [3] fornication or impurity in any of its forms, or promiscuity: this would hardly become the saints! •There must be no coarseness, or salacious talk and [4] jokes—all this is wrong for you; raise your voices in thanksgiving instead. •For [5] you can be quite certain that nobody who actually indulges in fornication or impurity or promiscuity—which is worshipping a false god—can inherit anything of the kingdom of God. •Do not let anyone deceive you with empty [6] arguments: it is for this loose living that God's anger comes down on those who rebel against him. •Make sure that you are not included with them. •You were [7/8] darkness once, but now you are light in the Lord; be like children of light, •for [9] the effects of the light are seen in complete goodness and right living and truth. Try to discover what the Lord wants of you, •having nothing to do with the futile [10/11] works of darkness but exposing them by contrast. •The things which are done [12] in secret are things that people are ashamed even to speak of; •but anything [13] exposed by the light will be illuminated •and anything illuminated turns into [14] light. That is why it is said:[b]

> Wake up from your sleep,
> rise from the dead,
> and Christ will shine on you.

So be very careful about the sort of lives you lead, like intelligent and not like [15] senseless people. •This may be a wicked age, but your lives should redeem it. [16] And do not be thoughtless but recognise what is the will of the Lord. •Do not [17/18] drug yourselves with wine, this is simply dissipation; be filled with the Spirit. Sing the words and tunes of the psalms and hymns when you are together, [19] and go on singing and chanting to the Lord in your hearts, •so that always and [20] everywhere you are giving thanks to God who is our Father in the name of our Lord Jesus Christ.

The morals of the home

Give way to one another in obedience to Christ. •Wives should regard their [21/22] husbands as they regard the Lord, •since as Christ is head of the Church and [23] saves the whole body, so is a husband the head of his wife; •and as the Church [24] submits to Christ, so should wives to their husbands, in everything. •Husbands [25] should love their wives just as Christ loved the Church and sacrificed himself

26 for her •to make her holy. He made her clean by washing her in water with a form
27 of words, •so that when he took her to himself she would be glorious, with no
28 speck or wrinkle or anything like that, but holy and faultless. •In the same way,
husbands must love their wives as they love their own bodies; for a man to love
29 his wife is for him to love himself. •A man never hates his own body, but he feeds
30 it and looks after it; and that is the way Christ treats the Church, •because it is
31 his body—and we are its living parts. •*For this reason, a man must leave his father*
32 *and mother and be joined to his wife, and the two will become one body.*[c] •This
mystery has many implications; but I am saying it applies to Christ and the
33 Church. •To sum up; you too, each one of you, must love his wife as he loves
himself; and let every wife respect her husband.

 ${}^{1}_{2}$ **6** Children, be obedient to your parents in the Lord—that is your duty. •The
first commandment that has a promise attached to it is: *Honour your father*
3 *and mother*, •and the promise is: *and you will prosper and have a long life in the land.*[a]
4 And parents, never drive your children to resentment but in bringing them up
correct them and guide them as the Lord does.

5 Slaves, be obedient to the men who are called your masters in this world,
6 with deep respect and sincere loyalty, as you are obedient to Christ: •not only
when you are under their eye, as if you had only to please men, but because you
7 are slaves of Christ and wholeheartedly do the will of God. •Work hard and
8 willingly, but do it for the sake of the Lord and not for the sake of men. •You
can be sure that everyone, whether a slave or a free man, will be properly rewarded
9 by the Lord for whatever work he has done well. •And those of you who are
employers, treat your slaves in the same spirit; do without threats, remembering
that they and you have the same Master in heaven and he is not impressed by one
person more than by another.

The spiritual war

 ${}^{10}_{11}$ Finally, grow strong in the Lord, with the strength of his power. •Put God's
armour on so as to be able to resist the devil's tactics. •For it is not against human
12 enemies that we have to struggle, but against the Sovereignties and the Powers
who originate the darkness in this world, the spiritual army of evil in the heavens.
13 That is why you must rely on God's armour, or you will not be able to put up any
resistance when the worst happens, or have enough resources to hold your
ground.

14 So stand your ground, with *truth buckled round your waist*, and *integrity*
15 *for a breastplate*,[b] •wearing for shoes on your feet *the eagerness to spread the*
16 *gospel of peace*[c] •and always carrying the shield of faith so that you can use it to
17 put out the burning arrows of the evil one. •And then you must accept *salvation*
from God to be your helmet and receive the word of God from the Spirit to use
as a sword.

18 Pray all the time, asking for what you need, praying in the Spirit on every
possible occasion. Never get tired of staying awake to pray for all the saints;
19 and pray for me to be given an opportunity to open my mouth and speak
20 without fear and give out the mystery of the gospel •of which I am an ambassador
in chains; pray that in proclaiming it I may speak as boldly as I ought to.

---

b. Zc 8:16   **c.** Ps 4:4 (LXX)
5 a. Ex 29:18   **b.** Presumably a quotation from a Christian hymn.   **c.** Gn 2:24
6 a. Ex 20:12   **b.** Is 59:17   **c.** Is 40:9

Personal news and final salutation

I should like you to know, as well, what is happening to me and what I am 21
doing; my dear brother Tychicus, my loyal helper in the Lord, will tell you
everything. •I am sending him to you precisely for this purpose, to give you 22
news about us and reassure you.

May God the Father and the Lord Jesus Christ grant peace, love and faith to 23
all the brothers. •May grace and eternal life be with all who love our Lord 24
Jesus Christ.

PHILIPPIANS

THE LETTER OF PAUL
TO THE CHURCH AT PHILIPPI

Address

1 From Paul and Timothy, servants of Christ Jesus, to all the saints in Christ
2 Jesus, together with their presiding elders and deacons. •We wish you the
grace and peace of God our Father and of the Lord Jesus Christ.

Thanksgiving and prayer

3
4 I thank my God whenever I think of you; and •every time I pray for all of you, I
5 pray with joy, •remembering how you have helped to spread the Good News
6 from the day you first heard it right up to the present. •I am quite certain that
the One who began this good work in you will see that it is finished when the Day
7 of Christ Jesus comes. •It is only natural that I should feel like this towards
you all, since you have shared the privileges which have been mine: both my
chains and my work defending and establishing the gospel. You have a permanent
8 place in my heart, •and God knows how much I miss you all, loving you as Christ
9 Jesus loves you. •My prayer is that your love for each other may increase more
and more and never stop improving your knowledge and deepening your
10 perception •so that you can always recognise what is best. This will help you to
11 become pure and blameless, and prepare you for the Day of Christ, •when you
will reach the perfect goodness which Jesus Christ produces in us for the glory
and praise of God.

Paul's own circumstances

12 I am glad to tell you, brothers, that the things that happened to me have
actually been a help to the Good News.

13 My chains, in Christ, have become famous not only all over the Praetorium but
14 everywhere, •and most of the brothers have taken courage in the Lord from these
chains of mine and are getting more and more daring in announcing the Message
15 without any fear. •It is true that some of them are doing it just out of rivalry
16 and competition, but the rest preach Christ with the right intention, •out of
nothing but love, as they know that this is my invariable way of defending the
17 gospel. •The others, who proclaim Christ for jealous or selfish motives, do not
18 mind if they make my chains heavier to bear. •But does it matter? Whether
from dishonest motives or in sincerity, Christ is proclaimed; and that makes me
19 happy; •and I shall continue being happy, because I know *this will help to save*

me,[a] thanks to your prayers and to the help which will be given to me by the Spirit of Jesus. •My one hope and trust is that I shall never have to admit defeat, 20 but that now as always I shall have the courage for Christ to be glorified in my body, whether by my life or by my death. •Life to me, of course, is Christ, but 21 then death would bring me something more; •but then again, if living in this 22 body means doing work which is having good results—I do not know what I should choose. •I am caught in this dilemma: I want to be gone and be with 23 Christ, which would be very much the better, •but for me to stay alive in this 24 body is a more urgent need for your sake. •This weighs with me so much that I feel 25 sure I shall survive and stay with you all, and help you to progress in the faith and even increase your joy in it; •and so you will have another reason to give 26 praise to Christ Jesus on my account when I am with you again.

Fight for the faith

Avoid anything in your everyday lives that would be unworthy of the gospel 27 of Christ, so that, whether I come to you and see for myself, or stay at a distance and only hear about you, I shall know that you are unanimous in meeting the attack with firm resistance, united by your love for the faith of the gospel •and 28 quite unshaken by your enemies. This would be the sure sign that they will lose and you will be saved. It would be a sign from God •that he has given you the 29 privilege not only of believing in Christ, but of suffering for him as well. •You and 30 I are together in the same fight as you saw me fighting before and, as you will have heard, I 'am fighting still.

Preserve unity in humility

2 If our life in Christ means anything to you, if love can persuade at all, 1 or the Spirit that we have in common, or any tenderness and sympathy, •then 2 be united in your convictions and united in your love, with a common purpose and a common mind. That is the one thing which would make me completely happy. •There must be no competition among you, no conceit; but everybody 3 is to be self-effacing. Always consider the other person to be better than yourself, so that nobody thinks of his own interests first but everybody thinks of other 4 people's interests instead. •In your minds you must be the same as Christ Jesus:[c] 5

> His state was divine, 6
> yet he did not cling
> to his equality with God
> but emptied himself 7
> to assume the condition of a slave.
> and became as men are;
> and being as all men are,
> he was humbler yet, 8
> even to accepting death,
> death on a cross.
> But God raised him high 9
> and gave him the name
> which is above all other names
> so that *all beings* 10
> in the heavens, on earth and in the underworld,
> *should bend the knee*[b] at the name of Jesus
> and that every tongue should acclaim 11

Jesus Christ as Lord,
to the glory of God the Father.

Work for salvation

12 ·So then, my dear friends, continue to do as I tell you, as you always have;
not only as you did when I was there with you, but even more now that I am no
13 longer there; and work for your salvation 'in fear and trembling'. ·It is God,
for his own loving purpose, who puts both the will and the action into you.
14 Do all that has to be done without complaining or arguing ·and then you will
15 be innocent and genuine, *perfect children of God among a deceitful and underhand*
16 *brood,*[c] and you will shine in the world like bright stars ·because you are offering
it the word of life. This would give me something to be proud of for the Day
of Christ, and would mean that I had not run in the race and exhausted myself
17 for nothing. ·And then, if my blood has to be shed as part of your own sacrifice
and offering—which is your faith[d]—I shall still be happy and rejoice with all of
18 you, ·and you must be just as happy and rejoice with me.

The mission of Timothy and Epaphroditus

19 I hope, in the Lord Jesus, to send Timothy to you soon, and I shall be
20 reassured by having news of you. ·I have nobody else like him here, as whole-
21 heartedly concerned for your welfare: ·all the rest seem more interested in
22 themselves than in Jesus Christ. ·But you know how he has proved himself by
working with me on behalf of the Good News like a son helping his father.
23 That is why he is the one that I am hoping to send you, as soon as
24 I know something definite about my fate. ·But I continue to trust, in the Lord,
that I shall be coming soon myself.

25 It is essential, I think, to send brother Epaphroditus back to you. He was sent
as your representative to help me when I needed someone to be my companion
26 in working and battling, ·but he misses you all and is worried because you heard
27 about his illness. ·It is true that he has been ill, and almost died, but God took
pity on him, and on me as well as him, and spared me what would have been one
28 grief on top of another. ·So I shall send him back as promptly as I can; you will
29 be happy to see him again, and that will make me less sorry. ·Give him a most
30 hearty welcome, in the Lord; people like him are to be honoured. ·It was for
Christ's work that he came so near to dying, and he risked his life to give me the
help that you were not able to give me yourselves.
3 1 Finally, my brothers, rejoice in the Lord.[a]

The true way of Christian salvation

It is no trouble to me to repeat what I have already written to you, and as far
2 as you are concerned, it will make for safety. ·Beware of dogs! Watch out for
3 the people who are making mischief. Watch out for the cutters.[b] ·We are the
real people of the circumcision, we who worship in accordance with the Spirit
of God; we have our own glory from Christ Jesus without having to rely on a
4 physical operation. ·If it came to relying on physical evidence, I should be fully

---

1 **a.** Jb 13:16 (LXX)
2 **a.** Vv. 6-11 are a hymn, though whether composed or only quoted by Paul is uncertain.
b. Is 45:23   **c.** Dt 32:5   **d.** Libations were common to Greek and Jewish sacrifices.
3 **a.** Paul's conclusion is interrupted by a long postscript.   **b.** A contemptuous reference to
the circumcisers comparing circumcision with self-inflicted gashes in pagan cults.

qualified myself. Take any man who thinks he can rely on what is physical: I am even better qualified. •I was born of the race of Israel and of the tribe of Benjamin, 5 a Hebrew born of Hebrew parents, and I was circumcised when I was eight days old. As for the Law, I was a Pharisee; •as for working for religion, I was a 6 persecutor of the Church; as far as the Law can make you perfect, I was faultless. But because of Christ, I have come to consider all these advantages that I had 7 as disadvantages. •Not only that, but I believe nothing can happen that will 8 outweigh the supreme advantage of knowing Christ Jesus my Lord. For him I have accepted the loss of everything, and I look on everything as so much rubbish if only I can have Christ •and be given a place in him. I am no longer trying for 9 perfection by my own efforts, the perfection that comes from the Law, but I want only the perfection that comes through faith in Christ, and is from God and based on faith. •All I want is to know Christ and the power of his resurrection 10 and to share his sufferings by reproducing the pattern of his death. •That is the 11 way I can hope to take my place in the resurrection of the dead. •Not that I have 12 become perfect yet: I have not yet won, but I am still running, trying to capture the prize for which Christ Jesus captured me. •I can assure you my brothers, 13 I am far from thinking that I have already won. All I can say is that I forget the past and I strain ahead for what is still to come; •I am racing for the finish, for 14 the prize to which God calls us upwards to receive in Christ Jesus. •We who are 15 called 'perfect' must all think in this way. If there is some point on which you see things differently, God will make it clear to you; •meanwhile, let us go forward 16 on the road that has brought us to where we are.

My brothers, be united in following my rule of life. Take as your models 17 everybody who is already doing this and study them as you used to study us. I have told you often, and I repeat it today with tears, there are many who are 18 behaving as the enemies of the cross of Christ. •They are destined to be lost. 19 They make foods into their god and they are proudest of something they ought to think shameful; the things they think important are earthly things. •For us, 20 our homeland is in heaven, and from heaven comes the saviour we are waiting for, the Lord Jesus Christ, •and he will transfigure these wretched bodies of ours 21 into copies of his glorious body. He will do that by the same power with which he can subdue the whole universe.

4 So then, my brothers and dear friends, do not give way but remain faithful 1 in the Lord. I miss you very much, dear friends; you are my joy and my crown.

Last advice

I appeal to Evodia and I appeal to Syntyche to come to agreement with each 2 other, in the Lord; •and I ask you, Syzygus,*a* to be truly a 'companion' and to 3 help them in this. These women were a help to me when I was fighting to defend the Good News—and so, at the same time, were Clement and the others who worked with me. Their names are written in the book of life.

I want you to be happy, always happy in the Lord; I repeat, what I want is 4 your happiness. •Let your tolerance be evident to everyone: the Lord is very 5 near. •There is no need to worry; but if there is anything you need, pray for it, 6 asking God for it with prayer and thanksgiving, •and that peace of God, which 7 is so much greater than we can understand, will guard your hearts and your thoughts, in Christ Jesus. •Finally, brothers, fill your minds with everything that 8 is true, everything that is noble, everything that is good and pure, everything that we love and honour, and everything that can be thought virtuous or worthy

9 of praise. •Keep doing all the things that you learnt from me and have been taught by me and have heard or seen that I do. Then the God of peace will be with you.

Thanks for help received

10 It is a great joy to me, in the Lord, that at last you have shown some concern for me again; though of course you were concerned before, and only lacked an 11 opportunity. •I am not talking about shortage of money: I have learnt to manage 12 on whatever I have, •I know how to be poor and I know how to be rich too. I have been through my initiation and now I am ready for anything anywhere: 13 full stomach or empty stomach, poverty or plenty. •There is nothing I cannot 14 master with the help of the One who gives me strength. •All the same, it was 15 good of you to share with me in my hardships. •In the early days of the Good News, as you people of Philippi well know, when I left Macedonia, no other 16 church helped me with gifts of money. You were the only ones; •and twice 17 since my stay in Thessalonika you have sent me what I needed. •It is not your gift that I value; what is valuable to me is the interest that is mounting up in 18 your account. •Now for the time being I have everything that I need and more: I am fully provided now that I have received from Epaphroditus the offering that you sent, *a sweet fragrance*—the sacrifice that God accepts and finds 19 pleasing. •In return my God will fulfil all your needs, in Christ Jesus, as lavishly 20 as only God can. •Glory to God, our Father, for ever and ever. Amen.

Greetings and final wish

21 My greetings to every one of the saints in Christ Jesus. The brothers who are 22 with me send their greetings. •All the saints send their greetings, especially those 23 of the imperial household.[b] •May the grace of the Lord Jesus Christ be with your spirit.

---

4 a. 'Companion' is the meaning of the proper name Syzygus.   b. I.e. in the service of the emperor.

COLOSSIANS

THE LETTER OF PAUL

TO THE CHURCH AT COLOSSAE

PREFACE

Address

1 From Paul, appointed by God to be an apostle of Christ Jesus, and from our 1
brother Timothy •to the saints in Colossae, our faithful brothers in Christ: 2
Grace and peace to you from God our Father.

Thanksgiving and prayer

We have never failed to remember you in our prayers and to give thanks for 3
you to God, the Father of our Lord Jesus Christ, •ever since we heard about 4
your faith in Christ Jesus and the love that you show towards all the saints
because of the hope which is stored up for you in heaven. It is only recently that 5
you heard of this, when it was announced in the message of the truth. The Good
News •which has reached you is spreading all over the world and producing the 6
same results as it has among you ever since the day when you heard about God's
grace and understood what this really is. •Epaphras, who taught you, is one of 7
our closest fellow workers and a faithful deputy for us as Christ's servant, •and 8
it was he who told us all about your love in the Spirit.

That will explain why, ever since the day he told us, we have never failed to 9
pray for you, and what we ask God is that through perfect wisdom and spiritual
understanding you should reach the fullest knowledge of his will. •So you will 10
be able to lead the kind of life which the Lord expects of you, a life acceptable
to him in all its aspects; showing the results in all the good actions you do and
increasing your knowledge of God. •You will have in you the strength, based on 11
his own glorious power, never to give in, but to bear anything joyfully, •thanking 12
the Father who has made it possible for you to join the saints and with them
to inherit the light.

Because that is what he has done: he has taken us out of the power of darkness 13
and created a place for us in the kingdom of the Son that he loves, •and in him, 14
we gain our freedom, the forgiveness of our sins.

I. FORMAL INSTRUCTION

Christ is the head of all creation

15 He is the image of the unseen God
and the first-born of all creation,
16 for in him were created
all things in heaven and on earth:
everything visible and everything invisible,
Thrones, Dominations, Sovereignties, Powers—
all things were created through him and for him.
17 Before anything was created, he existed,
and he holds all things in unity.
18 Now the Church is his body,
he is its head.

As he is the Beginning,
he was first to be born from the dead,
so that he should be first in every way;
19 because God wanted all perfection
to be found in him
20 and all things to be reconciled through him and for him,
everything in heaven and everything on earth,
when he made peace
by his death on the cross.

The Colossians have their share in salvation

21 Not long ago, you were foreigners and enemies, in the way that you used to
22 think and the evil things that you did; ·but now he has reconciled you, by his
death and in that mortal body. Now you are able to appear before him holy,
23 pure and blameless—·as long as you persevere and stand firm on the solid base
of the faith, never letting yourselves drift away from the hope promised by the
Good News, which you have heard, which has been preached to the whole human
race, and of which I, Paul, have become the servant.

Paul's labours in the service of the pagans

24 It makes me happy to suffer for you, as I am suffering now, and in my own
body to do what I can to make up all that has still to be undergone by Christ for
25 the sake of his body, the Church. ·I became the servant of the Church when God
26 made me responsible for delivering God's message to you, ·the message which
was a mystery hidden for generations and centuries and has now been revealed to
27 his saints. ·It was God's purpose to reveal it to them and to show all the rich glory
of this mystery to pagans. The mystery is Christ among you, your hope of glory:
28 this is the Christ we proclaim, this is the wisdom in which we thoroughly train
29 everyone and instruct everyone, to make them all perfect in Christ. ·It is for
this I struggle wearily on, helped only by his power driving me irresistibly.

Paul's concern for the Colossians' faith

1 2 Yes, I want you to know that I do have to struggle hard for you, and for
those in Laodicea, and for so many others who have never seen me face to
2 face. ·It is all to bind you together in love and to stir your minds, so that your

understanding may come to full development, until you really know God's secret •in which all the jewels of wisdom and knowledge are hidden. 3

I say this to make sure that no one deceives you with specious arguments. 4 I may be absent in body, but in spirit I am there among you, delighted to find you 5 all in harmony and to see how firm your faith in Christ is.

II. A WARNING AGAINST SOME ERRORS

Live according to the true faith in Christ, not according to false teaching

You must live your whole life according to the Christ you have received— 6 Jesus the Lord; •you must be rooted in him and built on him and held firm by the 7 faith you have been taught, and full of thanksgiving.

Make sure that no one traps you and deprives you of your freedom by some 8 secondhand, empty, rational philosophy based on the principles of this world instead of on Christ.

Christ alone is the true head of men and angels

In his body lives the fullness of divinity, and in him you too find your own 9 fulfilment, •in the one who is the head of every Sovereignty and Power.[a] 10

In him you have been circumcised, with a circumcision not performed by 11 human hand, but by the complete stripping of your body of flesh. This is circumcision according to Christ. •You have been buried with him, when you 12 were baptised; and by baptism, too, you have been raised up with him through your belief in the power of God who raised him from the dead. •You were dead, 13 because you were sinners and had not been circumcised: he[b] has brought you to life with him, he has forgiven us all our sins.

He has overridden the Law, and cancelled every record of the debt that we 14 had to pay; he has done away with it by nailing it to the cross;[c] •and so he got 15 rid of the Sovereignties and the Powers, and paraded them in public, behind him in his triumphal procession.[d]

Against the false asceticism based on 'the principles of this world'

From now onwards, never let anyone else decide what you should eat or drink, 16 or whether you are to observe annual festivals, New Moons or sabbaths. •These 17 were only pale reflections of what was coming: the reality is Christ. •Do not be 18 taken in by people who like grovelling to angels and worshipping them; people like that are always going on about some vision they have had, inflating themselves to a false importance with their worldly outlook. •A man of this sort 19 is not united to the head, and it is the head that adds strength and holds the whole body together, with all its joints and sinews—and this is the only way in which it can reach its full growth in God.

If you have really died with Christ to the principles of this world, why do you 20 still let rules dictate to you, as though you were still living in the world? •'It is 21 forbidden to pick up this, it is forbidden to taste that, it is forbidden to touch something else'; •all these prohibitions are only concerned with things that 22 perish by their very use—an example of *human doctrines and regulations*!• It may be argued that true wisdom is to be found in these, with their self-imposed 23 devotions, their self-abasement, and their severe treatment of the body; but once the flesh starts to protest, they are no use at all.

Life-giving union with the glorified Christ

3 1 Since you have been brought back to true life with Christ, you must look for the things that are in heaven, where Christ is, sitting at God's right hand.
2 Let your thoughts be on heavenly things, not on the things that are on the earth,
3 because you have died, and now the life you have is hidden with Christ in God.
4 But when Christ is revealed—and he is your life—you too will be revealed in all your glory with him.

III. EXHORTATION

General rules of Christian behaviour

5 That is why you must kill everything in you that belongs only to earthly life: fornication, impurity, guilty passion, evil desires and especially greed, which is
6 the same thing as worshipping a false god; •all this is the sort of behaviour that
7 makes God angry. •And it is the way in which you used to live when you were
8 surrounded by people doing the same thing, •but now you, of all people, must give all these things up: getting angry, being bad-tempered, spitefulness, abusive
9 language and dirty talk; •and never tell each other lies. You have stripped off
10 your old behaviour with your old self, •and you have put on a new self which will progress towards true knowledge the more it is renewed in the image of its
11 creator; •and in that image there is no room for distinction between Greek and Jew, between the circumcised or the uncircumcised, or between barbarian and Scythian, slave and free man. There is only Christ: he is everything and he is in everything.
12 You are God's chosen race, his saints; he loves you, and you should be clothed
13 in sincere compassion, in kindness and humility, gentleness and patience. •Bear with one another; forgive each other as soon as a quarrel begins. The Lord has
14 forgiven you; now you must do the same. •Over all these clothes, to keep them
15 together and complete them, put on love. •And may the peace of Christ reign in your hearts, because it is for this that you were called together as parts of one body. Always be thankful.
16 Let the message of Christ, in all its richness, find a home with you. Teach each other, and advise each other, in all wisdom. With gratitude in your hearts
17 sing psalms and hymns and inspired songs to God; •and never say or do anything except in the name of the Lord Jesus, giving thanks to God the Father through him.

The morals of the home and household

18
19 Wives, give way to your husbands, as you should in the Lord. •Husbands,
20 love your wives and treat them with gentleness. •Children, be obedient to your
21 parents always, because that is what will please the Lord. •Parents, never drive your children to resentment or you will make them feel frustrated.
22 Slaves, be obedient to the men who are called your masters in this world; not only when you are under their eye, as if you had only to please men, but
23 wholeheartedly, out of respect for the Master. •Whatever your work is, put
24 your heart into it as if it were for the Lord and not for men, •knowing that the

2 a. I.e. over the highest orders of angels.   **b.** God the Father.   **c.** Destroying our death warrant.   **d.** The tradition was that the Law was brought down to Moses by angels. **e.** Is 29:13

Lord will repay you by making you his heirs. It is Christ the Lord that you are serving; •anyone who does wrong will be repaid in kind and he does not favour 25 one person more than another. **4** Masters, make sure that your slaves are given 1 what is just and fair, knowing that you too have a Master in heaven.

The apostolic spirit

Be persevering in your prayers and be thankful as you stay awake to pray. 2 Pray for us especially, asking God to show us opportunities for announcing the 3 message and proclaiming the mystery of Christ, for the sake of which I am in chains; •pray that I may proclaim it as clearly as I ought. 4

Be tactful with those who are not Christians and be sure you make the best 5 use of your time with them. •Talk to them agreeably and with a flavour of wit, 6 and try to fit your answers to the needs of each one.

Personal news

Tychicus will tell you all the news about me. He is a brother I love very much, 7 and a loyal helper and companion in the service of the Lord. •I am sending him 8 to you precisely for this purpose: to give you news about us and to reassure you. With him I am sending Onesimus, that dear and faithful brother who is a fellow 9 citizen of yours. They will tell you everything that is happening here.

Greetings and final wishes

Aristarchus, who is here in prison with me, sends his greetings, and so does 10 Mark, the cousin of Barnabas—you were sent some instructions about him; if he comes to you, give him a warm welcome—•and Jesus Justus adds his greet- 11 ings. Of all those who have come over from the Circumcision, these are the only ones actually working with me for the kingdom of God. They have been a great comfort to me. •Epaphras, your fellow citizen, sends his greetings; this servant 12 of Christ Jesus never stops battling for you, praying that you will never lapse but always hold perfectly and securely to the will of God. •I can testify for him that 13 he works hard for you, as well as for those at Laodicea and Hierapolis. •Greetings 14 from my dear friend Luke, the doctor, and also from Demas.

Please give my greetings to the brothers at Laodicea and to Nympha and the 15 church which meets in her house. •After this letter has been read among you, 16 send it on to be read in the church of the Laodiceans; and get the letter from Laodicea for you to read yourselves. •Give Archippus this message, 'Remember 17 the service that the Lord wants you to do, and try to carry it out'.

Here is a greeting in my own handwriting—PAUL. Remember the chains I 18 wear. Grace be with you.

1 THESSALONIANS

THE FIRST LETTER OF PAUL
TO THE CHURCH IN THESSALONIKA

Address

1 1 From Paul, Silvanus and Timothy, to the Church in Thessalonika which is in God the Father and the Lord Jesus Christ; wishing you grace and peace.

Thanksgiving and congratulations

2,3 We always mention you in our prayers and thank God for you all, •and constantly remember before God our Father how you have shown your faith in action, worked for love and persevered through hope, in our Lord Jesus Christ.
4 We know, brothers, that God loves you and that you have been chosen,
5 because when we brought the Good News to you, it came to you not only as words, but as power and as the Holy Spirit and as utter conviction. And you observed the sort of life we lived when we were with you, which was for your
6 instruction, •and you were led to become imitators of us, and of the Lord; and it was with the joy of the Holy Spirit that you took to the gospel, in spite of the
7 great opposition all round you. •This has made you the great example to all
8 believers in Macedonia and Achaia •since it was from you that the word of the Lord started to spread—and not only throughout Macedonia and Achaia, for the news of your faith in God has spread everywhere. We do not need to tell other
9 people about it: •other people tell us how we started the work among you, how you broke with idolatry when you were converted to God and became servants
10 of the real, living God; •and how you are now waiting for Jesus, his Son, whom he raised from the dead, to come from heaven to save us from the retribution which is coming.

Paul's example in Thessalonika

1 2 You know yourselves, my brothers, that our visit to you has not proved ineffectual.
2 We had, as you know, been given rough treatment and been grossly insulted at Philippi, and it was our God who gave us the courage to proclaim his Good
3 News to you in the face of great opposition. •We have not taken to preaching
4 because we are deluded, or immoral, or trying to deceive anyone; •it was God who decided that we were fit to be entrusted with the Good News, and when we are speaking, we are not trying to please men but God, *who can read our inmost*

thoughts.[a] •You know very well, and we can swear it before God, that never at 5 any time have our speeches been simply flattery, or a cover for trying to get money; nor have we ever looked for any special honour from men, either from you or 6 anybody else, •when we could have imposed ourselves on you with full weight, 7 as apostles of Christ.

Instead, we were unassuming. Like a mother feeding and looking after her own children, •we felt so devoted and protective towards you, and had come to love 8 you so much, that we were eager to hand over to you not only the Good News but our whole lives as well. •Let me remind you, brothers, how hard we used to 9 work, slaving night and day so as not to be a burden on any one of you while we were proclaiming God's Good News to you. •You are witnesses, and so 10 is God, that our treatment of you, since you became believers, has been impeccably right and fair. •You can remember how we treated every one of you as a father 11 treats his children, •teaching you what was right, encouraging you and appealing 12 to you to live a life worthy of God, who is calling you to share the glory of his kingdom.

The faith and the patience of the Thessalonians

Another reason why we constantly thank God for you is that as soon as you 13 heard the message that we brought you as God's message, you accepted it for what it really is, God's message and not some human thinking; and it is still a living power among you who believe it. •For you, my brothers, have been like the 14 churches of God in Christ Jesus which are in Judaea, in suffering the same treatment from your own countrymen as they have suffered from the Jews, •the 15 people who put the Lord Jesus to death, and the prophets too. And now they have been persecuting us, and acting in a way that cannot please God and makes them the enemies of the whole human race, •because they are hindering us from 16 preaching to the pagans and trying to save them. They never stop trying *to finish off the sins they have begun,*[b] but retribution is overtaking them at last.

Paul's anxiety

A short time after we had been separated from you—in body but never in 17 thought, brothers—we had an especially strong desire and longing to see you face to face again, •and we tried hard to come and visit you; I, Paul, tried more than 18 once, but Satan prevented us. •What do you think is our pride and our joy? You 19 are; and you will be *the crown* of which we shall be *proudest* in the presence of our Lord Jesus when he comes; •you are our pride and our joy.   20

Timothy's mission to Thessalonika

3 When we could not bear the waiting any longer, we decided it would be best 1 to be left without a companion at Athens, and •sent our brother Timothy, 2 who is God's helper in spreading the Good News of Christ, to keep you firm and strong in the faith •and prevent any of you from being unsettled by the present 3 troubles. As you know, these are bound to come our way: •when we were with 4 you, we warned you that we must expect to have persecutions to bear, and that is what has happened now, as you have found out. •That is why, when I could 5 not stand waiting any longer, I sent to assure myself of your faith: I was afraid the Tempter[a] might have tried you too hard, and all our work might have been wasted.

Paul thanks God for good reports of the Thessalonians

6 However, Timothy is now back from you and he has given us good news of your faith and your love, telling us that you always remember us with pleasure
7 and want to see us quite as much as we want to see you. •And so, brothers, your faith has been a great comfort to us in the middle of our own troubles and sorrows;
8 now we can breathe again, as you are still holding firm in the Lord. •How can we
9 thank God enough for you, for all the joy we feel before our God on your account?
10 We are earnestly praying night and day to be able to see you face to face again and make up any shortcomings in your faith.

11 May God our Father himself, and our Lord Jesus Christ, make it easy for us
12 to come to you. •May the Lord be generous in increasing your love and make you
13 love one another and the whole human race*d* as much as we love you. •And may he so confirm your hearts in holiness that you may be blameless in the sight of our God and Father when our Lord Jesus Christ comes *with all his saints.*

Live in holiness and charity

1 4 Finally, brothers, we urge you and appeal to you in the Lord Jesus to make more and more progress in the kind of life that you are meant to live: the life
2 that God wants, as you learnt from us, and as you are already living it. •You have not forgotten the instructions we gave you on the authority of the Lord Jesus.
3 What God wants is for you all to be holy. He wants you to keep away from
4 fornication, •and each one of you to know how to use the body that belongs to
5 him*a* in a way that is holy and honourable, •not giving way to selfish lust like *the*
6 *pagans who do not know God.*b •He wants nobody at all ever to sin by taking advantage of a brother in these matters; the Lord always punishes sins of that sort, as
7 we told you before and assured you. •We have been called by God to be holy,
8 not to be immoral; •in other words, anyone who objects is not objecting to a human authority, but to God, *who gives you his* Holy *Spirit.*c

9 As for loving our brothers, there is no need for anyone to write to you about
10 that, since you have learnt from God yourselves to love one another, •and in fact this is what you are doing with all the brothers throughout the whole of Macedonia. However, we do urge you, brothers, to go on making even greater
11 progress •and to make a point of living quietly, attending to your own business
12 and earning your living, just as we told you to, •so that you are seen to be respectable by those outside the Church, though you do not have to depend on them.

The dead and the living at the time of the Lord's coming

13 We want you to be quite certain, brothers, about those who have died,*d* to make sure that you do not grieve about them, like the other people who have no hope.
14 We believe that Jesus died and rose again, and that it will be the same for those
15 who have died in Jesus: God will bring them with him. •We can tell you this from the Lord's own teaching, that any of us who are left alive until the Lord's coming
16 will not have any advantage over those who have died. •At the trumpet of God, the voice of the archangel will call out the command and the Lord himself will

---

2 a. Jr 11:20   **b.** 2 M 6:14
3 a. I.e. 'the one who puts you to the test'.
4 a. Lit. 'the vessel that is his': either his own body or his wife's.   **b.** Jr 10:25; Ps 79:6
c. Ezk 37:14   **d.** Lit. 'those who are sleeping'.

come down from heaven; those who have died in Christ will be the first to rise, and then those of us who are still alive will be taken up in the clouds, together 17 with them, to meet the Lord in the air. So we shall stay with the Lord for ever. With such thoughts as these you should comfort one another.　　　　　18

Watchfulness while awaiting the coming of the Lord

5 You will not be expecting us to write anything to you, brothers, about 'times 1 and seasons', •since you know very well that the Day of the Lord is going to 2 come like a thief in the night. •It is when people are saying, 'How quiet and 3 peaceful it is' that the worst suddenly happens, as suddenly as labour pains come on a pregnant woman; and there will be no way for anybody to evade it. But it is not as if you live in the dark, my brothers, for that Day to overtake 4 you like a thief. •No, you are all sons of light and sons of the day: we do not belong 5 to the night or to darkness, •so we should not go on sleeping, as everyone else 6 does, but stay wide awake and sober. •Night is the time for sleepers to sleep and 7 drunkards to be drunk, •but we belong to the day and we should be sober; let us 8 put on faith and love for a *breastplate*, and the hope of *salvation* for a *helmet*. God never meant us to experience the Retribution, but to win salvation through 9 our Lord Jesus Christ, •who died for us so that, alive or dead, we should still live 10 united to him. •So give encouragement to each other, and keep strengthening one 11 another, as you do already.

Some demands made by life in community

We appeal to you, my brothers, to be considerate to those who are working 12 amongst you and are above you in the Lord as your teachers. •Have the greatest 13 respect and affection for them because of their work.

Be at peace among yourselves. •And this is what we ask you to do, brothers: 14 warn the idlers, give courage to those who are apprehensive, care for the weak and be patient with everyone. •Make sure that people do not try to take revenge; 15 you must all think of what is best for each other and for the community. •Be 16 happy at all times; •pray constantly; •and for all things give thanks to God, 17/18 because this is what God expects you to do in Christ Jesus.

Never try to suppress the Spirit •or treat the gift of prophecy with contempt; 19/20 think before you do anything—hold on to what is good •and *avoid every* form of 21/22 *evil.*

Closing prayer and farewell

May the God of peace make you perfect and holy; and may you all be kept 23 safe and blameless, spirit, soul and body, for the coming of our Lord Jesus Christ. God has called you and he will not fail you.　　　　　24

Pray for us, my brothers.　　　　　25

Greet all the brothers with the holy kiss. •My orders, in the Lord's name, 26/27 are that this letter is to be read to all the brothers.

The grace of our Lord Jesus Christ be with you.　　　　　28

2 THESSALONIANS

THE SECOND LETTER OF PAUL
TO THE CHURCH IN THESSALONIKA

Address

1 From Paul, Silvanus and Timothy, to the Church in Thessalonika which is in
2 God our Father and the Lord Jesus Christ; •wishing you grace and peace
from God the Father and the Lord Jesus Christ.

Thanksgiving and encouragement. The Last Judgement

3 We feel we must be continually thanking God for you, brothers; quite rightly,
because your faith is growing so wonderfully and the love that you have for one
4 another never stops increasing; •and among the churches of God we can take
special pride in you for your constancy and faith under all the persecutions and
5 troubles you have to bear. •It all shows that God's judgement is just, and the
purpose of it is that you may be found worthy of the kingdom of God; it is for the
sake of this that you are suffering now.
6
7 God will very rightly repay with injury those who are injuring you, •and reward
you, who are suffering now, with the same peace as he will give us, when the Lord
8 Jesus appears from heaven with the angels of his power. •He will come *in flaming
fire* to impose the penalty on *all who do not acknowledge God*[a] and *refuse to accept*
9 the Good News of our Lord Jesus. •It will be their punishment to be lost eter-
nally, excluded *from the presence of the Lord and from the glory of his strength*
10 *on that day* when he comes *to be glorified among his saints* and *seen in his glory*[b]
by all who believe in him; and you are believers, through our witness.
11 Knowing this, we pray continually that our God will make you worthy of his
call, and by his power fulfil all your desires for goodness and complete all that
12 you have been doing through faith; •because in this way *the name* of our Lord
Jesus Christ *will be glorified* in you and you in him, by the grace of our God and the
Lord Jesus Christ.

The coming of the Lord and the prelude to it

1 To turn now, brothers, to the coming of our Lord Jesus Christ and how we
2 shall all be gathered round him: •please do not get excited too soon or
alarmed by any prediction or rumour or any letter claiming to come from us,
3 implying that the Day of the Lord has already arrived. •Never let anyone
deceive you in this way.

1 a. God's *coming in fire* is quoted from Is 66:15; the penalty on *those who do not acknowledge him* is a quotation from Jr 10:25. **b.** Quotations from Is 2:10-17; 49:3; 66:5.

It cannot happen until the Great Revolt has taken place and the Rebel, the Lost One, has appeared. •This is the Enemy, the one who claims to be so much 4 *greater than all* that men call 'god', so much greater than anything that is worshipped, that *he enthrones himself* in *God's* sanctuary and claims that he is God. Surely you remember me telling you about this when I was with you? •And you know, too, what is still holding him back*d* from appearing before his appointed time. •Rebellion is at its work already, but in secret,*e* and the one who is holding 7 it back has first to be removed •before the Rebel appears openly. The Lord 8 *will kill him with the breath of his mouth*ᵃ and will annihilate him with his glorious appearance at his coming.

But when the Rebel comes, Satan will set to work:*h* there will be all kinds of 9 miracles and a deceptive show of signs and portents, •and everything evil that 10 can deceive those who are bound for destruction because they would not grasp the love of the truth which could have saved them. •The reason why God 11 is sending a power to delude them and make them believe what is untrue •is 12 to condemn all who refused to believe in the truth and chose wickedness instead.

Encouragement to persevere

But we feel that we must be continually thanking God for you, brothers whom 13 the Lord loves, because God chose you from the beginning to be saved by the sanctifying Spirit and by faith in the truth. •Through the Good News that we 14 brought he called you to this so that you should share the glory of our Lord Jesus Christ. •Stand firm, then, brothers, and keep the traditions that we taught you, 15 whether by word of mouth or by letter. •May our Lord Jesus Christ himself, and 16 God our Father who has given us his love and, through his grace, such inexhaustible comfort and such sure hope, •comfort you and strengthen you in everything 17 good that you do or say.

3 Finally, brothers, pray for us; pray that the Lord's message may spread 1 quickly, and be received with honour as it was among you; •and pray that we 2 may be preserved from the interference of bigoted and evil people, for faith is not given to everyone. •But the Lord is faithful, and he will give you strength and 3 guard you from the evil one, •and we, in the Lord, have every confidence that 4 you are doing and will go on doing all that we tell you. •May the Lord turn your 5 hearts towards the love of God and the fortitude of Christ.

Against idleness and disunity

In the name of the Lord Jesus Christ, we urge you, brothers, to keep away from 6 any of the brothers who refuses to work or to live according to the tradition we passed on to you.

You know how you are supposed to imitate us: now we were not idle when 7 we were with you, •nor did we ever have our meals at anyone's table without 8 paying for them; no, we worked night and day, slaving and straining, so as not to be a burden on any of you. •This was not because we had no right to be, but in 9 order to make ourselves an example for you to follow.

We gave you a rule when we were with you: not to let anyone have any food if 10 he refused to do any work. •Now we hear that there are some of you who are 11 living in idleness, doing no work themselves but interfering with everyone else's. In the Lord Jesus Christ, we order and call on people of this kind to go on quietly 12 working and earning the food that they eat.

¹³
¹⁴   My brothers, never grow tired of doing what is right. • If anyone refuses to obey what I have written in this letter, take note of him and have nothing to do with

15   him, so that he will feel that he is in the wrong; • though you are not to regard him as an enemy but as a brother in need of correction.

Prayer and farewell wishes

16   May the Lord of peace himself give you peace all the time and in every way. The Lord be with you all.

17   From me, PAUL, these greetings in my own handwriting, which is the mark

18   of genuineness in every letter; this is my own writing. • May the grace of our Lord Jesus Christ be with you all.

2 a. Is 11:4

1 TIMOTHY

THE FIRST LETTER
FROM PAUL TO TIMOTHY

Address

1 From Paul, apostle of Christ Jesus appointed by the command of God our 1
saviour and of Christ Jesus our hope, •to Timothy, true child of mine in the 2
faith; wishing you grace, mercy and peace from God the Father and from Christ
Jesus our Lord.

Suppress the false teachers

As I asked you when I was leaving for Macedonia, please stay at Ephesus, to 3
insist that certain people stop teaching strange doctrines •and taking notice of 4
myths and endless genealogies; these things are only likely to raise irrelevant
doubts instead of furthering the designs of God*d* which are revealed in faith.
The only purpose of this instruction is that there should be love, coming out 5
of a pure heart, a clear conscience and a sincere faith. •There are some people 6
who have gone off the straight course and taken a road that leads to empty
speculation; •they claim to be doctors of the Law but they understand neither 7
the arguments they are using nor the opinions they are upholding.

The purpose of the Law

We know, of course, that the Law is good, but only provided it is treated 8
like any law, •in the understanding that laws are not framed for people who 9
are good. On the contrary, they are for criminals and revolutionaries, for the
irreligious and the wicked, for the sacrilegious and the irreverent; they are for
people who kill their fathers or mothers and for murderers, •for those who are 10
immoral with women or with boys or with men, for liars and for perjurers—and
for everything else that is contrary to the sound teaching •that goes with the 11
Good News of the glory of the blessed God, the gospel that was entrusted to me.

Paul on his own calling

I thank Christ Jesus our Lord, who has given me strength, and who judged 12
me faithful enough to call me into his service •even though I used to be 13
a blasphemer and did all I could to injure and discredit the faith. Mercy, however,
was shown me, because until I became a believer I had been acting in ignorance;
and the grace of our Lord filled me with faith and with the love that is in Christ 14
Jesus. •Here is a saying that you can rely on and nobody should doubt: that 15
Christ Jesus came into the world to save sinners. I myself am the greatest of them;

16 and if mercy has been shown to me, it is because Jesus Christ meant to make me the greatest evidence of his inexhaustible patience for all the other people
17 who would later have to trust in him to come to eternal life. •To the eternal King, the undying, invisible and only God, be honour and glory for ever and ever. Amen.

Timothy's responsibility

18 Timothy, my son, these are the instructions that I am giving you: I ask you to remember the words once spoken over you by the prophets, and taking them
19 to heart to fight like a good soldier •with faith and a good conscience for your weapons. Some people have put conscience aside and wrecked their faith in
20 consequence. •I mean men like Hymenaeus and Alexander, whom I have handed over to Satan to teach them not to be blasphemous.

Liturgical prayer

1 2 My advice is that, first of all, there should be prayers offered for everyone
2 —petitions, intercessions and thanksgiving—•and especially for kings and others in authority, so that we may be able to live religious and reverent lives
3/4 in peace and quiet. •To do this is right, and will please God our saviour: •he
5 wants everyone to be saved and reach full knowledge of the truth. •For there is only one God, and there is only one mediator between God and mankind,
6 himself a man, Christ Jesus, •who sacrificed himself as a ransom for them all.
7 He is the evidence of this, sent at the appointed time, and •I have been named a herald and apostle of it and—I am telling the truth and no lie—a teacher of the faith and the truth to the pagans.
8 In every place, then, I want the men to lift their hands up reverently in prayer, with no anger or argument.

Women in the assembly

9 Similarly, I direct that women are to wear suitable clothes and to be dressed quietly and modestly, without braided hair or gold and jewellery or expensive
10 clothes; their adornment is •to do the sort of good works that are proper for
11 women who profess to be religious. •During instruction, a woman should be
12 quiet and respectful. •I am not giving permission for a woman to teach or to
13 tell a man what to do. A woman ought not to speak, •because Adam was
14 formed first and Eve afterwards, •and it was not Adam who was led astray but
15 the woman who was led astray and fell into sin. •Nevertheless, she will be saved by childbearing, provided she lives a modest life and is constant in faith and love and holiness.

The elder-in-charge

1 3 Here is a saying that you can rely on: To want to be a presiding elder[a] is to
2 want to do a noble work. •That is why the president must have an impeccable character. He must not have been married more than once, and he must be
3 temperate, discreet and courteous, hospitable and a good teacher; •not a heavy drinker, nor hot-tempered, but kind and peaceable. He must not be a lover of
4 money. •He must be a man who manages his own family well and brings his
5 children up to obey him and be well-behaved: •how can any man who does not

3 a. The word *episcopos* used here by Paul had not yet acquired the same meaning as 'bishop'.

understand how to manage his own family have responsibility for the church of God? •He should not be a new convert, in case pride might turn his head 6 and then he might be condemned as the devil was condemned. •It is also 7 necessary that people outside the Church should speak well of him, so that he never gets a bad reputation and falls into the devil's trap.

Deacons

In the same way, deacons must be respectable men whose word can be 8 trusted, moderate in the amount of wine they drink and with no squalid greed for money. •They must be conscientious believers in the mystery of the faith. 9 They are to be examined first, and only admitted to serve as deacons if there 10 is nothing against them. •In the same way, the women must be respectable, 11 not gossips but sober and quite reliable. •Deacons must not have been married 12 more than once, and must be men who manage their children and families well.• Those of them who carry out their duties well as deacons will earn a 13 high standing for themselves and be rewarded with great assurance in their work for the faith in Christ Jesus.

The Church and the mystery of the spiritual life

At the moment of writing to you, I am hoping that I may be with you soon; 14 but in case I should be delayed, I wanted you to know how people ought to behave 15 in God's family—that is, in the Church of the living God, which upholds the truth and keeps it safe. •Without any doubt, the mystery of our religion is very 16 deep indeed:

> He was made visible in the flesh,
> attested by the Spirit,
> seen by angels,
> proclaimed to the pagans,
> believed in by the world,
> taken up in glory.

False teachers

4 The Spirit has explicitly said that during the last times there will be some 1 who will desert the faith and choose to listen to deceitful spirits and doctrines that come from the devils; •and the cause of this is the lies told by hypocrites 2 whose consciences are branded as though with a red-hot iron:*a* •they will say 3 marriage is forbidden, and lay down rules about abstaining from foods which God created to be accepted with thanksgiving by all who believe and who know the truth.*b* •Everything God has created is good, and no food is to be rejected, 4 provided grace is said for it: •the word of God and the prayer make it holy. 5 If you put all this to the brothers, you will be a good servant of Christ Jesus and 6 show that you have really digested the teaching of the faith and the good doctrine which you have always followed. •Have nothing to do with godless myths and 7 old wives' tales. Train yourself spiritually. •'Physical exercises are useful enough, 8 but the usefulness of spirituality is unlimited, since it holds out the reward of life here and now and of the future life as well'; •that is a saying that you can 9 rely on and nobody should doubt it. •I mean that the point of all our toiling and 10 battling is that we have put our trust in the living God and he is the saviour of the whole human race but particularly of all believers. •This is what you are to 11 enforce in your teaching.

12 Do not let people disregard you because you are young, but be an example to all the believers in the way you speak and behave, and in your love, your faith
13 and your purity. •Make use of the time until I arrive by reading to the people,
14 preaching and teaching. •You have in you a spiritual gift which was given to you when the prophets spoke and the body of elders laid their hands on you;
15 do not let it lie unused. •Think hard about all this, and put it into practice, and
16 everyone will be able to see how you are advancing. •Take great care about what you do and what you teach; always do this, and in this way you will save both yourself and those who listen to you.

Pastoral practice

1 Do not speak harshly to a man older than yourself, but advise him as you
2 would your own father; treat the younger men as brothers •and older women as you would your mother. Always treat young women with propriety, as if they were sisters.

Widows

3
4 Be considerate to widows; I mean those who are truly widows. •If a widow has children or grandchildren, they are to learn first of all to do their duty to their own families and repay their debt to their parents, because this is what
5 pleases God. •But a woman who is really widowed and left without anybody can give herself up to God and consecrate all her days and nights to petitions
6 and prayer. •The one who thinks only of pleasure is already dead while she
7 is still alive: •remind them of all this, too, so that their lives may be blameless.
8 Anyone who does not look after his own relations, especially if they are living with him, has rejected the faith and is worse than an unbeliever.
9 Enrolment as a widow is permissible only for a woman at least sixty years
10 old who has had only one husband. •She must be a woman known for her good works and for the way in which she has brought up her children, shown hospitality to strangers and washed the saints' feet, helped people who are in trouble
11 and been active in all kinds of good work. •Do not accept young widows because if their natural desires get stronger than their dedication to Christ, they want
12 to marry again, •and then people condemn them for being unfaithful to their
13 original promise. •Besides, they learn how to be idle and go round from house to house; and then, not merely idle, they learn to be gossips and meddlers in other people's affairs, and to chatter when they would be better keeping quiet.
14 I think it is best for young widows to marry again and have children and a home to look after, and not give the enemy any chance to raise a scandal about them;
15
16 there are already some who have left us to follow Satan. •If a Christian woman has widowed relatives, she should support them and not make the Church bear the expense but enable it to support those who are genuinely widows.

The elders

17 The elders who do their work well while they are in charge are to be given double consideration, especially those who are assiduous in preaching and
18 teaching. •As scripture says: *You must not muzzle an ox when it is treading out*
19 *the corn;*[a] and again: *The worker deserves his pay.*[b] •Never accept any accusation

4 a. Like runaway slaves.   **b.** The rejection of marriage was to be one of the hallmarks of Gnosticism; dietary regulations were more specifically Jewish.
5 a. Dt 25:4   **b.** Not traceable in the O.T.; but this is also to be found in Lk 10:7 where, again, it may be a quotation.

brought against an elder unless it is supported *by two or three witnesses.* •If any 20
of them are at fault, reprimand them publicly, as a warning to the rest. •Before 21
God, and before Jesus Christ and the angels he has chosen, I put it to you as a
duty to keep these rules impartially and never to be influenced by favouritism.
Do not be too quick to lay hands on any man, and never make yourself an 22
accomplice in anybody else's sin; keep yourself pure.

You should give up drinking only water and have a little wine for the sake 23
of your digestion and the frequent bouts of illness that you have.

The faults of some people are obvious long before anyone makes any 24
complaint about them, while others have faults that are not discovered until
afterwards. •In the same way, the good that people do can be obvious; but even 25
when it is not, it cannot be hidden for ever.

Slaves

6 All slaves 'under the yoke' must have unqualified respect for their masters, 1
so that the name of God and our teaching are not brought into disrepute.
Slaves whose masters are believers are not to think any the less of them because 2
they are brothers; on the contrary, they should serve them all the better,
since those who have the benefit of their services are believers and dear to
God.

The true teacher and the false teacher

This is what you are to teach them to believe and persuade them to do.
Anyone who teaches anything different, and does not keep to the sound teaching 3
which is that of our Lord Jesus Christ, the doctrine which is in accordance with
true religion, •is simply ignorant and must be full of self-conceit—with a craze 4
for questioning everything and arguing about words. All that can come of this
is jealousy, contention, abuse and wicked mistrust of one another; •and unending 5
disputes by people who are neither rational nor informed and imagine that
religion is a way of making a profit. •Religion, of course, does bring 6
large profits, but only to those who are content with what they have. •We brought 7
nothing into the world, and we can take nothing out of it; •but as long as we 8
have food and clothing, let us be content with that. •People who long to be rich 9
are a prey to temptation; they get trapped into all sorts of foolish and dangerous
ambitions which eventually plunge them into ruin and destruction. •'The love 10
of money is the root of all evils' and there are some who, pursuing it, have
wandered away from the faith, and so given their souls any number of fatal
wounds.

Timothy's vocation recalled

But, as a man dedicated to God, you must avoid all that. You must aim to 11
be saintly and religious, filled with faith and love, patient and gentle. •Fight the 12
good fight of the faith and win for yourself the eternal life to which you were
called when you made your profession and spoke up for the truth in front of
many witnesses. •Now, before God the source of all life and before Jesus Christ, 13
who spoke up as a witness for the truth in front of Pontius Pilate, I put to you
the duty •of doing all that you have been told, with no faults or failures, until 14
the Appearing of our Lord Jesus Christ,

> who at the due time will be revealed 15
> by God, the blessed and only Ruler of all,

the King of kings and the Lord of lords,
16 who alone is immortal,
whose home is in inaccessible light,
whom no man has seen and no man is able to see:
to him be honour and everlasting power. Amen.

Rich Christians

17 Warn those who are rich in this world's goods that they are not to look down on other people; and not to set their hopes on money, which is untrustworthy, but on God who, out of his riches, gives us all that we need for our happiness.
18 Tell them that they are to do good, and be rich in good works, to be generous
19 and willing to share—•this is the way they can save up a good capital sum for the future if they want to make sure of the only life that is real.

Final warning and conclusion

20 My dear Timothy, take great care of all that has been entrusted to you. Have nothing to do with the pointless philosophical discussions and antagonistic
21 beliefs of the 'knowledge' which is not knowledge at all; •by adopting this, some have gone right away from the faith. Grace be with you.

2 TIMOTHY

THE SECOND LETTER
FROM PAUL TO TIMOTHY

Greeting and thanksgiving

1 From Paul, appointed by God to be an apostle of Christ Jesus in his design 1
to promise life in Christ Jesus; •to Timothy, dear child of mine, wishing you 2
grace, mercy and peace from God the Father and from Christ Jesus our Lord.

Night and day I thank God, keeping my conscience clear and remembering 3
my duty to him as my ancestors did, and always I remember you in my prayers;
I remember your tears •and long to see you again to complete my happiness. 4
Then I am reminded of the sincere faith which you have; it came first to live in 5
your grandmother Lois, and your mother Eunice, and I have no doubt that it
is the same faith in you as well.

The gifts that Timothy has received

That is why I am reminding you now to fan into a flame the gift that God 6
gave you when I laid my hands on you. •God's gift was not a spirit of timidity, 7
but the Spirit of power, and love, and self-control. •So you are never to be 8
ashamed of witnessing to the Lord, or ashamed of me for being his prisoner;
but with me, bear the hardships for the sake of the Good News, relying on the
power of God •who has saved us and called us to be holy—not because of 9
anything we ourselves have done but for his own purpose and by his own grace.
This grace had already been granted to us, in Christ Jesus, before the beginning
of time, •but it has only been revealed by the Appearing of our saviour Christ 10
Jesus. He abolished death, and he has proclaimed life and immortality through
the Good News; •and I have been named its herald, its apostle and its teacher. 11

It is only on account of this that I am experiencing fresh hardships here 12
now;[a] but I have not lost confidence, because I know who it is that I have put
my trust in, and I have no doubt at all that he is able to take care of all that
I have entrusted to him until that Day.

Keep as your pattern the sound teaching you have heard from me, in the 13
faith and love that are in Christ Jesus. •You have been trusted to look after 14
something precious; guard it with the help of the Holy Spirit who lives in us.

As you know, Phygelus and Hermogenes and all the others from Asia refuse 15
to have anything more to do with me. •I hope the Lord will be kind to all the 16
family of Onesiphorus, because he has often been a comfort to me and has never
been ashamed of my chains. •On the contrary, as soon as he reached Rome, he 17
really searched hard for me and found out where I was. •May it be the Lord's 18

will that he shall find the Lord's mercy on that Day. You know better than anyone else how much he helped me at Ephesus.

How Timothy should face hardships

2 ¹ Accept the strength, my dear son, that comes from the grace of Christ Jesus. ² You have heard everything that I teach in public; hand it on to reliable people so that they in turn will be able to teach others.

³ Put up with your share of difficulties, like a good soldier of Christ Jesus. ⁴ In the army, no soldier gets himself mixed up in civilian life, because he must ⁵ be at the disposal of the man who enlisted him; •or take an athlete—he cannot ⁶ win any crown unless he has kept all the rules of the contest; •and again, it is ⁷ the working farmer who has the first claim on any crop that is harvested. •Think over what I have said, and the Lord will show you how to understand it all.

⁸ Remember the Good News that I carry, 'Jesus Christ risen from the dead, ⁹ sprung from the race of David'; •it is on account of this that I have my own hardships to bear, even to being chained like a criminal—but they cannot chain ¹⁰ up God's news. •So I bear it all for the sake of those who are chosen, so that in the end they may have the salvation that is in Christ Jesus and the eternal glory that comes with it.

¹¹ Here is a saying that you can rely on:

> If we have died with him, then we shall live with him.
> ¹² If we hold firm, then we shall reign with him.
> If we disown him, then he will disown us.
> ¹³ We may be unfaithful, but he is always faithful,
> for he cannot disown his own self.

The struggle against the immediate danger from false teachers

¹⁴ Remind them of this; and tell them in the name of God that there is to be no wrangling about words: all that this ever achieves is the destruction of those ¹⁵ who are listening. •Do all you can to present yourself in front of God as a man who has come through his trials, and a man who has no cause to be ashamed of his life's work and has kept a straight course with the message of the truth. ¹⁶ Have nothing to do with pointless philosophical discussions—they only lead ¹⁷ further and further away from true religion. •Talk of this kind corrodes like ¹⁸ gangrene, as in the case of Hymenaeus and Philetus, •the men who have gone right away from the truth and claim that the resurrection has already taken place. Some people's faith cannot stand up to them.

¹⁹ However, God's solid foundation stone is still in position, and this is the inscription on it: '*The Lord knows those who are his own*'[a] and 'All who *call on the name of the Lord*'[b] must avoid sin'.

²⁰ Not all the dishes in a large house are made of gold and silver; some are made of wood or earthenware: some are kept for special occasions and others ²¹ are for ordinary purposes. •Now, to avoid these faults that I am speaking about is the way for anyone to become a vessel for special occasions, fit for the Master himself to use, and kept ready for any good work.

²² Instead of giving in to your impulses like a young man, fasten your attention on holiness, faith, love and peace, in union with all those who call on the Lord

---

1 a. The second imprisonment at Rome.
2 a. Nb 16:5,26   b. Is 26:13

with pure minds. •Avoid these futile and silly speculations, understanding that 23
they only give rise to quarrels; •and a servant of the Lord is. not to 24
engage in quarrels, but has to be kind to everyone, a good teacher, and patient.
He has to be gentle when he corrects people who dispute what he says, never 25
forgetting that God may give them a change of mind so that they recognise the
truth and •come to their senses, once out of the trap where the devil caught 26
them and kept them enslaved.

The dangers of the last days

3 You may be quite sure that in the last days there are going to be 1
some difficult times. •People will be self-centred and grasping; boastful, 2
arrogant and rude; disobedient to their parents, ungrateful, irreligious; •heartless 3
and unappeasable; they will be slanderers, profligates, savages and enemies of
everything that is good; •they will be treacherous and reckless and demented 4
by pride, preferring their own pleasure to God. •They will keep up the outward 5
appearance of religion but will have rejected the inner power of it. Have nothing
to do with people like that.

Of the same kind, too, are those men who insinuate themselves into families 6
in order to get influence over silly women who are obsessed with their sins and
follow one craze after another •in the attempt to educate themselves, but can 7
never come to knowledge of the truth. •Men like this defy the truth just as 8
Jannes and Jambres defied Moses:[a] their minds are corrupt and their faith
spurious.•But they will not be able to go on any longer: their foolishness, like 9
that of the other two, must become obvious to everybody.

You know, though, what I have taught, how I have lived, what I have aimed 10
at; you know my faith, my patience and my love; my constancy •and the 11
persecutions and hardships that came to me in places like Antioch, Iconium and
Lystra—all the persecutions I have endured; and the Lord has rescued me from
every one of them. •You are well aware, then, that anybody who tries to live 12
in devotion to Christ is certain to be attacked; •while these wicked impostors 13
will go from bad to worse, deceiving others and deceived themselves.

You must keep to what you have been taught and know to be true; remember 14
who your teachers were, •and how, ever since you were a child, you have known 15
the holy scriptures—from these you can learn the wisdom that leads to salvation
through faith in Christ Jesus. •All scripture is inspired by God and can profit- 16
ably be used for teaching, for refuting error, for guiding people's lives and
teaching them to be holy. •This is how the man who is dedicated to God 17
becomes fully equipped and ready for any good work.

A solemn charge

4 Before God and before Christ Jesus who is to be judge of the living and the 1
dead, I put this duty to you, in the name of his Appearing and of his kingdom:
proclaim the message and, welcome or unwelcome, insist on it. Refute falsehood, 2
correct error, call to obedience—but do all with patience and with the intention
of teaching. •The time is sure to come when, far from being content with sound 3
teaching, people will be avid for the latest novelty and collect themselves a whole
series of teachers according to their own tastes; •and then, instead of listening 4
to the truth, they will turn to myths. •Be careful always to choose the right 5
course; be brave under trials; make the preaching of the Good News your life's
work, in thoroughgoing service.

Paul in the evening of his life

6 As for me, my life is already being poured away as a libation, and the time
7 has come for me to be gone. •I have fought the good fight to the end; I have run
8 the race to the finish; I have kept the faith; •all there is to come now is the
crown of righteousness reserved for me, which the Lord, the righteous judge,
will give to me on that Day; and not only to me but to all those who have longed
for his Appearing.

Final advice

9
10 Do your best to come and see me as soon as you can. •As it is, Demas has
deserted me for love of this life and gone to Thessalonika, Crescens has gone
11 to Galatia and Titus to Dalmatia; •only Luke is with me. Get Mark to come
12 and bring him with you; I find him a useful helper in my work. •I have sent
13 Tychicus to Ephesus. •When you come, bring the cloak I left with Carpus in
14 Troas, and the scrolls, especially the parchment ones. •Alexander the copper-
smith has done me a lot of harm; *the Lord will repay him for what he has done.*ᵃ
15 Be on your guard against him yourself, because he has been bitterly contesting
everything that we say.
16 The first time I had to present my defence, there was not a single witness to
support me. Every one of them deserted me—may they not be held accountable
17 for it. •But the Lord stood by me and gave me power, so that through me the
whole message might be proclaimed for all the pagans to hear; and so I was
18 *rescued from the lion's mouth.*ᵇ •The Lord will rescue me from all evil attempts
on me, and bring me safely to his heavenly kingdom. To him be glory for ever
and ever. Amen.

Farewells and final good wishes

19
20 Greetings to Prisca and Aquila, and the family of Onesiphorus. •Erastus
21 remained at Corinth, and I left Trophimus ill at Miletus.•Do your best to come
before the winter.
   Greetings to you from Eubulus, Pudens, Linus, Claudia and all the brothers.
22 The Lord be with your spirit. Grace be with you.

3 **a.** In Jewish tradition, the leaders of the Egyptian magicians and disciples of Balaam.
4 **a.** Ps 28:4 and 62:12; Pr 24:12   **b.** Ps 22:21

TITUS

THE LETTER FROM PAUL TO TITUS

Address

1 From Paul, servant of God, an apostle of Jesus Christ to bring those whom 1
God has chosen to faith and to the knowledge of the truth that leads to true
religion; •and to give them the hope of the eternal life that was promised so long 2
ago by God. He does not lie •and so, at the appointed time, he revealed his 3
decision, and, by the command of God our saviour, I have been commissioned to
proclaim it. •To Titus, true child of mine in the faith that we share, wishing you 4
grace and peace from God the Father and from Christ Jesus our saviour.

The appointment of elders

The reason I left you behind in Crete was for you to get everything organised 5
there and appoint elders in every town, in the way that I told you: •that is, each 6
of them must be a man of irreproachable character; he must not have been married
more than once, and his children must be believers and not uncontrollable or
liable to be charged with disorderly conduct. •Since, as president, he will be God's 7
representative, he must be irreproachable: never an arrogant or hot-tempered
man, nor a heavy drinker or violent, nor out to make money; •but a man who 8
is hospitable and a friend of all that is good; sensible, moral, devout and
self-controlled; •and he must have a firm grasp of the unchanging message of the 9
tradition, so that he can be counted on for both expounding the sound doctrine
and refuting those who argue against it.

Opposing the false teachers

And in fact you have there a great many people who need to be disciplined, 10
who talk nonsense and try to make others believe it, particularly among those
of the Circumcision. •They have got to be silenced: men of this kind ruin whole 11
families, by teaching things that they ought not to, and doing it with the vile motive
of making money. •It was one of themselves, one of their own prophets, who 12
said,[a] 'Cretans were never anything but liars, dangerous animals and lazy': •and 13
that is a true statement. So you will have to be severe in correcting them, and
make them sound in the faith •so that they stop taking notice of Jewish myths 14
and doing what they are told to do by people who are no longer interested in the
truth.

To all who are pure themselves, everything is pure; but to those who have been 15
corrupted and lack faith, nothing can be pure—the corruption is both in their
minds and in their consciences. •They claim to have knowledge of God but the 16
things they do are nothing but a denial of him; they are outrageously rebellious
and quite incapable of doing good.

Some specific moral instruction

2 It is for you, then, to preach the behaviour which goes with healthy doctrine.
The older men should be reserved, dignified, moderate, sound in faith and
3 love and constancy. •Similarly, the older women should behave as though they
were religious, with no scandalmongering and no habitual wine-drinking—they
4 are to be the teachers of the right behaviour •and show the younger women how
5 they should love their husbands and love their children, •how they are to be
sensible and chaste, and how to work in their homes, and be gentle, and do as
6 their husbands tell them, so that the message of God is never disgraced. •In the
7 same way, you have got to persuade the younger men to be moderate •and in
everything you do*a* make yourself an example to them of working for good: when
8 you are teaching, be an example to them in your sincerity and earnestness •and
in keeping all that you say so wholesome that nobody can make objections to it;
and then any opponent will be at a loss, with no accusation to make against us.
9 Tell the slaves that they are to be obedient to their masters and always do what
10 they want without any argument; •and there must be no petty thieving—they
must show complete honesty at all times, so that they are in every way a credit
to the teaching of God our saviour.

The basis of the Christian moral life

11 You see, God's grace has been revealed, and it has made salvation possible for
12 the whole human race •and taught us that what we have to do is to give up everything that does not lead to God, and all our worldly ambitions; we must be
13 self-restrained and live good and religious lives here in this present world, •while
we are waiting in hope for the blessing which will come with the Appearing of the
14 glory of our great God and saviour Christ Jesus.*a* •He sacrificed himself for
us in order to *set us free from all wickedness*b and *to purify a people so that it could
be his very own*c and would have no ambition except to do good.
15 Now this is what you are to say, whether you are giving instruction or
correcting errors; you can do so with full authority, and no one is to question it.

General instruction for believers

3 Remind them that it is their duty to be obedient to the officials and represent-
atives of the government; to be ready to do good at every opportunity; •not
to go slandering other people or picking quarrels, but to be courteous and always
3 polite to all kinds of people. •Remember, there was a time when we too were
ignorant, disobedient and misled and enslaved by different passions and luxuries;
we lived then in wickedness and ill-will, hating each other and hateful ourselves.
4 But when the kindness and love of God our saviour for mankind were revealed,
5 it was not because he was concerned with any righteous actions we might have
done ourselves; it was for no reason except his own compassion that he saved us,
by means of the cleansing water of rebirth and by renewing us with the Holy Spirit
6 which he has so generously poured over us through Jesus Christ our saviour.
7 He did this so that we should be justified by his grace, to become heirs looking
8 forward to inheriting eternal life. •This is doctrine that you can rely on.

---

1 **a.** Attributed to the Cretan poet Epimenides of Knossos.
2 **a.** Or 'our great God and our saviour, Christ Jesus'.   **b.** Ps 130:8   **c.** Ex 19:5

Personal advice to Titus

I want you to be quite uncompromising in teaching all this, so that those who now believe in God may keep their minds constantly occupied in doing good works. All this is good, and will do nothing but good to everybody. •But avoid 9 pointless speculations, and those genealogies, and the quibbles and disputes about the Law—these are useless and can do no good to anyone. •If a man disputes 10 what you teach, then after a first and a second warning, have no more to do with him: •you will know that any man of that sort has already lapsed and condemned 11 himself as a sinner.

Practical recommendations, farewells and good wishes

As soon as I have sent Artemas or Tychicus to you, lose no time in joining 12 me at Nicopolis, where I have decided to spend the winter. •See to all the travelling 13 arrangements for Zenas the lawyer and Apollos, and make sure they have everything they need. •All our people are to learn to occupy themselves in doing good 14 works for their practical needs as well, and not to be entirely unproductive.

All those who are with me send their greetings. Greetings to those who love 15 us in the faith. Grace be with you all.

PHILEMON

THE LETTER FROM PAUL TO PHILEMON

Address

1 From Paul, a prisoner of Christ Jesus and from our brother Timothy; to our
2 dear fellow worker Philemon, •our sister Apphia, our fellow soldier Archippus
3 and the church that meets in your house; •wishing you the grace and the peace
of God our Father and the Lord Jesus Christ.

Thanksgiving and prayer

4
5 I always mention you in my prayers and thank God for you, •because I hear
of the love and the faith which you have for the Lord Jesus and for all the saints.
6 I pray that this faith will give rise to a sense of fellowship that will show you all
7 the good things that we are able to do for Christ. •I am so delighted, and comforted, to know of your love; they tell me, brother, how you have put new heart
into the saints.

The request about Onesimus

8 Now, although in Christ I can have no diffidence about telling you to do
9 whatever is your duty, •I am appealing to your love instead, reminding you that
this is Paul writing, an old man now and, what is more, still a prisoner of Christ
10 Jesus. •I am appealing to you for a child of mine, whose father I became while
11 wearing these chains: I mean Onesimus. •He was of no use to you before, but he
12 will be useful[a] to you now, as he has been to me. •I am sending him back to you,
13 and with him—I could say—a part of my own self. •I should have liked to keep
him with me; he could have been a substitute for you, to help me while I am in the
14 chains that the Good News has brought me. •However, I did. not want to do
anything without your consent; it would have been forcing your act of kindness,
15 which should be spontaneous. •I know you have been deprived of Onesimus for
16 a time, but it was only so that you could have him back for ever, •not as a slave
any more, but something much better than a slave, a dear brother; especially
dear to me, but how much more to you, as a blood-brother as well as a brother
17 in the Lord. •So if all that we have in common means anything to you, welcome
18 him as you would me; •but if he has wronged you in any way or owes
19 you anything, then let me pay for it. •I am writing this in my own handwriting:
I, Paul, shall pay it back—I will not add any mention of your own debt to me,
20 which is yourself. •Well then, brother, I am counting on you, in the Lord; put
21 new heart into me, in Christ. •I am writing with complete confidence in your
compliance, sure that you will do even more than I ask.

a. A pun—'Onesimus' means 'useful'.

A personal request. Good wishes

There is another thing: will you get a place ready for me to stay in? I am hoping 22 through your prayers to be restored to you.

Epaphras, a prisoner with me in Christ Jesus, sends his greetings; ·so do my $^{23}_{24}$ colleagues Mark, Aristarchus, Demas and Luke.

May the grace of our Lord Jesus Christ be with your spirit.   25

THE LETTER TO THE
HEBREWS

A LETTER ADDRESSED
TO A JEWISH-CHRISTIAN COMMUNITY

PROLOGUE

The greatness of the incarnate Son of God

1 At various times in the past and in various different ways, God spoke to our
2 ancestors through the prophets; but •in our own time, the last days, he has
spoken to us through his Son, the Son that he has appointed to inherit everything
3 and through whom he made everything there is. · •He is the radiant light of God's
glory and the perfect copy of his nature, sustaining the universe by his powerful
command; and now that he has destroyed the defilement of sin, he has gone to
4 take his place in heaven at the right hand of divine Majesty. •So he is now as far
above the angels as the title which he has inherited is higher than their own name.

I. THE SON IS GREATER THAN THE ANGELS

Proof from the scriptures

5 God has never said to any angel: *You are my Son, today I have become your*
6 *father;*[a] or: *I will be a father to him and he a son to me.*[b] •Again, when he brings the
7 First-born into the world, he says: *Let all the angels of God worship him.*[c] •About
8 the angels, he says: *He makes his angels winds and his servants flames of fire,*[d] •but
to his Son he says: *God, your throne shall last for ever and ever;* and: *his royal*
9 *sceptre is the sceptre of virtue; •virtue you love as much as you hate wickedness.*
This is why God, your God, has anointed you with the oil of gladness, above all your
10 *rivals.*[e] •And again: *It is you, Lord, who laid earth's foundations in the beginning,*
11 *the heavens are the work of your hands; •all will vanish, though you remain, all*
12 *wear out like a garment; •you will roll them up like a cloak, and* like a garment
they will be changed. But yourself, you never change and your years are unending.[f]
13 God has never said to any angel: *Sit at my right hand and I will make your enemies*
14 *a footstool for you.*[g] •The truth is they are all spirits whose work is service, sent to
help those who will be the heirs of salvation.

1 a. Ps 2:7   **b.** 2 S 7:14   **c.** Dt 32:43   **d.** Ps 104:4   **e.** Ps 45:6-7   **f.** Ps 102:25-27
g. Ps 110:1

An exhortation

2 We ought, then, to turn our minds more attentively than before to what we ¹ have been taught, so that we do not drift away. •If a promise that was made ² through angels*ᵃ* proved to be so true that every infringement and disobedience brought its own proper punishment, •then we shall certainly not go unpunished ³ if we neglect this salvation that is promised to us. The promise was first announced by the Lord himself, and is guaranteed to us by those who heard him; God himself confirmed their witness with signs and marvels and miracles of all ⁴ kinds, and by freely giving the gifts of the Holy Spirit.

Redemption brought by Christ, not by angels

He did not appoint angels to be rulers of the world to come, and that world is ⁵ what we are talking about. •Somewhere there is a passage that shows us this. It ⁶ runs: *What is man that you should spare a thought for him, the son of man that you should care for him?* •*For a short while you made him lower than the angels; you* ⁷ *crowned him with glory and splendour.* • *You have put him in command of every-* ⁸ *thing.ᵇ* Well then, if he has *put him in command of everything,* he has left nothing which is not under his command. At present, it is true, we are not able to see that *everything has been put under his command,* •but we do see in Jesus one who was ⁹ *for a short while made lower than the angels* and is now *crowned with glory and splendour* because he submitted to death; by God's grace he had to experience death for all mankind.

As it was his purpose to bring a great many of his sons into glory, it was appro- ¹⁰ priate that God, for whom everything exists and through whom everything exists, should make perfect, through suffering, the leader who would take them to their salvation.ᶠ •For the one who sanctifies, and the ones who are sanctified, are of the ¹¹ same stock; that is why he openly calls them *brothers* •in the text: *I shall announce* ¹² *your name to my brothers, praise you in full assembly;ᶜ* or the text: •*In him I hope*; ¹³ or the text: *Here I am with the children whom God has given me.ᵈ*

Since all the *children* share the same blood and flesh, he too shared equally ¹⁴ in it, so that by his death he could take away all the power of the devil, who had power over death, •and set free all those who had been held in slavery all their ¹⁵ lives by the fear of death. •For it was not the angels that he took to himself; he ¹⁶ took to himself *descent from Abraham.ᵉ* •It was essential that he should in this way ¹⁷ become completely like his brothers so that he could be a compassionate and trustworthy high priest of God's religion, able to atone for human sins. •That is, ¹⁸ because he has himself been through temptation he is able to help others who are tempted.

II. JESUS THE FAITHFUL AND MERCIFUL HIGH PRIEST

Christ higher than Moses

3 That is why all you who are holy brothers and have had the same heavenly ¹ call should turn your minds to Jesus, the apostle and the high priest of our religion. •He was *faithful* to the one who appointed him, just like *Moses,* who ² stayed faithful *in all his house;* •but he has been found to deserve a greater glory ³ than Moses. It is the difference between the honour given to the man that built the house and to the house itself. •Every house is built by someone, of course; ⁴ but God built everything that exists. •It is true that Moses was *faithful in the* ⁵

house of God, as a servant, acting as witness to the things which were to be
6 divulged later; •but Christ was faithful as a son, and as the master in the house.
And we are his house, as long as we cling to our hope with the confidence that we
glory in.

How to reach God's land of rest

7
8   The Holy Spirit says: *If only you would listen to him today;* •*do not harden*
your hearts, as happened in the Rebellion, on the Day of Temptation in the
9 *wilderness,* •*when your ancestors challenged me and tested me, though they had*
10 *seen what I could do* •*for forty years. That was why I was angry with that generation*
11 *and said: How unreliable these people who refuse to grasp my ways!* •*And so, in*
12 *anger, I swore that not one would reach the place of rest I had for them.*[a] •Take care,
brothers, that there is not in any one of your community a wicked mind, so unbe-
13 lieving as to turn away from the living God. •Every day, as long as this 'today'
lasts, keep encouraging one another so that none of you is *hardened* by the lure of
14 sin, •because we shall remain co-heirs with Christ only if we keep a grasp on our
15 first confidence right to the end. •In this saying: *If only you would listen to him*
16 *today; do not harden your hearts, as happened in the Rebellion,* •those who
rebelled after they had *listened* were all the people who were brought out of Egypt
17 by Moses. •And those who made God *angry for forty years* were the ones who
18 sinned and whose *dead bodies were left lying in the wilderness.*[b] •Those that he
swore would never reach the place of rest he had for them were those who had been
19 disobedient. •We see, then, that it was because they were unfaithful that they
were not able to reach it.

1 **4** Be careful, then: the promise of *reaching the place of rest he had for them* still
2   holds good, and none of you must think that he has come too late for it. •We
received the Good News exactly as they did; but hearing the message did them no
3 good because they did not share the faith of those who listened. •We, however,
who have faith, shall reach a place of rest, as in the text: *And so, in anger, I swore*
that not one would reach the place of rest I had for them. God's work was undoubt-
4 edly all finished at the beginning of the world; •as one text says, referring to the
5 seventh day: *After all his work God rested on the seventh day.*[a] •The text we are
6 considering says: *They shall not reach the place of rest I had for them.* •It is established, then, that there would be some people who would reach it, and since those
7 who first heard the Good News failed to reach it through their disobedience, •God
fixed another day when, much later, he said 'today' through David in the text
already quoted: *If only you would listen to him today; do not harden your hearts.*
8 If Joshua had led them into this place of rest, God would not later on have spoken
9 so much of another day. •There must still be, therefore, a place of rest reserved
10 for God's people, the seventh-day rest, •since to *reach the place of rest* is to *rest*
11 *after your work,* as God did after his. •We must therefore do everything we can
to *reach this place of rest,* or some of you might copy this example of disobedience
and be lost.

2 a. The Law.   **b.** Ps 8:4-6 (LXX)   **c.** Ps 22:22   **d.** This, and the previous text, are from
Is 8:17-18.   **e.** Is 41:8-9
3 a. Ps 95   **b.** Nb 14:29
4 a. Gn 2:2

The word of God and Christ the priest

The word of God is something alive and active: it cuts like any double-edged 12 sword but more finely: it can slip through the place where the soul is divided from the spirit, or joints from the marrow; it can judge the secret emotions and thoughts. •No created thing can hide from him; everything is uncovered and open 13 to the eyes of the one to whom we must give account of ourselves.

Since in Jesus, the Son of God, we have the supreme high priest who has gone 14 through to the highest heaven, we must never let go of the faith that we have professed. •For it is not as if we had a high priest who was incapable of feeling 15 our weaknesses with us; but we have one who has been tempted in every way that we are, though he is without sin. •Let us be confident, then, in approaching the 16 throne of grace, that we shall have mercy from him and find grace when we are in need of help.

Jesus the compassionate high priest

5 Every high priest has been taken out of mankind and is appointed to act for 1 men in their relations with God, to offer gifts and sacrifices for sins; and so ↘ he can sympathise with those who are ignorant or uncertain because he too lives 2 in the limitations of weakness. •That is why he has to make sin offerings for 3 himself as well as for the people. •No one takes this honour on himself, but each 4 one is called by God, as Aaron was. •Nor did Christ give himself the glory of 5 becoming high priest, but he had it from the one who said to him: *You are my son, today I have become your father,*[a] •and in another text: *You are a priest of* 6 *the order of Melchizedek, and for ever.*[b] •During his life on earth, he offered up 7 prayer and entreaty, aloud and in silent tears, to the one who had the power to save him out of death, and he submitted so humbly that his prayer was heard. Although he was Son, he learnt to obey through suffering; •but having been $^8_9$ made perfect, he became for all who obey him the source of eternal salvation and was acclaimed by God with the title of high priest *of the order of Melchizedek.* 10

III. THE AUTHENTIC PRIESTHOOD OF JESUS CHRIST

Christian life and theology

On this subject we have many things to say, and they are difficult to explain 11 because you have grown so slow at understanding. •Really, when you should by 12 this time have become masters, you need someone to teach you all over again the elementary principles of interpreting God's oracles; you have gone back to needing milk, and not solid food. •Truly, anyone who is still living on milk cannot digest 13 the doctrine of righteousness because he is still a baby. •Solid food is for mature 14 men with minds trained by practice to distinguish between good and bad.

The author explains his intention

6 Let us leave behind us then all the elementary teaching about Christ and 1 concentrate on its completion, without going over the fundamental doctrines again: the turning away from dead actions and towards faith in God; •the teaching 2 about baptisms and the laying-on of hands; the teaching about the resurrection of the dead and eternal judgement. •This, God willing, is what we propose to do. 3

As for those people who were once brought into the light, and tasted the gift 4 from heaven, and received a share of the Holy Spirit, •and appreciated the good 5 message of God and the powers of the world to come •and yet in spite of this 6 have fallen away—it is impossible for them to be renewed a second time. They cannot be repentant if they have wilfully crucified the Son of God and openly 7 mocked him. •A field that has been well watered by frequent rain, and gives the crops that are wanted by the owners who grew them, is given God's blessing; 8 but one that grows brambles and thistles is abandoned, and practically cursed. It will end by being burnt.

Words of hope and encouragement

9 But you, my dear people—in spite of what we have just said, we are sure you 10 are in a better state and on the way to salvation. •God would not be so unjust as to forget all you have done, the love that you have for his name or the services 11 you have done, and are still doing, for the saints.[a] •Our one desire is that every one of you should go on showing the same earnestness to the end, to the perfect 12 fulfilment of our hopes, •never growing careless, but imitating those who have the faith and the perseverance to inherit the promises.

13 When God made the promise to Abraham, he *swore by his own self*, since it 14 was impossible for him to swear by anyone greater: •*I will shower blessings on* 15 *you and give you many descendants.*[b] •Because of that, Abraham persevered and 16 saw the promise fulfilled. •Men, of course, swear an oath by something greater than themselves, and between men, confirmation by an oath puts an end to all 17 dispute. •In the same way, when God wanted to make the heirs to the promise thoroughly realise that his purpose was unalterable, he conveyed this by an oath; 18 so that there would be two unalterable things in which it was impossible for God to be lying, and so that we, now we have found safety, should have a strong 19 encouragement to take a firm grip on the hope that is held out to us. •Here we have an anchor for our soul, as sure as it is firm, and reaching right *through* 20 *beyond the veil*[c] •where Jesus has entered before us and on our behalf, to become a high *priest of the order of Melchizedek, and for ever*.

A. CHRIST'S PRIESTHOOD HIGHER THAN LEVITICAL PRIESTHOOD

Melchizedek[a]

1 **7** You remember that *Melchizedek, king of Salem, a priest of God Most High, went to meet Abraham who was on his way back after defeating the kings*, and 2 *blessed him;* •and also that it was to him that Abraham gave *a tenth of all that he had*. By the interpretation of his name, he is, first, 'king of righteousness' and 3 also *king of Salem*, that is, 'king of peace'; •he has no father, mother or ancestry, and his life has no beginning or ending; he is like the Son of God. He remains a priest for ever.

5 a. Ps 2:7   **b.** Ps 110:4
6 a. The same phrase is used in Rm and 2 Co about a collection of money made for the church in Jerusalem.   **b.** Gn 22   **c.** Lv 16:2
7 a. Gn 14, from which the following quotation is made, is silent about any ancestors or descendants of Melchizedek, and about 'the beginning and ending' of his life.

Melchizedek accepted tithes from Abraham

Now think how great this man must have been, if the patriarch *Abraham paid* 4 *him a tenth of the treasure he had captured.*[b] •We know that any of the descendants 5 of Levi who are admitted to the priesthood are obliged by the Law to take tithes from the people, and this is taking them from their own brothers although they too are descended from Abraham. •But this man, who was not of the same 6 descent, took his tenth from Abraham, and he gave his blessing to the holder of the promises. •Now it is indisputable that a blessing is given by a superior to an 7 inferior. •Further, in the one case it is ordinary mortal men who receive the 8 tithes, and in the other, someone who is declared to be still alive. •It could be said 9 that Levi himself, who receives tithes, actually paid them, in the person of Abraham, •because he was still in the loins of his ancestor when *Melchizedek* 10 *came to meet him.*

From levitical priesthood to the priesthood of Melchizedek

Now if perfection had been reached through the levitical priesthood because 11 the Law given to the nation rests on it, why was it still necessary for a new priesthood to arise, one *of the same order as Melchizedek*[c] not counted as being 'of the same order as' Aaron? •But any change in the priesthood must mean a 12 change in the Law as well.

So our Lord, of whom these things were said, belonged to a different tribe, 13 the members of which have never done service at the altar; •everyone knows he 14 came from Judah, a tribe which Moses did not even mention when dealing with priests.

The abrogation of the old Law

This[d] becomes even more clearly evident when there appears a second 15 Melchizedek, who is a priest •not by virtue of a law about physical descent, but 16 by the power of an indestructible life. •For it was about him that the prophecy 17 was made: *You are a priest of the order of Melchizedek, and for ever.* •The 18 earlier commandment is thus abolished, because it was neither effective nor useful, since the Law could not make anyone perfect; but now this commandment is 19 replaced by something better—the hope that brings us nearer to God.

Christ's priesthood is unchanging

What is more, this was not done without the taking of an oath. The others, 20 indeed, were made priests without any oath; •but he with an oath sworn by the 21 one who declared to him: *The Lord has sworn an oath which he will never retract:* *you are a priest, and for ever.*[e] •And it follows that it is a greater covenant for 22 which Jesus has become our guarantee. •Then there used to be a great number of 23 those other priests, because death put an end to each one of them; •but this one, 24 because he remains *for ever*, can never lose his priesthood. •It follows, then, that 25 his power to save is utterly certain, since he is living for ever to intercede for all who come to God through him.

The perfection of the heavenly high priest

To suit us, the ideal high priest would have to be holy, innocent and 26 uncontaminated, beyond the influence of sinners, and raised up above the heavens; •one who would not need to offer sacrifices every day, as the other high 27 priests do for their own sins and then for those of the people, because he has done

28 this once and for all by offering himself. •The Law appoints high priests who are men subject to weakness; but the promise on oath, which came after the Law, appointed the Son who is made perfect *for ever.*

B. THE SUPERIORITY OF THE WORSHIP, THE SANCTUARY AND THE MEDIATION PROVIDED BY CHRIST THE PRIEST

The new priesthood and the new sanctuary

1 8 The great point of all that we have said is that we have a high priest of exactly this kind. He has his place *at the right* of the throne of divine 2 Majesty in the heavens, •and he is the minister of the sanctuary and of the true 3 *Tent* of Meeting which *the Lord*, and not any man, *set up.*[a] •It is the duty of every high priest to offer gifts and sacrifices, and so this one too must have something 4 to offer. •In fact, if he were on earth, he would not be a priest at all, since there 5 are others who make the offerings laid down by the Law •and these only maintain the service of a model or a reflection of the heavenly realities. For Moses, when he had the Tent to build, was warned by God who said: *See that you make everything according to the pattern shown you on the mountain.*[b]

Christ is the mediator of a greater covenant

6 We have seen that he has been given a ministry of a far higher order, and to the same degree it is a better covenant of which he is the mediator, founded on 7 better promises. •If that first covenant had been without a fault, there would have 8 been no need for a second one to replace it. •And in fact God does find fault with them; he says:

> *See, the days are coming—it is the Lord who speaks—*
> *when I will establish a new covenant*
> *with the House of Israel and the House of Judah,*
9 > *but not a covenant like the one I made with their ancestors*
> *on the day I took them by the hand*
> *to bring them out of the land of Egypt.*
> *They abandoned that covenant of mine,*
> *and so I on my side deserted them. It is the Lord who speaks.*
10 > *No, this is the covenant I will make*
> *with the House of Israel*
> *when those days arrive—it is the Lord who speaks.*
> *I will put my laws into their minds*
> *and write them on their hearts.*
> *Then I will be their God*
> *and they shall be my people.*
11 > *There will be no further need for neighbour to try to teach neighbour,*
> *or brother to say to brother,*
> *'Learn to know the Lord'.*
> *No, they will all know me,*

b. The regular tithe paid to levitical priests was a tenth.   **c.** Ps 110:4   **d.** What has been said in v. 12.   **e.** Ps 110:4
8 a. Nb 24:6 (LXX)   **b.** Ex 25:40

the least no less than the greatest,
since I will forgive their iniquities   12
and never call their sins to mind.^c

By speaking of a *new* covenant, he implies that the first one is already old. Now 13
anything old only gets more antiquated until in the end it disappears.

Christ enters the heavenly sanctuary

9 The first covenant also had its laws governing worship, and its sanctuary, 1
a sanctuary on this earth. •There was a tent which comprised two 2
compartments: the first, in which the lamp-stand, the table and the presentation
loaves were kept, was called the Holy Place; •then beyond the second veil, an 3
innermost part which was called the Holy of Holies •to which belonged the gold 4
altar of incense, and the ark of the covenant, plated all over with gold. In this
were kept the gold jar containing the manna, Aaron's branch that grew the buds,
and the stone tablets of the covenant. •On top of it was the throne of mercy, and 5
outspread over it were the glorious cherubs. This is not the time to go into
greater detail about this.

Under these provisions, priests are constantly going into the outer tent to 6
carry out their acts of worship, •but the second tent is entered only once a year, 7
and then only by the high priest who must go in by himself and take the blood to
offer for his own faults and the people's. •By this, the Holy Spirit·is showing that 8
no one has the right to go into the sanctuary as long as the outer tent remains
standing; •it is a symbol for this present time. None of the gifts and sacrifices 9
offered under these regulations can possibly bring any worshipper to perfection
in his inner self; •they are rules about the outward life, connected with foods and 10
drinks and washing at various times, intended to be in force only until it should
be time to reform them.

But now Christ has come, as the high priest of all the blessings which were to 11
come. He has passed through the greater, the more perfect tent, which is better
than the one made by men's hands because it is not of this created order; •and he 12
has entered the sanctuary once and for all, taking with him not the blood of goats
and bull calves, but his own blood, having won an eternal redemption for us.
The blood of goats and bulls and the ashes of a heifer are sprinkled on those who 13
have incurred defilement and they restore the holiness of their outward lives;
how much more effectively the blood of Christ, who offered himself as the 14
perfect sacrifice to God through the eternal Spirit, can purify our inner self from
dead actions so that we do our service to the living God.

Christ seals the new covenant with his blood

He brings a new covenant, as the mediator, only so that the people who were 15
called to an eternal inheritance may actually receive what was promised: his death
took place to cancel the sins that infringed the earlier covenant. •Now wherever 16
a will is in question, the death of the testator must be established; •indeed, it only 17
becomes valid with that death, since it is not meant to have any effect while the
testator is still alive. •That explains why even the earlier covenant needed 18
something to be killed in order to take effect, •and why, after Moses had 19
announced all the commandments of the Law to the people, he took the calves'
blood, the goats' blood and some water, and with these he sprinkled the book
itself and all the people, using scarlet wool and hyssop; •saying as he did so: *This* 20

21 *is the blood of the covenant that God has laid down for you.*[a] •After that, he sprinkled
22 the tent and all the liturgical vessels with blood in the same way. •In fact,
according to the Law almost everything has to be purified[b] with blood; and if
23 there is no shedding of blood, there is no remission. •Obviously, only the copies
of heavenly things can be purified in this way, and the heavenly things themselves
24 have to be purified by a higher sort of sacrifice than this. •It is not as though
Christ had entered a man-made sanctuary which was only modelled on the real
one; but it was heaven itself, so that he could appear in the actual presence of God
25 on our behalf. •And he does not have to offer himself again and again, like the
high priest going into the sanctuary year after year with the blood that is not his
26 own, •or else he would have had to suffer over and over again since the world
began. Instead of that, he has made his appearance once and for all, now at the
27 end of the last age, to do away with sin by sacrificing himself. •Since men only
28 die once, and after that comes judgement, •so Christ, too, offers himself only once
to take the faults of many on himself,[c] and when he appears a second time, it will
not be to deal with sin but to reward with salvation those who are waiting for
him.

SUMMARY: CHRIST'S SACRIFICE SUPERIOR TO THE SACRIFICES OF THE MOSAIC LAW

The old sacrifices ineffective

1 **10** So, since the Law has no more than a *reflection* of these realities, and no
finished picture of them, it is quite incapable of bringing the worshippers to
2 perfection, with the same sacrifices repeatedly offered year after year. •Otherwise,
the offering of them would have stopped, because the worshippers, when they had
3 been purified once, would have no awareness of sins. •Instead of that, the sins are
4 recalled year after year in the sacrifices. •Bulls' blood and goats' blood are useless
5 for taking away sins, •and this is what he said, on coming into the world:

> *You who wanted no sacrifice or oblation,*
> *prepared a body for me.*
6 > *You took no pleasure in holocausts or sacrifices for sin;*
7 > *then I said,*
> *just as I was commanded in the scroll of the book,*
> *'God, here I am! I am coming to obey your will.'* [a]

8 Notice that he says first: *You did not want* what the Law lays down as the things
to be offered, that is: *the sacrifices, the oblations, the holocausts and the sacrifices*
9 *for sin,* and *you took no pleasure* in them; •and then he says: *Here I am! I am*
coming to obey your will. He is abolishing the first sort to replace it with the
10 second. •And this *will* was for us to be made holy by the *offering* of his *body* made
once and for all by Jesus Christ.

The efficacy of Christ's sacrifice

11 All the priests stand at their duties every day, offering over and over again
12 the same sacrifices which are quite incapable of taking sins away. •He, on the

c. Jr 31:31-34
9 a. Ex 24:8 **b.** Many instances are given in Lv. **c.** Is 53:12
10 a. Ps 40:6-8 (LXX)

other hand, has offered one single sacrifice for sins, and then taken his place for ever, *at the right hand of God*, •where he is now waiting *until his enemies are made* 13 *into a footstool for him.*[b] •By virtue of that one single offering, he has achieved 14 the eternal perfection of all whom he is sanctifying. •The Holy Spirit assures us 15 of this; for he says, first:

> *This is the covenant I will make with them* 16
> *when those days arrive;*[c]

and the Lord then goes on to say:

> *I will put my laws into their hearts*
> *and write them on their minds.*
> *I will never call their sins to mind,* 17
> or their offences.

When all sins have been forgiven, there can be no more sin offerings. 18

IV. PERSEVERING FAITH

The Christian opportunity

In other words, brothers, through the blood of Jesus we have the right to enter 19 the sanctuary, •by a new way which he has opened for us, a living opening 20 through the curtain, that is to say, his body. •And we have the *supreme high priest* 21 over all *the house of God*. •So as we go in, let us be sincere in heart and filled with 22 faith, our minds sprinkled and free from any trace of bad conscience and our bodies washed with pure water. •Let us keep firm in the hope we profess, because 23 the one who made the promise is faithful. •Let us be concerned for each other, 24 to stir a response in love and good works. •Do not stay away from the meetings 25 of the community, as some do, but encourage each other to go; the more so as you see the Day drawing near.

The danger of apostasy

If, after we have been given knowledge of the truth, we should deliberately 26 commit any sins, then there is no longer any sacrifice for them. •There will be 27 left only the dreadful prospect of judgement and of *the raging fire* that is to *burn rebels.*[d] •Anyone who disregards the Law of Moses is ruthlessly *put to death on the* 28 *word of two witnesses or three;*[e] •and you may be sure that anyone who tramples 29 on the Son of God, and who treats *the blood of the covenant* which sanctified him as if it were not holy, and who insults the Spirit of grace, will be condemned to a far severer punishment. •We are all aware who it was that said: *Vengeance is* 30 *mine; I will repay.*[f] And again: *The Lord will judge his people*. •It is a dreadful thing 31 to fall into the hands of the living God.

Motives for perseverance

Remember all the sufferings that you had to meet after you received the 32 light, in earlier days; •sometimes by being yourselves publicly exposed to insults 33 and violence, and sometimes as associates of others who were treated in the same way. •For you not only shared in the sufferings of those who were in prison, but 34 you happily accepted being stripped of your belongings, knowing that you owned something that was better and lasting. •Be as confident now, then, since the reward 35

36 is so great. •You will need endurance to do God's will and gain what he has promised.

37   Only *a little while now, a very little while,*
     and the one that is coming will have come; he will not delay.[g]
38   *The righteous man will live by faith,*
     but if he draws back, my soul will take no pleasure in him.[h]

39 You and I are not the sort of people who *draw back*, and are lost by it; we are the sort who keep *faithful* until our souls are saved.

The exemplary faith of our ancestors

1   **11** Only faith can guarantee the blessings that we hope for, or prove the
2   existence of the realities that at present remain unseen. •It was for faith that our ancestors were commended.

3   It is by faith that we understand that the world was created by one word from God, so that no apparent cause can account for the things we can see.

4   It was because of his faith that Abel offered God a better sacrifice than Cain, and for that he was declared to be righteous when *God* made acknowledgement of *his offerings*. Though he is dead, he still speaks by faith.

5   It was because of his faith that Enoch was taken up and did not have to experience death: *he was not to be found because God had taken him.*[a] This was
6 because before his assumption it is attested that *he had pleased God.* •Now it is impossible to please God without faith, since anyone who comes to him must believe that he exists and rewards those who try tŏ find him.

7   It was through his faith that Noah, when he had been warned by God of something that had never been seen before, felt a holy fear and built an ark to save his family. By his faith the world was convicted, and he was able to claim the righteousness which is the reward of faith.

8   It was by faith that Abraham obeyed the call to *set out* for a country that was the inheritance given to him and his descendants, and that *he set out* without
9 knowing where he was going. •By faith he arrived, *as a foreigner*, in the Promised Land, and lived there as if in a strange country, with Isaac and Jacob, who were
10 heirs with him of the same promise. •They lived there in tents while he looked forward to a city founded, designed and built by God.

11   It was equally by faith that Sarah, in spite of being past the age, was made able to conceive, because she believed that he who had made the promise would be
12 faithful to it. •Because of this, there came from one man, and one who was already as good as dead himself, *more descendants than could be counted, as many as the stars of heaven or the grains of sand on the seashore.*[b]

13   All these died in faith, before receiving any of the things that had been
. promised, but they saw them in the far distance and welcomed them, recognising
14 that they were only *strangers and nomads on earth.* •People who use such terms about themselves make it quite plain that they are in search of their real homeland.
15 They can hardly have meant the country they came from, since they had the
16 opportunity to go back to it; •but in fact they were longing for a better homeland, their heavenly homeland That is why God is not ashamed to be called their God, since he has founded the city for them.

b. Ps 110   **c.** From the long quotation from Jr 31 made in ch. 8.   **d.** Is 26:11 (LXX)
e. Dt 17:6   **f.** Dt 32:35-36   **g.** Is 26:20 (LXX)   **h.** Hab 2:3-4 (LXX)
11 a. Gn 5:24   **b.** Gn 22:17, also quoted in Ex 32.

It was by faith that Abraham, *when put to the test, offered up Isaac.*[c] He offered 17 to sacrifice his only son even though the promises had been made to him •and he 18 had been told: *It is through Isaac that your name will be carried on.*[d] •He was 19 confident that God had the power even to raise the dead; and so, figuratively speaking, he was given back Isaac from the dead.

It was by faith that this same Isaac gave his blessing to Jacob and Esau for the 20 still distant future. •By faith Jacob, when he was dying, blessed each of Joseph's 21 sons, *leaning on the end of his stick as though bowing to pray.*[e] •It was by faith that, 22 when he was about to die, Joseph recalled the Exodus of the Israelites and made the arrangements for his own burial.

It was by faith that Moses, when he was born, *was hidden by his parents for* 23 *three months;* they defied the royal edict when they *saw* he was such a *fine* child. It was by faith that, *when he grew to manhood,* Moses refused to be known as the 24 son of Pharaoh's daughter •and chose to be ill-treated in company with God's 25 people rather than to enjoy'for a time the pleasures of sin. •He considered that 26 the insults offered to the Anointed were something more precious than all the treasures of Egypt, because he had his eyes fixed on the reward. •It was by faith 27 that he left Egypt and was not afraid of the king's anger; he held to his purpose like a man who could see the Invisible. •It was by faith that he kept *the Passover* 28 and sprinkled *the blood* to prevent *the Destroyer* from touching any of the first-born sons of Israel. •It was by faith they crossed the Red Sea as easily as dry land, 29 while the Egyptians, trying to do the same, were drowned.

It was through faith that the walls of Jericho fell down when the people had 30 been round them for seven days. •It was by faith that Rahab the prostitute 31 welcomed the spies and so was not killed with the unbelievers.

Is there any need to say more? There is not time for me to give an account 32 of Gideon, Barak, Samson, Jephthah, or of David, Samuel and the prophets. These were men who through faith conquered kingdoms, did what is right and 33 earned the promises. They could keep a lion's mouth shut, •put out blazing fires 34 and emerge unscathed from battle. They were weak people who were given strength, to be brave in war and drive back foreign invaders. •Some came back 35 to their wives from the dead, by resurrection; and others submitted to torture, refusing release so that they would rise again to a better life. •Some had to bear 36 being pilloried and flogged, or even chained up in prison. •They were stoned, 37 or sawn in half,[f] or beheaded; they were homeless, and dressed in the skins of sheep and goats; they were penniless and were given nothing but ill-treatment. They were too good for the world and they went out to live in deserts and 38 mountains and in caves and ravines. •These are all heroes of faith, but they did 39 not receive what was promised, •since God had made provision for us to have 40 something better, and they were not to reach perfection except with us.

The example of Jesus Christ

12 With so many witnesses in a great cloud on every side of us, we too, then, 1 should throw off everything that hinders us, especially the sin that clings so easily, and keep running steadily in the race we have started. •Let us not lose 2 sight of Jesus, who leads us in our faith and brings it to perfection: for the sake of the joy which was still in the future, he endured the cross, disregarding the shamefulness of it, and *from now on has taken his place at the right* of God's throne. Think of the way he stood such opposition from sinners and then you will not 3 give up for want of courage. •In the fight against sin, you have not yet had to 4 keep fighting to the point of death.

God's fatherly instruction

5　　Have you forgotten that encouraging text in which you are addressed as sons?
My son, when the Lord corrects you, do not treat it lightly; but do not get discouraged
6 *when he reprimands you.* •*For the Lord trains the ones that he loves and he punishes*
7 *all those that he acknowledges as his sons.*[a] •Suffering is part of your *training;*
God is treating you as his *sons.* Has there ever been any *son* whose father did not
8 *train* him? •If you were not getting this training, as all of you are, then you would
9 not be *sons* but bastards. •Besides, we have all had our human fathers who
punished us, and we respected them for it; we ought to be even more willing to
10 submit ourselves to our spiritual Father, to be given life. •Our human fathers
were thinking of this short life when they punished us, and could only do what
they thought best; but he does it all for our own good, so that we may share his
11 own holiness. •Of course, any punishment is most painful at the time, and far
from pleasant; but later, in those on whom it has been used, it bears fruit in peace
12 and goodness. •So *hold up your limp arms and steady your trembling knees*[b]. •and
13 *smooth out the path you tread;*[c] then the injured limb will not be wrenched, it will
grow strong again.

Unfaithfulness is punished

14　　*Always be wanting peace*[d] with all people, and the holiness without which no
15 one can ever see the Lord. •Be careful that no one is deprived of the grace of God
and that no *root of bitterness should begin to grow and make trouble;*[e] this can poison
16 a whole community. •And be careful that there is no immorality, or that any of
you does not degrade religion like Esau, *who sold his birthright* for one single
17 meal. •As you know, when he wanted to obtain the blessing afterwards, he was
rejected and, though he pleaded for it with tears, he was unable to elicit a change
of heart.

The two covenants

18　　What you have come to is nothing known to the senses: not a *blazing fire,*[f]
19 or a *gloom* turning to *total darkness,* or a *storm;* •or *trumpeting thunder* or the
great voice speaking which made everyone that heard it beg that no more should
20 be said to them. •They were appalled at the order that was given: *If even an animal*
21 *touches the mountain, it must be stoned.* •The whole scene was so terrible that
22 Moses said: *I am afraid,*[g] and was trembling with fright. •But what you have come
to is Mount Zion and the city of the living God, the heavenly Jerusalem where the
23 millions of angels have gathered for the festival, •with the whole Church in which
everyone is a 'first-born son' and a citizen of heaven. You have come to God
himself, the supreme Judge, and been placed with the spirits of the saints who have
24 been made perfect; •and to Jesus, the mediator who brings a new covenant and a
25 blood for purification which pleads more insistently than Abel's. •Make sure that
you never refuse to listen when he speaks. The people who refused to listen to the
warning from a voice on earth could not escape their punishment, and how shall
26 we escape if we turn away from a voice that warns us from heaven? •That time
his voice made the earth shake, but now he has given us this promise: *I shall make*

c. Gn 22:1-14　　**d.** Gn 21:12　　**e.** Gn 47:31　　**f.** Some apocryphal books say that this was
how King Manasseh had Isaiah executed.
12 a. Ps 3:11-12 (LXX)　　**b.** Is 35:3　　**c.** Pr 4:26 (LXX)　　**d.** Ps 34:14　　**e.** Dt 29:17
f. The quotations in vv. 18-20 are from Ex 19 (recalled in Dt 4).　　**g.** Dt 9:19

the earth shake once more and not only the earth but *heaven as well.*[h] •The words 27
once more show that since the things being shaken are created things, they are
going to be changed, so that the unshakeable things will be left. •We have 28
been given possession of an unshakeable kingdom. Let us therefore hold on to the
grace that we have been given and use it to worship God in the way that he finds
acceptable, in reverence and fear. •For our *God* is a *consuming fire.*[i]   29

APPENDIX

Final recommendations

13 Continue to love each other like brothers, •and remember always to 1
welcome strangers, for by doing this, some people have entertained angels 2
without knowing it. •Keep in mind those who are in prison, as though you were 3
in prison with them; and those who are being badly treated, since you too are in
the one body. •Marriage is to be honoured by all, and marriages are to be kept 4
undefiled, because fornicators and adulterers will come under God's judgement.
Put greed out of your lives and be content with whatever you have; God himself 5
has said: *I will not fail you or desert you,*[a] •and so we can say with confidence: 6
With the Lord to help me, I fear nothing: what can man do to me?[b]

Faithfulness

Remember your leaders, who preached the word of God to you, and as you 7
reflect on the outcome of their lives, imitate their faith. •Jesus Christ is the same 8
today as he was yesterday and as he will be for ever. •Do not let yourselves 9
be led astray by all sorts of strange doctrines: it is better to rely on grace for inner
strength than on dietary laws which have done no good to those who kept them.
We have our own altar from which those who serve the tabernacle have no right 10
to eat. •The bodies of the animals *whose blood is brought into the sanctuary* by the 11
high priest *for the atonement of sin are burnt outside the camp,*[c] •and so Jesus too 12
suffered outside the gate to sanctify the people with his own blood. •Let us go to 13
him, then, *outside the camp,* and share his degradation. •For there is no eternal 14
city for us in this life but we look for one in the life to come. •Through him, 15
let us offer God an unending *sacrifice of praise,*[d] a verbal sacrifice that is offered
every time we acknowledge his name. •Keep doing good works and sharing your 16
resources, for these are sacrifices that please God.

Obedience to religious leaders

Obey your leaders and do as they tell you, because they must give an account 17
of the way they look after your souls; make this a joy for them to do, and not a
grief—you yourselves would be the losers. •We are sure that our own conscience 18
is clear and we are certainly determined to behave honourably in everything we
do; pray for us. •I ask you very particularly to pray that I may come back to you 19
all the sooner.

EPILOGUE

News, good wishes and greetings

I pray that the God of peace, *who brought* our Lord Jesus *back*[e] from the dead 20
to become the great Shepherd of the sheep[f] by the blood that sealed an eternal

21 *covenant,*[h] •may make you ready to do his will in any kind of good action; and turn us all into whatever is acceptable to himself through Jesus Christ, to whom be glory for ever and ever, Amen.

22 I do ask you, brothers, to take these words of advice kindly; that is why I have written to you so briefly.

23 I want you to know that our brother Timothy has been set free. If he arrives 24 in time, he will be with me when I see you. •Greetings to all your leaders and to 25 all the saints. The saints of Italy send you greetings. •Grace be with you all.

h. Hg 2:6, probably influenced also by Ps 68:8.   i. Dt 4:24
13 a. Dt 31:6   b. Ps 118:6; Ps 27:1   c. Lv 16:27   d. Ps 50:14   e. Is 63:11   f. Ezk 34:23   g. Ezk 37:26

INTRODUCTION TO
THE LETTERS TO ALL CHRISTIANS

Seven letters not written by Paul are included in the New Testament and these, because they were addressed to the Church at large, have been known as 'the catholic epistles'. The three of them attributed to John have been briefly introduced in the introductory note to John's Gospel.

James

The traditional attribution of this letter to 'James, the brother of the Lord', is supported by internal evidence. Though it was written in Greek, the letter is full of hebraisms and its style of argument is characteristically semitic, and it was clearly intended for Jewish converts so familiar with the Old Testament that they would understand allusions to it without direct quotation. It is more a sermon than a letter and consists largely of moral exhortations, laying particular stress on the practical 'good works' expected of Christians and re-presenting much of the Jewish Wisdom tradition. It takes a different point of view from Paul's on the problem of relating faith to works, and may either be earlier than Galatians-Romans and written as early as A.D. 49, or it may be a rejoinder to what Paul had written and be placed at 57 or 58.

Jude

This is also a letter to Jewish Christians, probably written between A.D. 70 and 80. It denounces certain false teachers and threatens them with the punishments promised by Jewish tradition, and it quotes from apocryphal Jewish writings.

1 Peter. 2 Peter

1 Peter has from the earliest times been accepted as written by the apostle, though it may not have been first composed as a single letter. It is addressed to Christian churches largely made up of converts from paganism, and is in quite good Greek, perhaps through the help of the disciple Silvanus mentioned in it as secretary. The letter reflects a time of trial through which the churches were passing and contains much practical teaching under the dominating theme of fortitude in persecution.

2 Peter seems to date from later than Peter's death, though the writer may have had some claim to represent Peter and was possibly a disciple of his. One possibility is that he filled out one of Peter's writings by adopting the letter of Jude to make a chapter (ch. 2).

THE LETTER OF

JAMES

Address and greetings

1 From James, servant of God and of the Lord Jesus Christ. Greetings to the 1
twelve tribes of the Dispersion.[a]

Trials a privilege

My brothers, you will always have your trials but, when they come, try to treat 2
them as a happy privilege;[b] •you understand that your faith is only put to the 3
test to make you patient, •but patience too is to have its practical results so that 4
you will become fully-developed, complete, with nothing missing.

If there is any one of you who needs wisdom, he must ask God, who 5
gives to all freely and ungrudgingly; it will be given to him. •But he must ask 6
with faith, and no trace of doubt, because a person who has doubts is like the
waves thrown up in the sea when the wind drives. •That sort of person, in two 7
minds, wavering between going different ways, must not expect that the Lord 8
will give him anything.

It is right for the poor brother to be proud of his high rank, •and the rich 9
one to be thankful that he has been humbled, because riches last no longer than 10
the flowers in the grass; •the scorching sun comes up, and *the grass withers, the* 11
flower falls;[c] what looked so beautiful now disappears. It is the same with the rich
man: his business goes on; he himself perishes.

Happy the man who stands firm[d] when trials come. He has proved himself, 12
and will win the prize of life, the crown that the Lord has promised to those who
love him.

Temptation

Never, when you have been tempted, say, 'God sent the temptation'; God 13
cannot be tempted to do anything wrong, and he does not tempt anybody.
Everyone who is tempted is attracted and seduced by his own wrong desire. 14
Then the desire conceives and gives birth to sin, and when sin is fully grown, it too 15
has a child, and the child is death.

Make no mistake about this, my dear brothers: •it is all that is good, 16
everything that is perfect, which is given us from above; it comes down from the 17
Father of all light; with him there is no such thing as alteration, no shadow of a
change. •By his own choice he made us his children by the message of the truth 18
so that we should be a sort of first-fruits of all that he had created.

True religion

19   Remember this, my dear brothers: be *quick to listen'* but *slow* to speak and
20 slow to rouse your temper; •God's righteousness is never served by man's anger;
21 so do away with all the impurities and bad habits that are still left in you—accept
and submit to the word which has been planted in you and can save your souls.
22 But you must do what the word tells you, and not just listen to it and deceive
23 yourselves. • To listen to the word and not obey is like looking at your own features
24 in a mirror and then, •after a quick look, going off and immediately forgetting
25 what you looked like. • But the man who looks steadily at the perfect law of
freedom and makes that his habit—not listening and then forgetting, but actively
putting it into practice—will be happy in all that he does.
26   Nobody must imagine that he is religious while he still goes on deceiving
himself and not keeping control over his tongue; anyone who does this has the
27 wrong idea of religion. •Pure, unspoilt religion, in the eyes of God our Father
is this: coming to the help of orphans and widows when they need it, and keeping
oneself uncontaminated by the world.

Respect for the poor

1   **2** My brothers, do not try to combine faith in Jesus Christ, our glorified Lord,
2   with the making of distinctions between classes of people. • Now suppose a man
comes into your synagogue, *"* beautifully dressed and with a gold ring on, and at
3 the same time a poor man comes in, in shabby clothes, •and you take notice of the
well-dressed man, and say, 'Come this way to the best seats'; then you tell the
4 poor man, 'Stand over there' or 'You can sit on the floor by my foot-rest'. •Can't
you see that you have used two different standards in your mind, and turned
yourselves into judges, and corrupt judges at that?
5   Listen, my dear brothers: it was those who are poor according to the world
that God chose, to be rich in faith and to be the heirs to the kingdom which he
6 promised to those who love him. • In spite of this, you have no respect for anybody
who is poor. Isn't it always the rich who are against you? Isn't it always their
7 doing when you are dragged before the court? •Aren't they the ones who insult
8 the honourable name to which you have been dedicated? •Well, the right thing
to do is to keep the supreme law of scripture: *you must love your neighbour as*
9 *yourself;*[b] •but as soon as you make distinctions between classes of people, you are
committing sin, and under condemnation for breaking the Law.
10   You see, if a man keeps the whole of the Law, except for one small point
11 at which he fails, he is still guilty of breaking it all. • It was the same person who
said, ' *You must not commit adultery*' and ' *You must not kill*'.[c] Now if you commit
murder, you do not have to commit adultery as well to become a breaker of the
12 Law. •Talk and behave like people who are going to be judged by the law of
13 freedom, •because there will be judgement without mercy for those who have
not been merciful themselves; but the merciful need have no fear of judgement.

---

1 a. In O.T. days the 'Dispersion' (*diaspora*) meant the Jews who had emigrated from their
own country. The writer is using it here to mean the Jewish-Christians, living in the Graeco-
Roman world.   **b.** 'happy privilege' is a pun on the greeting formula in v. 1.   **c.** Is 40:6-7
d. Dn 12:12   **e.** Si 5:11
2 a. Jewish Christians may still have been attending synagogues, or the writer may have
adopted this word for the Christian assembly.   **b.** Lv 19:18   **c.** Ex 20

Faith and good works

Take the case, my brothers, of someone who has never done a single good 14
act but claims that he has faith. Will that faith save him? •If one of the brothers 15
or one of the sisters is in need of clothes and has not enough food to live on,
and one of you says to them, 'I wish you well; keep yourself warm and 16
eat plenty', without giving them these bare necessities of life, then what good is
that? •Faith is like that: if good works do not go with it, it is quite dead. 17

This is the way to talk to people of that kind: 'You say you have faith and I 18
have good deeds; I will prove to you that I have faith by showing you my good
deeds—now you prove to me that you have faith without any good deeds to show.
You believe in the one God—that is creditable enough, but the demons have the 19
same belief, and they tremble with fear. •Do realise, you senseless man, that faith 20
without good deeds is useless. •You surely know that Abraham our father was 21
justified by his deed, because he *offered his son Isaac on the altar*?[d] •There you see 22
it: faith and deeds were working together; his faith became perfect by what he did.
This is what scripture really means when it says: *Abraham put his faith in God,* 23
and this was counted as making him justified;[e] and that is why he was called 'the
friend of God'.

You see now that it is by doing something good, and not only by believing, 24
that a man is justified. •There is another example of the same kind:. Rahab the 25
prostitute, justified by her deeds because she welcomed the messengers and
showed them a different way to leave. •A body dies when it is separated from the 26
spirit, and in the same way faith is dead if it is separated from good deeds.

Uncontrolled language

3 Only a few of you, my brothers, should be teachers, bearing in mind that 1
those of us who teach can expect a stricter judgement.

After all, every one of us does something wrong, over and over again; the 2
only man who could reach perfection would be someone who never said anything
wrong—he would be able to control every part of himself. •Once we put a bit 3
into the horse's mouth, to make it do what we want, we have the whole animal
under our control. •Or think of ships: no matter how big they are, even if a gale 4
is driving them, the man at the helm can steer them anywhere he likes by
controlling a tiny rudder. •So is the tongue only a tiny part of the body, but it can 5
proudly claim that it does great things. Think how small a flame can set fire to a
huge forest; •the tongue is a flame like that. Among all the parts of the body, the 6
tongue is a whole wicked world in itself: it infects the whole body; catching fire
itself from hell, it sets fire to the whole wheel of creation. •Wild animals and birds, 7
reptiles and fish can all be tamed by man, and often are; •but nobody can tame the 8
tongue—it is a pest that will not keep still, full of deadly poison. •We use it to 9
bless the Lord and Father, but we also use it to curse men who are made in God's
image: •the blessing and the curse come out of the same mouth. My brothers, 10
this must be wrong—•does any water supply give a flow of fresh water and salt 11
water out of the same pipe? •Can a fig tree give you olives, my brothers, or a 12
vine give figs? No more can sea water give you fresh water.

Real wisdom and its opposite

If there are any wise or learned men among you, let them show it by their good 13
lives, with humility and wisdom in their actions. •But if at heart you have the 14
bitterness of jealousy, or a self-seeking ambition, never make any claims for

15 yourself or cover up the truth with lies —·principles of this kind are not the wisdom that comes down from above: they are only earthly, animal and
16 devilish. ·Wherever you find jealousy and ambition, you find disharmony, and
17 wicked things of every kind being done; ·whereas the wisdom that comes down from above is essentially something pure; it also makes for peace, and is kindly and considerate; it is full of compassion and shows itself by doing good; nor is
18 there any trace of partiality or hypocrisy in it. ·Peacemakers, when they work for peace, sow the seeds which will bear fruit in holiness.

Disunity among Christians

1 **4** Where do these wars and battles between yourselves first start? Isn't it precisely
2 in the desires fighting inside your own selves? ·You want something and you haven't got it; so you are prepared to kill. You have an ambition that you cannot satisfy; so you fight to get your way by force. Why you don't have what you
3 want is because you don't pray for it; ·when you do pray and don't get it, it is because you have not prayed properly, you have prayed for something to indulge your own desires.

4 You are as unfaithful as adulterous wives; don't you realise that making the world your friend is making God your enemy? Anyone who chooses the world
5 for his friend turns himself into God's enemy. ·Surely you don't think scripture is wrong when it says: the spirit which he sent to live in us wants us for himself
6 alone? ·But he has been even more generous to us, as scripture says: *God opposes*
7 *the proud but he gives generously to the humble.*[a] ·Give in to God, then; resist the
8 devil, and he will run away from you. ·The nearer you go to God, the nearer he will come to you. Clean your hands, you sinners, and clear your minds, you
9 waverers. ·Look at your wretched condition, and weep for it in misery; be
10 miserable instead of laughing, gloomy instead of happy. ·Humble yourselves before the Lord and he will lift you up.

11 Brothers, do not slander one another. Anyone who slanders a brother, or condemns him, is speaking against the Law and condemning the Law. But if you condemn the Law, you have stopped keeping it and become a judge over it.
12 There is only one lawgiver and he is the only judge and has the power to acquit or to sentence. Who are you to give a verdict on your neighbour?

A warning for the rich and the self-confident

13 Here is the answer for those of you who talk like this: 'Today or tomorrow, we are off to this or that town; we are going to spend a year there, trading, and
14 make some money'. ·You never know what will happen tomorrow: you are no
15 more than a mist that is here for a little while and then disappears. ·The most you should ever say is: 'If it is the Lord's will, we shall still be alive to do this or
16 that'. ·But how proud and sure of yourselves you are now! Pride of this kind is
17 always wicked. ·Everyone who knows what is the right thing to do and doesn't do it commits a sin.

1 **5** Now an answer for the rich. Start crying, weep for the miseries that are
2 coming to you. ·Your wealth is all rotting, your clothes are all eaten up by
3 moths. ·All your gold and your silver are corroding away, and the same corrosion will be your own sentence, and eat into your body. It was a burning fire that you
4 stored up as your treasure for the last days. ·Labourers mowed your fields, and

d. Gn 22:9   **e.** Gn 15:6
4 a. Pr 3:34 (LXX)

you cheated them—listen to the wages that you kept back, calling out; realise that the cries of the reapers have reached the ears of the Lord of hosts. •On earth 5 you have had a life of comfort and luxury; in the time of slaughter you went on eating to your heart's content. •It was you who condemned the innocent and 6 killed them; they offered you no resistance.

A final exhortation

Now be patient, brothers, until the Lord's coming. Think of a farmer: how 7 patiently he waits for the precious fruit of the ground until it has had the autumn rains and the spring rains! •You too have to be patient; do not lose heart, 8 because the Lord's coming will be soon. •Do not make complaints against one 9 another, brothers, so as not to be brought to judgement yourselves; the Judge is already to be seen waiting at the gates. •For your example, brothers, in sub- 10 mitting with patience, take the prophets who spoke in the name of the Lord; remember it is those who had endurance that we say are the blessed ones. You 11 have heard of the patience of Job, and understood the Lord's purpose, realising that *the Lord is kind and compassionate.*[a]

Above all, my brothers, do not swear by heaven or by the earth, or use any 12 oaths at all. If you mean 'yes', you must say 'yes'; if you mean 'no', say 'no'. Otherwise you make yourselves liable to judgement.

If any one of you is in trouble, he should pray; if anyone is feeling happy, he 13 should sing a psalm. •If one of you is ill, he should send for the elders 14 of the church, and they must anoint him with oil in the name of the Lord and pray over him. •The prayer of faith will save the sick man and the Lord will raise 15 him up again; and if he has committed any sins, he will be forgiven. •So confess 16 your sins to one another, and pray for one another, and this will cure you; the heartfelt prayer of a good man works very powerfully. •Elijah was a human 17 being like ourselves—he prayed hard for it not to rain, and no rain fell for three-and-a-half years; •then he prayed again and the sky gave rain and the earth 18 gave crops.

My brothers, if one of you strays away from the truth, and another brings 19 him back to it,•he may be sure that anyone who can bring back a sinner from 20 the wrong way that he has taken will be saving a soul from death and *covering up a great number of sins.*[b]

---

5 a. Ps 103:8　　**b.** Pr 10:12

1 PETER

THE FIRST LETTER OF PETER

Address. Greetings

1 1 Peter, apostle of Jesus Christ, sends greetings to all those living among foreigners in the Dispersion of Pontus, Galatia, Cappadocia, Asia and
2 Bithynia, who have been chosen, •by the provident purpose of God the Father, to be made holy by the Spirit, obedient to Jesus Christ and sprinkled with his blood. Grace and peace be with you more and more.

Introduction. The salvation of Christians

3 Blessed be God the Father of our Lord Jesus Christ, who in his great mercy has given us a new birth as his sons, by raising Jesus Christ from the dead, so that
4 we have a sure hope •and the promise of an inheritance that can never be spoilt or soiled and never fade away, because it is being kept for you in the heavens.
5 Through your faith, God's power will guard you until the salvation which has
6 been prepared is revealed at the end of time. •This is a cause of great joy for you, even though you may for a short time have to bear being plagued by all sorts of
7 trials; •so that, when Jesus Christ is revealed, your faith will have been tested and proved like gold—only it is more precious than gold, which is corruptible even though it bears testing by fire—and then you will have praise and glory and
8 honour. •You did not see him, yet you love him; and still without seeing him, you are already filled with a joy so glorious that it cannot be described, because
9 you believe; •and you are sure of the end to which your faith looks forward, that is, the salvation of your souls.

The hope of the prophets

10 It was this salvation that the prophets were looking and searching so hard for;
11 their prophecies were about the grace which was to come to you. •The Spirit of Christ which was in them foretold the sufferings of Christ and the glories that would come after them, and they tried to find out at what time and in
12 what circumstances all this was to be expected. •It was revealed to them that the news they brought of all the things which have now been announced to you, by those who preached to you the Good News through the Holy Spirit sent from heaven, was for you and not for themselves. Even the angels long to catch a glimpse of these things.

A call to sanctity and watchfulness

13 Free your minds, then, of encumbrances; control them, and put your trust in nothing but the grace that will be given you when Jesus Christ is revealed.

Do not behave in the way that you liked to before you learnt the truth; make 14
a habit of obedience: •be holy in all you do, since it is the Holy One who has 15
called you, •and scripture says: *Be holy, for I am holy.*[a] 16

If you are acknowledging as your Father one who has no favourites and judges 17
everyone according to what he has done, you must be scrupulously careful as long
as you are living away from your home. •Remember, the ransom that was *paid* 18
to free you[b] from the useless way of life your ancestors handed down was not paid
in anything corruptible, neither in *silver* nor gold, •but in the precious blood of a 19
lamb without spot or stain, namely Christ; •who, though known since before 20
the world was made, has been revealed only in our time, the end of the ages, for
your sake. •Through him you now have faith in God, who raised him from the 21
dead and gave him glory for that very reason—so that you would have faith and
hope in God.

Love

You have been obedient to the truth and purified your souls until you can 22
love like brothers, in sincerity; let your love for each other be real and from the
heart—•your new birth was not from any mortal seed but from the everlasting 23
word of the living and eternal God. •*All flesh is grass and its glory like the wild* 24
flower's. The grass withers, the flower falls, •*but the word of the Lord remains for* 25
ever.[c] What is this word? It is the Good News that has been brought to you.

Integrity

2 Be sure, then, you are never spiteful, or deceitful, or hypocritical, or envious 1
and critical of each other. •You are new born, and, like babies, you should 2
be hungry for nothing but milk—the spiritual honesty which will help you to
grow up to salvation—•now that you have *tasted the goodness of the Lord.*[a] 3

The new priesthood

He is the living stone, rejected by men but chosen by God and precious to him; 4
set yourselves close to him •so that you too, the holy priesthood that offers the 5
spiritual sacrifices which Jesus Christ has made acceptable to God, may be living
stones making a spiritual house. •As scripture says: *See how I lay in Zion a precious* 6
cornerstone that I have chosen and *the man who rests his trust on it will not be disap-*
pointed.[b] •That means that for you who are believers, it is precious; but for 7
unbelievers, *the stone rejected by the builders has proved to be the keystone,*[c] •*a* 8
stone to stumble over, a rock to bring men down.[d] They stumble over it because they
do not believe in the word; it was the fate in store for them.

But you are *a chosen race, a royal priesthood, a consecrated nation, a people set* 9
apart[e] to sing the praises of God who called you out of the darkness into his
wonderful light. •Once you were *not a people*[f] at all and now you are the People 10
of God; once you were *outside the mercy* and now *you have been given mercy.*

The obligations of Christians: towards pagans

I urge you, my dear people, while you are *visitors and pilgrims*[g] to keep your- 11
selves free from the selfish passions that attack the soul. •Always behave 12
honourably among pagans so that they can see your good works for themselves
and, when the day of reckoning comes, give thanks to God for the things which
now make them denounce you as criminals.

Towards civil authority

13 For the sake of the Lord, accept the authority of every social institution: the
14 emperor, as the supreme authority, •and the governors as commissioned by him
15 to punish criminals and praise good citizenship. •God wants you to be good
16 citizens, so as to silence what fools are saying in their ignorance. •You are slaves
    of no one except God, so behave like free men, and never use your freedom as an
17 excuse for wickedness. •Have respect for everyone and love for our community;
    fear God and honour the emperor.

Towards masters

18 Slaves must be respectful and obedient to their masters, not only when they
19 are kind and gentle but also when they are unfair. •You see, there is some merit
    in putting up with the pains of unearned punishment if it is done for the sake of
20 God •but there is nothing meritorious in taking a beating patiently if you have
    done something wrong to deserve it. The merit, in the sight of God, is in bearing
    it patiently when you are punished after doing your duty.

21 This, in fact, is what you were called to do, because Christ suffered for you
22 and left an example for you to follow the way he took. •He had not done anything
23 wrong, and *there had been no perjury in his mouth.*[h] •He was insulted and did not
    retaliate with insults; when he was tortured he made no threats but he put his
24 trust in the righteous judge. •He was *bearing our faults* in his own body on the
    cross, so that we might die to our faults and live for holiness; *through his wounds
    you have been healed.* You had *gone astray like sheep* but now you have come
    back to the shepherd and guardian[i] of your souls.

In marriage

1 **3** In the same way, wives should be obedient to their husbands. Then, if there
        are some husbands who have not yet obeyed the word, they may find them-
2 selves won over, without a word spoken, by the way their wives behave, •when
3 they see how faithful and conscientious they are. •Do not dress up for show:
4 doing up your hair, wearing gold bracelets and fine clothes; •all this should be
   inside, in a person's heart, imperishable: the ornament of a sweet and gentle
5 disposition—this is what is precious in the sight of God. •That was how the holy
   women of the past dressed themselves attractively—they hoped in God and were
6 tender and obedient to their husbands; •like Sarah, who was obedient to Abraham,
   and called him her *lord.* You are now her children, as long as you live good lives
   and do not give way to fear or worry.

7 In the same way, husbands must always treat their wives with consideration
   in their life together, respecting a woman as one who, though she may be the
   weaker partner, is equally an heir to the life of grace. This will stop anything
   from coming in the way of your prayers.

Towards the brothers

8 Finally: you should all agree among yourselves and be sympathetic; love the
9 brothers, have compassion and be self-effacing. •Never pay back one wrong
   with another, or an angry word with another one; instead, pay back with a

1 a. Lv 19:2   **b.** Is 52:3   **c.** Is 40:6-8
2 a. Ps 34:8   **b.** Is 28:16   **c.** Ps 18:22   **d.** Is 8:14   **e.** Is 43:20-21   **f.** Ho 1:9; the two
other quotations in this sentence are allusive references to Ho 2.   **g.** Ps 39:12   **h.** This
quotation, and the others in this paragraph, are from Is 53.   **i.** *episcopos.*

blessing. That is what you are called to do, so that you inherit a blessing yourself. Remember: *Anyone who wants to have a happy life and to enjoy prosperity must* 10 *banish malice from his tongue, deceitful conversation from his lips;* •*he must never* 11 *yield to evil but must practise good; he must seek peace and pursue it.* •*Because the* 12 *face of the Lord frowns on evil men, but the eyes of the Lord are turned towards the virtuous.*[a]

In persecution

No one can hurt you if you are determined to do only what is right; •if you 13 do have to suffer for being good, you will count it a blessing. *There is no need to* 14 *be afraid or to worry about them.*[b] •Simply *reverence the Lord*[c] Christ in your 15 hearts, and always have your answer ready for people who ask you the reason for the hope that you all have. •But give it with courtesy and respect and with a clear 16 conscience, so that those who slander you when you are living a good life in Christ may be proved wrong in the accusations that they bring. •And if it is the will of 17 God that you should suffer, it is better to suffer for doing right than for doing wrong.

The resurrection and 'the descent into hell'

Why, Christ himself, innocent though he was, had died once for sins, died for 18 the guilty, to lead us to God. In the body he was put to death, in the spirit he was raised to life, •and, in the spirit, he went to preach to the spirits in prison. 19 Now it was long ago, when Noah was still building that ark which saved only a 20 small group of eight people 'by water', and when God was still waiting patiently, that these spirits refused to believe. •That water is a type of the baptism which 21 saves you now, and which is not the washing off of physical dirt but a pledge made to God from a good conscience, through the resurrection of Jesus Christ, who has entered heaven and is at God's right hand, now that he has made the 22 angels and Dominations and Powers his subjects.

4 Think of what Christ suffered in this life, and then arm yourselves with the 1 same resolution that he had: anyone who in this life has bodily suffering has broken with sin, •because for the rest of his life on earth he is not ruled by human 2 passions but only by the will of God. •You spent quite long enough in the past 3 living the sort of life that pagans live, behaving indecently, giving way to your passions, drinking all the time, having wild parties and drunken orgies and degrading yourselves by following false gods. •So people cannot understand why 4 you no longer hurry off with them to join this flood which is rushing down to ruin, and then they begin to spread libels about you. •They will have to answer 5 for it in front of the judge who is ready to judge the living and the dead. •And 6 because he is their judge too, the dead had to be told the Good News as well, so that though, in their life on earth, they had been through the judgement that comes to all humanity, they might come to God's life in the spirit.

The revelation of Christ is close

Everything will soon come to an end, so, to pray better, keep a calm and sober 7 mind. •Above all, never let your love for each other grow insincere, since *love* 8 *covers over many a sin.*[a] •Welcome each other into your houses without grumbling. 9 Each one of you has received a special grace, so, like good stewards responsible 10 for all these different graces of God, put yourselves at the service of others. •If 11 you are a speaker, speak in words which seem to come from God; if you are a helper, help as though every action was done at God's orders; so that in everything God may receive the glory, through Jesus Christ, since to him alone belong all glory and power for ever and ever. Amen.

Recapitulation

12 My dear people, you must not think it unaccountable that you should be tested
13 by fire. There is nothing extraordinary in what has happened to you. •If you can have some share in the sufferings of Christ, be glad, because you will enjoy a much
14 greater gladness when his glory is revealed. •It is a blessing for you when they insult you for bearing the name of Christ, because it means that you have the
15 Spirit of glory, the Spirit of God resting on you. •None of you should ever deserve
16 to suffer for being a murderer, a thief, a criminal or an informer; •but if anyone of you should suffer for being a Christian, then he is not to be ashamed of it; he
17 should thank God that he has been called one. •The time has come for the judgement to begin at the household of God; and if what we know now is only the beginning, what will it be when it comes down to those who refuse to believe God's
18 Good News? •*If it is hard for a good man to be saved, what will happen to the wicked*
19 *and to sinners?*[b] •So even those whom God allows to suffer must trust themselves to the constancy of the creator and go on doing good.

Instructions: to the elders

1 Now I have something to tell your elders: I am an elder myself, and a witness to the sufferings of Christ, and with you I have a share in the glory that is
2 to be revealed. •Be the shepherds of the flock of God that is entrusted to you: watch over it, not simply as a duty but gladly, because God wants it; not for
3 sordid money, but because you are eager to do it. •Never be a dictator over any group that is put in your charge, but be an example that the whole flock can
4 follow. •When the chief shepherd appears, you will be given the crown of unfading glory.

To the faithful

5 To the rest of you I say: do what the elders tell you, and all wrap yourselves in humility to be servants of each other, because *God refuses the proud and will*
6 *always favour the humble.*[a] •Bow down, then, before the power of God now, and he
7 will raise you up on the appointed day; •*unload all your worries on to him,*[b] since
8 he is looking after you. •*Be calm but vigilant*, because your enemy the devil is
9 prowling round like a roaring lion, looking for someone to eat. •Stand up to him, strong in faith and in the knowledge that your brothers all over the world are
10 suffering the same things. •You will have to suffer only for a little while: the God of all grace who called you to eternal glory in Christ will see that all is well again: he
11 will confirm, strengthen and support you. •His power lasts for ever and ever. Amen.

Last words. Greetings

12 I write these few words to you through Silvanus, who is a brother I know I can trust, to encourage you never to let go this true grace of God to which I bear witness.
13 Your sister in Babylon, who is with you among the chosen, sends you greetings; so does my son, Mark.
14 Greet one another with a kiss of love.
Peace to you all who are in Christ.

3 a. Ps 34:12-16   b. Is 8:12-13 (LXX)   c. Pr 3:25   **4** a. Pr 10:12   b. Pr 11:31 (LXX)
5 a. Pr 3:34 (LXX)   b. Ps 55:22

2 PETER

THE SECOND LETTER OF PETER

Greetings

1 From Simeon Peter, servant and apostle of Jesus Christ; to all who treasure 1
the same faith as ourselves, given through the righteousness of our God and
saviour Jesus Christ. •May you have more and more grace and peace as you 2
come to know our Lord more and more.

A call to Christian living, and its reward

By his divine power, he has given us all the things that we need for life and for 3
true devotion, bringing us to know God himself, who has called us by his own
glory and goodness. •In making these gifts, he has given us the guarantee of 4
something very great and wonderful to come: through them you will be able to
share the divine nature and to escape corruption in a world that is sunk in vice.
But to attain this, you will have to do your utmost yourselves, adding goodness 5
to the faith that you have, understanding to your goodness, •self-control to your 6
understanding, patience to your self-control, true devotion to your patience,
kindness towards your fellow men to your devotion, and, to this kindness, love. 7
If you have a generous supply of these, they will not leave you ineffectual or 8
unproductive: they will bring you to a real knowledge of our Lord Jesus Christ.
But without them a man is blind or else short-sighted; he has forgotten how 9
his past sins were washed away. •Brothers, you have been called and chosen: work 10
all the harder to justify it. If you do all these things there is no danger that you will
ever fall away. •In this way you will be granted admittance into the eternal 11
kingdom of our Lord and saviour Jesus Christ.

The apostolic witness

That is why I am continually recalling the same truths to you, even though you 12
already know them and firmly hold them. •I am sure it is my duty, as long as 13
I am in this tent, to keep stirring you up with reminders, •since I know the time 14
for taking off this tent is coming soon, as our Lord Jesus Christ foretold to me.
And I shall take great care that after my own departure you will still have a 15
means to recall these things to memory.

It was not any cleverly invented myths that we were repeating when we 16
brought you the knowledge of the power and the coming of our Lord Jesus Christ;
we had seen his majesty for ourselves. •He was honoured and glorified by God 17
the Father, when the Sublime Glory itself spoke to him and said, 'This is my Son,
the Beloved; he enjoys my favour'. •We heard this ourselves, spoken from heaven, 18
when we were with him on the holy mountain.[a]

The value of prophecy

So we have confirmation of what was said in prophecies; and you will be 19
right to depend on prophecy and take it as a lamp for lighting a way

through the dark until the dawn comes and the morning star rises in your minds.
20 At the same time, we must be most careful to remember that the interpretation
21 of scriptural prophecy is never a matter for the individual. •Why? Because no
prophecy ever came from man's initiative. When men spoke for God it was the
Holy Spirit that moved them.

False teachers

1 2 As there were false prophets in the past history of our people, so you too will
have your false teachers, who will insinuate their own disruptive views and
disown the Master who purchased their freedom. They will destroy themselves
2 very quickly; •but there will be many who copy their shameful behaviour and the
3 Way of Truth will be brought into disrepute on their account. •They will eagerly
try to buy you for themselves with insidious speeches, but for them the Condemnation, pronounced so long ago, is at its work already, and Destruction is not
4 asleep. •When angels sinned, God did not spare them: he sent them down to the
underworld and consigned them to the dark underground caves to be held there
5 till the day of Judgement. •Nor did he spare the world in ancient times: it was
only Noah he saved, the preacher of righteousness, along with seven others, when
6 he sent the Flood over a disobedient world. •The cities of Sodom and Gomorrah,
these too he condemned and reduced to ashes; he destroyed them completely, as
7 a warning to anybody lacking reverence in the future; •he rescued Lot, however,
a holy man who had been sickened by the shameless way in which these vile people
8 behaved—•for that holy man, living among them, was outraged in his good soul
9 by the crimes that he saw and heard of every day. •These are all examples of how
the Lord can rescue the good from the ordeal, and hold the wicked for their
10 punishment until the day of Judgement, •especially those who are governed by
their corrupt bodily desires and have no respect for authority.

The punishment to come

Such self-willed people with no reverence are not afraid of offending against
11 the glorious ones, •but the angels in their greater strength and power make no
12 complaint or accusation against them in front of the Lord. •All the same, these
people who only insult anything that they do not understand are not reasoning
beings, but simply animals born to be caught and killed, and they will quite
13 certainly destroy themselves by their own work of destruction, •and get their
reward of evil for the evil that they do. They are unsightly blots on your society:
men whose only object is dissipation all day long, and they amuse themselves
14 deceiving you even when they are your guests at a meal; •with their eyes always
looking for adultery, men with an infinite capacity for sinning, they will seduce
any soul which is at all unstable. Greed is the one lesson their minds have learnt.
15 They are under a curse. •They have left the right path and wandered off to follow
the path of Balaam son of Beor, who thought he could profit best by sinning,
16 until he was called to order for his faults. The dumb donkey put a stop to that
17 prophet's madness when it talked like a man. •People like this are dried-up rivers,
fogs swirling in the wind, and the dark underworld is the place reserved for them.
18 With their high-flown talk, which is all hollow, they tempt back the ones who
have only just escaped from paganism, playing on their bodily desires with
19 debaucheries. •They may promise freedom but they themselves are slaves, slaves
to corruption; because if anyone lets himself be dominated by anything, then

1 a. At the transfiguration; Mt 17, Mk 9, Lk 9.

he is a slave to it; •and anyone who has escaped the pollution of the world once 20 by coming to know our Lord and saviour Jesus Christ, and who then allows himself to be entangled by it a second time and mastered, will end up in a worse state than he began in. •It would even have been better for him never to have 21 learnt the way of holiness, than to know it and afterwards desert the holy rule that was entrusted to him. •What he has done is exactly as the proverb rightly 22 says: *The dog goes back to his own vomit*[a] and: When the sow has been washed, it wallows in the mud.

The Day of the Lord; the prophets and the apostles

3 My friends, this is my second letter to you, and in both of them I have tried 1 to awaken a true understanding in you by giving you a reminder: •recalling to 2 you what was said in the past by the holy prophets and the commandments of the Lord and saviour which you were given by the apostles.

We must be careful to remember that during the last days there are bound 3 to be people who will be scornful, the kind who always please themselves what they do, and they will make fun of the promise •and ask, 'Well, where is this 4 coming? Everything goes on as it has since the Fathers died, as it has since it began at the creation.' •They are choosing to forget that there were heavens 5 at the beginning, and that the earth was formed by the word of God out of water and between the waters, •so that the world of that time was destroyed by 6 being flooded by water. •But by the same word, the present sky and earth are 7 destined for fire, and are only being reserved until Judgement day so that all sinners may be destroyed.

But there is one thing, my friends, that you must never forget: that with the 8 Lord, 'a day' can mean a thousand years, and *a thousand years is like a day*.[a] The Lord is not being slow to carry out his promises, as anybody else might be 9 called slow; but he is being patient with you all, wanting nobody to be lost and everybody to be brought to change his ways. •The Day of the Lord will come 10 like a thief, and then with a roar the sky will vanish, the elements will catch fire and fall apart, the earth and all that it contains will be burnt up.

Conclusion and doxology

Since everything is coming to an end like this, you should be living holy and 11 saintly lives •while you wait and long for the Day of God to come, when the sky 12 will dissolve in flames and the elements melt in the heat. •What we are waiting 13 for is what he promised: the new heavens and new earth, the place where right-eousness will be at home. •So then, my friends, while you are waiting, do your 14 best to live lives without spot or stain so that he will find you at peace. •Think of 15 our Lord's patience as your opportunity to be saved: our brother Paul, who is so dear to us, told you this when he wrote to you with the wisdom that is his special gift. •He always writes like this when he deals with this sort of subject, and this 16 makes some points in his letter hard to understand; these are the points that uneducated and unbalanced people distort, in the same way as they distort the rest of scripture—a fatal thing for them to do. •You have been warned about this, 17 my friends; be careful not to get carried away by the errors of unprincipled people, from the firm ground that you are standing on. •Instead, go on growing 18 in the grace and in the knowledge of our Lord and saviour Jesus Christ. To him be glory, in time and in eternity. Amen.

2 a. Pr 26:11
3 a. Ps 90:4

1 JOHN

THE FIRST LETTER OF JOHN

INTRODUCTION

The incarnate Word

1 1 Something which has existed since the beginning,
that we have heard,
and we have seen with our own eyes;
that we have watched
and touched with our hands:
the Word, who is life—
this is our subject.

2 That life was made visible:
we saw it and we are giving our testimony,
telling you of the eternal life
which was with the Father and has been made visible to us.

3 What we have seen and heard
we are telling you
so that you too may be in union with us,
as we are in union
with the Father
and with his Son Jesus Christ.

4 We are writing this to you to make our own joy complete.

I. WALK IN THE LIGHT

5 This is what we have heard from him,
and the message that we are announcing to you:
God is light; there is no darkness in him at all.

6 If we say that we are in union with God *a*
while we are living in darkness,
we are lying because we are not living the truth.

7 But if we live our lives in the light,
as he is in the light,
we are in union with one another,

---

1 a. In the translation, 'God' or 'Christ' has been used in several places, where the Greek has
a simple pronoun, in order to make the writer's meaning clear.

and the blood of Jesus, his Son,
purifies us from all sin.

First condition: break with sin

If we say we have no sin in us,   8
we are deceiving ourselves
and refusing to admit the truth;
but if we acknowledge our sins,   9
then God who is faithful and just
will forgive our sins and purify us
from everything that is wrong.
To say that we have never sinned   10
is to call God a liar
and to show that his word is not in us.

2 I am writing this, my children,   1
to stop you sinning;
but if anyone should sin,
we have our advocate with the Father,
Jesus Christ, who is just;
he is the sacrifice that takes our sins away,   2
and not only ours,
but the whole world's.

Second condition: keep the commandments, especially the law of love

We can be sure that we know God   3
only by keeping his commandments.
Anyone who says, 'I know him',   4
and does not keep his commandments,
is a liar,
refusing to admit the truth.
But when anyone does obey what he has said,   5
God's love comes to perfection in him.
We can be sure
that we are in God
only when the one who claims to be living in him   6
is living the same kind of life as Christ lived.
My dear people,   7
this is not a new commandment that I am writing to tell you,
but an old commandment
that you were given from the beginning,
the original commandment which was the message brought to you.
Yet in another way, what I am writing to you,   8
and what is being carried out in your lives as it was in his,
is a new commandment;
because the night is over
and the real light is already shining.
Anyone who claims to be in the light   9
but hates his brother
is still in the dark.
But anyone who loves his brother is living in the light   10

and need not be afraid of stumbling;
11 unlike the man who hates his brother and is in the darkness,
not knowing where he is going,
because it is too dark to see.

Third condition: detachment from the world

12 I am writing to you, my own children,
whose sins have already been forgiven through his name;
13 I am writing to you, fathers,
who have come to know the one
who has existed since the beginning;
I am writing to you, young men,
who have already overcome the Evil One;
14 I have written to you, children,
because you already know the Father;
I have written to you, fathers,
because you have come to know the one
who has existed since the beginning;
I have written to you, young men,
because you are strong and God's word has made its home in you,
and you have overcome the Evil One.
15 You must not love this passing world
or anything that is in the world.
The love of the Father cannot be
in any man who loves the world,
16 because nothing the world has to offer
—the sensual body,
the lustful eye,
pride in possessions—
could ever come from the Father
but only from the world;
17 and the world, with all it craves for,
is coming to an end;
but anyone who does the will of God
remains for ever.

Fourth condition: be on guard against the enemies of Christ

18 Children, these are the last days;
you were told that an Antichrist must come,
and now several antichrists have already appeared;
we know from this that these are the last days.
19 Those rivals of Christ came out of our own number, but they had
never really belonged;
if they had belonged, they would have stayed with us;
but they left us, to prove that not one of them
ever belonged to us.
20 But you have been anointed by the Holy One,
and have all received the knowledge.
21 It is not because you do not know the truth that I am writing to you
but rather because you know it already

and know that no lie can come from the truth.
The man who denies that Jesus is the Christ—   22
he is the liar,
he is Antichrist;
and he is denying the Father as well as the Son,
because no one who has the Father can deny the Son,   23
and to acknowledge the Son is to have the Father as well.
Keep alive in yourselves what you were taught in the beginning: 24
as long as what you were taught in the beginning is alive in you,
you will live in the Son
and in the Father;
and what is promised to you by his own promise   25
is eternal life.
This is all that I am writing to you about the people who are   26
       trying to lead you astray.
But you have not lost the anointing that he gave you,   27
and you do not need anyone to teach you;
the anointing he gave teaches you everything;
you are anointed with truth, not with a lie,
and as it has taught you, so you must stay in him.
Live in Christ, then, my children,   28
so that if he appears, we may have full confidence,
and not turn from him in shame
at his coming.
You know that God is righteous—   29
then you must recognise that everyone whose life is righteous
has been begotten by him.

II. LIVE AS GOD'S CHILDREN

3   Think of the love that the Father has lavished on us,   1
by letting us be called God's children;
and that is what we are.
Because the world refused to acknowledge him,
therefore it does not acknowledge us.
My dear people, we are already the children of God   2
but what we are to be in the future has not yet been revealed;
all we know is, that when it is revealed
we shall be like him
because we shall see him as he really is.

First condition: break with sin

Surely everyone who entertains this hope   3
must purify himself, must try to be as pure as Christ.
Anyone who sins at all   4
breaks the law,
because to sin is to break the law.
Now you know that he appeared in order to abolish sin,   5
and that in him there is no sin;
anyone who lives in God does not sin,   6

and anyone who sins
has never seen him or known him.

7   My children, do not let anyone lead you astray:
to live a holy life
is to be holy just as he is holy;

8   to lead a sinful life is to belong to the devil,
since the devil was a sinner from the beginning.
It was to undo all that the devil has done
that the Son of God appeared.

9   No one who has been begotten by God sins;
because God's seed remains inside him,
he cannot sin when he has been begotten by God.

Second condition: keep the commandments, especially the law of love

10   In this way we distinguish the children of God
from the children of the devil:
anybody not living a holy life
and not loving his brother
is no child of God's.

11   This is the message
as you heard it from the beginning:
that we are to love one another;

12   not to be like Cain, who belonged to the Evil One
and cut his brother's throat;
cut his brother's throat simply for this reason,
that his own life was evil and his brother lived a good life.

13   You must not be surprised, brothers, when the world hates you;

14   we have passed out of death and into life,
and of this we can be sure
because we love our brothers.

15   If you refuse to love, you must remain dead;
to hate your brother is to be a murderer,
and murderers, as you know, do not have eternal life in them.

16   This has taught us love—
that he gave up his life for us;
and we, too, ought to give up our lives for our brothers.

17   If a man who was rich enough in this world's goods
saw that one of his brothers was in need,
but closed his heart to him,
how could the love of God be living in him?

18   My children,
our love is not to be just words or mere talk,
but something real and active;

19   only by this can we be certain
that we are children of the truth
and be able to quieten our conscience in his presence,

20   whatever accusations it may raise against us,
because God is greater than our conscience and he knows everything.

21   My dear people,
if we cannot be condemned by our own conscience,
we need not be afraid in God's presence,

and whatever we ask him, 22
we shall receive,
because we keep his commandments
and live the kind of life that he wants.
His commandments are these: 23
that we believe in the name of his Son Jesus Christ
and that we love one another
as he told us to.
Whoever keeps his commandments 24
lives in God and God lives in him.
We know that he lives in us
by the Spirit that he has given us.

Third condition: be on guard against the enemies of Christ and against the world

4 It is not every spirit, my dear people, that you can trust; 1
test them, to see if they come from God,
there are many false prophets, now, in the world.
You can tell the spirits that come from God by this: 2
every spirit which acknowledges that Jesus the Christ has come
in the flesh
is from God;
but any spirit which will not say this of Jesus 3
is not from God,
but is the spirit of Antichrist,
whose coming you were warned about.
Well, now he is here, in the world.
Children, 4
you have already overcome these false prophets,
because you are from God and you have in you
one who is greater than anyone in this world;·
as for them, they are of the world, 5
and so they speak the language of the world
and the world listens to them.
But we are children of God, 6
and those who know God listen to us;
those who are not of God refuse to listen to us.
This is how we can tell
the spirit of truth from the spirit of falsehood.

III. LOVE AND FAITH

Love

My dear people, 7
let us love one another
since love comes from God
and everyone who loves is begotten by God and knows God.
Anyone who fails to love can never have known God, 8
because God is love.
God's love for us was revealed 9

when God sent into the world his only Son
so that we could have life through him;

10   this is the love I mean:
not our love for God,
but God's love for us when he sent his Son
to be the sacrifice that takes our sins away.

11   My dear people,
since God has loved us so much,
we too should love one another.

12   No one has ever seen God;
but as long as we love one another
God will live in us
and his love will be complete in us.

13   We can know that we are living in him
and he is living in us
because he lets us share his Spirit.

14   We ourselves saw and we testify
that the Father sent his Son
as saviour of the world.

15   If anyone acknowledges that Jesus is the Son of God,
God lives in him, and he in God.

16   We ourselves have known and put our faith in
God's love towards ourselves.
God is love
and anyone who lives in love lives in God,
and God lives in him.

17   Love will come to its perfection in us
when we can face the day of Judgement without fear;
because even in this world
we have become as he is.

18   In love there can be no fear,
but fear is driven out by perfect love:
because to fear is to expect punishment,
and anyone who is afraid is still imperfect in love.

19   We are to love, then,
because he loved us first.

20   Anyone who says, 'I love God',
and hates his brother,
is a liar,
since a man who does not love the brother that he can see
cannot love God, whom he has never seen.

21   So this is the commandment that he has given us,
that anyone who loves God must also love his brother.

5

1   Whoever believes that Jesus is the Christ
has been begotten by God;
and whoever loves the Father that begot him
loves the child whom he begets.

2   We can be sure that we love God's children
if we love God himself and do what he has commanded us;

3   this is what loving God is—

keeping his commandments;
and his commandments are not difficult,　　　　4
because anyone who has been begotten by God
has already overcome the world;
this is the victory over the world—
our faith.

Faith

Who can overcome the world?　　　　5
Only the man who believes that Jesus is the Son of God:
Jesus Christ who came by water and blood,[a]　　　　6
not with water only,
but with water and blood;
with the Spirit as another witness—
since the Spirit is the truth—
so that there are three witnesses,　　　　7
the Spirit, the water and the blood,　　　　8
and all three of them agree.
We accept the testimony of human witnesses,　　　　9
but God's testimony is much greater,
and this is God's testimony,
given as evidence for his Son.
Everybody who believes in the Son of God　　　　10
has this testimony inside him;
and anyone who will not believe God
is making God out to be a liar,
because he has not trusted
the testimony God has given about his Son.
This is the testimony:　　　　11
God has given us eternal life
and this life is in his Son;
anyone who has the Son has life,　　　　12
anyone who does not have the Son does not have life.

Conclusion

I have written all this to you　　　　13
so that you who believe in the name of the Son of God
may be sure that you have eternal life.

ENDING

Prayer for sinners

We are quite confident that if we ask him for anything,　　　　14
and it is in accordance with his will,
he will hear us;
and, knowing that whatever we may ask, he hears us,　　　　15
we know that we have already been granted what we asked of him.
If anybody sees his brother commit a sin　　　　16
that is not a deadly sin,
he has only to pray, and God will give life to the sinner

—not those who commit a deadly sin;
for there is a sin that is death,
and I will not say that you must pray about that.

17 Every kind of wrong-doing is sin,
but not all sin is deadly.

Summary of the letter

18 We know that anyone who has been begotten by God
does not sin,
because the begotten Son of God protects him,
and the Evil One does not touch him.

19 We know that we belong to God,
but the whole world lies in the power of the Evil One.

20 We know, too, that the Son of God has come,
and has given us the power
to know the true God.
We are in the true God,
as we are in his Son, Jesus Christ.
This is the true God,
this is eternal life.

21 Children, be on your guard against false gods.

5 a. The water and the blood from the side of Jesus, Jn 19:34, are here used as figures of his
'coming' to all Christians, through the water of baptism and through his sacrificial death.

2 JOHN

THE SECOND LETTER OF JOHN

From the Elder: my greetings to the Lady, the chosen one,[a] and to her 1
children, she whom I love in the truth—and I am not the only one, for so do all
who have come to know the truth—•because of the truth that lives in us and will 2
be with us for ever. •In our life of truth and love, we shall have grace, mercy and 3
peace from God the Father and from Jesus Christ, the Son of the Father.

The law of love

It has given me great joy to find that your children have been living the life of 4
truth as we were commanded by the Father. •I am writing now, dear lady, not to 5
give you any new commandment, but the one which we were given at the beginning, and to plead: let us love one another.

To love is to live according to his commandments: this is the commandment 6
which you have heard since the beginning, to live a life of love.

The enemies of Christ

There are many deceivers about in the world, refusing to admit that Jesus 7
Christ has come in the flesh. They are the Deceiver; they are the Antichrist.
Watch yourselves, or all our work will be lost and not get the reward it deserves. 8
If anybody does not keep within the teaching of Christ but goes beyond it, he 9
cannot have God with him: only those who keep to what he taught can have the
Father and the Son with them. •If anyone comes to you bringing a different 10
doctrine, you must not receive him in your house or even give him a greeting.
To greet him would make you a partner in his wicked work. 11

There are several things I have to tell you, but I have thought it best not to 12
trust them to paper and ink. I hope instead to visit you and talk to you personally,
so that our joy may be complete.

Greetings to you from the children of your sister,[b] the chosen one. 13

3 JOHN

THE THIRD LETTER OF JOHN

1 From the Elder: greetings to my dear friend Gaius, whom I love in the truth.
2 My dear friend, I hope everything is going happily with you and that you are as
3 well physically as you are spiritually. •It was a great joy to me when some brothers
   came and told of your faithfulness to the truth, and of your life in the truth.
4 It is always my greatest joy to hear that my children are living according to
   the truth.

5 My friend, you have done faithful work in looking after these brothers, even
6 though they were complete strangers to you. •They are a proof to the whole
   Church of your charity and it would be a very good thing if you could help them
7 on their journey in a way that God would approve. •It was entirely for the sake
   of the name that they set out, without depending on the pagans for anything;
8 it is our duty to welcome men of this sort and contribute our share to their work
   for the truth.

Beware of the example of Diotrephes

9 I have written a note for the members of the church, but Diotrephes, who
10 seems to enjoy being in charge of it, refuses to accept us. •So if I come, I shall
   tell everyone how he has behaved, and about the wicked accusations he has been
   circulating against us. As if that were not enough, he not only refuses to welcome
   our brothers, but prevents the other people who would have liked to from doing
11 it, and expels them from the church. •My dear friend, never follow such a bad
   example, but keep following the good one; anyone who does what is right is a
   child of God, but the person who does what is wrong has never seen God.

Commendation of Demetrius

12 Demetrius has been approved by everyone, and indeed by the truth itself.
   We too will vouch for him and you know that our testimony is true.

Epilogue

13 There were several things I had to tell you but I would rather not trust them
14 to pen and ink. •However, I hope to see you soon and talk to you personally.
15 Peace be with you; greetings from your friends; greet each of our friends by name.

THE LETTER OF
JUDE

Address

From Jude, servant of Jesus Christ and brother of James; to those who are 1
called, to those who are dear to God the Father and kept safe for Jesus Christ,
wishing you all mercy and peace and love.   2

The reason for this letter

My dear friends, at a time when I was eagerly looking forward to writing to 3
you about the salvation that we all share, I have been forced to write to you
now and appeal to you to fight hard for the faith which has been once and for all
entrusted to the saints. •Certain people have infiltrated among you, and they 4
are the ones you had a warning about, in writing, long ago, when they were
condemned for denying all religion, turning the grace of our God into immorality,
and rejecting our only Master and Lord, Jesus Christ.

The false teachers: the certainty of their punishment

I should like to remind you—though you have already learnt it once and for 5
all—how the Lord rescued the nation from Egypt, but afterwards he still
destroyed the men who did not trust him. •Next let me remind you of the angels 6
who had supreme authority but did not keep it and left their appointed sphere;[a]
he has kept them down in the dark, in spiritual chains, to be judged on the great
day. •The fornication of Sodom and Gomorrah and the other nearby towns was 7
equally unnatural, and it is a warning to us that they are paying for their crimes
in eternal fire.

Their violent language

Nevertheless, these people are doing the same: in their delusions they not 8
only defile their bodies and disregard authority, but abuse the glorious angels
as well. •Not even the archangel Michael, when he was engaged in argument 9
with the devil about the corpse of Moses, dared to denounce him in the language
of abuse; all he said was, 'Let the Lord correct you'. •But these people abuse 10
anything they do not understand; and the only things they do understand—just
by nature like unreasoning animals—will turn out to be fatal to them.

Their vicious behaviour

May they get what they deserve, because they have followed Cain; they have 11
rushed to make the same mistake as Balaam and for the same reward; they have
rebelled just as Korah did—and share the same fate. •They are a dangerous 12

obstacle to your community meals, coming for the food and quite shamelessly only looking after themselves. They are like clouds blown about by the winds and bringing no rain, or like barren trees which are then uprooted in the winter and so 13 are twice dead; •like wild sea waves capped with shame as if with foam; or like 14 shooting stars bound for an eternity of black darkness. •It was with them in mind that Enoch, the seventh patriarch from Adam, made his prophecy when he said, 'I tell you, the Lord will come with his saints in their tens of thousands, 15 to pronounce judgement on all mankind and to sentence the wicked for all the wicked things they have done, and for all the defiant things said against him by 16 irreligious sinners'. •They are mischief-makers, grumblers governed only by their own desires, with *mouths full of boastful talk*, ready with flattery for other people when they see some advantage in it.

A warning

17 But remember, my dear friends, what the apostles of our Lord Jesus Christ 18 told you to expect. •'At the end of time,' they told you 'there are' going to be people who sneer at religion and follow nothing but their own desires for 19 wickedness.' •These unspiritual and selfish people are nothing but mischief-makers.

The duties of love

20 But you, my dear friends, must use your most holy faith as your foundation 21 and build on that, praying in the Holy Spirit; •keep yourselves within the love of God and wait for the mercy of our Lord Jesus Christ to give you eternal life. 22 23 When there are some who have doubts, reassure them; •when there are some to be saved from the fire, pull them out; but there are others to whom you must be kind with great caution, keeping your distance even from outside clothing which is contaminated by vice.

Doxology

24 Glory be to him who can keep you from falling and bring you safe to his 25 glorious presence, innocent and happy. •To God, the only God, who saves us through Jesus Christ our Lord, be the glory, majesty, authority and power, which he had before time began, now and for ever. Amen.

---

a. Briefly mentioned in Gn 6:1-2, but elaborated in *The Book of Enoch*.

INTRODUCTION TO
THE BOOK OF REVELATION

A 'Revelation' (called *Apocalypse*, from the Greek term) is a distinct literary form; apocalyptic writing was very popular in some Jewish circles at the beginning of the Christian era. The framework of a Revelation is always a vision of hidden supernatural events; the language in which the vision is described is richly symbolic and so allusive that the message can be interpreted in more ways than one.

Thus the Book of Revelation is not to be accepted simply as an allegory which can be directly translated into other terms. It contains the author's vision of heaven and of the vindication of the Christian martyrs in the world to come, but it must be understood first and foremost as a tract for the times, written to increase the hope and determination of the Church on earth in a period of disturbance and bitter persecution, and prophesying the certain downfall and destruction of the Roman imperial power. The imagery, largely drawn from the Old Testament, especially Daniel, allows the author to allude to the enemy, Rome, under the disguise of the old enemy, Babylon; and to present the happenings of his own day, seen by their reflections in the heavens, as recapitulations or fulfilments of the great events of Israel's past.

The text contains difficulties: there are repetitions and interruptions, and there are passages out of context. One promising hypothesis is that the strictly prophetic part of the book is made up of two different 'apocalypses' written at different times and later conflated. The author cannot be identified with the author of the Gospel according to John, but we can say that the book was written inside the evangelist's immediate circle and is pervaded by his doctrine. Its date is generally estimated as A.D. 95, but there are some who believe that parts, at least, were composed as early as Nero's time, shortly before A.D. 70.

THE BOOK OF
REVELATION

Prologue

1 **1** This is the revelation given by God to Jesus Christ so that he could tell his
servants about the *things which are* now *to take place*[a] very soon; he sent his
2 angel to make it known to his servant John, •and John has written down
everything he saw and swears it is the word of God guaranteed by Jesus Christ.
3 Happy the man who reads this prophecy, and happy those who listen to him, if
they treasure all that it says, because the Time is close.

I. THE LETTERS TO THE CHURCHES OF ASIA

Address and greeting[b]

4 From John, to the seven churches of Asia: grace and peace to you from him
who is, who was, and who is to come, from the seven spirits in his presence before
5 his throne, •and from Jesus Christ, *the faithful witness, the First-born* from the
dead, *the Ruler of the kings of the earth.* He loves us and has washed away our
6 sins with his blood, •and made us a *line of kings, priests to serve* his God and
7 Father; to him, then, be glory and power for ever and ever. Amen. •It is he who
is coming on the clouds; everyone will see him, even *those who pierced
him,* and *all the races of the earth will mourn over him.* This is the truth. Amen.
8 'I am the Alpha and the Omega' says the Lord God, who is, who was, and who
is to come, the Almighty.

The beginning of the vision

9 My name is John, and through our union in Jesus I am your brother and share
your sufferings, your kingdom, and all you endure. I was on the island of Patmos[c]
10 for having preached God's word and witnessed for Jesus; •it was the Lord's day
and the Spirit possessed me, and I heard a voice behind me, shouting like
11 a trumpet, •'Write down all that you see in a book, and send it to the seven
churches of Ephesus, Smyrna, Pergamum, Thyatira, Sardis, Philadelphia and
12 Laodicea'. •I turned round to see who had spoken to me, and when I turned
13 I saw seven golden lamp-stands •and, surrounded by them, a figure *like a Son*

1 a. Dn 2:28   b. This section contains many O.T. allusions to the time of the Messiah.
The five direct quotations printed in italic are from: Ps 89:37,27; Is 55:4; Ex 19:6; Dn 7:13;
and Zc 12:10,14.   c. Patmos (10m. × 5m.) was used by the Romans as a penal colony.

of man,ᵈ dressed in a long robe tied at the waist with a *golden girdle.* •*His head* 14
and *his hair* were *white as white wool* or as snow, *his eyes* like a *burning* flame,
his feet like burnished bronze when it has been refined in a furnace, and *his voice* 15
like the sound of the ocean.ᵉ •In his right hand he was holding seven stars, out of 16
his mouth came a sharp sword, double-edged, and his face was like the sun
shining with all its force.

When I saw him, I fell in a dead faint at his feet, but he touched me with his 17
right hand and said, 'Do not be afraid; it is I, *the First* and *the Last;* I am the
Living One, •I was dead and now I am to live for ever and ever, and I hold the 18
keys of death and of the underworld. •Now write down all that you see of present 19
happenings and *things that are still to come.ᶠ* •The secret of the seven stars you 20
have seen in my right hand, and of the seven golden lamp-stands is this: the seven
stars are the angels of the seven churches, and the seven lamp-stands are the
seven churches themselves.

1. Ephesus

2 'Write to the angel of the church in Ephesus and say, "Here is the message 1
of the one who holds the seven stars in his right hand and who lives
surrounded by the seven golden lamp-stands: •I know all about you: how hard 2
you work and how much you put up with. I know you cannot stand wicked men,
and how you tested the impostors who called themselves apostles and proved
they were liars. •I know, too, that you have patience, and have suffered for my 3
name without growing tired. •Nevertheless, I have this complaint to make; 4
you have less love now than you used to. •Think where you were before you fell; 5
repent, and do as you used to at first, or else, if you will not repent, I shall come
to you and take your lamp-stand from its place. •It is in your favour, nevertheless, 6
that you loathe as I do what the Nicolaitans are doing. •If anyone has ears 7
to hear, let him listen to what the Spirit is saying to the churches: those who
prove victorious I will feed *from the tree of life set in* God's *paradise."ᵃ*

2. Smyrna

'Write to the angel of the church in Smyrna and say, "Here is the message of 8
the First and *the Last*, who was dead and has come to life again: •I know the trials 9
you have had, and how poor you are—though you are rich— and the slanderous
accusations that have been made by the people who profess to be Jews but are
really members of the synagogue of Satan. •Do not be afraid of the sufferings 10
that are coming to you: I tell you, the devil is going to send some of you to prison
to test you, and you must face an ordeal for *ten days.ᵇ* Even if you have to die,
keep faithful, and I will give you the crown of life for your prize. •If anyone has 11
ears to hear, let him listen to what the Spirit is saying to the churches: for those
who prove victorious there is nothing to be afraid of in the second death."

3. Pergamum

'Write to the angel of the church in Pergamum and say, "Here is the message 12
of the one who has the sharp sword, double-edged: •I know where you live, 13
in the place where Satan is enthroned, and that you still hold firmly to my name,
and did not disown your faith in me even when my faithful witness, Antipas, was
killed in your own town, where Satan lives.ᶜ

Nevertheless, I have one or two complaints to make: some of you are 14
followers of Balaam, who taught Balak to set a trap for the Israelites so that

15 they committed adultery by eating food that had been sacrificed to idols; •and
among you, too, there are some as bad who accept what the Nicolaitans teach.
16 You must repent, or I shall soon come to you and attack these people with the
17 sword out of my mouth. •If anyone has ears to hear, let him listen to what the
Spirit is saying to the churches: to those who prove victorious I will give the
hidden manna and a white stone[d]—a stone with *a new name* written on it,
known only to the man who receives it."

4. Thyatira

18 'Write to the angel of the church in Thyatira and say, "Here is the message
of the Son of God who has eyes like a burning flame and feet like burnished
19 bronze: •I know all about you and how charitable you are; I know your faith and
devotion and how much you put up with, and I know how you are still making
20 progress. •Nevertheless, I have a complaint to make: you are encouraging the
woman Jezebel[e] who claims to be a prophetess, and by her teaching she is luring
my servants away to commit the adultery of eating food which has been sacrificed
21 to idols. •I have given her time to reform but she is not willing to change her
22 adulterous life. •Now I am consigning her to bed, and all her partners in adultery
to troubles that will test them severely, unless they repent of their practices;
23 and I will see that her children die, so that all the churches realise that it is I who
search heart and loins and give each one of you what your behaviour deserves.[f]
24 But on the rest of you in Thyatira, all of you who have not accepted this teaching
or learnt the secrets of Satan, as they are called, I am not laying any special
25/26 duty; •but hold firmly on to what you already have until I come. •To those who
prove victorious, and keep working for me until the end, *I will give* the
27/28 authority over *the pagans[g]* •which I myself have been given by my Father, *to rule*
them with an iron sceptre and shatter them like earthenware. And I will give him
29 the Morning Star.[h] •If anyone has ears to hear, let him listen to what the Spirit
is saying to the churches."

5. Sardis

1 3 'Write to the angel of the church in Sardis and say, "Here is the message
of the one who holds the seven spirits of God and the seven stars: I know all
2 about you: how you are reputed to be alive and yet are dead. •Wake up; revive
what little you have left: it is dying fast. So far I have failed to notice anything in
3 the way you live that my God could possibly call perfect, •and yet do you
remember how eager you were when you first heard the message? Hold on to that.
Repent. If you do not wake up, I shall come to you like a thief, without telling
4 you at what hour to expect me. •There are a few in Sardis, it is true, who have
kept their robes from being dirtied, and they are fit to come with me, dressed
5 in white. •Those who prove victorious will be dressed, like these, in white robes;
I shall not blot their names out of the book of life, but acknowledge their names
6 in the presence of my Father and his angels. •If anyone has ears to hear, let him
listen to what the Spirit is saying to the churches."

d. The messianic figure in Dn; the descriptive quotations which follow are from Dn 7 and 10.
e. Ezk 43:2   **f.** Dn 2:28
2 a. Gn 2:9   **b.** I.e. of short duration.   **c.** I.e. 'where emperor-worship is practised.'
d. The manna hidden by Jeremiah (2 M 2:4-8), to be the food of those who are saved in the
heavenly kingdom; the white stone is a badge or token of admittance or membership.
e. By this name the writer is indicating a prophetess of the Nicolaitan sect.   **f.** Jr 11:20
g. Ps 2:8-9   **h.** Symbol of power and thus of the resurrection.

6. Philadelphia

'Write to the angel of the church in Philadelphia and say, "Here is the message 7 of the holy and faithful one who *has the key of David*, so that *when he opens, nobody can close, and when he closes, nobody can open*:[a] •I know all about you; 8 and now I have opened in front of you a door that nobody will be able to close—and I know that though you are not very strong, you have kept my commandments and not disowned my name. •Now I am going to make the synagogue of 9 Satan—those who profess to be Jews, but are liars, because they are no such thing—I will make them come and *fall at your feet*[b] and admit that *you are* the people *that I love*.[c] •Because you have kept my commandment to endure trials, 10 I will keep you safe in the time of trial which is going to come for the whole world, to test the people of the world. •Soon I shall be with you: hold firmly to what 11 you already have, and let nobody take your prize away from you. •Those who 12 prove victorious I will make into pillars in the sanctuary of my God, and they will stay there for ever; I will inscribe on them the name of my God and the name of the city of my God, the new Jerusalem which comes down from my God in heaven, and my own new name as well. •If anyone has ears to hear, let him 13 listen to what the Spirit is saying to the churches."

7. Laodicea

'Write to the angel of the church in Laodicea and say, "Here is the message of 14 the Amen, the faithful, the true witness, the ultimate source of God's creation: I know all about you: how you are neither cold nor hot. I wish you were one or 15 the other, •but since you are neither, but only lukewarm, I will spit you out of my 16 mouth. •You say to yourself, 'I am rich, I have made a fortune, and have 17 everything I want', never realising that you are wretchedly and pitiably poor, and blind and naked too. •I warn you, buy from me the gold that has been tested in 18 the fire to make you really rich, and white robes to clothe you and cover your shameful nakedness, and eye ointment to put on your eyes so that you are able to see. •I *am* the one *who reproves and disciplines all those he loves:*[d] so repent 19 in real earnest. •Look, I am standing at the door, knocking. If one of you hears 20 me calling and opens the door, I will come in to share his meal, side by side with him. •Those who prove victorious I will allow to share my throne, just as I was 21 victorious myself and took my place with my Father on his throne. •If anyone has 22 ears to hear, let him listen to what the Spirit is saying to the churches." '

II. THE PROPHETIC VISIONS

A. THE PRELUDE TO THE GREAT DAY

God entrusts the future of the world to the Lamb

4 Then, in my vision, I saw a door open in heaven and heard the same voice 1 speaking to me, the voice like a trumpet, saying, 'Come up here: I will show you *what is to come* in the future'. •With that, the Spirit possessed me and I saw 2 a throne standing in heaven, and the *One* who was *sitting on the throne*, •and 3 the Person sitting there looked like a diamond and a ruby. There was a rainbow encircling the throne, and this looked like an emerald.[d] •Round the throne in a 4 circle were twenty-four thrones, and on them I saw twenty-four elders sitting, dressed in white robes with golden crowns on their heads. •Flashes of lightning 5

were coming from the throne, and the sound of peals of thunder, and in front of the throne there were seven flaming lamps burning, the seven Spirits of
6 God. •Between the throne and myself was a sea that seemed to be made of glass, like crystal. *In the centre*, grouped round the throne itself, were *four animals*[b]
7 *with many eyes*, in front and behind. •*The first* animal was like *a lion, the second* like *a bull, the third* animal had *a human face*, and *the fourth* animal was like
8 a flying *eagle*. •*Each* of the four animals had *six wings* and *had eyes all the way round* as well as inside; and day and night they never stopped singing:

> '*Holy, Holy, Holy*
> *is the Lord God, the Almighty;*
> he was, he is and he is to come'.

9 Every time the animals glorified and honoured and gave thanks to the One sitting
10 on the throne, *who lives for ever and ever*, •the twenty-four elders prostrated themselves before him to worship the One *who lives for ever and ever*, and threw
11 down their crowns in front of the throne, saying, •'You are our Lord and our God, you are worthy of glory and honour and power, because you made all the universe and it was only by your will that everything was made and exists'.

1 5 I saw that in the right hand of the One sitting on the throne there was *a scroll*
2 *that had writing on back and front*[a] and was sealed with seven seals. •Then I saw a powerful angel who called with a loud voice, 'Is there anyone worthy
3 to open the scroll and break the seals of it?' •But there was no one, in heaven or on the earth or under the earth, who was able to open the scroll and read it.
⁴₅ I wept bitterly because there was nobody fit to open the scroll and read it, •but one of the elders said to me, 'There is no need to cry: *the Lion* of the tribe *of Judah, the Root*[b] of David, has triumphed, and he will open the scroll and the seven seals of it'.

6 Then I saw, standing between the throne with its four animals and the circle of the elders, a Lamb that seemed to have been sacrificed; it had seven horns, and it had seven eyes, which are the seven Spirits God has *sent out all over the*
7 *world.*[c] •The Lamb came forward to take the scroll from the right hand of the
8 One sitting on the throne, •and when he took it, the four animals prostrated themselves before him and with them the twenty-four elders; each one of them was holding a harp and had a golden bowl full of incense made of the prayers
9 of the saints. •They sang a new hymn:

> 'You are worthy to take the scroll
> and break the seals of it,
> because you were sacrificed, and with your blood
> you bought men for God
> of every race, language, people and nation
> and made them *a line of kings and priests,*[d]
> to serve our God and to rule the world'.

11 In my vision, I heard the sound of an immense number of angels gathered round the throne and the animals and the elders; there were *ten thousand times*

---

3 **a.** Is 22:22   **b.** Is 45:14   **c.** Is 43:4   **d.** Pr 3:12
4 **a.** For many of the descriptive details in this scene the writer draws on Ezk 1 and 10 and Is 6.   **b.** The angels or 'principles' which direct the physical world. Since Irenaeus, these four creatures have been used as symbols of the four evangelists.
5 **a.** Ezk 2:9   **b.** Gn 49:9; Is 11:10   **c.** Zc 4:10   **d.** Is 61:6

ten thousand of them^e and *thousands upon thousands*, ·shouting, 'The Lamb that 12
was sacrificed is worthy to be given power, riches, wisdom, strength, honour,
glory and blessing'. ·Then I heard all the living things in creation—everything 13
that lives in the air, and on the ground, and under the ground, and in the sea,
crying, 'To the One who is sitting on the throne and to the Lamb, be all praise,
honour, glory and power, for ever and ever'. ·And the four animals said, 'Amen'; 14
and the elders prostrated themselves to worship.

The Lamb breaks the seven seals

6 Then I saw the Lamb break one of the seven seals, and I heard one of the 1
four animals shout in a voice like thunder, 'Come'. ·Immediately a white 2
horse appeared, and the rider on it was holding a bow; he was given the victor's
crown and he went away, to go from victory to victory.

When he broke the second seal, I heard the second animal shout, 'Come'. 3
And out came another horse, bright red, and its rider was given this duty: to take 4
away peace from the earth and set people killing each other. He was given a huge
sword.

When he broke the third seal, I heard the third animal shout, 'Come'. 5
Immediately a black horse appeared, and its rider was holding a pair of scales;
and I seemed to hear a voice shout from among the four animals and say, 'A ration 6
of corn for a day's wages, and three rations of barley for a day's wages, but do not
tamper with the oil or the wine'.

When he broke the fourth seal, I heard the voice of the fourth animal shout, 7
'Come'. ·Immediately another horse appeared, deathly pale, and its rider was 8
called Plague, and Hades followed at his heels.

They were given authority over a quarter of the earth, *to kill by the sword,
by famine, by plague and wild beasts.*^a

When he broke the fifth seal, I saw underneath the altar the souls of all the 9
people who had been killed on account of the word of God, for witnessing to it.
They shouted aloud, 'Holy,. faithful Master, how much longer will you wait 10
before you pass sentence and take vengeance for our death on the inhabitants
of the earth?' ·Each of them was given a white robe, and they were told to be 11
patient a little longer, until the roll was complete and their fellow servants and
brothers had been killed just as they had been.

In my vision, when he broke the sixth seal, there was a violent earthquake 12
and the sun went as black as coarse sackcloth; the moon turned red as blood all
over, ·and *the stars of the sky fell*^b on to the earth *like figs* dropping from a fig 13
tree when a high wind shakes it; ·the *sky disappeared like a scroll rolling up* and all 14
the mountains and islands were shaken from their places. ·Then all the earthly 15
rulers, the governors and the commanders, the rich people and the men of
influence, the whole population, slaves and citizens, took to the mountains *to hide
in caves and among the rocks.*^c ·*They said to the mountains*^d and the rocks, '*Fall on us* 16
and hide us away from the One who sits on the throne and from the anger of
the Lamb. ·For *the Great Day of his anger* has come, *and who can survive it?*'^e 17

God's servants will be preserved

7 Next I saw four angels, standing at *the four corners of the earth,*^a holding the 1
four winds of the world back to keep them from blowing over the land or the
sea or in the trees. ·Then I saw another angel rising where the sun rises, carrying 2
the seal of the living God; he called in a powerful voice to the four angels

3 whose duty was to devastate land and sea, •'Wait before you do any damage on land or at sea or to the trees, until we have put the *seal on the foreheads*[b] of the
4 servants of our God'. •Then I heard how many were sealed: a hundred and forty-four thousand,[c] out of all the tribes of Israel.

5 From the tribe of Judah, twelve thousand had been sealed; from the tribe of
6 Reuben, twelve thousand; from the tribe of Gad, twelve thousand; •from the tribe of Asher, twelve thousand; from the tribe of Naphtali, twelve thousand;
7 from the tribe of Manasseh, twelve thousand; •from the tribe of Simeon, twelve thousand; from the tribe of Levi, twelve thousand; from the tribe of Issachar,
8 twelve thousand; •from the tribe of Zebulun, twelve thousand; from the tribe of Joseph, twelve thousand; and from the tribe of Benjamin, twelve thousand were sealed.

The rewarding of the saints

9 After that I saw a huge number, impossible to count, of people from every nation, race, tribe and language; they were standing in front of the throne and in front of the Lamb, dressed in white robes and holding palms in their hands.
10 They shouted aloud, •'Victory to our God, who sits on the throne, and to the
11 Lamb!' •And all the angels who were standing in a circle round the throne, surrounding the elders and the four animals, prostrated themselves before the throne, and touched the ground with their foreheads, worshipping God
12 with these words, 'Amen. Praise and glory and wisdom and thanksgiving and honour and power and strength to our God for ever and ever. Amen.'
13 One of the elders then spoke, and asked me, 'Do you know who these people
14 are, dressed in white robes, and where they have come from?' •I answered him, 'You can tell me, my lord'. Then he said, 'These are the people who have been through the great persecution,[d] and because they have washed their robes white
15 again in the blood of the Lamb, •they now stand in front of God's throne and serve him day and night in his sanctuary; and the One who sits on the throne will
16 spread his tent over them. •*They will never hunger or thirst* again; *neither the*
17 *sun nor scorching wind will ever plague them,* •because the Lamb who is at the throne *will be their shepherd and will lead them to springs of living water*;[e] and God *will wipe away all tears from their eyes*.'[f]

The seventh seal

1 8 The Lamb then broke the seventh seal, and there was silence in heaven for about half an hour.[a]

The prayers of the saints bring the coming of the Great Day nearer

2 Next I saw seven trumpets being given to the seven angels who stand in the
3 presence of God. •Another angel, who had a golden censer,[b] came and stood at the altar.[c] A large quantity of incense was given to him to offer with the prayers
4 of all the saints on the golden altar that stood in front of the throne; •and so

e. Dn 7:10
6 a. Ezk 14:21   b. Is 34:4   c. Ho 10:8   d. Is 2:10,18,19   e. Jl 2:11; 3:4
7 a. Ezk 7:2   b. Ezk 9:4 (see also Is 44:5).   c. Twelve (the sacred number) squared and multiplied by a thousand, representing the totality of the faithful.   d. Under Nero.   e. Is 49:10   f. Is 25:8
8 a. An awed silence; the 'coming of Yahweh' is preceded by silence in the prophetic writings.
b. In the shape of a shovel: the flat incense-vessel was also used for carrying live coals from the altar on which offerings were burnt.   c. The altar of incense.

from the angel's hand the smoke of the incense went up in the presence of God and with it the prayers of the saints. •Then the angel took the censer and *filled* 5 *it with the fire* from the altar, which he then threw down on to the earth; immediately there came peals of thunder and flashes of lightning, and the earth shook.

The first four trumpets

The seven angels that had the seven trumpets now made ready to sound them. 6 The first blew his trumpet and, with that, hail and fire, mixed with blood, were 7 dropped on the earth; a third of the earth was burnt up, and a third of all trees, and every blade of grass was burnt. •The second angel blew his trumpet, and it 8 was as though a great mountain, all on fire, had been dropped into the sea: a third of the sea turned into blood, •a third of all the living things in the sea were 9 killed, and a third of all ships were destroyed. •The third angel blew his trumpet, 10 and a huge star fell from the sky, burning like a ball of fire, and it fell on a third of all rivers and springs; •this was the star called Wormwood, and a third of all 11 water turned to bitter wormwood, so that many people died from drinking it. The fourth angel blew his trumpet, and a third of the sun and a third of the moon 12 and a third of the stars were blasted, so that the light went out of a third of them and for a third of the day there was no illumination, and the same with the night.

In my vision, I heard an eagle, calling aloud as it flew high overhead, 'Trouble, 13 trouble, trouble, for all the people on earth at the sound of the other three trumpets which the three angels are going to blow'.

The fifth trumpet

9 Then the fifth angel blew his trumpet, and I saw a star*a* that had fallen from 1 heaven on to the earth, and he was given the key to the shaft leading down to the Abyss.*b* •When he unlocked the shaft of the Abyss, *smoke poured up* out of 2 the Abyss *like the smoke from a* huge *furnace*^c so that the sun and the sky were darkened by it, •and out of the smoke dropped locusts which were given the 3 powers that scorpions have on the earth: •they were forbidden to harm any 4 fields or crops or trees and told only to attack any men who were without God's seal on their foreheads. •They were not to kill them, but to give them pain for 5 five months, and the pain was to be the pain of a scorpion's sting. •When this 6 happens, *men will long for death and not find it anywhere;*^d they will want to die and death will evade them.

To look at, these locusts were *like horses armoured for battle;*^e they had things 7 that looked like gold crowns on their heads, and faces that seemed human, •and 8 hair like women's hair, and *teeth like lions' teeth.* •They had body-armour like 9 iron breastplates, and the noise of their wings sounded like a great charge of horses and chariots into battle. •Their tails were like scorpions', with stings, 10 and it was with them that they were able to injure people for five months. •As 11 their leader they had their emperor, the angel of the Abyss, whose name in Hebrew is Abaddon, or Apollyon^f in Greek.

That was the first of the troubles; there are still two more to come.   12

The sixth trumpet

The sixth angel blew his trumpet, and I heard a voice come out of the four 13 horns of the golden altar in front of God. •It spoke to the sixth angel with the 14 trumpet, and said, 'Release the four angels that are chained up at the great river

15 Euphrates'. •These four angels had been put there ready for this hour of this
day of this month of this year, and now they were released to destroy a third of
16 the human race. •I learnt how many there were in their army: twice ten thousand
17 times ten thousand mounted men. •In my vision I saw the horses, and the riders
with their breastplates of flame colour, hyacinth-blue and sulphur-yellow; the
horses had lions' heads, and fire, smoke and sulphur were coming out of their
18 mouths. •It was by these three plagues, the fire, the smoke and the sulphur coming
19 out of their mouths, that the one third of the human race was killed. •All the
horses' power was in their mouths and their tails: their tails were like snakes,
20 and had heads that were able to wound. •But the rest of the human race, who
escaped these plagues, refused either to abandon *the things they had made with
their own hands*ᵍ—the *idols made of gold, silver, bronze, stone and wood*ʰ that can
21 neither see nor hear nor move—or to stop worshipping devils. •Nor did they give
up their murdering, or witchcraft, or fornication or stealing.

The imminence of the last punishment

1 **10** Then I saw another powerful angel coming down from heaven, wrapped in
a cloud, with a rainbow over his head; his face was like the sun, and his legs
2 were pillars of fire. •In his hand he had a small scroll, unrolled; he put his right foot
3 in the sea and his left foot on the land •and he shouted so loud, it was *like a lion
4 roaring*. At this, seven claps of thunder made themselves heard •and when the
seven thunderclaps had spoken, I was preparing to write, when I heard a voice
from heaven say to me, 'Keep the words of the seven thunderclaps secret and do
5 not write them down'. •Then the angel that I had seen, standing on the sea
6 and the land, *raised his right hand to heaven,*ᵃ •and *swore by the One who lives
for ever* and ever, *and made heaven and all that is in it*, and *earth and all it bears*,
7 and *the sea and all it holds*,ᵇ 'The time of waiting is over; •at the time when the
seventh angel is heard sounding his trumpet, God's secret intention will be
fulfilled, just as he announced in the Good News told to *his servants the prophets*'.

The seer eats the small scroll

8   Then I heard the voice I had heard from heaven speaking to me again. 'Go,'
it said 'and take that open scroll out of the hand of the angel standing on sea
9 and land.' •I went to the angel and asked him to give me the small scroll, and
he said, 'Take it and eat it; it will turn your stomach sour, but in your mouth it
10 will taste as sweet as honey'. •So I took it out of the angel's hand, and swallowed
it; it was as sweet as honey in my mouth, but when I had eaten it my stomach
11 turned sour. •Then I was told, 'You are to prophesy again, this time about
many different nations and countries and languages and emperors'.

The two witnesses

1 **11** Then I was given a long cane as a measuring rod, and I was told, 'Go and
measure God's sanctuary, and the altar, and the people who worship there;
2 but leave out the outer court and do not measure it, because it has been handed
3 over to pagans—they will trample on the holy city for forty-two months.ᵃ •But

---

9 a. A fallen angel.   **b.** Where fallen angels were imprisoned, to be released only to their
final punishment.   **c.** Ex 19:18   **d.** Jb 3:21   **e.** The descriptive details in vv. 7-9 owe much
to Jl 1 and 2.   **f.** 'Destruction'.   **g.** Is 17:8   **h.** Dn 5:4
10 a. Dt 32:40   **b.** Ne 9:6
11 a. This period, taken from Dn, is used as the symbol for any time of persecution.

I shall send my two witnesses to prophesy for those twelve hundred and sixty days, wearing sackcloth. •These are the *two olive trees*[b] and the two lamps *that stand* 4 *before the Lord of the world.*[c] •Fire can come from their mouths and consume 5 their enemies if anyone tries to harm them; and if anybody does try to harm them he will certainly be killed in this way. •They are able to lock up the sky so 6 that it does not rain as long as they are prophesying; they are able to turn water into blood and strike the whole world with any plague as often as they like. When they have completed their witnessing, the beast that comes out of the 7 Abyss *is going to make war on them and overcome them*[d] and kill them. •Their 8 corpses will lie in the main street of the Great City known by the symbolic names Sodom and Egypt, in which their Lord was crucified.[e] •Men out of every 9 people, race, language and nation will stare at their corpses, for three-and-a-half days, not letting them be buried, •and the people of the world will be glad about 10 it and celebrate the event by giving presents to each other, because these two prophets have been a plague to the people of the world.'

After the three-and-a-half days, *God breathed life into them and they stood up,*[f] 11 and everybody who saw it happen was terrified; •then they heard a loud voice 12 from heaven say to them, 'Come up here', and while their enemies were watching, they went up to heaven in a cloud. •Immediately, there was a violent earthquake, 13 and a tenth of the city collapsed; seven thousand persons[g] were killed in the earthquake, and the survivors, overcome with fear, could only praise the God of heaven.

The seventh trumpet

That was the second of the troubles; the third is to come quickly after it.   14

Then the seventh angel blew his trumpet, and voices could be heard shouting 15 in heaven, calling, 'The kingdom of the world has become the kingdom of our Lord and his Christ, and he will reign for ever and ever'. •The twenty-four elders, 16 enthroned in the presence of God, prostrated themselves and touched the ground with their foreheads worshipping God •with these words, 'We give thanks to 17 you, Almighty Lord God, He-Is-and-He-Was, for using your great power and beginning your reign. •*The nations were seething with rage*[h] and now the time has 18 come for your own anger, and for the dead to be judged, and for your servants the prophets, for the saints and for all who worship you, small or great, to be rewarded. The time has come to destroy those who are destroying the earth.'

Then the sanctuary of God in heaven opened, and the ark of the covenant 19 could be seen inside it. Then came flashes of lightning, peals of thunder and an earthquake, and violent hail.

The vision of the woman and the dragon

12 Now a great sign appeared in heaven: a woman, adorned with the sun, 1 standing on the moon, and with the twelve stars on her head for a crown. She was pregnant, and in labour, crying aloud in the pangs of childbirth. •Then $\frac{2}{3}$ a second sign appeared in the sky, a huge red dragon which had seven heads and ten horns, and each of the seven heads crowned with a coronet. •Its tail 4 dragged a third of *the stars from the sky and dropped them to the earth,*[a] and the dragon stopped in front of the woman as she was having the child, so that he could eat it as soon as it was born from its mother. •The woman brought *a male child* 5 *into the world*, the son who was *to rule all the nations with an iron sceptre,*[b] and the child was taken straight up to God and to his throne, •while the woman escaped 6

into the desert, where God had made a place of safety ready, for her to be looked after in the twelve hundred and sixty days.

7 And now war broke out in heaven, when Michael with his angels attacked the
8 dragon. The dragon fought back with his angels, •but they were defeated and
9 driven out of heaven. •The great dragon, the primeval serpent, known as the devil or Satan, who had deceived all the world, was hurled down to the earth
10 and his angels were hurled down with him. •Then I heard a voice shout from heaven, 'Victory and power and empire for ever have been won by our God, and all authority for his Christ, now that the persecutor, who accused our brothers
11 day and night before our God, has been brought down. •They have triumphed over him by the blood of the Lamb and by the witness of their martyrdom,
12 because even in the face of death they would not cling to life. •Let the heavens rejoice and all who live there; but for you, earth and sea, trouble is coming—because the devil has gone down to you in a rage, knowing that his days are numbered.'

13 As soon as the devil found himself thrown down to the earth, he sprang
14 in pursuit of the woman, the mother of the male child, •but she was given a huge pair of eagle's wings to fly away from the serpent into the desert, to the place where she was to be looked after for *a year and twice a year and half a year.*[c]
15 So the serpent vomited water from his mouth, like a river, after the woman,
16 to sweep her away in the current, •but the earth came to her rescue; it opened
17 its mouth and swallowed the river thrown up, by the dragon's jaws. •Then the dragon was enraged with the woman and went away to make war on the rest of her children, that is, all who obey God's commandments and bear witness for Jesus.

The dragon delegates his power to the beast

18
1   I was standing on the seashore. **13** Then I saw *a beast emerge from the sea:*[a] it had seven heads and ten horns, with a coronet on each of its ten horns, and its
2 heads were marked with blasphemous titles.[b] •I saw that the beast *was like a leopard*, with paws like *a bear* and a mouth like *a lion*;[c] the dragon had handed
3 over to it his own power and his throne and his worldwide authority. •I saw that one of its heads seemed to have had a fatal wound but that this deadly injury had healed and, after that, the whole world had marvelled and followed the beast.
4 They prostrated themselves in front of the dragon because he had given the beast his authority; and they prostrated themselves in front of the beast, saying, 'Who
5 can compare with the beast?[d] How could anybody defeat him?' •For forty-two months the beast was allowed *to mouth its boasts*[e] and blasphemies and to do
6 whatever it wanted; •and it mouthed its blasphemies against God, against his
7 name, his heavenly Tent and all those who are sheltered there. •It was allowed *to make war against the saints and conquer them, and given power* over every race,
8 people, language and nation; •and all people of the world will worship it, that

b. Zc 4:3,14, where they symbolise Joshua and Zerubbabel; here they probably represent Peter and Paul.   c. 2 K 1:10   d.˙ Dn 7:21   e. The 'Great City' or 'Babylon' in this book is Rome, whose actions were identified with Sodom's rejection of God's messengers and Egypt's oppression of God's people. The words 'in which their Lord was crucified' may be a gloss, or may be justified by the responsibility of the Roman authority for the crucifixion.   f. Ezk 37:5,10   g. That is, a great number of all classes.   h. Ps 2:1,5
12 a. Dn 8:10   **b.** Ps 2:9   **c.** Dn 7:25. Cf. 11:3.
13 a. Dn 7:3   **b.** Seven heads represent a succession of seven Roman emperors; ten crowned horns are ten subject kings.   **c.** Dn 7:4-6   **d.** A parody of the name Michael, 'Who-can-compare-with-God?'   **e.** Dn 7:8,11

is, everybody whose name has not been written down since the foundation of
the world in the book of life of the sacrificial Lamb. •If anyone has ears to hear, 9
let him listen: •*Captivity for those who are destined for captivity; the sword for* 10
those who are to die by the sword.[f] This is why the saints must have constancy
and faith.

The false prophet as the slave of the beast

Then I saw a second beast;[g] it emerged from the ground; it had two horns 11
like a lamb, but made a noise like a dragon. •This second beast was servant to 12
the first beast, and extended its authority everywhere, making the world and
all its people worship the first beast, which had had the fatal wound and had
been healed. •And it worked great miracles, even to calling down fire from 13
heaven on to the earth while people watched. •Through the miracles which it 14
was allowed to do on behalf of the first beast, it was able to win over the people
of the world and persuade them to put up a statue in honour of the beast that
had been wounded by the sword and still lived. •It was allowed to breathe 15
life into this statue, so that the statue of the beast was able to speak, and to have
anyone who refused to worship the statue of the beast[h] put to death. •He compelled 16
everyone—small and great, rich and poor, slave and citizen—to be branded on
the right hand or on the forehead, •and made it illegal for anyone to buy or sell 17
anything unless he had been branded with the name of the beast or with the
the number of its name.

There is need for shrewdness here: if anyone is clever enough he may interpret 18
the number of the beast: it is the number of a man, the number 666.[i]

The companions of the Lamb

14 Next in my vision I saw Mount Zion, and standing on it a Lamb who 1
had with him a hundred and forty-four thousand people, all with his name
and his Father's name written on their foreheads. •I heard a sound coming 2
out of the sky like the sound of the ocean or the roar of thunder; it seemed to be
the sound of harpists playing their harps. •There in front of the throne they were 3
singing a new hymn[r] in the presence of the four animals and the elders, a hymn
that could only be learnt by the hundred and forty-four thousand who had been
redeemed from the world. •These are the ones who have kept their virginity[a] 4
and not been defiled with women; they *follow* the Lamb wherever he goes;
they have been redeemed from amongst men to be *the first-fruits for God*[b] and
for the Lamb. •They never *allowed a lie to pass their lips*[c] and no fault can be 5
found in them.

Angels announce the day of Judgement

Then I saw another angel, flying high overhead, sent to announce the Good 6
News of eternity to all who live on the earth, every nation, race, language and
tribe. •He was calling, 'Fear God and praise him, because the time has come for 7
him to sit in judgement; worship *the maker of heaven and earth and sea*[d] and every
water-spring'.

A second angel followed him, calling, '*Babylon has fallen, Babylon the Great has* 8
fallen,[e] Babylon which gave the whole world *the wine of* God's *anger* to drink'.

A third angel followed, shouting aloud, 'All those who worship the beast and 9
his statue, or have had themselves branded on the hand or forehead, •will be made 10
to drink the wine of God's fury which is ready, undiluted, in his cup of anger;

in *fire and brimstone*[f] they will be tortured in the presence of the holy angels and
11 the Lamb •and *the smoke* of their torture *will go up for ever*[g] and ever. There will
be no respite, *night or day*, for those who worshipped the beast or its statue
12 or accepted branding with its name.' •This is why there must be constancy in the
13 saints who keep the commandments of God and faith in Jesus. •Then I heard
a voice from heaven say to me, 'Write down: Happy are those who die in the
Lord! Happy indeed, the Spirit says; now they can rest for ever after their work,
since their good deeds go with them.'

The harvest and vintage of the pagans

14 Now in my vision I saw a white *cloud* and, *sitting on it, one like a son of man*
15 with a gold crown on his head and a sharp sickle in his hand. •Then another angel
came out of the sanctuary, and shouted aloud to the one sitting on the cloud,
'*Put your sickle in* and reap: harvest time has come and *the harvest* of the earth
16 *is ripe*'.[h] •Then the one sitting on the cloud set his sickle to work on the earth, and
the earth's harvest was reaped.
17 Another angel, who also carried a sharp sickle, came out of the temple in
18 heaven, •and the angel in charge of the fire left the altar and shouted aloud to
the one with the sharp sickle, 'Put your sickle in and cut all the bunches off the
19 vine of the earth; all its grapes are ripe'. •So the angel set his sickle to work on
the earth and harvested the whole vintage of the earth and put it into a huge
20 winepress, the winepress of God's anger, •outside the city, where it was trodden
until the blood that came out of the winepress was up to the horses' bridles as
far away as sixteen hundred furlongs.

The hymn of Moses and the Lamb

1 **15** What I saw next, in heaven, was a great and wonderful sign: seven angels
were bringing the seven plagues that are the last of all, because they
2 exhaust the anger of God. •I seemed to see a glass lake suffused with fire, and
standing by the lake of glass, those who had fought against the beast and won,
and against his statue and the number which is his name. They all had harps
3 from God, •and they were singing the hymn of Moses, the servant of God,
and of the Lamb:

> 'How great and wonderful are all your works,
> Lord God Almighty;
> just and true are all your ways,
> *King of nations.*
4 *Who would not revere* and *praise your name, O Lord?*
> You alone are holy,
> *and all the pagans will come and adore you*
> for the many acts of justice you have shown.'[a]

f. Jr 15:2   g. Also called 'the false prophet', 16:13; 19:20; 20:10.   h. Dn 3:5-7,15   i. Codes
and riddles were made in both Greek and Hebr. by using numbers for letters, according to
their order in the alphabet. Some commentators have claimed that 666 is the total of the number-
values of 'Nero Caesar'.
14 a. As so often in the O.T., 'virginity' stands for faithfulness, and 'adultery' or 'fornication'
for idolatry.   b. Jr 2:2-3   c. Zp 3:13   d. Ex 20:11   e. Is 21:9. The *wine of* God's *anger*
is a phrase from Is 51:17, also used in Jr 25:15f.   f. Gn 19:28   g. Is 34:9-10   h. Jl 4:13;
Am 8:2
15 a. This hymn is nearer to the Psalms than to the Song of Moses in Ex 15. The two direct
quotations are from Jr 10 and Ps 86; the opening of it is reminiscent of Ps 92 and 98.

The seven bowls of plagues

After this, in my vision, the sanctuary, the Tent of the Testimony, opened 5 in heaven, •and out came the seven angels with the seven plagues, wearing pure 6 white linen, fastened round their waists with golden girdles. •One of the four 7 animals gave the seven angels seven golden bowls filled with the anger of God who lives for ever and ever. •*The smoke from the glory* and the power *of God* 8 *filled the temple so that no one could go into it*[b] until the seven plagues of the seven angels were completed.

16 Then I heard a voice from the sanctuary shouting to the seven angels, 1 'Go, and empty the seven bowls of God's anger over the earth'.

The first angel went and emptied his bowl over the earth; at once, on all the 2 people who had been branded with the mark of the beast and had worshipped its statue, there came disgusting and virulent sores.

The second angel emptied his bowl over the sea, and it turned to blood, like 3 the blood of a corpse, and every living creature in the sea died.

The third angel emptied his bowl into the rivers and water-springs and they 4 turned into blood. •Then I heard the angel of water say, 'You are the holy 5 He-Is-and-He-Was, the Just One, and this is a just punishment: •they spilt the 6 blood of the saints and the prophets, and blood is what you have given them to drink; it is what they deserve'. •And I heard the altar itself say, 'Truly, Lord 7 God Almighty, the punishments you give are true and just'.

The fourth angel emptied his bowl over the sun and it was made to scorch 8 people with its flames; •but though people were scorched by the fierce heat of it, 9 they cursed the name of God who had the power to cause such plagues, and they would not repent and praise him.

The fifth angel emptied his bowl over the throne of the beast and its whole 10 empire was plunged into darkness. Men were biting their tongues for pain, but instead of repenting for what they had done, they cursed the God of heaven 11 because of their pains and sores.

The sixth angel emptied his bowl over the great river Euphrates; all the water 12 dried up so that a way was made for the kings of the East[d] to come in. •Then 13 from the jaws of dragon and beast and false prophet I saw three foul spirits come; they looked like frogs •and in fact were demon spirits, able to work miracles, 14 going out to all the kings of the world to call them together for the war of the Great Day of God the Almighty.—•This is how it will be: I shall come like 15 a thief. Happy is the man who has stayed awake and not taken off his clothes so that he does not go out naked and expose his shame.—•They called the 16 kings together at the place called, in Hebrew, Armageddon.[b]

The seventh angel emptied his bowl into the air, and a voice shouted from 17 the sanctuary, 'The end has come'. •Then there were flashes of lightning and 18 peals of thunder and the most violent earthquake *that anyone has ever seen since there have been* men *on the earth*.[c] •The Great City was split into three parts 19 and the cities of the world collapsed; Babylon the Great was not forgotten: God made her drink the full winecup of his anger. •Every island vanished and 20 the mountains disappeared; •and hail, with great hailstones weighing a talent 21 each, fell from the sky on the people. They cursed God for sending a plague of hail; it was the most terrible plague.

B. THE PUNISHMENT OF BABYLON

The famous prostitute

1 **17** One of the seven angels that had the seven bowls came to speak to me, and said, 'Come here and I will show you the punishment given to the 2 famous prostitute*a who* rules *enthroned beside abundant waters,b* •the one with whom all the kings of the earth have committed fornication, and who has made 3 all the population of the world drunk with the wine of her adultery'.*c* •He took me in spirit to a desert, and there I saw a woman riding a scarlet beast which had seven heads and ten horns and had blasphemous titles written all over it. 4 The woman was dressed in purple and scarlet, and glittered with gold and jewels and pearls, and she was holding a gold winecup filled with the disgusting filth 5 of her fornication; •on her forehead was written a name, a cryptic name: 'Babylon the Great, the mother of all the prostitutes and all the filthy practices 6 on the earth'. •I saw that she was drunk, drunk with the blood of the saints, and the blood of the martyrs of Jesus; and when I saw her, I was completely 7 mystified. •The angel said to me, 'Don't you understand? Now I will tell you the meaning of this woman, and of the beast she is riding, with the seven heads and the ten horns.

The symbolism of the beast and the prostitute

8 'The beast you have seen once was and now is not;*d* he is yet to come up from the Abyss, but only to go to his destruction. And the people of the world, whose names have not been written since the beginning of the world in the book of life, will think it miraculous when they see how the beast once was and now 9 is not and is still to come. •Here there is need for cleverness, for a shrewd mind; the seven heads are the seven hills, and the woman is sitting on them.

10 'The seven heads are also seven emperors. Five of them have already gone, one is here now, and one is yet to come; once here, he must stay for a short while. 11 The beast, who once was and now is not, is at the same time the eighth and one of the seven, and he is going to his destruction.

12 '*The ten horns are ten kingsᵉ* who have not yet been given their royal power but will have royal authority only for a single hour and in association with the 13 beast. •They are all of one mind in putting their strength and their powers at the 14 beast's disposal, •and they will go to war against the Lamb; but the Lamb is *the Lord of lords and the King of kings,f* and he will defeat them and they will be defeated by his followers, the called, the chosen, the faithful.'

15 The angel continued, 'The waters you saw, beside which the prostitute was 16 sitting, are all the peoples, the populations, the nations and the languages. •But the time will come when the ten horns and the beast will turn against the prostitute, and *strip off her clothes and leave her naked;g* then they will eat her

---

b. 1 K 8:10-11
16 a. Of Parthia, the savage enemy dreaded by the Roman world.   **b.** 'Megiddo mountains'; Josiah's defeat at Megiddo, 2 K 23:29f, made this place a symbol of military disaster, cf. Zc 12:11.   **c.** Dn 12:1
17 a. Rome.   **b.** Jr 51:13, a literal description of Babylon, here applied metaphorically, as the author explains in v. 15.   **c.** I.e. the idolatry of emperor-worship.   **d.** The popular belief that Nero would return from the dead at the head of a Parthian army accounts for this parody of the divine title.   **e.** Dn 7:24; here they are kings of the satellite nations.   **f.** Dn 10:17
g. Ezk 16:37f

flesh and burn the remains in the fire. •In fact, God influenced their minds to do 17
what he intended, to agree together to put their royal powers at the beast's
disposal until the time when God's words should be fulfilled. •The woman you 18
saw is the great city which has authority over all the rulers on earth.'

An angel announces the fall of Babylon

18 After this, I saw another angel come down from heaven, with great 1
authority given to him; *the earth was lit up with his glory.*[a] •At the top of 2
his voice he shouted, '*Babylon has fallen*, Babylon the Great has fallen, and has
become *the haunt of devils*[b] and a lodging for every foul spirit and dirty, loathsome bird. •All the nations have been intoxicated by the wine of her prostitution; 3
every king in the earth has committed fornication with her, and every merchant
grown rich through her debauchery.'

The people of God summoned away

A new voice spoke from heaven; I heard it say, 'Come out, my people, away 4
from her, so that you do not share in her crimes and have the same plagues
to bear. •*Her sins have reached up to heaven,*[c] and God has her crimes in mind: 5
she is to be paid in her own coin.[d] She must be paid double the amount she exacted. 6
She is to have a doubly strong cup of her own mixture. •Every one of her shows 7
and orgies is to be matched by a torture or a grief. *I am the queen on my throne,*
she says to herself,[e] and *I am no widow* and shall never be in mourning. •For that, 8
within a single day, the plagues will fall on her: disease and mourning and famine.
She will be burnt right up. The Lord God has condemned her, and he has great
power.'

The people of the world mourn for Babylon

There will be mourning and weeping for her by the kings of the earth who 9
have fornicated with her and lived with her in luxury. They see the smoke as she
burns, •while they keep at a safe distance from fear of her agony. They will 10
say:

> 'Mourn, mourn for this great city,
> Babylon, so powerful a city,
> doomed as you are within a single hour'.

There will be weeping and distress over her among all the traders of the earth 11
when there is nobody left to buy their cargoes of goods; •their stocks of gold 12
and silver, jewels and pearls, linen and purple and silks and scarlet; all the
sandalwood, every piece in ivory or fine wood, in bronze or iron or marble; •the 13
cinnamon and spices, the myrrh and ointment and incense; wine, oil, flour and
corn; their stocks of cattle, sheep, horses and chariots, their slaves, their human
cargo.

'All the fruits you had set your hearts on have failed you; gone for ever, never 14
to return, is your life of magnificence and ease.'

The traders who had made a fortune out of her will be standing at 15
a safe distance from fear of her agony, mourning and weeping. •They will be 16
saying:

> 'Mourn, mourn for this great city;
> for all the linen and purple and scarlet that you wore,
> for all your finery of gold and jewels and pearls;
> your riches are all destroyed within a single hour'. 17

All the captains and seafaring men, sailors and all those who make a living
18 from the sea will be keeping a safe distance, •watching the smoke as she burns,
19 and crying out, 'Has there ever been a city as great as this!' •They will throw dust
on their heads and say, with tears and groans:

> 'Mourn, mourn for this great city
> whose lavish living has made a fortune
> for every owner of a sea-going ship;
> ruined within a single hour.

20 'Now heaven, celebrate her downfall, and all you saints, apostles and prophets:
God has given judgement for you against her.'
21   Then a powerful angel picked up a boulder like a great millstone, and as he
hurled it into the sea, he said, 'That is how the great city of Babylon is going
to be hurled down, never to be seen again.

22   'Never again in you, Babylon,
> will be heard the song of harpists and minstrels,
> the music of flute and trumpet;
> never again will craftsmen of every skill be found
> or *the sound of the mill*[f] be heard;
23   never again will shine *the light of the lamp*,
> never again will be heard
> *the voices of bridegroom and bride*.
> Your traders were the princes of the earth,
> all the nations were under your spell.

24 In her you will find the blood of prophets and saints, and all the blood that was
ever shed on earth.'

Songs of victory in heaven

1 **19** After this I seemed to hear the great sound of a huge crowd in heaven,
2 singing, 'Alleluia! Victory and glory and power to our God! •He judges
fairly, he punishes justly, and he has condemned the famous prostitute who
corrupted the earth with her fornication; he has avenged his servants that she
3 killed'. •They sang again, 'Alleluia! *The smoke* of her *will go up for ever* and
4 ever.' •Then the twenty-four elders and the four animals prostrated themselves
and worshipped God seated there on his throne, and they cried, 'Amen, Alleluia'.
5   Then a voice came from the throne; it said, 'Praise our God, you servants
6 of his and *all who, great or small, revere him*'. •And I seemed to hear the voices
of a huge crowd, like the sound of the ocean or the great roar of thunder,
7 answering, 'Alleluia! The reign of the Lord our God Almighty has begun; •let us
be glad and joyful and give praise to God, because this is the time for the marriage
8 of the Lamb. •His bride is ready, and she has been able to dress herself in dazzling
9 white linen, because her linen is made of the good deeds of the saints.' •The
angel said, 'Write this: Happy are those who are invited to the wedding feast of
the Lamb', and he added, 'All the things you have written are true messages
10 from God'. •Then I knelt at his feet to worship him, but he said to me, 'Don't
do that: I am a servant just like you and all your brothers who are witnesses to
Jesus. It is God that you must worship.' The witness Jesus gave is the same as
the spirit of prophecy.

18 a. Ezk 43:2   **b.** Is 34:11f   **c.** Jr 51:9   **d.** Jr 50:15   **e.** Is 47:8   **f.** Jr 25:10

C. THE DESTRUCTION OF THE PAGAN NATIONS

The first battle of the End

And now I saw heaven open, and a white horse appear; its rider was called ₁₁
Faithful and True; he is *a judge with integrity,*[a] a warrior for justice. •His eyes ₁₂
were flames of fire, and his head was crowned with many coronets; the name
written on him was known only to himself, •*his cloak was soaked in blood.*[b] He is ₁₃
known by the name, The Word of God. •Behind him, dressed in linen of dazzling ₁₄
white, rode the armies of heaven on white horses. •From his mouth came a sharp ₁₅
sword to strike the pagans with; he is the one *who will rule them with an iron
sceptre,*[c] and tread out the wine of Almighty God's fierce anger. •On his cloak and ₁₆
on his thigh[d] there was a name written: *The King of kings and the Lord of lords.*

I saw an angel standing in the sun, and he shouted aloud to all the birds that ₁₇
were flying high overhead in the sky, 'Come here. *Gather together at the great
feast*[e] that God is giving. •*There will be the flesh* of kings for you, and the flesh of ₁₈
great generals and heroes, the flesh of horses and their riders and of all kinds of
men, citizens and slaves, small and great.'

Then I saw the beast, with all the kings of the earth and their armies, gathered ₁₉
together to fight the rider and his army. •But the beast was taken prisoner, ₂₀
together with the false prophet who had worked miracles on the beast's behalf
and by them had deceived all who had been branded with the mark of the beast
and worshipped his statue. These two were thrown alive into the fiery lake
of burning sulphur. •All the rest were killed by the sword of the rider, which ₂₁
came out of his mouth, and *all the birds were gorged with their flesh.*

The reign of a thousand years

20 Then I saw an angel come down from heaven with the key of the Abyss ₁
in his hand and an enormous chain. •He overpowered the dragon, that ₂
primeval serpent which is the devil and Satan, and chained him up for a thousand
years. •He threw him into the Abyss, and shut the entrance and sealed it over him, ₃
to make sure he would not deceive the nations again until the thousand years
had passed. At the end of that time he must be released, but only for a short
while.

Then I saw some thrones, and I saw *those who are given the power to be judges*[a] ₄
take their seats on them. I saw the souls of all who had been beheaded for having
witnessed for Jesus and for having preached God's word, and those who refused
to worship the beast or his statue and would not have the brand-mark on their
foreheads or hands; they came to life, and reigned with Christ for a thousand
years. •This is the first resurrection; the rest of the dead did not come to life ₅
until the thousand years were over. •Happy and blessed are those who share ₆
in the first resurrection; the second death cannot affect them but they will be
priests of God and of Christ and reign with him for a thousand years.

The second battle of the End

When the thousand years are over, Satan will be released from his prison ₇
and will come out to deceive all the nations in the four quarters of the earth, ₈
Gog and Magog,[b] and mobilise them for war. His armies will be as many as the
sands of the sea; •they will come swarming over the entire country and besiege ₉
the camp of the saints, which is the city that God loves. But *fire will come down*

10 *on them from heaven*[c] and consume them. •Then the devil, who misled them, will be thrown into the lake of fire and sulphur, where the beast and the false prophet are, and their torture will not stop, day or night, for ever and ever.

The punishment of the pagans

11   Then I saw a great white throne and the One who was sitting on it. In his
12 presence, earth and sky vanished, leaving no trace. •I saw the dead, both great and small, standing in front of his throne, while the book of life was opened, and *other books opened* which were the record of what they had done in their lives, by which the dead were judged.

13
14   The sea gave up all the dead who were in it; •Death and Hades were emptied of the dead that were in them; and every one was judged according to the way in which he had lived. Then Death and Hades were thrown into the burning
15 lake. This burning lake is the second death; •and anybody whose name could not be found written in the book of life was thrown into the burning lake.

D. THE JERUSALEM OF THE FUTURE

The heavenly Jerusalem

1 **21** Then I saw *a new heaven and a new earth;*[d] the first heaven and the first
2 earth had disappeared now, and there was no longer any sea. •I saw the holy city, and the new Jerusalem, coming down from God out of heaven, as
3 beautiful as a bride all dressed for her husband. •Then I heard a loud voice call from the throne, 'You see this city? Here God lives among men. He will make *his home among them; they shall be his people,*[b] and he will be their God; his name
4 is *God-with-them.* •*He will wipe away all tears from their eyes;*[c] there will be no more death, and no more mourning or sadness. The world of the past has gone.'
5   Then the One sitting on the throne spoke: 'Now I am making the whole of creation new' he said. 'Write this: that what I am saying is sure and will come
6 true.' •And then he said, 'It is already done. I am the Alpha and the Omega, the Beginning and the End. I will give water from the well of life free to anybody
7 who is thirsty; •it is the rightful inheritance of the one who proves victorious;
8 and *I will be his God* and *he a son to me.*[d] •But the legacy for cowards, for those who break their word, or worship obscenities, for murderers and fornicators, and for fortune-tellers, idolaters or any other sort of liars, is the second death in the burning lake of sulphur.'

The messianic Jerusalem

9   One of the seven angels that had the seven bowls full of the seven last plagues came to speak to me, and said, 'Come here and I will show you the bride that the
10 Lamb has married'. •*In the spirit, he took me to the top of an enormous high mountain*[e] and showed me Jerusalem, the holy city, coming down from God out
11 of heaven. •It *had all the radiant glory of God*[f] and glittered like some precious
12 jewel of crystal-clear diamond. •The walls of it were of a great height, and had twelve gates; at each of the twelve gates there was an angel, and over the gates

19 a. Is 11:4   **b.** Is 63:1   **c.** Ps 2:9   **d.** I.e. the place where he wears his sword; so, perhaps, 'on his sword'.   **e.** Ezk 39:17
20 a. Dn 7:22   **b.** Ezk 38:2   **c.** Ezk 38:22
21 a. Is 65:17   **b.** Ezk 37:27   **c.** Is 8:8 and 25:8   **d.** 2 S 7:14   **e.** Ezk 40:2   **f.** Is 60:1-2

were written the names *of the twelve tribes of Israel; •on the east there were three* 13
*gates, on the north three gates, on the south three gates, and on the west three gates.*ᵉ
The city walls stood on twelve foundation stones, each one of which bore the 14
name of one of the twelve apostles of the Lamb.

The angel that was speaking to me was carrying a gold measuring rod 15
to measure the city and its gates and wall. •The plan of the city is perfectly 16
square, its length the same as its breadth. He measured the city with his rod and
it was twelve thousand furlongs in length and in breadth, and equal in height.
He measured its wall, and this was a hundred and forty-four cubits high—the 17
angel was using the ordinary cubit. •The wall was built of diamond, and the city 18
of pure gold, like polished glass. •The foundations of the city wall were faced 19
with all kinds of precious stone: the first with diamond, the second lapis lazuli,
the third turquoise, the fourth crystal, •the fifth agate, the sixth ruby, the seventh 20
gold quartz, the eighth malachite, the ninth topaz, the tenth emerald, the eleventh
sapphire and the twelfth amethyst. •The twelve gates were twelve pearls, each 21
gate being made of a single pearl, and the main street of the city was pure gold,
transparent as glass. •I saw that there was no temple in the city since the Lord 22
God Almighty and the Lamb were themselves the temple, •and the city did not 23
need the sun or the moon for light, since it was lit by the radiant glory of God
and the Lamb was a lighted torch for it. •*The pagan nations will live by its light*ʰ 24
and the kings of the earth will bring it their treasures. •*The gates of it will never* 25
be shut by day—and there will be no night there—•and *the nations will come,* 26
bringing their treasure and their wealth. •Nothing unclean may come into it: no 27
one who does what is loathsome or false, but only those who are listed in the
Lamb's book of life.

22 Then the angel showed me the river of life, rising from the throne of God 1
and of the Lamb and flowing crystal-clear •down the middle of the city 2
street. *On either side of the river were the trees of life, which bear twelve crops*
of fruit in a year, one in each month, and the leaves of which are the cure for the
*pagans.*ᵃ

*The ban will be lifted.*ᵇ The throne of God and of the Lamb will be in its place 3
in the city; his servants will worship him, •they will see him face to face, and his 4
name will be written on their foreheads. •It will never be night again and they 5
will not need lamplight or sunlight, because the Lord God will be shining on them.
They will reign for ever and ever.

The angel said to me, 'All that you have written is sure and will come true: 6
the Lord God who gives the spirit to the prophets has sent his angel to reveal
to his servants *what is soon to take place.* •Very soon now, I shall be with you 7
again.' Happy are those who treasure the prophetic message of this book.

I, John, am the one who heard and saw these things. When I had heard 8
and seen them all, I knelt at the feet of the angel who had shown them to me,
to worship him; •but he said, 'Don't do that: I am a servant just like you and 9
like your brothers the prophets and like those who treasure what you have written
in this book. It is God that you must worship.'

This, too, he said to me, 'Do not keep the prophecies in this book a secret, 10
because the Time is close. •Meanwhile let the sinner go on sinning, and 11
the unclean continue to be unclean; let those who do good go on doing good,
and those who are holy continue to be holy. •Very soon now, I shall be with you 12
again, *bringing the reward to be given to every man according to what he*
*deserves.*ᶜ •I am the Alpha and the Omega, *the First and the Last*, the Beginning 13

14 and the End. •Happy are those who will have washed their robes clean, so that they will have the right to feed on the tree of life and can come through the gates
15 into the city. •These others must stay outside: dogs, fortune-tellers, and fornicators, and murderers, and idolaters, and everyone of false speech and false life.'

EPILOGUE

16 I, Jesus, have sent my angel to make these revelations to you for the sake of the churches. I am of David's line, the root of David and the bright star of the morning.

17 The Spirit and the Bride say, 'Come'. Let everyone who listens answer, 'Come'. *Then let all who are thirsty come:*[d] all who want it may *have the water* of life, *and have it free.*

18 This is my solemn warning to all who hear the prophecies in this book: if anyone adds anything to them, God will add to him every plague mentioned in the
19 book; •if anyone cuts anything out of the prophecies in this book, God will cut off his share of the tree of life and of the holy city, which are described in the book.

20 The one who guarantees these revelations repeats his promise: I shall indeed *be with you* soon. Amen; come, Lord Jesus.

21 May the grace of the Lord Jesus be with you all. Amen.

g. Ezk 48:31-35　h. Is 60:3
22 a. Ezk 47:12　b. Zc 14:11　c. Ps 62:12　d. Is 55:1

CHRONOLOGICAL TABLE

	B.C.	
	B.C.	The census of Lk 2:1f? Cf. the *lapis Venetus* inscription, undated, giving evidence of a census in Apamea (Syria) by order of Quirinius 'legate in Syria'. Cf. Lk 2:2
QUINTILIUS VARUS, legate in Syria: 6-4		Birth of JESUS, about 7-6(?)
		End of March, beginning of April, 4 B.C., **death of Herod** at Jericho. Archelaus takes his body to the Herodion
ARCHELAUS ethnarch of Judaea and Samaria: 4 B.C.-6 A.D.		
HEROD ANTIPAS tetrarch of Galilee and Peraea: 4 B.C.-39 A.D.		
PHILIP tetrarch of Gaulanitis, Batanaea, Trachonitis, Auranitis and the district of Paneas (Ituraea): 4 B.C.-34 A.D.	A.D. 1	Between 5 and 10, birth of Paul at Tarsus; pupil of Gamaliel the Elder, Ac 22:3, cf. 5:34
6, Augustus deposes Archelaus who is exiled to Vienne (Gaul)		
6-41, **Judaea a procuratorial province** (with Caesarea as the capital)		
6, according to Josephus, QUIRINIUS legate in Syria(?)		
14 (19th August), death of Augustus. TIBERIUS emperor: 14-37		Valerius Gratus deposes Annas. Three other high priests follow, then JOSEPH CALLED CAIAPHAS: 18-36
VALERIUS GRATUS procurator: 15-26		
17-19, GERMANICUS, adopted son of Tiberius, in the East		About 27, Herod Antipas, married to the daughter of Aretas, marries Herodias, the wife of his brother Herod (son of Mariamne II)
26-36, PONTIUS PILATE procurator		Autumn of 27, the preaching of JOHN THE BAPTIST and the beginning of the ministry of Jesus. Cf. Lk 3:2 +

A.D.

The 15th year of Tiberius, Lk 3:1: 19th August 28 or 18th August 29, but according to the Syrian calculation: Sept.-Oct. 27 to Sept.-Oct. 28

30, on the eve of the Passover, i.e. 14th Nisan, a Friday, death of Jesus, Jn 19:31f. (The Passover fell on the Saturday, 8th April in 30 and 4th April in 33: the second date is too late, cf. Jn 2:20). Cf. Mt 26:17 +

30, **Pentecost**, outpouring of the Spirit on the Church, Ac 2. The first community. Ac 2:42, etc.

CALIGULA emperor: 37-41

36-37, winter (?), **martyrdom of Stephen** and dispersion of part of the community. A little later, **conversion** of PAUL. Cf. Ac 9:1 +

39, Caligula exiles Antipas to the Pyrenees and gives his tetrarchy to Agrippa I

Paul in 'Arabia', then in Damascus, Ac 9:19f; Ga 1:17f

About 39, Paul escapes from Damascus, 2 Co 11: 32f, and makes a first visit to the elders of the Church, Ga 1:18f (Cephas and James the brother of the Lord); Ac 9:25f

41-54, CLAUDIUS emperor. Agrippa I, now in Rome, contributes to his success; Claudius concedes him Judaea and Samaria. His brother Herod becomes king of Chalcis (41-48) and marries Berenice (daughter of Agrippa)

About 43, Paul and Barnabas at **Antioch** which becomes the centre for the hellenistic Christians. PETER in Samaria (Simon the magician) and in the coastal plain (the centurion Cornelius)

44, spring. On the death of Herod Agrippa I, Judaea again becomes a procuratorial province, 44-66

43 or 44, before the Passover, Agrippa I orders the beheading of JAMES, BROTHER OF JOHN (James the Great); during the feast he imprisons Peter. Ac 12

Between 45 and 49, **1st mission by Paul**: Antioch, Cyprus, Antioch in Pisidia, Lystra, ...Antioch, Ac 13:1f

AGRIPPA II, son of Agrippa I, king of Chalcis 48-53. In 49 he is named inspector of the Temple, with the right to nominate the high priest

About 48, famine in Judaea, worsened by the sabbatical year 47/48. Visit to Jerusalem, by HELEN, queen of Adiabene, a convert to Judaism; she brings relief to the population

49, Claudius 'drives from Rome the Jewish agitators stirred up by Chrestos' (Suetonius), cf. Ac 18:2

48-49, prophecy of Agabus and the aid given to the community at Jerusalem by that of Antioch. The **council of Jerusalem**: converts from paganism exempt from the Law, Ac 15:5f; Ga 2:1f

About the year 50, the oral tradition of the gospel is put into written form: the **Aramaic Matthew**, and the complementary **collection**. The **Letter of James** (or about 58)

50-52, **2nd mission by Paul**: Lystra (Timothy), Phrygia, Galatia, Philippi, Thessalonika, Athens (sermon on the Areopagus)

Winter of 50 to summer of 52, Paul in Corinth: the **Letters to the Thessalonians**; and, in the spring of 52, summoned to appear before Gallio. Summer 52, he goes to Jerusalem, Ac 18:22, and then to Antioch

53-58, **3rd mission by Paul**; APOLLOS at Ephesus and then at Corinth

A.D.

54-68, NERO emperor

55, Nero adds a part of Galilee and Peraea to the kingdom of Agrippa

54-57, after passing through Galatia and Phrygia, Paul stays at Ephesus for $2\frac{1}{4}$ years. After 56(?), **Letter to the Philippians**. About Passover 57, **1 Corinthians**. Then a quick visit to Corinth, 2 Co 12:14. Return to Ephesus and **Letter to the Galatians**

End of 57, passes through Macedonia. **2 Corinthians**

Winter 57-58, at Corinth, Ac 20:3, cf. 1 Co 16:6; **Letter to the Romans**

Passover 58, at Philippi, Ac 20:6, then, by sea, to Caesarea (Philip and Agabus)

Summer 58, in Jerusalem. JAMES THE BROTHER OF THE LORD heads the Judaeo-Christian community; his **Letter** to the Jews of the Dispersion (or possibly before 49)

Autumn of 60, Paul's voyage to Rome, the storm. he winters in Malta

61-63, Paul in Rome under military guard. His apostolate, **Letters to Colossians, Ephesians, Philemon** (and **to Philippians**?)

62, the High Priest Anan has **James** the brother of the Lord **stoned to death** (after the death of Festus and before the arrival of Albinus). SIMEON, son of Cleophas and of Mary (sister-in-law of the mother of Jesus), succeeded James as head of the church of Jerusalem (Eusebius)

63, Paul is set free, and possibly goes to Spain, Rm 15:24f

64, July, burning of Rome and persecution of the Christians

About 64, **1 Peter** and the **gospel of Mark**

64 (or 67), **martyrdom of Peter** in Rome

About 65, Paul at Ephesus, 1 Tm 1:3; in Crete, Tt 1:5; in Macedonia, whence he sends his **1st Letter to Timothy**, 1 Tm 1:3; and probably **Titus**

The **Greek gospel of Matthew**; the **gospel of Luke** and the Acts of the Apostles: before 70? or about 80?

About 67, **Letter to the Hebrews**. Paul, a prisoner in Rome, writes **2 Timothy**. A little later he is beheaded

68, April, GALBA emperor

68, June, suicide of Nero

69, January, OTHO proclaimed Emperor by the Praetorians and VITELLIUS by the legions in Germany

	A.D.	
69-79, VESPASIAN emperor. He entrusts the siege of Jerusalem to Titus		
End of 69, Vespasian in sole command of the empire		
		70, Passover. Many pilgrims in Jerusalem. **Titus lays siege** to the city with four legions. Tiberius Alexander is second in command
		70, 29th August, capture of the Inner Court and **burning of the Temple** (the 10th of Loos, i.e. the 10th of the 5th month, the day when Nebuzaradan set fire to the first Temple, Jr 52:12 and Josephus)
70, end of the year, Judaea an imperial province; under the rule of the legate of the Xth Legion based in Jerusalem. Caesarea a Roman colony		70, Sept., capture of the Upper City and the palace of Herod. The inhabitants killed, sold into slavery or condemned to hard labour
79-81, TITUS emperor		70-80, the **Letter of Jude**, then **2 Peter**. *2 Esdras* (apocryphal). About 78, the *Jewish War* (Josephus)
81-96, DOMITIAN emperor. Brother of Titus		About 95, John exiled to Patmos. Final text of **Revelation**. *Letter of St Clement*, bishop of Rome, to the Corinthians
96-98, NERVA emperor		**Gospel of John**; then **1 John** (**3 John** and **2 John** are possibly earlier). He opposes Cerinthus and his Docetism
98-117, TRAJAN emperor	100	At the beginning of Trajan's reign, **death of John at Ephesus**